TEACHING IN THE MIDDLE AND SECONDARY SCHOOLS

Fourth Edition

Joseph F. Callahan

Leonard H. Clark

Richard D. Kellough

Macmillan Publishing Company
New York

Maxwell Macmillan Canada
Toronto

Maxwell Macmillan International
New York Oxford Singapore Sydney

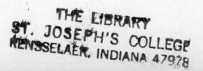

Cover Art: Leslie Bakshi
Editor: Robert B. Miller
Production Editor: Ben Ko
Art Coordinator: Raydelle M. Clement
Cover Designer: Robert Vega
Production Buyer: Patricia A. Tonneman

This book was set in Century Old Style by Waldman Graphics and was printed and bound by Semline. The cover was printed by Phoenix Color Corp.

Macmillan Publishing Company
866 Third Avenue
New York, New York 10022

Macmillan Publishing Company is part of the
Maxwell Communication Group of Companies.

Maxwell Macmillan Canada, Inc.
1200 Eglington Avenue East, Suite 200
Don Mills, Ontario M3C 3N1

Library of Congress Cataloging-in-Publication Data

Teaching in the middle and secondary schools
/[edited by] Joseph F. Callahan, Leonard H. Clark, Richard D.
Kellough.--4th ed.
        p.   cm.
    Includes bibliographical references and index.
    ISBN 0-02-318265-2
    1. High school teaching--United States. 2. Middle schools--United
States. I. Callahan, Joseph F. II. Clark, Leonard H.
III. Kellough, Richard D. (Richard Dean)
LB1737.U6T43 1992
373.11'02--dc20   91-23649
                                                                        CIP

Printing: 1 2 3 4 5 6 7 8 9   Year: 2 3 4 5

PREFACE

Like the preceding edition, this fourth edition continues to provide a basic self-instructional text on the methods of teaching in the middle and secondary schools. We continue to be mindful of the rationale for each of the various teaching techniques and attempt to illustrate how each of the methods discussed can be implemented in the classroom. Also, we continue to use the format of the self-teaching module as the mode of presentation in order to encourage reader participation in the learning, reader reaction to the text, and reader interaction with fellow students.

As students progress toward conceptual mastery, we expect that considerable self-motivation will be engaged. There should be a gradual development in confidence as the reader masters the concepts of each module, and this confidence should result in a desire to investigate the concepts further. For that purpose, the lists of sources at the end of each module augment the sometimes necessarily sketchy development in the module. We hope that skill in using the method will occur after intellectual mastery of the concept has been achieved.

Of course, expertise in methods and techniques comes from practice, particularly guided practice and experience. No one has ever become truly expert simply by studying a book and carrying out learning activities. These modules, however, provide the necessary background and basic knowledge that make early teaching practice and experience profitable. The modules should serve as effective springboards for laboratory experiences in teaching. We believe that instructors in methods courses can depend on the modules to provide some basic instruction so they can individualize their instruction and devote their time and attention to specific learning activities.

For this fourth edition, we paid closer attention to the differences between middle and secondary school teaching. We rewrote all or parts of every module, sometimes to add clarity and always to update content. All reading lists were updated. Previous users of the text will discover that some of the later modules of the previous edition have not only been rewritten but also have been relocated, creating a more logical sequence. The modules are now organized into seven major divisions of the textbook called parts. Part I, "Introduction to Teaching in Middle and Secondary Schools," consists of the first module and is designed to bridge foundations in education courses with the rest of the modules of this methods book. Part II, "Planning for Instruction," consists of four modules covering different aspects of instructional planning. Part III, "Motivating the Students and Managing the Classroom," consists of two modules. Part IV, "Selecting and Implementing Instructional Strategies," consists of five modules. Part V, "Preparing and Using Instructional Aids," consists of two modules. Part VI, "Preparing for Measurement, Evaluation, and Grading," consists of two modules, and Part VII, "Becoming a Professional," contains the final module.

For this edition the exercises have assumed a greater importance. To improve utilization their format has been modified, and all of the exercises have been rewritten, with many new ones added and a few old ones deleted. Whereas in the previous edition exercise answers—when provided—were located at the end of the module, they now are found on the bottom of the second page of each exercise. Some exercises now depend upon a school site visitation, including Exercises 1.2, 1.4, and 8.5 Each of the exercises is contained on a perforated tearsheet, designed for easy use by the reader.

Also for this fourth edition, we have provided a more detailed table of contents and have added a glossary at the end of the text. The index is now separated into a name index and a subject index. In addition, there is now an instructor's manual available for instructors who use the book. We believe that these changes make this fourth edition of the text even more user friendly.

We wish to acknowledge those who helped in the writing of certain modules for the first edition as well as those writers and publishers who have graciously granted their permissions to use materials that are included in this fourth edition. We continue to be grateful for suggestions that have come from our students, the reviewers, and the users of previous editions. Specifically, we acknowledge the following persons who have provided significant contributions to this book:

Leo Auerbach, Jersey City State College, for writing the module on reading and study skills for the first edition.

Raydelle Clement, our Art Coordinator from Macmillan, who magically translated our scribbles into actual art work.

Nedra A. Crow, University of Utah, for a very usable review for this edition.

Roger T. Cunningham, Ohio State University, for his insightful and practical review for this edition.

Dan Duffee, Springfield, Ohio, for his brilliant editing of the manuscript for this fourth edition.

William B. Fisher, Jersey City State College, for contributing the module on teacher-centered strategies for the first edition.

Leigh Chiarelott, Bowling Green State University, for her valued suggestions for the entire book.

Louise E. Hock, New York University, for contributing the module on discussion and group strategies for the first edition.

Ben Ko, our Production Editor at Macmillan, whose friendliness and efficiency made the final stages of publication almost enjoyable for us.

William J. Meisner, Jersey City State College, for contributing the module on lesson planning for the first edition.

Robert B. Miller, our Senior Editor at Macmillan, for his belief in the value of this book and for his confidence in our ability to put it together.

Ronald E. Peake, University of West Florida, for his astute review and helpful suggestions for this edition.

Isobel L. Pfeiffer, University of Akron, for contributing the modules on measurement and evaluation and on grading for the first edition.

J. Bernard Smith, Duquesne University, for an attentive review of a previous edition.

Mack Welford, Roanoke College, for his constructive review of a previous edition.

As always, we assume full responsibility for any shortcomings that exist in this fourth edition. We hope you find the book professionally valuable and interesting to read.

CONTENTS

PART IV
SELECTING AND IMPLEMENTING INSTRUCTIONAL STRATEGIES

Module 14
Projected and Recorded
Instructional Aids   **427**

PART VI
Preparing for Measurement,
Evaluation, and Grading   **459**

Module 15
Measurement and Evaluation   **461**

Module 16
Grading   **489**

PART VII
BECOMING A PROFESSIONAL   **523**

Module 17
BECOMING A Professional   **525**

TO THE READER

Welcome to an adventure in learning. Now that you have begun to think about and plan your career in teaching, it is our guess that you will find adventures of this sort very helpful in planning to meet the excitement and the challenges that await you in the classroom. It seems safe to predict that not only will you increase your background in educational theory and methodology as you work your way through this textbook, but also you will improve your chances of becoming an effective teacher when the time arrives to put theory learned into practice.

Probably you have not encountered many books organized as this one, calling for such active participation on your part. From this point forward, you are expected to become a sensitive, self-motivated learner engaged in making frequent and sound judgments and decisions about your learning and teaching. For the most part, you will control your rate of progress through the various modules of this book, and you will decide when you have mastered the knowledge presented in each and are ready to continue to the next module. To assist you we have (1) listed the objectives for each module, (2) provided a comprehensive set of questions to test your mastery at the close of each module, and (3) provided an answer key for your use in evaluating your progress. Exercises requiring your active learning are found in each module. Some of these are self-check exercises, others will be compared with responses of your classmates, and in some cases discussed with your instructor. Students who have little time to spend on study can move through the various modules and finish quickly so long as they study attentively and demonstrate the mastery called for on each posttest. Slower-paced individuals, who wish to ponder and probe various areas and who decide to read extensively from the selected readings listed at the end of each module, can establish a pace that suits their purposes.

It is not intended that any student will be able to prepare for a teaching career solely by completion of this kind of study program. Teaching is a human activity. It deals with people, with children, parents, and fellow professionals. It involves various kinds of knowledge, judgments, and decision making; it requires communications skills, human relations techniques, and a host of other attributes for the cultivation of which human interaction and professional expertise are inseparable necessities. But faithful and zealous use of this learning tool will add depth and meaning to your classroom sessions in education course. Mastery of these modules will carry you beyond the initial steps of preparation so you may place into context more of the campus lectures about education that you hear, and ask questions about schools and students that go beyond the layperson's level of significance.

The chapters of this book are called modules; essentially they are self-contained units that have cognitive values by themselves. Each module contains a rationale, a list of specific objectives, the module text, exercises, a posttest, a list of suggested readings, and the answer key to the posttest.

The rationale attempts to establish the purpose of each module and, in some cases, the link with other aspects of pedagogical knowledge. The objectives inform you very specifically what you should know and be able to do as a consequence of your study of the module. You can think of the rationale and objectives as being useful in establishing a mind set. The list of suggested readings points out other sources of information by which to deepen and broaden your understanding of the topic. The posttest and key inform you of your progress toward module mastery. The general study plan recommended is as follows:

1. Read the rationale to acquaint yourself with the task you are addressing and, if possible, with how this module fits among the others that you have studied or will study.

2. Examine carefully the module objectives. Find out what will be expected of you upon completion of your study of the module.

3. Read through the module, checking back from time to time to see how well you are mastering the objectives. Review what you do not understand. As a quick reference to the meaning of specific terms a glossary is provided at the end of the text. Also, because certain topics may be discussed in some detail or another in more than one module, you will occasionally want to check the index for a specific topic you are reading about and see if it is discussed in another module. If it is, then you may benefit by moving to that other module and continue reading about the topic there. By doing so, you may improve your comprehension of that particular topic.

4. Do the exercises in each module, both to check your understanding and to clinch your learning. Some of the exercises are self-check exercises, i.e., answers to the exercises are included at the end of each exercise. Others are more divergent and will necessitate the sharing of your responses with others in your class for their feedback and evaluation.

5. Try out your knowledge by exposing yourself to some of the suggested readings.

6. Take the posttest at the end of the module, then check your answers against those as provided for each module at the end of the text. Review if necessary.

Enjoy your quest! Become a great teacher.

PART I
Introduction to Teaching in Middle and Secondary Schools

The single module of Part I provides an orientation to middle and secondary school teaching by:

□ Reviewing the differences between the middle school and the secondary school.

□ Discussing the teacher as a decision maker.

□ Introducing variables that need consideration during instructional planning.

□ Presenting information about teaching style.

□ Introducing ten characteristics of the effective teacher.

□ Introducing a pattern for teaching.

Our greatest national resource is the minds of our children.
—Walt Disney

We must return to the basics, but the "basics" of the 21st century are not only reading, writing, and arithmetic. They include communication and higher problem-solving skills, and scientific and technological literacy— the thinking tools that allow us to understand the technological world around us.
—Educating Americans for the 21st Century

MODULE 1
Theoretical Considerations

RATIONALE

SPECIFIC OBJECTIVES

MODULE TEXT

Teaching as Decision Making
The Role of Content
The Nature of the Student
The Nature of Learning
> *Learning and the Brain*
> *Learning as an Individual Matter*
> *Learning Style*
> *Learning and Motivation*
> *Important Principles of Learning for the Twenty-First Century*
> *Learning Modes*
> *Concept Presentation*
> *Skill Development*
> *Attitude Development*
> *Readiness*
> *Retention and Transferability*
> *Time on Task*

Direct Versus Indirect Instruction
The Nature of Groups
Developing a Teaching Style
A Pattern for Teaching

SUMMARY

SUGGESTED READING

POSTTEST

RATIONALE

Although this book is designed to explain the *know-how* of teaching more than it is the *why*, to use teaching methods well requires some understanding of the *whys*. Consequently, this module reviews basic ideas that serve as a foundation for the selection of strategies and techniques.

Our reason for reviewing these ideas is simple: to be competent, a teacher must not only know how to teach but also understand why one approach is likely to be more effective than another for a given purpose or situation. To be competent, teachers must understand their options and utilize the best strategies and techniques for the accomplishment of their goals. This module reviews some of those ideas necessary for selecting the strategies and techniques presented in subsequent modules.

SPECIFIC OBJECTIVES

At the completion of this module, you should be able to:

1. Define teaching.
2. Identify factors that affect a competent teacher's choice of teaching methods.
3. Describe the role of subject matter in teaching.
4. Describe how the nature of students influences teaching methods.
5. Describe how the nature of learning influences teaching methods.
6. Describe how the workings of the brain affect teaching methods.
7. Describe how learning style affects teaching methods.
8. Describe how the nature of groups influences teaching methods.
9. Describe how the differences between direct and indirect teaching affect teaching methods.
10. Describe how one's own teaching style affects teaching methods.
11. Describe the characteristics typical of effective teachers.
12. Describe the five-step teacher pattern.
13. Describe ways in which middle schools differ from junior and senior high schools.

MODULE TEXT

Teaching is not telling something to a group of listeners, or explaining some concept, or demonstrating a mastery of an important topic. Rather, teaching is helping students learn. Of course, when you are helping students learn, you may engage in telling, explaining, or demonstrating, but you do these only as a means to accomplish an end. In the final analysis your success as a teacher is determined by how well your students have learned.

For better or worse, however, teaching in schools constitutes more than just helping students learn. There teachers must ensure that students learn designated material—the content that comprises the planned curriculum. Theoretically, this material is arranged to help students learn by building on what has been learned before and preparing the way for what is to come. Yet no matter how strictly a curriculum must be followed, every teacher faces the necessity of selecting from several alternatives those strategies and tactics that most likely will result in the desired learning. Although the outcome may not always meet your expectations, you should experience a high degree of success if the content and methods you select are appropriate.

Teaching as Decision Making

Although pedagogy is based on scientific principles, classroom teaching is as much an art as a science. Few rules apply to every classroom situation. In fact, the content, the instructional objectives, the materials of instruction, the teaching procedures, the evaluation techniques, and the instructional follow-ups in most teaching situations are the result of subjective judgments. Although many of these decisions are made at leisure during preinstruction planning, many others must be made intuitively on the spur-of-the-moment. Once class has begun, there is often precious little time for making carefully reasoned judgments. As best you can, you base teaching decisions on your knowledge of pedagogical research, the subject matter, and the students in your classes. But you must also base many more decisions on intuition, feeling, impulse, and prior experience. The better your understanding of the subject and the students and the greater your repertoire of teaching techniques, the more likely your decisions will result in effective student learning. Still, no matter how well versed you are in pedagogical knowledge, your choice of teaching methods must be subjective.

There is no one best method of teaching that will always generate a high degree of student learning. Rather, there are any number of strategies, tactics, and techniques that may or may not be effective in a particular situation. **Strategy** refers to a general approach or plan, **tactic** refers to the method used to carry out strategies in particular situations, and **technique** refers to the procedure used to implement the tactic. The competent teacher selects the teaching method that best suits each situation. In deciding which method to use, you will be influenced by a number of factors.

The objective of the instruction is the first factor. The tactics and strategies selected to teach information, for example, are not necessarily those you might use to teach concepts or skills. Students can absorb information from lectures and other teacher presentations. Students learn concepts, however, by considering the idea in a number of contexts; and students develop skills through practice, preferably guided practice. Among the many tactics and techniques available to you, some are suited for presenting new information, whereas others are suited for showing students how to do things, influencing attitudes, motivating students, guiding work in progress, or arousing emotions.

The students comprise a second factor. Competent teachers adapt their teaching methods to their students, using approaches that interest the students, that are neither too difficult nor too easy, and that are relevant to the students' lives. This adaptation process is complicated because each student is different from every other. All do not have the same interest, abilities, backgrounds, or learning styles. As a matter of fact, students not only differ from one another but each individual student changes from day to day. What appeals to a student today may not have the same appeal tomorrow. Therefore, a teacher needs to consider both the nature of students in general and each student in particular.

The nature of each specific group constitutes a third factor. A teacher needs to know something of group dynamics and their application to the structure and processes of particular groups. Teaching strategies that work well with one class of students may not be at all effective with another class. Furthermore, strategies that work well with certain high school groups may not be appropriate for those of middle or junior high school.

"'Middle schools' are schools that have been planned for students ranging in age from 9 through 14. Middle schools generally include grades five through eight (with grades six through eight being the most popular organization), although many varied patterns exist. For example, a school might include grades seven and eight, which is typical of junior high schools, but still be a middle school. Although middle schools vary considerably in organization, generally the fifth and sixth grades are each self-contained (each class has one teacher for all or most of the day), while seventh and eighth grades are departmentalized, i.e., students in these grades may meet each day for a homeroom class, then go to other rooms and teachers for other subjects."[1] Figure 1.1 reviews the characteristics of the middle school.

The nature of the subject matter to be taught is a fourth factor. For example, the strategy used to teach literature should not be the same as the one used to teach a scientific formula. Teachers must select teaching methods best suited to the structure and role of the subject matter being taught.

---

[1]From Eugene C. Kim and Richard D. Kellough, *A Resource Guide for Secondary School Teaching: Planning for Competence*, 5th ed. (New York: Macmillan, 1991), p. 3. By permission of Macmillan Publishing Company.

FIGURE 1.1
Characteristics of the
Middle School

1. Historical Development. Whereas the junior high school emerged as a recommendation from the Committee of Ten (1918) to separate secondary school into a junior stage and a senior stage, the middle school did not appear until the 1960s, as a result of several factors, most notably:
   a. Overcrowding of existing junior high schools.
   b. Recognition of the need to attend to the needs of the 10–14 age-group by providing a more effective transition for students from the self-contained classrooms and child-centered caring of elementary teachers to the program-centered, departmentalized schedule of junior and senior high schools.
   c. Recognition that because these age-years may be for many students their final substantive educational experience, innovative efforts need to be made to encourage students to stay in school to continue their formal education.
2. Emerging trends characteristic of middle school education:
   a. Articulation with and involvement of parents or guardians in the education of their children.
   b. Interdisciplinary teaching, especially in language arts, social studies, mathematics, and science.
   c. Involvement of teachers in making positive emotional connections with students. Middle schools tend to have longer advising (or homeroom periods) than do junior high schools (which tend to use more full-time counselors, like high schools).
   d. More variation in instructional methodology than in junior or senior high schools, with perhaps more use of strategies for cooperative learning.

The technology and materials available constitute a fifth factor. You cannot use materials, equipment, and techniques that you do not have. Further, some techniques and media suitable for one objective or group may not be suitable in another setting.

Finally, a teacher's personal skills and preferences comprise a sixth factor. Because teachers' styles, personalities, and competencies differ, the approach that is effective for you may not work well for your colleague in the adjacent classroom.

In short, the strategy and tactics chosen for any given teaching situation should be fitted to the objectives, the students, the group, the subject matter, the available technology and materials, and the skills and personality of the teacher. A perfect fit for all these factors is, of course, impossible. Yet they all should be considered when selecting strategies and tactics for a particular situation.

Now do Exercise 1.1 and Exercise 1.2.

The Role of Content

Subject content is the substance of teaching. Without it there would be no teaching or learning. Content cannot really be separated from method because it is not solely a matter of information. The subject matter of your teaching field consists of facts, concepts, skills, attitudes, and appreciations. The skills and appreciations may be more important than the factual content. If students do not learn such intellectual skills as critical thinking, problem solving, and clearly expressing their thoughts, the intellectual value of the instruction may be minimal. Remember, knowing how is as much a part of the curriculum content as knowing what: "To know something is not just to have received information but also to have interpreted it and related it to other knowledge. To be skilled is not just to know how to perform some action but also to know when to perform it and to adapt the performance to varied circumstances."[2]

---

[2]Lauren B. Resnick and Leopold E. Klopfer, eds., "Toward the Thinking Curriculum: An Overview," in *Toward the Thinking Curriculum: Current Cognitive Research*, 1989 ASCD Yearbook (Alexandria, VA: ASCD, 1989), p. 4.

EXERCISE 1.1 TEACHERS AND THEIR METHODS OF INSTRUCTION

The purpose of this exercise is for you to reflect on how you have been taught (throughout your schooling) and share those reflections with your classmates, looking for differences as well as commonalities.

1. The following is a list of teaching methods. Rate each according to your familiarity and experiences with it, using this rating scale: A = very familiar and with good learning experiences; B = somewhat familiar; C = never experienced; D = familiar but with bad learning experiences.

_____ Assignments		_____ Laboratory investigation
_____ Committee		_____ Lecture
_____ Computer-assisted		_____ Library work
_____ Cooperative learning		_____ Mock up
_____ Debate		_____ Panel
_____ Demonstration (student)		_____ Problem solving
_____ Demonstration (teacher)		_____ Project, independent study
_____ Discovery		_____ Questioning
_____ Discussion		_____ Review and practice
_____ Drama		_____ Role play
_____ Drill		_____ Self-instructional package
_____ Expository		_____ Simulation
_____ Field trip		_____ Slides (35 mm)
_____ Film		_____ Socratic questioning
_____ Game		_____ Study guide
_____ Group work (small)		_____ Symposium
_____ Guest speaker		_____ Telecommunication
_____ Homework		_____ Term paper
_____ Individualized instruction		_____ Textbook
_____ Inquiry		_____ Tutorial
_____ Jury		_____ Videodisc

2. Now list the methods in four columns according to the rating you gave to each.

A Methods   *B* Methods   *C* Methods   *D* Methods

3. In small groups, share your columns with your classmates. Are there methods that seem to show up consistently in certain columns? If so, try and analyze why. Questions that you might discuss in your groups are:

□ In what ways have your teachers' teaching styles differed?

□ Which have appealed to you most?

□ What qualities did they have that you would most like to emulate? Avoid?

□ Did they seem to rely more on certain strategies, tactics, and techniques?

EXERCISE 1.2 TEACHER AS DECISION MAKER

In this exercise, you will observe a middle school, junior high school, or senior high school teacher for one class period, tabulate the number of decisions the teacher of that classroom makes for that one period, and then share your results with your classmates. Obtain permission from a cooperative teacher by explaining the purpose of your observation. A follow-up thank you would be appropriate.

School, teacher, and class observed: _____

1. Use the following format for your tabulations. You may initially want to tabulate on a blank sheet of paper and then later organize and transfer your tabulations to this page. Tabulate and identify each decision. To tabulate the decisions made prior to class, confer with the teacher before the class begins.

   Decisions made prior to class:
   Examples:
   (objectives)
   (amount of time devoted to question and answer period)

   Decisions made during class:
   Examples:
   (called upon Juan to answer question)
   (teacher remained silent until students in back row got quiet)

2. What was the total number of decisions made by this one teacher prior to class___
   and during class _____?
   Compare your results with those of others in your class.

3. Did you share your results with the cooperating teacher? His or her reaction?

4. What percentage of all teacher decisions were planned? _____
   Spontaneous? _____

5. Your conclusions from this exercise?

Much of the content of academic disciplines is transient, because the growth of knowledge is so rapid that what seems basic today may be obsolete tomorrow. Therefore, teachers should select course content and teaching methods that will give students the skills and understandings necessary for assimilating further knowledge and applying their learning to new situations.

All fields contain more content than anyone could possibly teach. Consequently, teachers must select the content that seems most likely to be important to the students. This principle is sometimes called the **doctrine of contingent value**, that is, thorough coverage of the most important and useful content is more desirable than covering everything superficially. In general, a teacher should regard content not as an end in itself but as a means to knowledge. Learning that is not available for use is of little value.

Teachers sometimes forget that how a subject is taught affects content. For example learning a concept through a lecture is not the same as learning it through experimentation. Thus, to an extent, method is content. Therefore, when fitting a method to the content, you must consider what effect the method will have on a student's understanding, appreciation, and acquisition of skills.

The Nature of the Student

Middle school, junior high, and senior high school students are in the process of changing from children to adults. This change is so dramatic in the middle school years that educators call middle school students **transecents**. In a dramatic growth spurt transecents change from little boys and girls to gawky adolescents with new secondary sex characteristics and all the problems that come with new life roles. This growing up continues until the adolescent becomes a young adult—a process not finished until the post–high school years.

During transecence and the rest of adolescence, individual differences in physical, intellectual, social, and emotional growth are striking. Not only do individuals differ from one another but each seems to change markedly from day to day, for this is not only a period of growth but also a period of instability and insecurity. Becoming an adult is not an easy task. Although boys and girls desire opportunities to act independently, they generally need and want security and support. Because of these contrasting needs both for security and for escape from adult domination, young people tend to band together for mutual support as they experiment with new sociosexual roles. To find security, they often become conformists, extremely susceptible to peer pressure. Nevertheless, adolescents normally are self-motivated, active, and interested in novelty. Their intellectual growth causes them to be interested in ideas and allows them to cope with formal intellectual operations and abstract ideas. These desires cause some adolescents to adopt idealistic causes and cause others to try adventures and roles that can get them into trouble. Adolescence, including transecence, is a period of change, of new experiences, of learning new roles, of uncertainty and instability—undoubtedly one of the most trying times in life. Schools and teachers should provide opportunities for adolescents to explore and experiment in a stable, supportive atmosphere. An increasing number of middle schools have recognized that students in those early adolescent years need a special educational experience to nurture them through this unstable time, including interdisciplinary teaching teams and supportive guidance activities. Simply making minor changes in grade-level representation and changing the name of a school from "junior high" to "middle school" is ineffective. To be effective, techniques for teaching these students must be distinguishable from those that are commonly used in high school teaching.

Now proceed to do Exercises 1.3 and 1.4.

The Nature of Learning

Learning and the Brain

Learning is largely a function of the brain. Thus, your teaching should be compatible with the way it works. If recent research is accurate, much of traditional teaching practice may not meet that test. For instance, the age-old practices of sitting still, listening, doing only what one is told to do, and generally being a quiet recipient of imparted knowledge are probably not the most effective ways to learn. Rather, learning requires an active and stimulating environment, because the brain is naturally an aggressive problem solver that creates patterns out of the many inputs provided by the senses, confusing and complex as those inputs may be. Therefore, the richer the environment, the better the chances that the learner will develop good concepts, skills, and problem solutions.

Furthermore, to work best, the brain needs a supportive climate. Fear and threats tend to shut down the cerebral mechanisms that foster high-level thinking. Although a harsh, fear-dominated classroom may permit learning by rote memorization, such an environment cuts off creativity, original thinking, problem solving, and the understanding of major concepts. To make your classes most effective, you must provide a class atmosphere that is rich and challenging but not threatening.

LEARNING AS AN INDIVIDUAL MATTER

Students differ in their ability to learn, their readiness to learn, their learning skills, and their learning styles. Some of these differences may be innate, but most are the result of how the students have learned to learn, for skill in learning is learned. Teachers should take great care to teach the skills of learning—to teach students how to learn. Later modules detail procedures for doing this.

Teachers should also take into account and make adjustments for individual differences in orientation and learning style. Research has shown that how a person learns is connected to the differences in the left and right hemispheres of the brain. Verbal learning, logical thinking, and the academic cognitive processes seem dominated by the left hemisphere, whereas affective, intuitive, spatial, emotional, and visual elements seem dominated by the right hemisphere. Some people, it seems, tend to be oriented toward their right cerebral hemisphere, and others toward the left hemisphere. Therefore, teachers find that some students learn better through verbal teaching approaches, whereas others learn better through more visual or emotional instruction. As a result, some students are alienated by traditional academic instruction and so never progress to their full potential. To prevent this from happening, teachers in every classroom should include both affective and cognitive learning in their teaching, attempting to challenge the students' learning in each of these areas. All subject matter has both affective and cognitive elements. In early learning, it may be wise to cater to the orientation of the individual student. Later, it is best to provide opportunities for students to participate in a variety of activities that involve both types of learning.[3]

LEARNING STYLE

Such orientation is one of the elements that make up **learning style**, that is, the way individuals concentrate on, absorb, and retain new or difficult information or skills. According to one educator, learning style consists of "a combination of environmental, emotional, sociological, physical, and psychological elements that permit individuals to receive, store, and use knowledge or abilities."[4] This combination of elements in one's learning style is different for each person. Thus, some students are more comfortable in self-contained classes featuring direct, teacher-centered expository teaching; others react better in a mix of large-group, small-group, and independent study; others are best served by small discussion groups; and still others are most productive in independent study. Some students learn best in classes that emphasize logical presentations, others do better in classes that emphasize imagery. There are probably as many

---

[3]Thomas R. Blakeslee, "Brain Behavior Research," in *Student Learning Styles and Brain Behavior* (Reston, VA: National Association of Secondary School Principals, 1982), pp. 185–195.

[4]Rita Dunn, "Learning Style and Its Relation to Exceptionality at Both Ends of the Spectrum," *Exceptional Children* (April 1983), **49**:496–506.

EXERCISE 1.3 PERSONAL CHARACTERISTICS OF STUDENTS AND THE EFFECTS OF THOSE UPON THE EDUCATION AND LEARNING OF STUDENTS

Describe any evidence or feelings that you have that your own social class, race, subculture, or gender has affected your personal educational experiences and learning. Describe whether the effect has been positive or negative.

Share this with others in your class.
Follow up: Describe what you learned from this exercise.

EXERCISE 1.4   OBSERVATION AND COMPARISON OF SENIOR HIGH AND MIDDLE SCHOOL STUDENTS

In this exercise you will observe and compare the physical and behavioral patterns of senior high and middle school students. Select two classes, similar in subject (e.g., English, mathematics, social science, science), one of eleventh or twelfth grade students, the other of fifth, sixth, or seventh grade students. Make prior arrangements for your classroom observations; a follow-up thank you to the cooperating teachers and school principals would be appropriate. Record your observations by answering the following questions about the two sets of students, and then compare your responses with those of your classmates. (Try to visit both classes on the same day to avoid variables caused by day of week or the weather.)

	HIGH SCHOOL	**MIDDLE SCHOOL**
Name of school visited?	_____	_____
Grade level?	_____	_____
Subject of class?	_____	_____
Variation in height?	_____	_____
Variation in weight?	_____	_____
Variation in secondary sex characteristics?	_____	_____
Attentiveness to class?	_____	_____
Distractions by peers?	_____	_____

Variation in dress?   _____   _____

Variation in
appearance?   _____   _____

Apparent friendships in
class?   _____   _____

Cutting of peers?   _____   _____

Reactions to peers of
opposite sex?   _____   _____

Responses to peers of
same sex?   _____   _____

Physical contact with
peers?   _____   _____

Physical contact with
teacher?   _____   _____

Noise level of class?   _____   _____

Responses to teacher?   _____   _____

varieties of learning styles as there are individual students. Silver and Hanson, however, have divided learners according to four types:

1. The sensing-thinking learner who is practical, matter-of-fact, and work-oriented.
2. The sensing-feeling learner who is sympathetic and friendly and works for group harmony.
3. The intuitive-thinking learner who is theoretical, intellectual, and knowledge-oriented.
4. The intuitive-feeling learner who is curious, insightful, imaginative, and creative.[5]

Each of these types of learner needs an instructional approach that suits his or her learning style. Also, each learning style is more effective in certain learning situations than in others. When teachers match their teaching styles to students' learning styles—and when students learn to match their learning styles to the learning task—students' attitudes toward schoolwork and their achievement both improve.

Nevertheless, a teacher should not overly cater to student learning-style preferences. For instance, some students are scanners, whereas other students are focusers. Scanners are better in English; focusers are better in mathematics. Thus, students must be taught both styles if they are to be successful in both English and in mathematics. Perhaps the most useful approach you can make would be to follow these rules:

☐ Cater to individual styles as much as possible, particularly in the early stages of study.

☐ Use a mix of teaching styles so that students with different learning styles will have an opportunity to work in their preferred style at least some of the time.

☐ Teach students how to use different styles of learning suitable to the teaching situation, subject matter, and learning objectives.

Learning and Motivation

Learning also depends on student motivation. All learning takes place in relation to some student goal. If students' goals are not in harmony with the teacher's objectives, teaching becomes difficult. To make instruction most effective, teachers must utilize the students' natural goals or entice them to accept goals suitable to the instruction. Motivational techniques are discussed in Module 6. Now do and share Exercises 1.5 and 1.6.

Important Principles of Learning for the Twenty-First Century

Exercises 1.5 and 1.6 are designed to impress upon you certain important and basic principles of learning, principles that have evolved from studies of recent years. Three important principles are:

1. Students must be actively involved in their own learning and in the assessment of that learning.
2. Teachers must hold high expectations for the learning of each student.
3. Teachers must provide constant, steady, understandable, and reliable feedback to students about their learning.

Learning Modes

The mode of learning determines what is learned. A person does not learn to write by learning to recognize grammatical constructs of sentences. Neither does a person learn to swim by listening to a lecture on the Australian crawl. School learning becomes superficial when the teaching methods used are inappropriate for the understanding,

---

[5]Mary Alice Gunter and Phyllis Riley Hotchkiss, "Yuk, Peanut Butter Again: Avoiding Instructional Monotony," in *Action in Teacher Education* 7 (Fall 1985), pp. 31–35; citing H. F. Silver and R. J. Hanson, *Teaching Styles and Strategies* (Morristown: NJ: Institute for Cognitive and Behavioral Studies, 1982), pp. 6–7.

skills, and attitudes desired. Memorizing, for instance, is not the same as understanding. Yet, many students do little more than memorize information. The result is verbalism, the mouthing of little-understood words and sentences. To make learning real to students, teachers should use direct and realistic experiences whenever feasible. Vicarious experiences, such as those from reading about pyramids, are necessary to provide students with knowledge otherwise unattainable; however, direct experience of the real thing—when all the student's senses and all learning modalities are engaged—is more powerful.

Learning modalities are the sensory channels through which learners receive and retain information. They are the keys to learning. Organizing instruction around one or more of these channels is called modality-based instruction.[6] The modalities of importance to the classroom teacher are the visual (seeing), the auditory (hearing), tactile (touching), and the kinesthetic (moving). Teaching strategies that engage all four modalities will reach more students, and the student learning will be longer lived.

Concept Presentation

In presenting a concept, a teacher should provide numerous examples, thereby letting the students consider the idea from various perspectives in order to establish relationships and draw conclusions. Remember, a teacher cannot simply give concepts to a student in the same way that a teacher imparts information. The understanding of a concept requires the student's active participation.

Skill Development

Skills are best learned through experience. At the beginning, the teacher must teach the students how to perform the skill, and teacher explanations and demonstrations can be very effective. In this process, showing how is usually more useful than telling how. But the skill itself is best learned through guided practice. Teachers can take difficult skills apart so that students can practice the hard-to-master portions separately, but complete mastery can come only with extended practice of the entire skill, under supervision. Only through guided practice can a student eliminate improper procedures and perfect the techniques, and this is true of both psychomotor and cognitive skills.

In middle, junior, and senior high schools, perhaps most important are the academic and thinking skills. And student failure is often the result of teachers' neglecting to teach their students how to study, how to take tests, how to do their assignments, and how to learn in general. All teachers should give students instruction in these skills. Teachers should also develop classes and courses that give students plenty of opportunities to practice such thinking skills.

Attitude Development

Teachers can teach attitudes by providing both a conducive atmosphere and models that students can emulate. Acquiring knowledge and developing understanding can enhance the learning of attitudes. Nevertheless, changing an attitude is often a long process, requiring the commitment of the teacher and the provision of numerous experiences that will guide students to new convictions.

Readiness

No matter what you want to teach, instruction cannot be effective until the students are ready to learn that content. In simple terms, **readiness** is the combination of maturity, ability, motivation, and prior learning that makes it possible for a person to learn something. For instance, a kindergartner is not ready to read *The Tempest*. Students' lack of readiness can create problems for teachers. In some cases, when a lack of maturity is the problem, the only solution may be to direct efforts elsewhere until the student is ready. In other cases, when the student lacks a skill or prerequisite

---

[6]*See* Walter B. Barbe and Raymond H. Swassing, *Teaching Through Modality Strengths: Concepts and Practices* (Columbus, OH: Zaner-Bloser, Inc., 1988).

EXERCISE 1.5   MY PERCEPTIONS OF HOW I LEARN
Sources of Motivation

The purpose of this exercise is for you to explore your present understanding of what motivates you to learn. Answer the following questions and then share those answers with your colleagues. When answering these questions, don't concern yourself with whether your answers are "right" or "wrong."

1. How do you define what is learning?

2. Do you think there is any difference in the way you personally learn for short-term retention as opposed to the way you learn for long-term retention? If so, explain that difference.

3. Identify and rank order (from most important to least important) what you believe to be at least three sources of motivation for your own learning. For each, identify by writing either *I* or *E* in the blank whether you believe that source is Intrinsic (within yourself) or Extrinsic (grades, rewards, expectations of others, etc.).

_____ a.

_____ b.

_____ c.

_____ d.

_____ e.

4. Did you ever learn something that you previously had thought you could never have learned? Explain, describing what motivated you and helped you to learn it.

EXERCISE 1.6   MY PERCEPTIONS OF HOW I LEARN
Techniques Used

The purpose of this exercise is for you to explore your present understanding of how you learn best. Answer the following questions and then share those answers with your colleagues. When answering these questions, don't concern yourself with whether your answers are "right" or "wrong."

1. When in a class, how do you study for an examination? Check each of the following techniques you use, then elaborate with an example that will help you explain it to others. For each technique that you use, circle *S* or *L* to indicate that you believe you use this technique primarily for short-term (S) or long-term (L) retention.

_____ a. *Outline* material?   S   L

_____ b. Use *mnemonic* devices?   S   L

_____ c. Make *connections* (i.e., build bridges) of the new material with your prior knowledge, experiences, attitudes, beliefs, or values (this is known as elaboration)?   S   L

_____ d. Write *summaries* of important ideas?   S   L

_____ e. Construct *visual (graphic) representations* (e.g., charts, graphs, maps, or networks) of verbal material to be learned?   S   L

_____ f. Participate in *cooperative study* groups?   S   L

_____ g. *Teach others* what you have learned or are learning?   S   L

_____ h. Other?   S   L

2. From your selections and descriptions to the first question, do you believe that there is any difference in how you learn, depending on whether you are learning for short-term or long-term retention? If so, in a paragraph describe this difference.

3. Now share your answers to questions one and two with your colleagues, and compare their results with your own. How do they compare?

4. From this exercise, what can you conclude? What have you learned about your own learning? About how others learn?

knowledge, a teacher can solve the problem by correcting the deficiency—that is, by making the student ready.

Retention and Transferability

For learning to be of value to the learner, it must be retained and also be transferable. Solid, thorough learning helps a person remember what has been learned and provides a basis for transferring what has been learned to new situations. Frequent renewal and reinforcement of the learning also aid in retention and transferability. And the more a person uses what has been learned, the better a person can remember and transfer it. Teachers can further facilitate transfer by pointing out uses in various circumstances, both during the initial teaching and later during the renewal, reinforcement, or review teaching.

Time on Task

How time is used by the teacher and by that teacher's students is more important than is the amount of time allocated for instructional time. Students learn less in a class in which the teacher spends a great deal of time in noninstructional or noninteractive activities. Students achieve less in a class in which the teacher sits and grades papers or works on lesson plans while the students sit quietly reading or working on assignments. Students learn less in a class in which there is a considerable amount of instructional time wasted on discussion of behavior problems or in making instructional transitions. Therefore, teachers must make sure that in their classes students have real learning activities to do and—except for breaks at opportune moments—are actually engaged in those activities. What counts more is not the amount of time allowed for learning activities but the amount of time the students spend actively and interactively engaged.

Direct Versus Indirect Instruction

Both direct (or didactic or traditional) and indirect (or experiential) instruction have a place in a teacher's repertoire. Direct instruction is primarily teacher-centered—typically large-group, highly structured expository teaching focused on academic content. It features lecture and explanation, controlled practice, and question-answer sessions as well as other highly teacher-directed activities. In this type of teaching the teacher provides students with feedback in the form of criticism, comments, questions, hints, suggestions, and, where appropriate, praise. Direct instruction covers a large amount of content and aims to keep students actively engaged. Teachers using this type of teaching monitor students' work to encourage an optimum of profitable student time on task. In the controlled discussions teachers emphasize questions on factual information—moving from the simple to the more difficult—and follow with teacher commentary and criticism. In direct instruction, teachers maintain virtually complete control of the content, pace, sequence, and processes of the instruction.

Generally, indirect instruction is more student-centered than direct instruction (though it does include teacher talk in which the teachers indirectly influence students.) The teacher attempts to get the students themselves to discover things and develop ideas. Indirect instruction includes open discussions, inquiry and discovery lessons, individual and small-group work, and various projects, as well as numerous multitask activities in which students largely control the conduct of their learning activities. In these activities the teacher does not give the students knowledge as much as attempt to guide the students in their own search for knowledge.

You need to be able to conduct both direct and indirect instruction. Direct instruction seems most useful for teaching fundamental skills and knowledge. Indirect instruction often works better when teaching higher-order and affective content.

The Nature of Groups

In schools almost all teaching is done in groups. Such teaching proves most effective when the climate of the group is positive, that is, when the students and the teacher know and accept one another and work harmoniously toward common group goals. A positive climate works because feelings of personal worth, belonging, and security tend to support learning. This classroom condition is most likely to occur when the group is cohesive and diffusely structured. Diffusely structured groups are those free from in-group concerns—self-esteem is spread evenly throughout rather than concentrated in a few stars or favorites. Communications in diffusely structured groups are generally open, and the class norms allow for a wide range of behavior, thus creating an atmosphere of tolerance and good feeling. Groups with these characteristics tend to develop feelings of cohesiveness and togetherness. When such an atmosphere is coupled with the cooperation of the natural student leaders in the class, teaching and learning usually progress smoothly and efficiently.

Developing a Teaching Style

Every teacher develops a personal style of teaching with which the teacher feels most comfortable. This teaching style includes a combination of personal traits as well as the amount of expertise a teacher has in methodology, subject matter, and pedagogical theory. The most effective teachers can vary their styles—that is, their styles are flexible enough to encompass a great number of strategies and tactics and are therefore readily adaptable to the different sorts of situations that may develop. Effective teachers can modify their styles by selecting and using the strategy that is most appropriate, thus securing active student involvement and the greatest amount of student achievement. Highly effective teaching of this sort requires both expertise in a wide variety of methods and a feeling for the appropriate situation in which to use each method, as well as a good command of the subject matter and an understanding of the students being taught. This may sound like a large order, but many beginning teachers become adept at this kind of teaching style and do so surprisingly quickly.

Thus, to be an effective teacher you should: (1) master a large repertoire of techniques—both direct and indirect—in order to be prepared for many contingencies; and (2) develop an open style of teaching that allows you to be flexible and adaptable.

In addition, you will want to incorporate into your teaching style the characteristics of the most effective teachers. The following are ten characteristics of effective teachers:

1. The effective teacher knows the students, their styles, their strengths and weaknesses, their knowledge and skills, and how they learn best.

2. The effective teacher is well prepared, that is, a master of content who carefully plans the lessons.

3. The effective teacher is well organized. That teacher's classes move along smoothly and briskly, with a minimum of confusion, overlapping, dead spots, irrelevancies, sudden shifts in direction without appropriate transitions, and inappropriate behavior.

4. The effective teacher is businesslike and conducts a businesslike class in which each student's class time is concentrated on accomplishing learning tasks.

5. The effective teacher is a good manager. The students know what they are supposed to do and do it because from the very first day the teacher carefully maps out the rules of behavior and the consequences of inappropriate behavior, sets up definite and clearly understood routines for classroom procedures, and makes clear and relevant assignments, pointing out what the students are to do, how they are to do it, and why they do it.

6. The effective teacher makes manifest by his or her behavior to the students that each student is respected by the teacher, that the teacher is sincerely concerned about each student's progress and welfare, and that the teacher confidently expects each student to do well.

7. The effective teacher adjusts the teaching method to fit the subject matter, the objectives, the group, and the individual students.

8. The effective teacher monitors student performance carefully and continually, providing frequent comprehension checks, giving students individual and constructive feedback about their work and progress, and taking particular care to recognize individual student accomplishment, however slight.

9. The effective teacher is an effective communicator, who uses thoughtfully selected words, carefully planned questions, expressive voice inflections, useful pauses, meaningful gestures, and productive and expressive body language.

10. The effective teacher is quick to recognize a student who may be in need of special attention, knows where and how to refer a student whose behaviors indicate a need for more specialized attention, and can do so with minimal class disruption or embarrassment to the student.

These characteristics will be developed more fully in the remaining modules of the book.

A Pattern for Teaching

You should also incorporate into your teaching style the following five-step pattern that comprises a model for effective teaching. The steps of this model are:

1. Diagnosis

2. Preparation

3. Guidance of learning

4. Evaluation of learning

5. Follow-up (or follow through)

Diagnosis refers to the initial assessment of the situation. In this step, the teacher assesses the students' present state of knowledge as well as their needs and desires as a basis for determining what should be done.

In the next step, the teacher gets ready for the instruction. Preparation includes planning lessons, devising motivational strategies, gathering materials and equipment, and arranging the setting for instruction.

Guidance of learning includes the actual instruction—showing students how, presenting information, and providing constructive feedback to students about their work.

In the fourth step, the teacher evaluates students' progress and, in so doing, the success of the instruction. Evaluation, an ongoing process, provides information to both the teacher and the students about where they have made progress and where they have not. Evaluation is the basis for determining the next step.

In the final step of this five-step pattern, the teacher follows up the instruction by helping students fill in what they have missed and building on what they have learned.

These five steps tend to merge together. The evaluation and follow-up for one unit or lesson may become the diagnosis, preparation, and guiding-learning phases for the next one. But, even if truncated, this five-step sequence is always evident in good teaching.

SUMMARY

In this module we have outlined the theoretical principles for effective secondary and middle school teaching. Imbedded in these principles and critical to the effectiveness of a teacher is that teacher's planning for instruction, the topic of the next module.

SUGGESTED READING

Alexander, W. M. "The Middle School: What? Why? How? How Well?" *California ASCD Journal for Supervision and Curriculum Development* 2(3):6–13 (Spring-Summer 1989).

Caine, R. N., and Caine, G. "Understanding a Brain-Based Approach to Learning and Teaching." *Educational Leadership* 48(2):66–70 (October 1990).

Caught in the Middle: Educational Reform for Young Adolescents in California Public Schools. Report of the Superintendent's Task Force. Sacramento: California State Department of Education, 1987.

Curry, L. "A Critique of the Research on Learning Styles." *Educational Leadership* 48(2):50–56 (October 1990).

Derry, S. A. "Putting Learning Strategies to Work." *Educational Leadership* 46(4):4–10 (December 1988/January 1989).

Dunn, R., and Griggs, S. A. *Learning Styles: Quiet Revolution in Secondary Schools.* Reston, VA: National Association of Secondary School Principals, 1988.

Eichhorn, D. H. *The Middle School.* New York: Center for Applied Research in Education, 1966.

Fenwick, J. J. *The Middle School Years.* San Diego, CA: Fenwick Associates, 1986.

Gazzaniga, M. *Mind Matters: How the Mind and Brain Interact to Create Our Conscious Lives.* Boston: Houghton Mifflin, 1988.

George, P. S., and Oldaker, L. L. *Evidence for the Middle School.* Columbus, OH: National Middle School Association, 1985.

Johnston, J. H., and Markle, G. C. *What Research Says to the Middle Level Practitioner.* Columbus, OH: National Middle School Association, 1986.

Keefe, J. W. "Learning Style: Where are we going?" *Momentum* 21(1):44–48 (Feb 1990).

Klivington, K. *The Science of Mind.* Boston: MIT Press, 1989.

McCarthy, B. "Using the 4MAT System to Bring Learning Styles to Schools." *Educational Leadership* 48(2):31–37 (October, 1990).

Moss, T. C. *Middle School.* Boston: Houghton Mifflin, 1969.

Mosston, M., and Ashworth, S. *The Spectrum of Teaching Styles.* White Plains, NY: Longman, 1989.

Newman, J. W. *America's Teachers: An Introduction to Education.* White Plains: Longman, 1990.

Ornstein, A., and Levine, D. U. *Foundations of Education.* 4th ed. Boston: Houghton Mifflin, 1989.

Resnick, L. B., and Klopfer, L. E. (eds.) *Toward the Thinking Curriculum: Current Cognitive Research.* 1989 ASCD Yearbook. Alexandria, VA: Association for Supervision and Curriculum Development, 1989.

Springer, S., and Deutsch, G. *Left Brain, Right Brain.* New York: W. H. Freeman, 1989.

Titus, T. G. et al. "Adolescent Learning Styles." *Journal of Research and Development in Education* 24(3):165–171 (September 1990).

Tye, K. *The Junior High School: A School in Search of a Mission.* Lanham, MD: University Press of America, 1985.

U.S. Department of Education. *What Works: Research About Teaching and Learning.* Washington, D.C.: U.S. Department of Education, 1986.

Weinstein, C. E.; Bridley, D. S.; Dahl, T.; and Weber, E. W. "Helping Students Develop Strategies for Effective Learning." *Educational Leadership* 46(4):17–19 (December 1988/January 1989).

Wiles, J., and Bondi, Jr. *Making Middle Schools Work.* Alexandria, VA: Association for Supervision and Curriculum Development, 1987.

Matching   Match the steps in column I with the tasks listed in column II. A step may include more than one task. All entries in column II should be used, and some will be used more than once.

I	II
_____ 1. Diagnosis	a. Lesson planning
_____ 2. Preparation	b. Testing
_____ 3. Guidance of learning	c. Pretesting
_____ 4. Evaluation of learning	d. Reteaching
_____ 5. Follow-up	e. Instruction
	f. Room arrangement
	g. Beginning the next lesson
	h. Estimating students' prior knowledge

Check   Check the statements that accurately complete this sentence: Effective teachers _____ .

_____   6. are masters of the subject content

_____   7. use a variety of teaching methods

_____   8. run permissive laissez-faire classes

_____   9. expect their students to do well

_____ 10. monitor student performance carefully

_____ 11. know their students' strengths and weaknesses

_____ 12. avoid routinizing classroom procedures

_____ 13. can use both direct and indirect instructional strategies

_____ 14. demonstrate respect for their students

_____ 15. adjust method to content

_____ 16. insist on absolutely quiet classes

_____ 17. provide students with individual feedback about their learning

Multiple Choice   Place the letter of the best answer in the blank provided. If two or more of the choices seem correct, select the one most applicable to the situation.

_____ 18. To encourage retention of learning, you should
  a. use memory drills.
  b. use mnemonic devices.
  c. emphasize thorough learning.
  d. emphasize transfer values.

_____ 19. One would expect to ascertain a student's readiness to learn in which of the following steps?
  a. Diagnosis
  b. Preparation
  c. Evaluation
  d. Follow-up

_____ 20. Learning skills are
  a. learned.
  b. innate.
  c. inherited.
  d. instinctive.

_____ 21. Transecence is a period of
  a. stability.
  b. self-confidence.
  c. change.
  d. independence from peer pressure.

_____ 22. According to the doctrine of contingent value, the teacher should
   a. accentuate the subject matter that is most likely to be valuable to the students.
   b. accentuate content that is relevant to students now.
   c. accentuate the basics.
   d. accentuate the eternal values.

_____ 23. When selecting teaching methods you should remember that
   a. indirect methods are superior to direct methods.
   b. problem solving is the heart of all good teaching.
   c. the method you use will to some extent determine the content the students learn.
   d. exposition is the best type of teaching method.

_____ 24. To establish a positive group climate, try to make the group
   a. centrally structured.
   b. cohesive.
   c. elitist.
   d. teacher-centered.

_____ 25. Your teaching style should be
   a. teacher-centered.
   b. student-centered.
   c. eclectic.
   d. indirect.

_____ 26. True middle schools are
   a. no longer in existence in the United States.
   b. those schools designed for students ranging in age 9 to 14.
   c. those schools that used to be known as junior high schools.
   d. those schools that house departmentalized seventh and eighth grades.

_____ 27. It is recommended that you develop a larger repertoire of teaching techniques so that
   a. you can utilize more fully the strategies of direct instruction.
   b. you can utilize more fully the strategies of indirect instruction.
   c. you can cover the subject matter more easily.
   d. you can better adapt your teaching to particular teaching-learning situations.

_____ 28. Middle school students are usually
   a. children.
   b. transecents.
   c. adolescents.
   d. young adults.

_____ 29. Teaching is best described as
   a. forming students' minds.
   b. helping students learn.
   c. guiding study.
   d. instructing students.

_____ 30. The real test of one's teaching is
   a. the excellence of the planning.
   b. the degree the lesson interests people.
   c. how well the students have learned.
   d. the teacher's classroom control.

_____ 31. In selecting teaching methods it is important to remember that
   a. students differ from each other.
   b. students prefer easy assignments.
   c. high school students cannot think abstractly.
   d. vicarious experience is preferable to direct experience.

_____ 32. Time on task refers to
     a. the length of the lesson.
     b. time allotted for a learning activity.
     c. time students spend actually working on a learning activity.
     d. estimated time to complete a unit of study.

_____ 33. Which of the following is most typical of indirect teaching?
     a. controlled practice.
     b. teacher-centered methods.
     c. expository teaching methods.
     d. open discussion.

_____ 34. To make your teaching successful, you should
     a. teach each student in the same way.
     b. match your teaching to each student's learning style.
     c. use a mix of teaching strategies so as to accommodate different learning styles.
     d. emphasize deep-focus learning styles.

_____ 35. To teach skills the teacher should emphasize
     a. supervised practice.
     b. inductive learning.
     c. indirect learning.
     d. rote learning.

_____ 36. For learning, the brain responds best when
     a. the input is strict and harsh.
     b. the input is threatening.
     c. the input is complex.
     d. the input is simple.

_____ 37. To promote higher-order learning it is best to
     a. make classes challenging.
     b. insist on absolute quiet.
     c. concentrate on right-brain learning.
     d. concentrate on direct teaching.

_____ 38. In teaching it is best to
     a. concentrate on right-brain learning.
     b. concentrate on left-brain learning.
     c. cater to the student's preference.
     d. teach toward both hemispheres.

_____ 39. Learning style is
     a. an indication of one's intelligence.
     b. genetic.
     c. unchangeable.
     d. different from individual to individual.

_____ 40. Students learn best in
     a. a challenging atmosphere.
     b. a very strict, repressed atmosphere.
     c. a very permissive atmosphere.
     d. quiet surroundings.

PART II
PLANNING FOR INSTRUCTION

Part II, consisting of four modules, deals with your understanding of the:

□ Reasons for advertent planning for instruction.

□ Essential elements of instructional planning.

□ Available resources for planning.

□ Value of cooperative planning.

□ Preparation of a course plan.

□ Types of instructional objectives.

□ Process of preparing instructional objectives.

□ Types and formats of unit and lesson plans.

□ Process of preparing your own unit and lesson plans.

□ Importance of individualizing the instruction.

□ Process of beginning your resource file.

There is probably only one person's behavior we have the power to control, train, and modify: our own!

—Art Costa

Imagination is more important than knowledge.

—Albert Einstein

MODULE 2
Principles of
Instructional Planning

RATIONALE

Planning is a large part of every teacher's job, and each teacher is responsible for planning at three levels: the planning of courses, the planning of units, and the planning of lessons. Throughout your career you and your fellow teachers will be engaged almost continually in the process of planning on one of these three levels. Thus the importance of mastering the process at the very start of your career cannot be overemphasized.

A **course** can be defined as a complete sequence of instruction that presents to the students a major division of subject matter or a discipline. A **unit** is a major subdivision of a course, comprising planned instruction about some central theme, topic, issue, or problem for a period of several days to a maximum of three weeks. Units that last much longer than three weeks tend to lose their effectiveness as recognizable units of learning. A **lesson** is a subdivision of a unit, usually taught in a single period or, on occasion, two or three successive periods.

Courses may be laid out for a year, a semester, a quarter, or, in the case of minicourses, a few weeks. Units ordinarily are shorter than courses. A minicourse is, in effect, a free-standing unit and should be treated as a unit as far as planning is concerned. In many school systems, teachers as members of curriculum-planning committees and workshops also participate in the planning of the entire curriculum.

Although careful planning is a critical skill for a teacher, a well-developed plan for teaching will not guarantee the success of a lesson or unit or even the overall effectiveness of a course. But the lack of a well-developed plan will almost certainly result in failure. Like a good map, a good plan facilitates reaching the goal with more confidence and with fewer wrong turns.

The heart of planning is decision making. For every plan, you must decide what your objectives are, what specific subject matter should be taught, what materials of instruction are available and appropriate, and what methods and techniques you should use to accomplish your objectives. Making such decisions is complicated because there are almost as many different teaching variations as there are teachers. Therefore, you must be familiar with the principles that undergird good lesson, unit, and course planning. That the principles of all educational planning are much the same makes mastering the necessary planning skills easier than it might be.

This module describes the importance of teacher planning, what that planning involves, and how it is done. In Module 3 you will learn how to write objectives, in Module 4 you will learn different types of unit plans, and then in Module 5 you will put it all together and prepare your own unit plan, complete with daily lessons.

SPECIFIC OBJECTIVES

At the completion of this module, you should be able to:

1. Explain why planning is essential to good teaching.
2. Explain the dangers of teaching without a plan.
3. Describe the essential elements in any plan: deciding what one wishes to accomplish and how to accomplish it.
4. Describe the purposes and values of general and specific objectives.
5. Describe the criteria that one should use in selecting learning experiences to include in the teaching plans.
6. Identify the principal resources available for use in planning.
7. Explain the purpose and procedures of teacher planning.
8. Explain the rationale for teacher-student planning.

MODULE TEXT   **The Importance of Planning**

A teacher who has not planned or has planned poorly will fail. Careful planning is essential for effective teaching. It helps produce well-organized classes and a purposeful classroom atmosphere because it reduces the likelihood of problems in classroom management and control. Also, planning helps guarantee that the teacher knows the subject, for in planning carefully the teacher becomes master of the material and the methods of teaching it. No teacher can know all there is to know about the subject matter of any course, but careful planning keeps the teacher from fumbling through half-digested, half-understood content, making errors along the way. Planning is likely to make classes more lively, more interesting, more accurate, and more relevant.

Teachers who do not plan carefully are asking for trouble. Teaching without adequate written planning is likely to be sloppy and ineffective because the teacher has not thought out exactly what to do and how to do it. Even plans that were previously done and successfully implemented need constant revision in order to update the content, to make it relevant to the current students, and to make the best use of new technology and instructional materials.

Essential Elements

Two elements are necessary in any plan: (1) deciding what one wishes to accomplish and (2) deciding how to go about accomplishing it. They require that you as the teacher (and perhaps your students as well) ask yourself such essential questions as:

1. What do I want to accomplish?
2. How can I accomplish it?
3. Who is to do what?
4. When and in what order should events occur?
5. What resources are available, and where are they?
6. What materials and equipment are needed, and where are they?
7. How will I get things started?
8. How will I follow up?
9. How can I tell whether I have accomplished the goals?

Before continuing with the text, do Exercise 2.1, to review the elements of planning.

There is at least one important question missing from the preceding list. Perhaps you identified it or it surfaced during your discussion of Exercise 2.1. That question is "Why?" Why should students learn the content? Why do you want them to achieve these objectives? It is important that you always understand the why. When a student asks you, "Why do I have to learn this stuff?" you should have at the tip of your tongue a legitimate reason, one thought out long before the question was asked. All too frequently, teachers have not the slightest idea why students should study the content of their courses (except, perhaps, because it is in the textbook or is on the state-administered standardized tests). This lack contributes to the perception that much of what is taught in school is irrelevant to the lives and needs of both the students and the larger community. To avoid that perception, you as teacher should prepare a statement of rationale for every unit you teach in which you explain what the students are to learn and why they are to learn it. And before beginning the unit, you should share the rationale with your students.

Before continuing with the text, do Exercise 2.2.

At this stage in your professional development, the previous list of nine questions may seem formidable or even overwhelming. But be assured that as you begin to use them in planning for your classes, they will soon become an automatic part of your teaching style.

Let us begin our study of planning techniques by considering the first of the two elements identified earlier—what one wishes to accomplish, that is, the objectives of the instruction.

Objectives and Planning

Just as it is difficult to overemphasize the importance of planning, it is also difficult to overemphasize the importance of well-conceived and clearly stated objectives. In one sense, it is impossible to do any real planning until you have decided what you want to do. In teaching, deciding on the objectives means deciding what you hope the students will learn: What facts? What concepts? What skills? What attitudes? What appreciations? What ideals? The objectives are the foundation on which the teacher builds the plan of action. They provide the basis for your decisions regarding the choice of content, material, and methods and techniques that make up your strategy for teaching the course, unit, or lesson.

For example, suppose you are in New York City and want to go to San Francisco. Your objective is to go to San Francisco. Having this objective in mind, you then decide on a plan of action, a strategy for achieving your objective. You might decide to leave on Monday or Friday or maybe next month. You might decide to drive or go by train, bus, or airplane. You might decide to go by the shortest route possible or take the long scenic route or even to go by way of the Panama Canal. All of these alternatives would bring you to your objective, San Francisco. But notice that without the objective, the various alternatives would have no meaning. Perhaps subobjectives exist that can help eliminate certain of your alternatives. For instance, you may want to stop enroute to visit your aunt in St. Louis. That subobjective would certainly eliminate some of the alternatives, making your decision-making process somewhat less complicated. The unavailability of certain resources, such as money, might also help in your decision making.

For another example closer to the teaching profession, suppose your objective in a history course is to teach students basic concepts underlying democratic freedom. You must plan a course that would best serve that objective. You might decide that the content should include the Magna Charta, the Bill of Rights, and similar documents. Or you might decide that to concentrate on modern examples of freedom, fairness, rights, and responsibilities would be more effective. You might decide that it would be best to lecture, or to show videos, or to use role playing, or to allow free discussion, or perhaps to combine several of these. You might decide that the students ought to study original documents, scholarly discussions, popular reading, textbooks, or learning-activity packets. When it comes to deciding what to do to achieve a teaching objective, an effective teacher's options sometimes seem limitless. Every option, though, should be based on achieving the objective.

As you select objectives and the teaching strategies, there are several things you must consider in order to make reasonable decisions. One consideration is the curriculum. A second consideration is the nature of the learners: are they bright or slow, mature or immature, advantaged or disadvantaged? What are their interests, goals, and general tendencies of behavior? A third consideration is what you have to work with: materials, equipment, software, texts, and reading materials. A fourth consideration is the nature of the community, its resources and its expectations. And a final consideration is the nature of the subject matter or discipline to be taught.

Before continuing with the text, do Exercise 2.3.

Generally, educators speak of two types of objectives: general objectives and specific objectives. **General objectives**, sometimes referred to as goals, are broad concepts, skills, attitudes, appreciations, and ideals, such as "to develop an appreciation for music" or "to develop the habit of reflective thinking in specific situations." **Specific objectives**, in contrast, are narrower, the achievement of which will bring about the general objectives. An example of a specific objective is "at the conclusion of the unit, students will be able to demonstrate three techniques for checking the validity of a hypothesis." Course plans are usually built around goals (general objectives), lesson plans around specific objectives, and unit plans around a combination of the two.

EXERCISE 2.1   REVIEWING THE ELEMENTS OF PLANNING

In this exercise you will review the elements of planning. Review the list of nine essential questions for instructional planning by answering the following, and review your responses with your classmates.

1. Is each of the questions important? Explain why or why not for each.

2. Identify other questions that you think you should ask yourself when planning a lesson, unit, or course.

3. Review your responses with your classmates and then clearly identify what you have learned from this exercise.

EXERCISE 2.2 ANALYZING CONTENT FOR RATIONALE

The purpose of this exercise is to analyze content as found in student textbooks for the subject(s) you intend to teach. Select one or more textbooks in your subject field, textbooks used by students of middle school, junior high, or senior high school. (Textbooks for this exercise may be borrowed from your college or university library collection, or from teachers in the field, perhaps those whom you met while doing Exercises 1.2 and 1.3.) From each book select one chapter and respond to the following questions.

Textbook title _____ Grade level _____

Chapter title _____

1. After reading the selected chapter, identify *specifically* what, if anything, you would want a student to know as a result of studying that chapter.

2. Write a statement of rationale that addresses why the student should know this material.

3. What reasons can you give as to why a student should study your subject field as a whole?

4. There is much talk and activity about the importance of the "basics." What are the basics in your subject field?

5. Share your responses to the previous four questions with others in your class, then identify what you have learned from this exercise.

EXERCISE 2.3 PLANNING FOR A COURSE

In this exercise, you will begin thinking about preparing to teach a course. Answer the following two questions, then share your responses with your classmates. Assume that you are teaching a ninth-grade course in your major field.

Identify the course by title: _____

1. What specifics would you need to know about the curriculum, students, resources, and the like, in order to plan the course?

2. We hear a lot about making teaching relevant. Is this really important? If so, what do you need to know in order to make your teaching relevant?

A Plan for Action

As already noted, the bulk of any plan consists of the content and methods the teacher has decided to use to meet the objectives. The content and the teaching methods must be designed so that they contribute to the achievement of the goal. For instance, if your goal is to teach students to be skillful in thinking scientifically, then you must design course content and procedures that actually give students training and practice in thinking scientifically. Memorizing formulas and learning the textbook by rote will not achieve that goal, because such tasks will not give students a chance to think scientifically. Similarly, if you wish to teach students to express themselves well in writing, you must provide them with experiences in writing. Learning rules of grammar may help, but that will not do the entire job. Sometimes teachers seem to forget this basic fact: if you want students to learn something, your content and procedures must be appropriate for what you want them to learn.

Before continuing with the text, do Exercise 2.4.

Of course, in selecting your content and methods there are a number of other considerations you must keep in mind. Among them are degree of difficulty, interest levels, suitability for students' backgrounds, and feasibility.

Evaluating the Plan

Effective teachers evaluate their plans to find out how these plans succeeded and in what ways they can be improved. By always saving the good plans and the good parts of mediocre plans, as well as by revising (or discarding) the poor plans or poor parts of mediocre plans, you will steadily build a collection of sound plans and a repertoire of effective teaching procedures. No plan, however, should ever be set in concrete. Even the most effective plans eventually have to be revised, because students change, the available technology and materials change, and content changes.

Resources for Planning

Planning courses, units, and lessons is time-consuming work, but such planning is often enjoyable and not really too difficult. Usually, you need not do it entirely from scratch, alone and unassisted. You can make your beginning years in the classroom easier by starting a file of material and ideas while you are in your professional training. (Exercise 2.6 will get you started in building your resource file.) In addition, once you begin to teach, department heads, supervisors, and other teachers are usually ready to give you the benefit of their experiences. Some school systems have prepared curriculum guides, courses of study, and syllabuses for the courses offered in their schools (for high school accreditation, these are required). These documents, written by teachers, are generally explanations and outlines of the courses in the curriculum. They usually suggest topics to be included in courses, general goals for courses, specific objectives for units, and materials and methods that might be used, as well as a helpful bibliography. Use them. In some school systems, teachers are expected to follow them closely. In fact, in some districts a teacher may be released from his or her teaching duties for not following the prescribed course of study.

In other school districts, the guides, courses of study, and syllabuses are merely suggestions that you may or may not use. You should study them and use what seems to be good for your purposes. During your student teaching as well as your initial years as a teacher, you need to know what the district expects of you with respect to following the courses of study.

Some school systems have adopted standardized curriculums that include course outlines, prepackaged text material, exercises, assignments, audiovisual materials, and locally standardized tests. When these are provided, much of your planning has been taken care of. But these materials will not teach! Many teachers have found it necessary to change and adapt them. When change is needed, supervisors, department heads, and other teachers will undoubtedly advise you. Some school systems have published resource units for particular units of study. **Resource units** (as opposed to actual teaching units) are general plans for a unit or a particular topic designed to be used as the basis for building a teaching-unit plan. Resource units are usually rich in suggestions for teaching the unit. In them you will find suggestions for objectives, content, methods, readings, audiovisual resources, community resources, and other teaching materials suitable for that unit.

Some schools may provide no guide, syllabus, or course of study. In that case, the beginning teacher has several options to choose from. One is to use curriculum guides, syllabuses, courses of study, and resource units from other school systems. These may be just as helpful to you as to the teachers in the other school system, though they should never be followed slavishly. These can usually be found in the central office or curriculum centers of city, regional, county, or school administrative districts, as well as at the curriculum libraries of teacher-preparation colleges and universities. Other sources usually available in curriculum libraries are the curriculum materials on various topics published by state departments of education, large city school systems, professional organizations, the federal government, and commercial publishing houses. Some of the resource units published by organizations and governmental agencies are especially helpful. The more of these resources you have available, the better off you will be. Therefore, if possible, become familiar with the curriculum and teaching resources at your college or in the district where you now live. And begin to collect materials for the day when you will need them in your own classroom.

For secondary school teachers, particularly those teaching in high schools, the most common of the resources for course, unit, and lesson planning is the textbook. In addition to its expository role, the textbook usually provides both an organized outline of the subject matter field and such teaching aids as study questions, exercises, test questions, and suggestions for learning activities and further study. Most middle, junior high, and senior high school textbooks on the market today provide instructor's manuals that can be of great help in the planning process.

Beware, however, of becoming a slave to the textbook. You, the teacher, should be the master. Undoubtedly you are more familiar with your own teaching goals and skills; the students' needs, abilities, and inclinations; and the local school requirements than a textbook author living far away. Use the textbook as a base—secondary school students generally need a single textbook for the course—but do not let the textbook prevent you from the creative, flexible teaching that will best suit your students and your instructional goals. Remember, the textbook may be a source of inspiration for your instructional objectives, but those instructional objectives should determine what you teach and how you teach it.

Other resources close at hand are your college textbooks. Although these are likely to be written at a level unsuitable for your students, they can sometimes be an excellent source of ideas, pictures, charts, and other information adaptable for use in your own classes.

Before continuing the text, do Exercise 2.5 and Exercise 2.6.

Cooperative Planning

Team Planning

In some schools teachers plan together in teams. These teams may be teaching teams in which teachers share the teaching of a block course, a course that may meet for a couple of hours each morning. Block courses are common for certain cross-discipline studies in early middle school grades. For example, a team might consist of an English teacher, a mathematics teacher, a science teacher, and a social studies teacher. The team meets regularly once to several times a week to plan together and to coordinate activities and assignments. Teams of this type are quite common in middle schools.

In high schools, planning teams often consist of all teachers who teach the same course. For example, all teachers of biology may convene on a regular basis to plan a common curriculum for all sophomore biology classes.

EXERCISE 2.4 PRACTICE IN SELECTING STRATEGIES TO MATCH A GOAL

In this exercise, you will practice selecting strategies that match your educational goal. Suppose you want to teach students to be good citizens. Make a list of ten specific actions that you would do with your students that you think would help them to become good citizens. Share and discuss these with your classmates.

1.

2.

3.

4.

5.

6.

7.

8.

9.

10.

EXERCISE 2.5   EXAMINING CURRICULUM DOCUMENTS

In this exercise, you will familiarize yourself with existing curriculum documents currently available for your study. Visit the curriculum library of your college or a nearby school system (teachers and department heads are possible sources as well). Study several curriculum guides, resource units, state curriculum bulletins, teacher's editions of school textbooks, and other curriculum materials described in this module. Make several photocopies of this exercise and complete the exercise for each document. Share and discuss the results with your classmates.

Title of document: _____

Source (local school, state, other): _____

Date of publication of document: _____

		Yes	No
1.	Does the document contain the following components?		
	a. Statement of philosophy	_____	_____
	b. Evidence of needs assessment	_____	_____
	c. Goals and objectives	_____	_____
	d. Scope and sequence articulation	_____	_____
	e. Recommended procedures (learning activities)	_____	_____
	f. Recommended resource materials	_____	_____
	g. Evaluation procedures	_____	_____
2.	Does the document list expected learning outcomes?	_____	_____
3.	Does the document contain detailed unit plans?	_____	_____
4.	Does the document contain initiating activities (activities for starting a unit or lesson)?	_____	_____
5.	Does it contain enrichment activities?	_____	_____
6.	Does it contain culminating activities?	_____	_____
7.	Does it provide activities for learners with special needs?	_____	_____
8.	Does it provide bibliographic entries?	_____	_____
9.	Does it list audiovisual and other materials needed?	_____	_____
10.	Does it provide information regarding resource ideas?	_____	_____
11.	Does it help you understand what you are expected to teach?	_____	_____
12.	Does it help you understand how to do it?	_____	_____
13.	Are there questions you have that are not answered by your study of this document? If so, list them here for class discussion.		

EXERCISE 2.6   BEGINNING A RESOURCE FILE

In this exercise, you will begin your own resource file, either on your computer or on file cards. Organize your file in whatever way makes the most sense to you. Consider including the following for each entry: (a) name of resource; (b) how, when, and where available; (c) how to use, including name of teaching unit; (d) evaluative comment. This file can build throughout your professional career. You may wish to cross-reference your filing system to accommodate various categories of items, such as:

1. Articles from magazines, newspapers, and periodicals
2. Computer programs
3. Copies of student worksheets
4. Examination question items
5. Free and inexpensive materials, sources of
6. Games and games sources
7. Guest speakers and other community resources
8. Laser videodisc sources
9. Media catalogs
10. Motivational ideas
11. Pictures, posters, and other stills
12. Resources to order
13. Supply catalogs
14. Videocassette sources
15. Miscellaneous

Planning procedures are about the same as in any other planning, except that the team members plan together. After the team has completed its planning, each teacher must plan specifically for his or her role in the team teaching or for that teacher's own segment of the overall plan. One advantage of team planning is that teachers can easily coordinate their activities; another is that it gives teachers a chance to share ideas. But successful team planning may demand even more careful and detailed planning than solo teaching does.

Teacher-Student Planning

Many teachers encourage students to participate in the planning of their learning activities, units, and courses. Such participation tends to give students a proprietary interest in the activities, maybe increasing their motivation. What students have planned themselves often seems more relevant to them than what others have planned for them. And they like to see their own plans succeed. Thus teacher-student planning can be an effective motivational aid.

In spite of these merits, teacher-student planning can be risky. Therefore, the teacher must provide the students with adequate guidance. Be cautious about asking students to make decisions for which they are poorly equipped.

SUMMARY

In this module we presented the rationale for instructional planning and the principles of instructional planning. You have learned of the variety of documents and resources that are at your disposal for that planning. Modules that follow lead you further into the specific knowledge and processes necessary to develop your own effective teaching plans.

SUGGESTED READING

Brandt, R. S., ed. *Content of the Curriculum.* 1988 ASCD Yearbook. Alexandria, VA: Association for Supervision and Curriculum Development, 1988.

Johnson, D. W., and Johnson, R. T. *Learning Together and Alone.* Englewood Cliffs, NJ: Prentice-Hall, 1987.

Kim, E. C., and Kellough, R. D. *A Resource Guide for Secondary School Teaching: Planning for Competence,* 5th ed. New York: Macmillan, 1991.

Tyson-Bernstein, H. *A Conspiracy of Good Intention: America's Textbook Fiasco.* Washington, DC: Council for Basic Education, 1988.

POSTTEST

Short Answer

1. Identify two dangers of teaching without a plan.

_____

_____

_____

2. Identify the two most important decisions in planning, according to this module.

_____

_____

_____

3. According to this module, what questions must you ask yourself when planning?

_____

_____

_____

_____

4. Much of what is taught seems irrelevant. What might be the reason for this, according to this module?

_____

_____

5. When planning, what considerations are important in the selection of objectives?

_____

_____

6. According to this module, what is the most important criterion for the selection of learning activities for a course, unit, or lesson?

_____

7. If you were to test the adequacy of certain subject matter for inclusion in a particular course, unit, or lesson, what would be your chief criterion?

_____

8. Identify what you should expect to find in a course of study.

_____

_____

_____

_____

9. Identify one advantage of team planning.

_____

_____

10. Of what value is a textbook when planning?

_____

_____

11. How is cooperative team planning different from solo planning?

_____

_____

12. Identify one argument in favor of using teacher-student planning.

_____

_____

13. What is a resource unit?

_____

_____

14. How would you use the student textbook as a planning resource?

_____

_____

_____

15. Identify five reasons why planning is an essential element in effective teaching.

_____   _____

_____

_____

MODULE 3
Setting Objectives

RATIONALE

Aimless activity seldom pays off. To be effective and efficient, you must have a reasonably clear notion of what it is you wish to accomplish when beginning any endeavor. Otherwise, you have no way of knowing what approach to take, what methods and materials to use, or what has been accomplished in the end. Teaching is no different from other activities in this respect. Unless well aimed, teaching will be ineffectual, for neither you nor the students will clearly know what they should be learning. Therefore, you must learn how to formulate teaching objectives that will be useful to you as well as clearly understood by your students.

As a rule, teaching objectives are best written out. Otherwise, they are likely to be ambiguous, too comprehensive, or too general. To make objectives definite and precise, you should usually write them in behavioral terms. By pinpointing just what behavior is expected as a result of the instruction, such objectives will both give your teaching direction and establish criteria for measuring success.

In this module, we show you how to select and formulate clear teaching objectives. When you have finished this module, you should be able to identify and prepare general and specific objectives in the descriptive, behavioral, and covert categories.

SPECIFIC OBJECTIVES

At the completion of this module, you should be able to:

1. Define, identify, and construct each of the following:
   a. General objective
   b. Specific objective
   c. Behavioral objective
   d. Simple behavioral objective
   e. Criterion-referenced objective
   f. Covert behavioral objective

2. Explain the role of general and specific objectives.

3. Define and describe the cognitive, affective, and psychomotor taxonomies of educational objectives and their significance.

4. Write objectives suitable for the various levels of the three domains.

MODULE TEXT

Ways of Stating Objectives

Teachers can state objectives in a number of ways. One way is to prepare a statement or descriptive phrase that describes the skill, concept, appreciation, attitude, or ideal to be learned. Examples of descriptive objectives include:

☐ Concept (or generalization)
  Weather affects nearly all of people's enterprises.
☐ Skill (or ability)
  The ability to recognize the difference in spelling of masculine and feminine nouns and adjectives.
  The ability to find synonyms in *Roget's Thesaurus* quickly and easily.
☐ Attitude
  An attitude of respect toward other people.
  A strong desire to look at all sides of an issue before making a decision.

Teachers frequently use descriptive objectives in curriculum guides, resource units, and other curriculum documents. Such a formulation is useful for describing general goals and objectives but is likely to be too general for pinpointing the specific learning behaviors of units and lessons.

Another common way to write objectives is to begin with an infinitive, such as:

☐ To discover the most common cause of accidents in the home.
☐ To appreciate the contributions of immigrants to American life.

☐ To practice good citizenship.

☐ To develop skill in the use of the micrometer.

Note that objectives written with infinitives usually lack specifics, and for this reason they should not be used for most purposes. There is no reason, however, why they cannot be used for general objectives. For instance, major aims of education are often written in this fashion. But infinitive phrases are usually too ambiguous to be useful as course goals or as unit and lesson objectives.

Because descriptive objectives and objectives written with infinitives both lack specificity, teachers should usually write objectives that focus on specific behavior at the end of instruction. The sections that follow are primarily concerned with the preparation of behavioral objectives—specific statements of what the student will be able to do as a result of the learning experience.

Behavioral Objectives

A **behavioral objective** is a statement that describes what the student will be able to do once the instruction has been completed. Note that a behavioral objective describes the student behavior that results from the instruction. That behavior is called **terminal behavior,** for it is the behavior expected when the instruction ends, or terminates. This behavior is not terminal in the sense that all learning stops at that point—the terminal behavior at the end of one unit may well be the jumping-off point for learning new behavior in the next unit.

Note also that the behavior described is the terminal behavior of the student, not the teacher. Behavioral objectives do not describe what the teacher is going to do. Rather, they describe what the teacher or the school expects the student to do or be able to do as a result of being taught (consequently, behavioral objectives are also referred to as performance objectives). In this sense, behavioral objectives are teacher goals. Student goals may also be behavioral, but those will be discussed later.

Behavioral objectives, then, are descriptions of the student terminal behavior expected to result from the instruction. The basic formula for writing a behavioral objective is to use these phrases: *At the end of the instruction* (lesson, unit, course, or school curriculum), *the students will* (or will be able to). . . . These phrases (or similar phrases) usually distinguish behavioral objectives from nonbehavioral objectives.

Any objective that describes terminal behavior of the students is a behavioral objective. One source of confusion is that many writers of behavioral objectives use the present tense rather than the future tense. Maybe objectives should always be written in the future tense because an objective is something the teacher hopes to achieve in the future, but educational practices are not always so logical.

Now do Exercise 3.1 and test your ability to recognize objectives that are behaviorally stated.

Covert Versus Overt Behavior

Notice that certain of the behavioral objectives in Exercise 3.1 called for the students to "understand" or "appreciate" at the conclusion of the instruction. Although such objectives describe terminal behavior, they call for a different type of behavior than behavioral objectives that require students to solve problems or use some formula. Understanding, knowing, feeling, and appreciating are types of behaviors that cannot be observed directly, because these occur within a person. A student may understand perfectly without giving any outward sign of understanding. Such behavior is said to be covert. Behavioral objectives that call for covert behavior that cannot be observed directly are called covert behavioral objectives.

Of the objectives in Exercise 3.1, these are covert behavioral objectives:

☐ The students will understand that the basic issue that resulted in secession was the extension of slavery. (1)

☐ The students will understand that vibrating bodies provide the source of all sound and sound waves. (6)

□ The students will appreciate the problems faced by those who have emigrated from Southeast Asia to the United States. (9)

In the answer key to Exercise 3.1, suggestions were made about how these covert behavioral objectives could have been written. If followed, those suggestions would have changed the statements into overt behavioral objectives. The other behavioral objectives in the exercise (5, 7, and 8) called for students to convert from one scale to another, read bus schedules, and solve problems. Such behavior is said to be overt, because it is observable by someone else. To judge whether a person can read a bus schedule successfully, you can give that person a bus schedule and see if he or she can read it. Other examples of observable behavior include such activities as telling, explaining, describing, writing, running, and spelling. Objectives that call for overt terminal behavior are called overt behavioral objectives.

These are further examples of overt behavioral objectives:

□ As a result of the study of this course, the student will refrain from making final conclusions until he or she has carefully examined the data.

□ The students will treat members of other races with respect and consideration.

□ The students will listen to classical recordings of their own choosing.

Both covert and overt behavioral objectives are useful in education, but each has its drawbacks. Because you cannot observe covert activity directly, the only way you can judge how well a student has achieved a covert objective is to observe an overt behavior that can indicate whether the student has reached the covert objective. For a covert objective to be useful in a specific situation, a teacher must derive from it related overt behavioral objectives, which can then be used as a basis for determining how well students have achieved the covert objective. The changes suggested in the explanation of objectives 1, 6, and 9 in Exercise 3.1 are examples of this process.

For instance, consider this objective: "Upon completion of this unit, the students will understand why North Africa and the Middle East are rapidly changing in today's world." A teacher cannot directly observe how well the students have achieved the objective, or how well they understand. But a teacher can estimate how well they "understand" by measuring their achievement of related overt objectives, such as: "The students will be able to explain the impact that the discovery and exploitation of the Middle East oil fields has had on the development of the area." Frequently, several overt behavioral objectives are needed in order to get a good sampling of the behavior encompassed by a single covert behavioral objective.

The trouble with covert behavioral objectives, then, is that you cannot observe them directly. In contrast, the trouble with overt behavioral objectives often is that teachers tend to dredge up trivial objectives in an effort to find ones that are readily observable. After all, it is difficult to write overt behavioral objectives that adequately describe major cognitive or affective goals. Consequently, writers of objectives tend to concentrate on the less important details and forget the big picture. This tendency to emphasize the unimportant at the expense of the important has been true of teaching throughout history. And if we are to accept, for example, what a recent survey of high school seniors had to say about teachers, the tendency remains.[1] Many teachers have tended to concentrate on isolated, unrelated facts rather than on ideas, appreciations, and attitudes. A search for easily observable and measurable objectives has made this tendency even stronger. Some current lists of behavioral objectives reveal an emphasis on petty and inconsequential learning.

Behavioral Objectives and Evaluation

One purpose of setting objectives is to be able to evaluate with some precision whether the teaching has brought about the desired terminal behavior. Evaluation presents no great problem when the desired terminal behavior is overt, but when the activity is

---

[1]*See* David L. Clark's "High School Seniors React to Their Teachers and Their Schools," in *Phi Delta Kappan* 68(7): 503–509 (March 1987).

EXERCISE 3.1 RECOGNIZING BEHAVIORAL OBJECTIVES
A Self-Check Exercise

Place a check mark before the objectives that describe an anticipated terminal behavior of students—that is, check the behavioral objectives. Compare your answers against the answer key that follows. Discuss any problem areas with your classmates.

_____ 1. The students will understand that the basic issue that resulted in secession was the extension of slavery.

_____ 2. Digestion is the chemical change of foods into particles that can be absorbed.

_____ 3. To explain what an acid is and what an acid's properties are.

_____ 4. Introduction to vector qualities and their use.

_____ 5. The students will be able to convert Celsius temperatures to Fahrenheit.

_____ 6. The students will understand that vibrating bodies provide the source of all sounds and sound waves.

_____ 7. At the end of the lesson, with at least 90 percent accuracy, the students will be able to read a bus schedule well enough to determine at what time buses are scheduled to arrive and leave at designated stations.

_____ 8. Given a number of quadratic equations with one unknown, the students will be able to solve the equations correctly in 80 percent of the cases.

_____ 9. The students will appreciate the problems faced by those who have emigrated from Southeast Asia to the United States.

_____ 10. A study of the external features and internal organs of the frog through video films of dissections.

_____ 11. To discuss the reasons why the field of philosophy was well developed by the ancient Greeks.

_____ 12. Animals' physical adaptation to their environments.

ANSWER KEY TO EXERCISE 3.1

1. This is a behavioral objective. Although another verb might be more appropriate (e.g., *recognize*), understanding is a kind of behavior. In this case, understanding that slavery was the basic issue that brought about secession is the terminal behavior the teacher expects of the students.

2. This is not a behavioral objective. Rather, it is a description of a concept and does not describe an expected terminal behavior.

3. This is not a behavioral objective. It describes teacher behavior rather than student terminal behavior. It is more a teaching procedure than an objective.

4. This is not a behavioral objective—or even an objective of any type. It is a topic or title.

5. This is a behavioral objective. It describes clearly what the students will be able to do as a result of the instruction; it describes their expected terminal behavior.

6. This is a behavioral objective. The objective is rather broad, and another verb might have been more useful. Understanding is a kind of terminal behavior, but the objective might have been more measurable had the teacher used a verb other than *understanding*. A better formulation would have been: "The students will be able to recall that . . ." or "The students will be able to demonstrate that. . . ."

7. This is a behavioral objective. It is specific and very clear about the teacher's expectation of student behavior at completion of the lesson.

8. This is a clearly written behavioral objective.

9. This is a behavioral objective. Although the terminal behavior described is vague and general, it is nevertheless a terminal behavior. Perhaps a clearer formulation would have been: "The students will demonstrate an appreciation of the problems faced by those who have emigrated from Southeast Asia to the United States by recalling the many problems the people faced before, during, and following that emigration."

10. This is not a behavioral objective. It describes no behavior of any kind. It is the title of a topic with a mention of methods.

11. This is not a behavioral objective. It is not an objective at all, but rather a description of the teaching procedure to be used.

12. This is not a behavioral objective. Again, this is a title of a topic. It describes no behavior and no objective.

covert, evaluation becomes more difficult. Since covert terminal behavior cannot be observed directly, the only way to tell whether the objective has been achieved is to observe behavior that might indicate the presence of the covert terminal activity. Thus, for purposes of evaluation, a teacher should whenever possible formulate objectives in terms of overt behavior. Moreover, a good behavioral objective identifies precisely the standard of behavior required for satisfactory performance. Behavioral objectives that indicate the standard of performance expected are called **criterion-referenced** behavioral objectives.[2]

General and Specific Objectives

In education, objectives are what teachers hope students will learn as a result of instruction. As in other pursuits, objectives may range from the general to the specific. Consider this extremely general statement of the major purposes of public education in the United States:

> As a result of their schooling, the youth of the United States will be good citizens;
> think clearly and rationally;
> use their leisure time in a worthwhile manner;
> live a healthful life;
> earn a good living at their vocations;
> appreciate beauty in art, music, nature, and the community.

For contrast, consider these very specific lesson-plan objectives:

□ The student will be able to recite from memory without error the first stanza of A. E. Housman's "Loveliest of Trees."

□ Given a topographical map of the area, the student will be able to find the altitude of the block house on Signal Mountain to the nearest five feet.

Most teaching objectives fall somewhere between these extremes (Figure 3–1). As the continuum implies, objectives are not general or specific in absolute terms; rather, some objectives are more general or more specific than others. The continuum in reality represents a sequencing of objectives. In practice, the sequence is this: you can expect your courses to be aimed at broad general objectives, your units to be focused on general objectives supported by specific objectives, and your lessons to be guided by specific objectives.[3] (When you see a general objective in a lesson plan, it is usually a general objective of the unit or perhaps a course goal doubling as a unit general objective.) General objectives can be useful when shared with students as advance mental organizers. The students will then know what to expect and begin to prepare mentally to learn the appropriate material.[4] Check your comprehension of this concept of a continuum of objectives by doing Exercise 3.2.

In well-ordered school systems, the more specific objectives combine to support the more general ones. Thus, the learning required by the specific objectives of several lessons will combine to bring about the learning that makes up a general unit objective,

---

[2]Sometimes these are called performance objectives. In some school systems the educational goals are set up as competencies (i.e., competency-based, or outcome-based education) that the students are supposed to achieve. These goals are divided into specific performance objectives, or sometimes referred to as goal indicators. If the students can perform the competencies called for by these specific goals, their education is considered successful; if not, it is not. School curricula, teacher performance, and student achievement may all be evaluated by these criteria.

[3]Educational authorities have not standardized the terminology to be used for designating the various types of objectives. In the literature, the most general objectives of education are often called educational aims; the general objectives of schools, curricula, and courses are called goals; the objectives of units and lessons are called instructional objectives; and extremely narrow objectives are called drill objectives. The implication of this scheme is that educational aims are more general than goals, goals are more general than general objectives, general objectives are more general than specific objectives, and drill objectives are the most specific of specific objectives.

[4]The value of stating learning objectives in behavioral terms and in providing advance organizers is well documented by recent research. *See* Thomas L. Good and Jere E. Brophy, *Looking in Classrooms,* 4th ed. (New York: Harper & Row, 1987), p. 334.

FIGURE 3.1
Continuum of Teaching
Objectives

Most General	Very General		General	Specific
Nationwide education goals	Schoolwide goals	Course objectives	Unit objectives	Lesson objectives

several unit objectives will combine to build a course objective, or certain course objectives will combine to produce a schoolwide goal. For instance, the schoolwide goal "The students will become good citizens" might be supported by such subordinate curriculum or course goals as:

□ The students will understand their duties and responsibilities as citizens.

□ The students will understand the legislative process and how it works.

□ The students will take an active part in community affairs.

In planning your courses you should first select the general objectives that are to be the course goals and then break down these course goals into the general objectives that are to be the unit goals. Finally, you should divide these into the specific objectives for the lessons in the unit. The specific lesson plans will support the general objectives of the unit, the unit objectives will support the course goals, and the course goals will support the schoolwide objectives (Figure 3.2).

Since teaching objectives describe the terminal behavior (performance) that teachers expect of students at the end of instruction, those objectives may be written in terms of covert or overt activity. As a rule, however, only broad curricula and course goals should be written as covert behavior. Unit and lesson specific objectives probably should always describe overt behavior. As a matter of fact, since there seems to be a tendency for some teachers to emphasize petty behavioral objectives, it may be wise to write your general objectives or goals as covert objectives, supported by several more specific overt behavioral objectives.

For example, in a unit, one of the general objectives might be:

The student understands the difference between common and proper nouns.

Subordinate, specific objectives whose achievement would result in attainment of this general objective might be:

1. The student can define both proper and common nouns.

2. The student can pick out the proper and common nouns in a passage with 90 percent accuracy.

3. The student capitalizes proper nouns but not common nouns when he or she writes.

In practice, you should set your general goals first and then derive a number of subordinate specific objectives that together would accomplish those goals. It may then be necessary to derive still more specific objectives to accomplish the initial specific objectives, which thus become lower-level general goals.

For example, you might select the following as a unit objective:

The students will understand the difference between the two temperature scales, Fahrenheit and Celsius.

You might decide that a good way to get the students to understand the difference between the two scales would be to teach them to convert from one scale to the other and to interpret the meaning of readings on either of the two scales. You then derive the following subordinate objectives:

1. The students will be able to convert from Fahrenheit to Celsius.

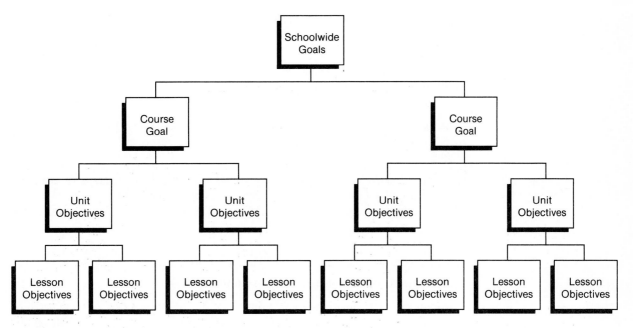

FIGURE 3.2
General and Specific Objectives

2. The students will be able to convert from Celsius to Fahrenheit.

3. The students will be able to recall the formulas for converting from one scale to the other.

4. The students will be able to interpret verbally the temperature as indicated on either a Celsius or Fahrenheit scale.

If you choose your subordinate objectives well, the students presumably will have achieved the unit objective once they have achieved the subordinate objectives. However, some worthwhile goals are so elusive that it is almost impossible to write specific behavior that indicates whether the students have truly achieved the goal. Therefore, you should probably write most of your cognitive and affective course goals and unit general objectives as covert objectives, reserving overt behavioral objectives for the specific objectives of your units and lessons.[5]

Objectives that address attitudes and feelings (i.e., affective objectives) may be either overt or covert behavioral objectives, though setting specific overt objectives at the unit or lesson level is usually unwise because it is so difficult to judge attitudes and feelings by examining overt behavior. There can be no fixed rule about any of this, however. As in almost everything in teaching, you must learn to adjust the objectives to the circumstances. As a professional, such adjustment is—or should be—your prerogative to do.

Check your understanding of these concepts by doing Exercise 3.3 and Exercise 3.4.

Simple or Criterion-Referenced Behavioral Objectives

Behavioral objectives may be either simple or criterion-referenced. A simple objective states only what the student will be able to do after the instruction, whereas a criterion-referenced objective states not only the terminal behavior expected but also what standard of performance students should attain. (In Exercise 3.1, objectives 7 and 8 are stated as criterion-referenced.)

---

[5]One can also use criterion-referenced behavioral objectives (i.e., behavioral objectives that specify how well the students should perform) as goal indicators (competencies) for school and curriculum goals, but ordinarily these will be established by curriculum committees.

This is a simple behavioral objective:

At the end of the lesson the student will be able to read a bus schedule.

It states what the student should be able to do at the end of the instruction. To make a criterion-referenced behavioral objective, you would have to add the standard of performance to be attained:

At the end of the lesson, the student will be able, *with at least 90 percent accuracy,* to read a bus schedule to determine at what time buses are to arrive and leave designated points.

The acceptable standard of performance (in this instance, 90 percent) is an arbitrary standard determined by the teacher (or by a curriculum committee).

Criterion-referenced objectives may also give the conditions under which the student is expected to meet the standard:

Given an interurban bus schedule at the end of the lesson, the student will be able, with at least 90 percent accuracy, to read the schedule to determine at what time buses are to arrive and leave designated points.

Notice that the conditions—and, consequently, the severity of the standard—of the previous criterion-referenced objective differ from the conditions set forth in the next example:

Given excerpts from a bus schedule at the end of the lesson, the student will be able, with at least 90 percent accuracy, to determine at what time buses are to arrive and leave the designated points contained in the excerpts.

Presumably, reading excerpts from the bus schedule would not be as difficult as reading the bus schedule itself.

Thus, criterion-referenced behavioral objectives usually contain these three essential elements:

1. An observable, and therefore measurable, behavior that the students will be able to perform at the completion of instruction.
2. The standard at which the students are expected to perform.
3. The conditions under which the students are expected to perform in order to meet the standard.

Some critics think that inclusion of these three essential elements tends to make the objective trivial—the instruction emphasizes bits and pieces of information at the expense of large understandings and appreciations. No doubt this is a danger, but the wary teacher can avoid that pitfall. With care, you can make the performance standards and conditions broad and strong. Furthermore, understandings, appreciations, and attitudes are composed of clusters of narrower behaviors. By selecting a good sampling of subordinate criterion-referenced objectives for each understanding or appreciation you wish to teach, you can attain the larger goal and have evidence that you have done so. For these reasons, the specific objectives that you use in teaching probably should be criterion-referenced behavioral objectives.

Because criterion-referenced behavioral objectives call for much more specific terminal behavior than do simple behavioral objectives and because they provide a definite standard by which to judge student performance, they are more useful for test building, evaluation, diagnosis, and feedback than are other types of objectives. Since the early 1970s this type of objective has been popular with educational experts, particularly those whose interests center on tests and evaluation, programming, and systematizing instruction.

Cognitive, Affective, and Psychomotor Objectives

Objectives address three main areas, or domains: (1) the cognitive, which encompasses concepts, ideas, factual knowledge, or intellectual skill; (2) the affective, which encom-

EXERCISE 3.2   THE CONTINUUM OF TEACHING OBJECTIVES
A Self-Check Exercise

In this exercise, you will reinforce your understanding of the continuum of teaching objectives. On the continuum of Figure 3.1, where would you place each of the following objectives? Use the following code: MG = most general, VG = very general, G = general, S = specific. Check your responses with the answer key. Discuss any differences with your classmates.

_____ 1. The student will appreciate the problems faced by those who emigrate to the United States.

_____ 2. The student will demonstrate the scientific attitude.

_____ 3. The student will understand that various species of birds have different types of beaks and that these differences in type of beak are related to what the birds feed on.
    a. The students will be able to identify from pictures the beaks of woodpeckers, birds of prey, ducks, seed eaters (finches, grosbeaks), insect eaters, pelicans, herons, crossbills, and sandpipers.
    b. The students will be able to explain the functions of each type of beak listed.

ANSWER KEY TO EXERCISE 3.2

According to our thinking, in this list Objective 2 is Most General, Objective 1 is Very General, Objective 3 is Specific. Do you agree?

EXERCISE 3.3   SEQUENCING INSTRUCTIONAL OBJECTIVES
Individual Work

In this exercise, you will check your understanding of the importance of sequencing instructional objectives.

1. Select a common schoolwide goal.

    Schoolwide goal:

2. From that goal (step 1) write a sequence of related objectives from the most general to the most specific as related to your subject field.

    Course objective:

    Unit objective:

    Lesson objective(s):

3. Share this sequence with your classmates for their feedback.

EXERCISE 3.4 SEQUENCING INSTRUCTIONAL OBJECTIVES
Small-Group Work

In this exercise, you will work in groups of four. The following are some sample general goals for courses in various subject fields. For each goal, identify specific objectives that must be achieved before the general goal can be attained. Each group should share its list of specific objectives with the entire class.

1. Students will be able to distinguish the major characteristics of tragedy and comedy.

2. Students will write clear, expository prose.

3. Students will understand the place of the planet Earth in the galaxy.

4. Students will understand that the basic nature of society is rooted in its values.

5. Students will be able to discuss differences that exist among microorganisms, plants, and animals.

6. Students will understand that humans' need for sociality is a factor in implementing change.

7. Students will appreciate that the earth's resources are not infinite.

passes appreciation, ideals, attitudes, or morals; and (3) the psychomotor, which encompasses gross motor and finer movement skills, communication skills, and the creativity that coordinates all skills in all domains. In each of these domains, objectives may range from those calling for the simplest tasks to those requiring the most complex ideas, skills, or reactions. Several authorities have attempted to arrange the objectives in each of the domains into taxonomies (systematic classifications) according to the complexity, intensity, or sophistication of the activities involved. These taxonomies are useful for judging the depth of teaching.

The Cognitive Domain

In a taxonomy of objectives that has become widely accepted, Bloom and his associates arranged cognitive educational objectives into classifications according to the complexity of the skills and abilities embodied in the objectives.[6] The resulting taxonomy portrays a ladder ranging from the simplest to the most complex mental processes.[7] The six major categories (or levels) in Bloom's taxonomy of cognitive objectives are:

1. *Knowledge* (the recognition and recall of information)
2. *Comprehension* (the understanding of the meaning of the information)
3. *Application* (the ability to use information)
4. *Analysis* (the ability to dissect knowledge into component parts and see their relationships)
5. *Synthesis* (the ability to put the parts together to form new ideas)
6. *Evaluation* (the ability to judge the worth of an idea, notion, theory, thesis, proposition, information, or belief)

Bloom's taxonomy also includes various subcategories, though these are not emphasized in this module. It may be less important that an objective be absolutely classified than it is for the teacher to be cognizant of hierarchies of levels of thinking and to understand the importance of attending to student development from lower to higher levels of operation, in all three domains.

A discussion of each of Bloom's six categories follows.

1. Knowledge.   The basic element in Bloom's taxonomy concerns the acquisition of knowledge—that is, the ability to recognize and recall information. Although this is the lowest level of the six categories, the information to be learned may not itself be of a low level. In fact, the information may be of an extremely high level. Bloom and his associates include at this first level knowledge of principles, generalizations, theories, structures, and methodology, as well as knowledge of specifics and ways and means of dealing with specifics.

Action verbs appropriate for this category include: *choose, complete, define, describe, identify, indicate, list, locate, match, name, outline, recall, recognize, select, state.* (Note that some verbs may be appropriately used at more than one cognitive level.)

The following are examples of simple objectives in this knowledge category. Note especially the verb used in each example. From this point on, in order to conserve space, TSWBAT stands for "the student will be able to . . . ," the initial phrase of simple objectives. Examples include:

☐ TSWBAT list the principal parts of speech.

☐ TSWBAT complete the conjugation of the Latin verb *amare.*

---

[6]Benjamin S. Bloom, ed. *Taxonomy of Educational Objectives, Book I: Cognitive Domain* (White Plains, NY: Longman, 1984).

[7]Rather than an orderly progression from simple to complex mental operations as illustrated by Bloom's taxonomy of cognitive objectives as illustrated in this text, other researchers prefer an identification of cognitive abilities that range from simple information storage and retrieval, through a higher level of discrimination and concept attainment, and to the highest cognitive ability to recognize and solve problems, as organized by Robert M. Gagné, Leslie Briggs, and Walter Wager, *Principles of Instructional Design,* Third Edition (New York: Holt, Rinehart and Winston, 1988).

☐ TSWBAT name the logical fallacies.

☐ TSWBAT state the Pythagorean theorem.

☐ TSWBAT recall which criteria are recommended for testing certain hypotheses.

☐ From a list of formulas, TSWBAT identify the formula for sulfuric acid.

☐ TSWBAT define the following: axiom, reflexive, symmetric, transitive substitute theorem, equivalent.

☐ Given a selection of common working tools. TSWBAT identify each by name and purpose.

☐ TSWBAT describe the procedure for diagnosing the cause of a stalled engine.

☐ TSWBAT recall the stages of mitosis.

☐ Given a drawing of a skeleton, TSWBAT correctly label the names of the various bones listed.

☐ Given a drawing of a sewing machine, TSWBAT label the different parts.

☐ TSWBAT name the positions of offensive players on a football team.

Beyond the first category (knowledge), the remaining five categories of Bloom's taxonomy of the cognitive domain have to do with using the knowledge that has been remembered. They encompass the educational objectives aimed at developing cognitive skills and abilities, including comprehension, application, analysis, synthesis, and evaluation of information.

2. Comprehension.   The skills and abilities in the next higher category are those of comprehension. These include the ability to translate or explain knowledge, to interpret that knowledge, and to extrapolate from it to address new situations.

Action verbs appropriate for this category include: *change, classify, convert, defend, describe, estimate, expand, explain, generalize, infer, interpret, paraphrase, predict, recognize, summarize, translate.*

Examples of simple objectives in this category are:

☐ TSWBAT describe each of the principal parts of speech.

☐ TSWBAT translate the conjugation of the Latin verb *amare*.

☐ TSWBAT recognize the logical fallacies.

☐ TSWBAT derive the Pythagorean theorem.

☐ TSWBAT predict which criteria are recommended for testing certain hypotheses.

☐ TSWBAT recognize the formula for sulfuric acid.

☐ TSWBAT describe each of the following: axiom, reflexive, symmetric, transitive substitute theorem, equivalent.

☐ Given a selection of common working tools, TSWBAT recognize each by purpose.

☐ TSWBAT describe the procedure for diagnosing the cause of a stalled engine.

☐ TSWBAT generalize about each stage of mitosis.

☐ Given drawings of skeletons, TSWBAT infer information about the type of animal of each skeleton.

☐ Given a drawing of a sewing machine, TSWBAT explain the functions of the different parts.

☐ TSWBAT explain the job of the positions of offensive players on a football team.

3. Application.   The next higher category on the taxonomy includes the skills of application. Once students can understand the information, they should be able to apply it. Doing so represents a somewhat higher level of cognitive ability than comprehension.

Action verbs appropriate for this category include: *apply, compute, demonstrate, develop, discover, modify, operate, participate, perform, plan, predict, relate, show, use.*

Examples of simple objectives in the application category are:

☐ TSWBAT demonstrate in complete sentences each of the listed principal parts of speech.

☐ TSWBAT use in complete sentences the conjugations of the Latin verb *amare*.

☐ TSWBAT differentiate the logical fallacies.

☐ TSWBAT perform a problem using the Pythagorean theorem.

☐ TSWBAT apply the criteria recommended for testing certain hypotheses.

☐ TSWBAT compute the formula for sulfuric acid from knowledge of its components.

☐ TSWBAT differentiate each of the following: axiom, reflexive, symmetric, transitive substitute theorem, equivalent.

☐ Given a selection of common working tools, TSWBAT demonstrate how each is used.

☐ TSWBAT demonstrate the procedure for diagnosing the cause of a stalled engine.

☐ TSWBAT discuss each stage of mitosis.

☐ Given parts of a skeleton, TSWBAT correctly predict the type of animal.

☐ Given a sewing machine, TSWBAT demonstrate its operation.

☐ TSWBAT relate how the different positions of offensive members of a football team depend upon each other.

4. Analysis. The next higher category includes objectives that require students to utilize the skills of analysis. These skills include analysis of elements, analysis of relationships, and analysis of organizational principles.

Action verbs appropriate for this category include: *analyze, break down, categorize, classify, compare, contrast, debate, deduce, diagram, differentiate, discriminate, identify, illustrate, infer, outline, relate, separate, subdivide.*

Examples of simple objectives in this category are:

☐ TSWBAT identify inconsistencies in television commercials.

☐ TSWBAT analyze the logical fallacies.

☐ TSWBAT debate the criteria recommended for testing certain hypotheses.

☐ TSWBAT discriminate among the following: axiom, reflexive, symmetric, transitive substitute theorem, equivalent.

☐ TSWBAT illustrate each stage of mitosis.

☐ TSWBAT identify the major themes of a novel.

☐ TSWBAT spot bias in a news story.

☐ TSWBAT diagnose the reason an engine is inoperative.

5. Synthesis. The synthesis category of cognitive objectives includes objectives that involve such skills as designing a plan, proposing a set of operations, and deriving a set of abstract relations.

Action verbs appropriate for this category include: *arrange, categorize, classify, combine, compile, constitute, create, design, develop, devise, document, explain, formulate, generate, modify, organize, originate, plan, produce, rearrange, reconstruct, revise, rewrite, summarize, synthesize, tell, transmit, write.*

Examples of simple objectives in this category of the taxonomy are:

☐ TSWBAT write clear directions for performing a simple task.

☐ TSWBAT propose a suitable method for determining the chemical consistency of an unknown solution.

☐ TSWBAT create a logical outline of a proposition preparatory for writing an essay.

☐ Given the necessary data, TSWBAT construct a graph showing the rise and fall of the GNP of the past decade.

□ TSWBAT design a plan for a community survey.

□ Given a hypothesis, TSWBAT design an experiment suitable for testing the hypothesis.

□ Given the necessary information concerning income, exemptions, deductions, and withholding tax, and the appropriate IRS 1040 instruction booklet, TSWBAT fill out an IRS Form 1040 without error.

6. Evaluation.   The highest cognitive category of Bloom's taxonomy is evaluation. This includes offering opinions and making judgments according to internal criteria and external criteria.

Action verbs appropriate for this category include: *appraise, argue, assess, compare, conclude, consider, contrast, criticize, decide, discriminate, evaluate, explain, interpret, judge, justify, rank, rate, relate, standardize, support, validate.*

Examples of simple objectives in this category are:

□ TSWBAT distinguish between a well-developed character and one that is stereotypical.

□ TSWBAT write a critique of a television drama showing merits and faults in its plot and characterization.

□ TSWBAT judge which form—1040EZ, 1040A, or 1040—is appropriate in a given situation of tax reporting.

□ TSWBAT determine which picture best meets the stated criteria.

□ TSWBAT contrast decision making and problem solving.

At this point, you should check your understanding of Bloom's taxonomy by working through Exercise 3.5.

The Affective Domain

Krathwohl, Bloom, and Masia developed a useful taxonomy of the affective domain. The following are their major categories (or levels), from least internalized to most internalized:[8]

1. *Receiving* (awareness of the affective stimulus and the beginning of favorable feelings toward it)

2. *Responding* (taking an interest in the stimulus and viewing it favorably)

3. *Valuing* (tentative belief in the value of the affective stimulus becomes commitment to it)

4. *Organization* (organization of values into a system of dominant and supporting values)

5. *Characterized by a value or value complex* (determination of one's conduct, beliefs, and, finally, character or philosophy of life)

The following paragraphs describe more fully the types of objectives that fit these categories of the affective domain. Although there is considerable overlap from one category to another, they do give a basis by which to judge the quality of objectives and the nature of learning in this domain.

1. Receiving.   In this category, the least internalized, the student exhibits willingness to give attention to particular phenomena or stimuli, and the teacher is able to arouse, hold, and direct that attention.

Action verbs appropriate for this category include: *ask, choose, describe, differentiate, distinguish, hold, identify, locate, name, point to, recall, recognize, reply, select, use.*

---

[8]David R. Krathwohl, Benjamin S. Bloom, and Bertram B. Masia, *Taxonomy of Educational Goals, Handbook II: Affective Domain* (New York: David McKay, 1964).

EXERCISE 3.5   IDENTIFICATION OF COGNITIVE LEVELS
A Self-Check Exercise

The following cognitive objectives were taken from plans prepared by teachers. For each, identify the highest category required of the Bloom taxonomy of the cognitive domain. Then check your decision against the key that follows. If you do not agree with the key, turn back to the discussion of the taxonomy and study it again. Then if you still disagree, discuss the matter with your classmates and instructor. Classifications are sometimes ambiguous—it could be that your answer is as right as that in the key.

Use the following codes for your answers: 1 = knowledge; 2 = comprehension; 3 = application; 4 = analysis; 5 = synthesis, 6 = evaluation.

_____ 1. The student will be able to detect faulty logic in advertising propaganda.

_____ 2. The student will be able to differentiate fact and opinion in news stories.

_____ 3. Given the facts of the political situation, the student will be able to draw reasonable hypotheses concerning the causes of the Persian Gulf War.

_____ 4. The student will be able to devise a workable plan for investigating a social phenomenon.

_____ 5. The student will write an original short story.

_____ 6. At the end of the lesson, the students will perceive the moods of melancholy and retreat in Byron's *The Ocean*.

_____ 7. You will be able to define *corporation* in your own words.

_____ 8. Given the requisite tools and materials—electric drill and bit, knife, screwdriver, ruler, soldering gun, wire strippers, solder, and flux—the student will construct a portable testing device for repair of motors and sealed-in units.

_____ 9. Given a list of five solids, five liquids, and five gases, students will be able to describe the physical and chemical properties of each.

_____ 10. You will be able to devise a method to prove a ray to be the bisector of an angle.

ANSWER KEY TO EXERCISE 3.5

1, category 6; 2, category 4; 3, category 4; 4, category 5; 5, category 5; 6, category 2; 7, category 2; 8, category 3; 9, category 1; 10, category 5.

Examples of objectives in this category are:

☐ TSWBAT pay close attention to the directions for enrichment activities.

☐ TSWBAT listen attentively to the classroom lectures.

☐ TSWBAT demonstrate sensitivity to the concerns of others.

2. Responding.   In this category, students respond to the stimulus they have received. They may do so because of some outside pressure, or they may do so voluntarily because they find it interesting or because responding gives them satisfaction.

   Action verbs appropriate for this category include: *answer, applaud, approve, assist, comply, command, conform, discuss, greet, help, label, perform, play, practice, present, read, recite, report, select, spend (leisure time in), tell, write.*

   Examples of objectives in this category are:

☐ TSWBAT show interest in the subject by doing extra reading.

☐ TSWBAT volunteer in classroom recitation.

☐ TSWBAT enthusiastically participate in classroom discussions and projects.

☐ TSWBAT seek out examples of good art.

☐ TSWBAT read for recreation.

☐ TSWBAT select high-quality classical music to listen to.

☐ TSWBAT willingly cooperate in group activities.

☐ TSWBAT find pleasure in studying nature in the field.

☐ TSWBAT voluntarily write a letter to the editor of the local newspaper taking a stand on a particular social issue.

3. Valuing.   Objectives in the valuing category have to do with students' beliefs, attitudes, and appreciations. The simplest objectives concern a student's acceptance of beliefs and values. Higher objectives concern a student's learning to prefer certain values and finally becoming committed to them.

   Action verbs appropriate for this category include: *argue, assist, complete, describe, differentiate, explain, follow, form, initiate, invite, join, justify, propose, protest, read, report, select, share, study, support, work.*

   Examples of these objectives are:

☐ TSWBAT demonstrate concern about racial injustices.

☐ TSWBAT recognize the value of the freedom of the press.

☐ TSWBAT argue for the need for a more pollution-free environment.

☐ TSWBAT exhibit problem-solving attitudes.

☐ TSWBAT withhold judgment until all evidence has been considered.

☐ TSWBAT demonstrate appreciation for language by trying to speak and write precisely.

☐ TSWBAT show appreciation of poetry by selecting poetry for recreational reading.

☐ When faced with new evidence on an issue, TSWBAT demonstrate a willingness to change his or her position.

4. Organization.   This fourth category in the affective-domain taxonomy concerns the building of a person's value system. In this category the student begins to conceptualize values and arrange them into a value system that recognizes priorities and relative importance of the various values one faces in life.

   Action verbs appropriate for this category include: *adhere, alter, arrange, balance, combine, compare, defend, define, discuss, explain, generalize, identify, integrate, modify, order, organize, prepare, relate, synthesize.*

Examples of objectives in this category are:

☐ TSWBAT form judgments concerning proper behavior in school and community.

☐ TSWBAT decide what values are most important to him or her.

☐ TSWBAT form judgments concerning the type of life he or she would like to lead in view of his or her own abilities, interests, and beliefs.

☐ TSWBAT form judgments concerning what his or her life work should be.

☐ TSWBAT establish personal standards of behavior to guide his or her own behavior.

5. Characterized by a Value or Value Complex.   This is the final and highest category in the affective domain. At this level the learner's behaviors are consistent with his or her internalized values.

Action verbs appropriate for this category include: *act, complete, display, influence, listen, modify, perform, practice, propose, qualify, question, revise, serve, solve, use, verify.*

Examples of objectives in this category are:

☐ TSWBAT regularly cooperate in group activities.

☐ TSWBAT be meticulous about his or her personal grooming.

☐ TSWBAT work independently and diligently.

☐ TSWBAT live up to a well-defined ethical code of behavior.

☐ TSWBAT be precise in speech by being accurate in the use of language expression and thought.

☐ When confronted by a word he or she is not sure how to spell, TSWBAT demonstrate interest by looking it up in a dictionary.

The Psychomotor Domain

Whereas identification and classification within the cognitive and affective domains are generally agreed upon, there is less agreement on the classification within the psychomotor domain. Originally, the goal in this domain was simply that of developing and categorizing proficiency in skills, particularly those dealing with gross and fine muscle control. Consequently, the objectives were arranged in a hierarchy from simple gross locomotor control to the most creative and complex, requiring originality and fine locomotor control—for example, from simply threading a needle to designing and making a piece of clothing on the sewing machine. From Harrow is the following taxonomy of the psychomotor domain.[9] Below each category are sample objectives as well as a list of possible action verbs for that category. The categories are:

MOVEMENT (GROSS COORDINATION)
☐ TSWBAT demonstrate jumping rope without missing.

☐ TSWBAT grasp the golf club correctly.

Actions verbs include: *adjust, carry, clean, locate, obtain, walk.*

MANIPULATING (FINER COORDINATION)
☐ TSWBAT build a kite.

☐ TSWBAT play the B-flat scale on the violin.

Action verbs include: *assemble, build, calibrate, connect, thread.*

COMMUNICATING (COMMUNICATION OF IDEAS AND FEELINGS)
☐ TSWBAT demonstrate active listening skills.

☐ TSWBAT describe his or her own feelings about the abortion controversy.

Action verbs include: *analyze, ask, describe, draw, explain, write.*

---

[9]A. J. Harrow, *Taxonomy of the Psychomotor Domain* (New York: Longman, 1977).

CREATING (COORDINATION OF ALL SKILLS FROM ALL THREE DOMAINS)

☐ TSWBAT write and perform a musical composition.

☐ TSWBAT create and perform new dance patterns.

☐ Action verbs include: *create, design, invent.*

Using the Taxonomies

Theoretically, the taxonomies are so constructed that students achieve each lower level before being ready to move to the higher levels. But this theory does not always hold in practice, particularly when categories overlap. The taxonomies are important in that they point out the various levels to which instruction must aspire. If education is to be worthwhile, teachers must formulate and achieve objectives in the higher categories of the taxonomies as well as in the lower categories. If you aim for these higher objectives sufficiently often, your teaching will not be focused on the trivial. Many teachers, however, do not include a sufficient percentage of objectives from the higher categories of the domains. Indeed, considering the objectives and test questions that teachers write, it would appear that many never expect to move student learning from the lowest levels of simple recall and recognition of factual information.

In writing your objectives, remember that the point is not so much to write objectives at any particular level as it is to formulate the best objectives you can for the job you have to do. Use the taxonomies to make sure that your teaching does not concentrate on the trivial. Writing effective objectives is essential to the preparation of good items for the evaluation of student learning. Effectively communicating your behavioral expectations to students and then measuring their learning against those expectations will make your teaching efficient and effective.

Writing Objectives

Writing Criterion-Referenced Objectives

To write good criterion-referenced behavioral objectives can be both difficult and time-consuming. In fact, some critics feel that writing such objectives is not worth the time or effort. But criterion-referenced behavioral objectives do make for precise objectives, especially as a basis for evaluation and feedback. Perhaps teachers should always use them for the specific objectives of units and lessons. If a teacher keeps the taxonomy of educational objectives in mind and remembers the need for some objectives from the higher categories of the domains, the teacher can avoid a proliferation of objectives that can make the content petty and trivial.

A complete criterion-referenced behavioral objective (or performance objective) consists of a four-part statement that includes:

1. Who will perform the behavior (i.e., the student or the *audience*).

2. The overt *behavior* that will be performed.[10]

3. The *conditions* under which the behavior will be performed.

4. The standard of performance expected (sometimes referred to as the level or *degree* of performance).

The italicized words in the preceding list can help you remember the four parts, or ingredients, of a criterion-referenced behavioral objective. In preparing an objective, you should think of the ABCDs of its formation—the *a*udience, the *b*ehavior, the *c*onditions, and the *d*egree of performance.

Therefore, in writing out the criterion-referenced objectives, first you designate the person who is going to do the performing called for by the objective. That is the student. If the objective is addressed to the learner, especially in individualized instruction, use the word *you.*

---

[10]Some authorities divide this into two categories: the act (or behavior) and the product. Thus in the objective "The student will be able to write an essay describing the causes of the revolution," *write* is the behavior and *an essay describing the causes of the revolution* is the product. We think combining the two is preferable.

Second, describe what the behavior or performance will be. To do this you will need an action verb and its object, such as the following: "will write a poem," "will describe the plan," "will run the mile," "will build a desk." In this type of behavioral objective, the verb must be an action verb that describes overt action that can be observed and is measurable. Action that is covert is useless to you as a teacher preparing criterion-referenced objectives.

Overt behavioral objectives generally use such verbs as *solve, convert, read, explain,* and *describe.* Covert objectives generally use less active verbs, such as *understand, appreciate, know, feel, think,* and *believe.* The test by which you determine whether behavior is overt or covert is to check whether the verb describes action that can be observed directly. Now, with Exercise 3.6, try your skill at recognizing verbs that can be used in preparing overt behavioral objectives.

The third part in the four-part statement concerns the conditions under which the behavior will occur. These conditions include: the information, tools or equipment, and materials and supplies that will or will not be available to the student; any limitations of time and space; and other restrictions that may be applicable. In writing this portion of the objective, it is wise to try to visualize what conditions would be present in a "real life" performance, duplicating those conditions as much as you can in the objective.

Examples of conditions include such introductory phrases as "in a 30-minute written multiple choice test," "given a ruler and protractor," "given excerpts from the interurban bus schedule," "completely without notes," "in a new and strange situation," and "from a set of pictures." These conditions should be clear enough so that conditions are standard for everyone. If they are vague and fuzzy, one student may have a more difficult task to perform than another, though the basis for behavior and standards may seem the same. This point is especially important to keep in mind when working with students of diverse cultural backgrounds.

Finally, the standard of performance is the last part of the objective to write. Here you state what will be the level of behavior (degree of performance) you will accept as satisfactory. Your criterion may be the minimum number acceptable ("at least five reasons," "all ten reasons"), the percent or proportion acceptable ("with 90 percent accuracy," "in eight of ten cases"), acceptable limits of tolerance ("within plus or minus five degrees"), acceptable limits of time ("within a period of 15 minutes"), or some other standard. Usually this standard is set rather arbitrarily on the basis of the teacher's prior experience and current expectations. But when individualizing or teaching for mastery learning, the standard of expectation for individual students should be no less than 85 percent.

Now check your understanding of the four parts of a criterion-referenced behavioral objective by doing Exercise 3.7, Exercise 3.8, and Exercise 3.9.

Writing Simple Behavioral Objectives

Simple behavioral objectives are easier to formulate than criterion-referenced objectives—you simply must write what has to be done and who has to do it. The procedure for writing simple behavioral objectives is the same as that for writing criterion-referenced behavioral objectives, except that parts 3 and 4 are omitted. In simple objectives, you may use the less active verbs such as *know, understand, appreciate, comprehend, learn,* and *enjoy.* Remember that simple behavioral objectives may be covert objectives; criterion-referenced objectives may not. You may use simple behavioral objectives when formulating general objectives and goals, unless your instructors do not want you to use covert objectives at all, as is the case in some teacher preparation programs.

Writing Affective Behavioral Objectives

As already suggested, writing behavioral objectives in the affective domain is difficult because attitudes and feelings are covert. You cannot always tell how a person feels from that person's behavior. Sometimes, a person's behavior does not represent his or her real feelings. Quite frequently the person dissimulates—whistles a happy tune

EXERCISE 3.6   RECOGNIZING VERBS FOR OVERT
BEHAVIORAL OBJECTIVES
A Self-Check Exercise

From the following list of verbs circle those that *should not* be used in overt behavioral objectives—that is, those verbs that describe covert behaviors that are not directly observable and measurable. Check your answers against the answer key that follows. Discuss any problems with your classmates and instructor.

1.	apply	16.	grasp
2.	appreciate	17.	identify
3.	believe	18.	illustrate
4.	combine	19.	indicate
5.	comprehend	20.	infer
6.	compute	21.	know
7.	create	22.	learn
8.	define	23.	name
9.	demonstrate	24.	outline
10.	describe	25.	predict
11.	design	26.	realize
12.	diagram	27.	select
13.	enjoy	28.	solve
14.	explain	29.	state
15.	familiarize	30.	understand

Answer Key to Exercise 3.6

The following should be circled: 2, 3, 5, 13, 15, 16, 19, 21, 22, 26, 30. If you missed more than a couple, then you need to read the previous sections again and discuss your errors with your classmates and instructor.

EXERCISE 3.7   RECOGNIZING THE PARTS OF CRITERION-REFERENCED BEHAVIORAL OBJECTIVES
A Self-Check Exercise

In the following two objectives, identify the parts of the objectives by underlining once the *audience,* twice the *behavior,* three times the *conditions,* and four times the *performance level* (degree or standard of performance). Check against the answer key that follows; discuss any problems with your classmates and instructor.

1. You will write a 500-word account of the battle between the forces of Gondor and its allies against those of Mordor and its allies, as related in *The Lord of the Rings,* completely from memory. This account will be accurate in all basic details and include all the important incidents of the battle.

2. Given an interurban bus schedule, at the end of the lesson the student will be able to read the schedule well enough to determine at what time buses are scheduled to leave randomly selected points, with at least 90 percent accuracy.

ANSWER KEY TO EXERCISE 3.7

	OBJECTIVE 1	**OBJECTIVE 2**
Audience	You	The student
Behavior	will write a 500-word account of the battle between the forces of Gondor and its allies against those of Mordor and its allies	will be able to read the schedule
Conditions	completely from memory	given an interurban bus schedule
Performance level	This account will be accurate in all basic details and include all the important incidents of the battle.	well enough to determine (and) with at least 90 percent accuracy

EXERCISE 3.8   WRITING CRITERION-REFERENCED OBJECTIVES FROM HYPOTHETICAL TEACHING SITUATIONS

Part I

For each of the following hypothetical teaching situations, write one criterion-referenced objective. When completed, share your objectives with your classmates for their feedback and evaluation.

1. You are a typing teacher. By the end of the semester you believe that each student should be able to type at least 40 words per minute with no more than one error per minute.

2. You are teaching a unit on map reading, and you hope that at the end of the unit your students will be able to locate places on the globe by giving latitude and longitude to the nearest degree (plus or minus three) in at least 75 percent of the examples you set for them as a unit test.

3. You are teaching English literature. At the end of the unit you hope that at least half of your students will like Shakespearean comedy enough that they will continue to read some on their own.

4. You are teaching mathematics. You expect that at the end of the unit each student will be able to do two-digit multiplication and division with 90 percent accuracy.

5. You are teaching French. You expect all your students to be able to read with comprehension high school level-three French prose by the end of the semester.

Part II

Answer each of the following questions, check against the answer key that follows, and discuss any problems with your classmates and instructor.

1. Of the previous five hypothetical situations, teacher expectations for one is within the affective domain. Which one? _____

2. Of the same five situations, teacher expectations for two objectives include behaviors from two separate domains. Which two situations? _____ and which two domains? _____

Answer Key to Exercise 3.8, Part II

1. Situation 3

2. Situation 1 and Situation 2; psychomotor and cognitive.

EXERCISE 3.9   RECOGNIZING CRITERION-REFERENCED BEHAVIORAL OBJECTIVES
A Self-Check Exercise

Of the following ten objectives, circle the numbers of those that are unequivocally criterion-referenced behavioral objectives—the ones that have all four ingredients. Check your work against the answer key that follows. Discuss any problems with your classmates and instructor.

1. The student will be able to solve equations with one unknown.

2. Given examples of the type X^5/X^3, the student will solve the examples by subtracting exponents correctly in at least nine out of ten cases.

3. The student will be able to describe the differences between the policies followed by Lincoln and Johnson and those followed by the Radical Republicans in Congress.

4. Given a paper triangle, the student will be able to determine the center of gravity of the triangle by the paper-folding technique.

5. The student will be able to spell correctly each of the following common contractions: *doesn't, wouldn't, he's, you're, isn't, aren't, I'd, what's, hadn't, there's, they're, hasn't, you'll,* and *don't.*

6. Given a new and strange situation, the student usually attempts to examine all the available data before arriving at a conclusion.

7. The student can accurately define both mitosis and meiosis.

8. Given a specified word processing program, the student can use it unhesitatingly to write a research report.

9. The student can run a hundred yards in twelve seconds.

10. Given a dozen examples of rocks, the student can identify them without making more than three errors.

Answer Key to Exercise 3.9

Items 2, 9, and 10 are unequivocally criterion-referenced. Item 4 is also, assuming that the writer expects a 100 percent errorless performance. Items 6, 7, and 8 are criterion-referenced, though the criteria (*usually, accurately,* and *unhesitatingly*) are too subjective and liable to interpretation. Items 1 and 3 are not criterion-referenced. Items 1, 3, 4, and 5 are really simple behavioral objectives.

so no one will see fear or sadness. If people could not hide their real feelings, social relations would soon break down. Moreover, sometimes people do not know what their real attitudes are. Under periods of stress, attitudes carefully suppressed can suddenly appear. Also, a person's attitudes and feelings may be transitory and selective. The scientist who is carefully objective in the laboratory may be quite emotional, prejudiced, and irrational when making social judgments.

Another consideration is that the development and transformation of attitudes, ideals, and appreciations are usually long processes, taking months and years rather than the days or weeks of lessons and units. Finally, students often say and do what they think the teacher wants, keeping their real feelings, attitudes, and beliefs to themselves. After all, it is each person's individual right to keep such things private and personal.

For these reasons, writing behavioral objectives for the affective domain may be pointless. For the affective domain, covert objectives may serve our purposes just as well in the average classroom situation. Nevertheless, it is possible to write useful affective behavioral objectives. In doing so, you use much the same procedure as in writing other behavioral objectives, except that you add a statement about what effect (feeling, attitude) the behavior is supposed to indicate. The following example illustrates the suggested format:

> The student demonstrates a growing interest in operatic music by regular listening to the weekly radio programs of the Metropolitan Opera Company for recreational purposes.

In this objective, the elements are

☐ Who? The student.

☐ Behavior? Listen to the radio programs of the Metropolitan Opera Company.

☐ Conditions? For recreational purposes.

☐ How often? Regularly.

☐ Indicating what? The student's interest in opera.

A teacher can only assume that the student's listening to the radio broadcasts does, in fact, indicate that the student has become interested in opera. Here are other examples of behavioral objectives in the affective domain:

☐ The student exhibits a willingness to revise his or her conclusions on the basis of new evidence.

☐ The student shows an interest in history by borrowing and reading library books on history.

☐ The student exhibits civic responsibility by participating in civic projects.

☐ The student maintains meticulous records of his or her spending.

☐ The student reads Shakespearean plays for recreation.

☐ The student associates freely with peers without regard to their race or social class.

Writing Covert Behavioral Objectives

To write covert behavioral objectives you use the same formula as for simple overt behavioral objectives: that is, who does what? The difference is that the activity described is not observable and the verb used is not an action verb. Verbs that might be used in covert objectives include: *appreciate, believe, comprehend, enjoy, feel, know, learn, like, recognize, think* and *understand.* They are most useful for describing emotional or instructional goals and affective objectives.

As discussed in this module, objectives may be (a) overt or covert, (b) general or specific, and (c) simple or criterion-referenced. Also, in some cases these categories tend to overlap, and the categories may be combined in a number of ways.

SUMMARY

Objectives range from the very general to the very specific. Course goals, for instance, are usually quite general, while unit and lesson objectives represent specific elements of the course goals. These fairly specific objectives address overt behavior. Ordinarily, course goals and broad educational aims are written as covert behavioral objectives, as sometimes are affective objectives for unit and lesson plan use. Specific unit and lesson objectives, however, should be overt behavioral, sometimes simple and sometimes criterion-referenced.

You will have to use all the possible combinations of characteristics in the behavioral objectives you prepare for courses, units, and lessons when you teach. When you write the objectives for courses, units, and lessons, you will want to follow a procedure similar to the following:

1. Set up your course goals. Usually, these will have to be quite general. Therefore, you will probably need to make them simple, and in many cases you will find it easier and more rewarding to make them covert. (Can you see why general, simple, covert statements may be most useful as overall course objectives?) Overt behavioral objectives, simple or criterion-referenced, may also be useful. In some cases criterion-referenced objectives are a necessity. This is particularly likely to be the case in skill-centered subjects and under accountability systems.

2. Once your course objectives have been formulated, you should establish your units and set up the general objectives for each of your units. When doing so, be sure that these unit objectives, together, make up the course objectives. No necessary ingredient should be left out or short-changed. These objectives may be overt or covert, simple or criterion-referenced, depending on your evaluation of what is most desirable.

3. Now you need to set the specific objectives for each unit. These may be objectives for specific lessons if the unit is organized on a day-by-day lesson basis, or they may simply be unit subdivisions if you are using the laboratory or module approach. In any case, these objectives should all add up to the learning products called for in the general objectives. Remember, the specific examples can only be a sampling of all the subordinate objectives that could be combined to make up the general objectives. The general objectives can be broken down into many specific objectives. But because you can select only a limited number, you must try to get a good sampling of specific objectives for every general objective. Usually, you will want to make these specific objectives criterion-referenced behavioral objectives, but simple objectives may be preferable at times. Covert behavioral objectives are seldom useful for specific objectives.

When writing objectives you should remember to:

1. Try to get a good spread among the various levels of the three domains: cognitive, affective, and psychomotor. It is much too easy to get caught up with trivia, expecting learning that never gets beyond that of simple cognitive recall. To build specific, criterion-referenced behavioral objectives that call for use of the higher mental processes is not easy and it does take time. No one ever said that effective teaching was easy! But knowledge is not simply a collection of separate facts. The lists of action verbs presented in this module may help you write specific objectives that call for important learning.

2. Write each goal as a statement that describes the behavior sought, in such general terms as *understands, comprehends, knows,* and *appreciates.*

3. State each behavioral objective, general or specific, in terms of student performance rather than teacher performance.

4. Describe the terminal behavior of the student rather than the subject matter, the learning process, or the teaching procedure.

5. State each behavioral objective at the proper level of generality.

6. Define each general objective or goal by a sampling of specific behavioral objectives that describe terminal behavior and that show when the objective has been reached.

7. Provide a sufficient sampling of relevant specific behavioral objectives to demonstrate that each of the more general objectives or goals has been achieved.

8. Include in your objectives an adequate sampling of the high-level cognitive, affective, and psychomotor goals that are frequently omitted because they are difficult or time-consuming to write.

9. Limit each specific behavioral objective to only one learning product rather than a combination of learning products.

Although in this module we have talked only of objectives formulated by teachers, those objectives are likely to be fruitless unless accepted by the students. Students act not to fulfill a teacher's objectives but their own objectives. Therefore, you must take steps to guarantee that students buy into your objectives. One way to do this is to inform them early in the course, unit, or lesson of what you hope they will learn. If they consider the learning to be desirable and decide to work for that goal, you will be well on your way toward success. For that reason, it may be wise to select goals that are attractive to your students and to sell those goals as being worthwhile. In addition, for many courses students have a good notion of what learning they would enjoy or profit from most. Research indicates that student participation in the selection of objectives can be highly motivating. Knowing the goals set for a course and having good feedback concerning one's progress toward these goals are strong motivating devices. When the students know clearly what they are supposed to do, why they are doing it, and how much progress they are making, they will usually try to attain the goals. That is why, if teachers set clear behavioral objectives that seem reasonable, students will accept them and work toward them.

SUGGESTED READING

Alvino, J., et al. "Building Better Thinkers." *Learning 90* 18(6): 40–55 (February 1990).

Anderson, J. R. *Cognitive Psychology and Its Implications.* San Francisco: Freeman, 1985.

Bloom, B. S., ed. *Taxonomy of Educational Objectives, Handbook I: Cognitive Domain.* White Plains, NY: Longman, 1984.

Gagné, R. M. *Instructional Technology: Foundations.* Hillsdale, NJ: Lawrence Erlbaum, 1987.

Gronlund, N. E. *Stating Objectives for Classroom Instruction.* 3rd ed. New York: Macmillan, 1985.

Harrow, A. J. *Taxonomy of the Psychomotor Domain.* White Plains, NY: Longman, 1977.

Krathwohl, D. R., Bloom, B. S., and Masia, B. B. *Taxonomy of Educational Objectives: Handbook II: Affective Domain.* New York: David McKay, 1964.

Mager, R. F. *Preparing Instructional Objectives.* Rev. 2d ed. Belmont, CA: David S. Lake, 1984.

Martin, B. L., and Briggs, L. J. *The Affective and Cognitive Domains.* Englewood Cliffs, NJ: Educational Technology Publications, 1986.

Thompson, D. G. *Writing Long-Term and Short-Term Objectives, A Painless Approach.* Champaign, IL: Research Press, 1977.

Weinstein, C. E., et al. "Helping Students Develop Strategies for Effective Learning." *Educational Leadership,* 46(4): 17–19 (December 1988/ January 1989).

POSTTEST

Analyze Label the overt behavioral objectives *B*, the covert objectives *C*, other objectives *D*, and items that are not objectives *X*.

_____ 1. The students will realize that Romanticism was and is sentimental.

_____ 2. You will be able to read altitudes by the use of contour lines on a topographical map.

_____ 3. To encourage students to be neat and accurate in their work.

_____ 4. To discuss the reasons for the Protestant Reformation.

_____ 5. In this course we will examine the great works of Renaissance art.

_____ 6. An appreciation of modern music.

_____ 7. To cultivate the scientific attitude.

_____ 8. The students will be able to type at least thirty words a minute with no more than five errors.

Write *A* beside those verbs that describe covert activities and *B* beside those that describe overt behaviors.

_____ 9. appreciate	_____ 13. comprehend	_____ 17. define
_____ 10. estimate	_____ 14. identify	_____ 18. organize
_____ 11. predict	_____ 15. realize	_____ 19. recognize
_____ 12. solve	_____ 16. understand	_____ 20. write

Which of the following are general objectives? Which are specific objectives? Mark the general objectives *G* and the specific objectives *S*.

_____ 21. You will be able to speak French well enough to carry on a simple conversation.

_____ 22. The student will develop marketable vocational skills.

_____ 23. Given an appropriate sample of verse, the student will be able to identify the alliteration in it.

_____ 24. The student will appreciate the role economics plays in our national life.

_____ 25. The student will be able to define ionization.

_____ 26. The student will be able to convert yards to meters.

_____ 27. The student will speak correct idiomatic English.

Which of the following objectives are covert? Which are overt behavioral objectives? Mark the covert objectives *C* and the overt behavioral objectives *B*.

_____ 28. The students will realize the contributions of various ethnic groups.

_____ 29. The students will enjoy listening to good music.

_____ 30. You will be able to identify correctly the tools in an ordinary woodworking shop.

_____ 31. The students will be able to use the card catalog easily and accurately.

Check each complete criterion-referenced objective in the following list.

_____ 32. You will be able to write a summary of the plot of *The Wife of Bath*.

_____ 33. Given a diagram of an internal combustion engine, the student will be able to correctly label at least 80 percent of the components.

_____ 34. You will be able to list the steps for troubleshooting a Tecumseh motor without error.

_____ 35. Given a right triangle with the length of sides indicated, the student will specify the sine of one of the acute angles as a fraction in four out of five cases.

Using numbers 1 (lowest) through 6 (highest), rank the following in correct order from lowest to highest mental processes according to Bloom's taxonomy.

_____ 36. Analysis

_____ 37. Application

_____ 38. Comprehension

_____ 39. Evaluation

_____ 40. Knowledge

_____ 41. Synthesis

Multiple Choice   Place the letter of the best answer in the space provided.

_____ 42. What is the major relationship between general and specific objectives?
     a. A general and a specific objective are necessary for every lesson plan.
     b. General objectives must be written as overt behavioral objectives; specific objectives should not be.
     c. Specific objectives should always support a general objective.
     d. Specific objectives should be written as descriptive objectives; general objectives should not be.

_____ 43. Descriptive objectives are most useful for describing
     a. drill objectives.
     b. performance objectives.
     c. specific lesson objectives.
     d. general aims and goals.

_____ 44. The purpose of the taxonomies, according to this module, is to point out
     a. proper teaching strategies.
     b. levels to which instruction should aspire.
     c. standards for curriculum improvement.
     d. standards for student evaluation.

_____ 45. Covert objectives describe
     a. unobserved terminal activity.
     b. terminal behavior.
     c. performance standards.
     d. terminal student competencies.

The following is a list of elements that may or may not appear in objectives. Mark elements that according to the module may appear in: (1) overt behavioral objectives, B; (2) covert behavioral objectives, C; (3) affective objectives, A; (4) psychomotor objectives, S; (5) cognitive objectives, X; (6) criterion-referenced objectives, R. Note that each element may appear (probably does) in more than one type of objective.

_____ 46. Who will perform the behavior.

_____ 47. The behavior to be performed.

_____ 48. The standard of performance to be accepted.

_____ 49. The conditions under which the behavior will be performed.

_____ 50. The purpose of the behavior.

Short Answer

51. Define criterion-referenced behavioral objective.

_____

_____

52. Give two arguments for using behavioral objectives.

_____

_____

53. Define terminal behavior.

_____

_____

54. What is meant by "covert behavioral objective"?

_____

_____

55. Explain the value of a taxonomy of objectives.

_____

_____

56. A complete criterion-referenced objective consists of four parts. What are they?

_____

_____

_____

_____

57. What fifth part is often added to an affective objective?

_____

58. It is sometimes recommended that objectives in the affective domain not be written as overt behavioral objectives. Why is this so?

_____

_____

59. Explain the value of descriptive objectives.

_____

_____

60. What relationships should specific objectives have to general objectives and goals?

_____

_____

61. A broad objective, such as to understand the scientific method, is called a _____ objective.

62. Curriculum planners write objectives as infinitive phrases, as statements describing the learning product (the skill, concept, attitude, appreciation, or ideal to be learned), as covert behavioral objectives, and as overt behavioral objectives. According to this module, which of these is preferable for specific objectives?

_____

_____

Indicate the taxonomic category level of each of the following.

63. The student will be able to play the piano well enough to perform professionally.

_____

64. The student demonstrates concern about racial injustice by that student's relationships with others.

_____

65. When listening to a debate, the student can distinguish between valid and invalid arguments.

_____

66. The student will be able to describe the meaning of "the web of life."

_____

67. The student shows a love for fine literature by his or her selection of recreational reading.

_____

68. The student will be able to read and interpret the stock market reports.

_____

69. Given the topographic map of an area, the student will be able to identify the drainage system of the district.

_____

MODULE 4
Unit and Course Planning

RATIONALE

This module deals with the planning of units and courses. It shows how to carry out the two essentials of planning—(1) determining suitable goals and objectives and (2) selecting learning activities that will accomplish these goals and objectives.

Unit and course planning have a much greater scope than lesson planning. A course plan lays out the objectives, content, and organization for an entire semester or year. Unit plans lay out the objectives, content, and organization for course subdivisions that last from several days to three weeks. (A unit plan longer than three weeks is not recommended because beyond three weeks it begins to lose its effectiveness as a distinct unit of study.) Unit plans set forth the major goals toward which the instruction will be directed. Lesson plans, in contrast, set forth only the daily objectives and activities by which the teachers hope to bring about the learning that makes up the course or unit objectives. For this reason the direction and validity of the specific objectives and content of daily lesson plans are determined by the general goals and content outlined in the unit and course plans. In short, unit and course planning determines both what students should study in their daily lessons and what the impact of the entire curriculum should be, whereas the specific objectives and procedures of the daily lessons lead to the ultimate achievement of the long-term goals of the unit and the course. Thus, while lesson planning sets forth a sequence of what teachers and students will do in their daily lessons, unit and course planning determines the overall learning.

SPECIFIC OBJECTIVES

At the completion of this module, you should be able to:

1. Identify the four types of units described in this module.
2. Describe the distinguishing characteristics of each of the four types of units.
3. Describe the procedures for planning each of the four types of units.
4. Explain what considerations should be kept in mind when selecting:
   a. Goals
   b. Activities
   c. Content
   d. Materials
   e. Evaluation procedures
5. Describe the five principles of course organization as discussed in this module.
6. Explain what is meant for a course to be psychologically organized.
7. Describe the basic procedures of course planning.
8. Explain the steps one can take in course planning so as to increase the course's value for retention and transfer of knowledge.
9. Describe a procedure for building a plan for a continuous progress course.
10. Describe how to conduct teacher-student planning for units and courses.

MODULE TEXT

Units

As a rule, courses are divided into units. In effect, each unit is a long assignment in which—for a period of several days and up to three weeks—the instruction centers on a topic, theme, or major concept. By centering on a topic, theme, or concept, units serve to organize the course into manageable divisions that bring cohesiveness and focus to students' learning. Centering the instruction facilitates the development of general principles and understandings, avoiding the fractionalization and trivialization of course content that would result from a succession of unrelated or poorly articulated lessons. Such a strategy also serves to center the course on its important elements and to bring out the relationships among these elements. Course content divided into units is more usable and more meaningful than it would be if divided only into lessons. For example, if you were going to study the modern automobile (the course), you would want to organize your study into a natural sequence of units—one unit might be the drivetrain, another the fuel system, and yet another the components of the auto interior. Such organization would be preferable to an unrelated series of daily lessons in which one day students would study the fuel injectors and the next day they would study the types of driving lights. Organizing a course into sequential and teachable units of instruction facilitates student learning as well as the application and transfer of that learning.

As presented in this module, units can be organized in four basic ways:

1. An ordinary unit
2. A true or laboratory type unit
3. A learning package or module
4. A contract unit

Each of these is discussed in more detail later. Basically, however, an ordinary unit consists of a series of lessons centered on a topic, theme, major concept, or block of subject matter. A true or laboratory unit consists of a variety of learning experiences centered around long-term assignments rather than a series of separate lessons. A learning package or module is designed for individualized or modularized self-instruction. A contract unit is an individualized unit plan for which a student agrees (contracts) to carry out certain activities during the unit.

General Unit Planning Procedure

The steps for planning units are much the same for all four types of units:

1. *Select a suitable topic or theme.* Often these are already laid out in your course of study or textbook.
2. *Select the unit's general objectives.* The objectives should be written as an overview or rationale, covering what the unit is about and what the students generally are to learn. They may, however, be written as descriptive or behavioral objectives (as discussed in Module 3). When you plan these objectives, you should:
   a. become as familiar with the topic and materials on the topic as you can
   b. consult courses of study, other curriculum documents, and resource units for ideas
   c. decide what you believe the students should learn from the study of the topic and how you should best approach it
   d. write out a general statement or overview in which you summarize what you hope the students will have learned about the topic at the completion of the unit
   e. make sure that your unit objectives are congruent with the course objectives
3. *Select suitable specific learning objectives.* In so doing:
   a. include understandings, skills, attitudes, appreciations, and ideals
   b. be specific, avoiding vagueness and generalizations
   c. use behavioral objectives when feasible
   d. be sure that the specific objectives will contribute to the major learning described in your general statement or overview
4. *Detail the instructional procedures by which you will teach the topics.* These procedures will include the subject content and the learning activities, set up as a series of lessons or as a unit of work. No matter which approach you take, you will have to follow these same general steps in your initial planning:
   a. Gather ideas for learning activities that might be suitable for the unit. Refer to curriculum guides, textbooks, resource units, and other curriculum documents. Do not forget to use other teachers as resources for learning activities.
   b. Check these learning activities to make sure that they would actually contribute to the learning designated in your objectives. Discard any ideas that do not contribute directly to your goals.
   c. Check to make sure that the learning activities are feasible in your situation. Can you afford to give them the time, effort, and expense necessary? Do you

have the necessary materials and equipment? Are they suited to the maturity level of your students?

   d. Check the resources available to be certain that they support the content and learning activities.

   e. Decide how to introduce the unit of work. Provide for introductory activities that will:

     (1) arouse the students' interest

     (2) inform the students of what the unit is about

     (3) help you learn about your students—their interests, their abilities, and their present knowledge about the topics

     (4) show the relationship with preceding units and courses

     (5) give students opportunities to plan what they will do during the unit

   f. Plan developmental activities, providing activities that will:

     (1) maintain student interest

     (2) provide for individual differences

     (3) promote the learning cited in your specific objectives

   g. Plan culminating activities, including activities that will:

     (1) summarize what has been learned

     (2) bring together any loose ends

     (3) apply what has been learned to new situations

     (4) provide a transfer to the unit that follows

5. *Plan for the evaluation of students' learning.* Evaluating student progress should permeate the entire unit. Make plans to gather information in several ways, including informal observations, student performance, and paper and pencil evaluations. Be certain that your plan for evaluating the progress of your students matches well with the specific learning products or terminal behaviors of your unit objectives.

6. *Provide for materials of instruction.* Your units cannot function without materials. Therefore, you must plan long before the unit begins for audiovisual equipment and materials, bibliographies, reading material, reproduced materials, and community resources. For example, reading material that is not available to the students is not much help to them, even if it is in your bibliography.

THE ORDINARY UNIT PLAN

First, the word *ordinary* does not mean *blah*. An ordinary unit plan is the type of unit plan most commonly described for beginning teachers. An **ordinary unit** is a series of lessons centered on a topic, theme, major concept, or block of subject matter. This series of lessons hangs together because the lessons are all aimed at accomplishing the unit objectives and because each of the lessons is related to the others. In an ordinary unit each lesson builds on the previous lesson by contributing additional subject matter, providing further illustrations, and supplying more practice or other added instruction, all of which are aimed at bringing about mastery of the knowledge and skills on which the unit is centered. Usually these lessons are teacher-centered, expository, and supplemented by student recitations, discussions, reports, and projects.

Preparing the Ordinary Unit Plan

Preparing a plan for an ordinary unit consists of the following steps:

Step 1. Select a topic, such as Water, the Skeletal System, the Crisis in the Middle East, the Civil War, or Introduction to Equations. This should be an easy task, since the topics for the course already are laid out in your course plan.

Step 2. Select general and specific objectives that represent what you hope the students will learn about the topic. These unit objectives should be such that they contribute to the course objectives. As a rule, unit objectives are general in nature, pointing out the major concepts, skills, attitudes, and appreciations at which the unit is aimed. In an ordinary unit, specific objectives are usually reserved for lesson plans. These general objectives may be stated as major concepts to be learned, such as "The divergent paths of the American People: 1800–1850." They may also be stated as covert behavioral objectives, such as "The students will demonstrate an appreciation for the difficulties pioneers experienced as they moved westward." They may also begin with an infinitive, such as "Students will develop an understanding of the essential ingredients of a short story: plot, character, and ending."

Step 3.   Plan a sequence of daily lesson plans that will cause students to reach your objectives. You do not have to build these lessons in their entirety now, but you should note what you expect their content and procedure to be. These lessons make up the "procedure" of the ordinary unit. They include the following:

- □ **Introductory lessons**, lessons that tie this unit to the preceding ones, point out the objectives and reason for studying this unit, provide for preassessment and diagnostic activities, set the tone for the lessons to follow, and generally motivate the students.

- □ **Developmental lessons**, lessons that build the learning that makes up the unit objectives and content. In most ordinary units the learning activities in these lessons are largely of the teacher-centered expository type, although not necessarily so. Small-group work, seatwork, discussion, practice sessions, and inquiry activities may all be included in the lessons of the developmental section of the ordinary unit.

- □ **Culminating lessons**, lessons that tie together what has been learned in the developmental lessons, making the learning secure. These may include teacher recapitulations, review lessons, student reports, and transfers to the next unit, usually ending in a unit test.

Step 4.   Decide on any major activities, projects, or other assignments (e.g., field trips and written assignments) and incorporate them in appropriate locations in your lessons.

Step 5.   Provide a scheme as well as the instruments that will evaluate student progress. Usually this step includes the unit test mentioned earlier. Since the purpose of the unit test is to determine how well students have mastered the unit's content, the test questions are based on that content. The unit test is given at completion of the unit. In addition to this unit test, frequent learning and comprehension checks should be built into the lessons of the unit in order to gauge and reinforce the learning taking place. Some of these comprehension checks may be used for grading purposes.

Step 6.   Provide the necessary materials to support the instruction.

The Laboratory-Type Unit

A **laboratory-type unit**, sometimes called a true unit, differs from an ordinary unit in that it is much more cohesive and, at the same time, allows for much more individualization. Most of the teaching takes place in an individualized, problem-solving, laboratory fashion rather than in daily lessons. The bulk of the teaching is of the inquiry rather than the expository type. Thus, during much of the unit the student is engaged more in active personal research than in listening to the recitation of the teacher. In such a unit, some but not all activities and experiences are required of every student. There may be a number of optional activities that students can choose to do or not do as they please, depending on individual interests, needs, and goals. The required activities or experiences are called **core** or **basic activities**. The optional activities are called **optional related activities**. In a laboratory-type unit the students do a considerable amount of the planning themselves. For the students to have the freedom to proceed at their own speed and in their own direction, they are provided a study guide that allows them to begin and carry out activities—under supervision—without being heavily dependent on the teacher. The following description of a laboratory-type unit in action may clarify what teaching through this approach encompasses:[1]

---

[1]Originally published in Leonard H. Clark and Irving S. Starr, *Secondary School Teaching Methods*, Fourth Edition (New York: Macmillan, 1981), p. 144. Adapted by permission of Macmillan Publishing Company.

Mr. Jones teaches Problems of Democracy at Quinbost High School. In his course outline he has listed a unit on minority groups. Mr. Jones always tries to make his course interesting and challenging, stimulating and motivating to his students. On the day he was to introduce the unit, he came to the classroom seemingly in an angry mood, tossed his books on the desk, and glared at the class. He then began a tirade on a particular minority group, telling the class of something that a member of that group had done to him the day before, and concluding by saying that all members of that particular group were alike.

Immediately, his class began to challenge him, disagreeing, telling him he was unfair to generalize on the basis of one incident and that he shouldn't talk like that. Seizing upon this reaction, Mr. Jones then asked the class whether or not they had ever expressed such feelings about any particular group. As the animated discussion continued, the class members began to see what Mr. Jones was doing. Almost as one body they said that they wanted to discuss minority groups as a class topic.

The stage had been set! Mr. Jones had fired their interest; the students' desire to study the topic was keen. He then set the class to discussing what subject matter should be discussed and what outcomes there should be. This led to general teacher-student planning. Soon students were choosing committees and projects on which to work. Then, with the aid of prepared teacher-made study guides and their committees and project assignments, individual students completed tentative plans for their roles in the unit.

The study guide they used consisted of three parts:

1. The first part noted questions and problems for which every student was to find answers and also suggested where the students might look to find these answers.

2. The second part listed a number of readings and activities that the students might find interesting. All students were expected to do some of these, but no one had to do any particular one. These activities were optional. In none of these activities or the required problems and questions was the student held to any prescribed reading or procedure. All the student was asked to do was to carry out the activity, solve the problem, or find the information; there was free choice about the ways and means.

3. The third part of the study guide was a bibliography.

Once the teacher and students had finished their planning, they began to work. Except for two periods that Mr. Jones used for showing videos, the next two weeks were devoted to laboratory work. The committees met; the researchers investigated; the students carried out their plans.

Then the committees and researchers began to report. Some of the groups presented a panel discussion. Another group presented a play. Another conducted a question-and-answer game that they had invented. In all of these activities students tried to share what they had learned. In between these reports, Mr. Jones and the students discussed the implications of the findings and other points they thought pertinent and important.

Finally, the unit ended with everyone's setting down his or her ideas concerning the treatment of minority groups, and with a short objective test, based on the teacher's objectives as shown in the questions of the study guide.

Thus, after a little over three weeks, the unit was finished.

A close examination of this unit shows that it was actually divided into four phases. First, Mr. Jones introduced the unit to the students and tried to "fire their interest" in the topic. Second, the students worked individually and in small groups in a laboratory fashion. Third, the committees and individual researchers reported on what they had accomplished and then discussed their findings. Fourth, Mr. Jones tried to assess the students' growth by means of evaluative devices and evaluative procedures. These four phases are called: (1) the introductory phase, (2) the laboratory phase, (3) the sharing phase, and (4) the evaluative phase. In laboratory-type units, the phases may appear in order or they may not. When a unit is successfully individualized, all the phases of the unit may be in progress simultaneously.

Introductory Phase

In the introductory phase the purpose is to get the unit off to a good start. If your introductory activities work well, they should: arouse the students' interest; inform the students of what the unit is about; help the teacher learn more about the students, their interests, their abilities, and their present knowledge; show how the unit relates to earlier units and courses; and provide an opportunity for the students to plan how they will study the unit. This important phase sets the tone for the entire unit—a bright, breezy, stimulating start may make all the difference. Therefore, the teacher should strive to find introductory activities that will challenge the students' curiosity, arouse their interest, and set them to thinking about the topic. Since the students will likely plan their work cooperatively, the teacher must make sure that all students have the necessary background. Introductory teacher talks, videos, and video discs may give just the orientation the students need. To help the students actually plan their own activities, the best method probably is to distribute a study-and-activity guide or a list of possible activities, letting students choose and organize for themselves under the teacher's guidance. Once they have decided what to do, individual students could fill out a plan such as the one shown in Figure 4.1.

Laboratory Phase

During the laboratory phase, the students implement the plans they have made, including both the required activities and the selected optional activities. Most of the work in this phase is done individually or in small cooperative learning groups, at the students' own speed and in their own ways. Nevertheless, the teacher reserves class time for any whole-class activities that may be necessary or that seem advantageous. During this phase, most of the students' direction for carrying out activities comes from their study-and-activity guides as well as from special study guides provided for optional related activities. Although all students will not do the same activities in the same way during the laboratory phase, all students will learn much the same things— that is, the learning products set forth in the objectives. For this reason, the required activities are usually set up as problems that all students must attempt to solve in one way or another. The optional activities should be related somehow to the required activities. By this process, all students should achieve the same objectives despite reading different books or solving the problems in different ways.

FIGURE 4.1
Sample Form for a Work Plan

Name _____   Class _____
Unit _____   Date _____

Activities I plan to do:

Committees I plan to work with:

Materials I plan to read:

Things I plan to make:

Sharing Phase

The sharing phase consists of opportunities for students to pool what they have individually learned. This sharing does not imply a series of reports, though there should be some reporting. Since the activities have all been aimed at the same set of objectives, the students' learning should have much in common. Therefore, there should be much to discuss and debate, through which students pool their ideas and share what they have discovered. In addition, the students might share their experiences through panels, dramatizations, demonstrations, exhibits, class newspapers, jury procedures, and similar techniques.

Evaluative Phase

Effective teachers evaluate continually, not just at the end. Nevertheless, the end of the unit makes an excellent occasion for taking stock. At this point, the teacher needs to know how well the students have done in order to evaluate the success of the unit, prepare for whatever remedial follow-up seems necessary, and then move smoothly into the next unit. For the most practical value, the measurement devices you use in the evaluation should be of the diagnostic type.

PLANNING THE LABORATORY-TYPE UNIT

When you plan a laboratory-type unit you must provide for the following elements:

1. *Introduction*, including topic, time duration, course title, grade level, justification, and place in the course or curriculum.

2. *The general objective*, often written as an overview or rationale, telling what the unit is about and what students are expected to learn.

3. *The specific objectives*, covering the skills, understandings, attitudes, ideals, and appreciations the students will be expected to learn. These should be written as learning products or as behavioral objectives (current opinion favors the use of behavioral objectives).

4. *The actual unit of work or unit assignment*, the required and related optional activities in which the students will engage. Frequently, these activities are categorized as introductory activities, developmental activities, and culminating activities. The introductory activities are used in the introductory phase, the developmental activities in the laboratory and sharing phases, and the culminating activities in the sharing and evaluative phases. Note that the activities of the sharing phase can be either developmental or culminating. Culminating activities are those that tie material together and bring the unit to closure in high style. Activities in which students pool and share experiences are excellent for this purpose, as is an end-of-the-unit test—the idea is for the unit to start with a bang and end with a boom. A calendar scheduling when various activities and audiovisuals are to occur is a handy tool for implementing the unit.

5. *The general study-and-activity guide*, containing the instructions for carrying out the core activities to be done individually and in small groups.

6. *Special study-and-activity guides*, containing the instructions for carrying out the optional related activities and various special activities, such as field trips.

7. *Evaluative procedures*, with details of the procedures and instruments that will be used to measure and evaluate student progress and the success of the unit. These must adequately test both the general and specific objectives.

8. *A list of readings*, for student use.

9. *A list of materials*, anything needed for students to do the activities.

10. *A bibliography*, for teacher use.

Some teachers also include an outline of the subject content. In order to provide for each of these elements adequately, you should use the following procedure.

Step 1. Selecting the Topic.   As implied in the discussion of an ordinary unit, the topic of the unit is for all practical purposes the name of the unit. The topic is usually a portion of subject matter, though it might be a problem or a theme. Ordinarily, it is one in a sequence of topics already outlined in the course plan. To be usable, a topic should: (a) center on some major understanding, problem, issue, or theme; (b) both fit the course objectives and further the course plan; (c) be relevant to students' lives and to the society in which they live; (d) be manageable, not too difficult, too big, or too demanding of time and resources; and (e) be suitable to students' abilities and interests.

Step 2. Writing the Unit Objectives.   The general objective can be written as an overview describing the major concept that the students should learn. For example, the overview for Mr. Jones's unit on minority groups was:

> Every citizen should understand what our minority problems are. Citizens should analyze their feelings about different minority groups. All should evaluate the contributions of each of these groups to the development of the United States. We must try to understand the importance of cooperation among all groups.

Other examples of unit overviews are:

> The learning products sought for each student are (1) the ability to make a screwdriver involving the use of those common hand tools peculiar to the machine shop; (2) the ability to operate the engine lathe, drill press, and milling machine with the dividing or indexing hand; (3) some understanding and appreciation of the source, characteristics, and proper-ties of tool steel (water quench), machinery steel, and hard maple from the standpoint of the consumer; (4) some understanding and appreciation of the place of the metalworking industry in present-day society from the standpoint of materials and processes employed, products produced, and the effect of these materials, processes, and products on the worker and on the consuming public; and (5) some understanding and appreciation of the work performed by those employed in a variety of occupations in the metalworking indus-tries and related shops from the standpoint of the opportunities and requirements for em-ployment in these industries.

>   Well-written adventure stories appeal to seventh-grade readers because of their ex-citing, suspenseful plots, their heroic characters, and interesting settings.

The purpose of the overview or the general objectives is to give the unit a focal point. (Examples of overviews are those found in the Rationale section at the beginning of each module of this text.) In addition, the general objectives of the unit should list the general skills, attitudes, appreciations, and ideals that the students should acquire from studying the unit.

The specific learning products may be written as descriptions of the concepts, attitudes, or skills to be learned, such as:

☐ The guilt for starting World War I was shared by many nations.

☐ The perimeter of any figure is simply the distance around the figure.

They are probably best written as behavioral objectives, such as:

☐ Upon completion of this unit the student will be able to explain, with 100 percent accuracy, the role that each nation played in starting World War I.

☐ Upon completion of this unit the student will be able, with 100 percent accuracy, to determine the perimeter of (a) triangles, (b) squares, (c) rectangles, (d) parallelo-grams, (e) trapezoids, and (f) general polygons.

There are two important concerns in writing the specific objectives: (1) they must contribute to the larger goal and (2) they must be specific enough and clear enough for both teacher and the students to understand what the objectives are. In addition, the objectives must be achievable in the time allotted and with the resources available, be worthwhile in the minds of the students, and be neither too difficult nor too easy to achieve. Specific objectives should also allow for differences in students' abilities, interests, backgrounds, needs, and goals. Teachers often find it helpful to list separately the different categories of specific objectives (concepts, skills, appreciations, attitudes). Note that in a laboratory-type unit the specific objectives cannot be relegated to lesson plans as in an ordinary unit.

Step 3. Planning the Unit of Work.   Once the objectives are written, you then prepare the plan for the unit of work. The first step is to identify potentially good activities. To gather potentially useful activities you might search curriculum documents, textbooks, books on teaching in the discipline, and the professional periodical literature. Then the activities must be culled: Are they really suitable for the objectives? If not, can they be adapted so as to make them suitable? Are they feasible in view of the time, material, equipment, and other resources available? Are they worth the time and effort? Are they too difficult or too easy? Which will do the job best? At this point, check the resources available and make a list of them. The list should include audiovisual media, library resources, equipment, and supplies. It is embarrassing and frustrating after concocting elaborate plans to find that you do not have the materials and supplies you need.

Now divide the activities into two categories: those that should be required of all students and those that should be optional. In each unit there should be enough optional work to give each student a chance to do something he or she can enjoy and do well.

Next, decide how to introduce the unit. Try to find introductory activities that will both tell the students what the unit is about and arouse their interest. If you intend to have students cooperate in planning the unit, include cooperative planning in your introductory activities.

Next, plan the developmental activities and the culminating activities. These should include: (1) provisions for committee and individual laboratory types of work; (2) opportunities for students to share what they have learned with one another; and (3) whole-class activities, such as videos, guest speakers, field trips, and teacher talks. For activities that need scheduling, set definite (even if tentative) times. In your scheduling, remember to allow students enough time to complete both their required and their optional work.

Then prepare a study guide for the students to follow during the laboratory phase, when they are working alone or in small groups. In addition to using this study guide in the laboratory phase, the students will find it helpful in their personal planning during the introductory phase.

Finally, plan how you will evaluate the students' work. Build tests, quizzes, rating scales, and other instruments and devices that you will need for the evaluative phase.

The following is an excerpt from a plan designed for an industrial-arts unit (for which the overview was presented as an example in the discussion of Step 2):

Unit of Work: (Tentative time allotment is five forty-four-minute periods per week for five weeks.[2] Four periods each week are given to manipulative and observational experiences in the machine shop; one period each week to witnessing demonstrations, listening to brief lectures and illustrated talks, participating in discussions, and in other forms of individual and group activity in the industrial arts related laboratory.)

A. Introduction: Illustrated lecture, discussion, test, and demonstration.
1. Explain the threefold nature of the unit study: (a) to learn how to make a useful and practical screwdriver from both wood and steel in preparation for doing more advanced work that permits the learner to select, under the guidance of the instructor, those projects that best meet immediate and anticipated needs of the students; (b) to learn about the various branches of the metalworking industry, related industries, and their services to society through readings and through visual aids, such as the films, "The Tool and Diemaker," "The Drama of Steel," "Grits That Grind," "Magnesium," and "Files on Parade"; (c) to learn how to buy and care for the tools and products of metalworking and related industries.

---

[2]Units that are longer than the recommended maximum of three weeks are acceptable and not uncommon in shop, physical education, music, and other highly activity-oriented subject fields.

2. Demonstrate the correct and safe use of each tool and machine in the elementary situations in which the students will use it.
3. Give a test of multiple-response, completion, matching, and identification questions to discover what the students already know about the meanings and insights to be developed.
4. Hand out the "List of Readings and References" and activity guide (Job Breakdown) for the Screwdriver Ferrule, and explain the uses of the list of readings and references and the more detailed guides (Job Breakdowns) to follow.

B. Laboratory Work
   (Note: items that follow are part of a general study and activity guide or job breakdown.)
   1. Make a useful screwdriver with a wooden handle as per assembly print to be furnished by the instructor.
      a. Study the sample screwdriver, completed component parts, and the assembly print submitted by the instructor, and develop the necessary working detail sketches, scale of two to one, of the screwdriver ferrule, blade, and handle. (Ask the teacher for a special study and activity guide showing good sketches and giving suggestions for making them.)
      b. After the sketches for the screwdriver have been completed and initialed by the instructor, prepare a bill of materials needed for making the project. (Ask the teacher for a special study and activity guide for making out a bill of materials.) Calculate how much the article will cost to produce. Obtain the teacher's approval on your bill of materials and estimated cost.
      c. Select and cut to length on the power hacksaw the stock that you will need for making the screwdriver. (Ask for the special study and activity guide.)
      d. Machine the stock to overall finished length and break all sharp edges. (Ask for the special study and activity guide or breakdown.)
      e. Machine and fabricate screwdriver ferrule and blade to blueprint (B/P) specifications. (Ask for the special study and activity guides or job breakdowns.)

Step 4. Preparing the General Study-and-Activity Guide.   The purpose of the general study-and-activity guide is to give the students information they need to perform the required activities and to select the optional activities they want to pursue. The activities should largely be of the problem-solving or inquiry type. The instructions should be explicit enough that the students can guide themselves through the activities without heavy dependence on the teacher. The guide is useful because it gives the student: (1) a source to which the student can refer if an assignment is forgotten, (2) a definite assignment so the student can proceed to new activities without waiting for a new assignment from the teacher, and (3) definite instructions that should eliminate both misunderstandings about assignments and excuses for incomplete or unattempted assignments.

   The following are excerpts from a general study guide accompanying a unit on adventure stories (for which the overview was presented as an example in the discussion of Step 2):

   1. Read Jack London's story, "The Lost Poacher" (1:312–321). [Read pages 312–321 of the first reference appearing at the end of the study guide.] What chance has "Bub" Russell to become a hero in the eyes of his mates? What makes a person a hero? Study the questions appearing in 1:380–381. (Note: These references are keyed to the bibliography furnished with the study guide. The number preceding the colon refers to a book; the numbers following the colon are the page references.)

   3. Read Jeannette Eaton's story of David Livingstone's life (1:176–186). As you read, think how Livingstone's life differs from that of "Bub" Russell. If you could change places with either of these people, which would you prefer to be? Write a short paragraph explaining why. Be prepared to discuss the story using the questions appearing in the study guide.

   5. Read "Old Slewfoot" from *The Yearling* by Marjorie Kennan Rawlings (2:109–120). What sort of person is Penny to the other people and animals in the story?

6. Prepare an adventure poem to recite to the class as a committee. Part of the poem might be recited in chorus. Examples of poems your committee might recite are "Casey at the Bat," "Clara Burton," "The Cremation of Sam McGee," and "The Highwayman." Be prepared to show why the selection is a good adventure poem.

8. Read "Treasure" by Mark Twain (1:65–75) and "Mafatu Stout Heart" by Armstrong Sperry (1:91–100). Which had the more exciting existence, Mafatu or Tom Sawyer? Back up your answer with evidence from the story.

10. Read "One Minute Longer," by Albert Payson Terhune (1:240–249). How does the author build suspense in this story?

11. Read Stephen Meader's "Escape from the River of the Wolves" (1:250–260). Notice how the excitement is carried through the story. How does the author maintain this excitement?

Step 5. Preparing Special Study-and-Activity Guides. The study-and-activity guides you prepare need not follow any particular form. Just be sure they explain to students how to carry out the study or activity concerned. Some of the things you might want to include in a special study-and-activity guide are:

☐ The purpose of the activity

☐ Background information

☐ Directions for carrying out the activity

☐ Exercises and drill material

☐ Fact or problem questions

☐ Problems to solve

☐ Suggested readings

☐ Self-correcting tests and exercises

☐ Follow-up activities

The following are two examples of special study-and-activity guides. This first example is a guide for a discussion:[3]

12th Grade Social Studies
Factors in the consideration of Means and Ends

1. Can necessity create its own law?
2. Can "ends" be judged without previous standards of judgment?
3. Who decides, or how is it decided, that an "end" is good?
4. Are the "means" employed toward making an "end" good?
5. When is necessity "real," when is it "imagined"?
6. Can we separate "means" from "ends"?
7. Are the "means" to be judged before or after the "ends" are achieved?
8. Is the question of the "ends" justifying the "means" for both individuals and states?
9. Do the means determine the ends?
10. Does the pinch of necessity preclude any national consideration of means?
11. How do we consider degrees of "necessity"?
12. How can we determine whether some ends are better than others?
13. Are certain types of means and ends peculiar to specific aspects of society?
14. Are certain means improper, criminal, etc., even when they are not employed?
15. Can means and ends ever be considered moral?
16. Is law a fact only when it can be enforced?

---

[3]From a Cheltenham (PA) 12th grade social studies unit.

17. Can evil means be employed toward a good end?

18. How can we evaluate abstract ends?

19. How is the concept of what constitutes an end to be reached?

20. Can ends exist independent of the individual?

This second example is a guide for a recording:

Listening Questions for The Phoenician Traders (Note: The following are illustrative of the type of questions one might use in a special study guide for use with this recording. They represent different levels and types of questions. In using such study guides the teacher must guard against merely mechanical exercises.)

1. What seems to be the major business of the Phoenicians?

2. What seems to be the relationship between Tyre and Carthage?

3. What can you learn about the trade routes of the Phoenicians?

4. What was life like on a caravan?

5. What can you note about Phoenician ships and seamanship?

6. What did you learn about Phoenician trade? How did they carry it on? How did they keep accurate accounts and so on? In what way did they trade?

7. How nearly accurate is the reconstruction of Phoenician life? If you do not know, how can you find out?

8. Prepare a list of questions that would emphasize or bring out the important idea expressed in this recording.

Step 6. Developing a Scheme for Evaluation.   Because evaluation of student progress must take place continually throughout the unit, you must incorporate evaluating procedures and devices into the unit. Reports, papers, classwork, and progress tests are among the types of activities that make up this continual evaluation. In addition, each unit should probably culminate in a diagnostic test. Such a culmination helps tie together the various threads in the unit and reveal how well you have achieved your teaching goals. A diagnostic test is essential for determining what you should do next.

Step 7. Preparing a List of Readings for the Students' Use.   Here you should list the important references for the students' study. Number the works listed so they may be keyed to the exercises, problems, and other activities listed in the unit of work or the unit assignment. Check to be sure the readings are available to the students. This list should be duplicated and issued to the students for their own use.

Step 8. Deciding and Listing What Instructional Materials and Resources Will Be Needed.   Long before the unit of work begins, it is essential that you know (1) what audiovisual materials, duplicated materials, community resources, and the like, you will need and (2) the availability of these needed materials. The list you make should be attached to the student's general study-and-activity guides.

Step 9. Preparing a Teacher's Bibliography.   Here you record references that you might find helpful for reference, information, and ideas as the unit proceeds. This list is for your use, not for student use.

The Learning Activity Packet

A learning activity packet (also called a learning packet, learning activity package, or instructional package) is designed for independent, individual study. The packet consists of instruction, references, exercises, problems, self-correcting materials, and all the other information and materials that a student needs to carry out a unit of work independently. Consequently, students can work on learning packets individually at their own speed, and different students can be working on different packets at the same time. Students who successfully finish a packet can move on to another unit of work without waiting for the other students to catch up. Such packets are essential ingredients of continuous-progress courses. To prepare a learning activity packet, you follow nearly the same procedures as for other types of units. The principal difference is that the learning activity packet is designed for independent, individual self-instruction. One type of learning packet is the self-instructional package, which is different from unit packages in that the self-instructional package is designed to teach less content than is typical of units. The exercise that follows will guide you through the process of preparing a self-instructional package for your own teaching. To prepare a learning activity packet, you would follow essentially the same steps, except that this package is designed to last longer and to cover more content material.

PLANNING A LEARNING CONTRACT

The learning contract is another variation of the unit. The procedure for planning a contract unit is about the same as that for an ordinary unit, except that in the learning-contract plan the student agrees to fulfill certain requirements during the unit. The basic procedure for planning a contract unit is:

1. Establish objectives and activities whereby students may achieve the objectives.
2. Decide what the unit requirements will be.
3. Decide whether the contract will have a variable-letter-grade agreement built in.
4. Decide what activities will be required.
5. Decide which activities will be optional.
6. Provide a written study-and-activity guide describing the activities.
7. Allow each student to decide how to meet the requirements.
8. Require that each student prepare or sign a written contract based on the decisions made with the teacher.

All contracts involve an element of *quid pro quo*. Some contracts are simply student-teacher agreements of what the student must do and the teacher will accept for satisfactory completion of the unit. Other contracts have a variable-letter-grade agreement built into them. The sample contract shown in Figure 4.2 does not contain such an element. It could be made to do so by adding the requirements for a certain grade, as in Figure 4.3.

Another system for planning a contract is to decide what activities and quality of work performance will be required for each of the grade levels (A, B, C, and D) and to specify these requirements on the contract or in the study-and-activity guide. For example:

To pass with a D, you must complete activities 1–10 and pass the posttest.
For a grade of C, you must complete activities 1–10, receive at least a C on the posttest, and satisfactorily complete two optional related activities.

FIGURE 4.2
Sample General Contract

GENERAL CONTRACT

Student _____ Date to be completed _____

During the unit, I will:

☐ Read Chapter III of the text.

☐ Do the problems on Worksheet A.

☐ Participate in the panel on the Panama Canal.

☐ Pass the unit test.

☐ Demonstrate that I can perform all the requirements of Group C.

Student signature _____

EXERCISE 4.1   PREPARING A SELF-INSTRUCTIONAL PACKAGE

This purpose of this exercise is to guide you through the process of preparing a self-instructional package for use in your own teaching. The exercise continues for several pages; it is important that you follow it step-by-step, beginning with the following boxed-in "cover page."

Self-Instructional Package Number: *1*
Instructor's Name: Professor Richard D. Kellough
School: California State University, Sacramento
Course: General Secondary and Middle School Methods
Intended Students: Students in Teacher Preparation
Topic: How to Write a Self-Instructional Package
Estimated Working Time: 10 hours

For the challenge of today's classroom . . .

THE SELF-INSTRUCTIONAL PACKAGE

You are about to embark upon creating and writing a perfect lesson plan. The result of your hard work will be an instructional module in which you will take a lot of pride. More important, you will have learned a technique of teaching that absolutely assures that learning takes place. For what more could you ask?

Let us get to the essence of what this self-instructional package (S.I.P.) is: this S.I.P. is about "how to write the S.I.P." The general objective is to guide you gently through the process of preparing and writing your first S.I.P. Let's begin the experience with background about the history of the S.I.P.

Exercise 4.1 copyright 1991 by Richard D. Kellough.

A History

Research evidence indicates that student achievement in learning is related to time and to the *quality of attention* being given to the learning task. You knew that already! In 1968, Benjamin Bloom developed a concept of individualized instruction called **mastery learning**, based on the idea that students need sufficient time-on-task to master content before moving on to new content. Did you know that? _____. (Please read along with a pencil and fill in the blanks as you go.)

Although Bloom is usually given credit for the concept of mastery learning, the idea did not originate with him. He reinforced and made popular a model developed earlier by John Carroll. In 1968, Fred Keller developed a similar model called the Keller Plan, or the Personalized System of Instruction (P.S.I.). The P.S.I. quickly became a popular teaching technique in the community and four-year colleges. In about 1972, enter Johnson and Johnson (not of the Band-Aid family, but Rita and Stuart Johnson), who developed their model of mastery learning and called it the Self-Instructional Package (S.I.P.). Since 1972 I (Richard D. Kellough) have been developing an improved version, which you are now experiencing. As you will learn, *frequent comprehension checks and corrective instruction* are important to the effectiveness of the S.I.P.

One other thing. There are several devices available to individualize instruction, but the S.I.P. has the flexibility to be adaptable for use at all grade and subject levels, from kindergarten through college. Let me give you what I believe to be are the reasons for the popularity of this strategy.

- ☐ The S.I.P. allows the instructor to *create an experience that absolutely assures learning*. Creating makes you feel good; when your students learn, you feel good—two reasons for the S.I.P.'s popularity.

- ☐ The S.I.P. is truly *individualized*, because it is a package written for an individual student, with that student in mind as it is being written.

- ☐ Although it takes time to prepare, the S.I.P. *requires little financial expenditure*, a fact important to today's teacher.

- ☐ Once you have prepared your first S.I.P., it is possible that you will see that you have a series begun. Subsequent packages are easier to do, and you may see value in having a series available.

- ☐ With today's emphasis on the *basics*, the S.I.P. is particularly helpful for use in remediation.

- ☐ When you finish your S.I.P. you will have completed the content that could be used for a *computer program*.

- ☐ With today's *large and mixed-ability classes*, teachers need help! Here is time and cost-effective help!

- ☐ With emphasis today on competency-based instruction, the S.I.P. makes sense.

How are we doing so far? _____ Are your interest and curiosity aroused? _____ Do you have questions? If so, write them down, then continue.

Questions: _____

_____

What Is the Self-Instructional Package and Why Use It?

The S.I.P. is a learning package designed for an individual student; it is self-instructional (i.e., if you, the teacher, drop dead—heaven forbid—the student can continue to learn), and *it requires about 30–50 minutes of learning time.* The final package can be recorded on tape, video, or computer disc, or it can be written in booklet form, or it can exist in any combination of these.

Here are ways that teachers have found the S.I.P. to be useful:

☐ As an *enrichment* activity for an accelerated student.

☐ As a strategy for make-up for a student who has been absent.

☐ As a strategy for a student in need of *remediation*.

☐ As a strategy for introducing basic information to an entire class, freeing the teacher to work with individual students, making the act of teaching more *time-efficient,* a particularly significant value of the S.I.P.

☐ As a learning experience especially coordinated with manipulatives, perhaps in connection with a science experience, library work, a computer, a tape-recording, a videotape, a videodisc, or hands-on materials for an activity, or any combination of these.

One other point before we stop and check your comprehension: *The single most important characteristic of the S.I.P. is that it uses small sequential steps followed by immediate and corrective feedback to the learner.* In that respect, the S.I.P. resembles programmed instruction.

 Stop the action!

Let's check your learning with the review questions and instructions that follow.

Comprehension Check 1:

Answer the following three questions, then check your responses by reviewing Feedback Check 1. If you answer all three questions correctly, continue the package; otherwise back up and review.

---

1. How would you define what is an S.I.P.? _____

_____

2. What is the single most important characteristic of the S.I.P.? _____

_____

3. What is one way that the S.I.P. could be used in your own teaching, a way that currently stands out in your thinking? _____

_____

Feedback Check 1:

1. Although we will continue development of the definition, at this point it should resemble this: The S.I.P. is an individualization of learning-teaching strategy that teaches toward mastery learning of one relatively small bit of content by building upon small, sequential steps and providing corrective feedback throughout.

2. Referring to the small, sequential steps, followed by immediate and corrective feedback.

3. Your answer is probably related to one of those listed earlier, but could differ.

How Does the S.I.P. Differ from Other Kinds of "Learning Packages?"

Another characteristic of the S.I.P. is the *amount of learning contained in one package.* Each S.I.P. is designed to teach a relatively small amount of material, but to do it well. *This is a major difference in the S.I.P. from other types of learning activity packages.*

And, in case you have been wondering about what the S.I.P. can be designed to teach, I want to emphasize that it *can be designed*

☐ For any topic

    ☐ In any discipline

        ☐ For cognitive understanding

            ☐ For psychomotor development

                ☐ For affective learning.

That probably brings to your mind all sorts of thoughts and questions. Hold them for a moment and let's do another comprehension check.

 Stop the action and check your learning.

Comprehension Check 2:

Answer the following two questions, then check your responses in the feedback box that follows.

---

1. How does the S.I.P. differ from other self-contained learning packages? _____

    _____

2. Although teachers frequently emphasize learning that falls within the cognitive domain, is it possible for the S.I.P. to be written to include learning in the psychomotor and affective domains? Yes or no? _____

Feedback Check 2:

1. Length of learning time is shorter for the S.I.P., and it is written with an individual student in mind. It is written to teach one thing well, to one student.
2. The S.I.P. *can* be written for any domain, although evaluation is trickier for the affective and for the highest level psychomotor.

Perhaps we should now say a word about what we mean when we use the expression *teach one thing well*—that is, to explain what is meant by mastery learning. Theoretically, if the package is being used by an individual student, performance level expectation is 100%. In reality performance level will most likely be between 85 and 95%, particularly if you are using the S.I.P. for a group of students rather than an individual. That 5–15% difference allows for human errors, as can occur in writing and in reading.

Now that you have learned what is the S.I.P.—and how this learning strategy differs from other learning activity packages—it is time to concentrate on development of your S.I.P. Please continue.

S.I.P. DEVELOPMENT

How Do I Develop a Self-Instructional Package?

As with any good lesson plan, it takes time to develop an effective S.I.P. Indeed, preparation of your first S.I.P. will test your imagination and writing skills! Nevertheless, it will be time well spent; you will be proud of your product. *It is important that you continue following this package, step-by-step; do not skip parts, or we will assume no responsibility for your final product! Understand?* _____ Development of your S.I.P. emphasizes the importance of:

☐ Writing the learning objectives clearly, precisely, and in behavioral terms.

☐ Planning the learning activities in small, sequential steps.

☐ Providing frequent practice and learning comprehension checks.

☐ Providing immediate feedback, corrective instruction, and assurance to the learner.

☐ Preparing evaluative questions that measure against the learning objectives.

As you embark on preparing what may be the most perfect lesson plan you have ever prepared, keep in mind the following two points:

1. Prepare your first S.I.P. so it will take no more than

30–50 minutes of student time.

---

2. Use a *conversational tone* in your writing. Write in the first person, as though you are talking directly to the student for whom it is intended. For example, when speaking of the learning objectives, use *You will be able to* rather than *The student will be able to*. Keep in mind that you are communicating to one person rather than to an entire class (even though you may be preparing your package for entire class use). It helps to pretend that you are in a one-on-one situation tutoring the student at the writing board.

   Stop the action, and again check your learning.

Comprehension Check 3:

Answer the following two questions, then check your responses in Feedback Check 3.

---

1. What maximum learning time duration is recommended? _____

2. What major item of importance has been recommended for you to keep in mind as you write your S.I.P.? _____

Feedback Check 3:

1. Approximately 30–50 minutes, depending upon the grade and achievement level.
2. Write in the first person, as if you are speaking directly with the student.

Now that we have emphasized the *length of learning time, and the personalization of your writing,* here are other important reminders.

3. Make your S.I.P. attractive and stimulating. Consider using cartoons, puns, graphics, scratch-and-sniff stickers, interesting manipulatives. Use your creative imagination! Use both cerebral hemispheres!

Add sketches, diagrams, models, pictures, magazine clippings, humor, and a conversational tone, as students appreciate a departure from the usual textbooks and worksheets.

4. Use colleagues as resource persons, brainstorming ideas as you proceed through each step of package production.

During production, use your best cooperative learning skills.

5. The package should not be read (or heard) like a lecture. It <u>must</u> involve small sequential steps with frequent practice and corrective feedback instruction (as modeled in this package).

". . . and with the course material broken down into small self-instructional units, students can move through at individual rates."

6. The package should contain a variety of activities, preferably involving all three learning modalities—<u>visual, auditory, tactile and kinesthetic</u>.

7. Vary margins, indentations, fonts, etc.

     so the final package does not have   the usual textbook or worksheet appearance with which students are so familiar. Build into your package the "Hawthorne Effect."

Note about the cosmetics of your S.I.P.: My own prejudice about the S.I.P. is that it should be spread out more than the usual textbook page or worksheet. Use double-spaced lines, varied margins, etc. Make cosmetic improvements after finishing your final draft. Write, review, sleep on it, write more, revise, add that final touch. This package that you are using has been "toned down" and modified for practical inclusion in this textbook.

---

8. Your S.I.P. does not have to fit the common 8½ × 11 size. You are encouraged to be creative in the design of your S.I.P.'s shape, size, and format.

9. Like all lesson plans, the S.I.P. is subject to revision and improvement after use. *Write, review, sleep on it, write more, revise, test, revise. . . .*

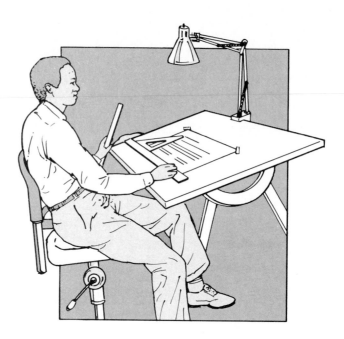

Those are nine points to remember as you prepare your package. Perhaps before proceeding, it would be useful to review them. Remember, too, the well-written package *will assure learning.* Your first S.I.P. will take several hours to produce, but it will be worth it!

Proceed with the steps that follow.

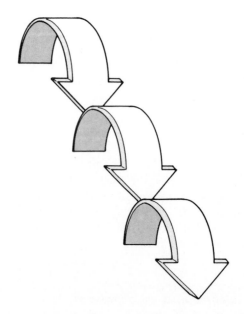

STEPS FOR DEVELOPING YOUR S.I.P.

Instructions: It is important that you proceed through the following package development step-by-step.

One thing you will notice is that immediately after writing your learning objectives you prepare the evaluative test items; both steps precede the preparation of the learning activities. That is not the usual order followed by a teacher when preparing lessons, but it does help to assure that test items match objectives. Now, here we go! *Step-by-step,* please.

Note: From here on, write on separate paper for draft planning.

Step 1. Prepare the cover page. It should include the following items:

- ☐ Instructor's name (that is you)
  - ☐ School (yours)
    - ☐ Class or intended students (who it's for)
      - ☐ Topic (specific but not wordy)
        - ☐ Estimated working time

For a sample, refer to the beginning of this package. You can vary the design of the cover page according to your needs.

Step 2. Prepare the instructional objectives. For now, these should be written in specific behavioral terms. Later, when writing these into your package introduction, you can phrase them in more general terms.

Recommended is the inclusion of at least one attitudinal (affective) objective, such as "Upon completion of this package you will tell me your feelings about this kind of learning."

---

*Step 3. **Comprehension Check 4:***

Share with your colleagues what you have accomplished (with Steps 1 and 2) to solicit their valuable feedback and input.

Step 4. Depending on feedback (from step 3), *modify items 1 and 2* if necessary. For example, after listing the learning objectives, you may find that you really have more than one package in preparation, and within the list of objectives you may find a natural cut-off between packages "1" and "2." You may discover that you have a *series* of modules begun.

Step 5. Prepare the pretest. If the learner does well on the pretest, there may be no need for the student to continue the package. Some packages (like this one) may not include a pretest, though most will. And if this is your first S.I.P. writing experience, we think you *should* include a pretest.

Suggestion: The pretest need not be as long as the posttest, but a limited sample of questions to determine whether the student already knows the material and need not continue with the package. A pretest also serves to mentally set the student for the S.I.P.

Step 6.   Prepare the posttest. The pretest and posttest could be identical, but usually the pretest is shorter. It is important that both pretest and posttest items actually test against the objectives (of Step 2). Try to keep the items objective (e.g., multiple-choice type), avoiding as much as possible the use of subjective test items (e.g., essay type), but do include at least one item measuring an affective objective (see boxed item in Step 2).

Important reminder: If your package is well-written, the student <u>should</u> achieve 85–100% on the posttest.

Step 7.   **COMPREHENSION CHECK 5:**

Share with colleagues your pretest and posttest items (providing a copy of your objectives) for suggested improvement changes before continuing to the next step.

Use the following space to write notes to yourself about ideas you are having, and regarding any materials you may need to complete your package.

Dear Self —

Good work so far! Before continuing, take a break.

It is time to stop working for a while . . .   *. . . and go play!*

Step 8.   Okay, enough play, it is time to prepare the text of your S.I.P. This is the "meat" of your package, what goes between the pretest and the posttest. It is the INSTRUCTION. Reminder: For the S.I.P. to be self-instructional, the learner should be able to work through the package with little or no help from you.

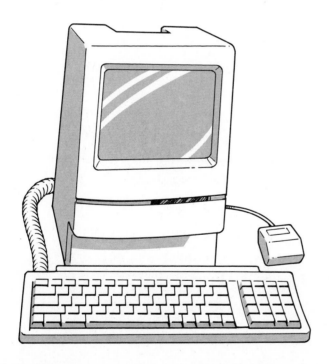

An important ingredient in your package is the <u>directions</u>. The package should be self-directed and self-paced therefore, each step of the package should be clear to the learner, making you, the instructor, literally unnecessary. *Everything needed by the learner to complete the package should be provided with the package.*

Use small, sequential steps with frequent practice cycles, followed by comprehension checks and corrective feedback. Make it fun and interesting with a variety of activities for the student, activities that provide for learning in several ways, from writing to reading, from viewing a videotape to drawing, from listening to a tape-recording to doing a hands-on activity. And be certain the activities correlate with the learning objectives. The learning cycles should lead to satisfaction of the stated objectives, and the posttest items *must* measure against those objectives.

Step 9.   **Comprehension Check 6:**

Test your package. Try it out on your colleagues as they look for content errors, spelling and grammar errors, clarity, and offer suggestions for improvement. Duplicate and use the Packet Evaluation Form provided at the end of this exercise.

Stop the Action
Congratulations on the development of your first S.I.P.!
However, two additional steps need your consideration.

Step 10.   *Revise if necessary.* Make appropriate changes to your S.I.P., as a result of the feedback from your colleagues. Then you are ready to give your S.I.P. its first real test—try it out on the student for whom it is intended.

Step 11.   *Further revisions.* This comes later, after you have used it with the student for whom it was originally intended. Like any other well-prepared lesson or unit plan, it should always be subject to revision, to improvement, never "set in concrete."

S.I.P. PACKET EVALUATION FORM

---

1. Packet Identification

      Author:

      Title of S.I.P.:

2. Packet

Objectives: Do they tell the student
    a. what the student will be able to do?

    b. how the student will demonstrate this new knowledge or skill?

Is there a clear statement (overview or introduction) of the importance, telling the learner what will be learned by completing the packet?

3. Pretest

4. Activities (Practice Cycles)

      Are small sequential steps used?

      Are there frequent practice cycles, with comprehension checks and corrective feedback to the learner?

5. Posttest: Does it test against the objectives?

6. Clarity and Continuity of Expression

7. Is the Packet Informative, Attractive, and Enjoyable?

8. Additional Comments Useful to the Author of This Packet

```
┌─────────────────────────────────────────────────────────────┐
│              PERFORMANCE LEVEL CONTRACT                        │
│                                                                │
│  Student _____ Unit to be completed by _____  │
│                                                                │
│  During this unit I will:                                      │
│                                                                │
│  1. Read chapter III of the text.                              │
│  2. Do the problems on Worksheet A.                            │
│  3. Participate in the panel on the Panama Canal.              │
│  4. Pass the unit test with a mark of at least B.             │
│  5. Demonstrate that I can perform all the requirements in     │
│     Group C.                                                    │
│                                                                │
│  The terms of this contract may be renegotiated by mutual      │
│  agreement.                                                     │
│                                                                │
│      Student signature _____               │
│      Teacher signature _____               │
│                                                                │
└─────────────────────────────────────────────────────────────┘
```

FIGURE 4.3
Sample Performance Contract

For a grade of B, you must complete activities 1–10 plus satisfactorily complete four of the optional related activities, and receive a grade of no less than a B on the posttest.

For a grade of A, you must complete activities 1–10 plus satisfactorily complete six of the optional activities, and receive no less than a B on the posttest.

Planning the Course

The responsibility for what goes on in your course is yours as teacher. In some schools, you will be provided with courses of study, syllabi, and curriculum guides that provide suggestions about course objectives, content, sequences, procedures, and materials of instruction. In some schools, you may be expected to provide students with a major role in charting the course. In others, you will be left alone to cope the best you can. No matter what policy the school follows, the ultimate responsibility for the course and for how well the students learn is yours.

Even when course plans are rigidly laid out by the school authorities, the teacher determines what actually is taught. As teacher, you determine content and process emphases, interpretations, and methods of presentation. You also adapt the course to suit your students. You put your stamp on the course by such procedures as changing the unit sequence, modifying the time to be spent on topics, using different teaching methods, supplementing the prescribed content, and providing for individualized assignments and projects. Even such a simple thing as the way you field questions makes a difference in what you teach in your course.

Basic Principles for Course Planning

The procedures for planning a course are not difficult. In general, they consist of the following steps:

1. Determine the overall course goals (what it is you hope the students will learn) and principal supporting objectives.
2. Determine what content to incorporate into the course in view of your objectives. This step includes selecting the topics to be studied, arranging them into an appropriate sequence, and deciding how much emphasis to place on each topic.
3. Decide how much time to spend on each topic.
4. Determine your approach—including basic strategies, major assignments, references, texts, and so on—in view of the goals and topics you have selected.
5. Determine procedures for evaluating student attainment of course objectives.

In implementing these steps you should keep in mind several important principles:

1. The course should be psychologically organized.
   a. Its organization should be based on the nature of the students and how they learn.
   b. It should meet students at their own levels of maturity and be relevant to their current needs, interests, and concerns.
   c. It should allow for differences among students, recognizing that students do not all have the same needs, backgrounds, interests, and concerns. Neither are an individual's needs, interests, and concerns constant. Consequently, effective teachers not only try to select topics that have intrinsic interest for the students but also try to provide variation for individuals within the topics by providing ways in which students may skip, add, or substitute topics if it should seem desirable.
   d. It should be selective. The course does not try to cover all of the subjects—which no course could really do—but it includes the content most valuable and relevant to the student and to the course goals, and it omits content not necessary for those purposes.
   e. It should encourage the development of logical memory as opposed to rote memory, skill in the use of the tools of learning, and the ability to think critically and to solve problems.
   f. It should use a combination of both vicarious and direct learning experiences in proportions suitable to the ability levels of the learners. Ordinarily, younger, less able, less experienced, and less sophisticated students will profit more from direct experiences, and older, more able, more experienced, and more sophisticated students learn well from vicarious experiences, such as lectures and reading. In any case, the course does not limit itself to book learning and worksheets.

2. The course should be compatible with the resources available. If you do not have, or cannot get, the things you need to implement your plans, the course will prove fruitless.

3. The course content organization and approach should be selected because of their value in securing transfer and retention of knowledge. Unless the content stays with the learner and can be used by the learner in new situations, it is not of much value. Retention and transfer are most likely when:
   a. The learner sees the value of the learning and how to use it in other situations and the learning situation is similar to the using situation.
   b. The learning is thorough.
   c. The learning is reviewed by frequent use in which the learner applies what has been learned and adds the new learning to previous learning.
   d. The learner draws generalizations that can aid in the application of the learning to new situations.

4. The course content, organization, and instructional approaches should contribute to achieving the course objectives. This is such an obvious requirement that it seems hardly worth repeating, but teachers sometimes ignore it. You must plan your course so it contributes to your objectives. For example, if your objective is to create skill in writing, your course must give plenty of practice in writing. Practice in reading may be excellent for some things, but it cannot take the place of writing if the goal is excellence in writing. Surprisingly often, course content has nothing to do with what the teacher claims to be the objectives.

5. The course content, organization, and teaching strategies must reflect the nature of the discipline or subject matter. Not all subject matter can be learned in the same way. The structures of disciplines, and portions of a discipline, differ. In planning courses, you must respect these differences and reflect the structures of the disciplines in the organization of courses and the strategies for teaching them.

Selecting the Goals

In many school districts, the course goals are prescribed by the school authorities in a course of study, curriculum guide, or syllabus. When this is the case, you should make use of the goals provided. But even in that case, you still must think through what it is you would like your students to learn. You may want them to master certain subject matter, believing that other subject matter is relatively less important. Or you may believe the most important goal should be the development of certain skills or attitudes. The important thing is that you should know what you want the students to learn and why you want them to learn it. All too often what is taught in school has little value to the students. (To some degree or another, this has always been true: the Roman philosopher Seneca complained about it in Nero's time.)

Your overall course goals should be—and of necessity will be—quite general. This is not the time to formulate specific objectives, though some general objectives may refer to rather specific criteria. Specific objectives should be used for planning of units and lessons. The specific form the course goals eventually will take is also not important at this point. Whether or not they should be simple or criterion-referenced is a matter for you to decide (unless, of course, the school district specifies otherwise). Ordinarily, general descriptions of the learning will suffice.

The following are a few examples of course objectives gleaned from courses of study:

ADVANCED BIOLOGY II

Objectives:

1. To achieve a working knowledge of the skills, mental and physical, necessary to perform scientific experimentation safely and correctly.
2. To learn the use of statistical analysis in the study of experimental results.
3. To learn the use of scientific literature when attempting to solve problems.
4. To achieve a deeper knowledge in some areas of biology studied in previous courses.

CREATIVE WRITING I

A. To learn to tighten sentence structure.
B. To learn to use concrete sensory words.
C. To express feelings about experiences.

FRENCH III

To develop reading and writing skills (in French) to the point that the student can read and write anything he or she can express orally.

To check your understanding of general course objectives, work through Exercise 4.2 and Exercise 4.3.

Planning the Sequence of Topics

After deciding on the general objectives for a course, it becomes necessary to select the basic content and the teaching approaches. Perhaps the best way to proceed is to outline the content and divide it into broad course topics that you expect can be covered in one to three weeks each. Then arrange these topics into a logical, psychological sequence and allocate an amount of time for each. At this point you should also decide on a general teaching approach for the topics. This decision is important because your teaching approach may make a considerable difference in the amount of time needed for teaching a topic. In establishing a schedule for the course, you should allow some 10 days of leeway for assemblies, examinations, storms, miscalculations, and so forth. You should also decide on any major assignments, such as term papers and projects, so you can provide time for them on the calendar.

The basic criterion in deciding the sequence of topics and approaches is whether or not they contribute to the course objectives, though you must also consider other criteria such as transfer value, interest level, and relevance. These topics are, in effect, the titles of the units that will comprise the course.

As a beginning teacher you will find that you need assistance in setting up a sequence of topics. You can usually find all the assistance you need in courses of study, curriculum guides, syllabi, teacher's manuals, and textbooks. For instance, a Wisconsin teacher's manual for a single-semester senior high school psychology course outlines the following sequence of units, with commentary on how each should be taught:

I.	The Science of Psychology	2 weeks
II.	Learning	3 weeks
III.	Understanding Human Behavior	3 weeks
IV.	Patterns of Behavior	3 weeks
V.	Mental Health	4 weeks
VI.	Family and Small Group Behavior	2 weeks
VII.	You and Society	1 week

Some schools and districts do not provide outlines or do not suggest time allocations in their outlines. If you have no such outline provided by your school or district, do not hesitate to consult the courses of other school districts. Another aid is the table of contents of a good textbook. Following a textbook has the advantage of giving you a carefully built structure on which to lean until you become more confident. If you select to go this route, however, you should remember that all the topics (chapters or units) included in the text are probably not equally as important—following a text too closely reduces your chances to make your course creative, flexible, innovative, and relevant to your own students' needs. It seldom pays to "marry" the textbook. If you find that you have to plan this way at first, you should try to "divorce" yourself from the text as soon as you can. It is particularly important to remember that it is not necessary to cover everything just because it is in the text. Remember, to cover everything in a subject is impossible.

Keep in mind that all course plans are of necessity tentative. Therefore, make your plans in outline. You can and should fill in the details later, when you plan your units. If you plan to order films or similar aids, however, you ought to have firm dates in order to get those aids when you need them.

Check your understanding of how to prepare a course outline by doing Exercise 4.4.

CONTINUOUS-PROGRESS COURSE PLANNING

In continuous-progress courses, students continue through courses at their own speeds and according to their own individual needs. A student who finishes a module is free to go on to another; a student who is having difficulty with a module may keep at it even though other students have moved on. Students who demonstrate that they have already mastered the content of a module may be excused from that module; students who demonstrate they need more help may be steered into additional modules in the area where they need help. In short, continuous-progress courses provide a mode for individualizing students' course work according to their demonstrated abilities and needs.

The only difference between preparing a continuous-progress, individualized course and an ordinary course is that when preparing the continuous-progress course, you must divide the course into modules and give the students self-instructional packets or learning activity packets so they can guide their own learning. Follow this procedure for teaching such courses:

1. Divide the course into modules and try to make the modules of fairly equal length.

2. Prepare behavioral objectives with standards of competence performance.

3. Prepare a learning activity packet for each module. Each packet should contain (a) the rationale for studying the module; (b) the objective of the module, stated as

EXERCISE 4.2   EXAMINING GENERAL COURSE OBJECTIVES

Examine the examples of course objectives presented in the text for courses in advanced biology, creative writing, and French. In your group, discuss how much guidance each gives the teacher who is about to plan the sequence of topics, subject matter content, and instructional approaches. From this discussion, what did you and your group conclude about preparing general course objectives?

EXERCISE 4.3   PREPARING GENERAL COURSE OBJECTIVES

For a course that you intend to teach in middle, junior, or senior high school, prepare a list of no less than three general course objectives that you think are most important for that course. Share your list with other teacher candidates from your field. After discussion, you may modify your list if you choose.

Course and grade level for which objectives are planned: _____

Objective 1:

Objective 2:

Objective 3:

EXERCISE 4.4   PREPARING A COURSE TOPIC OUTLINE

For a course you intend to teach at the middle, junior high, or senior high school level, prepare a sequence of topics for one school year (assume a 180-day school year). Be sure that (a) all the topics necessary for fulfilling your course objectives are covered, (b) enough time is allocated for each topic, and (c) the sequence of topics makes sense logically and psychologically. Take your time with this assignment—you may need to do some juggling before it satisfies you. When you are satisfied, have your outline evaluated by classmates of related subject fields. The question they should keep in mind while evaluating your outline is, "Will the outline really do what it is intended to do?" After it has been evaluated by your classmates, you may make changes in it; then present it to your course instructor for that instructor's evaluation.

Course objectives (from Exercise 4.3):

Course Outline   Weeks (for each topic)

behavioral objectives; (c) the materials necessary for students to have as they work on the module, or directions for getting the materials and equipment needed; and (d) the directions they need to carry out the activities in the module.

4. Prepare a plan for evaluating the students' learning for each module. This plan should provide for pretests, progress tests, and final mastery tests. Provisions should be made so students can "test out" of modules or parts of modules in which they are already competent.

5. Set students to work on their modules in laboratory fashion.

6. Supervise the students as they work on the modules.

7. Determine when the students are ready to progress from one module to another. Students who fail to achieve the standards of performance in the mastery test should be asked to restudy the module, taking mastery tests until they can meet the standard. For this reason each student should take a diagnostic pretest before beginning a module. Note that the mastery tests should be criterion-referenced, though they need not be written tests. Performance tests are often more satisfactory. Note also that in many instances there is no need for students to follow the same sequence. Students may be allowed to select which module they will do and when they will do it, as long as you agree that their selection is a reasonable one that will allow them to meet the criteria established by you in step 2.

Work with individual students as they progress through their modules. Students should not have to stand around waiting to find out what they should do next; neither should they have to struggle along trying to do work they do not understand. When students need help, they should get it! Consequently, plan to give all your class time to supervising and guiding while students are working on their modules. In order to save time, it may be helpful to gather students who are having the same or similar problems or who are doing the same activities in a particular module for small-group discussion.

In such a sequence, students can work through the modules at their own speed, selecting or omitting modules (under your guidance) as seems most desirable. This freedom makes it possible for each student to have, in effect, an individual course of study.

Teacher-Student Cooperative Planning

Students should enter into the planning of units, lessons, and courses. But no matter how much they contribute, the ultimate responsibility for the plan is the teacher's.

There are two approaches to teacher-student planning. In the first approach the teacher does the basic planning but provides options for the students, who then plan their own work by selecting those options they will pursue. The simplest form of this approach is the standard practice of encouraging students to select and implement projects, reports, outside reading, and similar independent activities. In the second approach, students must select activities from a study guide, which lists required and optional activities. In this approach, the class participates in the formulation of the original plan. They may go as far as selecting the goals, content, procedures, sequences, and materials to be studied, though usually they have a smaller role. There are also various combinations of these two approaches.

Whatever approach you use, you should address teacher-student planning cautiously. Students should not be expected to take on their planning role without instruction and guided practice by the teacher. Always begin teacher-student planning slowly, maybe with such minor questions as "Would you prefer to have the test on Monday or Tuesday?" or "Which story would you like to read next?" You may begin by allowing students to select which activities they prefer from a list of activities. Another beginning approach to teacher-student planning is to issue study guides that call for students to plan and complete their learning activities in laboratory fashion.

After such a beginning, you can gradually increase the students' role in planning the units. At first the students might be encouraged to identify their personal learning objectives and plans for achieving those objectives. Later, students might work together to plan unit goals, content, and learning activities and to establish standards for their own work until they are finally ready to take major responsibility for unit and course planning. If you introduce teacher-student planning in a step-by-step fashion and show students how to carry out each step before proceeding to the next, you can expect gratifying results.

SUMMARY

In this module we discussed planning the course and presented several ways of developing your units. In the module that follows you will learn how to prepare the daily lessons that comprise those units.

SUGGESTED READING

Brandt, R. S., ed. *Content of the Curriculum.* 1988 ASCD Yearbook. Alexandria, VA: Association for Supervision and Curriculum Development, 1988.

Kim, E. C., and Kellough, R. D. *A Resource Guide for Secondary School Teaching: Planning for Competence.* 5th ed. New York: Macmillan, 1991.

Resnick, L. B., and Klopfer, L. E. *Toward the Thinking Curriculum: Current Cognitive Research.* 1989 ASCD Yearbook. Alexandria, VA: Association for Supervision and Curriculum Development, 1989.

Russell, J. D. *Modular Instruction.* Minneapolis, MN: Burgess, 1974.

Stinard, T. A., and Dolphin, W. D. "Which students benefit from self-paced mastery instruction and why." *Journal of Educational Psychology* 73(5): 754–758 (Oct. 1981).

Want, M. C., and Wahlbert, H. J., eds. *Adapting Instruction to Individual Differences.* Berkeley, CA: McCutchan, 1985.

POSTTEST

Multiple Choice

_____ 1. According to this module, in an ordinary unit one would expect to find
   a. a series of lessons centered on a topic.
   b. a laboratory plan.
   c. a contractual agreement between teacher and student.
   d. a packet of learning materials.

_____ 2. According to this module, a true unit differs from an ordinary unit in that it
   a. is more cohesive and allows for more individualization.
   b. does not provide a scheme for student evaluation.
   c. provides wider general objectives.
   d. does not provide optional activities.

_____ 3. In preparing objectives for a unit, what types of objectives would be acceptable?
   a. criterion-referenced objectives
   b. covert objectives
   c. simple behavioral objectives
   d. any or all of the above

_____ 4. In a true unit all students must engage in the required activities
   a. at the same time.
   b. in the same way.
   c. in sequence.
   d. as need and interest dictate.

_____ 5. In the laboratory phase of the unit students engage in
   a. individual activities.
   b. small-group activities.
   c. whole-class activities.
   d. any or all of the above.

_____   6. Which of the four unit plans discussed gives students the least freedom?
  a. ordinary unit
  b. the true unit
  c. the learning activity packet
  d. the contract unit

_____   7. To introduce cooperative teacher-student planning to your classes it is recommended that you
  a. run a wide-open class from the start.
  b. initiate teacher-student planning in small steps.
  c. do not interfere with students' planning; let them learn from their mistakes.
  d. start with a discussion in which you plan the course objectives.

_____   8. The self-instruction packet concept was first introduced by
  a. Bloom
  b. Carroll
  c. Johnson and Johnson
  d. Keller

_____   9. Ultimately, who decides what is actually taught in a course?
  a. students
  b. teacher
  c. principal
  d. superintendent of schools

_____ 10. In a psychologically organized course
  a. the course sequence is based on the structure of the disciplines.
  b. the course covers the subject.
  c. the course allows for differences among students.
  d. the course centers around direct experiences as opposed to vicarious experiences.

_____ 11. To give the course transfer value you should
  a. provide complete coverage of the subject.
  b. provide for much extrinsic interest.
  c. provide variation by giving students opportunities to skip, add, or substitute topics.
  d. provide opportunities for applying the learning to new situations.

_____ 12. The basic criterion for selecting unit topics is whether or not they
  a. contribute to course objectives.
  b. are interesting.
  c. have transfer value.
  d. follow logical course organization.

Short Answer

13. In preparing the objectives for an ordinary unit, what types of objectives should you use, general or specific? Why?

_____

_____

_____

_____

14. Is it necessary to set up a time schedule when planning a unit? Why or why not?

_____

_____

_____

15. Should a plan for an ordinary unit contain provisions for tests and other major assignments? Explain why or why not.

_____

_____

_____

16. Should the specific objectives for a true unit be written as statements describing the learning products or as behavioral objectives? Explain your answer.

_____

_____

_____

_____

17. Identify and describe four criteria for selecting the topic for a unit.

_____

_____

_____

_____

18. Identify and describe four criteria for good, specific unit objectives.

_____

_____

_____

_____

19. Ordinarily, what type of activities would you expect to find in the introductory phase of a unit? Why?

_____

_____

_____

_____

20. Do all the required activities in the unit have to be done by all students
    a. at the same time? Why or why not?

_____

_____

    b. in the same way? Why or why not?

_____

_____

21. Identify the principal difference between a learning packet and a laboratory unit.

_____

_____

_____

_____

22. Explain the essential differences between writing objectives
    a. for a unit and a learning packet.

_____

_____

    b. for a unit and a contract plan.

_____

_____

23. Explain the simplest way to set up a learning contract in a contract plan.

_____

_____

24. Identify and describe what you would expect to find in a study guide for a laboratory unit.

_____

_____

_____

_____

25. Identify and describe what you should include in a learning packet you constructed.

_____

_____

_____

_____

26. Identify five principles one should keep in mind when carrying out the steps for course building.

_____

_____

_____

_____

_____

27. According to this module there are five basic steps in planning a course. Identify and describe them.

_____

_____

_____

_____

_____

_____

_____

28. Unless a course plan facilitates students' retention and transfer of what is studied in it, it will be unsuccessful. Describe what you can do in planning the course to aid retention and transfer. (Identify at least three possibilities.)

_____

_____

_____

_____

_____

_____

29. Outline the procedure recommended for building a continuous progress course.

_____

_____

_____

_____

_____

30. Identify and describe procedures recommended for cooperative student-teacher planning of courses.

_____

_____

_____

_____

_____

31. Describe how the self-instructional package differs from other types of learning activity packages.

_____

_____

_____

_____

32. For writing a self-instructional package, identify and describe at least five guidelines to follow.

_____

_____

_____

_____

_____

MODULE 5
Lesson Planning

RATIONALE

Seldom can a teacher enter a class unprepared and yet teach effectively. Spur-of-the-moment teaching rarely results in forceful, meaningful, logically presented lessons from which students develop clear understanding of knowledge, skills, or concepts. Such lessons require careful thought and preparation. The teacher must decide which aspects of the subject should be the focus of a lesson, how a topic should be adapted to a particular audience, how a lesson should follow up on preceding lessons, and how a lesson should prepare students for lessons to come. Without careful attention to these matters, lessons tend to be dull, drifting aimlessly toward no good purpose.

This module is designed to acquaint you with the basic components and procedures necessary for developing effective lesson plans. It includes both examples and suggestions that should prove helpful. Ultimately, however, you, as the teacher, will have to adapt, alter, and adjust these suggestions to meet the needs of your students. You will have to develop a lesson plan style that is comfortable for you, usable in your classroom, and effective in helping students learn.

SPECIFIC OBJECTIVES

At the completion of this module, you should be able to:

1. Describe the various formats for lesson planning.
2. Explain the role of the daily lesson plan.
3. Describe the basic components of the daily lesson plan and their functions.
4. Construct a daily lesson plan.

MODULE TEXT

The Daily Lesson Plan

Effective teachers are always planning. For the long range, they plan the scope and sequence of courses and develop content for courses. Within courses they develop units, and within units they design the activities to be used and the tests to be given. They familiarize themselves with textbooks, materials, audiovisual resources, and innovations in their field. Yet—despite all this planning—the daily lesson plan remains pivotal to the planning process.

Assumptions

Not all teachers need elaborate written plans for every lesson. Sometimes effective and skilled teachers need only a sketchy outline. Sometimes they may not need written plans at all. Old hands who have taught the topic many times in the past may need only the presence of a class to stimulate a pattern of presentation that has often been successful before (though frequent use of old patterns may lead one into the rut of unimaginative teaching).

Considering this apparent diversity among teachers, certain assumptions might be made before exploring lesson planning further:

1. Not all teachers need elaborate written plans for all lessons.
2. Beginning teachers need to prepare detailed written lesson plans.
3. Some subject matter fields and topics require more detailed planning than others do.
4. Some experienced teachers have clearly defined goals and objectives in mind even though they have not written them into lesson plans.
5. The depth of knowledge a teacher has about a subject or topic influences the amount of planning necessary for the lessons.
6. The skill a teacher has in following a trend of thought in the presence of distraction will influence the amount of detail necessary when planning activities.
7. A plan is more likely to be carefully plotted when it is written out.

8. There is no particular pattern or format that all teachers need to follow when writing out plans. (Some teacher-preparation programs have agreed on certain lesson-plan formats for their student teachers; you need to know if this is the case for your program.)

9. All effective teachers have a planned pattern of instruction for every lesson, whether that plan is written out or not.

Written Plans

Well-written lesson plans have many uses. They give a teacher an agenda or outline to follow in teaching a lesson. They give a substitute teacher a basis for presenting appropriate lessons to a class. They are certainly very useful when a teacher is planning to use the same lesson again in the future. They provide the teacher with something to fall back on in case of a memory lapse, an interruption, or some distraction, such as a call from the office or a fire drill. Above all, they provide beginners security, because with a carefully prepared plan a beginning teacher can walk into a classroom with a confidence gained from having developed a sensible framework for that day's instruction.

Thus, as a beginning teacher you should make considerably detailed lesson plans. Naturally, this will require a great deal of work for at least the first year or two, but the reward of knowing that you have prepared and presented effective lessons will compensate for that effort. Since most teachers plan their daily lessons only a day or two ahead, you can expect a busy first year of teaching.

Some prospective teachers are concerned with being seen using a written plan in class—they think it may suggest that the teacher has not mastered the field. On the contrary, a lesson plan is a visible sign of preparation on the part of the teacher. A written lesson plan shows that thinking and planning have taken place and that the teacher has a road map to work through the lesson no matter what the distractions. Most experienced teachers agree that there is no excuse for appearing before a class without evidence of careful preparation.

A Continual Process

Experienced teachers may not require plans as detailed as those necessary for beginning teachers (after all, experienced teachers often can develop shortcuts to lesson planning without sacrificing effectiveness). Yet lesson planning is a continual process even for them, for there is always a need to keep materials and plans current and relevant. Because no two classes are ever exactly the same, today's lesson plan will probably need to be tailored to the peculiar needs of each class. Also, because the content of a course will change as new developments occur or new theories are introduced, your objectives and the objectives of the students, school, and teaching staff will change.

For these reasons, lesson plans should be in a constant state of revision. Once the basic framework is developed, however, the task of updating and modifying becomes minimal. If you maintain your plans on a computer, making necessary changes from class to class and from year to year becomes even easier.

The daily lesson plan should provide a tentative outline of the class period but should always remain flexible. A carefully worked-out plan may have to be set aside because of unforeseen circumstances, such as a delayed school bus, an impromptu assembly program, or a fire drill. A daily lesson planned to cover six aspects of a given topic may end with only three of the points having been considered. These occurrences are natural in the school setting, and the teacher and the plans must be flexible enough to accommodate this reality.

The Problem of Time

A lesson plan should provide enough materials and activities to consume the entire class period. Since planning is a skill that takes years to master, a beginning teacher should overplan rather than run the risk of having too few activities. When a lesson plan does not provide enough activity to occupy the entire class period, a beginning teacher often loses control of the class and discipline problems develop. Thus, it is best to prepare more than you likely can accomplish in a given class period. Students are very perceptive when it comes to a teacher who has finished the plan for the period and is attempting to bluff through the remaining minutes. If you ever do get caught short—as most teachers do at one time or another—one way to avoid embarrassment is to spend the remaining time in a review of material that has been covered that day or in the past several days.

The Daily Plan Book

At this point, a distinction should be made between actual lesson plans and the book of daily plans that many schools require teachers to maintain and even submit to their supervisors a week in advance. A daily-plan book is most assuredly not a daily lesson plan. Rather, it is a layout sheet on which the teacher shows what lessons will be taught during the week, month, or term. Usually the book provides only a small lined box for each class period for each day of the week. These books are useful for outlining the topics, activities, and assignments projected for the week or term, and supervisors sometimes use them to check the adequacy of teachers' course plans. They can also be useful for substitute teachers, who must try to fill in for you when you are absent. But they are not daily plans. Teachers who believe that the notations in the daily-plan book are lesson plans are fooling themselves. Student teachers should not be allowed to use these in place of real lesson plans.

CONSTRUCTING A DAILY LESSON PLAN

Each teacher perhaps should develop a personal system of lesson planning—the system that works best for that teacher. But a beginning teacher probably needs a more substantial framework from which to work. For that reason, this module provides a preferred lesson-plan format as well as several alternative formats. Nothing is sacred about any of these formats, however. Each has worked for some teachers in the past. As you review them, determine which appeals to your style of presentation and use it with your own modifications until you find a better model.

Whatever the format, however, all plans should be written out in an intelligible style. There is good reason to question teachers who say they have no need for a written plan because they have their lessons planned "in their heads." The periods in a school day are many, as are the numbers of students in each class. When multiplied by the number of school days in a week, a semester, or a year, the task of keeping so many things in one's head becomes mind-boggling. Until you have considerable experience behind you, you will need to write and keep detailed daily plans for guidance and reference.

Components of a Daily Lesson Plan

As a rule, your written lesson plan should contain the following basic elements. These components need not be present in every written lesson plan, nor must they be presented in any particular format. As a beginning teacher, however, you would be wise to consider the suitability of each format before attempting to construct a plan. The basic elements are:

1. Control and identification data
   a. Name of course and grade level
   b. Unit
   c. Topic within unit
2. General objectives (the course or unit objective to which this lesson contributes)
3. Specific objectives of this lesson
4. The subject-matter content
5. Key points

6. The procedure (the learning activities)
   a. Introduction
   b. Lesson development
   c. Conclusion
   d. Timetable
7. Materials of instruction
8. Assignment
9. Special notes and reminders
10. Comprehension checks
11. Evaluation of lesson

The following sections consider in some detail each of these elements. As you read about them, remember these three reasons for writing detailed lesson plans: (1) to clarify to yourself what you wish to accomplish, (2) to set forth what you plan to do to achieve your objectives, and (3) to remind yourself what it was you intended so that you will not forget, make mistakes, and omit important details.

Control and Identification Data

Control and identification data are presented as the heading of the lesson plan both for the benefit of supervisors who may check over your work and for your own benefit if you save the plan for future use. These data include:

1. *Name of course and grade level.* These merely serve as headings for the plan, and facilitate orderly filing of plans. Examples are:

                    United States History I   Grade 11
                          Science   Grade 7

2. *Name of the unit.* Inclusion of this facilitates the orderly control of the hundreds of lesson plans a teacher constructs. For example:

       United States History I   Grade 11   Unit: The Civil War
           Science   Grade 7   Unit: Science and Measurement

3. *Topic to be considered within the unit.* This is also useful for control and identification. For example:

       United States History I   Grade 11   Unit: The Civil War
                          Topic: Main Causes
          Science   Grade 7   Unit: Science and Measurement
                      Topic: Metric Scavenger Hunt

General Objectives

Ordinarily the general objective noted in the daily lesson plan is a broad unit objective that is supported by the lesson, though sometimes the general objective may apply only for two or three days' work rather than for a two- or three-week unit. A lesson usually supports only one general objective, but a lesson occasionally may contribute to more than one broad unit objective. You should state general objectives in your daily lesson plans to guarantee that specific lesson goals are consistent with your major overall goals. Remember that general objectives are often not stated in behavioral terms and are more closely related to concept development. Examples include:

☐ To develop an understanding of the reasons for the division between the strict constructionists and loose constructionists points of view at the Philadelphia Convention in 1787.

☐ To understand the concepts of length, area, volume, mass, and time.

☐ To appreciate the effect that the lifestyle of Edgar Allan Poe had on his writing.

Specific Objectives

Specific objectives should identify the major aims of the daily lesson plan. Ordinarily, these objectives should be specific enough to be accomplished within a class period, though sometimes the development of a specific objective must occur over time. When writing these objectives you should consider them as outcomes, understandings, appreciations, attitudes, special abilities, skills, and facts. Remember that you need to keep in mind how you will evaluate whether your objectives have been achieved. These specific objectives are your expectations of what students will be able to do as a result of this lesson—not what the teacher will do. As discussed earlier, your specific objectives might be covert or overt or a combination of both. Examples include:

☐ The student will be able to add, subtract, multiply, and divide two-digit numbers using a hand calculator. [overt, cognitive]

☐ The student will be able to identify the major internal organs of *Rana pipiens*. [overt, cognitive]

☐ The student will demonstrate appreciation for the symbolism in *Lord of the Flies*. [covert, affective]

☐ The student will demonstrate an understanding of the underlying cause of the Civil War as it relates to the stated causes. [covert, cognitive]

☐ The student will be able to list and define the steps in the scientific method. [overt, cognitive]

Setting specific objectives is a crucial step in any lesson plan. It is at this point that many lessons go wrong. In writing specific objectives teachers sometimes mistakenly list what they intend to do—such as "cover the next five pages" or "do the next 10 problems"—and fail to focus on just what their objective in these activities truly is. When you approach this step in your lesson planning, ask yourself, "What do I want my students to learn from these lessons?" Your answer to that question is your objective!

CONTENT

To make sure your lesson actually covers what it should, you should write down just what content you want covered. This material may be placed in a separate section or combined with the procedure section. The important thing is to be sure that your information is written down so you can refer to it quickly and easily when you need to.

If, for instance, you are going to introduce new material using the lecture method, you will want to outline the content of that lecture. The word *outline* is not used casually—you need not have pages of notes to sift through; nor should you read declarative statements to the class. You should be familiar enough with the content so that an outline (in detail, if necessary) will be sufficient to carry on the lesson as in the following example. (Note: Detailed information about using the lecture as a teaching strategy is found in Module 8.) This is an example of a content outline:

1. Causes of Civil War
   A. Primary causes.
      1. Economics.
      2. Abolitionist pressure.
      3. Slavery
      4. _____
   B. Secondary causes.
      1. North-South friction.
      2. Southern economic dependence.
      3. _____ .

If you intend to conduct the lesson through discussion, you should write out the key discussion questions. For example:

☐ What do you think Golding had in mind when he wrote *Lord of the Flies*?

☐ What did the conch shell represent? Why did the other boys resent Piggy?

Since it is unlikely that you could remember all aspects of a topic while responding to student discussion, be sure that these aspects are well noted in your content section. If there are opposing sides to topics, for instance, your plan should include the pros and cons of each in order to prompt student discussion. For example:

III. Capital punishment

Pro	Con
A. Deterrent	A. Not a deterrent
B. Saves money	B. Rehabilitation
C. Eye for eye	C. Morally wrong

Similarly, if activities such as debates or simulations are to be used, your plan should spell out the details of the activity. For example:

IV. Simulation: War and Peace
   A. Read directions
   B. Break class into nation groups
   C. Elect spokesperson
   D. Read directions for Phase I
   E. Begin Phase I

Key Point

Not every lesson has a key point, though most probably do. Ask yourself if there were one thing in the lesson that you most want the students to retain, could you identify it? If not, there is no need to include this component in the plan. On the other hand, if there is a pivotal point around which the entire lesson revolves, you may wish to identify that point—not only for yourself, but for the class as well. This key point could be effectively used as an introduction or as a conclusion or as both. It could also be emphasized in the content of the lesson. Examples include:

□ Key Point: Although there were many causes, primary and secondary, for the Civil War, the main cause for this war (as for all wars) was economics.

□ "Today we shall see that. . . ." [Used as an introduction]

□ "Today we have seen. . . ." [Used as a conclusion]

The Procedure

The procedure is the section in which you establish what you and your students will do during the lesson. Ordinarily, you should plan this section of your lesson as an organized entity having a beginning, a middle, and an end to be completed during the lesson. This structure is not always needed, because some lessons are simply parts of units or long-term plans and merely carry on activities spelled out in those long-term plans. Still, most daily lessons need to include in their procedure:

□ An introduction

□ A lesson development

□ A lesson conclusion

□ A timetable (probably)

Because a written lesson plan can serve as a ready reference, not only should the procedure section of your plan be written down, but it should also be written in a format you can easily follow. Therefore, write down your lesson development so you can read it easily and find your place quickly. This usually means write in large print and in an outline format. (Note: With the increasing use of personal computers many teachers find it helpful to put their lesson plans onto a computer disk; for this portion of their lesson plan they use a large font.)

Introduction to the Lesson.   Like any good performance, a lesson needs an effective introduction. In many respects the introduction sets the tone for the rest of the lesson by alerting the class that the business of learning is to begin. After all, you must have students' attention before you can teach them anything. The introduction should be an attention-getter. If it is exciting, interesting, or innovative, it can create a favorable mood for the class. In any case, a well-done introduction serves as a solid indication that you are thoroughly prepared. Although it is difficult to develop an exciting introduction to every lesson, there is always a variety of options available by which to spice up the launching of a lesson. You might, for instance, begin the lesson by briefly reviewing yesterday's lesson, showing how it relates to today's lesson. This serves two purposes—introducing today's lesson and reviewing yesterday's. Another possibility is to review vocabulary words from previous lessons and to introduce new vocabulary. A third approach might be to review a concept developed in the previous day's lesson. Still another possibility is to use the key point of the day's lesson as an introduction and then again as the conclusion. Brief examples of introductions are:

☐ "As we have seen by yesterday's demonstration, the gravitational pull on the earth's surface affects the tides. Today we will consider different types of tides. . . ."

☐ "Juan, what is meant by *factor*? Suzy, what do we mean when we say *interpolate*?"

☐ "We have seen that, despite the claims of national unity, the period of the 1820s was actually a time of great regional rivalry."

In short, you can use the introduction of the lesson to review past learning, tie the new lesson to the previous lesson, introduce new material, point out the objectives of the new lesson, or—by showing what will be learned and why the learning is important—induce in students a mindset favorable to the new lesson.

The Lesson Development.   The developmental activities, which comprise the bulk of the lesson plan, are the ways by which you hope to achieve your lesson objectives. They include activities that present information, demonstrate skills, provide reinforcement of previously learned material, and provide other opportunities to develop understanding and skill. These activities should be described in some detail so you will know exactly what it is you plan to do. At this point in the plan, generalities usually do suffice. Teachers often think that they need only determine the principal line of the lesson development. Yet, simply to decide that in a certain lesson you will "discuss the XYZ affair," for instance, will not be sufficient. You will also need to know what principal points should be considered, what key questions should be used, what sequence should be followed, and what conclusions the discussion should focus on. Otherwise the class will likely drift aimlessly.

To assure that plans for these activities are clearly laid out, they should ordinarily be carefully written out—and in some detail. This will guarantee that you have a firm plan of action (too often, plans not written out are dreams without substance). Writing the plan down will also serve as a reminder or reference. During the stress of a class it is easy to forget details of your plan and your subject, and for this reason you should note the answers to the questions you intend to ask and the solutions to problems you intend your students to solve.

Lesson Conclusion.   Having a clear-cut conclusion (also known as closure or culminating activity) is as important as having a strong introduction. The lesson closure complements the introduction. The closing activity should summarize and bind together what has ensued in the developmental stage and should reinforce the principal point. One way to accomplish these ends is to restate the key point of the lesson. Another is to briefly outline the major points of the lesson development. Still another is to repeat the major concept that was your objective. No matter what the way, this concluding activity should be brief and to the point.

The Timetable.   To estimate the time factors in any lesson can be difficult. A good procedure is to gauge the amount of time needed for each learning activity and note that time alongside the activity and strategy in your plan. For example:

1. Introduce film (10 min)
   a. Why do you suppose Ghandi was so popular?
   b. What do you think Ghandi was trying to do?
   c. Why do you think his methods were so successful?
2. Show film (25 min)
3. Review film's major points (10 min)
4. Comments about tomorrow's assignment (5 min)

Placing too much faith in your time estimate may be foolish—an estimate is more for your guidance in planning than for anything else. Beginning teachers frequently find that their discussions and lectures do not last as long as was expected. To avoid being embarrassed by running out of material, try to make sure that you have planned enough work to consume the entire class period. If you plan too much, you can use the remainder for the next day's lesson. Sometimes, you might plan an extra activity to use if the lesson runs short. Also, as mentioned earlier, if your lesson runs short, you can spend time on review or on introducing the next day's lesson. In any case, remember that to overplan is better than to underplan.

Materials and Equipment to Be Used

This section of your lesson plan is a reminder that you will need to have certain materials ready for the lesson. For instance, for a certain lesson you may need an opaque projector and some pictures. There is no need to list items that are already or constantly in your classroom—the purpose of this section of the plan is simply to guarantee that you know what is needed for the lesson and that you have it ready when needed. Audiovisual equipment and materials may need to be ordered well in advance of the day you want to use them.

Assignment

If a homework assignment is to be given, you should make note of it somewhere in your lesson plan. When to present the assignment to the class is optional—except that it should never be verbally given as an afterthought as the students begin exiting the room at the end of the period. Many teachers like to write the day's assignment at a regular place on the board at the beginning of the class or an entire week's assignments on the board each Monday, drawing student attention to this early in the class or regularly each Monday. Others prefer to wait until the end of the lesson each day. Either method is acceptable, though mentioning the assignment each Monday or regularly at the beginning of each period (or both) minimizes the chance of your forgetting about it. Still other teachers prefer to write out the assignments for a period of a week or more, distributing copies to the students at regular intervals.

Whatever way you present assignments, you must allow enough time to explain the assignment clearly and to ensure that the students understand what they must do and how they should do it. In preparing an assignment, you should ensure that it:

☐ Is clear

☐ Is definite

☐ Is reasonable, neither too long nor too difficult

☐ Gives students background necessary for them to complete it successfully

☐ Shows students how to do it sufficiently well that they will not flounder needlessly

☐ Provides for individual student differences

In the written plan you usually need only include a short notation concerning the assignment, such as: *Assignment:* Read pp. 234–239, and answer questions 1, 5, 8.

Special Notes

You should provide a place in your lesson plan for special notes and reminders to yourself. Most of the time you will not need such reminders, but when you do, it helps to have reminders in a special place so you can refer to them readily. In this section you can place reminders concerning such things as announcements to be made, school programs, makeup work for certain students, and so on. These things may or may not be important, but they do need to be remembered.

Comprehension Checks

You must include in your lesson details of how you will evaluate how well students are learning and how well they have learned. Comprehension checks for determining how well they are learning can be in the form of questions you ask and the students ask during the lesson. Questions you intend to ask should be built into the developmental section.

For determining how well they have learned, teachers typically use review questions at the end of a lesson (as a closure) or the beginning of the next lesson (as a review or transfer introduction), independent practice at the completion of a lesson, and tests. Again, questions for checking for comprehension should be detailed in your lesson plan.

Evaluation of the Lesson

This section is reserved for the teacher to make notes or comments about the lesson. It can be particularly useful if you plan to use the lesson again. When you look at the lesson the following year, you likely will not recall if the lesson went well or not, so jotting down some notes at the conclusion of a taught lesson will help you make the next presentation more effective. Criteria for evaluating a lesson plan are listed in Figure 5.1.

Before continuing with the text, read Exercise 5.1 and begin to use what you have learned so far about lesson plans.

FIGURE 5.1
Lesson Plan Checklist

Does your lesson plan:

☐ Provide a tie-in to previous lessons?

☐ Provide an adequate set induction?

☐ Clearly identify the objectives for the students?

☐ Provide for a clear presentation of the learning content?

☐ Provide an adequate demonstration or illustration?

☐ Provide for checking for student comprehension during the lesson?

☐ Provide for checking for student comprehension after the lesson?

☐ Provide for preparing students for their homework assignment?

☐ Provide an adequate summary and follow up?

☐ Provide for the elimination of dead spots during the class period?

☐ Make adequate provisions for individual and small-group activities?

☐ Provide for student individual differences?

☐ Provide adequately for materials and equipment for instruction?

☐ Provide a lead-in for the next lesson?

EXERCISE 5.1 PREPARING A TWO-WEEK UNIT PLAN, COMPLETE WITH A SEQUENCE OF TEN DAILY LESSON PLANS

This exercise provides you the opportunity to practice what you learned in this and previous modules about planning—putting it all together to make a complete unit plan. Select a topic that you are likely to teach and then prepare a two-week unit plan, complete with a ten-day sequence of daily lesson plans. Your unit plan should include the components for an ordinary or laboratory-type unit plan (as presented in Module 4). Your daily plans should follow the guidelines presented in this module, but over the period of ten days they should include a variety of teaching strategies, such as lecture, discussion, simulation, inquiry, and the use of audiovisuals. You may need to refer to later modules of this text as you plan the development and phases of the daily lessons and the evaluation tools for the unit (a presentation of various lesson plan formats concludes this module).

Upon completion of your unit plan, share it with your classmates for their feedback, make appropriate modifications, and then hand it in for your instructor's feedback and evaluation.

Your course instructor may have additional guidelines or requirements for this exercise.

LESSON PLAN FORMATS

There is no mandatory basic lesson plan format and no irreplaceable list of lesson plan components. You should select a format that you find easy to work with, adapting it to the various lessons you teach. The format preferred by the authors of this text is the outline format that follows. In this format the content of the lesson is incorporated into the procedure, though the major concept or key point is listed separately.

PREFERRED LESSON PLAN FORMAT

Class: United States History   **Grade:** 11
Unit: The New Nation
Topic: Hamilton's Financial Plan
Unit objective: The students will understand the major problems faced by the new nation.
Specific objective: The students will be able to explain the financial dilemma faced by the new nation.
Key point: The diversity of means of exchange helped confuse financial matters in the United States during the Revolution and under the Articles of Confederation.
Procedure:

1. Introduction by teacher to set scene. Make following points and show samples of each. (8 minutes).
   a. Back country and West—barter system.
      (1) Put word "barter" on board
      (2) Ask "What does it mean"?
   b. After 1764 no paper money could be printed but some still in circulation.
   c. British, French, and Spanish coins in demand.
   d. Virginia—tobacco warehouse receipt used as money.
   e. IOUs to soldiers from Continental Congress.
   f. Promissory notes to European creditors.
   g. Each state had own paper money under Articles of Confederation.

2. Role Play. (20 minutes)
   a. Have students play parts of:
      (1) Merchants (3 sts.)
      (2) Soldiers (3 sts.)
      (3) Continental Congress officials (6 sts.)
      (4) European creditors (3 sts.)
      (5) Residents of different states (10 sts.)
   b. Merchants sell to Continental Congress.
   c. Soldiers receive pay from Continental Congress.
   d. Continental Congress go to European creditors (who sit at a distance).
   e. Residents of different states go back and forth trying to buy and sell.
   f. Easterners go to Kentucky and try to use cash where only barter is used and vice versa.
   g. In all cases—each uses own money and much trouble develops over various forms of currency.

3. Enter Alexander Hamilton [select responsible student] (5 minutes)
   a. Speech outlining financial policy.
      (1) Debts of previous government ($12 million foreign, $44 million domestic, $25 million state).
      (2) Where get money for new government?
      (3) How to strengthen credit?

4. Discussion. (12 min.)
   a. Ask individuals what they learned from role playing.
   b. What were characteristics of system? (List on board.)
      Elicit from class:
         confusion
         diversity
         separateness of each political entity
         animosity among people
         much debt
   c. What effect would Hamilton's program have on these characteristics? (List on board.)
      Elicit from class:
         clear up confusion
         unify nation
         sound credit

Materials: play coins; play paper money; replicas of colonial and Revolutionary currency; handmade IOUs; promissory notes; tobacco warehouse receipt; objects for trade.

Assignment: Read Thomas Jefferson's reaction to Hamilton's plan. What was his position and why?

Note: Speak to "Alexander Hamilton" before class.

Evaluation of lesson:

Alternative Format 1

You or the school system for which you work may require other formats. Other commonly used lesson-plan formats are illustrated in the following pages. The first of these alternative formats follows the outline of the preferred format, except that it lists the content and procedures separately.

Lesson Topic _____ Date _____

Unit _____ Grade _____

1. Lesson Objective

2. Content

3. Procedure

4. Instructional Materials

5. Evaluation

ALTERNATIVE FORMAT 2

The second alternative format is virtually the same as the first, except that it provides a column for notes about the items in the content and procedure sections. It also has a special section for evaluation and questions. In this format, *Evaluation* refers to a test or some other evaluative devices of the students' work, whereas *Questions* refers to the questions the teacher would use in the class recitation or discussion.

Teacher _____ Course Topic ___ Date _____

Unit _____

Objectives

CONTENT	NOTES

Procedures

Evaluation and Questions

Assignment

Materials of Instruction

Evaluation

ALTERNATIVE FORMAT 3

The third alternative format is most suited to a recitation or lecture-question lesson. In this format, following a space for noting the introductory activities, the teacher writes the content in outline form in one column. In a second column, the teacher writes the key questions to be asked in connection with the items in the content column. This section is followed by a space for a summary. Although the word *procedure* is not mentioned, this format provides for a procedure section of three parts: introduction, development, and conclusion.

Unit _____ Course _____ Date _____	
Lesson Topic _____	
Objective _____	
Introduction	
CONTENT	KEY QUESTIONS

Summary

Materials

Assignment

Evaluation

Alternative Format 4

A fourth alternative format commonly used lists the objectives in one column and the activities that are to bring about these objectives in another column. This format has the advantage of pointing out which activity is designed to bring about each objective, and thus incidentally guarantees that each activity is designed to address some objective. But this format may be difficult to use in class because it does not lend itself to a step-by-step outline of the procedure, as in the preferred lesson plan format.

Lesson _____ Course _____ Date _____

Objectives	**Activities**
1. Bargain and compromise were the principal methods of solving political difficulties about 1850.	1. Map study. Review the new territory added to United States.
	2. What was slave? What free?
	3. On map find slave states.
2. etc.	4. etc.

Materials of Instruction Needed

Assignment

Evaluation

Alternative Format 5

The fifth alternative format is often used partly as a supervisory device. It provides spaces for detailed identification data, aims, understandings, special notes, and assignments, as well as columns for the teacher's timetable, outline of content, and the methods to be used to teach the content. Although the form may appear complicated, the fact that the three columns of the "procedure" are listed according to time sequence makes the format easy to follow during class.

School _____ Teacher _____

Grade _____ Date _____ Day _____

Period(s) or Module(s) _____ Room(s) _____ Week Ending _____

Daily Lesson Plan

Day's Aims and Objectives Major Understandings:	Routines (general housekeeping reminders)
Skills to Be Developed:	Student Assignment(s) (for one or more days)
Attitudes:	

Chronological Time Sequence (minute by minute or number of minutes to be used in each part of outline)	Outline of Content to Focus upon in Order to Achieve Aims and Objectives	Teaching Methods, Techniques (and needed materials)

Evaluation

Sample Lesson Plans

The preceding pages have presented the fundamental components that go into the development of a daily lesson plan. It is important for the beginning teacher to note that some components will bear more strikingly on certain subject matter fields. Some can be modified to relate more specifically to a given subject, topic, or class of students. The essential point to remember, however, is that a daily lesson plan should be a flexible instrument that can be effectively used by the classroom teacher. A plan is valueless if simply prepared to meet an administrative requirement that plans be filed in the main office. Similarly, a plan is valueless if constructed so rigidly that departures are impossible. Examples of lesson plans in various formats follow.

Sample Lesson Plan 1—Algebra

1. **Course:** Algebra 1, Grade 9, Average Group
2. **Topic:** Factoring polynomials having common factors.
3. **Content:**
   a. Vocabulary: *Old* Factor, product, polynomial, monomial.
   New Common factor, greatest common factor.
   b. Concepts: *Old* Distributive law.
   New Factoring polynomials that have common factors is the inverse process of multiplying a polynomial by a monomial.
   c. Skills: *Old* Using the distributive law, multiplying a polynomial by a monomial.
   New Finding the greatest common factor.
4. **Method of presentation:** Teacher-student discussion
   Time schedule: 10 min—review homework.
   15 min—present new material.
   15 min—guided practice and supervised study.
   Assignment: Read pp. 244–245; p. 245, 1–29: all odd numbered problems.
5. **Objectives:**
   a. Students will be able to demonstrate that factoring polynomials having common factors is the inverse process of multiplying a polynomial by a monomial.
   b. Students will be able to find the greatest common factor.
6. **Evaluation:**

7. **Materials:** none

Procedure
1. Review:
   a. What is a product?
   b. What is a factor?
2. Given the problem: $3a + 4b$ what are the factors?
   $\times\ 4a$ how do we find the products?
   what is the product?
3. Can we write this problem another way?

   $4a(3a - 4b) = 12a^2 - 16ab.$

   What gives us the right to do the problem this way? (Dist. Law)

   What is the Distributive Law?

4. Give examples: $2a(m + 3n)$; $3x(2x - 1)$; $a^2(a^2 + b^2)$.

5. $a(x + y + z) = ax + ay + az$.

    What law is this?

    When multiplying a polynomial by a monomial, what may be said about the product? (The monomial is seen in each term of the product.)

    We may say that a is what to each term in the product? (common).

6. In $2ax + 2ay =$ what is the common factor? ($2a$).

    Where do you think we would put the common factor?

    What do we do to each term in the product? (divide it by the common factor and put quotient in parentheses).

    Just as division is the inverse of multiplication, what can we say the relationship between factoring polynomials and the process of multiplying a polynomial by a monomial is? (the inverse).

7. $6m + 6n = 6(m + n)$
   $mn + m = m(n + 1)$
   $3a^2 - 3a = 3a(a - 1)$

    For each problem, what is its common factor?

    Where do I put it?

    What do I do to each term in the product?

8. $4a^2 + 12a = 4a(a + 3)$

    Could I write $4a^2 + 12a = 4(a^2 + 3a)$? Why?

    What is $4a$ called? (greatest common factor).

9. What is the greatest common factor in these problems?

    Where do I put it?

    What do I do to each term in product?

    $6xy - 3x^2 = 3x(2y - x)$.

    $2a + 4ab + 2ac = 2a(1 + 2b + c)$.

10. Given the example: $6a^2b - 15ab^2 = ?\ 3ab(2a - 5b)$.

    This check could still be valid if G.C.F. had not been chosen, ex. $3a$ instead of $3ab$. Therefore, what should we do to check for G.C.F.? (Inspect each term in the polynomial to make sure no single number or letter is seen in each term.)

Sample Lesson Plan 2—Social Studies

Social Studies II: United States History and Problems.

Unit: Evolving a Foreign Policy.

Topic: The Changing Relationship of Puerto Rico to the United States in the Twentieth Century.

Objectives: Students will be able to:

1. Outline the evolution of the political and economic ties between Puerto Rico and the United States over a specified period of time.

2. Demonstrate an appreciation for the unique role of Puerto Rico in current inter-American affairs.

3. Relate current problems to their historical antecedents.

Procedure

1. Conclude unfinished business: an oral report comparing life in Maryland suburbia with life in rural North Dakota.

2. Review by means of puzzle.

3. Establish purposes for listening to oral reports by offering listening guide questions. Present reports sequentially to trace the changing relationship of Puerto Rico to the United States.
   a. The Island of Puerto Rico Before 1898.
   b. Political and Economic Change, 1898–1940.
   c. Luis Muñoz Marin and Operation Bootstrap.
   d. Puerto Rico: The Cultural Bridge Between the Americas.
   e. Teodoro Muscoso and the Alliance for Progress.

4. Summarize by means of special assignment, which the students will copy from the board upon entering the classroom.

Assignment: Read "Crisis in Latin America," a speech made by the governor of Puerto Rico. Keep these questions in mind:

1. Why does the author caution us about the use of political "labels"?

2. In what ways is the term "Latin America" really an unsuitable expression?

3. What are the particular problems that Latin America faces?

4. In the Alliance for Progress, what roles does the author hope the United States will play?

5. Why is there stress on the phrase "Operation Seeing-Is-Believing"?

6. What unique function does the governor feel his own island can play in the Alliance for Progress?

Evaluation:

Materials: Copies of puzzle for review

SAMPLE LESSON PLAN 3—SCIENCE

Physical Science, Grade 7.
Unit: Science and Measurement
Topic: The Metric Scavenger Hunt
Objectives: Students will estimate length in metric units within a 10 percent accuracy.
Materials: Metric Scavenger Hunt worksheet; metric rulers.
Procedure

1. Anticipatory set: Introduce this as a great activity. (5 min)
   How many have ever gone on a scavenger hunt?

2. Give instructions, rules for Metric Scavenger Hunt. (5 min)

3. Check for understanding. (5 min)

4. Divide class into groups of four (cooperative learning groups) and embark on hunt. (5 min)

5. During hunt, check individuals for understanding. (20 min)

6. Check for group results. Debrief. (10 min)

Evaluation for future use:

Now that you have read through the sample lesson plans, study them more closely by working through Exercise 5.2.

SUMMARY

There is no single best way to organize a daily plan, no fool-proof formula that will guarantee a teacher an effective lesson. With experience and the increased competence that comes from experience, you will develop your own style, your own methods of implementing that style, and your own formula for preparing a "teaching map." This teaching map charts the course, places markers along the trails, pinpoints danger areas, highlights areas of interest and importance along the way, and ultimately brings the traveler to the successful completion of the objective.

SUGGESTED READING

Henak, R. M. *Lesson Planning for Meaningful Variety*. Washington, DC: National Education Association, 1980.

Johnson, D. W., and Johnson, R. T. *Learning Together and Alone*. Boston, MA: Allyn and Bacon, 1991.

Kim, E. C., and Kellough, R. D. *A Resource Guide for Secondary School Teaching: Planning for Competence*. 5th ed. New York: Macmillan, 1991.

Romiszowski, A. J. *Producing Instructional Systems: Lesson Planning for Individualized and Group Learning Activities*. New York: Nichols, 1984.

EXERCISE 5.2   EXAMINATION OF SAMPLE LESSON PLANS

Examine the three sample lesson plans presented in this module. Answer the following questions about them and share your responses with others in your class.

1. What is your opinion about each of them?

2. Do they measure up to the criteria listed in Figure 5.1?

3. Would a substitute teacher be able to follow each one?

4. Specifically how could each be improved?

   a. Algebra lesson plan:

   b. Social studies lesson plan:

   c. Science lesson plan:

True-False   Write *T* or *F*. If you consider the statement false or iffy, explain why.   **POSTTEST**

_____ 1. A good daily lesson plan guarantees an effective lesson.

_____ 2. All teachers, regardless of their experience, should prepare daily lesson plans.

_____ 3. It is quite acceptable for beginning teachers who are firm in their grasp of the subject matter to keep their lesson plans only in their heads.

_____ 4. Each teacher should develop a personal style of lesson planning that is appropriate for her or his needs.

_____ 5. Students should never see a teacher using a lesson plan.

_____ 6. Most teachers develop the knack of perfect timing after several months; that is, they can bring a class right up to the bell with a lesson plan.

_____ 7. Lesson plans should be in a constant state of revision from one use to the next.

_____ 8. Lesson plans are the single most important element in all the planning a teacher does.

_____ 9. General objectives usually refer to larger goals than those sought in the daily lesson.

_____ 10. A lesson should begin when the bell rings and end when the bell rings.

_____ 11. A teacher should never use the same lesson plan twice.

_____ 12. Formats for lesson plans should be tailored to meet student and teacher goals.

_____ 13. If a lesson plan falls short of the time limit, giving the class a study hall is the best remedy.

_____ 14. A lesson plan should be flexible; it should lend itself to sudden, unforeseen occurrences.

_____ 15. The content of a lecture should be written in prose in your lesson plan.

_____ 16. Every lesson plan should be designed to stress a key point.

_____ 17. In a lesson plan the student learning objectives should be stated in behavioral terms.

_____ 18. The subject content of a lesson plan should be written in long and detailed paragraphs.

_____ 19. The content of your lesson plan should spell out details you might otherwise forget.

_____ 20. The lesson plan should provide a strong conclusion to that lesson.

_____ 21. To be acceptable, a lesson plan must contain an outline of the content in the procedure section of the plan.

_____ 22. As a beginning teacher you should prepare an elaborately detailed lesson plan for every lesson you teach.

_____ 23. The lesson plan book frequently made available to teachers in a school is nothing more than a layout sheet.

_____ 24. In some schools, teachers are required to submit their written lesson plans to their supervisor or principal.

_____ 25. Good lesson plans should be saved for subsequent use.

_____ 26. Every lesson plan should follow the same format.

_____ 27. Every lesson plan should contain an introduction, a lesson development section, and a conclusion.

_____ 28. Key questions that you are going to ask students in class should be written into your lesson plan.

_____ 29. It is wise to include the answers to important questions and problems in your lesson plan.

_____ 30. It is more important for elementary school teachers to prepare detailed lesson plans than it is for secondary school teachers to do so.

Short Answer

31. Describe the relationship between learning activities of the lesson plan and the specific objectives of the lesson plan.

_____

_____

32. Describe the role of the key point in the lesson plan.

_____

_____

33. Give two major reasons for writing out your lesson plan in some detail.

_____

_____

34. What could you do if your lesson plan falls short in time?

_____

_____

35. When and how is it best to give the assignment for the next day?

_____

_____

PART III
Motivating the Students and Managing the Classroom

Part III, consisting of two modules, deals with your understanding of:

☐ Education motivational theory.

☐ Techniques for providing a supportive classroom environment.

☐ Techniques for getting to know your students as people.

☐ The importance of providing positive modeling behaviors.

☐ Today's concept of classroom control.

☐ Guidelines for establishing rules for classroom behavior.

☐ Guidelines for efficient and effective classroom management.

☐ Guidelines for dealing with difficult students.

Remember that "Help us grow this grass" is a far more effective sign than "Keep off the grass."

—Norman Vincent Peale

Nothing makes people so worthy of compliments as occasionally receiving them. One is more delightful for being told one is delightful—just as one is more angry for being told one is angry.

—Katharine F. Gerould

MODULE 6
Motivation for Learning

RATIONALE

Of major importance to effective classroom management—and consequently to effective teaching—is motivation. Students who are well motivated to learn usually do learn if lessons are reasonably well designed. When students' attitudes are antagonistic toward school, school learning, teachers, or classes, teachers' efforts will not likely be fruitful. Therefore, teachers often have the responsibility of convincing students that learning well in their classes is the thing to do. The teachers who know individual students are better able to accomplish this task, through adapting lessons and courses to student needs and interests and tempting them by making the course seem valuable to them personally.

This module presents concepts and strategies that will help you as you learn to enhance student motivation in ways that are favorable to their learning, and to make efficient the management and control of your classes.

SPECIFIC OBJECTIVES

At the completion of this module, you should be able to:

1. Discuss education motivational theory.
2. Describe student perceptions about the classroom and about their learning that are necessary for the expected learning to occur.
3. Describe resources and devices you can use to learn more about your students.
4. Describe a dozen general procedures for improving students' motivation toward their school work.
5. Describe how you can use the principles of positive reinforcement for the motivation of student learning.

MODULE TEXT

Student Perceptions

A modern theory of motivation holds that the effort a student is willing to spend on a task is a product of (1) the degree to which that student believes he or she can successfully complete the task and achieve the rewards of that completion and (2) the degree of value the student places on that reward. This axiomatic concept is referred to as the **expectancy × value theory.**[1] For teachers, the importance of this concept is that both aspects must be present for student learning to occur—that is, the student must see a value in the experience and the student must feel that he or she can achieve the intended outcome of the experience.[2] A student will be less likely to try to learn if that student sees little or no value in the material; a student will likely not try to learn when that student believes he or she is incapable of learning the material. Before students do, they must feel they can do, and before students do, they must feel that the doing is important. In this module we provide strategies that can help you demonstrate to students that they can and should achieve your intended learning outcomes.

Regardless of the instructional and motivational strategy chosen, certain perceptions by students must be in place to support the successful implementation of that strategy. These perceptions are:

1. Students must feel that the classroom environment is supportive of their efforts.
2. Students must feel welcomed in the classroom and accepted by the teacher.
3. Students must perceive the expected learning as being challenging but not impossible.
4. Students must perceive the expected learning outcomes as being worthy of achieving.

---

[1]N. Feather (ed.), *Expectations and Actions* (Hillsdale, NJ: Erlbaum, 1982).
[2]Thomas L. Good and Jere E. Brophy, *Looking in Classrooms* (New York: Harper & Row, 1987), p. 309.

This module offers strategies a teacher can use to help instill these perceptions, thus allowing maximum learning to take place. Regardless of the effectiveness with which the teacher selects and implements motivating instructional strategies, however, classroom management problems will occur. The next module addresses the topic of effective classroom management.

Providing a Supportive Classroom Environment

To promote motivation and learning the teacher should "accentuate the positive" and "catch them being good." Teachers whose classes are pleasant and positive find that their students learn and behave better than students of teachers whose classes are harsh, repressive, and negative. The following are specific suggestions for making the atmosphere supportive of student learning.

Getting to Know Your Students

If classes are to move forward smoothly and efficiently, they should fit the students' abilities, needs, aptitudes, interests, and goals. Therefore, you need to know your students well enough to provide classroom learning activities they will find interesting, valuable, and motivating. There are a number of specific steps you can take to get to know your students.

Prepare and Use a Seating Chart to Assist You in Quickly Learning Student Names. Like everyone else, students appreciate being recognized and addressed by their names. Quickly learning and using their names is an important motivating strategy. One technique for learning names quickly is to use a seating chart. A way to do this is to prepare slips of paper bearing the names of your students, and then as you call your roll, place the name slips into the proper spots in a pocket-type seating chart. Some schools provide these pocket-type charts; if not, you can easily make one yourself. You can also make a blank seating chart on which you write in the names during roll call or when students are doing seat work. Many teachers prefer to assign permanent seats and then make seating charts from which they can unobtrusively check the roll while students are doing seat work. It is usually best to get your students into the lesson before taking roll and doing other housekeeping chores.

Many teachers assign permanent seats in this way: on the first day of school tell your students that they can sit wherever they want but by Friday of that first week they should be in a permanent seat, from which you will make a permanent seating chart. Other teachers prefer to assign permanent seats on the first or second day of school so they can begin learning student names even more quickly. Whichever way you proceed, a seating chart assists in your quickly learning names and in taking daily roll unobtrusively.

Addressing students by name every time you speak to them will also help you remember their names. (Be sure to learn to pronounce their names correctly; that helps in making a good impression.) Another way to learn student names is to return their papers each day yourself, calling their names and then handing the papers to them, paying careful attention to look at each student and making mental notes that may help you to associate names with faces.

Get to Know Your Students as People.   None of us is motivated when we feel recognized only as a statistic or a number. Each of us is a distinct person, and we feel much more positive about a formal setting (such as a classroom and a doctor's office) when we feel recognized as being important and unique individuals. With your own students, learn about each as much and as quickly as you can—about their personalities, characters, ability levels, interests, and home life. The best way to learn about a person is to spend a great deal of time with that person, talking together, socializing together, and working together. Unfortunately, the structure of high schools (and to a lesser extent middle schools) makes it difficult to know students well. The daily teacher load is often quite heavy (100–150 students per teacher) and the teacher's time is limited.

Consequently, teachers must utilize various shortcuts, tips, clues, and other techniques to get to know their students. The most useful techniques for learning about your students include:

□ *Classroom Sharing.* One technique that is not only motivating during that first week of school but also helpful in getting to know more about each of your students is to spend some time during the first week of class asking each student to share a bit about him- or herself. These are the kind of questions you might ask:

   What name would you like us to call you by?

   Where did you attend school last year?

   What are your out-of-school interests or hobbies?

   What is one thing you would especially like us to know about you?

How the student answers such questions may be as revealing about that student as is the information (or the lack thereof) that the student does share. From what is revealed during this sharing, you sometimes get clues about additional information you would like to solicit from the student in private or to find out from school sources.

□ *Observations.* Observing the students in class, on the athletic field, and at lunch may give additional information about their personalities, friendships, interests, and potentialities. For instance, you may find that a student who seems phlegmatic, lackadaisical, or uninterested in the classroom is a real fireball on the playing field or at some other student gathering.

□ *Conversations.* Conversations between you and individual students before, during and after class, as well as at other times in school, can be helpful in conveying the important message that you are interested in each student as a unique and valued individual. Keep in mind that students who feel they have been betrayed by prior adult associations may at first be distrustful of your sincerity. Be patient, but do not hesitate to take advantage of the opportunity afforded by talking with individual students outside of class time. Investing a few minutes of time in a positive conversation between you and a student, during which you indicate a genuine interest in that student, can pay real dividends when it comes to that student's learning in your classroom.

□ *Conferences with Students.* Conferences with a student, that student's parent or guardian, and with that student's other teachers can also be useful for data gathering. Conferences with students can be formal, structured, one-on-one interactions scheduled by you for the purpose of learning more about each individual student. In such a setting as this, it is helpful if you follow these suggestions:

1. Ask only open-ended questions. Encourage the student to talk freely. Listen to what the student says.

2. Don't moralize, judge, or condemn, but accept a student's opinions and values as what they are—his or her opinions and values.

3. Let the student do most of the talking.

4. As soon as possible after the conference, record your observations. Your personal file concerning the students you teach should by year's end contain hunches about actions you have seen as well as direct quotations of statements you have heard that seem to have some bearing on the student's behavior. Failure to record such revelations quickly may result in your forgetting them or, worse yet, remembering them incorrectly.

Remember, your purpose is to try to learn more about each individual student so you can better facilitate the learning of each student in your class. When a student is aware that you are genuinely interested in him or her as a person, that student is likely to be better motivated to learn in your class.

□ *Conferences with Parents or Guardians.* Parent or guardian conferences can reveal a lot about the student and that student's interests, abilities, goals, and support from home. This information may be volunteered directly by the parent or be gleaned through answers to your questions. Just as often, though, you may be able to draw inferences from unintentional clues. A parent's speech pattern, for example, may reveal the source of a student's mispronunciations. Aggressive or meek behavior by a parent or guardian may suggest reasons for the child's behaviors.

□ *Student Writing.* What a student writes for your class can be as revealing as what the student says and does. You should read everything a student writes for your class and ask for clarification whenever you need it.

□ *Questionnaires.* Some teachers find valuable the use of interest-finding and autobiographical questionnaires. In an interest-finding questionnaire the student is asked to answer questions such as:

When talking to your friends at lunch, what do you usually discuss?

Do you like to read?

What kind of books do you read in your spare time?

Do you read the daily newspaper?

If so, which section do you read first?

What kind of movies do you enjoy seeing?

Do you watch television often?

If so, what are your favorite shows?

Do you have any hobbies?

If you had free choice, what course would you most like to take at this school?

In an autobiographical questionnaire the student is asked to answer questions such as:

What do you plan to do when you finish high school?

Do you have a job? If so, what is it? Do you like it?

How do you like to spend your leisure time?

Do you like to read? What do you like to read?

Do you have a hobby? What is it?

Answers to student questionnaires can provide ideas about how to tailor assignments for individual students.

□ *Cumulative Record Files.* These record files are held in the school office or counseling department. They include data recorded annually by teachers, administrators, and counselors and contain information about the student's academic background, standardized test scores, and extracurricular activities. Use caution with your use of any conclusions that may have been drawn by others—a student's past should not be held against that student.

□ *Test Results.* Both standardized and teacher-made tests can help match the learning activities to the present knowledge and capabilities of the students. Diagnostic tests are especially useful for this purpose, and many excellent ones are available commercially. However, it is quite possible to build useful diagnostic tests of your own. Unit tests should almost always be diagnostic, unless they are end-of-term tests. To build such a diagnostic test:

1. Establish the specific learning products, information, concepts, skills, attitudes, ideas, and appreciations for which you wish to test. These will be most useful when they are written as specific behavioral objectives.

2. Write test items that test each of these objectives. To utilize such tests for diagnostic purposes, it is necessary to analyze the test results to find where the students do well and where they do not. This analysis can sometimes be done

by inspection, but often it is essential to use some form of test analysis. In your analysis, identify which items each student answered correctly and which incorrectly. You can assume that students who answered the items having to do with an objective correctly have achieved that objective and that students who missed those items did not. Work through Exercise 6.1 for a better understanding of this concept. More on the topic of test item construction and analysis is found in Modules 15 and 16.

Creating a Positive Classroom Atmosphere

The classroom should be a pleasant place to be and to learn. All students should feel welcomed in the classroom and accepted by the teacher. The following are suggestions for making your classroom a place where all of your students want to be.

Guarantee That All Students Feel Welcomed into Your Classroom.   The academic classroom is no place for prejudice of any sort. You should personalize the teaching by demonstrating to each student that he or she is welcomed and accepted into your classroom. You can do this by being positive in your comments and mannerisms to each and every student, by modeling behaviors that represent trust and respect and that are characteristic of an open, accepting classroom environment. You may need to learn how to demonstrate dislike for a specific student behavior without demonstrating nonacceptance of that student as a person. Students sometimes need help in understanding that denial of a specific behavior is not denial of them as worthwhile persons. To increase a student's feelings of self-worth and acceptance in your classroom, you might want to consider each of the following:

□ Mark the number right instead of the number wrong.

□ Use correcting pens with colors other than red.

□ Reward positive behaviors rather than punish negative behaviors.

□ Send positive notes home.

□ Teach students cooperative learning procedures.

□ Check the roll at the end of each week and ask yourself if there are students that you should give some special positive attention to during the next week.

Try to emphasize the "dos" rather than the "don'ts," the rewards rather than the punishments, the joy of learning and knowing rather than the pain of studying and the fear of failure. Let the students know that you want them to do their best. Give them time and support their efforts. Reward their successes and honest attempts. This may mean modifying your own concept of what a success actually is. Especially avoid punishing a student who is trying but has not yet succeeded.

Pay Attention to Your Classroom's Physical Appearance.   This is easier for teachers who have their own classroom for the entire day than for those who move from one classroom to another. Nevertheless, there are things that all teachers can do to create a hospitable classroom environment. A pleasant, neat, comfortable, and bright classroom helps provide a climate favorable to learning—when the room looks nice, the tendency for everyone is to keep it that way. Therefore, make the classroom as attractive as possible. It is surprising how much you and your students can do to make even the most drab classroom a pleasant place.

An initial step in improving a classroom's appearance—and student attitudes—is to keep the classroom neat and orderly. Provide a place for everything and try to keep everything in its place. Tidy up, clean up, and put things away after using them. Improve the classroom atmosphere by brightening it up. Use displays, murals, bulletin boards, posters, and pictures. If you lack tackboards or display areas, be creative: use adhesives that allow you to fasten things directly to the wall without marring its finish, or cover the wall with murals drawn on wrapping paper. You might cover the walls with wrapping paper and let your graffiti artists decorate them (be sure not to use paint or ink that will stain through and mark the walls). Use lots of pictures. Preferably,

EXERCISE 6.1 DIAGNOSIS FROM AN ITEM ANALYSIS

The following chart represents a sample nine-item analysis of the results of a test that was designed to measure the student learning associated with three different specific objectives. Assume that the small sample of that item analysis as shown in the chart is typical of the entire analysis, and answer the questions that follow the chart. Code: ✔ = correct answer: 0 = incorrect answer.

SAMPLE ITEM ANALYSIS

Objective	Item	Alicia	Bill	Jamaal	David	Ellen
1	1	✔	0	✔	✔	✔
	2	✔	0	✔	✔	✔
	3	✔	0	✔	✔	✔
2	4	0	0	0	0	0
	5	0	✔	0	0	0
	6	✔	✔	0	0	0
3	7	✔	✔	✔	✔	0
	8	✔	0	0	✔	0
	9	✔	✔	✔	✔	✔

1. What, if anything, needs to be taught again?

2. Do any of the students need remedial work? If so, who and what?

these should all be pertinent to what you are teaching and should be changed for each unit in order to keep the classroom bright, interesting, and up-to-date. But purely decorative pictures are better than no pictures at all.

Pay Attention to Your Students' Creature Comforts.   Students find studying difficult when they are physically uncomfortable. To the extent possible, attend to the lighting, heating, cooling, and ventilation in the classroom. A hot and stuffy classroom can destroy motivation and control; so too can classrooms that are too dark or in which students are facing a glare. Young adolescents in particular cannot sit for long periods of time. Try to vary the instruction so that they will not have to sit and listen quietly for long periods of time.

Teachers, Students, and Staff Must Realize That Classroom Instruction Is an Important School Activity.   Unfortunately, the behavior of some schools seems to teach students that the least important thing happening in the school is the classroom instruction. Classes are too often interrupted by announcements or by students arriving with unimportant messages from the office, or they are dismissed for last-minute pep rallies and other assemblies and activities. Noises and activities from outside the classroom often distract students, and you may not have much control over such things. The weather may be too warm to close doors and windows to eliminate the sounds and sights of these distractions. For example, it is all-too-common to visit schools and hear loud noises from lawn maintenance crews operating their hedge clippers and lawn mowers right outside of classroom windows—noises so loud that classroom discussions and activities have to be suspended. Teachers should appeal to their administrators that class disruptions, interruptions, and outside distractions must be kept to a minimum. Why can't lawn crews do those things before or after school? Why can't schools enact policies that announcements and messages be delivered only during the first or last five minutes of each class period? A school that seems to place little importance on the teacher's classroom instruction diminishes student motivation for learning.

Try to Run a Happy Ship.   Try to make what you have to teach seem attractive to learn. Fun and humor both relaxes tension and enhances student motivation and learning. A teacher who can admit to mistakes, and even laugh at them, is more motivating than one who never admits to a mistake, never laughs when appropriate, and never seems to enjoy having fun with the students. Of course, fun and humor should not ever be at the expense of an individual student in the class.

Encourage Students' High Levels of Aspiration and Self-Esteem.   Success raises aspirations, whereas failure lowers them. Therefore, try to see that each student experiences success in your class. Provide creative, interesting, and challenging but reasonable assignments. Treat mistakes positively, and use them as opportunities to teach the students the value of errors. Students need successes so they will not become discouraged and give up. Set high standards, however. Be certain that your students know what your standards are and that you are confident of their ability to meet those standards. Take time to make your expectations clear, and help the students meet these expectations by showing them what they do well and what they could do differently to improve their work.

Diffusely Structure Your Class.   Try to build group cohesiveness in your class by encouraging cooperative student involvement and participation. Cooperative learning procedures get all students into the act of learning, disallowing any in-group from dominating the class. Your class should act as a group working for a common cause with shared responsibilities rather than as a bunch of competing individuals. Rewards for progress can be given to teams on the basis of the team's achievement rather than given to individual students.

Use Interesting Strategies and Tactics.   Today's students have been growing up in an electronic age saturated with multimillion-dollar television, stage, and screen productions; fast-paced, computer-controlled arcade games; and instant communication and information retrieval systems made available by modern electronics—an age unlike any previous generation of school children. When these young people step into your classroom and experience something short of a high-budget production—without an eye-catching and sensory-stimulating "commercial break"—it may seem difficult to motivate them or maintain their attention for longer than 10 minutes. By the time these students have reached middle school, however, they are aware of the realities of school teaching and have experienced past teachers and classes that were not particularly motivating. Because of that awareness and their prior experiences, you will have ample opportunity to plan courses that will stimulate and motivate your students into productive learning. The following is a list of some teaching strategies that can be used to arouse interest and increase motivation (each is discussed in detail in subsequent modules):

☐ Special projects, both individual and group.

☐ Real-life situations in which students do real things.

☐ Simulations and role-playing.

☐ Educational games.

☐ Solving real problems, perhaps those of the school or community.

☐ Building real things.

☐ Discussion and decision-making on real topics and problems.

☐ Modern audiovisual equipment, such as laser videodiscs, interactive computer programs, multipurpose writing boards, and telecommunications.

☐ Imaginative use of traditional audiovisual equipment, such as the chalkboard and the overhead and opaque projectors.

☐ Imaginative assignments, both for individual and group work.

☐ Creative introduction of topics, such as the use of "magic" to introduce topics, especially in mathematics, science, and social science.

☐ Real-life examples to which the students can relate.

Reflect on your own school experiences by doing Exercise 6.2.

Providing Positive Modeling and Examples

Students learn behavior by imitating others. If teachers can provide students with good and honorable models from which they can pattern themselves, then the conditions are right for them to achieve the kind of behavior teachers seek. It may be possible to use students' admiration for older students, highly regarded students, natural peer-group leaders, and such personalities as sports stars, movie stars, and world figures. Yet, such personalities are not always reliable as good models of behavior. Fictional and historical characters, however, are always available in books and other media, and it may be possible to use such characters to advantage in your teaching.

Perhaps the most reliable and influential model is a pleasant teacher whose classroom personality is characterized by "empathy, warmth and genuineness."[3] Such a teacher does not take him- or herself too seriously. Self-centered teachers—those who worry about how they will appear and how classroom incidents will affect them—are much more likely to have difficulty than teachers whose interests center on their students and on how classroom incidents will affect their students. Therefore, go in there and teach the very best you can. Act with confidence but without arrogance and everything will probably go well. If you concentrate on teaching well and if your plans and procedures are reasonably good, you will less likely experience problems in classroom control. As mentioned before, you would do well to develop an active interest in your students, a friendly attitude, an interesting personality, and a healthy sense of humor. Above all, demonstrate that you enjoy teaching, studying, and working with

---

[3]Duane Brown, *Changing Student Behavior: A New Approach to Discipline* (Dubuque, IA: William C. Brown Company, 1971), p. 12.

EXERCISE 6.2   REFLECTIONS ON MY OWN SCHOOL EXPERIENCES

The purpose of this exercise is for you to reflect on your own educational experiences and ask yourself what your teachers did that made their classes interesting to you. Answer the following first three questions and then, in small groups, share your responses with your classmates. After sharing your responses, in your small groups answer questions 4 and 5. Share those with the entire class, and then individually answer question number 6.

1. Recall two teachers that have motivated you the most. Identify them by the class and year of schooling.

     Teacher A:

     Teacher B:

2. What specifically did each teacher do that motivated (or interested) you?
     Teacher A:

     Teacher B:

3. Do you think most kids in their classes were motivated by these teachers' actions? Why or why not? Describe.

After sharing your responses, in groups answer the following questions.

4. Were there any common responses among your answers to questions 1 and 2? If there were, describe them here.

5. Was there a common response to your individual responses to question 3? If there was describe it here.

6. After sharing all responses in your large group, what did you learn as a result of this exercise?

your students. Attitudes are contagious. If you demonstrate that you are enthusiastic about what you teach and teach joyously, your students may become enthusiastic too. Approach your teaching with pleasure and with confidence. If you concentrate on teaching in a businesslike, confident manner, you will probably be well on the road to having the kind of classroom control you desire.

A word of caution is necessary: although every teacher should be friendly with students, becoming too chummy could be detrimental to the classroom atmosphere. Avoid entangling alliances, teacher's pets, and favored companionships. Teachers should behave as responsible adults and socialize with adults—students will often like and respect them more that way. And keeping the proper distance diminishes the danger of being accused of playing favorites or of a student's attempting to take advantage of or being hurt by a friendship.

In the final analysis, you should set a good example and be a good model. Your behavior should be consistent with that expected of your students. For example, the teacher should return homework papers in timely fashion when timeliness is expected of students. The teacher should arrive promptly to class meetings when such promptness is expected of students. The teacher should spell correctly and write clearly and legibly when those things are expected of students.[4] If the students realize that you are trying to serve them well and that you really care about them as persons of dignity, they will be more likely to respond positively to your teaching.

Making the Learning Seem Worthwhile

Be sure the learning and activities seem worthwhile. Show the students how the material they are studying can be useful to them now, as well as in the future. Provide an assortment of activities, materials, and content that will appeal to the variety of interests and learning styles present in the class. Find special projects for special individual students. Encourage students to cooperate with you in the planning of their own learning activities. Above all, select content that is relevant to their lives and the needs of the community, and be sure they know why that content is important and relevant for them personally. Never start them on an activity without being certain they know why they are going to do it.

Take advantage of the students' motives. Use their interests, ideals, goals, and attitudes. Appeal to their curiosity, pride, desire for fun, need for achievement, and social interests. Try to use the concerns of your students as vehicles of teaching. Focus on the present and future more than on the past. Utilize job-related applications of the content being taught. Take advantage of situations that occur outside the classroom. In this connection remember that intrinsic causes of motivation (i.e., incentives that come from within the learner) are usually more powerful than extrinsic sources (i.e., sources from without, external rewards). Students will usually work harder to learn something because they want to learn it than they will merely to earn some extrinsic prize or reward.[5]

Reinforcing Positive Behaviors

One theory of psychology holds that people tend to behave in ways that have rewarded them in a way they find valuable. This is called reinforcement theory, because it is based on the belief that rewards or gratifying results strengthen a tendency to behave in a certain fashion, and lack of reward weakens the tendency to act in that fashion. For instance, if a student is promised free time for his or her own purposes when that student has worked well for a certain period, the student may work toward that reward and develop higher standards for work in the future. In disagreeing with this theory, some argue that once the extrinsic reward is removed, the student's motivation dampens and the student ceases the desired behavior. Perhaps the real truth lies somewhere

---

[4]Kim and Kellough, p. 223.
[5]*See* E. L. Deci and R. M. Ryan, *Intrinsic Motivation and Self-Determination in Human Behavior* (New York: Plenum Press, 1985).

in between. Teaching in a classroom is less than ideal. Not all activities are going to be intrinsically motivating. But activities that are interesting and intrinsically rewarding will not be further served by the addition of external rewards. Evidence indicates that to add external incentives to activities that are already highly interesting tends to reduce motivation. In the development of skills, where much repetition is needed and boredom is likely to ensue, the use of rewards is probably particularly useful.

The reinforcement theory seems to hold many implications for the motivation and control of student behavior. Unfortunately, this theory has been honored in the breach in all too many cases. Teachers often unintentionally reinforce the wrong behavior. When the student who is seeking attention (that student's immediate goal) misbehaves (that student's goal-seeking behavior), the teacher might reprimand the student, thus giving the student the attention desired. But when the same student behaves well, the teacher ignores that behavior. Thus, the teacher reinforces the student's negative behavior and neglects the positive behavior. As a result, the teacher strengthens the student's tendency to misbehave and weakens the student's inclinations to behave well. Therefore, take care to reinforce the type of activity you want to encourage. Try not to reinforce untoward behavior; rather, accentuate the positive. Catch students being good! Look for successful efforts to commend rather than failures to berate.

There is no need for you to place much faith in grades and marks for student reinforcement. They are not dependable for several reasons:

1. Not all students place much value on high grades.
2. Not all students can expect to receive high grades or marks. High-ability students who try usually receive high grades, but low-ability students who try seldom do.
3. Because the efforts of low-ability students so seldom pay off in high marks no matter how hard they try, "those students who need to try hardest are given the least incentive to do so."[6]

Rather than depending on grades to provide motivation, it would ordinarily be more profitable to adjust the lessons and the curriculum, making them appeal more to students' intrinsic motives, or to use such techniques as computer-assisted instruction, continuous promotion, or pass-fail marking.

Now reinforce your understanding of rewards by doing Exercise 6.3.

Building Trust

Try to build students' trust in you. Careful preparation, hard work, enthusiastic teaching, empathy, respect for your students, fairness, and justice will help you in developing a trusting relationship with your students. Trust is something you cannot force; it is given when deserved. Trust is probably the greatest resource you can have when it comes to generating desirable student motivation and furthering their learning.

SUMMARY

Students are less likely to learn when they do not feel that the learning is important or worth the time. In this module we described student motivation for learning and some of the sources for motivation, extrinsic and intrinsic. In addition, we presented suggestions for teacher behaviors that will help to increase your students' desires to learn in your classroom. Concomitant to specific attempts to motivate your students is how you manage your classroom, what strategies you select, and how those strategies are implemented. Classroom management is the topic of the next module, followed by several modules on the selection and implementation of particular strategies.

SUGGESTED READING

Ames, C., and Ames, R. eds. *Research on Motivation in Education, Vol. II: The Classroom Milieu.* Orlando, FL: Academic Press, 1985.

Brophy, J. "Synthesis of research on strategies for motivating students to learn." *Educational Leadership* 45(2):40–48 (October 1987).

---

[6]J. W. Michaels, "Classroom Reward Structure and Academic Performance," *Review of Educational Research* 47:95 (Winter, 1977).

EXERCISE 6.3   REWARDS AS REINFORCEMENT

In this exercise, you begin preparing how you will use rewards as motivational reinforcement in your own teaching. There are several types of rewards that can be used to reinforce desirable student behavior, including tangible rewards (such as athletic passes), recognition rewards (such as a certificate for achievement), material rewards (such as food or script money), social rewards (such as being assistant coach or teacher), activity rewards (free time), and intrinsic rewards (deriving pleasure from doing an activity).

1. For the subject and grade level you intend to teach, list examples of rewards in each category that you think would be appropriate:

   a. Tangible rewards:

   b. Recognition rewards:

   c. Material rewards:

   d. Social rewards:

   e. Activity rewards:

   f. Intrinsic rewards:

2. Now, observe a class (or think back on your own classroom experiences) and answer the following:

a. What behaviors were rewarded? And how?

b. What behaviors were not rewarded?

c. Were there examples of students being rewarded for being quiet, for being cooperative, and so on?

d. Were there examples of students being rewarded for misbehaving?

e. Remember, sometimes a punishment can be a reward. From your observations or experiences, were there examples of this?

Deci, E. L., and Ryan, R. M. *Intrinsic Motivation and Self-Determination in Human Behavior.* New York: Plenum Press, 1985.

Emmers, A. P. *After the Lesson Plan: Realities of High School Teaching.* New York: Teachers College Press, 1981.

Gage, N. L., and Berliner, D. C. *Educational Psychology*, 3d ed. Boston: Houghton Mifflin, 1984.

Kim, E. C., and Kellough, R. D. *A Resource Guide for Secondary School Teaching: Planning for Competence*, 5th ed. New York: Macmillan, 1991.

Perrone, V. *A Letter to Teachers.* San Francisco: Jossey-Bass, 1991.

POSTTEST

Analyze Which of the following are recommended for the teacher's use in motivating students? Mark those recommended in this module *R*; those not recommended *X*.

_____ 1. Give clear instructions.

_____ 2. Provide a variety of activities.

_____ 3. Be enthusiastic about your teaching and about learning.

_____ 4. Provide interesting set induction to lessons.

_____ 5. Emphasize marks and grades.

_____ 6. Try to fit your teaching to the students' present goals.

_____ 7. Allow students complete freedom to do what they want.

_____ 8. Utilize real-life situations in which students do real things.

_____ 9. Diffusely structure your class.

_____ 10. Establish high standards and expectations.

_____ 11. Reward and reinforce desirable student behavior.

_____ 12. Utilize individual student projects.

_____ 13. Threaten punishment for inappropriate behavior.

_____ 14. Establish assignments that are challenging but not impossible.

_____ 15. Treat students as individuals.

_____ 16. Be a buddy of each student.

_____ 17. Try to provide each student with successes.

_____ 18. Be very strict.

_____ 19. Come down hard on students who make mistakes.

_____ 20. Catch them being good.

Short Answer

21. What sorts of information would you expect to find in a cumulative record folder?

_____

_____

22. According to reinforcement theory, which teacher action is usually preferable, to reward or to punish? Why?

_____

_____

23. Describe the expectancy × value theory.

_____

_____

24. What does the following excerpt from an item analysis of a diagnostic test tell you?

Objective	Item	STUDENT				
		Jesus	Joe	Latisha	Betty	John
1	1	✔	✔	✔	0	✔
	2	✔	✔	✔	0	✔
	3	✔	✔	✔	0	✔

MODULE 7
Classroom Management

RATIONALE

Effective teaching requires a well-organized, businesslike classroom in which motivated students work diligently at their learning tasks, free from distractions and inappropriate behavior. Providing such a setting for learning is called effective classroom management.

Essential for effective classroom management is the maintenance of **classroom control**, that is, the process of controlling student behavior in the classroom. This classroom control is similar to the old concept of "classroom discipline." Modern classroom control involves:

☐ Steps for preventing student misbehavior

☐ Ideas for handling student misbehavior

The control aspect of teaching is frequently the most worrisome to beginning teachers—and they have good cause to be concerned. Even experienced teachers sometimes find control difficult, particularly at the junior high school and high school levels, where teachers have so many students that it is difficult to get to know them all well, and where so many students have been alienated by bad experiences in earlier school years.

Another part of effective classroom management is good organization and administration of activities and materials. In a well-managed class students know what to do, have the materials to work with, and keep on task; the class atmosphere is supportive, the assignments clear, the materials of instruction current and readily available, and the classroom proceedings businesslike. At all times the teacher is in control, seeing that students are spending time on appropriate tasks. For your teaching to be effective you must be skilled in classroom management procedures.

SPECIFIC OBJECTIVES

At the completion of this module, you should be able to:

1. Describe the modern concept of effective classroom control.

2. Define permissiveness, democratic control, and self-discipline.

3. Explain several strategies and tactics that should help create self-discipline in your students.

4. Show how each of the following contributes to effective classroom control: a positive approach, well-planned lessons, a good start, classroom rules, enforcement of rules, correction of misbehavior, and classroom management.

5. Describe specific procedures for establishing the conditions and carrying out the actions necessary to establish and maintain classroom control.

MODULE TEXT

Effective Classroom Management

Effective classroom management is the process of organizing and conducting a class so that it results in maximum student learning. To manage your class successfully, you need to plan your lessons carefully; provide students with a pleasant, supportive climate for learning; create interest; instill a desire to learn and achieve; establish control; prevent distractions and disturbances; deal quickly and quietly with distractions and disturbances that are unavoidable; and, in general, promote effective student learning. While certain of these teacher skills were discussed in the previous module, others are discussed here or in subsequent modules.

What is a well-managed, effectively controlled class? In today's schools, the classroom atmosphere is more likely to be, in the words of the lyricist, "more free and easy," and teachers, "more bright and breezy" than they were in the days of our grandparents when "reading and writing and 'rithmetic" were "taught to the tune of a hickory stick." Nevertheless, this swing toward pleasantness and "permissiveness" does not mean that students are free to behave as they please. Although silence is no longer a *sine qua non* and repressive classes are considered taboo, every teacher is charged with the responsibility of providing a classroom atmosphere that is favorable to learning. Learning does not usually occur in classrooms that are disorderly and noisy. The degree of quiet and kind of order necessary depend on the type of class. Laboratory sessions allow for conversation and movement; lecture sessions require quiet attention; and discussions, purposeful conversation. Work sessions in school rooms resemble work sessions in business or industry, periods in which many things are happening, most of which, it is desired, will be productively directed toward the job at hand.

Sometimes, beginning teachers misunderstand today's philosophy of classroom atmosphere and assume that the permissive classroom atmosphere means that anything goes. Such teachers are way off base; the students will soon tag them out. Orderliness is essential. Permissiveness, as used in today's context, means that the teaching should support the students in their efforts to learn and not clamp them down tightly in a pattern that would keep them from thinking for themselves. In a permissive class, students are encouraged to seek out and express their own ideas without fear of reprisals because of honest mistakes, but there are accepted rules for behavior, and breaking these rules cannot be tolerated any more than it would have been in a traditional class. Since use of the word *permissiveness* often delivers different connotations, perhaps rather than speaking of permissive classrooms we should talk of supportive classrooms.

Another notion that seems to confuse beginning teachers is that correction and strict control is harmful to the mental health of students. Quite the contrary is true. Students benefit from the maintenance of high standards and adherence to democratic rules; laissez-faire teaching, in contrast, can be downright harmful. Mental health is best fostered by democratic teaching in the environment of a controlled classroom.

In short, you, as the teacher, must establish yourself as the person in charge of your classroom. Students should not have any doubt that you are in charge and that their behavior is governed by your rules or rules that have been established with your approval. Your classes should be democratic, not chaotic.

Getting Organized

In classroom management a good beginning may make all the difference. Therefore, you should appear at your first class, and every class thereafter, as well prepared and as confident as possible. Perhaps you will feel nervous and apprehensive, but being ready and well prepared will probably help you at least to look confident. Then, if you proceed in a businesslike, matter-of-fact way, the impetus of your well-prepared beginning will cause the day to proceed as desired.

Planning

Since a good beginning is so important, you should take great care with your planning. Poorly planned classes that wander—or classes that provide students with nothing to do, or that seem worthless, or that are dull and drab—contain the seeds of control problems. Ad lib teaching is sloppy teaching, and sloppy teaching leads to control and learning problems. To prevent or minimize problems of this sort, you need to take care in planning. Although planning is addressed in detail in Module 5, here are some suggestions that can help in this task:

☐ Students should be furnished with enough purposeful activities that they are kept busy and active throughout the class period. Avoid dead spots, spots of time where some or all of the students have nothing to do. Plan ahead so all materials are available and ready for distribution and student use.

☐ Limit the time spent in teacher talk (lectures). As a general rule, no more than one-fifth of class time should be devoted to such activity. If you must lecture—and sometimes it may be the only practical procedure—then plan your lecture with key questions, audiovisuals, and other interest-catching activities. (Details on the use of the lecture and other specific strategies follow in the next modules of this text.)

☐ Provide for individual differences and for instruction in how to study the particular lesson, how to use the equipment or materials, and how to do the assignment.

☐ Your plan should be flexible enough that you can make minor last-minute adjustments when what you had planned does not seem to fit the class predisposition for that day.

☐ Be reasonable in your expectations. For example, absolute quiet from students who are excited about the learning activity is not a reasonable expectation.

☐ Provide for good motivation. The lesson planned should seem interesting, challenging, and valuable to the students. Avoid planning lessons that repeat the same deadly routine day after day after day.

☐ Understand that not all of your lessons can be exciting and stimulating. Your students need to understand that, too. For less-than-exciting lessons you may want to consider the use of awards for appropriate behavior and for jobs done well or on time.

☐ Spice up your assignments. Assignments should be worthwhile, interesting, relevant, and challenging. Sometimes, by necessity, assignments are drills, which tend to be dull and boring. For those you may want to increase student motivation by the use of rewards for jobs well done. Be sure that you explain clearly what is to be done and how to do it. Sometimes, you will have to go into detail, giving examples and demonstrating proper procedures, to make everything clear. When students are not clear on what to do or how to do it, they tend to give up.

☐ Routinize the organizational and administrative details of classroom management in order to eliminate dead spots and avoid disorderly breakdowns in classroom decorum. Students respond better when they know what to expect, when these housekeeping tasks are routinized. These routines should be part of your lesson plan.

☐ To make your planning and management easier on yourself, have a standard plan or ritual for your lesson organization. This does not mean that you should use the same strategies and tactics in all your classes—quite the contrary. But you should check to see which of your standard sections are necessary for a particular lesson and whether you have adequately provided for each of these necessary sections.

Various lesson plan formats are discussed in Module 5. The following is a restatement of the basic sections that should be considered when you are organizing your lesson:

1. Set introduction (your introduction of the lesson or activity, designed to motivate and to stimulate a mind set)
2. Clarification of objectives for the students (what they are to learn and why)
3. Tie-in with prior lessons
4. Presentation of the new content
5. Presentation follow-up (checking for understanding, guided practice, independent practice)
6. Small group and independent laboratory-type study
7. Closure (culminating activity that ties together the set, the presentation, the follow-up activities, and sometimes a transfer to the next day's lesson)
8. Materials and equipment of instruction (to be certain that you have these things ready for the lesson)
9. Assignment
10. Notes and reminders (including evaluative items and suggestions for next use of this lesson)

Establishing Classroom Behavior Rules

Part of your preclass preparation should be the determination of your expectations for student classroom behavior as well as the establishment of your classroom behavior rules (CBRs). Your rules must seem reasonable to your students, and you must enforce your rules. But sometimes the rules can be a cause of trouble. To avoid this difficulty, you should establish only the minimum number of rules necessary for order in the classroom. Too many rules may confuse students and make the classroom atmosphere too repressive. By establishing and sticking to a few rules, you can leave yourself some room for judgments and maneuvering. Ordinarily, your rules should be quite specific so that students will know what is acceptable and what is not.

When you decide what your classroom rules will be, you should also decide what the consequences for violating those rules will be, as well as how you will implement those consequences. Do not paint yourself into a corner, but establish what you will do in the face of inappropriate student behavior. Your students also need to understand the consequences of inappropriate behavior. Completely extemporaneous decisions—those not based on prior thought—may lead to unnecessary, undesirable complications.

Explain your rules and consequences to students early in the course—preferably on the first day. (Try to state your rules in positive terms, i.e., stressing the "dos" rather than the "don'ts.") When establishing your classroom behavior rules consider the following things that students need to know:[1]

□ *How to correctly obtain your attention and help.* Most teachers who are effective classroom managers ask that students raise their hands and only until the teacher acknowledges (usually by a nod) that he or she has seen the student's hand. With that acknowledgment, the student may lower his or her hand. To prevent that student from becoming bored with waiting, it is important that the teacher attend to that student as quickly as possible.

□ *How to correctly enter and leave the classroom.* When the class (tardy) bell rings, and prior to the final dismissal bell, teachers who are effective classroom managers expect students to be in their seats and to be attentive to the teacher. Students work best when the expectations are clear to them, and when there is an established routine. Teachers must plan carefully how they will spend the first and final few minutes of each class period or school day. This means establishing and maintaining a regular routine.

□ *How to correctly store personal belongings.* Students need to know where, when, and how to properly store, retrieve, and care for their coats, books, pencils, medicine, and other items. Classroom control is best when items that students need for class activities are neatly arranged and located in places that require minimum foot traffic.[2]

□ *How to correctly go to the drinking fountain and to the bathroom.* Once again, we emphasize the importance of establishing a regular routine, and at the same time we should point out that teachers who are effective class managers avoid having the entire class line up at the same time to do something—whenever the entire class is forced into off-task time (e.g., standing in line), problems are most certain to occur.

□ *How to behave during a class interruption.* Unfortunately, class interruptions do occur: For some important reason, the principal or some other person from the office may need to interrupt the class to see the teacher or a student or to make an announcement to the entire class. Students need to know what behavior is expected of them during such interruptions.

□ *How to correctly obtain and to use papers, books, the pencil sharpener, and other materials, supplies, and equipment available for their use in the classroom.* Classroom management is easiest to maintain when there is the least amount of foot traffic, when there are established routines that students clearly expect and understand, when there is the least amount of student off-task time, and when items that students need for class activities are neatly arranged and located in nearby places. Therefore,

---

[1]E. C. Kim and R. D. Kellough, *A Resource Guide for Secondary School Teaching: Planning for Competence,* 5th ed. (New York: Macmillan, 1991), pp. 346–47.

[2]Thomas L. Good and Jere E. Brophy, *Looking in Classrooms,* 4th ed. (New York: Harper & Row, 1987) p. 232.

plan the room arrangement, equipment and materials storage, preparation of equipment, materials, and transitions between activities so that you avoid needless delays and confusion.[3]

□ *What to do when they are late to school, or when they will be leaving school early.* Understand the school policies regarding early dismissals and tardy students, and follow them. With regard to school policies, routinize your own procedures so that students clearly understand what they are to do if they must leave school early (e.g., a medical appointment) or are tardy.

Think about your own classroom rules by doing Exercise 7.1.

Organizing and Arranging the Classroom

When it is time for class to start, you should be all ready to go. Get together all the instructional materials you will need ahead of time. Have the room and materials arranged for orderly and efficient use. Be sure the bulletin boards are set, any boardwork ready, all needed equipment set up and working, and any necessary supplies at hand.

In most classrooms the seats are arranged in rows. This linear arrangement is fine for lectures and most audiovisual presentations, but rows do not encourage discussion and student involvement. You may find it more satisfactory to arrange your class in a hollow square, a double horseshoe, or a circle (see Figure 7.1). If you plan to use committee or small-group work, small circles usually work best. Although adjusting classroom seating arrangements to the type of activity is generally a good idea, it may be better to go along with an existing arrangement rather than cause a large commotion by moving furniture once a class has started.

Conducting the Class

As soon as the bell rings, you should begin your class without delay, confusion, or dead time. Experts generally recommend that you require your students to report to their assigned classroom stations at the beginning of the class period, so you can take attendance and perform other routine administrative tasks quickly. Once these details are completed, the students can move to ad hoc work stations suitable for that day's learning activities.

Keeping Things Moving

Once the class has started, it should move forward briskly and steadily. The pace should be vigorous enough to keep students alert, but not so brisk as to lose those who are trying. Each student should feel some pressure to do well. This pressure should not be oppressive, but everyone should realize it exists. Let it be known by word and by your actions that you expect everyone to be on task and to do his or her

FIGURE 7.1
Seating Arrangements

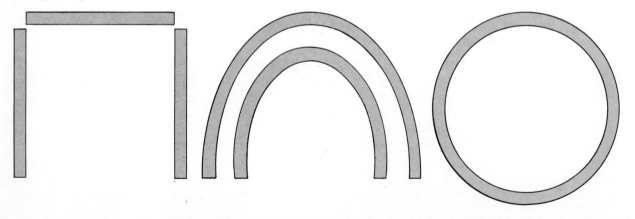

---

[3]Good and Brophy, p. 232.

EXERCISE 7.1   PREPARING CLASSROOM BEHAVIOR RULES

The purpose of this exercise is to start you thinking about your own list of classroom behavior rules that you will use for your teaching. Prepare a list of rules that you will insist on when you teach. Will your list vary according to whether you are teaching middle school, junior high school, or high school? If it will, then prepare separate lists. Then share your list(s) with your classmates for their responses.

best, and that you do not tolerate dawdling, disturbances, time wasting, or other inappropriate behavior. To promote this businesslike atmosphere, try to make sure that everyone has something worthwhile to do, that the students all know how to do what they are supposed to be doing, and that the students all have the materials they need. At no time should any student be standing around with nothing to do or be kept waiting for equipment, materials, or attention. Be alert for any student who has a hand raised for your attention, acknowledge that student, and attend to the question as quickly as possible.

MOVEMENT MANAGEMENT

To keep things moving briskly and smoothly and to minimize distractions, utilize the principles of movement management.[4] Movement management refers to the process of keeping the class moving forward at a brisk pace without side trips or interruptions. The first of these principles is that by starting your class the moment the bell rings, you can eliminate the fooling around and time wasting that often occurs before a lesson begins. The second is that the class should move forward steadily and purposefully. Transitions from one activity to the next should be natural and unobtrusive. Each activity should start promptly without confusion and continue briskly to a definite, planned conclusion. Movement around the class should be controlled, orderly, and routinized. In short, movement management is keeping the class on track. To ensure that your movement management is effective, be careful that not even you interrupt the smooth progress of the class. For example:

☐ When your students are busy and on task, avoid interrupting them with instructions, statements, or announcements.

☐ When you do have announcements, instructions, or statements to make, be sure that the students are ready to hear you. A class of 28 students always needs mental time to prepare for any transition.

☐ Be sure an activity is finished before you start a new one. Students should not be left dangling on an unfinished activity while the teacher starts off on a new direction. Be sure they know when you end one activity and begin the next, and make the transitions smooth and logical.

☐ Avoid interrupting yourself. Avoid getting off the topic. If you start discussing one thing, keep to it until you are finished. Avoid jumping around from one topic or activity to another and then back again. A class of 28 students cannot be expected to make those kinds of cognitive leaps.

☐ Try not to be distracted by the irrelevant. Never interrupt the class's progress by harping on matters not pertinent to the task at hand. Avoid public harangues. Admonishments to individual students should always be done quietly and privately, without interrupting the rest of the class.

☐ Avoid making mountains out of molehills. Avoid talking an activity to death. Once you have said what is necessary, stop.

☐ Avoid providing too much detail. If something can be done in a few steps or explained in a few words, then so explain.

☐ Maintain a logical sequence. An outline on a transparency on the overhead or on the writing board is often helpful to teacher and students both.

☐ Involve your students in your teaching.

☐ Avoid the overuse of workbooks and other humdrum seat work. Activities afforded by workbooks and quiet seat work are best reserved for reinforcing and assessing knowledge and skills that have already been taught.

---

[4]Jacob S. Kounin, *Discipline and Group Management in the Classroom* (New York: Holt, Rinehart and Winston, 1970), pp. 102–8.

The teacher should not breach any of these ten rules, otherwise the teacher's infraction will cause student misbehavior to occur and impede the efficiency of that class's movement management. Pay particular attention when planning and implementing small-group work.

Small-Group Work

Small-group activities (three to five students) are useful for teaching students to handle ideas and for helping students to learn from each other.[5] Examples of activities that lend themselves to small-group work are: brainstorming; oral reports; sharing, editing, and reacting to each other's work; and joint projects. Unless these are well managed and monitored, however, small-group activities may bog down and become time wasters.

To make small-group work run smoothly and efficiently, the groups need to be carefully structured and the activities clearly planned. The structure of a group, or learning team, can be based on interests or specific skills. Within a group, students may be mixed according to abilities.[6] Group learning that emphasizes cooperation within the group is particularly useful in that it can "meet student needs for belonging, power, fun, and freedom, while providing the bonus of higher achievement and better attitudes among the majority of students."[7] Hence, because it attends to students' basic needs, group learning provides a strong motivator for students to achieve.

For groups to function well, the students within a group need to understand their individual roles (e.g., summarizer, monitor, recorder, encourager, researcher), their tasks, the procedures, routines, and the group's responsibilities. It is sometimes helpful to appoint a monitor to check the group's progress and to answer questions about the assignment. You may want to ask that students who have questions consult with other students before questioning you.

In evaluating group work, group achievement is rewarded. Some teachers assign two grades, one grade for the group's achievement and another for how well the group worked together. Additionally, achievement testing will measure and allow for individual achievement.

Clarifying by Routinizing

Routinizing the humdrum day-after-day tasks will ease movement management. Students are more likely to do things without argument or disruption when they are used to doing them and doing them in a certain way. If you establish routines for various everyday functions, students will always know what they are supposed to do. In this way, you can reduce fuss and confusion. Just what routine you select matters little as long as it is reasonably efficient.

Among the common tasks that need routinizing are: taking attendance, distributing equipment and supplies, collecting and passing papers, starting and stopping class, attending to interruptions caused by a classroom visitor, requesting the teacher's attention, leaving the room for an emergency, arriving to class late, and needing to sharpen a pencil or go to the wastebasket. Therefore, take time to see that your students understand the classroom rules and procedures expected of them. Ordinarily the time to teach such routines occurs when the routine is first introduced. Soon the routines should become so automatic that students follow them without prompting or interruptions.

With-it-ness and Overlapping

Two teaching skills important for effective classroom management are (1) **with-it-ness** (as Kounin called it), the teacher's knowing at all times what is going on every-

---

[5]For more about the value of team learning, a particularly useful reference for teachers is William Glasser's *Control Theory in the Classroom* (New York: Perennial Library, 1985).

[6]*See* Robert E. Slavin, *Using Student Team Learning*, rev. ed. (Baltimore: Johns Hopkins Press, 1980).

[7]C. M. Charles, *Building Classroom Discipline: From Models to Practice*, 3rd ed. (New York: Longman, 1989), p. 148.

where in the classroom and (2) **overlapping**, the teacher's ability to attend to more than one matter at a time.

With-it-ness might be thought of as "having eyes in the back of your head." In addition to being aware of everything going on in the classroom at all times, there are two other characteristics of the teacher who is "with it." One is the teacher's timing, and the other is the teacher's ability to attend to the right culprit. It is important that you attend to potentially disruptive student behavior quickly and with the least amount of class disturbance, and it is important that you attend to the right student. In effectively managing your classroom, your movement and nonverbal behaviors in the classroom are important. Disrupting the entire class with a reprimand to two misbehaving students (and perhaps only one of those is guilty) is a poor teaching technique—perhaps an even more disrupting behavior than that of the two students being reprimanded.

To develop your with-it-ness skills, you should:

1. Keep the entire class under surveillance all the time. Look around the room frequently. Move around the room. Be on top of potential misbehavior and redirect student attention before the misbehavior occurs or gets out of control.

2. Keep students alert by calling on them randomly, asking questions and then calling on an answerer, circulating from group to group during team learning activities, and frequently checking on individual progress.

3. Keep all students in the act. Avoid becoming too involved with any one student or group. Avoid the temptation to concentrate only on those students who seem most interested or responsive.

4. Quietly redirect the behavior of a misbehaving student.

5. If two or more errant behaviors are occurring simultaneously but in different locations in the classroom, treat the most serious first.

6. Above all, maintain a high level of student interest by introducing variety and sparkle into your teaching.

The teacher's ability to attend to more than one matter at a time is referred to as the teacher's overlapping ability. Overlapping is a prerequisite to effective with-it-ness. The teacher who can effectively attend to more than one matter at once uses body language, body position, and hand signals to communicate with students. Consider the following examples of overlapping ability:

☐ While working with a small group of students, a student in another part of the room has his hand raised wanting the teacher's attention. While continuing to work with the group of students, the teacher signals with her hand to the student, an acknowledgment that she is aware that he wants her attention and will get to him quickly.

☐ While attending to a visitor who has walked into the room with a written message from the office and while reading the message, the teacher demonstrates verbally or by gestures to the class that she expects them to continue their work.

☐ Without missing a beat in his lecture, by gesture, eye contact, or moving closer to the student, the teacher aborts the behavior of a potentially disruptive student.

☐ Rather than being seated at the teacher's desk and allowing students to come to the desk with their papers and problems, the teacher expects students to remain seated and raise their hands, while the teacher moves around the room monitoring and attending to individual students.

Effective classroom management depends on the teacher's constant awareness and monitoring of all students and class activities. Monitoring requires constant checking and feedback. Among the things to check are:

Is everyone attending to business?

Does everyone have something purposeful to do?

Does everyone understand the assignment?

Does everyone understand how to proceed?

Does everyone have the materials to work with?

Are teacher directions clear?

Is the content too difficult?

Is the work challenging enough?

Are the physical conditions all right?

Does everyone understand the expected standards of behavior and workmanship?

Are the students progressing as well as they should? Are they using the proper procedures?

It is absolutely imperative that you continually check students' work and provide feedback. By so doing you can catch and correct errors before they become a problem, as well as find opportunities to provide specific praise for good work. Careful monitoring can prevent problems now and in the future, and it also helps guarantee a businesslike learning climate.

In summary, you need to make sure that your class moves briskly from the first to the final ringing of the bell. To achieve this goal, you must pay particular attention to your preparation, organization, movement management, with-it-ness, and overlapping, and, perhaps above all, to your monitoring.

Maintaining Control

Most beginning teachers find group control their most worrisome problem. As a rule, however, teachers who establish good motivation and classroom management are not greatly troubled by problems with classroom control. Even in the "worst" schools in the "worst" neighborhoods, some teachers run efficient, effective classrooms with hardly any control problems at all.

Why Students Misbehave

Misbehavior is any behavior considered inappropriate in the classroom or school setting. Students misbehave for many reasons. One is the sheer deviltry of it. Another is for the attention received as a result of the misbehavior. Classrooms are usually somewhat unnatural and restrictive, so students like to relieve the tension. Other reasons for misbehavior may stem from a student's family and community background or from a student's emotional well-being. Some misbehavior is simply an unrestrained outburst of the restlessness, rowdiness, and exuberance of youth. On the other hand, much student misbehavior is school-caused or teacher-caused. Classes may be tedious and boring. The curriculum may seem worthless and irrelevant to anything that is important to youth. When their schooling is far removed from their lives, they can lose interest and become inattentive, the resolution of which is to direct their energies into what seems to them more fulfilling activities.

Some teachers never have discipline problems; others have constant problems. The guidelines presented in this book, if followed, can provide you with the skills necessary to prevent discipline problems from occurring in your classroom—though no teacher can avoid the occasional discipline problems. That being the case, in addition to guidelines for preventive discipline, the guidelines here will assist you in knowing what to do at the first sign of potential misbehavior and how you can positively redirect misbehavior that has occurred.

Sometimes a teacher is confronted at school with major problems of misbehavior that have ramifications outside of the classroom or that start outside and spill over into the classroom. Those types of control problem will be addressed later in this module.

In other instances a misbehavior is so minor and of such short duration that the teacher is advised to ignore it, because not to ignore it would create an even greater distraction from the lesson. From Emmer, examples of behaviors of this type include "occasional callouts during discussions; brief whispering among students during a lesson; or short periods of inattentiveness, perhaps accompanied by visual wandering or daydreaming. There is no point in worrying about such trivial behaviors as long as they are not disruptive; they do not significantly affect student cooperation or involvement in learning activities. To attempt to react to them would consume too much of your energy, interrupt your lessons constantly, and detract from your classroom's climate."[8]

Types of Misbehavior

From Charles are these five broad types of misbehavior that teachers may have to contend with, and listed here in their order of seriousness:[9]

1. *Aggression.* Occasionally, aggressive students physically or verbally attack teachers or other students. By law this can be a punishable offense, and you are best advised to find out what your own state and local laws are with respect to physical and verbal attacks by students upon teachers and students. A teacher should never have to put up with this type of student misbehavior. Whenever you are in doubt about what action to take, you should discuss your concern about a student's aggressive behavior with the school counselor or an administrator. In some instances you may need to send for help immediately.

2. *Immorality.* This type of misbehavior includes cheating, lying, and stealing. A student who habitually exhibits such behavior may need to be referred to specialists. Whenever you have good reason to suspect immoral behavior of a student, you should discuss your concerns with that student's school counselor.

3. *Defiance of authority.* This is when a student refuses, perhaps hostilely, to do what the teacher tells that student to do. Defiance is worthy of temporary or permanent removal from the class—at least until there has been a conference about the situation, a conference perhaps that involves the student, the teacher, a parent or guardian, and a school official.

4. *Class disruptions.* This type includes talking loudly, calling out, walking about the room, clowning, and tossing objects, all of which the student knows are unacceptable behaviors in the classroom. In dealing with these kinds of misbehaviors it is important that the teacher has communicated to students the consequences of such inappropriate behaviors, and then deal promptly and consistently with the misbehavior. You must not ignore minor infractions of this type, for if you do they will escalate beyond your worst expectations.

5. *Goofing off.* This least serious type includes those misbehaviors that are most common to the classroom: fooling around, not doing the assigned tasks, daydreaming, and just generally being off task. Fortunately, in most instances, with this type of misbehavior all it takes to get the student back on task is a quiet redirection from the teacher.

Gauge your understanding of student misbehaviors and how teachers should react by doing Exercises 7.2 and 7.3.

Preventive Discipline

The most fruitful steps you can take to achieve well-disciplined classes are preventive steps. These steps were considered in the earlier discussion of motivation and classroom management. Basically, the premise is that when motivation and classroom management are well taken care of, problems in classroom control are minimal.

Encouraging Self-Control

Generally students want to behave properly and acquire the approval of the teacher. Usually, a student misbehaves for some specific reason, and the task for the teacher

[8]Edmund T. Emmer et al., *Classroom Management for Secondary Teachers*, 2nd ed. (Englewood Cliffs, NJ: Prentice-Hall, 1989), p. 105.

[9]C. M. Charles, *Building Classroom Discipline: From Models to Practice*, 3rd ed. (New York: Longman, 1989), p. 2.

is to understand that reason and help the student regain self-control. The best control of student behavior is self-control. If you help students learn to take responsibility for their own learning and to carry out this responsibility, you will have accomplished much. Some of the ways teachers work to help students with their self-control include the following.

Help Students Establish a Code of Conduct for Themselves.   Doing so has the advantage of acquainting students with what acceptable behavior is and why such behavior is necessary for the success of the group or of society. To be successful, this code should not be dictated by the teacher, but worked out together to the mutual satisfaction of all concerned.

Help Students Improve Their Own Standards of Conduct.   This must be a slow process. It is accomplished by making students aware of optional behaviors, of high standards, and of the disadvantages of the lower standards. Classroom discussions of behaviors can be helpful in the process. Teachers have had success by talking out behavior problems with the students, so the students can see why a particular behavior is unacceptable, what the students should do about it as penance, and what actions could remedy the fault.

Use the Enforcement of Rules as a Tool.   Sometimes, enforcing rules helps students learn to discipline themselves. Both enforcing the rules fairly and making students follow the rules tend to support the habit of desirable behavior. In some classes students enforce many of the rules themselves. Although this procedure works well for mature groups, it is likely to throw too much burden on younger students. In most cases, the teacher should probably assume the responsibility for rule enforcement.

Support Student Self-Control.   When a teacher assumes control over a student's behavior—by using aggressive verbal orders or punitive measures—the teacher may momentarily cease a disruptive behavior, but such action is usually counterproductive to the encouragement of self-control. Techniques that can be used by a teacher to encourage and support student self-control are those whereby the teacher quietly refocuses student attention to an on-task behavior, with techniques such as the following:

☐ Use of nonverbal signals sent to the student. These signals can be sent by eye contact, the hand, or facial expressions. They indicate the teacher's with-it-ness and communicate to the student that the teacher wants the student behavior back on task.

☐ Use of proximity control. When a teacher moves closer to a misbehaving student, the student will usually get back on task.

☐ Showing interest in a student's work when the student begins to lose interest in the class activity. The teacher can simply walk over to the restless student and ask to see the student's work. Making a positive statement about that work as well as suggesting further improvement will usually redirect the student's behavior.

☐ Humor and a smile will usually redirect student off-task behavior. This communicates two important things to the student: (1) the teacher is aware and uncomfortable with the student's inattentive behavior and wants the student back on task, and (2) while not being entirely happy with the student's inattentive behavior the teacher still accepts the student as a worthwhile individual.

☐ Use of academic time-outs. Sometimes, when a student has become bored and inattentive, the student's misbehavior can be redirected by giving the student a minor responsibility, such as delivering materials to the office or doing some paper work for you in the classroom. However, a word of caution is in order: the student's time-out activity must not be seen by the student as an incentive for future misbehavior. Upon completion of the time-out activity, a quiet word from the teacher to the student is in order, such as, "Thank you for helping me. Now I would like

EXERCISE 7.2   IDENTIFYING TEACHER BEHAVIORS THAT CAUSE STUDENT MISBEHAVIOR

The purpose of this exercise is for you to become aware of the kinds of teacher behaviors to avoid, because they tend to reinforce or cause student misbehavior. Place a check next to each of the following situations you believe are indicative of teacher behaviors that cause student misbehavior. Then identify what the teacher should do instead. Share your responses with your classmates. An answer key follows.

_____   1. The teacher is always late in arriving to the classroom, and class never begins until at least five minutes past the ring of the tardy bell.

_____   2. The teacher ignores brief whispering between two students during a quiet classroom activity.

_____   3. The teacher ignores brief talking between two students during a teacher lecture.

_____   4. During a classroom discussion one student appears to be daydreaming and just staring out the window.

_____   5. During quiet study time the teacher stops all activity and reprimands two students for their horsing around, and then writes out a referral for each of the two students.

_____   6. The teacher advises the students to pay attention during the showing of the film or else he will give them a quiz over the film's content.

_____   7. The teacher tells a student that because he has disturbed the class today he must come in after school and remain with that teacher for the same amount of time that he disturbed the class.

_____ 8. The teacher observes a student cheating on a test, so the teacher walks over to the student, picks up the student's test paper and tears it up.

_____ 9. While delivering a lecture, the principal walks into the classroom. The teacher stops the lecture and walks over to see what the principal wants.

_____ 10. The teacher begins a conversation with several students in the rear of the room while a student learning team is giving its oral report to the class.

ANSWER KEY

Situations 1, 3, 5, 6, 7, 8, 9, and 10 should be checked as teacher behaviors that reinforce or cause student misbehavior, for reasons explained below. You may not agree, particularly since specific circumstances might vary. But you should talk about these and arrive at understandings within your group.

1. The teacher must model his or her expectations of students; in this case, arriving and starting class on time.
2. Minor infractions are sometimes best ignored.
3. This should not be ignored. Students are expected to give attention to the teacher or whoever has the floor at the moment—that is common courtesy. By not attending to these students (perhaps by eye contact, proximity control, or use of name dropping during the lecture) the teacher is saying it is okay to talk when the teacher is lecturing.
4. Minor infractions are sometimes best ignored.
5. By disrupting the class learning activity, the teacher is reinforcing the very kind of behavior that the teacher finds unacceptable from the students.
6. Threats are unacceptable behaviors, from the students or the teacher. And tests should never be administered as punishment.
7. By giving the student even more individual time after school, the teacher is likely reinforcing and rewarding the student's misbehavior that caused the student problem in the first place. Besides, this is not a safe thing for the teacher to do. Detention hall, run by someone other than this teacher, is a better alternative.
8. This teacher, who has taken no time to diagnose and prescribe, is reacting too hastily and with hostility. This kind of teacher behavior reinforces the notions that you are guilty until proven innocent and that the process is more important than the individuals.
9. The teacher's lesson is more important; otherwise, the lesson learned is that disruptions are okay.
10. This is disrespectful, and the teacher and class should be giving full attention to the students giving their report.

EXERCISE 7.3   RESOLVING A DISCIPLINE PROBLEM
Brainstorming Ideas

The purpose of this exercise is to assist you in developing a repertoire of ideas about what you might do in a situation where a student is misbehaving. You can work on this exercise in small groups, or alone whenever you have a student that is causing problems in your classroom. Completion of this exercise will generate ideas about what you might do in certain situations. Follow each step closely.

1. *Statement of the problem.* Identify a specific discipline problem that you have experienced as a student, or one that you are now having as a teacher. State as clearly as you can what the problem is, such as the student is disruptive to classroom learning, the student just sits and does nothing, the student is ridiculed by others in the class, and so on.

2. *Identification of what you have observed about or that is related to this student.* List everything you know and have observed about this student, whether you believe it to be relevant or not. Include student behaviors, physical characteristics, grade level, subject, grades, attendance, hobbies, special talents, disabilities, how the student is getting along with other teachers, and so on.

3. *List of things tried.* List everything you have tried with this student and their results, such as isolation in the classroom, referrals, talk with parent or guardian, rewards, discussions with the student in or out of class, discussions with the student's other teachers, the student's counselor, and so on.

4. *Share steps one through three with your colleagues.* During the sharing discussion you may get new ideas about the student, the student's behavior, and things that you might try in order to work more positively with the student. As the ideas are generated, write them down—that is the next step.

5. *New things to try with this student.* As you complete the previous steps you will almost certainly gain ideas about new ways to work with this student. As those ideas are generated, write them down.

6. *Follow-up report of new strategy that was tried and the results.* At some later date, perhaps in a week or two, list here (and perhaps report to your group) what you tried and describe the results.

1. Statement of problem:

2. Observations about the student:

Adapted from Kim and Kellough, pp. 381–2. By permission of Macmillan Publishing Company.

3. Things I have tried and results:

4. Sharing:

5. New ideas:

6. New strategy tried and results:

you to finish your work and show it to me when it is done." In that way the student gets back on task after the brief time-out.

Enforcing Rules

No matter how well motivated, managed, and self-controlled your classes are, problems will arise. Therefore, you should be particularly attentive to rule enforcement. What you do when someone breaks the rules is more important than the rule breaking itself.

Reasonably strict enforcement of rules can have a salutary effect on the class and the classroom atmosphere, because enforcement has a positive ripple effect. When students see that you take swift, fair but firm action against infractions by other students, they are less likely to misbehave. The ripple effect is especially powerful when you show that you can control students who have high status in their peer group. Conversely, when students see that others are getting away with breaking the rules, they lose respect for both the rules and the teacher—and that can have a negative ripple effect. To gain the most advantage of a positive ripple effect, you must start a policy of strict enforcement on the very first day. Being lax in the beginning courts disaster. It is much easier to relax a policy of strict enforcement later than it is to turn a class around.

In any case, rule enforcement should be fair and consistent. Fairness and consistency in enforcement does not mean mindless conformity to an enforcement pattern. Justice should sometimes be tempered with mercy, and the nature of the punishment should sometimes be adjusted to the nature of the offender, as well as to the nature of the offense. But when this is done, the action taken should seem reasonable to all concerned. Ordinarily, measures such as the following, many of which have been previously discussed, will be more effective than negative ones:

☐ Let students know what you expect of them.

☐ Correct inappropriate behavior at once.

☐ Use nonintensive corrective measures, such as movement toward the source of trouble, hand signals, eye contact, and frowns.

☐ Handle all minor problems and punishments yourself.

☐ Treat the problem rather than the person.

☐ If at all possible, use alternatives rather than punishment. If necessary, punishment should be swift, sure, impressive, and appropriate to the "crime."

☐ Try to relieve tensions. Talk things over with the students. Show them how to improve. Emphasize what they are doing well. Inject a bit of humor and good feeling.

☐ When the class begins to become restless, switch activities.

☐ When you foresee that a student is about to get into trouble, attend to that student and redirect the student's attention, such as with the techniques discussed in the previous section on self-control.

☐ Plan periodically to make new seating assignments, perhaps on a regular basis, though not too often.

☐ If you must deny a student request, explain why.

☐ Keep student movement in the classroom to a minimum.

☐ Avoid dead time during the period, time when individual students have nothing to do.

☐ Have an alternative lesson plan in case the original plan is not working.

On the whole, negative methods of rule enforcement are not effective. You should avoid the following:

☐ *Nagging.* Continual or unnecessary scolding or criticizing of a student succeeds only in upsetting the student and arousing the resentment of other students.

☐ *Threats and ultimatums.* Avoid painting yourself into a corner. Once you have made a threat or given an ultimatum, you are stuck if the students call you on it. In maintaining control, threats become promises. Once made, they must be carried out or you will lose control. If students learn that your threats are empty, they will disregard them and you. In addition, a threat such as "If you do not pay attention to this film I will give you a quiz on it" is unacceptable in effective teaching. If you are going to give a quiz on the film, then you should prepare the quiz, announce it, and give it, regardless of the students' behavior during the film. They are two separate matters. A test should never be used as a form of punishment. And, in this particular instance, the teacher is threatening punishment of the entire class, though some students, threat or no threat, may well pay attention to the film and not cause any trouble.

☐ *Hasty judgments and actions.* Although your responses to behavior problems should be prompt, do not be overly hasty. Impulsive reactions on your part could lead to greater problems than you can even imagine.

☐ *Overreaction to minor incidents.* Avoid treating minor incidents as major ones. Otherwise they may develop into real problems. Minor problems of misbehavior can usually be resolved by the use of the techniques discussed in the previous section about self-control. When those don't work, then the teacher may need to assume control, using punishment, removal of rewards, detention, or even referral to a counselor or some school authority.

☐ *Arbitrary, capricious, inconsistent enforcement of rules.* If a teacher is inconsistent, students will test that teacher to see what they can get away with. Inconsistency also causes student resentment, confusion, and mistrust.

☐ *Loud talk, yelling, and screaming.* Never try to talk over your class. Yelling and screaming simply add to the commotion. Teachers who yell and scream or try to talk over their class are part of the problem; loud talk, yelling, and screaming never solve anything.

☐ *Harsh, unusual, and inconsistent punishment.* Flogging, beating, tongue-lashing, and humiliation are both ineffective and indicative of a teacher who has lost control. Although some students may occasionally need to be reprimanded, hurting or humiliating them may do much more harm than good. Punishment is discussed in more detail in the next section.

Correcting Misbehavior

The goal of classroom control is to motivate and shape the students in such a way that they do not create discipline problems. Thorough planning, positive motivation, and efficient classroom management are preventive measures that are the real keys to classroom control. When students are working well, control and discipline take care of themselves. Nevertheless, even in the best of classroom situations, the behavior of some students will be less than desirable and will need to be turned into more positive directions.

Theoretically, there are five basic methods to stop anyone from behaving in an undesirable way. One method is to keep the offender at it until he gets sick of it (the satiation principle). A second method is to make sure that the undesirable behavior is not rewarded in any way and in that way dies out (the extinction principle). A third method is to provide an alternative that is incompatible with the undesirable behavior, and to see to it that the alternative behavior is rewarded while the undesirable behavior is not (the incompatible alternative principle). A fourth method is to create an aversive situation that the person can relieve only by giving up the undesirable behavior (the negative reinforcement principle). A fifth method calls for punishment or results supposedly so unpleasant that the person will not willingly repeat the misbehavior again (the punishment principle). Satiation and extinction are not practical measures for correcting misbehavior in the classroom. Therefore, teachers can depend only on incompatible alternatives, negative reinforcement, and punishment to correct misbehavior. The incompatible alternative and the negative reinforcement methods are usually more successful than punishment.

In the incompatible alternative method, the teacher establishes an alternative behavior that is so rewarding the student forsakes the misbehavior. To find extremely strong, usable rewards suitable to the classroom situation is not always easy, but it can be done. The catch, of course, is that the reward for the alternative behavior must be so powerful that it overshadows the reward derived from the misbehavior.

The negative reinforcement method is much more subtle. In this method, the teacher sets up an aversive situation designed to plague the student as long as he or she misbehaves. As soon as the student stops misbehaving, the plaguing stops. The student who stops misbehaving is rewarded by relief from pain or annoyance. This approach is a more effective way to correct student misbehavior than punishment.

At times a teacher must fall back on punishment in an attempt to cure misbehavior. When this time comes, a teacher should attempt to make the punishment appropriate to the misdeed and also swift, sure, and impressive—definitely a punishment and not a reward. The student should have no doubt about the severity of the punishment, why the punishment has been inflicted, and the types of behavior that will prevent future punishment. Among the punishments often used are isolation, reprimands, extra work, deprivation of privileges, and detention. None is very effective in the long term. In the short term, however, they may shake up the student enough so that more positive measures can be applied with greater chances of success. Now consider some of the punishments used by teachers and the recommendations for their use or disuse.

Verbal Punishment

You will often have to reprimand a student. As often as possible, your reprimand should be a declarative statement that is brief and to the point, and as private as possible. Redirecting student attention with the use of questions such as "Katrina, why are you doing that?" is seldom effective. Also, verbal reprimands that the entire class can hear are disruptive to student concentration and work and thus are counterproductive to an effective learning atmosphere. Loud, public, and frequent reprimands do not create a favorable learning environment, and they may do more harm than good. When you must call a student to task, quietly point out the inappropriate behavior and spell out the corrective behavior. There is no point in hurting the student's feelings, in causing resentment, and in building an unpleasant atmosphere with harsh words. The consequences of misbehavior should already be well understood, so if the student persists in the inappropriate behavior, then you proceed to step two of your consequences, which might be a detention.

Detention

Although detention has not proven to be particularly effective, keeping students after school is one of the most common types of punishment. Since it does have a mildly unpleasant effect on students, it is of some value as a deterrent. For many students, however, detention is such a mild inconvenience that they take it in stride as part of the regular responsibilities of being a student. In contrast, for students who work after school, detention may cause distress out of proportion to the misbehavior. And if the students just sit around during the detention period, detention becomes another complete waste of time for everyone concerned, reinforcing their concept of school as being a waste of time.

Detention after school, alone with the teacher in that teacher's classroom, is not recommended for several reasons. First, such detention might be perceived by the student as a reward rather than a punishment for the student's misbehavior. Second, such detention creates safety and liability problems for the teacher. Third, such detention is often more a punishment for the teacher than for the student.

To be profitable, detention probably should be combined with individual conferences, makeup work, tutoring, or some other educational activity. In some schools, being assigned to detention means to be assigned to a schoolyard clean-up detail. Liability could be an issue in such instances. What if the student is injured while serving on the work detail?

Loss of Privileges

Loss of privileges seems to be one of the most effective forms of punishment. It probably works best when combined with a system that grants rewards for good behavior. Then, if the privileges lost seem valuable to the student, loss of privileges demonstrates to the student that inappropriate behavior is costly while appropriate behavior pays off.

Examples of privileges that have worked for teachers are a trip to a pizza parlor with the teacher as host, a trip to an ice cream parlor with the teacher as host, and free-choice time in class each Friday.

Restitution and Reparation

A time-honored belief in the American tradition is that "the punishment should fit the crime." This notion is the basis for the use of restitution and reparation as punishment. Punishment of this type has several advantages. It associates the punishment with the offense in a natural way. It teaches misbehaving students that they are responsible for their misdeeds and that willful damage should be compensated for. It can be administered fairly and with impartiality. Most importantly, it teaches offenders that their actions affect the welfare of others and that they must accept the responsibility for making things right, by paying back others for the inconvenience and expense caused by the inappropriate behavior.

Punishing the Group

A teacher should never punish—nor threaten to punish—the entire class for the misbehavior of a few. Doing so only aligns the class against the teacher, creating a hostile atmosphere that is counterproductive to the establishment of a positive and effective climate for learning.

Assigning Extra Work

Assigning extra class work to offenders is another punishment you should avoid using. It has no worthwhile advantages, and furthers the notion that schoolwork is just that, work.

Lowering Academic Marks

To lower students' academic marks as a punishment is a misuse of the grading system. Academic marks should be only an indicator of academic achievement. To mark a student down for his or her behavior when the student has learned well gives a false index of that student's academic progress. Schools have separate marks for classroom behavior—the citizenship grade. Citizenship marks represent the teacher's subjective opinion of the student's behavior in that teacher's classroom.

Physical Activity as Punishment

Except perhaps for physical education classes, where the punishment clearly fits the subject matter and can be carefully supervised, physical punishment (e.g., doing push-ups or running around the track) should not be used by the classroom teacher.

Writing as Punishment

Academic work should never be used as punishment or seen by students as being punishment for their misbehavior. Requiring students to write sentences on the board or in their notebooks as a punishment is unacceptable in effective teaching. Writing should never be assigned as punishment. Note well: using writing as punishment will also alienate you from the teachers of the English department.

Corporal Punishment

A teacher should never strike, push, shove, or manhandle a student in any way for any reason. Corporal punishment (e.g., spanking) is now illegal in many states. Physical handling of a student is disallowed in many school districts. There are many instances where physical punishment has resulted in student injury and in subsequent legal action against the teacher and school. In other cases students have reacted violently, injuring the administering teacher or administrator. A good rule of thumb is that if you get really angry at a student, back off until you have cooled off. If you want the student temporarily out of your sight, you can send the student to the vice-principal's office for a cooling-off period. Find out what the policy is in your own school for sending a student to the office for such a time out.

When a Class Is out of Control

That a class would get totally out of your control is very unlikely if you carefully follow the guidance presented in this book. But if a class does get out of control, the following tactics should help:

1. Get help if you feel the situation is potentially dangerous—from a teacher nearby or from the office—but do not leave the room yourself.

2. Remain calm. If you feel a bit panicky, keep quiet for a while.

3. Try to get the students' attention, but without shouting. Do not add to the confusion. Different tactics may help here. For instance, one teacher sat on the floor in the middle of the room until the class got quiet. Another flicked the light switch a few times. Another blew a whistle.

4. Ask that all students take their seats (or remain standing quietly).

5. Redirect the activity of individual students, one at a time. Try to start with those students you know will respond positively to your request.

6. As soon as things have come under better control, quietly begin a lesson.

Handling Major Offenses

If you are ever confronted with a major offense, such as students' carrying weapons, using drugs, vandalizing property, leaving the room without authorization, or fighting, first try to stop the misbehavior. Then report it immediately to the principal's office.

Remember, you are neither a law-enforcement officer nor a psychiatrist. Major problems require outside assistance from professionals. As a professional teacher, you have the right to request and receive assistance from principals, parents, and other school personnel.

Check your understanding of measures of control by doing Exercises 7.4 and 7.5.

SUMMARY

As a school classroom teacher you should not be expected to solve all the societal woes that can spill over into your classroom. But, on the other hand, you as a professional have certain responsibilities, including: to properly and thoroughly prepare for your classes; to professionally manage and control your classes; and to be able to diagnose, prescribe, and remedy those learning difficulties, disturbances, and minor misbehaviors that are the norm for classrooms and for the age group with whom you are working. If you follow the guidelines that have been provided in this and in previous modules for planning and for managing your classroom teaching, you will be well on your way to developing a teaching style and a management system that, for the most part, should run smoothly and without serious control problems.

It is important to select the most appropriate strategies to accompany your teaching plans and management procedures. Modules that follow present guidelines for your selection of specific strategies.

SUGGESTED READING

Cangelosi, J. S. *Classroom Management Strategies.* White Plains, NY: Longman, 1988.

Canter, L. "Assertive Discipline—More Than Names on the Board and Marbles in the Jar." *Phi Delta Kappan* 71(1):57–61 (September 1989).

Charles, C. M. *Building Classroom Discipline.* 3d ed. White Plains, NY: Longman, 1989.

Dreikurs, R.; Grunwald, B.; and Pepper, F. *Maintaining Sanity in the Classroom.* New York: Harper & Row, 1982.

Emmer, E. T., et al. *Classroom Management for Secondary Teachers.* 3d ed. Englewood Cliffs, NJ: Prentice-Hall, 1989.

Emmer, E. T., et al. *Organizing and Managing the Junior High Classroom.* Austin, TX: University of Texas, Classroom Organization and Effective Teaching Project, Research Development Center for Teacher Education, 1982.

Englander, M. *Strategies for Classroom Discipline.* New York: Praeger Publishing, 1987.

Gervais, R. L., and Dittburner, D. A. *What to Do When . . . ? A Handbook for Classroom Discipline Problems with Practical and Positive Solutions.* Lanham, MD: University Press of America, 1985.

Glasser, W. *Control Theory in the Classroom.* New York: Perennial Library, 1985.

Good, T. L., and Brophy, J. E. *Looking in Classrooms.* 4th ed. New York: Harper & Row, 1987.

Harvey, K. *Classroom Management.* Glenview, IL: Foresman, 1985.

Hill, D. "Order in the Classroom." *Teacher* 1(7):70–77 (April 1990).

Jones, F. *Positive Classroom Discipline.* New York: McGraw-Hill, 1987.

Kounin, J. *Discipline and Group Management in Classrooms.* New York: Holt, Rinehart and Winston, 1977.

Lemlech, J. K. *Classroom Management: Methods and Techniques for Elementary and Secondary Teachers.* 2d ed. White Plains, NY: Longman, 1988.

Long, J. D.; Frye, V.; and Long, E. W. *Making It Till Friday: A Guide to Successful Classroom Management.* 3d ed. Princeton, NJ: Princeton Book Co., 1985.

Sanford, J. P., and Emmer, E. T. *Understanding Classroom Management: An Observation Guide.* Englewood Cliffs, NJ: Prentice Hall, 1988.

Sprick, R. S. *Discipline in the Secondary Classroom: A Problem-by-Problem Survival Guide.* West Nyack, NY: The Center for Applied Research in Education, 1989.

Wolfgang, C. H., and Glickman, C. D. *Solving Discipline Problems: Strategies for Classroom Teachers.* 2d ed. Needham Heights, MA: Allyn & Bacon, Longwood Division, 1987.

EXERCISE 7.4   APPLYING MEASURES OF CONTROL

The purpose of this exercise is for you to determine when you might use each of the various options available when there is a student behavior problem in your classroom. For each of the following, as specifically as possible identify a situation in which you would and you would not use that measure. Then share your responses with those of others in your class.

1. Eye contact and hand signal to the student.
   Would:

   Would not:

2. Send student immediately to the office of the vice-principal.
   Would:

   Would not:

3. Ignore the student.
   Would:

   Would not:

4. Assign the student to detention.
   Would:

   Would not:

5. Send a note home to parent or guardian about the student's misbehavior.
    Would:

    Would not:

6. Touch a student on the shoulder.
    Would:

    Would not:

7. Provide candy as rewards.
    Would:

    Would not:

8. Provide time out from academic time.
    Would:

    Would not:

9. Verbally redirect the student's attention.
   Would:

   Would not:

10. Use a verbal reprimand.
    Would:

    Would not:

EXERCISE 7.5   SELECTING MEASURES OF CONTROL

The purpose of this exercise is to provide situations to help you in determining which measures of control you would apply in similar situations. For each of the following, state what you would do in that situation. Then share your responses with your colleagues.

1. A student reveals a long knife and threatens to cut you.

2. During a test a student appears to be copying answers from a neighboring student's answer sheet.

3. Although you have asked a student to take his seat, he refuses.

4. While talking with a small group of students you observe two students on the opposite side of the room tossing paper airplanes at each other.

5. During small-group work one student seems to be aimlessly wandering around the room.

6. Although chewing gum is against your classroom rules, at the start of the class period you observe a student chewing what appears to be gum.

7. During band rehearsal you (as band director) observe a student about to stuff a scarf down the saxophone of another student.

8. During the viewing of a film two students on the side of the room opposite you are quietly whispering.

9. At the start of the period, while about to take her seat a boy pulls the chair from beneath the student. She falls to the floor.

10. Suddenly, for no apparent reason, a student gets up and leaves the room.

Analyze For practices that are recommended in this module, mark an *R*; for practices not recommended mark an *X*.

_____ 1. At the first class do a great deal of teacher-student planning.

_____ 2. Make your classes completely nondirective.

_____ 3. Provide for individual student differences.

_____ 4. Plan to lecture at least half of the period during each lesson, if possible.

_____ 5. Routinize ordinary administrative procedures.

_____ 6. Talk over the reasons for the various rules you establish.

_____ 7. Avoid setting rules until you are sure you have the students under your control.

_____ 8. Start classes immediately when the bell rings and continue until the final bell.

_____ 9. Use a great deal of positive reinforcement, but use strong individual praise in public sparingly.

_____ 10. Maintain a brisk enough pace during class that students feel some pressure.

_____ 11. Use cooperative learning teams that are comprised of about four students of varying abilities and interests.

_____ 12. From time to time, change the membership of the learning teams.

_____ 13. Monitor your classes constantly by the use of eye contact and the location of your body in the classroom.

_____ 14. Emphasize self-discipline.

_____ 15. The responsibility for rule enforcement should be given to the students.

_____ 16. Encourage student participation in the establishment of classroom behavioral standards.

_____ 17. At the beginning of the school year student movement in the classroom should be kept to a minimum.

_____ 18. Show-offs should be isolated in the classroom.

_____ 19. When in doubt about who is misbehaving, it is okay to punish the entire class.

_____ 20. Take care of all minor discipline problems yourself, but in the case of major problems do not hesitate to ask for help from the principal's office.

Short Answer

21. Why should teachers avoid laissez-faire teaching?

_____

_____

22. Identify one strategy that might help students to improve their own standards of behavior in the classroom.

_____

_____

23. What is probably the most common cause of student misbehavior in the classroom?

_____

_____

24. A beginning teacher was advised not to smile in her classes before Christmas. Was this sound advice? Why or why not?

_____

_____

25. Should a beginning teacher set up a long list of rigid rules? Why or why not?

_____

_____

26. Which is preferred, and why: to be very strict at first and then relax when your control has been established, or to be relaxed at first and then tighten the ship later if students misbehave?

_____

_____

27. Describe the difference, if any, between permissive and laissez-faire teaching.

_____

_____

28. Explain the difference between the teacher's use of praise and the use of positive reinforcement. Which, if either, should be used most often and why?

_____

_____

_____

29. Identify at least four teacher behaviors you can use in the classroom each day to minimize the chance of discipline problems.

_____

_____

_____

_____

30. Explain the concept of movement management.

_____

_____

_____

_____

31. As a classroom teacher, what forms of punishment should you avoid using?

_____

_____

_____

_____

PART IV
Selecting and Implementing Instructional Strategies

Part IV, consisting of five modules, facilitates your selection and implementation of particular instructional strategies by:

☐ Providing skill development in the use of questioning.

☐ Providing exercises for the improvement of your own teaching skills.

☐ Providing guidelines for teaching thinking skills.

☐ Providing descriptions of the access and delivery modes.

☐ Providing guidelines for the use of the lecture.

☐ Providing descriptions of problem solving, inquiry, and discovery methods.

☐ Providing guidelines for your use of discussion, demonstrations, the textbook, assignments, recitation, review, projects, group work, and other strategies.

☐ Providing guidelines for helping students develop their reading, writing, and study skills.

☐ Providing guidelines for dealing with student differences.

☐ Providing additional guidelines for individualizing the instruction.

After several years of intensive work on these matters, the improvements in students' higher mental process learning and achievement became very pronounced. These and other approaches made it clear that most students could learn the higher mental processes if they became more central in the teacher-learning process.

—Benjamin Bloom

Give me a fish and I will eat today. Teach me to fish and I will eat for a lifetime.

—Chinese proverb

MODULE 8
Teacher-centered Instructional Strategies

RATIONALE

As professionals, competent teachers know what they want and ought to do, as well as how to do it. Therefore, if you are to become a professional, it is important that you have well-defined educational goals at which to aim. Basically, those goals should be to arouse your students to think for themselves and to awaken their power to observe, remember, reflect, and combine.

To achieve these basic goals, you must develop skill in teaching because, in spite of clichés, most effective teachers are made, not born. Aptness for teaching, the cliché holds, is a native endowment, an instinct like that of a robin, which can build a perfect nest the first time it needs one. Nonsense! The ability to teach, like the ability to do anything else, is primarily an acquired power derived from a correct knowledge of what needs to be done. If there are exceptions to this rule, they are quite uncommon. Of course, teachers vary in their ability to execute instructional plans effectively, and to some extent these variations derive from differences in innate skills. But the seeming variations in innate ability are more likely the product of the personal skills and personality traits that a teacher has developed during the normal course of growing up. Therefore, the way to become a competent teacher is to study carefully the how and why of the educational processes and to practice diligently, according to the best that research has to offer. Each teacher can most effectively harness whatever innate skills he or she may possess only through careful definition of objectives, thoughtful planning, and effective implementation of those plans.

Knowledge of these procedures can be learned. The skills can be developed. And thus you must master the skills required for giving interesting and informative lectures, for using questions to build concepts and stimulate thinking, and for presenting lessons that will both drive concepts home and increase students' skills.

In this module we consider teaching methods that are basically expository in nature. These are the time-honored methods used by teachers to share knowledge and to stimulate thinking and learning. We also discuss methods used in skill development and in fixing knowledge. All these methods are largely teacher-centered. Their basic technique is to give learners information and then ensure remembering. Their role is to provide students with a foundation for higher thinking. At the conclusion of your study of this module, you should be able to demonstrate how various methods—specifically the lecture, the question, the practice activities, and the recitation—can be used to help students learn and achieve.

SPECIFIC OBJECTIVES

At the completion of this module, you should be able to:

1. Describe a general strategy for expository teaching.
2. Explain how to use the lecture method effectively.
3. Demonstrate an effective lecture.
4. Describe techniques for improving recitation.
5. Explain how to conduct an open-text recitation.
6. Explain how to conduct show-how teaching activities.
7. Explain how to conduct effective practice and drill.
8. Explain how to help students memorize effectively.
9. Describe the Socratic technique.
10. Demonstrate effective questioning techniques.
11. Describe the use of different types of questions.
12. Demonstrate how to handle student questions.
13. Describe procedures for conducting review sessions.

Expository Methods

Of all the teaching methods available, probably the most commonly used in middle schools, as well as in junior and senior high schools, are the expository techniques. These include informal and formal teacher talks, the latter being the lecture. Teacher talk is an important, valuable, and unavoidable teaching tool.

You should be aware of the two risks associated with teacher-talk strategies. One is the danger of the teacher's talking too much. On many occasions the teacher does need to explain and describe things, but this must not be overdone. Instead of telling, a teacher is better advised to probe the students, ask questions, pose problems, seek comments, and solicit questions. When students discuss and develop explanations, they may learn more than they would from a teacher's talk.

The second risk is the danger of the teacher's believing that the students have learned something just because they have been told. A pedagogical rule that has the force of law is that whenever possible, students will misunderstand, misinterpret, or miss altogether what teachers tell them. Follow up your talks with questions designed to check for student comprehension.

A General Strategy

When you use lectures and other teacher talks, you will find it helpful to proceed along the following general guidelines:

1. Begin by presenting an **advance organizer,** a brief presentation of preinstructional cues about the main ideas you hope to get across in your talk. This may or may not be in writing. It could be an outline to introduce your topic, or it could be a type of introduction that mentally prepares students for your talk.

2. After the advance organizer you then proceed with the body of your talk. As you do, explain unfamiliar terms. Writing them down on the board or on a study-guide sheet will help students recognize and understand those terms. In giving your talk, try to move forward smoothly and surely. Proceed in an orderly fashion, making the relationship between the various facts and ideas clear and avoiding unnecessary words, frills, and embellishments.

3. As your talk progresses, actively encourage students to participate. Ask occasional questions that make students think about what is being said. These questions should cause students both to recall information and to discriminate among the facts and ideas being presented. Provide immediate feedback to the student responses so students will know where they are right and where they are off track, and thus by comparison and contrast build better understanding.

4. As you talk, try to ensure your effectiveness by carefully monitoring for signs of confusion, boredom, misunderstanding, and mind wandering. Build redundancy into your talk. Remember the advice of a famous speaker: tell them what you are going to tell them, tell them, and then tell them what you told them.

5. Follow up your talk with another activity that will help clinch the learning.

Informal Teacher Talks

Most of your teacher-talk activities should be short, informal extemporary explanations or descriptions rising out of the needs of the occasion—such as during a class discussion or student questions, or in the giving of an assignment. Such talks are usually most effective when they are interwoven with questions and discussion.

Informal talks will probably be one of your most common modes of teaching. Learn to use them well. Because of their short length and informality, they need not be planned as carefully as a lecture (a formal talk), but they should be planned. Be sure, as discussed in Module 5, to get all the important points down in your lesson plan and provide for supporting aids and materials that will be needed or be helpful.

A particular risk of short, briefly planned, informal talks is the danger of the teacher's saying something or doing something impulsively that is not true or creates a problem. Because of this danger, teachers—and beginning teachers in particular—are encouraged to prepare detailed plans, even for those portions of the lesson plan set aside for informal talks. Careful and detailed preparation will help, though nothing can ensure that you will never do or say something that you will regret.

LECTURES (FORMAL TALKS)

With the lecture method the teacher tries to give the learners knowledge that the teacher possesses and the learners do not. This definition is true as far as it goes, though it is something of an oversimplification. The lecture, when done well, is more than just the teacher's telling students things they do not know. Skillful teachers use lectures to arouse student interest and motivation, to set students to thinking and wondering, to open new vistas, to bring together isolated facts and ideas, to summarize and synthesize quickly, and to review previous lessons.

Not all lecturers are as skillful as they could be. Consequently, students do not learn from the lecture as well as they might. One reason lectures sometimes fail is that they tend to make students passive learners. Physical passivity does not necessarily indicate mental inactivity, but unless a teacher provides opportunities for interaction during the lecture, the students may just sit, sometimes without even listening. And unless the lecturer takes special precautions, the lecture provides little reinforcement by which to drive home understanding. Consequently such lectures result in only superficial learning, low-level simple recall, or, most likely, in no learning at all. The result of all this is that ordinary lectures are too often long and boring—ineffective for teaching most classes in middle school, junior high, and high school.

When to Use the Lecture.   For the most part, lectures are of limited usefulness for secondary school and middle school teaching. In many classes, especially in middle school and junior high school, they probably should never be used. And in most classes where lectures are used, they should be limited to 10 to 15 minutes. Formal lectures are often fairly abstract in their approach, and they provide students little opportunity to inquire or explore. Lectures are also generally not effective for changing attitudes, and they seldom exercise students' higher mental abilities or lead students directly to the attainment of the higher cognitive goals.

Yet, lectures do have their usefulness. You might use a lecture for any of the following purposes:[1]

- Introduce a unit of study.
- Present a problem.
- Summarize a problem.
- Explain an inquiry.
- Provide "cutting edge" information otherwise unobtainable to students.
- Share the teacher's experiences.
- Promote student inquiry or critical thinking.
- Provide a transition from one unit of study to the next.

In spite of the difficulties and limitations, the lecture can be a valuable strategy in your instructional repertoire. Consider the following guidelines for effectively implementing this instructional strategy.

---

[1]E. C. Kim and R. D. Kellough, *A Resource Guide for Secondary School Teaching: Planning for Competence,* 5th ed. (New York: Macmillan, 1991), p. 248. By permission of Macmillan Publishing Company.

Planning the Lecture.   For planning a lecture, use these guidelines:

1. State the purpose and major theme of the lecture clearly.

2. Avoid covering too much content in one lecture. The lecture is the quickest way to present material that cannot be given in writing or by film, but if the lecturer moves too fast, its impact will be lost. Including only a few important points is usually quite enough. Too often, especially with the beginning teacher, a lecture consists of pouring into the students every fact that occurs to the teacher—as many facts as possible in a limited time. Such lecturing is analogous to force-feeding, which can cause loathing for the food. A lecture with too much content may extinguish students' intellectual curiosity in that teacher's class.

3. Develop the lecture content in a logical sequence that students can follow.

4. Tailor the lecture for your unique class of students. It is very important that you plan your lecture around the interests, maturity, and prior learning of the students for whom the lecture is intended.

5. Include clues that emphasize the logical development of the content step by step.

6. Plan your lecture's introduction. Begin the lecture with an interest-catching device. Experienced lecturers often recommend puzzling the listeners a little at first in order to catch their interest and entice them to listen carefully.

7. Repeat important points—repetition is the main means of reinforcement available to the lecturer.

8. Provide for questions, both real and rhetorical, to check students' comprehension and to revive their interest at strategic points.

9. In your lecture notes, mark those things that you wish to stress by writing them in capital letters, by underlining, or by placing a symbol (such as a star) in the margin. You should also mark symbols in the margin as reminders when you are to refer to an audiovisual or are going to ask a planned question.

10. Make the lecture as brief as possible. Include questioning and the use of visuals, especially when the lecture must extend beyond 10 minutes.

11. Incorporate humor to keep the students interested.

12. Provide concrete examples.

13. Use audiovisual materials.

14. Prepare an outline for students to follow. You could plan to put the main points of the outline on the board or overhead projector, or you could pass out copies to all students.

15. Provide a useful and powerful summary.

Giving the Lecture.   During the lecture, the transfer of knowledge should be an exhilarating experience to the listeners. It should develop in the learner a sense of putting things together. To produce this feeling, the skillful lecturer learns to read the audience, feel its reaction, and adjust the lecture to the response of that audience. Use these guideline: for giving a lecture:

1. Be alert to signs of restlessness, boredom, or confusion, and provide some attention getters when such signs occur.

2. Include recapitulation as an aid to the students.

3. Point out clues that will help students follow the steps in the development of the content of the lecture.

4. Use your voice to emphasize and dramatize. Remember that the teacher who lectures is on stage and must use any device that will captivate the audience.

5. Use other strategies to complement the lecture. Study guides and outlines that

the students may follow during the lecture may help. Any device that you can use to capture your students' attention and put across your points is going to be useful. On occasion, you may wish to use a silent demonstration to bolster your lecture presentation, as in the following example:

For a lecture on the relationship of gas volume to temperature change, a lecturer prepared a system consisting of a Bunsen burner heating a retort [glass vessel] to which a balloon was attached. He did not explain the purpose of this system. However, as he lectured on the concept that the heating of a gas tends to increase its volume, the size of the balloon attached to the heated retort increased until finally the balloon burst. By this technique, the lecturer hoped to give the students a visual example of the concept that was being developed verbally. This technique not only made the concept concrete for the students, but also dramatized it. The bursting of the balloon particularly brought forth a strong class response to what might otherwise have been an obscure abstraction.

6. Use incomplete outlines that the students complete as the lecture goes on so as to make an active learning situation out of a passive one.

7. Throw in a question, real or rhetorical, from time to time to whet students' interest and encourage their thinking.

8. Use audiovisual aids. The use of the writing board, the overhead projector, pictures, maps, graphs, and realia, not only adds life to your lecture but usually also makes your ideas clearer. It is easier to understand what you can both see and hear than what you can only hear.

9. Keep your language clear, concise, and as simple as you reasonably can, keeping in mind who your audience is. Avoid sounding pompous.

10. Try to keep to the point. Digressions, reminiscences, and trivia will sometimes obscure the message.

11. Encourage questions and reactions from students during the lecture. When you see a hand raised, acknowledge with a nonverbal gesture and then call upon that student as quickly as you can find a good place to pause in the lecture.

12. Above all, try to excite a spirit of inquiry and to create in each student a desire to know and discover more on his or her own. Remember that you cannot think for a student or give a student an idea before that student has been given an opportunity to explore the idea alone. The teacher whose purpose is simply to impart information is thinking of the mind of the student as something like a two-gallon bottle into which the teacher can pour the contents. The mind can act as a bottle—but what is poured in today will be diluted by a part of what is poured in tomorrow, and that again will be diluted by what is poured in the next day. At the end, there will be little of the original left. A process of lecturing students into boredom and passivity is altogether too frequently practiced, and intelligent teachers should consider the consequences before they pursue this method further.

Following up the Lecture.   After the lecture is completed, you should follow up with related activities in order to secure the learning. Hold the students responsible for the content of the lecture. Students should take notes during the lecture and study them afterward. After the lecture you should check their notes and the students' comprehension of the lecture. Use follow-up discussions, student summaries, projects, tests, quizzes, and other activities in order to fix the important ideas and to build those ideas into larger concepts through thought and inquiry.

Note Taking.   Some students do not learn from lectures as well as they might because no one has ever really taken the time to teach them how to listen and to take notes. To ensure that your students learn these skills, you should monitor their note taking and then, for those students for whom it is difficult, teach them how.

Check your understanding of the formal lecture by doing Exercise 8.1.

EXERCISE 8.1   THE LECTURE
Summary Review and Practice

The purpose of this exercise is to provide a summary review to check your comprehension of this important, often used, and often abused teaching strategy. Answer each of the following questions and then share your responses with your classmates.

1. How does the lecture differ from informal teacher talk?

2. Although sometimes a useful technique, lecturing should be used sparingly in high school classes and even less for junior high and middle school classes. Why is it not as useful as some other strategies?

3. Specifically, when might you use a formal lecture?

4. What can a lecturer do to arouse and maintain interest in the lecture?

5. While planning a lecture, what principles should be kept in mind?

6. Identify at least five things you can do to make a lecture successful.

7. Thinking back to the classes given by the best lecturer in your college experience, what did that professor do that made his or her lectures better than average?

8. Thinking of a lecture or informal talk given by one of your current professors or colleagues, what use of aids did the lecturer use to spice up the lecture? What devices might have been used that were not? If you were the lecturer, would you have done it differently? If so, explain how.

9. For a specific grade level (identify) prepare a major behavioral objective for a topic in your field. Identify the major points that you would try to make and how you would try to get those points across in a lecture designed to support that major objective.

   Field: _____

   Grade level: _____

   Topic: _____

   Major objective: _____

   Major points: Method of achieving:

   _____   _____

   _____   _____

   _____   _____

   _____   _____

   _____   _____

   _____   _____

   Estimate of amount of time needed to present this lecture:

10. Now, implement the lecture of the previous item (number 9) to a group of your peers and obtain their feedback, using the criteria of number 8 for that feedback. If the equipment is available, you may wish to video tape your lecture so you can watch it and evaluate it yourself. Upon completion of implementing the lecture and obtaining evaluative feedback about it, prepare a self-evaluation of the lecture, again using the criteria of number 8. Share this self-evaluation with your course instructor.

Questioning

Questioning, an important technique employed by most teachers, can be used for so many purposes that it is difficult to see how a teacher can persevere unless skilled in this strategy. Therefore, as a beginning teacher you should learn the rationale for different questioning techniques and then practice these techniques.

Among the many purposes for which a teacher might use questioning are:[2]

1. To give instructions (e.g., "Why don't we form a circle?").
2. To find out something the teacher did not know.
3. To find out whether the student knows something.
4. To develop the student's thinking.
5. To motivate student learning.
6. To provide drill and practice.
7. To help students organize materials.
8. To help students interpret materials.
9. To emphasize important points.
10. To show relationships, such as cause and effect.
11. To discover student interests.
12. To develop appreciation.
13. To provide review.
14. To give practice in expression.
15. To reveal mental processes.
16. To show agreement or disagreement.
17. To establish rapport with the class.
18. To diagnose.
19. To evaluate.
20. To gain the attention of wandering minds.

Effective teachers try to adapt the type and form of each question they ask to the purpose for which they ask it. Consequently, the questions designed to find out whether students know something may be quite different from those designed to initiate student thinking about something.

Types of Questions

There are many ways of categorizing questions. For example, questions may be broad or narrow. Whereas narrow questions usually seek recall of fact or specific correct answers consisting of responses of a single word or phrase, the answers to broad questions are more complicated and seldom can be answered by a single word or phrase. Broad questions often require the answerer to arrive at an independent conclusion. Thus, by causing students to think at higher mental levels and to provide original answers, broad questions widen the scope of the learning and stimulate interaction and involvement among the students.

Questions can also be categorized as convergent questions and divergent questions. Convergent questions are designed to seek a predictable and singularly correct response, though they sometimes require high-level mental processing. They stimulate convergent thinking. In contrast, divergent questions are wide open and designed to stimulate divergent thinking. Their answers are less predictable and not necessarily singularly correct. Divergent questions more likely stimulate intuitive and creative thought.

---

[2]Numbers 2–20 adapted from Leonard H. Clark and Irving S. Starr, *Secondary and Middle School Teaching Methods*, 6th ed. (New York: Macmillan, 1991), p. 219.

Examples of convergent questions include:

☐ If the radius of a circle is 10 feet, what is the circumference of that circle?

☐ What is the name of the organelle that contains DNA?

In those examples the teacher is asking for simple recall of information already learned. Examples of divergent questions include:

☐ Suppose that the thirteen American colonies had not separated themselves from England. What do you think the map of North America would look like today?

☐ What steps do you think the government should take to improve the economic situation?

☐ What do you suppose the ozone concentration in the atmosphere will be in the year 2050?

It is not always easy to differentiate about whether a question is convergent or divergent, nor is it always important to be able to do so. For example, if the mathematics students had not yet learned how to find the circumference of a circle when knowing the radius, then a higher-level convergent question would be appropriate. This question would still have one correct answer but it would be close to being divergent, such as: "Knowing the radius, do you suppose it might be possible to determine the circumference?"

Some types of questions, whether convergent or divergent, require students to place a value on something, and these are sometimes referred to as evaluative questions. If the teacher and the students all agree on certain premises, then the evaluative question would also be a convergent question. If original assumptions differ, then the response to the evaluative question would be more subjective, and therefore that evaluative question would be divergent in type. Examples of evaluative questions include:

☐ Which do you consider to be the better practice?

☐ Should President Nixon have been impeached?

☐ What kind of character was Othello?

☐ Should the United States have sent troops to the Persian Gulf?

It is important for teachers to use a balance of different types of questions. Such a balance helps motivate students and stimulate higher levels of learning. Furthermore, you should always try to use the type of question best suited for your purpose. This probably means that you should use more divergent and evaluative questions than most teachers do.

Probing and Socratic Questions

Probing questions are the type used to follow up student responses, to encourage them to think more thoroughly, to request clarification to ill-considered answers or notions, and to ferret out solid answers to only partially answered questions. For example, if a student says that everyone in a democracy must speak the same language if the country is to remain viable, the teacher may request clarification by asking: "What about Switzerland?" "Is that fact or opinion?" "Can you cite specific instances?" "What is the factual basis for such a belief?" "Can you help us further understand what you mean, perhaps by giving an example?"

Other types of probing questions simply go further into the topic. If, for instance, a student says that every citizen of the United States has the right of free speech, the teacher might ask: "What gives them the right to free speech?" "Does the right of free speech include the right to spread malicious, libelous gossip?"

Still another type of probing question is the use of Socratic questioning, an important tool in discovery and inquiry teaching (discussed in Module 10). The ancient Greek philosopher Socrates used this approach to try to get his students to improve their

EXERCISE 8.2   RECOGNIZING QUESTION TYPES
A Self-Check Test

Read each of the following questions and classify each with this code: *B* for Broad or *N* for Narrow, *C* for Convergent or *D* for Divergent, and *E* for Evaluative. For each question you will have at least two marks; and for some, three marks. The first two are marked for you. Check against the answer key that follows and discuss any problems or discrepancies with your classmates and instructor.

BD   1. Do you agree with Maria, John?

BDE   2. How does the repetition in the Bolero affect you?

_____   3. Do you believe that argument will help in the case of Swaziland?

_____   4. What must I multiply by in order to clear the fractions in this equation?

_____   5. Did O'Henry's trick ending make the story more interesting?

_____   6. How would you end the story?

_____   7. Who came out of the door, the lady or the tiger?

_____   8. How do the natural resources of the United States compare with those of the Soviet Union?

_____   9. If you were setting up the defenses of the colonies, where would you put the forts?

_____ 10. In view of all the information we have, do you believe the union's sending out seventy thousand letters asking voters to defeat the six assemblymen was justified?

_____ 11. What difference did an Equal Rights Amendment make?

_____ 12. Who was Otto Jespersen?

_____ 13. Should a teacher who earns $28,000 a year be entitled to unemployment benefits during the summer months when school is not in session?

_____ 14. What would you do in this situation if you were governor?

_____ 15. What would have happened if Washington had decided to attack New Brunswick rather than Quebec?

_____ 16. What would happen if you used H_2SO_4 instead of HCl?

_____ 17. How would you set up the equation?

_____ 18. Why did you like this poem better than the previous one?

_____ 19. Which type of cell, animal or plant, has a cell wall?

_____ 20. When $2N - 10 = 0$, what does N equal?

Answer Key

3. BDE	9. BD	15. BD
4. NC	10. BDE	16. NC
5. BDE	11. BDE	17. NC
6. BD	12. NC	18. BDE
7. NC	13. BDE	19. NC
8. BD	14. BD	20. NC

EXERCISE 8.3 PREPARING QUESTION TYPES

For a course and grade level that you intend to teach, prepare five questions for each of the following types. Share your questions with your colleagues for their feedback.

Course: _____ Grade level: _____

1. Divergent questions:

    a. _____
    _____

    b. _____
    _____

    c. _____
    _____

    d. _____
    _____

    e. _____
    _____

2. Evaluative questions:

    a. _____
    _____

    b. _____
    _____

    c. _____
    _____

    d. _____
    _____

    e. _____
    _____

thinking. Socrates' idea was that one should never tell a student what to think, but that by means of questioning one should act as a midwife assisting at the birth of students' ideas. In general, the procedure for the use of Socratic questioning is to:

1. Elicit from the students a statement of belief or opinion. This can be done by asking students to respond to some sort of expository statement or to express their own belief or opinion.
2. Examine a situation, belief, or opinion by the use of probing questions.

When examining a situation, belief, or opinion:

□ Try to elicit certain answers.

□ Challenge students to examine their own ideas and beliefs.

□ Ask your questions in a logical sequence.

□ Aid students in their development of their own ideas as a result of your questioning.

□ Lead students to a predetermined goal, concept, or belief.

Levels of Questions

Your questions can be adjusted to fit the levels of Bloom's taxonomy of cognitive objectives (see Module 3). You will recall that in that taxonomy the levels run from the lowest (simple recall of information) through comprehension, application, analysis, and synthesis to the highest (evaluation). Examples of questions at these levels are:

Knowledge.	What is the formula for water?
Comprehension.	What does *market value* mean?
Application.	In the Northern Hemisphere, in which direction should your heat-energy gathering device face?
Analysis.	In what ways does this advertisement violate common sense?
Synthesis.	What measures could we take that might improve the traffic problem at Thomas Jefferson Middle School?
Evaluation.	In view of the arguments presented by Senator Merlino and the National Rifle Association, do you think that the government should ban Saturday night specials?

In adjusting questions to these cognitive levels, the premise is that the teacher should ask questions at the higher levels only after being sure that the students understand and can perform at the lower levels. In asking questions in a sequential order—from lower order to higher order—the teacher raises the level of student operation and thinking, important to teachers who want to help their students develop skills in critical thinking. In practice this kind of questioning is difficult and often impractical, but there is no doubt that teachers should attempt to use questions both to expand students' understandings and to lift them to higher cognitive levels of operation. You can do this by:

□ Planning your question sequence carefully.

□ Including your question sequence in your lesson plan.

□ Following low-level questions and acceptable responses with higher-level questions.

For instance, after you ask the provisions of a decision, you might follow up with additional questions on what impact these provisions would have. This follow-up can be done by asking students both to elaborate on their answers or to comment on or expand the answers of other students. Questions at the synthesis level are usually difficult to carry off in the ordinary class discussion. Nevertheless, sometimes they can form the nucleus for a rousing class discussion, as when a Jersey City high school class brought forth numerous suggestions on how a decaying downtown area could be rejuvenated.

When using questions, rather than bothering to try and deal with all six levels in Bloom's taxonomy, it may be easier and more practical to think in terms of these three levels of questions[3]:

1. *Low-level questions.* These questions, designed to gather and recall information, are sometimes referred to as input questions because they are designed to retrieve information that has been stored (put) in memory. Sample key words and desired behaviors are: *complete, count, define, describe, identify, list, match, name, observe, recall, recite, select.*

2. *Intermediate-level, processing questions.* At this level students are required to process information by drawing relationships between cause and effect, as well as to synthesize, analyze, summarize, compare, contrast, or classify data. Sample key words and desired behaviors are: *analyze, classify, compare, contrast, distinguish, explain, group, infer, organize, plan, synthesize.*

3. *Highest level of applying and evaluating in new situation.* Questions at this level encourage students to think imaginatively and creatively and to apply what they already know to novel situations, often by having to expose their values or to make judgments. Key words and desired behaviors include: *apply, build, evaluate, extrapolate, forecast, generalize, hypothesize, imagine, judge, predict.*

Now try your skills at recognizing the levels of questions by doing Exercises 8.4 and 8.5.

Guidelines for Questioning Techniques

The levels of questions that you use in class discussions and on tests is a major cue to the level of thinking and learning that you expect of your students. As a classroom teacher your major goal should be to help your students learn how to solve problems, make decisions, and think creatively and critically—not just to fill their memories with facts. How you formulate your questions and how you implement your questioning strategy will be important to the successful fruition of this goal.

To develop skill in questioning is not difficult, but it does require attention to detail. The following guidelines will be useful as you build your skill in the use of this important teaching strategy.

GENERAL GUIDELINES

1. Questions should be clear, and not too wordy.

2. Questions should be used to stimulate thinking and to produce an extended answer.

3. A question should not contain the answer.

4. Questions should rarely call for a simple yes or no response.

5. Questions should lead students toward the development of a concept.

GUIDELINES FOR PRESENTING QUESTIONS

1. Try to anticipate questions that you will use and write key questions into your lesson plan.

2. Evaluate your questions according to clarity, level, and relevancy.

3. Ask the question first, pause, and then call on a student to answer it.

4. After asking a question, allow for think time by waiting for at least three seconds before calling on a student.

5. If a partial answer is given, pose another question to expand that answer.

6. Involve as many students as possible—avoid falling into the habit of calling on the same students or only those who you know will give a correct answer.

---

[3]Adapted from Arthur L. Costa, *The Enabling Behaviors* (Orangevale, CA: Search Models Unlimited, 1989), pp. 7–9. Copyright by Arthur Costa. By permission.

EXERCISE 8.4   IDENTIFYING THE COGNITIVE LEVELS OF QUESTIONS
A Self-Check Test

The purpose of this exercise is to test your comprehension and recognition of the three levels of questions. Mark each of the following questions with a 1, 2, or 3. Check your answers against the key that follows. Resolve problems by sharing with your classmates and instructor.

1 = the lowest level, gathering and recalling information.

2 = the intermediate level, requiring students to process information.

3 = the highest level, requiring students to apply or to evaluate data in a new situation.

_____ 1. John, do you agree with Maria?

_____ 2. How does the repetition in the Bolero affect you?

_____ 3. Do you believe that argument will hold up in the case of Swaziland?

_____ 4. What must I multiply by in order to clear the fractions in this equation?

_____ 5. Did O'Henry's trick ending make the story more interesting?

_____ 6. How would you end the story?

_____ 7. Who came out of the door, the lady or the tiger?

_____ 8. How do the natural resources of the United States compare with those of the Soviet Union?

_____ 9. If you were setting up the defenses of the colonies, where would you put the forts?

_____ 10. In view of all the information we have, do you believe the union's sending out seventy thousand letters asking voters to defeat the six assemblymen was justified?

_____ 11. What difference has an Equal Rights Amendment made?

_____ 12. Who was Otto Jespersen?

_____ 13. Should a teacher who earns $28,000 a year be entitled to unemployment benefits during the summer months when school is not in session?

_____ 14. What would you do in this situation if you were governor?

_____ 15. What would have happened if Washington had decided to attack New Brunswick rather than Quebec?

_____ 16. What would happen if you used H_2SO_4 instead of HCl?

_____ 17. How would you set up the equation?

_____ 18. Why did you like this poem better than the previous one?

_____ 19. Which type of cell, animal or plant, has a cell wall?

_____ 20. When $2N - 10 = 0$, what does N equal?

Answer Key

1. 2 (analyze, compare)
2. 3 (evaluate)
3. 3 (evaluate)
4. 1 (recall)
5. 3 (evaluate)
6. 3 (design)

7. 1 (recall)
8. 2 (compare)
9. 3 (hypothesize)
10. 3 (evaluate)
11. 3 (generalize)
12. 1 (recall)
13. 3 (judge)

14. 3 (design)
15. 3 (hypothesize)
16. 3 (predict)
17. 2 (explain)
18. 3 (evaluate)
19. 1 (recall)
20. 1 (simple recall)

EXERCISE 8.5 RECOGNIZING THE LEVELS OF CLASSROOM QUESTIONS

The purpose of this exercise is to develop your skill in recognizing the levels of class-room questions. Arrange to visit a secondary or middle school class, and in the spaces provided tally the times you hear questions (or statements) that cause students: to gather or recall information, to process information, or to apply or evaluate information in a new situation. In the left-hand column you may want to write key words to assist your memory. After your observation, compare and discuss this exercise with your colleagues.

School and class visited:_____

Date of observation: _____

	Tallies of Level of Question or Statement
At **recall level**. Key words: *complete, count, define, describe,* and so on.	
At **processing level**. Key words: *analyze, classify, compare,* and so on.	
At **application level**. Key words: *apply, build, evaluate,* and so on.	

7. Acknowledge a good response.

8. Handle incorrect responses positively. Try to rephrase the question in such a way that the student will arrive at an acceptable response. Reinforce any correct part of a partially correct response. Build on student responses, whether correct, incorrect, or partially correct.

9. Encourage students not to accept answers that they believe are incorrect, whether from you or from other students. This encourages listening and higher-level thinking.

Handling Student Questions

To create the proper atmosphere for productive interaction and involvement, you must be careful in not only how you use questions but also how you respond to students' questions and answers. According to an old proverb, "What I hear, I forget. What I see, I remember. What I say and do, I understand." What students say and do can also cause them to think in an inquiring manner. They may question each other; they may question the teacher, who should be able to respond with other questions that can guide students toward the educational goals. Therefore, try to develop a classroom atmosphere in which students are encouraged to ask questions and seek answers to their questions.

The questions of students present teachers with a persistent dilemma: how much should you as a teacher help the students *versus* how much should you as teacher require students to work things out on their own? The nature of teaching seems to indicate that students should be taught to depend on their own resources. Therefore, it is unwise both to let students acquire the habit of running to you as soon as a slight difficulty presents itself and to discourage students who need assistance and clarification. Often, the best procedure is to suggest clues that will help students solve their problems themselves. Refer the student to principles that have previously been learned but perhaps forgotten. Call the student's attention to some rule or explanation previously given to the class. Go just as far as to enlighten the student and get the student on the right track. There is great satisfaction in discovering the solution to a difficult problem for one's self. Not only is the problem solved, but the process of doing it alone also goes far in adding to the student's self-esteem.

Additional hints on handling student questions and promoting student interaction and the development of individual student self-esteem include:

☐ Use student questions as springboards for further questions, discussions, and investigations.

☐ Consider all relevant questions that students ask. Some you may answer yourself, some others you may refer to the class or to specific individuals, and some you may have to look up or have someone look up.

☐ Encourage students to ask questions that challenge the textbook or other persons' statements, such as "What was the authority or basis for that statement?" or "Can you provide evidence to support that to be the case?"

☐ Handle trivial and irrelevant questions kindly, courteously, and firmly.

☐ Avoid allowing particular students to dominate. Counsel privately students who do tend to dominate and take up too much of the time. Let them know that you appreciate their contributions but that you want to give equal time to all students.

Check your understanding of student questions by doing Exercises 8.6 and 8.7.

Recitation

The old-fashioned recitation method continues to be very much in vogue, perhaps because it is one of the simplest teaching methods to understand. Theoretically, it should be one of the easiest to conduct, for essentially it consists of only three steps:

1. The teacher assigns students something to study.
2. The students study it.
3. The teacher asks the students (in a whole-class situation ordinarily) about what they have studied in order to see if they have got it right.

The method has merit. Because of its long history, it is pretty well known and accepted by students. The question-and-answer technique both provides reinforcement for what has been learned and gives students feedback about accuracy. The expectation of having to face questions in class has motivational value as well. Finally, recitation provides opportunities for students to learn from each other.

As practiced too frequently, though, the recitation method has more faults than merits. Too much of the questioning, for example, is of simple cognitive recall. As a result, when poorly used the method tends to yield only superficial understanding, even discouraging the development of higher mental processes, including attitudes, appreciations, ideals, and skills. When used by an unskilled teacher, recitation tends to be boring and to create an unfriendly, anti-intellectual class atmosphere.

Recitations, however, need not be stifling. To liven them up, focus them on interesting and thought-provoking questions. Present these questions to the students in the initial assignment so that the questions are before them as they study. Then use the questions as the basis for the recitation. Plan your questioning procedures in advance of the class so that the questions focus on thinking and sharing of ideas rather than only on recall. Because of the de-emphasis on rote memorization and the emphasis on using the higher intellectual processes, students can be—and perhaps should be—allowed to consult their texts as the recitation is carried on. It might sometimes be advantageous for student learning to have students study in teams of three or four, where the teams are made of students of varying abilities and knowledge of the subject.[4]

Open-Text Recitation

The open-textbook recitation is really a discussion in which the students may consult their books and other materials to back up their arguments and justify their opinions. The procedure for conducting an open-text recitation is basically the same as that outlined in the previous section. The teacher first makes a study assignment that includes suggestions and questions designed to encourage students to think and draw inferences about what they are to read and study. Then the recitation is focussed on open-ended, thought-provoking questions of the Socratic, divergent, or evaluative type. Lower-order recall and convergent questions should be used as well, but ordinarily they do not play as important a role as broader, open-ended questions. As the recitation proceeds, the teacher encourages students both to challenge and respond to others' statements and to express their own interpretations, inferences, and conclusions. At any time the students are free to consult their texts, notes, or other materials to support their arguments. Finally, someone, the teacher or a student, provides a summary. In many instances, no final decisions or arguments are necessary or desirable—the summary simply cites the positions and arguments taken. At other times, the facts of the case and the nature of the subject matter may require a definite conclusion.

This technique has many advantages. It frees the class from overemphasis on simple recall of facts and opens it up to higher levels of thinking. It helps students realize that facts are means to ends—the ends being concepts, ideas, understandings, and the ability to think critically. It gives students practice in checking and documenting. In the best of circumstances, it shows them the importance of getting the facts straight, of listening to and respecting the opinions of others, and of suspending judgments until sufficient data are in. All in all, this is an excellent means of teaching students to use

---

[4]Some parents resent the concept of cooperative learning, and in some schools have gone as far as to request that teachers not use the technique. To avoid controversy, you might prefer to use the phrase *team learning* rather than *cooperative learning*.

EXERCISE 8.6   AN ANALYSIS OF GOOD, FAIR, AND POOR QUESTIONS
A Self-Check Test

Evaluate each of the following questions by checking the *Poor, Fair,* or *Good* column for each question. Use the following code in the right column to indicate your reasons why:

A = Calls for no answer and is a pseudo question.

B = Asks for recall but little or no thinking.

C = Challenging, stimulating, or discussion-provoking type of question that calls for high-level thinking, including reason and problem solving.

Upon completion check your responses against the answer key and discuss any problems with your colleagues and instructor.

Questions	Poor	Fair	Good	Why?
1. In what region are major earthquakes located?				
2. According to the theory of isostasy, how would you describe our mountainous regions?				
3. What mineral will react with HCl to produce CO_2?				
4. What kind of rock is highly resistant to weathering?				
5. Will the continents look different in the future? Why?				
6. Who can describe what is a continental shelf?				
7. What caused the Industrial Revolution?				
8. What political scandal involved President Harding?				
9. This is a parallelogram, isn't it?				
10. Wouldn't you agree that the base angles of an isosceles triangle are congruent?				
11. In trying to determine the proof of this exercise, what would you suggest we examine at the outset?				
12. What conclusion can be drawn concerning the points of intersection of two graphs?				
13. Why is pure water a poor conductor of electricity?				
14. How do fossils help explain the theory of continental drift?				
15. If Macbeth told you about his encounter with the apparitions, what advice would you have offered?				
16. Who said, "If it were done when 'tis done, then 'twere well if it were done quickly"?				
17. In the poem "The Sick Rose," what do you think Blake means by "the invisible worm"?				

Questions	Poor	Fair	Good	Why?
18. Should teachers censor the books that students read?				
19. Explain the phrase "Ontogeny recapitulates phylogeny."				
20. Name the ten life functions.				
21. What living thing can live without air?				
22. What is chlorophyll?				
23. Explain the difference between RNA and DNA.				
24. Who developed the periodic table based on the fact that elements are functions of their atomic weight?				
25. Johnny, why aren't you in your seat?				

Answer Key

1. F, B	6. P, A	11. G, C	16. F, B	21. F, B
2. G, C	7. G, C	12. G, C	17. G, C	22. F, B
3. F, B	8. F, B	13. F, B	18. G, C	23. G, C
4. F, B	9. P, A	14. G, C	19. G, C	24. F, B
5. G, C	10. P, A	15. G, C	20. F, B	25. P, A

EXERCISE 8.7   A COOPERATIVE LEARNING EXERCISE IN THE USE OF QUESTIONING

The purpose of this exercise is to practice preparing and implementing questions designed to lead student thinking from the lowest level to the highest. Prior to class, prepare a *five-minute lesson* for the purpose of posing questions that will guide the learner from lowest to highest levels of thinking. Teaching will be one-on-one, in groups of four, with each member of the group assuming a particular role—teacher, student, judge, or recorder. Each of the four members of your group will play each of the roles once, five minutes each time. The exercise takes approximately 30 minutes to complete. (If there are only three members in a group, the roles of judge and recorder can be combined during each five-minute lesson.)

Suggested lesson topics:

□ Teaching styles

□ Evaluation of student achievement

□ A skill or hobby

□ My developing teaching competencies

□ A particular teaching strategy

In class, divide into groups of four:

Teacher: Pose recall, processing, and application-level questions related to one of the topics above, or any topic you choose.

Student: Respond to the questions of the teacher.

Judge: Identify the level of each question or statement used by the teacher and the corresponding level of thinking demonstrated by the student.

Recorder: Tally the number of each level of question or statement used by the teacher (S = sender); also tally the level of student responses (R = receiver). Record any problems encountered by your group

TALLY SHEETS FOR EXERCISE 8.7

	Min.	Input	Processing	Output
Sender _____	1 S			
Receiver _____	R			
	2 S			
	R			
	3 S			
	R			
	4 S			
	R			
	5 S			
	R			

	Min.	Input	Processing	Output
Sender _____	1 S			
Receiver _____	R			
	2 S			
	R			
	3 S			
	R			
	4 S			
	R			
	5 S			
	R			

	Min.	Input	Processing	Output
Sender _____	1 S			
Receiver _____	R			
	2 S			
	R			
	3 S			
	R			
	4 S			
	R			
	5 S			
	R			

	Min.	Input	Processing	Output
Sender _____	1 S			
Receiver _____	R			
	2 S			
	R			
	3 S			
	R			
	4 S			
	R			
	5 S			
	R			

their higher mental faculties, because the basic technique is to use broad divergent and evaluative questions and to bounce follow-up questions around the class until the group begins to discuss the question freely. It is an excellent technique for use in the approaches discussed in Module 10.

Show-How Techniques

So far this module has been concerned with telling and questioning, but one of the most important methods of teaching is showing learners how. As emphasized earlier, students do not always learn from what teachers tell them. Showing them how or running through a practice session may be much more effective. That is why you should take sufficient time to show students how to study your subject, how to conduct experiments, how to set up equations, how to use the library, how to take notes, and so on. After showing them, you should allow sufficient practice time to master that learning.

Show-how teaching deals mostly with skill development, a necessity in teaching both intellectual and physical skills. Usually a show-how operation starts off with an introduction describing the procedure, its purposes, its merits, and warnings against any potential safety hazards or problems. This introduction is normally followed by a demonstration, either by the teacher or aide or by some audiovisual device, such as a videotape. In any case, the presentation should be accompanied by an explanation of what is happening. Ordinarily, the demonstrator should run through the complete procedure first and then demonstrate the steps in the procedure separately and sequentially. Thus, in teaching a library skill, it might be advantageous after a short introduction to show a film clip of the procedure to be learned and then to go through the procedure step by step. In carrying out the demonstration, follow these guidelines.

GUIDELINES FOR USING A DEMONSTRATION

1. Be sure everyone can see. A demonstration some cannot see is not much help to them.

2. Proceed slowly. If you go through it too quickly, students will not be able to understand the procedure. Sometimes it is good to go through the procedure at normal speed and then repeat it in slow motion.

3. If the procedure is complex, after demonstrating the complete procedure, break it down into steps and demonstrate each step separately.

4. Repeat the demonstration or portions of it as necessary until students understand what is to be done. Repeating demonstrations after students have started practicing is usually effective.

5. In demonstrating, remember that when you are facing the students, right and left are reversed for them. When important, try to assume a position that will allow students to see the demonstration in proper perspective.

6. Be sure to prepare for any aspect of the demonstration that could be dangerous.

After the demonstration, it may be advantageous to have the students walk through the steps "by the numbers" as you explain and demonstrate. Thus, in teaching a dance routine you explain the first step, then demonstrate how to do it, and then have your students do it as you observe. Repeat this process for the second step and for each step thereafter. At each step you or an aide should check to see that students are performing correctly. Similarly, when teaching map-reading skills, the teacher might first explain contour lines, then demonstrate their use, and then give the students a simple exercise in reading contour lines, checking their comprehension as they go.

Another important aspect of showing students how is that of showing them how to learn, especially in your field. Students need to be conscious and in control of their own thinking, a concept called **metacognition**. When a person's metacognition is employed, that person is aware of what he or she is thinking during the process of performing a task, and this awareness is used to control what he or she does. As a teacher, you can help students learn by interacting with individual students who are engaged in learning, asking about what the student is thinking at that moment. As a student becomes more conscious of his or her thought processes during learning, the student is likely to become more self-directed toward that learning. To further help students in metacognition you can help each student become better aware of how the student best acquires information, how the student processes that information, and how the student processes information to resolve problems.

Specifically, ways of showing students how to learn include the following:

☐ Demonstrate to students your own thought processes as you pursue a problem in your field or some other problem.

☐ Ask individual students questions that require them to verbalize their thoughts as they are pursuing a problem.

☐ Require that students submit a written plan of action before attacking a problem. Give feedback about their plans, such as making a suggestion for an intermediate process where the student's plan indicates a leap between one step and the next.

☐ Have students work in teams to solve a problem, where one student describes his or her thoughts out loud while another student listens, observes, and provides critical feedback to the problem-solving student (students reverse roles with each subsequent problem).

When students understand the procedure or the processes, start practice activities, using the guidelines outlined in the following section.

Drill and Practice

Sometimes you learn things quite thoroughly in one attempt. More frequently, you need repetition if learning is to be thorough or lasting. That is why teachers must count on drill and practice for students to master skills and to increase understanding. You should use drill and practice to consolidate, clarify, strengthen, and refine what students have already learned as well as to give students additional opportunities to learn thoroughly. The procedures for drill and practice activities described in the section on show-how techniques are equally useful for teaching and reinforcing the learning and for the retention of cognitive skills, facts, and understandings. The procedure outlined in the following guidelines should be useful both for teaching and reinforcing learning and for retention of psychomotor skills, cognitive skills, facts, and understandings.

1. Be sure that students have the proper tools and work under satisfactory conditions.
2. Keep practice highly motivated.
   a. Eliminate unnecessary drill and practice.
   b. Vary the kind of practice to make concepts fuller and practice less boring. Early practice should be concrete; later sessions can become increasingly more abstract. Use devices such as games and contests.
   c. Use short practice periods. As students improve, the periods can become longer with longer spaces of time between them.
   d. Keep the practice moving swiftly while being careful not to sacrifice accuracy for speed.
   e. Apply some pressure.
   f. Include only pertinent and important material so the practice lesson will not become dull.
   g. Make practice meaningful. Be sure the students understand what they have to do, why they have to do it, and how to do it. Be sure they have a goal and standards of excellence to shoot for. Point out why the drill is needed.
   h. Let students contribute to the planning and evaluating of their own practice activities.
   i. Provide students with knowledge of their progress. In order not to dampen student motivation, try to be positive with your feedback about their progress.

3. Keep practice as real and lifelike as possible. Simulations are useful for this purpose.

4. Carefully supervise drill and practice sessions. Point out errors and show how to correct them, while being positive and encouraging. Encourage students to criticize and evaluate their own work, while soliciting from them ways they can improve.

5. Structure the practice sessions. It is often necessary to pull skills out of context for formal practice. Use the part-whole method—practice the whole operation, but take difficult parts out of context and practice them separately when necessary.

6. Individualize practice. Use diagnosis as the basis of each student's practice. Focus practice on an individual student's weaknesses and gaps in learning. Use materials that can be automated. Self-correcting material, such as learning activity packages and computer programs (either purchased or homemade), can be very useful. Also excellent are exercises in which students work in pairs or small groups to help each other and correct one another.

7. Make practice part of the regular work. Do not separate it for special instruction unless necessary. Use the regular schoolwork for practice material. Keep it simple. In the beginning it may be necessary to take practice out of context and concentrate on it alone for short periods.

8. Use a variety of materials. Homemade copied material, workbooks, and other purchased exercises are all useful. Develop your resource file of such materials by saving exercises, workbook materials, programmed materials, and so on. Organize these materials in file folders according to topics or units.

Memorization

Sometimes students must memorize things. There is even a time for memorization without much understanding. For example, to learn a language you must first memorize the alphabet. To learn to play the trumpet you must memorize the fingering. To learn mathematics you must first learn the numbering system. In the study of chemistry, you should know the symbols for the common elements. The alphabet, the fingering on the trumpet, numbers, and symbols are all kinds of tools. In mathematics certain assumptions must be memorized before other concepts can be developed. In fact, in all the disciplines, there are basic points that must be memorized before a learner can understand the major concepts. To review what must be memorized in your discipline, do Exercise 8.8.

When teaching through memorizing, remember that memorization is really a special case of practicing. In general, the techniques suggested for conducting practice sessions hold for memorizing sessions. Nevertheless, perhaps the following five guidelines will be of additional help:

1. Avoid overuse of memorizing. Be sure there is a purpose for the memorizing and that the students see what that purpose is. Have students memorize only those things that are absolutely essential to memorize.

2. If possible, have students study for meaning before memorizing. Some things must be memorized, meaningful or not, such as German word order or Greek letters, whose shape seem arbitrary. These are tools of the trade, and they must be mastered to move on. But it is much easier to memorize those things that have meaning if you understand the meaning. For instance, for someone who does not know Latin it is probably much easier to remember "There is no accounting for taste" than to remember "*De gustibus non disputandum est.*"

3. When students are memorizing long pieces, they should use the part-whole method.

4. Utilize the recall method, where students study and then try to recall without prompting.

5. Encourage the use of **mnemonics** to aid students in their memorization, devices students invent or ones supplied by you. Examples of common mnemonic devices include:

a. The notes on a treble staff are *FACE* for the space notes and *E*mpty *G*arbage *B*efore *D*ad *F*lips (EGBDF) for the line notes. The notes on the bass staff are *A*ll *C*ows *E*at *G*ranola *B*ars or *G*rizzly *B*ears *D*on't *F*ly *A*irplanes.

b. The periods of the Paleozoic Era are *C*avemen *O*bject *S*trenuously *D*uring *M*ost *P*olite *P*arties (Cambrian, Ordovician, Silurian, Devonian, Mississippian, Pennsylvanian, and Permian).

c. The order of the planets from the Sun are *M*y *V*ery *E*ducated *M*other *J*ust *S*erved *U*s *N*ine *P*izzas (Mercury, Venus, Earth, Mars, Jupiter, Saturn, Uranus, Neptune, and Pluto).

d. The hierarchy of the biological classification system is *K*indly *P*rofessors—or *D*octors—*C*an *O*nly *F*ail *G*reedy *S*tudents (Kingdom, Phylum—or Division, Class, Order, Family, Genus, and species).

Review

In any class of students, frequent reviews are necessary, because memory is aided by repetition and by association and because understanding is improved by review. In the sciences, for instance, many concepts cannot be fully understood in isolation. Neither can all the scientific terms be fully appreciated until they are seen in the context of later topics. Frequently, notions that were understood only dimly the first time they were studied become much clearer when revisited later while studying other topics.

In conducting reviews, the teacher must be aware both of the character of the students and of the discipline being pursued. In mathematics and in foreign languages, where so much depends upon every link in the great chain, frequent reviews are often necessary. It is profitable to recall, almost daily, some principles that were previously studied. In disciplines where the parts have less direct connection, such as geography, the reviews may be given at larger intervals, though daily review helps to keep students on their toes.

Here again the techniques of questioning come into play. As far as possible, the review should lead from facts to concepts to principles applied to practical life. Experience in thinking is often more profitable than the knowledge itself.

It is always advantageous to have a general review at the close of any particular study, such as at the end of a unit or of a semester of study. This enables you to detect any false notions that the students entertained during the study. You now can present the subject as a whole and view one part in the light of another. In human physiology, for instance, much more understanding is gained about the process of growth after a person has studied absorption and secretion. Similarly, the economy of respiration is much clearer when viewed in connection with the circulation of the blood.

A general review can be an enlightening process and is always profitable, with perhaps one exception: when the review is instituted solely as preparation for a written examination. Then, review may degenerate into a mere device for passing the exam. The purpose of reviewing should be to master the subject for its own sake—to unify concepts—and not for the purpose of being able to talk about it on one special occasion.

In summary, a review is an opportunity for the students to look at a topic again. It is a "re-view," a repeat look. It is not the same as drill or practice, though sometimes a teacher can use the same methodology. Review is useful every day as a means for tying the day's lesson to preceding lessons. At this time you can summarize points that should have been made and establish relationships with past and future lessons. End-of-unit and end-of-term reviews are useful, but it is important that reviewing be more frequent than only at the end of a unit or term. Frequent reviews are more effective. Besides, end-of-unit and end-of-term reviews tend to become preparations for examinations.

Almost any technique can be used in review sessions, though the common oral quiz in which the teacher goes around the room asking one fact question after another can become pretty boring. If you do use this type of review, use some scheme to mix up the questions to keep students alert. Tactics that you might want to consider are

EXERCISE 8.8   WHAT MUST BE MEMORIZED IN MY DISCIPLINE?

For your discipline, identify content that must be memorized before a student can proceed in the development of an understanding of major concepts. List these things, identifying some ways you might be able to facilitate student memorization of that content. Then discuss this with colleagues in your discipline.

CONTENT TO BE MEMORIZED   **SUGGESTED WAYS TO MEMORIZE IT**

student summaries, quiz games, dramatizations, student-provided test questions, discussion, broad questioning, and application problems. Techniques that require students to use what they should have learned are good because those techniques may not only serve as review but also provide motivation by opening new vistas for students.

SUMMARY

In this module we have discussed and provided guidelines for the use of a number of rather traditional teaching strategies that generally are centered on the teacher and involve a lot of teacher talk. The use of lectures, questions, recitations, open-text recitations, show-how techniques, drill and practice, memorization, review, and other teacher-centered strategies discussed in this module all have stood the test of time. You are advised to learn well how to use them, and to enlarge your repertoire of teaching techniques by developing your understanding and skill in the use of strategies that are less teacher-centered, some of which are presented in the modules that follow.

SUGGESTED READING

Broadwell, M. M. *The Lecture Method of Education.* Englewood Cliffs, NJ: Educational Technology Publications, 1980.

Brookfield, S. D. *The Skillful Teacher.* San Francisco: Jossey-Bass, 1990.

Dillon, J. T. *Teaching and the Art of Questioning.* Fastback 194. Bloomington, IN: Phi Delta Kappa Educational Foundation, 1983.

Friedman, P. G. *Listening Processes: Attention, Understanding, Evaluation.* Washington, DC: National Education Association, 1983.

Sudman, S., and Bradburn, N. M. *Asking Questions.* San Francisco: Jossey-Bass, 1982.

POSTTEST

Multiple Choice   In each of the following place the letter of the best response in the space provided.

_____ 1. The Socratic method of teaching uses
      a. lecture.
      b. drill.
      c. simulation.
      d. probing questions.

_____ 2. In conducting an open-text recitation you should center the discussion on
      a. the use of open-ended questions.
      b. memory questions.
      c. drill questions.
      d. fact questions.

_____ 3. A divergent question calls for
      a. a set answer.
      b. the recall of specific facts.
      c. a creative or thoughtful answer.
      d. knowledge or generalizations.

_____ 4. When conducting a demonstration it is recommended that the teacher
      a. go through it slowly step by step, then run through it quickly.
      b. after showing the procedure in its entirety, walk through it in slow motion, step by step.
      c. always face the students.
      d. ask high-level questions as you conduct the demonstration.

_____ 5. Recommending that students remember PAW for "pour acid into water" is an example of the use of
      a. metacognition.
      b. mnemonics.

        c. divergent thinking.

        d. symbolism.

_____ 6. The use of review is recommended

        a. at frequent intervals.

        b. at the end of the semester.

        c. at the end of a unit of study.

        d. only for preparation for an examination.

_____ 7. Metacognition is

        a. being aware and thinking about one's own thinking.

        b. a device used for memorizing factual information.

        c. not recommended for secondary school students.

        d. a technique used in open-book recitations.

Short Answer

8. Can a lecture be a useful teaching strategy for teaching secondary or middle school students? If so, identify key guidelines.

9. Distinguish among each of these types of questions: convergent, divergent, input, processing, application.

10. When a student answers your question incorrectly, what should you do?

11. Should you encourage students to ask questions that challenge their textbook?

12. Should it ever be permissible to allow students to use their books during a class recitation or discussion?

13. Describe what you can do to improve the effectiveness of student recitations.

14. Describe the risks in the use of teacher-centered strategies.

15. What is meant by an advance organizer?

_____

_____

16. Identify five key guidelines for using questioning as a teaching strategy.

_____

_____

_____

_____

_____

17. Is it important for students to understand how and what they are thinking? If so, why and how can a teacher help them with this understanding?

_____

_____

_____

_____

_____

18. Within your own field, differentiate and give examples of what are facts, what are concepts, and what are processes.

_____

_____

_____

_____

19. In your field, which of the three items in the previous question are most important for your students to learn? Why?

_____

_____

_____

20. Describe when, if ever, students need to memorize content in your discipline.

_____

_____

_____

_____

MODULE 9
Student-centered Instructional Strategies

RATIONALE

Today, theorists and practitioners want to make what goes on in the classroom consistent with the reality of the world outside the classroom. They urge teachers to give recognition to the various skills needed to function in society as a human being, worker, citizen, consumer, and parent; to develop a more sophisticated awareness of the uses of knowledge; and to become concerned not only with knowing about but also in knowing how.

Teachers are urged to accept the principle that learning is an active process. They are told that the goals of education encompass not only the acquisition of knowledge but also the guidance of every person to his or her fullest potential. Such guidance involves development of a multitude of skills, such as the skills of critical thinking, of independent inquiry and problem solving, and of group participation. Teachers are also urged to consider the role of the school as a humanizing experience and to provide openness in the educative process—an openness of objectives, curriculum, methodology, evaluation, and environment. In many ways, these two objectives of openness and humanism can be traced to an earlier era when some progressive educators were suggesting that the normal educational experience was not good preparation for life and that learning should be involved in living here and now.

As those ideas have gained new support and fresh interpretation, the nature of teaching itself has continued to undergo critical scrutiny, with a broadening of the processes, techniques, and procedures used by many teachers as they try to cope with vastly expanded objectives. Illustrative of such expanded objectives is the modern interest in students' developing skills of active participation in group endeavors.

Group activity is a part of life—in the circles of family and friends, as well as in the civic, religious, economic, governmental, and social recreational realms. In one way or another, at one time or another, everyone is involved in activities with others, either as a participant or an observer. These activities include legislative committee operations, collective negotiations in business and labor, radio and television talk shows, discussion and round-table sessions, religious and club activities, various symposia, panels, and Town Hall meetings on the cultural circuit, and many more.

Participants in such group activities assume multiple roles, depending on the nature and purpose of the activity and the personal predilection of individual participants. In addition to the obvious leader-follower dichotomy, participants' roles in group activity include questioners, clarifiers, problem solvers, compromisers, advocates, facilitators, catalysts, evaluators, and synthesizers.

Group participatory skills are learned skills, not innate skills, and the school has a role to play in the development of social skills, both by encouraging awareness and analysis and by experiential approaches. Therefore, teacher-centered strategies alone are insufficient—teachers need to add to their repertoire of strategies a variety of techniques that provide students with opportunities to interact with one another. Such techniques also provide experience in analysis of group behavior and human interaction, as well as the development of individual skills along those lines. The range of these techniques is wide and varied, including debates, forums, panels, symposia, committee work, buzz sessions, small-group and cooperative learning activities, and role-playing.

The task of the prospective teacher is threefold: (1) to acquire the skills needed to participate in such activities, (2) to comprehend the principles and theory underlying effective use of such activities, and (3) to develop the skill to use group experiences with learners and the ability to guide students toward effective functioning in participatory activities.

The techniques and procedures described in this module are ones that all teachers can use, whatever the educational situation. In other words, teachers in traditional classroom settings will find them useful as part of their repertoire, and teachers in more innovative settings will find them especially appropriate to the participatory nature of such learning situations.

At the completion of this module, you should be able to:

1. Describe the various techniques for discussion and group work available for instructional purposes.
2. Analyze the advantages and disadvantages of each technique.
3. Show how to conduct each of these techniques.
4. Select the specific discussion or other group-work technique appropriate for your specific purposes, students, and content.
5. Describe the roles of the teacher and various participants in group activities.

The schools in the United States have long accepted as a major function the socializing of the individual person—the guidance of the child from a self-centered, immature, dependent state to that of a mature, self-directive, interdependent individual able to live and work with others in responsible fashion. This function assumes greater significance as participatory democracy continues to spread throughout the world. The increased sophistication of such participation requires the use of highly developed skills of communication, cooperation, self-direction, critical judgment, and problem solving. Such skills can and should be taught in schools.

Fortunately, as a teacher you will have at your disposal a wide and varied range of participatory techniques. These activities can be formal or informal. Their purposes can be information giving, opinion sharing, or value clarifying. The participants can number two or many times that number. The time involved can vary from a few minutes to many sessions continuing over a period of days or weeks. To begin thinking about these activities, reflect on your own experience by doing Exercise 9.1.

Total Class as a Group Enterprise

To start thinking about processes of participation and group interaction, it is helpful to view the class as a group. In efforts to provide discussion and group experiences for learners, teachers sometimes overlook the opportunity to make the total class sessions more interactive. You should not find it difficult to move from a lecture or teacher-centered type of classroom to one involving various discussion approaches.

Consider for a moment some readily evident characteristics of these two major instructional approaches. The stereotypic—and prevalent—recitation-type strategy suggests:

☐ Teacher-led and teacher-dominated sessions.

☐ A questioning approach of a relatively superficial, information-seeking nature.

☐ Repeating or restating (reciting) what was learned, studied, memorized.

☐ The "hearing" of lessons to detect right and wrong answers.

☐ The teacher checking to see if students have done their work.

☐ A one-to-one relationship between the questioner and hearer and between the teller and answerer.

☐ All decision making in the hands of the teacher regarding purposes, content, process, and participation.

A flowchart of participation in such a session would probably reveal a significant number of tallies for the teacher, with a smaller number distributed over a relatively small number of students selected by the teacher to participate (Figure 9.1). The major mode of operation would tend to be a question and an answer, with an occasional comment relative to the accuracy or character of student response. There might be the occasional lecture or minilecture.

FIGURE 9.1
Diagram showing the type of flow of interaction found in a typical recitation. Note that the interaction is between the teacher and individual students only. There is no cross flow between student and student.

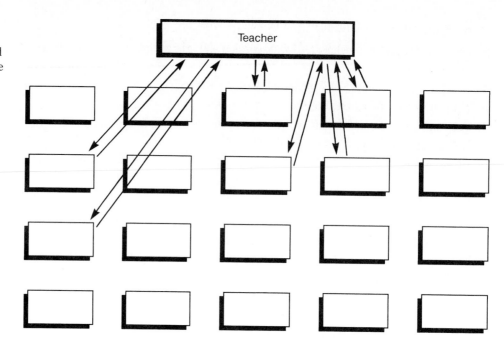

In contrast, consider the possibilities inherent in the concept of such total class activity viewed as genuine discussion, with student interactive participation and the focus not on hearing lessons but on inquiry and discovery (Figure 9.2). When viewed this way, class sessions are characterized by:

FIGURE 9.2
Diagram showing the type of flow interaction in a whole class discussion. In this class, students have been arranged in a hollow square. Arrows pointing to the center of the square indicate that the person was speaking to the group as a whole. Arrows pointing to individuals indicate the person the speaker was addressing. Note that the conversation includes much cross talk beween student and student, and much talk addressed to the group as a whole. The teacher's role in the discussion is minimal.

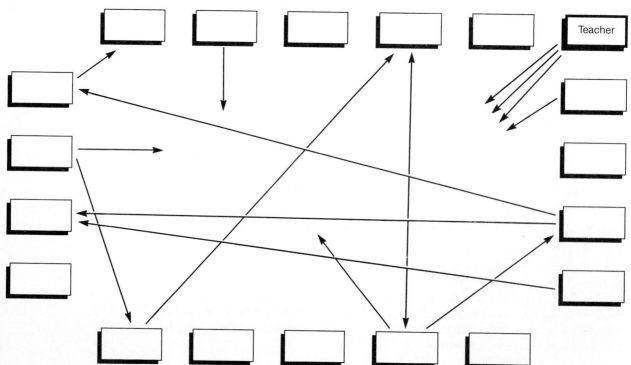

EXERCISE 9.1   A REFLECTION ON MY PAST INVOLVEMENT WITH STUDENT-CENTERED INSTRUCTIONAL ACTIVITIES

The purpose of this exercise is for you to reflect on your own past involvement in participatory activities. Here is a list of such activities:

1. For each write *F* if you are *familiar* with it, *E* if you have observed it *effectively used* by a teacher, and *L* if as a student it was an activity that *you liked*. You may use any one, a combination of any two, or all three of the letter codes, *F, E,* and *L*.

   _____ Brainstorming   _____ Forum   _____ Simulation
   _____ Buzz session   _____ Jury trial   _____ Small cooperative
   _____ Committee   _____ Panel   group learning
   _____ Debate   _____ Role playing   _____ Sociodrama
   _____ Discussion   _____ Round table   _____ Symposium
   _____ Fishbowl

2. Share your marks and experiences with your classmates in small groups.

3. As you study this module, try to engage in various group activities with your classmates. Assume various roles. Keep records of involvement and interaction. Perhaps ask someone to serve each time as observer to help you analyze the process and its effectiveness. As you gain knowledge and experience about these activities, consider how you might use them in your own teaching.

- ☐ Probing exploration of ideas, concepts, and issues.
- ☐ Building upon student responses in a ̕evelopmental flow.
- ☐ Interaction among participants.
- ☐ Shifting leadership among participants.
- ☐ Questioning, sharing, differing, conjecturing on the part of all.
- ☐ Student participation in decision making.
- ☐ Hypothesizing and problem solving.

The essential difference between the two types of classroom is that the first tends to view knowledge as consisting of a series of correct answers, whereas the second tends to view knowledge as the product of creative inquiry and active student participation in the learning process. Only through genuine student involvement and interaction can hypotheses be tested, views expressed, questions raised, controversy examined, and insights developed, along with other desirable cognitive processes.

A helpful way to begin analyzing the differences between the two approaches is to use an interaction analysis system, such as the Flanders approach or the Amidon-Hunter Verbal Interaction Category System. These systems attempt to record in easily recognizable and quantifiable ways the nature of classroom interaction, providing a clear indication of the relative proportion of teacher talk and student talk, along with varying degrees of analysis about the nature of the interaction and exchange. Any teacher wishing to move toward more participatory discussion might well start with such an analysis to determine the present character of the classroom sessions. Steps can then be taken to improve the amount and quality of student involvement. (See Module 17 for a discussion of the Flanders interaction analysis system.)

What is your own experience in group activities? Exercise 9.2 will help you reflect on that subject. Analyze group interaction in Exercise 9.3.

Various Techniques of Interaction

In addition to total class discussion, teachers have at their disposal a varied repertoire that provides many opportunities for students to participate actively in the learning process. The tactics and strategies can be broadly classified into two categories: (1) the relatively formal, planned, short-term, presentation-type technique, and (2) those group strategies that involve more student interaction and work of a long-term nature with varied purposes, including the analysis of the group process itself.

Presentation-Type Techniques

The first category of group discussion techniques includes the use of panels, symposia, debates, forums, round-table discussions, and similar ways of involving students in their own learning. All these possibilities provide opportunities for student presentation of ideas, opinions, and information as well as for the expression of differing viewpoints. They all involve a degree of structure and the need for some planning. But they vary in the degree of formal preparation involved, as the following definitions show:[1]

- ☐ *The round table.* An informal group of usually five or fewer participants, who sit around a table and converse among themselves and with the audience.
- ☐ *The panel.* A fairly informal setting in which four to six participants with a chairperson discuss a topic among themselves, followed by a give-and-take with the class. Each participant makes an opening statement, but there are no speeches.
- ☐ *The forum.* A type of panel approach in which panel members interact with the audience.

---

[1]Based on Leonard H. Clark and Irving S. Starr, *Secondary and Middle School Teaching Methods,* 6th ed. (New York: Macmillan, 1991), p. 251.

□ *The symposium.* A more formal setting in which the participants present speeches representing different positions and then open up for questions from the floor.

□ *The debate.* A very formal approach consisting of set speeches by participants of two opposing teams and a rebuttal by each participant.

□ *The British-style debate.* A somewhat less formal approach in which principal presentations are given by spokespersons of each side. The floor is then opened for comment and questions from members of each side alternately.

□ *The jury trial.* An approach in which the class simulates a courtroom.

Symposia, debates, jury trials, and forums require thoughtfully prepared and well-organized materials, whether in the form of written papers or outlines or in the form of well-conceived remarks. Panels and round-table discussions usually benefit from advanced preparation, but they can be utilized along more informal lines, permitting the chance for spontaneous exchange of views, free-flowing exposition of ideas, and even rap sessions of a wide-open character.

Such techniques are widely adaptable to a variety of subject areas. As you read the examples of the varying uses of these methods in different subjects, try to think of how you could utilize these or similar tactics in courses you expect to teach.

A symposium might be held in a science class to present and discuss current developments or to present differing viewpoints on certain controversial issues, such as the use of nuclear power and the elimination of nuclear waste material. In a home economics class or a home and family living course, a panel of students could discuss views on family roles and responsibilities. A variation of this could have each student reacting in a particular role, as parent, child, peer-group friend, or nonparental adult. Or a panel might consist of a group of invited participants, parents, community leaders, and law-enforcement officers who would exchange their views on the meaning and character of family life today.

In a social studies class, students could engage in a panel discussion of the causes and manifestations of racism in society and in their own lives and experience. Or a symposium could examine the problem of racism from several aspects—historical, economic, social, moral, and ethical. Or a debate could be held on a topic such as, "There is less racism today than there was in the 1960s."

Another variation could be to adapt the format of a popular television talk show for the exploration of important ideas and developments. Students could take turns playing the moderator and the guests; the entire class could become involved in the questioning.

Other examples should come readily into mind for English and foreign language classes, as well as for other areas of the curriculum. There are manifold opportunities throughout the instructional program for the use of such techniques for student participation.

It should be emphasized that all of these techniques also permit development of certain specific skills, such as exposition, discussion, listening, analysis, and critical thinking. For example, debates require skills of critical analysis, the art of persuasion, rapid rebuttal skills, and the ability to suspend judgment until all points are heard. Panels, forums, jury trials, and symposia provide opportunity for learning how to organize material, as well as for learning the listening and communication skills necessary to any informal interaction. Round-table discussions provide experience in effective exchange of ideas, opinions, and viewpoints, in active listening and responding, and in rapid, spontaneous, and responsive interaction.

These techniques are helpful one-shot approaches to be used whenever appropriate to the content and purposes. Teachers should not take for granted that students know how to handle such procedures. The skills involved in individual preparation and presentation are acquired skills and thus can be taught. Students need to be taught how to gather information, take notes, select major points, organize material, present a position succinctly, and engage in dialogue and debates with one another. These are

EXERCISE 9.2   A REFLECTION ON MY OWN PARTICIPATION WITHIN GROUPS

Answer each of the following questions and then share your responses with others in your class.

1. List the groups to which you currently belong (in which you have been active during the past two weeks) and the skills needed to function effectively in each group.

Name of group	Active, inactive	Skills needed

2. Select one of the groups you listed as active and analyze your own participation in a recent activity of that group.
   a. Describe the nature of your own participation.

   b. What role(s) did you perform?

    c. How effective was your participation?

    d. Describe how your own participation might have been made more effective.

EXERCISE 9.3   ANALYZING GROUP INTERACTION

1. Select three talk shows currently on television and analyze the nature of each.
   Name of three shows:

   a = _____ b = _____

   c = _____

   The nature of the group interaction.
   Show a:

   Show b:

   Show c:

   The quality of the interaction.
   Show a:

   Show b:

   Show c:

   The form of discussion.
   Show a:

   Show b:

Show c:

The roles of participants.
Show a:

Show b:

Show c:

Other relevant characteristics.
Show a:

Show b:

Show c:

2. Share your responses to the three talk shows with your colleagues. Compare responses.

3. What are your conclusions about talk shows and the interaction on those shows as a result of this exercise?

4. What are some analogies with respect to guidelines for the use of total class interaction in your teaching?

skills that can be taught by the teacher, sometimes in class sessions as a whole and sometimes with individual guidance, as students begin to participate in a variety of such activities. The use of such techniques helps students learn to avoid verbatim copying of material and memorization of presentations, which should be eliminated from the classroom.

These techniques can be used effectively for many purposes, such as:

☐ To report the findings of committees, research, and investigation. This is perhaps the most common use of formal discussions. Panels may consist of representatives of several committees or a single committee.

☐ To present the findings of individual inquiry.

☐ To add a measure of student participation to large-group instruction.

☐ To vary the pace of the class.

☐ To furnish springboards for beginning a discussion or class investigation.

☐ To obtain differing viewpoints and information before the class. Formal discussions are excellent when used as a strategy for making students aware of many sides of an issue or for presenting the differing points of view, beliefs, and opinions on matters of all sorts. They are also useful for presenting a fair picture of the various positions concerning a controversial matter.

☐ To provide a culminating activity that reviews and brings closure to what has been learned in a unit of study.

In general, all of these methods follow a similar pattern. The common procedure of this general pattern is that first, several participants present positions, arguments, points of view, or reports, and then the other members and the audience ask questions and discuss the topic. In large groups, this discussion is usually only a question-and-answer period, but in smaller groups, it may be a truly open discussion.

Use Exercise 9.4 to investigate presentation-type techniques further.

Panels, Symposia, Round Tables, and Forums. Suggestions for conducting presentation-type discussions, panels, symposia, round tables, and forums include the following:

1. Let students cooperate in selecting the topic with your help and guidance.
2. Select the panel members. They may be representatives of small groups, persons having special interests, self-selected persons, or persons who would do well or need the experience.
3. Help the students to prepare the presentation.
   a. If the panel members are committee or group representatives, supervise the committee or group work as you would any other committee. Otherwise, treat the gathering and organizing of material as you would in any other report or research study.
   b. Help panel members develop their presentations. Work with them as they build their presentation plans, prepare their notes, and so on. In some cases you should rehearse the students and coach them in their delivery.
   c. Brief students on their procedures and their roles. Be sure they know what to do. Let them talk their plans over, but there should be no rehearsal of the entire panel (except in the case of formal presentations at assemblies, PTOs, and the like).
   d. Be sure the chairperson is well briefed and knows how to
      (1) Introduce the topic, prepare the audience, and explain the procedures.
      (2) Introduce the panelists.
      (3) Ensure that the panelists do not talk too long.
      (4) Solicit questions from the audience. Students can also be assigned to make up questions for homework.

(5) Accept questions and refer them in such a way as to encourage more questions.

(6) Sum up when necessary.

(7) Redirect the flow of discussion when necessary.

(8) Close the discussion.

4. Conduct the presentation. To involve students, ask them to take notes on the panel and the discussion following, to summarize the major points taken, pro, con, and in-between, and to evaluate the arguments and logic of the panel members (but not their manner or skill of presentation).

5. Follow the presentation with a class discussion. Call for questions from the floor, additional comments, criticisms of the positions taken, and the like. Sometimes it is wise to have questions planted in addition to the questions and comments that should naturally arise.

6. Follow up and tie up loose ends. Have the chairperson or members of the class summarize the important points and positions.

Formal Debate.   The most formal of all discussion techniques is the debate. It is so formal that many teachers doubt its effectiveness in ordinary classrooms. Other teachers advocate it, because debate (1) provides depth study of a controversial matter, (2) gives two sides of an issue, (3) can be very interesting, and (4) clarifies the controversy at issue. On the other hand, these advantages are offset by its formality, its emphasis on black-and-white thinking, its involvement of only a few students, and its tendency to focus on skill in debating rather than on discovering the truth.

To conduct a debate, it is necessary to have a proposition, such as: Resolved: that the entire cost of public schools in every school district should be borne by the states. You also need two teams of debaters, one arguing for the proposition and one arguing against it, and a formal procedure in which each team member makes a formal presentation for a set number of minutes and later a rebuttal to the arguments of the other team. The order of presentation and rebuttal is: first speaker for; first speaker against; second speaker for; second speaker against; first rebuttal for; first rebuttal against; second rebuttal for; second rebuttal against. After the final rebuttal, there is usually a general discussion. This discussion is conducted by a moderator who also introduces the topic of the debate, introduces the speakers, and closes the meeting. Because most formal debates outside the classroom are held as contests between debating teams, it may be advantageous to have the class or a panel of judges decide which team presented the better case. Many teachers, however, feel that this competition detracts from the classroom atmosphere and therefore do not recommend it.

British-Style Debate.   Some of the disadvantages of the formal debate are avoided in the British-style debate, patterned after procedures made famous by the British Parliament. Briefly, it consists of having principal spokespersons on each side present their cases pro and con and then inviting questions and comments from the other members of each team alternatively. When you use this technique:[2]

1. Select a question or proposition to be debated.

2. Divide the class into two teams, one for the proposition, the other against it.

3. Select two principal speakers for each team.

4. Direct the first principal speaker of each team to present the team's argument in a five-minute talk.

5. Direct the second speaker for each team to present the team's argument in a three-minute talk.

---

[2]Clark and Starr, p. 254. By permission of Macmillan.

EXERCISE 9.4 INVESTIGATION OF PRESENTATION-TYPE TECHNIQUES

In groups of four, use a library to investigate in detail the distinctive characteristics of (1) debate, (2) forum, (3) round-table discussion, (4) symposium, and (5) any other similar type that you find.

Following your library research, compile your research findings within your group. Then through your small-group discussion derive examples of appropriate uses for each type of activity, relative to teaching specific content in your subject area. Share your findings and examples with the entire class.

6. Throw the question open to comments, questions, and answers from the other team members. In order to keep things fair, alternate between the members of the pro and con teams.

7. Let one member of each team summarize its case. Often this is done by the first speaker, but if a third principal speaker does the summarizing, it makes for better class participation.

8. Follow up with general discussion.

Class Discussions

Among other things, class discussions can be used in problem solving, developing and changing attitudes, value clarification, development of communication skills, and building sensitivity to other people's viewpoints. They directly involve students in their own learning by making them responsible for their learning. They give students opportunities to develop self-confidence, self-reliance, and poise as they learn to organize, present, and defend their own views.

To carry out a class discussion, you should first prepare for the discussion. Be sure that the topic selected is discussable. The best topics are controversial problems or issues that can be resolved or clarified through discussion. Make up a plan for the discussion to follow. Include an agenda, time limits, and topic boundaries. Be sure the students are well informed on the topic. In an opening statement, brief the students on the purpose of the discussion and its ground rules. Try to create a pleasant physical environment.

Next, start off the discussion with some lively springboard, such as an anecdote, role playing, a series of open-ended questions, a film, or a contrived incident.

Once the discussion has begun, try to keep it moving. Keep it on track by restating the problem; summarizing; redirecting the course of the discussion; and stopping inefficient, immaterial, impertinent, or emotional discussion when necessary. Use open-ended questioning. Throw questions around in order to involve many class members. Use questions such as "Do you agree?" and "Would you like to make a comment?" Sometimes such questions will draw out the shy, reserved pupils. Encourage cross discussion.

Try to elicit a high order of thinking. Challenge inconsistencies, faulty logic, and superficiality by careful questioning. Ask students why they say what they say and believe what they believe. Make them consider consequences of their position. In other words, force them to examine their own ideas and the ideas of their colleagues critically. Do not allow unexamined opinions to go unchallenged. See to it that mistakes in fact are corrected. If necessary, supply the correct information yourself.

Finally, try to bring the discussion to a conclusion. Keep the discussion open-ended, but try to stimulate the students to integrate and synthesize the point discussed into logical conclusions. These conclusions should be theirs, not yours. End the discussion with a good summarizing activity. The following checklist provides guidelines for conducting discussions and evaluating your discussion techniques.

Checklist for Discussion Leader

☐ Did I lead rather than monopolize?

☐ Did I introduce the topic well?

☐ Did I keep the discussion moving?

☐ Did I keep the group on the topic?

☐ Did I give everyone a chance to participate? Did I encourage everyone to participate?

☐ Did I draw out the shy ones? Did I keep the atmosphere permissive?

☐ Did I prevent anyone from monopolizing?

☐ Did I handle the overtalkative tactfully and kindly?

☐ Did I keep the discussion open? Did I encourage fresh new ideas?

□ Did I discourage time-wasting side issues?

□ Did I clarify issues and questions?

□ Did I summarize as needed?

□ Did I close when we were finished?

□ Did the group accomplish its objectives satisfactorily?

□ Was it a good discussion?

Generate your own list of potential topics for class discussion by doing Exercise 9.5.

Committees and Small Groups

The use of small-group work for a particular task requires longer involvement of perhaps two, three, or even more sessions. Sometimes these groups are considered committees and may function for a week or two or longer. Whatever the length of time, such group work is distinguished from the buzz group techniques (discussed later in the module) by the specific task orientation, a planned involvement of all, and a more formal outcome through an activity, project, or presentation.

Such group work can be used for: (1) planning activities for various purposes, such as a party or field trip; (2) cooperative project work; and (3) actual study of a specific unit of work.

The background experience of the students should guide the teacher in determination of the nature and extent of group work. With students who have had little or no experience in working together, it is wise to start with activities of interest that have an immediate or early visible result. For example, students might work in small groups on the planning of party or music activities. In classes where field trips are involved, whether to museums, theaters, civic centers, or historical monuments, the various aspects of planning can be handled by the students in small groups, each of which is responsible for one aspect of the trip.

Another early type of experience might involve discussion and decision making about matters of genuine interest to the class. For example, as students become more experienced in working together, they might engage in developing criteria for grading in their particular class situation or actually prepare evaluative instruments for various aspects of their course work.

With more experience, students can accept responsibility for projects that span a longer time period but still are of a direct nature and involve visible progress. In a science class, for example, small groups can be established for: (1) the care of terrariums; (2) fish raising; (3) care and study of hamsters and mice; (4) care and study of various plants, among other possibilities. Students can take care of their respective projects, study various aspects of growth and development, observe, and make regular progress reports to the entire class. Similarly, students can work together in small groups on various ecology projects, or in activities focused around study of nutrition vis-à-vis cost and advertising, or any number of consumer education projects. In such projects, there are usually clearly defined goals and clear-cut procedures for achieving them. The results of such study will have meaning for the entire class.

In English and social studies classes, group work can be used to help students acquire knowledge of the mass media—especially newspapers, radio, and television— including the various kinds of writing and production involved and the roles of various personnel. Students could engage in the actual production of a class newspaper or magazine. In such an endeavor, the class could be so organized that certain students would be made responsible for editing, reporting, editorializing, writing columns, obtaining and writing advertisements, and similar duties. Students could specialize in reporting and writing about medicine, education, leisure activities, national and international affairs, or local and state issues.

A variation of the activity could be the production of a television news program or a documentary focusing on a specific issue of current interest. As with the class news-

EXERCISE 9.5   IDENTIFYING TOPICS FOR CLASS DISCUSSION

The purpose of this exercise is to generate possible topics, issues, or problems in your discipline suitable for genuine class discussion. First, identify some potential topics on your own. Then in your subject-matter groups, talk about possible topics and generate a group list of at least 10 clearly identified topics. Then share that list with the entire class for class members' responses and input.

Our group's list of topics for genuine class discussion:

1.

2.

3.

4.

5.

6.

7.

8.

9.

10.

paper, students will gain rich insights into the processes of news gathering and reporting, as well as much knowledge about the substantive matters being reported.

As students gain more experience with group procedures and acquire more sophisticated skills, they can begin to handle more substantive aspects of course content through working together in genuine inquiry. More advanced skills of planning, hypothesizing, decision making, investigating, organizing, sharing, and reporting are involved. In addition to providing opportunities for inquiry and genuine interaction in important content areas, small-group work makes possible the study of a wider variety of topics, issues, and problems than does a course conducted along more typical lines of total class attention to the same content.

Several examples of more substantive topics will help illustrate the value of such group involvement. In a study of transportation in a science class, groups might be formed according to the various means of transportation. One group studying the development of the automobile could investigate the internal combustion engine, the Wankel engine, and electric cars. A group investigating air travel could study the various types of lighter or heavier aircraft—balloons, prop and jet planes, and rockets. A study of sea travel could involve analysis of the use of wind, steam, diesel, atomic power, and various types of seacraft.

In a social studies class, groups organized along similar lines might focus on the historical development of the various means of transportation and their social and economic impact, with critical analysis of various issues related to transportation today. History teachers wishing to develop a sophisticated insight into the nature of revolution might set up several groups, each of which could develop broad guidelines in advance so that the separate groups will proceed in ways that will yield common bases for comparison at the conclusion of the group investigations. Thus, each group's investigation and report might be designed to include such considerations as long-term causes, immediate causes, class of people who instigated the revolt, method of revolt, and results.

Sociodrama and Role Playing

Another type of experience in participation and interaction is that of sociodrama and role playing. Examples of this type of activity include mock trials and portrayals of town meetings, United Nations sessions, Congressional hearings, and similar types of civic portrayals. A more imaginative form of dramatic involvement would be acting out "You Are There" types of scenes in which students portray various figures from history or fiction. Reference has already been made to the possibilities of role-playing adaptations of various television programs, such as "Meet the Press" or "Nightline."

Such dramatic role-playing activities have several advantages. They permit students to use information in the light of the particular perceptions of the role being played. They make it possible to examine concepts and ideas from different viewpoints expressed in the role playing. They help promote understanding and deepen insights through the necessity of thinking as the character being portrayed. They can provide opportunity for greater understanding by having students act out roles and positions different from those they would tend to favor and approve. Such reversal of roles helps to deepen the awareness of the complex, controversial nature of much knowledge and of many issues. Suggestions for conducting role playing and simulation can be found in Module 10.

Buzz Sessions and Group Work

Another broad category of student involvement includes strategies of buzz sessions, group work of a relatively short-term span, and committee work of longer duration. The buzz session can serve many useful purposes and functions as the name implies. It is an opportunity to meet together briefly in relatively small groups of four to seven to share with each other opinions, viewpoints, and reactions. These sessions rarely last more than 15 minutes and require no advance formal preparation or lengthy follow-up.

A teacher can use the buzz session at the beginning of the school year to help students get to know one another. In such situations, the students can talk about themselves, their interests, hobbies, travel, and other matters of concern to young people. There need be no reporting back to the class from such a session, although a brief summary of the group activity might occasionally be desirable.

Buzz sessions can be used for informal discussion of certain aspects of the course content. In an English class, students can meet in small groups to discuss various short stories, essays, or books that they have read on an individual basis. In this way, they not only share reactions and opinions but also become acquainted with a wide variety of literary material. Similarly, buzz sessions can be used to discuss comparisons of two or three literary works that have been studied by the entire class. In a foreign language class, buzz sessions can be used to give students practice in conversing and communicating in the specific language under study. The substance of the sessions will depend on the purposes desired and the content under study. The ideas and topics being discussed can range from opinions on certain films to discussions of travels at home and abroad, as well as critiques of literary works in the language being studied.

Buzz sessions in a social studies class could be used in such situations as:

☐ After a study of a given problem or issue, students could share views as to the single most effective way of coping with the problem, whether it be pollution, transportation, or any similar matter of current importance.

☐ Students can share their reading of newspapers and newsmagazines to provide exchange of views on current events.

☐ Sessions can focus on hypothetical thinking: what would have happened if . . . ? or what would happen if . . . ?

Whatever the substantive nature of such discussions, these buzz sessions serve many other purposes. They provide an opportunity for all to participate in a way that is not possible in a total class situation. They help students learn the skills of listening as well as of talking. They can be used to let off steam when students seem restless or bored or are in some way not responsive to the larger class session of the day. They help students learn to think in action while interacting with each other.

Guidelines for conducting buzz groups include:

1. Form buzz groups arbitrarily by some such procedure as counting off, drawing cards, or simply "you six in the rear right-hand corner," "you six in the first three seats of the first and second rows," and so on.

2. Appoint a leader and recorder for each group.

3. Brief the group on what they are to do. Be sure they understand.

4. Let them discuss for five to ten minutes or so. It is better if the discussion is too short than too long.

5. Follow up with a whole-class exercise—a class discussion, a fishbowl-type panel by the group representatives, a panel of recorders, or the like.

Brainstorming

Another technique for generating ideas and stimulating meaningful discussion and problem-solving activity is called brainstorming. In this technique the leader introduces a topic or problem and asks group members for their ideas, solutions, or comments. Group members respond with whatever comes to mind—no holds are barred. All comments, no matter how farfetched, are accepted and recorded, anonymously, on the board or on a transparency. No discussion or comments on the various contributions are allowed until all the group members have expressed every idea that they can think of, for the purpose of the brainstorming session is to get as many ideas as possible on the floor. Later in a discussion the members may cull the responses and decide next steps, but during the brainstorming there should be no restraints except those of decency and decorum. The ideas generated make excellent springboards for discussion, research, problem solving, small group, and other inquiry and discovery techniques.

Fishbowl Technique

A form of group technique sometimes used in group decision making or conflict resolution—as well as to develop skills in participation—is the fishbowl technique. Guidelines for conducting the fishbowl technique include:

1. Confront the class with a problem, issue, or conflict that requires a solution or decision.
2. Divide the class into subgroups and arrange the groups around a circle.
3. For each group, select or have them select a representative who will argue the group's position.
4. Give the group members five or six minutes to discuss and take a position on the problem, issue, or conflict under consideration.
5. Have the representatives of the various groups meet in the center of the circle and argue the case in accordance with their instructions. No one else can talk, but group members may pass instructions to their representatives by written notes.
6. Allow any representative or group to call a recess for group-representative consultation, if it seems necessary.
7. End the fishbowl after a set period of time or when the discussants have reached a decision or resolved the conflict.
8. Follow up the discussion with a critique.

Jury Trial Technique

The jury trial technique combines elements of group work, research, study, and panel presentation. It uses simulated courtroom procedures to discuss an issue or problem. Examples include: Should the draft be re-established? Should there be a mandatory 55 mile-per-hour speed limit? Guidelines for conducting a jury trial are:

1. Select an issue or problem to judge.
2. Have all students research the issue or problem.
3. Select students to act as lawyers, researchers, and writers, both pro and con.
4. Have the lawyers, witnesses, and researchers prepare arguments and plan for arguing the case.
5. Conduct the trial.
   a. Let the teacher, an administrator, or a visiting teacher act as judge. If you elect to have a student judge, you must plan to act as the judge's coach.
   b. Let the attorneys present their opening statements.
   c. Call the witnesses pro and con to testify.
   d. Attorneys question and cross examine. Researchers feed the attorneys information and questions that they can use.
   e. The attorneys from each side interpret the evidence and argue that it favors their side in a final statement.
   f. As the trial proceeds, the judge points out fallacious arguments, errors in fact, and other obvious errors.
   g. The class, acting as the jury, votes to see who won the case.
   h. Follow up with general discussion, if it seems desirable.

Role of the Teacher

Whatever the activity or project, it is important to keep in mind the need to teach the skills of group functioning. The process of guiding student growth in participatory experiences is a major responsibility of the teacher. The teacher must come to know each student well, must always be aware that participatory skills must be learned, and must be perceptive in guiding group activities.

The teacher's role is significant at every stage of the process. It begins with a commitment to the value of group instructional procedures. The attitude of teachers is important. The effective teacher knows that skills of group work must be taught, and so builds upon students' present levels of experience and skill. The effective teacher understands the difference between the verbal noise that signifies purposeful group activity and the noisy interaction that suggests group disintegration. The effective teacher is aware of the many decisions involved in the use of group techniques and has the data and insights upon which to make such decisions.

For example, your first decision might concern the appropriateness of a particular group procedure for the content under study and the purposes to be achieved. Subsequent decisions might concern the readiness of students for group work, the size of the groups, the placement of students in particular groups, and the degree of help and guidance you must provide. For students who have had little or no experience with group activities, you should begin with frequent buzz-group sessions of short duration to help students become familiar with verbal interaction among themselves. You can then move toward the establishment of groups or committees for relatively easy, direct, clearly defined tasks. As students gain experience and expertise, more sophisticated involvement can be expected of them.

The degree of direction and help you supply should vary from student to student, from group to group, and situation to situation. Again, if group work is a relatively novel experience, you may have to set specific guidelines at first—such as requiring the selection of a leader and recording secretary—and provide alternative suggestions regarding procedures and division of responsibility in the groups. It is helpful to circulate from group to group, assuming whatever role seems appropriate at any given time— observer, resource, mediator, or participant—until students gain experience and confidence in handling group strategies. Of course, you will have a variety of materials and resources available, as well as a fund of possibilities to suggest when asked.

An important responsibility of the teacher has to do with the placement of students in group situations. For group work to be most effective, you should use a variety of approaches to such placement.

When buzz groups are set up, it is wise to use different techniques of student assignment so that over a period of time students will get to talk and work with all classmates. You might ask the five people in the corner to make up a buzz group on one occasion; on the next occasion, the five people in the row next to the board; or the next, every fifth student as we "count off" around the room.

Membership in groups or committees might be based on student choice of classmates they would like to work with, or the task, responsibility, or topic they would like to work on, as well as teacher assignments. If you decide to make the assignment yourself, you should always keep in mind student preferences, abilities, and inclinations.

Under most circumstances, the results of group work will be more productive if students can participate in groups of their own selection. However, there will be times when you will wish to assign students on the basis of some criterion. A student's self-selection over many months may not have included a certain kind of group process or project. To provide a breadth of experience, you may decide to assign the students to a specific type of group. In other instances, you may believe it wise to break up certain pairings or clustering of students to broaden their contacts with others, to avoid or break down dependency relationships, or to find out more about a student's ability to function with different people.

Throughout the group-work experience, you as teacher have a valuable role to perform. It is helpful at the very beginning to circulate from one group to another to be available for questioning, to provide necessary guidance, or to get a "feel" for the interaction and progress within each group. After group plans are underway, individual students may need teacher advice and guidance relative to their particular responsibilities. Keeping in close touch also permits you to detect any potential difficulties or trouble spots and makes possible wise decisions regarding occasional shifting of students from one group to another.

There are many skills involved in group procedures—planning skills, research skills, search for appropriate materials and references, note-taking and reporting techniques—for which you can be an ever-ready resource. Reporting techniques can be the kind of sharing with fellow group members that helps keep all abreast of progress, and the kind of sharing in which students report the result and products of their group endeavor to the entire class. For students who have had no experience in such group reporting, you may have to suggest a number of possibilities or meet with the group frequently as students explore their own thinking.

For group work of relatively long duration, two weeks or more, the use of student progress reports can be very helpful. Use them to help students become aware of their use of time, to assess the degree of accomplishment, to reappraise their plans, and to share with the rest of the class various problems encountered or bring helpful suggestions to the attention of other groups. The progress report can be oral or written and can vary in form in relation to the nature of the group work. A simple statement reporting how the group is getting along may be quite sufficient.

An important aspect of group work is the evaluative process, which should accompany it at all stages but especially at the conclusion of the endeavor. Not only results and accomplishments but also the process engaged in throughout the group work needs assessment. In such appraisal sessions, students can identify areas of weakness and think through ways of improving group activities another time. The role of the teacher in helping students evaluate effectively and purposefully is crucial. During students' initial experience with group activities, the teacher will have to assume strong leadership in guiding evaluative sessions and procedures. As students gain experience in group work, they will be able to assume more and more responsibility for evaluation, as well as for all other aspects of group processes.

Some Caveats

It would be misleading to give the impression that once a decision has been made to use a particular discussion or group technique all will go well. Often that is not the case. As with all other learning activities, there will be successes and failures, progress and retrogression. It is during times of trouble that the role of the teacher becomes crucial.

Many problems arise as a result of unwarranted and exaggerated expectations of teachers relative to students' ability to handle group procedures and processes of inquiry. Teachers tend to overestimate the level of skill, degree of competence, and background of experience of the students. As a result, the teacher often does not provide for gradual involvement in such work, moving from the relatively easy to the more difficult. Frequently, the teacher does not provide sufficient help at the start of any such study or the continuous guidance students need as the work proceeds.

It is important to recall that students in all likelihood will confront two types of problems, those associated with the processes of working together, and those involving the substantive aspects of an inquiry approach to learning. The first set of problems will require the teacher's help in guiding toward consensus and compromise, in helping to resolve personality differences, and in coping with overt behavior problems.

The second kind of problem requires constant attention to the many aspects of the discovery or inquiry approach—locating information, effective use of materials and resources, note-taking and organizational skills, and effective communication. You should not assume that once the rudiments of these skills are taught little more needs to be done. Rather, as students confront different and more complex challenges in their discussion and group work, their prior learnings need to be reinforced and more sophisticated insights and skills need to be taught. Teaching, therefore, becomes a continuous, ongoing process.

A helpful procedure you might follow is to involve the students in direct discussion of such problems as often as seems appropriate and desirable. One of the objectives of participatory experiences is that of guiding students toward skill in analysis and evaluation of their own functioning and accomplishments. The more students can analyze and assess the problems they face, the more likely they will be to arrive at sensible solutions. Such evaluation is part of the process of learning to work with others.

Another kind of problem likely to arise is that of individual students who in one way or another pose difficulties. There will be the reluctant student—the loner who cannot or will not engage in group endeavors. There will be the aggressive, dominating type of student, ever eager to impose his or her will upon others. There will be the retiring, reserved student, content to do what is asked, but not likely to exhibit initiative or imagination. There will be the student whose abilities are of such a low order that much understanding, direction, and help will be required of fellow group members and of the teacher.

There is, of course, no one way to cope with any of these problems. You will have to be guided by your knowledge of the individual involved (as well as of the other students), by the nature of any given situation, by the past record of performance, by the objectives to be achieved, and by many other factors that will contribute to wise handling of problem cases.

Some Guidelines

In summary, the following guidelines may be helpful:

□ Start where the students are, assess their readiness for group activity, and plan accordingly.

□ Be alert throughout the process, and be ready to vary your own involvement as the occasion requires, at times being a dominant figure, at other times a retiring one.

□ Assume a variety of roles—leader, resource, guide, mediator—as needed.

□ Have a multitude of materials and resources available and be ready to suggest others.

□ Provide a variety of opportunities throughout the year for student participation in discussion and group activities.

□ Keep helpful records of the nature of the group work used during the year and of each student's participation. Anecdotal records about individual students may be especially helpful.

□ Encourage students to keep records, perhaps even a diary or portfolio, of their experiences throughout the year in discussion and group work.

□ Be an active observer at all times, diagnosing, assessing, appraising, evaluating, and planning for improvement and progress.

Means and Ends

The uses of discussion techniques and group procedures can be viewed in terms of means and ends, for they serve both purposes. As means, they are processes and strategies used to achieve some specific instructional objective related to course content or substance. As ends, they are valuable learning experiences in themselves, providing their own rationale for use and analysis.

Means

As has been pointed out earlier, the use of various discussion techniques serves a number of purposes in the teacher's overall instructional strategy. They can be an appropriate means of achieving specific content knowledge and comprehension. They can provide variety in learning activity and a needed change of pace. They can serve to reduce tension or resolve conflict. They can promote independent thinking and help to clarify beliefs and values. They provide opportunities for cooperative action as well as for independent study.

You should view the use of the various techniques as a continuum that provides opportunities ranging from the relatively elementary to the highly sophisticated. For example, panels and buzz sessions can make possible the sharing of a wide range of opinions and views, and can provide a setting for the conveying of information, telling about, or exposition. Forums, debates, and round-table discussions are appropriate techniques for highlighting controversy and for expression of differing viewpoints. A science class could utilize them effectively in probing an issue, such as the ecology movement in contrast to traditional concepts of progress in technology and society.

Small groups and committees can operate at a more sophisticated level in exploring, probing, and examining complex issues, such as the morality of nuclear energy or nerve warfare, or various solutions to the energy crisis. As students acquire skills in group action, they can engage in problem-solving and research activities of an advanced nature through small group and committee planning and activity.

Ends

As ends, the process dimension of discussion and group work takes priority. The techniques and procedures can be viewed as ends in themselves, as learning experiences utilized to acquire skills of participation and cooperative action. Learning the ways of discussion is an important aspect of education. As such, the experiences help students acquire skills in expression, argumentation, exposition, planning, execution of plans, and cooperation. Direct appraisal and evaluation are important in helping students gain insights relative to participant roles, their own functioning, their typical tendencies, strengths, and weaknesses. Skillful use of discussion and group work provides many opportunities for self-knowledge and self-actualization as an integral part of the participatory experience.

Analysis of Student Roles

In order to conduct discussion and group work well one needs to understand the nature of the various roles assumed by participants. Already familiar are the formal roles of leader—whether as moderator, chairman, or designated leader of a small-group endeavor—and the informal role of leadership assumed by various participants as discussion, planning, and sharing shifts from one student to another. Similarly, the role of cooperative participant or follower is a familiar one to all of us who find this often more comfortable than exerting leadership. Then, there is the frequent role designation of recording secretary for certain types of group sessions.

Even a cursory observation of group process reveals a multitude of other roles, reflected either subconsciously as an outgrowth of individual traits and characteristics, or assumed deliberately in an effort to facilitate or block group process. Several such roles can be readily identified. There is the facilitator, the group member whose contributions generally try to move forward the discussion or planning. There is the blocker, who tends to object, challenge, hold back, disrupt, or in other ways interfere with orderly progress. There is the mediator or compromiser, who attempts to help the group out of an impasse or controversy. There is the loner, who can be either a nonparticipant or one who seeks to do his or her own thing, rarely engaging in general cooperative action. There is the observer type who participates little but at appropriate times comments on the procedures of the group. The observer can help to clarify for the group its particular stage of development and progress, as well as the ways in which it has been functioning.

Many more roles could be identified, but several important points might well be made, whatever the number and types of roles delineated. If students are to be guided toward effective, cooperative activity, they need to be helped toward an understanding of these roles and of their own type of participation. They need to be encouraged to try different positive roles and need to be helped to change more negative behavior. Especially to be noted are the dangers inherent in assuming dependency roles, whether the student becomes dependent on the teacher, on a specific classmate, on the leader, or on the entire group. One of the values of group techniques is the opportunity for growth in independent functioning. As teacher, therefore, you must be a perceptive observer at all times in order to help students move in positive directions toward positive, effective, and productive roles.

Desirable Outcomes

Involvement in group work seems to result in greater participation when all students come together again in the total class situation. The participation in small groups seems to build confidence, develop verbal skills, and promote thinking and doing. As a result, these characteristics seem to carry over to behavior in large-class situations.

Another promising aspect of the use of these processes is their contribution to growth in various affective realms. Group activities seem conducive to developing openness to ideas, acceptance of others, and sensitivity to people and beliefs, all qualities for which education claims to accept some responsibility.

A third desirable outcome is the generally more cooperative atmosphere in the classroom as a result of the more cooperative attitude of students. Genuine discussion and group work tends to promote a *we* feeling, a willingness to work together on common goals and projects. Such attitudes become a welcome substitute for the more usual competitive *I* versus *you* atmosphere of much of educational practice.

Some Concepts to Be Explored

It should be obvious that there is more to participatory activities than mere verbalization. In fact, there are many areas of inquiry devoted to rigorous study of key aspects of effective participation. Two that might be noted here are in the realm of group dynamics and in communication theory.

Group dynamics, or the study of human behavior in groups, is a provocative area for investigation and one that pays rich dividends for teachers. The teacher who wishes to become skillful in the use of discussion and group techniques could gain much help from the principles of group dynamics and the research that has been done in that area.

Similarly, an understanding of communication theory offers rich insights into the complexities of the act of communication. The saying "I know you think you heard what I said, but . . ." illustrates the complex relationship between sender, message, and receiver. If discussion and group work are to reach their full potential in classroom practice, teachers need to bring to their work with students the insights and understandings to be gained from serious study of communication theory. Students need to be helped to acquire these same insights as they increasingly participate in an active way in the entire educational process.

SUMMARY

In this module we have presented, discussed, and given examples of the use of various teaching strategies, strategies in which students rather than the teacher are at the center of the learning activity. To use these strategies effectively the teacher needs skills in functioning as a participant in such activities, to comprehend the principles and theory underlying effective use of student-centered activities, skill in the implementation of these activities, and insight and understandings in group dynamics. For the beginning teacher this module has provided a start.

SUGGESTED READING

Brookfield, S. D. *The Skillful Teacher.* San Francisco: Jossey-Bass, 1990.

Gage, N. L. *Educational Psychology,* 3d ed. Chapter 20. Boston: Houghton Mifflin, 1984.

Gall, M. D., and Gall, J. P. "The Discussion Method," in N. L. Gage, ed., *The Psychology of Teaching Methods–The Seventy-fifth Yearbook of the National Society for the Study of Education, Part I.* Chicago: University of Chicago Press, 1976.

Hill, W. F. *Learning Through Discussion.* Beverly Hills, CA: Sage, 1977.

Johnson, D. W., et al. *Circles of Learning: Cooperation in the Classroom*. Alexandria, VA: Association for Supervision and Curriculum Development, 1984.

Johnson, D. W., and Johnson, R. T. *Learning Together and Alone*. 3rd ed. Boston: Allyn and Bacon, 1991.

Kahney, H. *Problem Solving: A Cognitive Approach*. Milton Keynes: Open University Press, 1986.

Schmuch, R. A., and Schmuch, P. A. *Group Processes in the Classroom*. Dubuque, IA: W. C. Brown, 1971.

Sharon, S. "Cooperative learning in small groups: Recent methods and effects on achievement, attitudes, and ethnic relations." *Review of Educational Research* 50(2):241–271 (Summer 1980).

Stanford, G. *Developing Effective Classroom Groups: A Practical Guide for Teachers*. New York: Hart, 1977.

Multiple Choice   Select the most appropriate response to each of the following.   **POSTTEST**

_____ 1. The major justification for helping students develop skills in discussion and group process is
   a. the inclusion of speech in the language arts curriculum.
   b. the failure of parents to accept responsibility for teaching these skills.
   c. the necessary respite that such activities provide from the more cognitive aspects of the instructional program.
   d. the prevalence of group activity and human interaction in everyday life and experience.

_____ 2. The use of small-group or committee work techniques is most appropriate in relation to
   a. acquisition of specified information.
   b. development of psychomotor skills.
   c. promoting individual creative talents.
   d. an inquiry approach to learning.

_____ 3. All but *one* of the following are characteristic of total class sessions involving student interaction and an emphasis on inquiry:
   a. student involvement in decision making.
   b. teacher checking of lessons to determine right and wrong answers.
   c. probing analysis of concepts and issues.
   d. shifting leadership roles among the participants.

_____ 4. Fundamental to the importance of teaching group skills in the classroom is the view that the school
   a. exists solely for the transmission of knowledge.
   b. is intended to provide salable skills and career preparation.
   c. has a major responsibility to help socialize the individual.
   d. should concentrate on teaching students how to think.

_____ 5. The least formal of the following group discussion techniques is
   a. round-table discussion.
   b. symposium.
   c. debate.
   d. forum.

_____ 6. The greatest value in role-playing activities lies in
   a. enhancing the acting skills of talented students.
   b. permitting ego gratification on the part of some students.
   c. promoting the creative instincts of students.
   d. deepening insights and understandings relative to the issues and personalities involved.

_____ 7. To gain skill in spontaneous conversation in a foreign language, the most appropriate technique would be
   a. panels.
   b. debates.
   c. buzz groups.
   d. simulated TV programs.

_____ 8. The least important purpose of buzz sessions is
   a. acquisition of specific information.
   b. greater participation of all students.
   c. the opportunity for a change of pace and reduction of tension.
   d. sharing of many individual views and opinions.

_____ 9. Committee work differs from the buzz group techniques largely on the basis of
   a. involvement of more students.
   b. greater focus on expressive skills.
   c. well-organized outcome relative to a specific task.
   d. more direct teacher involvement.

_____ 10. For students inexperienced in small-group work, the best type of activity to start with would be
   a. production of a class magazine.
   b. planning of a field trip to a local museum.
   c. a survey of community consumer habits.
   d. committee study of several different revolutions.

_____ 11. In group-work activities, it is important for the teacher to be an active observer at all times in order to
   a. assess and guide individual and group growth in participatory skills.
   b. prevent errors and misjudgment on the part of students.
   c. select appropriate leaders.
   d. direct student plans for class presentations.

_____ 12. The least likely outcome of small-group and committee work is
   a. increased confidence on the part of individual students.
   b. increased competition among students.
   c. increased skill in self-direction.
   d. increased sensitivity to others.

_____ 13. Which of the following would be most useful in presenting the research of individuals or committees?
   a. A buzz session.
   b. A brainstorming session.
   c. A panel.
   d. A fishbowl.

_____ 14. Which of the following would you recommend as a means for group decision making?
   a. Panels.
   b. Symposia.
   c. Formal debate.
   d. Fishbowl.

_____ 15. In what way does the British-style debate differ from the formal debate?
   a. There must be more than two sides.
   b. Each side has a chance for rebuttal.
   c. Team members other than presenters may ask questions or make comments.
   d. Each side presents its case by set speeches.

_____ 16. To make small-group work productive the teacher should
      a. keep rigid control of the group process.
      b. teach students how to work as groups.
      c. let students do as they will.
      d. limit small-group work to committee projects.

_____ 17. Which of the following flowchart diagrams best pictures an excellent discussion?

_____ 18. One virtue of group techniques is that they
      a. tend to foster an openness to ideas and acceptance of others.
      b. are teacher centered.
      c. present facts more vividly.
      d. save time.

_____ 19. The discussion leader can stimulate discussion by
      a. asking open-ended questions.
      b. using a springboard.
      c. asking divergent questions.
      d. all of the above.

_____ 20. Which of these roles should the teacher assume when conducting discussions and group activities?
      a. Resource person.
      b. Guide.
      c. Mediator.
      d. All of the above.

MODULE 10
Problem Solving, Discovery, and Inquiry

This module examines a number of teaching strategies that all have the element of problem solving in common. These teaching methods require students to draw conclusions, learn concepts, and form generalizations through induction, deduction, observation, or application of principles. The premises underlying these methods are (1) that a person learns to think by thinking and (2) that knowledge gained through self-discovery is more meaningful, permanent, and transferable than knowledge learned from teachers using expository techniques.

At the completion of this module, you should be able to:

1. Differentiate between and discuss the relationship among problem solving, inquiry, and discovery.
2. Define thinking, identify skills involved in good thinking, and describe ways the teacher can help students become good thinkers.
3. Differentiate between and discuss the relationship among facts, concepts, and generalizations.
4. Describe the procedures advocated for teaching by each of the following techniques: discovery, inquiry, problem solving, project, research project, case study, Socratic discussion, open-text recitation, role-playing, simulation, springboard, value discussion, problem-solving discussion, moral dilemma discussion, and value clarification techniques.
5. Discuss the advantages and disadvantages of using each of the methods listed.
6. Describe the procedures for conducting the study of controversial issues.
7. Describe procedures for building morals and values.

Intrinsic to the methods described in this module is the assumption that students should actively seek out knowledge rather than receive knowledge through lectures, demonstrations, or textbook reading and reciting, and so on. Ordinarily, methods that involve inquiry, discovery and problem solving have several advantages over expository methods. Perhaps foremost, they better motivate students to learn. They give students opportunities to learn and practice intellectual skills, to learn to think rationally, to see relationships and disciplinary structure, to understand intellectual processes, and to learn better how to learn. In addition, retention from inquiry learning is superior to that from most other teaching strategies, and the highly personal involvement of the learners contributes to feelings of self-worth.

Inquiry, discovery, and problem solving can also have several disadvantages. They are usually costly in time and effort, with no guarantee that the cost will pay off. When using these methods, classroom control can be a riskier proposition than when using expository methods. When students are actively learning, they are just that—active. Active students are usually noisy students, and for some teachers noise can be a problem. Furthermore, the truths that students discover for themselves are sometimes far removed from those the teachers have in mind. Slipshod thinking and investigating can prove difficult to eliminate or correct. When students reach erroneous conclusions, reteaching may be more difficult than had expository teaching been used in the first place. Although teaching by inquiry, discovery, and problem solving when done well is usually more effective in the long run, it is not always more efficient. How much time students should take to rediscover well-known facts and principles is problematical, particularly in a time when there is so much to learn.

Thus, considering these conflicting advantages and disadvantages, what does a beginning teacher need to know about the use of problem solving, discovery, and inquiry? Should these techniques be used at all? If so, when? And how? An attempt to answer these questions is made in this module.

Problem Solving

Learning encompasses much more than simply the learner's acquiring information and developing an understanding of concepts. At its highest, learning involves transferring and applying that knowledge to new situations. The processes of transfer and application are accomplished through what is known as **problem solving,** or the ability "to define or describe a problem, determine the desired outcome, select possible solutions, choose strategies, test trial solutions, evaluate the outcome, and revise these steps where necessary."[1] Thus, problem solving is not a teaching strategy but a behavior that facilitates learning. What a teacher can and should do is to provide opportunities for students to solve problems.

Providing students with activities that develop their problem-solving skills is certainly not a new idea. In 1938, John Dewey stressed the importance of providing students with opportunity and skills in identifying and solving problems that are real and relevant to them.[2] For Robert Gagné problem solving is at the top of the scale of intellectual activity. Gagné stresses that the ability to solve problems is dependent upon prior knowledge and skill development.[3]

As emphasized before in this text, teachers should help students develop cognitive skills in order for them to operate at higher levels of cognition. The question is how to do it. Expository methods—the use of receptive learning—may or may not do an adequate job. The techniques presented here will. Teaching strategies a teacher can use to encourage the development of problem-solving skills are explained in the remainder of this module.

When presenting students with the opportunity to solve problems, some problems are closed, or convergent, because there is only one right solution or answer. Other problems are open-ended, or divergent; they have many possible answers or solutions.

Method of Problem Solving

One method of problem solving is the IDEAL method.[4] In the IDEAL method, the first step is *i*dentification of the problem. In a math story problem, for instance, students must identify the problem being posed. In a real-world problem, actual recognition that a problem exists as well as a clear identification of that problem are two difficult steps in the process of problem solving. Perhaps students are not given enough opportunity to recognize and identify problems. In the classroom, problem recognition and identification are often already done for the students.

In the IDEAL method, the next step is *d*efinition of the problem. Defining a problem means stating it or restating it in terms that are understandable to the problem solver. Defining the problem provides a clearer outline of the problem and its extent.

After the problem is defined, the next step is *e*xploration of possible solutions. Possibilities might range from working backward to using metaphors to brainstorming. Students need awareness of these different ways of solving problems.

After exploring possible strategies, problem solvers *a*ct on their ideas and *l*ook for the effects of their actions on resolving the problem. Inherent in successful problem solving are certain predispositions representing values and attitudes that can be encouraged, modeled, and fostered by teachers. These include: respect for evidence, ability to suspend judgment, tolerance for ambiguity, open-mindedness, and sensitivity to others. Students will have difficulty in solving real problems when these attitudes and values are not embraced.

---

[1]Arthur L. Costa (ed.), *Developing Minds: A Resource Book for Teaching Thinking* (Alexandria, VA: ASCD, 1985), p. 312.

[2]John Dewey, *Experience and Education* (New York: Macmillan, 1938).

[3]Robert M. Gagné, *The Conditions of Learning* (New York: Holt, Rinehart and Winston, 1977).

[4]J. D. Bransford and B. S. Stein, *The IDEAL Problem Solver* (New York: Freeman, 1984). From *Teaching as Decision Making: Instructional Practices for the Successful Teacher* by Marvin Pasch et al., p. 209. Copyright © 1991 by Longman Publishing Group. Reprinted by permission of Longman.

Problem solving involves thinking, decision making, and discovery, processes that are addressed next.

Thinking

One of the principal goals of education is to develop skill in thinking. Among other definitions, thinking can be thought of as the mental process by which a person makes sense out of experience.[5] Beyer divides the process into two categories—the cognitive and the metacognitive (both of which have been discussed in previous modules).

In young people, thinking skills are not yet fully developed. They must be instilled and cultivated. Consequently, educators have created numerous programs for instilling and cultivating thinking skills. Many of these programs are set apart from the standard school curriculum and teachers who want to use them may need special training in the techniques and strategies of the individual program.[6]

Fortunately, thinking skills can and should be taught in regular classes. Skillful use of discovery, inquiry, and problem-solving approaches allows teachers to teach students to learn and practice basic thinking skills, such as:

☐ Recognizing, identifying, and defining problems.

☐ Finding evidence.

☐ Observing accurately and without prejudice.

☐ Interpreting and reporting correctly.

☐ Detecting faulty arguments, polemics, bias, prejudice, poor logic, and other evidences of faulty reasoning.

☐ Detecting relationships, seeing parts in relationship to the whole, tying elements together, and recognizing similarities and differences.

☐ Choosing between alternatives.

☐ Making inferences and drawing conclusions.

☐ Analyzing.

☐ Separating fact from fiction.

☐ Using knowledge as a departure point for building new knowledge, ideas, and thought.

Unless students develop their thinking skills, they are doomed to be impulsive, prejudiced, ill-informed, and narrow-minded. If students are to become good thinkers, courses should not only include thought-provoking content but direct interaction in various teaching techniques as well. Among the many learning skills that can be taught directly, Kaplan has identified the following 12:[7]

1. *Think about what the lesson or problem means to you.* The teacher should help students connect their learning experiences to their own lives.

2. *Estimate how long it will take to complete the lesson or project.* The teacher should help students make realistic appraisals of the time it will take to do a project.

---

[5]Barry K. Beyer, *Practical Strategies for the Teaching of Thinking* (Boston: Allyn & Bacon, 1987).

[6]Examples of such programs for middle school, junior high school, or high school students include Building Thinking Skills (Midwest Publications, P.O. Box 448, Pacific Grove, CA); ICE (Institute for Creative Education, 700 Hollydell Ct., Sewell, NJ 08080); CoRT (Cognitive Research Trust, 2030 Addison St., Suite 400, Berkeley, CA 94794); IE (Instrumental Enrichment, 1211 Connecticut Ave., NW, Washington, DC 20036); SOI (Structure of Intellect, 45755 Goodpasture Rd., Vida, OR 97488); California Writing Project (Office of Teacher Education, University of California at Irvine, Irvine, CA 92717); and Creative Problem Solving (437 Franklin St., Buffalo, NY). For a review of programs and a listing of additional programs, *see* Robert Baum, "10 Top Programs," *Learning 90,* 18(6): 51–55 (February 1990); and "Programs for Teaching Thinking," in Part VIII of Arthur L. Costa (ed.), *Developing Minds: A Resource Book for Teaching Thinking* (Alexandria, VA: ASCD, 1985).

[7]From Sandra N. Kaplan, "12 Learning-to-Learn Skills," *Learning 90* 18(6):42–43 (February 1990). By permission of *Learning 90* and the Springhouse Corporation.

3. *Transfer what you have learned to other situations.* The teacher should help students find continuity between the previous and the new materials.

4. *Push your thinking to the limits and take a chance.* The teacher should encourage students to try new tasks and to take risks, letting the students know that failing at something new can be a learning experience in itself.

5. *Organize a task into its essential parts.* Students profit from learning how to focus on a task or problem step by step.

6. *Determine or estimate what materials you will need for an assignment or problem resolution before starting on it.* This is an important skill for efficient time and organizational management.

7. *Decide how you can collaborate with others on the assignment or problem resolution.* The teacher should encourage students to work together on assignments and problems. Lessons here can be learned from industry and research, where collaboration is a key to problem resolution.

8. *Learn to work to please yourself—rather than others.* Kaplan suggests asking students to chart their satisfaction levels for various tasks on a scale of 1 to 10, then having them think about why one task has a higher rating than another. This information can then be used by students both to find ways they can explore their interests and to find sources of motivation for the completion of tasks that formerly have been of low interest.

9. *When you feel frustrated, stop and regroup.* Students need to know that frustration is a part of learning, that perseverance is a virtue, and that sometimes everyone needs to put a job aside, step back and reflect, and then attack it with renewed vigor.

10. *Realize that there are choices when you get stuck on a task or problem.* As Kaplan says, students need to make the final decision, but they also need to know that when they get stuck they have three options: to give up; to go around it; or go through it, do their best, and learn from the experience.

11. *Discussion is a give-and-take process.* Teachers can help students realize the value not only in explaining their views to others but also in listening to the opinions of others. They can learn how to disagree without being disagreeable.

12. *Separate your self-worth from your work.* As emphasized in previous sections of this text, students must learn that another person's evaluation of their work is not a comment on their worth as human beings. Teachers need to model this skill, so that when they evaluate the work of an individual student, that student does not feel less worthy as a person.

Kaplan suggests creating your own "Think First" chart of items such as these and then posting that chart as thinking reminders to your students.

To teach thinking skills, the teacher should begin by teaching them directly. First, the teacher should both explain and demonstrate the skill. Second, the teacher should provide examples of the skill well done. For instance, a teacher might point out an excellent use of the technique employed by one of the students or show an example of proper execution of the skill in a film.

Teachers might also use such techniques as probing questions to shape students' abilities to think logically and to recognize, define, and solve problems. If possible, the teacher should stimulate the students to think about both their thought processes and their behavior, encouraging the students to try different and more effective ways to proceed. An example of a cooperative-learning activity that can be useful is having pairs of students examine each other's thinking processes listing the strategies and tactics used and describing changes that might improve thinking.

Once students have understood the how and why of the thinking skills, they should then have plenty of practice in using those skills. At first, this practice should be limited to comparatively easy problems with plenty of instructional aids to help them remember what to do and how to do it. Here the teacher can take advantage of timely moments to prompt students into selecting and executing improved thinking procedures. For this purpose many teachers recommend the use of pairs or small groups in which one student goes through the process while the other(s) provides feedback. If students take the opportunity to examine their own thinking and behavior—especially in the light of feedback from their peers or teachers—they should be able to sharpen their thinking skills considerably.

Finally, students should reinforce their learning by applying their thinking skills to a variety of assignments and life situations, both to increase their proficiency and to enhance their ability to transfer thinking skills. In this phase of learning, as in the practice phase, the students need plenty of feedback to capitalize on their successes and errors.

To introduce the teaching of specific thinking skills, some teachers recommend the following approach:

1. *Select the skill to be taught.* Presumably, as in the teaching of any other skill, the teacher should build the "greater skills" on "lesser skills." Thus, the inclusion of thinking skills in any curriculum or course should follow a definite sequence. When you teach thinking skills in your courses, you should make sure that the students in your classes are equipped with the skills and knowledge necessary to provide a foundation for the new skill.

2. *Identify the main attributes of the skill to be taught.* You should make sure that you understand what the skill is, what its purpose is, what skills and knowledge are prerequisite, how to carry out the skill step by step, and so on. This task may require of you some hard thinking and studying.

3. *Introduce the skill.* The skill should be introduced when it will be a meaningful addition to the course content—if the skill is not relevant to the course at a certain point, introducing it at that point will not be fruitful. When the time is right to introduce the skill, first explain what the skill is and why it should be learned. When you are sure they understand, explain how to implement the skill step by step, and then demonstrate the whole procedure and its steps. Once students have caught on to what is expected and how to do it, put them to work using the skill. As they work, let them analyze their procedures and provide them with feedback on their progress.

4. *Provide practice.* Students should have opportunity to practice until they attain mastery. At first, practice sessions should be guided and rather carefully monitored. At this stage, peer criticism as well as teacher guidance may be beneficial. Later, as soon as students seem ready, independent practice should prove profitable.

5. *Continue review and practice sessions throughout the course.* After a skill has been mastered, it should be used as the occasion demands throughout the school year. Skills that are not practiced from time to time will soon disappear. Such practice sessions should be closely tied to normal course content.[8]

Discovery and Inquiry

Problem solving can be distinguished from discovery and inquiry in this way: whereas problem solving is a way of thinking and behaving, discovery and inquiry are teaching strategies that utilize active student thinking and problem solving. Within discovery and inquiry strategies, the teacher incorporates student problem recognition, problem definition, problem solving, and decision making.

Discovery can be thought of as the result of seeking knowledge. **Inquiry** can be thought of as an open-ended and creative way of seeking knowledge.

---

[8]Roberta M. Jackson, "Thumbs up for Direct Teaching of Thinking Skills," *Educational Leadership* (May 1986), 43:33–36 describes how teachers in a Virginia middle school are using this type of approach to teach thinking skills directly.

FIGURE 10.1
Levels of Inquiry (E. C. Kim and R. D. Kellough, *A Resource Guide for Secondary School Teaching: Planning for Competence,* 5th ed., New York: Macmillan, 1991, p. 253. By permission of Macmillan Publishing Company.)

	Level I	Level II	Level III
Problem Identification	Identified by teacher or textbook	Identified by teacher or textbook	Identified by student
Process of Solving Problem	Decided by teacher or textbook	Decided by student	Decided by student
Identification of Tentative Solution to Problem	Resolved by student	Resolved by student	Resolved by student

In education, there is no singular definition of discovery learning. For Bruner, discovery is the act of finding out for one's self.[9] For Gagné, discovery results from problem solving and is the final step in a hierarchy of learning steps that combines previously learned rules into a new and higher order.[10] Whereas Bruner placed emphasis on the importance of inductive learning, Gagné placed greater emphasis on the importance of deductive learning. For true inquiry, both are undoubtedly important, though induction is given high priority.

Both discovery learning and inquiry learning actively involve students in two important activities—problem solving and decision making. To distinguish strategies for inquiry teaching from those of discovery teaching, the teacher should use these two criteria: (1) who recognizes and identifies the problem and (2) the amount of decision making done by students.

Figure 10.1 identifies three levels of inquiry according to how much is expected of the student.

What is referred to as Level I inquiry is traditional, didactic, "cookbook" teaching, in which a problem is defined for the student, who then works through the problem to an inevitable solution. If the "program" is well designed, the end result is inevitable because the student "discovers" what was intended. This level of inquiry is also referred to both as guided inquiry and as discovery, because the students are carefully guided through the investigation to "discovery."

Level I inquiry is highly manageable, and the learning outcome is predictable. It is probably best for teaching fundamental concepts and principles. But students who never experience learning beyond Level I are missing an opportunity to engage their highest mental operations, and they never get to experience more motivating, real-life problem solving. Furthermore, those students may come away with the false notion that problem solving is a linear process, which it is not. True inquiry is cyclic rather than linear. The inquiry cycle is illustrated in Figure 10.2. One enters the inquiry cycle whenever a discrepancy or problem is observed and recognized, and that can occur at any point in the cycle.

By the time students reach junior and senior high school, they should be provided experiences for true inquiry, which begins with Level II, where students actually design the processes for their inquiry. In true inquiry teachers emphasize the tentative nature of conclusions, which makes an activity more like real-life problem solving, where decisions are always subject to revision.

---

[9]Jerome Bruner, "The Act of Discovery," *The Harvard Educational Review,* 31(1):21 (1961).

[10]Robert Gagné, "Varieties of Learning and the Concept of Discovery." In L. S. Shulman and E. S. Keislar (Eds.), *Learning by Discovery: A Critical Appraisal* (Chicago: Rand McNally, 1968).

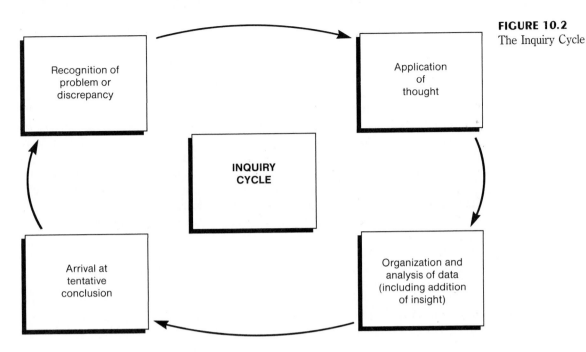

FIGURE 10.2
The Inquiry Cycle

In Level III inquiry, students identify the problem as well as decide the processes and reach a conclusion. When using individual projects and independent study as instructional strategies, teachers are usually engaging their students in this level of inquiry.

The Processes

In true inquiry, the students generate ideas and then design ways to test those ideas. The various processes students use represent the many critical thinking skills. Some of these skills are concerned with generating and organizing data, whereas others are concerned with building and using ideas. Figure 10.3 provides four main categories of these thinking processes and their place within the inquiry cycle.

Some processes in the cycle are discovery processes and others are inquiry processes. Inquiry processes include the more complex mental operations (including

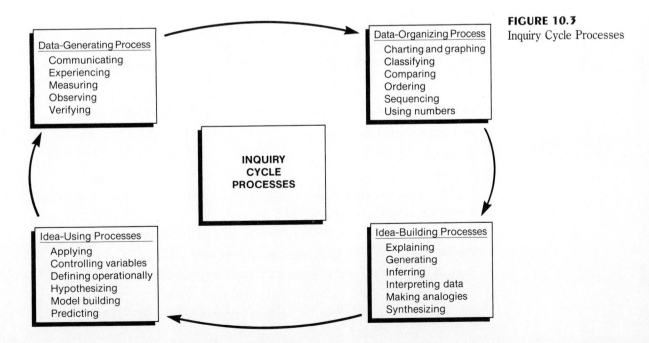

FIGURE 10.3
Inquiry Cycle Processes

all of those in the idea category). Adolescents, who are in the process of developing their thinking capabilities, should be provided experiences that require the more complex, higher-level inquiry skills. Such is certainly the case for secondary school students.

Inquiry learning is a higher-level mental operation that introduces the concept of the **discrepant event** or using the element of surprise to help learners develop skills in observing and being alert for discrepancies. This strategy provides opportunities for students to investigate their own ideas about explanations. Inquiry, like discovery, is a problem-solving strategy; the difference between the two is in the amount of decision-making responsibility given to the students. Inquiry also helps students understand the importance of suspending judgment and the tentativeness of "answers" and "solutions." Students eventually are better able to deal with ambiguity.

For centuries educational theorists have thought that learning is more meaningful, thorough, and usable when students actively seek out and discover knowledge rather than just being receivers of knowledge. This position is implicit in the strategies of such master teachers as Socrates and Jesus of Nazareth, in the theories of such thinkers as Rousseau and Pestalozzi, and in the ideas of twentieth-century educational philosophers such as John Dewey. Many practitioners today are convinced that this position is correct, and they use discovery and inquiry teaching as the heart of their teaching approaches. But students also learn from being shown, told, or conditioned. It is neither necessary nor wise for teachers to insist that students rediscover all the knowledge encompassed by the curriculum. Some of that knowledge is best learned from expository methods and some by discovery and inquiry. Effective teachers use the teacher-centered or student-centered strategy that seems best suited to a particular learning-teaching situation.

There are many ways to introduce student-centered techniques into your teaching. Among the more common examples are Socratic and guided discussions, research and other student projects, case studies, and the various types of action learning and community involvement activities.

Teacher's Role in Discovery and Inquiry Teaching

Since discovery and inquiry imply problem solving and decision making by students, your role becomes that of guiding their learning rather than that of dictating and giving them direct instruction. In this role you must propose problems, raise issues, and ask questions designed to catch student interest, to start them thinking, and to encourage their own investigation. In addition, you must establish a classroom environment that encourages guessing, skepticism, and intuitive thinking. This kind of classroom environment requires planning, self-control, cooperation, and trust; allows for serendipity; and places a value on mistakes and on diversity. It takes conviction, careful planning, practice, and skill for a teacher to effectively use discovery and inquiry. To get you started in the use of these techniques, keep the following guidelines in mind:.

1. Be supportive and accepting.
2. Accentuate the positive.
3. Provide clues.
4. Encourage the exchange of ideas.
5. Encourage students to hypothesize.
6. Provide opportunity for students to investigate their hypotheses.
7. Provide assistance when students seem to lose their way.
8. Help students analyze and evaluate their ideas, interpretations, and thinking.
9. Foster free debate and open discussion, and urge students to try to think things out with no threat of reprisals when their thinking does not conform to the expected or to the norm.

Facts, Concepts, and Understandings

Except for playing a parlor game such as "Trivial Pursuit," factual knowledge is useful only when it leads to general understanding (principles, theories, and laws). Concepts, major ideas that share a common set of attributes, are the essential building blocks of understanding within a discipline. Although concepts cannot be taught directly, factual knowledge and generalizations can, and learning these things adds to the student's developing understanding of the major themes of a discipline. For example, the United States is a democracy. That statement is an example of a fact. *Democracy* is an example of a concept—in this instance, a rather abstract one. Whereas facts and generalizations take the form of statements, concepts may often take the form of just one word. This is an example of a generalization about democracy: "In a democracy, such as the United States, the decision-making power is placed in the hands of the majority, while at the same time the rights of the minority are protected." A generalization often binds two or more concepts.

Inquiry and discovery are valuable strategies for helping students understand major concepts, especially abstract ones, because with these strategies students can, in some degree or another, actually live what they are learning about. In contrast, students might better learn about a generalization through knowledge of the generalization's component parts—the facts and notions about the concepts. Often such knowledge is best taught by an expository technique.

A person develops an understanding of a notion or concept by becoming familiar both with the ideas, beliefs, artifacts, or objects that are examples and with those that are not examples. A child, for instance, learns by observation that certain characteristics signify that an animal is not a dog by observing both dogs and animals that are not dogs. A child learns that certain characteristics signify being free and others signify not being free by seeing and hearing about instances when people or animals are free and not free. The teacher's job, in these instances, is to provide students with the opportunities to observe, name, classify, and practice, as well as to ask appropriate probing questions in the process.

Exercise 10.1 explores how you could introduce a generalization to your students.

The Use of Thought Questions

Teaching through use of discovery and inquiry depends on the skillful use of thoughtful and probing questions. You should practice these questions until their use becomes second nature. Students also need to develop their skills in questioning. The techniques (described in Module 8) essentially include:

1. Emphasizing how and why.
2. Following up leads and developing ideas through additional probing, clarifying questions.
3. Encouraging students to acquire facts before venturing too far into flights of fancy.
4. Asking divergent questions.
5. Encouraging students to discuss one another's thinking and thinking processes.
6. Utilizing Socratic questioning.

Work through Exercise 10.2 to get a feel for the use of probing questions.

Springboards

Springboard techniques are excellent for launching problem solving. Springboards include anything that lends itself to such questions as: "How come?" "So what?" "If so, then what?" Examples of such techniques are role-playing, movies, dramatizations, pictures, and models. The great teachers of ancient and modern times have used parables to stimulate original thought. In this method those teachers told a simple story, such as the story of the good Samaritan, and then asked their students to use this story as a springboard or jumping-off for building conclusions or generalizations. Springboards are helpful in setting the stage for problem recognition.

Suitability of Problems

When students have recognized and identified problems they want to investigate, the teacher then has the responsibility to approve the problem's suitability for student investigation. Among the criteria you can use are:

☐ Is it pertinent to the course objectives?

☐ Is it relevant to students' lives and to community life?

☐ Is it feasible? Do we have the necessary resources? Can we complete it in the time available? Can the student handle it?

☐ Is it worth the effort?

When students have identified a problem they want to investigate and you do not believe that it fits these criteria, you can usually guide them in reidentifying or narrowing the problem so that it does fit these criteria. Exercise 10.3 (p. 301) will help you understand how to identify the suitability of problems.

Projects

In education, the word *project* has come to mean any activity, individual or group, involving the investigation and solution of problems that is planned and carried to a conclusion by students under the guidance of the teacher. Originally, a project was conceived as being of significant practical value and resulting in some tangible product of personal value to the learner, such as the raising and marketing of a calf. To be worthy of the name, a project must be truly a problem-solving activity. In a true project the student plans, executes, and evaluates the entire undertaking. The teacher's role is simply to help, advise, and guide the learning.

Although ideally all projects should derive from students' interests, students usually have trouble finding and selecting suitable projects. You can help them in this in several ways. You might provide lists of suggestions or maybe try to stimulate ideas by class discussion. You could tell students what others have done in the past, or you could have last year's students come to the class on a consulting basis to describe their successful projects. No matter how students get the ideas, when they finally choose their projects, they should check those projects for suitability. The criteria that should be met are that (1) the project should make a real contribution to a worthwhile learning objective; (2) the project should result in some worthwhile end; and (3) the project should be reasonable insofar as time, effort, cost, and availability of resources are concerned.

To conduct a project requires a combination of restraint and guidance from the teacher. The students need to accept most of the responsibility for their projects, but they should not be allowed to flounder unnecessarily. The teachers must make themselves available to assist the students when necessary and must from time to time check their progress without interfering. Taking the middle course between too much and too little requires both tact and good judgment.

Research Projects

The research project is an interesting variety of the genre. In this type of project, the student, independently or as a member of a committee, investigates some matter and then reports on it. As a rule this type of project is best done by the more academically talented students. Yet although students with little academic talent or interest usually do not take to this type of activity well, they can accomplish appropriate projects reasonably well when the projects are interesting enough to them, when they have the necessary guidance, and when the roles given to them are reasonable for persons of their abilities. Often they can also make significant contributions to group research

EXERCISE 10.1 TEACHING TOWARD UNDERSTANDING OF GENERALIZATIONS

Identify one basic concept or generalization in your teaching field. Then identify experiences you could provide students so that they would discover from examples of positive and negative characteristics what the concept or generalization is and what it is not, and thus define the concept or generalization in their own thinking. Try to organize these experiences in a logical sequence. Then share your responses with your colleagues for their feedback.

My teaching field: _____

1. Concept or generalization:

2. Experiences to be provided:

EXERCISE 10.2 USE OF PROBING QUESTIONS

Review Exercise 10.1 to see if you included in your list the use of probing questions. If not, identify here a sequence of probing questions that you could use to help students in their understanding of the generalization identified in that exercise.

My teaching field: _____

1. Concept or generalization:

2. Sequence of probing questions:

EXERCISE 10.3   PROBLEMS SUITABLE FOR STUDENT INVESTIGATION

Identify interesting and suitable problems for secondary and middle school student investigations in your teaching field. List 10 if possible, and identify why each would be suitable. Share your list with your colleagues for their feedback. After sharing with your colleagues you may modify or add to your list ideas obtained from that sharing process.

My teaching field: _____

Problem	Rationale
1.	
2.	
3.	
4.	

5.

6.

7.

8.

9.

10.

projects; however, less able students should not be forced to do research projects. They can usually gain more benefits from other types of activities.

The process used in a research project is that of any problem-solving activity:[11]

1. Decide exactly what it is that one is to try to find out.

2. Define the problem so that it is manageable in the time available and with the materials and personnel available.

3. Decide what tasks must be done to get the necessary data and who will do each job.

4. Gather the materials and equipment necessary.

5. Perform the data-gathering tasks.

6. Review and analyze the data gathered.

7. Draw conclusions and generalizations from the data gathered.

8. Report the findings and conclusions.

Perhaps, as applied to research projects, these steps need some explanation. Selecting a topic for research can be somewhat bothersome. Most students find it difficult to select a problem on which they can really focus. To be worthwhile, the research should be aimed at a specific problem. Large, diffuse, ill-defined topics seldom result in anything worthwhile. Help students select topics of manageable proportions. Gathering the information requires that the students have mastered certain skills and are aware of certain materials. Too many research projects are simply data and information cribbed from an encyclopedia. Help students develop skill in looking up and finding pertinent references. They also need help in developing research techniques. Few students take adequate notes unless teachers instruct them in the art of note taking. Students also have great trouble with such research skills as use of scientific equipment, sampling, analyzing data, testing for fact, and interpreting statistics unless they receive special instruction and supervision. Research is not easy, and proficiency in the use of scholarly procedures and intellectual tools is difficult to attain unless students are carefully schooled and supervised in their use. Students also need help in seeing the significance of their data and in drawing valid conclusions and generalizations from their research. Special class sessions for teaching these intellectual skills are helpful and should be utilized, but most of the skill development in this area must be taught by supervising the individual effort of student researchers.

Research projects usually are best conducted as individual or small-group activities. Very few of them are truly successful when conducted as whole-class activities, though sometimes projects such as community surveys or the investigation and preparation of a report on a community problem can be very rewarding. The students in one New Jersey high school class, for instance, were concerned about racial prejudice in that school and community. As a class, they studied a number of references on the problem of prejudice, developed a questionnaire, gave the questionnaire to citizens in the community, analyzed the findings, and published the results. Some of the data and conclusions resulting from this study may be suspect in several ways (after all, the study was the work of beginners), but the students discovered much about race prejudice and their community, and developed some familiarity with research techniques. Because the teacher carefully supervised the project and frequently criticized the students' efforts, errors were kept to a minimum, and the students learned through their mistakes as well as their successes.

Learn more about what projects are suitable for students by doing Exercise 10.4.

---

[11]L. H. Clark and I. S. Starr, *Secondary and Middle School Teaching Methods,* 6th ed. (New York: Macmillan, 1991), p. 284.

SURVEYS

Surveys of the community or of the school population are among the most interesting types of research projects. If well planned and well conducted, they can teach the students much, but if poorly conceived and executed, they can lead to confusion, miseducation, and an upset community. Before launching into a community survey, be sure that the students know well both the topic they are to investigate and the procedure they are to use. This can be achieved by direct teaching and practice in the class.

Gathering the Information.   There are many ways to gather data, such as interviews, questionnaires, or observation. It is, of course, important to pick the right data-gathering technique and to aim it directly at the correct goal. To be sure that the technique is suitable and well aimed, you and your students must carefully examine the problem to see exactly what data are needed for its solution. Then the students, under your guidance, must design a strategy to obtain that information. If this strategy involves a questionnaire or opinion sampling, then the students must design the instrument. Although the development of an instrument may not be so necessary if the strategy adopted involves interviewing or observation, probably the results will be more profitable and dependable if a data-gathering instrument such as a rating scale or checklist is used. The students must be instructed and practiced in the use of these instruments so they will not waste the time of the respondents and also so the data gathered will be what was wanted.

Processing the Data.   Once the data have been gathered, they must be interpreted. This part of the research can be somewhat tricky. Most persons are tempted to make generalizations and conclusions that are not justified by the data. You should help students set up criteria by which to distinguish between significant and insignificant data. In some cases, to interpret the data, students may have to use simple statistics, but usually for class use careful inspection will suffice. The important point is to extrapolate cautiously. It is much safer to say that of the people we asked, 10 percent said yes, 70 percent said no, and 20 percent did not answer, than to say that the people of the community reject the proposition. In this regard, students should be made aware of the difficulties of sampling, the need of an adequate sample, and techniques for analyzing and interpreting their data. It is probably best to record the data in tabular form without comment. For example: Question 1. Do you prefer Plan A or Plan B? Total, 50 (100 percent). A, 5 (10 percent). B, 30 (60 percent). No Answer, 15 (30 percent).

Publishing the Results.   Publishing the results of a survey usually should be reserved for classroom use only. Only exceptionally good surveys rate publishing more widely and even they should not be published until cleared by school officials. There is no reason to publish anything that will not enhance the school's image or reputation as a scholarly institution.

Building the Instrument.   As many college and university graduate students have found out to their sorrow, to build an effective questionnaire is not an easy task. The following suggestions may help students who attempt to use questionnaires or opinion samplings in research projects.

1. Be sure to include in the questionnaire only those things that are needed. If you can find the information in another way with reasonable ease, do so.

2. Be sure the questions are clear. Check them for ambiguities. To be sure that they are unambiguous, try them out on other students and teachers. You may find that you ought to rewrite many of them or explain the terms or references you are using.

3. Be sure the questions are easy to answer. Yes-no, one word checklists, or multiple choice questions are the easiest and quickest both to answer and to interpret.

EXERCISE 10.4   PROJECTS SUITABLE FOR STUDENT INVESTIGATION

Identify by title five projects in your field that would be suitable for middle school students as well as five for high school students. The questions to keep in mind are: Would the projects be valuable to students who do them? Are they practicable in time, costs, materials, and abilities of the students? Share your lists with your colleagues for their feedback.

My subject field: _____

Middle School Student Projects

1.

2.

3.

4.

5.

High School Student Projects

1.

2.

3.

4.

5.

However, be sure to give the respondent a chance to comment. It is maddening to a respondent not to be able to say that the answer is "yes, but . . ." or "well, it depends on . . . ." Forced choice items have no place in questionnaires written by public school students; they should be reserved for use by professionals or by graduate students.

4. Be sure to set up the questionnaire so that it will be easy to tally the answers. For instance, if the answers can be arranged so that they appear in a column on the right (or left) side of the sheet, it makes tabulating much easier. Additional remarks and comments cannot be made easy to tabulate, but space should be provided for them. Be sure to give the respondent room enough to write a reasonably long, but not too long, comment.

Interview Procedure.   To be sure that students conducting interviews ask the questions they should without taking up too much of the interviewee's time, or garbling the questions, or omitting necessary questions, the interview questions should be planned and written out before the interview. A written plan is necessary also because, if one hopes to get comparable data from the interviews, the students must ask all the respondents the same questions in the same way. Therefore, it is wise to develop a formal procedure, such as the following suggested by Popkewitz:[12]

> My name is _____ . My class is doing a survey about student participation. I will be speaking to many students in your school and other schools. I would like to ask you a few questions.
> A. Do you often discuss school issues with
>   1. Friends?
>   2. Class officers?
>   3. School officials?
> B. Have you ever attended a meeting (church, school board, union, etc.) in which school policy was discussed?
> C. Have you ever taken an active part regarding school issues, such as writing a letter or presenting a petition?

This format makes it easy for students to record answers to their questions. They should record the answers of the respondent immediately. If they try to depend on memory, they will get mixed up, forget, and, therefore, bring in incorrect data.

Observation Techniques.   If research involving the use of observation techniques is to be successful, the students must be well prepared to observe carefully and profitably. The observation must be planned and the observers trained so that they see and report the data in the same way. For this purpose, the students should decide exactly what it is they must look for. In some instances, this means that they will have to decide upon the standards for establishing the presence or absence of the phenomenon, or for deciding the criteria for such categories as *much, some,* and *little.* They will also need to devise an instrument on which to record their observations. Frequently this instrument should be a checklist in which the observers merely note the presence or absence of phenomena, as in the following:

   1. Check the applicable item.
      a. Student selected a hot dish.
      b. Student selected a dessert.
      c. Student selected a coke.

---

[12]Thomas S. Popkewitz, *How to Study Political Participation,* How to Do It Series No. 27 (Washington, D.C.: National Council for the Social Studies, 1974), p. 5.

Or the instrument may be a rating scale in which the student records his or her judgment of the amount or quality of the phenomenon present, as in the following:

The students' conduct in the cafeteria line was
                    very orderly   fairly orderly   disorderly
The students' conduct at their tables was
                    very orderly   fairly orderly   disorderly

In the constructing of these devices, teachers should try to help students concoct procedures that make observing, recording, and interpreting the data as simple and as easy as possible. When observing, recording, or interpreting becomes unnecessarily complicated, the devices are usually accompanied by unnecessary errors.

Case Study Method

The case study is a special type of problem-solving method. It consists of a searching, detailed study of a particular situation, institution, decision, or issue from which students draw generalizations concerning the type. The case study can give students considerable understanding of difficult, complex matters.

Although the procedures for conducting case studies are quite simple, they are usually difficult to carry out. In general, they include the following steps:

1. Select and define a topic or problem to investigate. The topic should be a specific case so typical of a larger subject that studying it would throw light on that entire subject.

2. Identify, collect, and make ready the materials needed for studying the case in depth. Usually, most will be reading material, but do not forget that sometimes films, pictures, or audio and video tapes may be better for your purpose. So may laboratory or field work.

3. Now that you have the things to work with, you are ready to begin the case study. Start with any good introduction. In the introduction, the students should get an understanding of the problem or issue before them, what they are attempting to find out, and the method of attack. This is the time when you sell the case study to the students, so make your introduction persuasive. At this point, it may be wise to give out a study guide that the students can use as they investigate the case. The bulk of the study of the case can be done individually by students investigating individually with the study guide for a base. If you wish, it is possible to proceed on a group or whole-class basis through the use of discussions and the like. But the really important part of this phase of the case study approach is to study the particular case in depth, learn as much as one can about it, and draw conclusions.

4. Now the students share their findings and conclusions. They can do this in many ways; perhaps the most profitable is the free discussion. Role-playing, panels, and symposia may also prove very useful. In these discussions, the students should be encouraged to draw inferences from the case study, as they have been doing right along about the class of things the case study represents.

Gain practice in preparing a case study by doing Exercise 10.5.

Field Trip

One of the very best ways to make instruction real is to take the students out in the field to see and do things, such as to go to the theater to see a production of *Macbeth*, to go down to the swamp to see ecological problems firsthand, to go to the museum to see the works of great art, or to visit the site of a battle. Field trips, carefully planned and executed, can pay off in increased motivation and meaningful learning, but they require careful planning. In fact, of all the possible instructional activities, they probably require the most careful planning. To prepare for a particular field trip, you should:

1. Talk over the trip with your principal and department head.

EXERCISE 10.5   PREPARING A CASE STUDY

Prepare a case study for use in your teaching. Upon completion share it with your colleagues for their reactions and input.

My teaching field: _____

1. Topic or problem of case study:

2. Listing of materials needed:

3. The Case Study (identification of type): _____

   Grade level for which the case can be used: _____

4. Prepare the case study.

2. Take the trip yourself, if feasible, to see how to make it most productive and to see what arrangements should be made.

3. Arrange for details at the place to be visited. These arrangements include: a schedule; the briefing of the host, or tour personnel, on what you want and what type of group you are; provisions for eating and rest rooms; and so on. Obtain clear information about fees.

4. Arrange for permissions from the school authorities and parents.

5. Arrange for schedule changes, excuses from other classes, and so on.

6. Arrange for transportation.

7. Arrange for the collection of funds, payments, and so on.

8. Arrange for the safety of students.

9. Arrange the itinerary, including all stops—rest stops, meals, and so on. Do not plan to rush. Allow plenty of time. Figure that someone will get lost, or be late, or something!

10. Establish rules of conduct.

11. Brief the students. Give them directions: what to do if lost or left behind, what to take along, what they are going to do, what they should look for, what notes they should take, what materials they should bring back. Give them a copy of the study guide.

12. Provide for follow-up activities. Taking along tape recorders and cameras will allow you to bring back a record of what you did and saw. Tape record interviews, talks, questions and answers, and take pictures of the people, places, and things seen as the basis of a class follow-up.

13. Take steps to see that no one is left out because of lack of money, race, religion, or ethnic background.

14. Arrange for other teachers and parents to help you.

Figure 10–4 is a worksheet used for planning and reporting field trips at a New Jersey junior high school. Notice the meticulous detail that the board of education expects of teachers who conduct field trips. As you examine this form, ask yourself why the school board and school administrators have required each of the items they have listed.

Another type of field trip is when students go into the field (as in life science, biology, or earth science class, for instance) to record observations, or generally to gather data useful for their class assignments. Field work of this type tends to tie instruction to reality as well as make learning more active and interesting.

Action Learning

Field trips and surveys are examples of community involvement activities. Such activities allow students to observe and study realities outside the schoolroom. Action learning activities tend to carry such learning a step further. In these activities students actually become involved in community affairs or community service projects. In Jersey City (N.J.), for instance, students participated in a local political campaign; and in a Vermont village a science class investigated and brought to the attention of the local officials a problem concerning water pollution. Such activities effectively extend the classroom into the community. By so doing they quite often get at objectives that other learning activities fail to reach. In action learning, what in the classroom is academic becomes real and vivid. To prepare students for such activities, use the technique suggested for community involvement and research projects discussed in the preceding section.

FIGURE 10.4
Worksheet for Field Trip

Date _____

TEACHER'S WORKSHEET ON FIELD TRIP

This worksheet is intended both as a teacher's guide and a report. It should be handed in after the completion of the trip. Check applicable items as completed.

Trip to _____

Teacher _____ Subject _____ Date of trip _____

Group or section _____ Alternate date _____

Planning on Part of Teacher

_____ Are the educational values of the proposed trip definite and clear? State them briefly:

_____ Figure the cost: Transportation $_____

Admissions $_____

Meals $_____

Total $_____

_____ Is the total cost figure sufficient, reasonable, and within the reach of most of the group?

_____ Secure approval of the principal and turn in Permission for School Excursion (Form 132).

_____ Check school calendar with vice-principal and sign for date.

_____ Make arrangements with bus company, after securing at least two bids.

_____ Have the places you intend to visit been "scouted," either by you or someone you know?

_____ Chaperones to be secured: two adults per bus, one of whom must be a licensed teacher.

_____ If the trip takes two hours or more, is a bathroom stop available en route?

_____ Have teachers made arrangements with the vice-principal for students left behind or for teachers' duties left "uncovered"?

Preparation of the Class

_____ Discuss purposes of trip with the class.

_____ Each student who is going must have Field Trip Permit signed by parents (Form 126).

_____ Discuss proper clothes to be worn by the students.

_____ Discuss conduct on bus, including:

_____ No arms or heads to be out of windows.
_____ Remain in seats except by permission.
_____ Trash to be placed in paper bags.
_____ Nothing to be thrown out of bus windows.
_____ Students remain in seats on bus at destination until teacher gets off first.
_____ Listen to teacher's directions for dismounting at destination.

_____ Discuss the method of control which is to be used during the trip:

_____ "Buddy System"—students are paired up and given numbers (1A-1B, 2A-2B, etc.) The pair must remain together. If they leave the main group, they must tell another pair where they are going. Students must immediately report the loss of a "buddy." Each chaperone will supervise so many sets of buddies.
_____ Or "Group system"—divide a busload into two or three squads, with a student leader *and* a chaperone in charge of each. Attendence to be taken by each group frequently.
_____ Or other system of control as planned by teacher and approved by principal.

_____ Eating arrangements to be explained to pupils. Need for staple foods, rather than a day of candy and soda, should be discussed.

_____ On day before trip, class should make a list of things to be looked for on trip.

On the Morning of the Trip

_____ Proper attendance taken in homeroom or classroom.

_____ Correct absentee cards sent to office.

_____ Correct list of those remaining behind turned in to office.

_____ Permission slips (Form 126) filed in main office.

_____ Students reinstructed on bus safety rules.

_____ Take first-aid kit; also empty paper bags for car sickness.

_____ Check attendance *on the bus* immediately before leaving. Teacher in charge reports discrepancies to the attendance secretary in main office.

Follow-Up

_____ Has the trip been followed up by the class with evaluation—either written or oral—of ideas and facts learned?

_____ Write a brief evaluation of the trip: What were its values? Would you take a group on it next year? Other comments. Use space below.

_____
Signature of Teacher

Discussion and Discovery

Socratic Method

Socratic questioning has been treated in an earlier module of this text. It is one of the very oldest of discovery methods of which we have any record. According to Plato, Socrates' method was to ask a series of questions by which he hoped to cause his pupil to examine beliefs, upset preconceptions, and then draw new conclusions. The secret of the method was in the use of questions that were both challenging and leading. This questioning requires a great amount of skill and a thorough knowledge, because the questioner must be ready to follow with a new appropriate question wherever the student may lead. When you use Socratic questioning, think out beforehand the type of questions you should ask. In fluid situations, it is impossible to anticipate what the answers will be and to be prepared for all contingencies. Probably that was why Socrates depended so much upon leading questions, such as, All people want to be happy, don't they? Handled by an expert, such as Socrates was, the Socratic method can be a superb instrument for examining and discovering ideas, as the following excerpt from the *Meno* illustrates:[13]

Socrates: Now boy, you know that a square is a figure like this?

(Socrates begins to draw figures in the sand at his feet. He points to the square A B C D.)

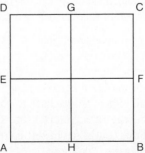

_____
[13]From *Plato: Protagoras and Meno*, translated by W. K. C. Guthrie (London: Penguin Books, 1965), pp. 133–137. Reprinted by permission of the publisher.

Boy: Yes.

Socrates: It has all these four sides equal?

Boy: Yes.

Socrates: And these lines which go through the middle of it are also equal? (*The lines* EF, GH.)

Boy: Yes.

Socrates: Such a figure could be either larger or smaller, could it not?

Boy: Yes.

Socrates: Now if this side is two feet long, and this side the same, how many feet will the whole be? Put it this way. If it were two feet in this direction and only one in that, must not the area be two feet taken once?

Boy: Yes.

Socrates: But since it is two feet this way also, does it not become twice two feet?

Boy: Yes.

Socrates: And how many feet is twice two? Work it out and tell me.

Boy: Four.

Socrates: Now could one draw another figure double the size of this, but similar, that is, with all its sides equal like this one?

Boy: Yes.

Socrates: How many feet will its area be?

Boy: Eight.

Socrates: Now then, try to tell me how long each of its sides will be. The present figure has a side of two feet. What will be the side of the double-sized one?

Boy: It will be double, Socrates, obviously.

Controlled or Guided Discussion

The controlled or guided discussion is an attempt to adopt the Socratic method to the necessities of large classes found in most schools. Basically it consists of the following three steps:

1. Select certain generalizations to be learned.
2. Furnish students with information by means of lectures, reading, film, or other expository techniques.
3. Utilize probing questions to guide students as they draw principles and generalizations from the information they have been given or have found in their reading or study. This method is not a true discussion or a true inquiry. As usually conducted, it is very teacher-centered and seldom open-ended. In carrying it out, the teacher continually asks students challenging, thought-provoking questions, designed to arouse their thinking in an attempt to persuade them to arrive at the conclusions or generalizations the teacher has set up as goals.

For an example of how one might use a guided discussion to develop a generalization, let us use the Oregon Trail as an example. Suppose that the teacher wished to have students realize that the terrain has considerable impact on the location of routes. The teacher could then initiate a lesson in map study and perhaps a reading, describing travel along the trail. Then, in discussion, the teacher could ask questions such as (1) What seems to be the most direct route from Missouri to Oregon? (2) What are the disadvantages of this route? (3) In setting out to select a route to Oregon, what factors would you, as a pioneer, look for?

As a result of this type of questioning, it is hoped that the teacher will be able to draw the conclusion that, in setting out a route, a person must consider such elements as slope, water, and attitudes of the natives. To reinforce these ideas, the teacher might compare the route selected for the Oregon Trail with the routes selected for super tankers bringing oil from the Arabian oil fields to the East Coast of the United States.

Open-Text Recitation

In the controlled discussion, there is no reason that students should not have before them the information to be used in drawing their conclusions. Controlled discussions should not be exercises in remembering, but in discovering. In the lesson we have just seen, the maps and written information provided are resources that can make the lesson more meaningful and productive if the students can refer to them during the class. This sort of class, often called an open-textbook recitation, has already been discussed in Module 8. The point in this type of lesson is to develop a discussion in which students can defend their ideas, justify their contributions, and check on proposals while the class is in progress. Such discussions may or may not be open-ended. Although the open-textbook recitation is ordinarily conducted as a controlled discussion, there is absolutely no reason why textbooks and references should not be used in true discussions. Probably it would be preferable in many instances if many open-textbook recitations were conducted as true discussions rather than as controlled discussions. Figure 10.5 shows the difference in the flow of conversation between a controlled and a true (open) discussion.

Problem-Solving Discussion

Discussion can be used both as a means of inquiry and intellectual discovery if the problem under discussion is important to the students and if conducted so that it is free and permissive, yet also disciplined and orderly. Rap sessions or bull sessions will not suffice, but well-conducted discussions are excellent for solving problems, because they bring out so many ideas from so many different people. Group members usually have many differing values, biases, insights, standards, conclusions, and beliefs. Open discussion reveals these differences and frees group members to examine, or at least to defend, their own values and beliefs and consider the values and beliefs of others. Because it is difficult to maintain narrow stereotypic thinking in such circumstances, the discussion tends to open group members to new ideas, to stimulate new thinking, and, perhaps, to create answers to the problems to be solved. In this connection brainstorming and the fishbowl technique discussed in the preceding module can be especially useful.

The procedures for conducting a discussion aimed at solving a problem are just about the same as those for carrying on any other type of discussion. Although they, or other discussions, seldom keep strictly to the line prescribed by the most logical development, they should follow the general patterns of the problem-solving process.

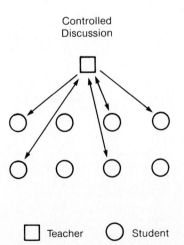

Controlled
Discussion

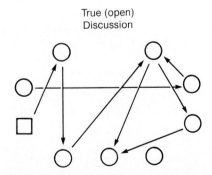

True (open)
Discussion

FIGURE 10.5
Flow of Conversation in
Discussions

☐ Teacher   ◯ Student

As adapted for discussion groups by Burton, Kimball and Wing, these procedures include the following points:[14]

1. The group becomes aware of a problem that it believes can be solved by talking it out.

2. The group defines the problem. This defining process may be quite difficult and time-consuming.

3. The group analyzes and explores the problem so that all will understand it. The process includes (a) determining what the facts are; (b) becoming acquainted with the values, backgrounds, and levels of maturity of the various group members; and (c) discovering the hidden objectives, if any, of individual group members.

4. The group thinks the problem through together. This process will undoubtedly be slow and orderly. Errors will be made and time consumed, but the procedure is necessary.

5. The group brings resources to help explore the problem. A pooling of ignorance solves no problems, so the group seeks out the information it needs from whatever sources promise to be most fruitful.

6. The group develops the "machinery and organization" necessary for cooperative thinking as it goes along. These are not set up in advance.

7. The group continually summarizes, casts straw votes, and projects tentative solutions as the discussion goes along so as to delay making premature final conclusions and to bring about the consensus of all its members.

8. The group continually evaluates its progress, both as to process and to substance.

9. The group comes to a tentative conclusion that it tries out in an actual situation.

You recognize, of course, that these are the procedures used by all successful committees, society meetings, town meetings, and the like to solve problems brought before them.

Formal Discussion

The formal discussion methods discussed in Module 9—panels, forums, symposiums, debates, British-style debates, and the like—are not so much inquiry methods as they are methods for reporting and clarifying what has been inquired into and discovered. The procedures that lead up to these presentations are ordinarily inquiry or problem-solving techniques. Panels, forums, round tables, and British-style debates can be the capstones for projects and case studies, for example. They can be used to give a project or case study a visible reason for being. See Module 9 for procedures for carrying out these strategies.

Developing Values and Morals

It is evident that the lay people of the community hold the schools responsible for teaching students the morals and values that they perceive to be essential to the good life in a democratic country.[15]

Traditional Approaches

For years the methods used by teachers to help students adopt certain values have been as follows.

---

[14]Adapted from William H. Burton, Roland B. Kimball, and Richard L. Wing, *Education for Effective Thinking* (New York: Appleton-Century-Crofts, 1960), p. 328.

[15]This section has been adapted in part from Module 11, "Teaching Values," *Teaching in the Elementary School* (New York: Macmillan Publishnig Co., 1977), Joseph F. Callahan and Leonard H. Clark, eds. The original module was written by John C. Turpin of Baldwin-Wallace College.

Models and Modeling.   Either by their own behavior or by selecting outstanding examples of virtue among the adult world, living or dead, the teachers drew attention to the practice of values that they looked upon as acceptable.

This was the purpose behind Plutarch's *Lives* and the numerous biographies of exemplary Americans such as George Washington (who supposedly never told a lie) and Honest Abe Lincoln. It was also the reason that in decades past townspeople expected exemplary behavior of teachers, preachers, and other professional persons.

The force of this strategy should not be underestimated. Modeling is the source of a major share of our beliefs and attitudes. We tend to imitate those we admire. Therefore, you should try to provide students with admirable exemplars to pattern after.

Persuasion.   By presenting arguments carefully, teachers traditionally hoped to prevail upon students to accept selected sets of values that were approved by segments of the adult population. In short, they tried to sell certain beliefs and attitudes to the students. This is the approach used by the advertisers and propagandists in the press, radio, and television. It works well when it is sufficiently convincing and alternatives are not too enticing.

Limiting Choice.   By eliminating attractive but unacceptable value choices from the options offered to students, teachers attempted to provide practice in judgment making. They offered, for example, two "goods," so that despite the selection made, no conflict with society resulted. Or they stacked the deck and offered choices, one of which was so obnoxious that there was little doubt about the option to be exercised.

Inspiration.   Through the use of fable, myth, biography, and history, teachers highlighted and made attractive the values they wished to inculcate. The influence of examples set by historical characters have already been mentioned. It remains only to mention the influence of song and story. Students' behavior, beliefs, and attitudes are frequently the direct result of what they have read, what they have seen on stage, screen, or television, or what they have heard in the songs of the times. For modern teachers, this influence can be a mixed blessing.

Rules and Regulations.   The intent of these rules was the control of behavior by rewards and punishments until the stage of automatic "correct" response had been reached. The influence of these approaches can be seen in some of the modern behavior modification techniques discussed in the modules on discipline and control.

Tradition and Religious Dogma.   Acceptance of values was encouraged on the grounds that holy people or heroic people of the past had practiced them. Many people behave the way they do because they have been convinced that that is the way one ought to act. That is why for years so many men and women rigorously followed a code of honor. The power of religious dogma and historical tradition can be seen in the behavior of members of various religious groups and societies.

Appeal to Conscience.   By indicating the shame or guilt associated with one way of behavior, teachers cultivated behavior of the opposite sort in accordance with the values they supported.

Indoctrination.   Using their position of esteem and authority gained from their training and superior knowledge, teachers informed their students what values, beliefs, and behavior were important with the expectation that students would accept their dictates without much debate.

Value Clarification

During the 1960s, two additional strategies for teaching values and moral development became popular. These strategies are value clarification and the discussion of moral dilemmas. Some teachers and theorists have come to believe that these approaches are much more effective than the traditional ones and should therefore be used by teachers. But teachers should not be too quick to give up the traditional techniques and their modern counterparts. They have worked well in the past and are working well now all over the world. Nevertheless, value clarification deserves a close look.

As described by Raths, its principal proponent, **value clarification** "is a way of interacting with a student so that he considers what he has chosen, what he prizes, or what he is doing. It stimulates him to clarify his thinking and behavior and thus to clarify his values."[16] Its purpose is to help students to accept, and become committed to, proper high-level values. The basic method is to question, to challenge, and without moralizing to help students look at what they have chosen, or are prizing, or are doing. The object is not to dictate values but to encourage each student to look at his or her own behavior and make decisions from the alternatives that exist, and by so doing create a mood in which students have an opportunity to modify the direction of their lives.

Of course, if no acceptable options for students are available, value-clarification techniques are not appropriate. In such situations you should specifically direct the students concerning how they should behave. When, however, options are available, you must avoid trying to influence the students to accept particular values. Thus, in matters when no choice is permissible—such as setting a fire in the classroom waste-basket or using profane language during class—you should be clear and forceful in denying choice to students, because an unwise choice cannot be tolerated by the policies that govern the group behavior. After all, some behavior is proper and some behavior is wrong, and students should understand which is which. But in matters that are less crucial, when choice is possible, you must be willing to give students the freedom to choose, if values are to result.

The use of value clarification has other limitations also. John Stewart complains that value clarification is too much dependent on peer pressure and so "may possibly cause more harm than good." Stewart is also concerned that, in his opinion, value clarification being based on moral relativism may be "inadequate, ineffective, and possibly even dangerous."[17] Is it not possible that when a teacher has students clarify their own values without making a value judgment about the correctness of that judgment the teacher is as much as saying, "Whatever you believe is all right"? And, of course, that simply is not true. In fact, the student may be adopting a value that is destructive to that student as an individual. In some cases citizens have objected strenuously to the use of value clarification and moral dilemma techniques—even to the extent of going to court to protest their use.

Nevertheless, value clarification has a number of strengths. Raths, for instance, believes that value clarification will be beneficial to students having manifestly idiosyncratic behavior patterns—apathy, flightiness, drift, overconformity, or underachievement, for instance—that may be caused by confusion of values. Another strength of value clarification is that much of the time it is a personal and private prodding of students to look at themselves, their attitudes, their behavior, and their ideas that helps them to a better understanding and, possibly, a reshaping of themselves. Because of its supportive nonjudgmental aspect, it creates an atmosphere conducive to learning and change. Because of its emphasis on choosing, it helps to develop skill in decision making.

Now consider a number of the techniques used in value clarification.

Clarifying Response.   Clarifying responses are short, informal interchanges, mostly spur of the moment, in which the teacher asks the student to reconsider what he or she has said or has done. They consist of such teacher questions as: "Do you really

---

[16]Louis E. Raths, Merrill Harmin, and Sidney B. Simon, *Values and Teaching, Working with Values in the Classroom* (Columbus, Oh.: Charles E. Merrill Publishing, 1966), p. 51.

[17]John S. Stewart, "Clarifying Values Clarification: A Critique," *Phi Delta Kappan*, (June 1975), 684–688.

believe that?" "What makes you take that position?" "Does your remark apply to everyone?" "Would it apply in such and such a situation?" The teacher tries to raise questions in the student's mind and to cause the student to think further about the bases of what he or she has said or done.

Value-Clarifying Discussions.   Short, informal discussions of the discovery type are also useful for helping students discover and understand values, for they give students a chance to examine their own views and compare them with those of others. Frequently, value-clarification discussions can arise naturally out of the class situation. At other times you may wish to use a springboard that will present a value judgment or a conflict. Possible springboards include provocative questions, anecdotes, cartoons, pictures, tape recordings, news items, and the like. As in problem-solving discussions, the teacher should encourage students to think freely. To create and maintain a supportive class climate that will stimulate thought, you should avoid the use of leading questions, preaching, informing students that their opinions are wrong, and other tactics that cut off thinking, or force students into giving lip service to positions that they may not believe in, or that impede the consideration of alternative positions. Insofar as possible, keep the value clarifying discussion open-ended, nonjudgmental, and pressure-free, for your purpose is to enhance understanding, not to sell a belief.[18]

Value Sheets.   A value sheet consists of a series of questions about an issue. The issue may be presented on the value sheet, or by a role-playing incident, a simulation, a dramatization, a tape recording, a reading selection, or some other manner. After the students have seen, heard, or read the presentation of the issue, have them write answers to the questions on the value sheet. Then follow up with one of the following procedures:[19]

1. Have students discuss their answers in small groups without your being present.
2. Have students turn in their completed value sheets to you. Read selected portions to the class aloud. Do not identify the writers of the papers unless they want you to.
3. Have students turn in their completed value sheets to you. Read them privately. Return them with comments but without grading them.
4. Have students turn in the papers to a committee that will select papers representing various positions for posting or to be read aloud.
5. Use the value sheets as a basis for a class discussion.

Moral Dilemmas.   Discussions of moral dilemmas are used to develop a high standard of intelligent moral behavior in students. In this procedure the teacher tries to raise students' moral levels by presenting them with challenging moral problems or dilemmas by means of an anecdote, a story, a news item, a parable, or the like. Then one asks the students to consider what one ought to do in a given situation and why. Their responses and their implications can be worked into an open discussion of what is the right and proper thing to do under the circumstances.

Role-Playing and Simulation

Role-Playing

Role-playing and simulation can be used effectively in inquiry and discovery teaching. By attempting to simulate a real problem, students may get real insight into the nature of a problem situation. Role-playing may be used to clarify attitudes and concepts; demonstrate attitudes and concepts; deepen understandings of social situations; prepare for real situations (such as practicing the interview procedures to be used in a survey); plan and try out strategies for attacking problems; test out hypothetical so-

---

[18]Raths, op. cit., p. 115
[19]Ibid., pp. 107–109.

lutions to problems; and practice leadership and other skills. Role-playing has a number of drawbacks, however. Role-playing is slow; is often not realistic enough so that false concepts result; and although serious business, is often thought of as entertainment.

As you already know, role-playing is an unrehearsed dramatization, in which the players try to clarify a situation by acting out the roles of the participants in the situation. To carry out a role-playing session, the following procedures are recommended:

1. Pick a simple situation, not a complicated one, to role-play. Two to four characters usually are quite enough.

2. Select a cast who will do the job. Use volunteers, if feasible, but only if the volunteers are equal to the task. It is preferable to sacrifice self-selection for effectiveness. Sometimes it is helpful to select several casts and run through the role-playing several times, each time with a different cast. Different interpretations of the parts should give the audience more data from which to draw their inferences and make their discoveries.

3. Be sure that the characters in the cast understand the situation, the purpose of the role-playing, and their roles. To this end, brief the players well and then discuss their roles with them. Sometimes it is helpful to outline the general line they should follow and to rehearse the first few lines. However, too much direction and too much warmup can ruin the role-playing by stereotyping the interpretations.

4. Brief the audience. Be sure everyone understands what the players are supposed to be trying to do.

5. Stage the role-playing. Let the role-players interpret freely. However, if they get hopelessly lost, it may be necessary for you to stop the role-playing and reorient the players.

6. If it seems desirable, repeat the role-playing with reversed roles or with different role-players.

7. Follow up the role-playing with a discussion about what happened in the role-playing and its significance. At this point, the teacher should encourage students to come to some conclusions and make some generalizations (although it may be more satisfactory to leave the discussion open-ended). Sometimes the discussion may reveal new or different interpretations and concepts that warrant a replaying of the roles and further discussion and analysis.

Simulation

A simulation differs from role-playing in that the former is an enactment of a make-believe episode as much like the real thing as possible, but with some of the dangerous and complicating factors removed. The beginning truck driver does not suffer dire results from a mistake if he or she pulls in front of a speeding bus when driving the driver education simulator, the beginning aviator crashes with impunity when the plane stalling is simulated, and the soldier who mishandles a new weapon in a dry run without live ammunition kills no one. Simulations of this sort, although in our examples largely aimed at developing skills, can be useful for helping students gain insights into difficult matters. The young, aspiring lawyer who tries a case in a simulated courtroom not only gains skill in legal practice but also gains insight into the law of the case being tried. In the social studies classroom, the students simulating the management of a business are learning what happens when they overbuy, overprice, and make strategic errors.

In these simulations, students go through the process in what they were learning in a real way. That is the value of simulation. By taking roles in the simulated activity, the students may come to understand the real situation and how to act in it.

Simulations differ from role-playing in that the scenarios must be carefully drafted. In these scenarios the students are assigned definite roles that require them to take specific action in a well-defined situation, and the students are confronted by simulated, real-life situations that require them to take actions just as they would have to in real life (or at least as close to real life as feasible). These actions may lead to new predicaments that require new actions. In taking actions, the players are not free but must stay in character and keep their actions within the limits prescribed by the roles they have assumed and by the realities of the simulated situation.

If you are to produce a simulation, the following procedure may prove useful:

1. Prepare the material, equipment, and props that will be needed.

2. Introduce the plan to the students. Explain the purpose of the simulation. Give the directions for playing it.

3. Assign roles. Probably it is best to pick the players yourself. Accepting volunteers or selecting students by chance may result in disastrous miscasting.

4. Brief the students in their roles. Be sure they understand them.

5. Conduct the simulation. Follow the scenario to the letter.

6. Follow up with a critique in which students have a chance to discuss what they have done and to draw generalizations.

Controversial Issues

The content of topics most suitable for the methods described in this module may sometimes be controversial. Teaching controversial issues can be something of a problem. Students, parents, and the local public often feel very strongly about them. It is wise to treat them gingerly or your teaching may do more harm than good.

In the first place, because controversial issues can be so touchy, you should be careful to select topics that will throw more light than heat. There is no point in introducing into your courses topics so controversial that they upset your effectiveness. Therefore, before you commit yourself to any controversial topics, consider the following criteria.

1. Is the topic pertinent to your course and your course goals?

2. Are you knowledgeable enough and neutral enough to handle it fairly and impartially?

3. Is it worth the time and effort?

4. Are the students sufficiently mature and informed to cope with it?

5. Is there sufficient material available to allow students adequate consideration of the various points of view?

6. Can it be discussed without overemotionalism? Will it be upsetting to the people in the community?

After you select a controversial topic, you must be careful to teach it fairly and honestly. Controversial issues are open-ended questions and should be treated as such. Ordinarily they do not have "right answers" or "correct solutions"—otherwise there would be no controversy. Therefore your focus, when teaching controversial matters, should be on process rather than content. Your goal should be to show students how to deal with controversial issues so as to make wise decisions on the basis of carefully considered information.

To achieve this end you should teach your students what the issues are, how to sort out facts from propaganda and myth, how to evaluate the positions of the various sides, and how to draw their own conclusions. To do this you will have to teach students how to check out sources of information and facts, to identify sources of information, and to test these sources for authority, accuracy, objectivity, and timeliness by using such questions as: "What is the basis for this statement?" "Is this 'authority' really in a position to know?" "Is it corroborated by other evidence?" "Is the information current?" To build reasoning skills, provide pupils with questionable statements and show them how to prove or disprove them. To help students separate fact from opinion, keep a fact-opinion table on the chalkboard (Figure 10.6). You should also help students from getting hung up on the meaning of words. Often the emotional connotations of

FIGURE 10.6
Fact-Opinion Table

FACT	OPINION

words obscure their meaning and prevent logical evaluation of facts and arguments. So do students' values. Such techniques as value-clarifying responses, value sheets, and value discussions help students discover and evaluate their own values. So that the students may understand just what community value conflicts are involved in the issue being studied, it is sometimes helpful for students to conduct an opinion survey on the topic. In any case you should encourage the students to use research-type activities to dig out facts, opinions, and values, and to place them on the table for all to see and evaluate.

When teaching controversial issues, you should try not to become too involved in the controversy. Certainly you should not advocate one position or another. This is another reason for using research or problem-solving activities as a basis for the study of controversial issues. Nevertheless, at times you may find that in order to give students a chance to look at all sides of the controversy, you may have to present some aspects of the topic yourself. Otherwise students may never understand the complexity of the issue, the variety of positions, the divergence in values, or the moral, ethical, political, financial implications, and the like. Sometimes it may be necessary to play the devil's advocate. When you do, try not to give the impression that you are advocating one side or another. Use expressions such as "some people say," "other people believe," and so on.

Everyone in a class should have the right to express an opinion on the issue to be studied. Problem-solving, research-type activities followed by discussion activities provide good media for obtaining nearly universal student involvement. Debates, panels, dramatics, role-playing, and simulations are other examples of activities that let students present their points of view. Simulated town meetings, jury trials, council meetings, legislatures, or party conventions can be especially useful.

When using such discussion modes for teaching controversial issues, you should first establish some ground rules. For example:

☐ All facts must be supported by authority.
☐ Everyone must be given an opportunity to be heard.
☐ No one should interrupt (except perhaps the leader to keep the discussion on track).
☐ Personal remarks are forbidden.

To get the study of the issue started and to arouse interest, sometimes a free-for-all introductory discussion in which students may express themselves without restraint is helpful, but ordinarily you should apply the ground rules so as to promote orderly thinking and to keep the discussion from getting too hot. To keep rash opinion statements under control, sometimes teachers ask students to present arguments contrary to their own point of view. Doing so may help students to understand and respect the opinions of others and to realize the complexity of the issue.

In short, to teach controversial issues well, you must see to it that students learn how to identify what is the basis for the controversy, what is at stake, what value conflicts are involved, what the facts are, and what their own values and beliefs are so that they can make informed decisions and take intelligent stands now and in the future.

Exercise 10.6 will help you explore how you might teach a controversial issue.

EXERCISE 10.6 TEACHING ABOUT CONTROVERSIAL ISSUES

The purpose of this exercise is for you to discover before teaching what some of the possibilities are for controversial issues in your field, and for you to consider what you can and will do with the issues. This exercise should first be completed by you and then shared with members of your class who share your discipline interest.

1. Your discipline: _____

2. Spend some time in the library studying current periodicals in your subject field, and also talk with your colleagues in the schools, and list two or three potential controversial issues that are likely to come up during your teaching.

Issue   **Resource**

3. Take one of these issues and identify "sides" and "current resources."

4. Identify your own position on this issue with a statement of your rationale.

5. How accepting can you be of students who take an opposing position?

6. Share the above with other teacher candidates from your field. Note any comments of theirs that you find helpful or enlightening.

Kim and Kellough, p. 113. By permission of Macmillan Publishing Company.

SUMMARY

This module has examined a number of teaching strategies, all of which have elements of problem solving and are designed to engage students in higher levels of thinking, combined here under the heading of problem solving, discovery, and inquiry. These teaching methods have in common that the students are expected to draw conclusions, concepts, and generalizations from some form of induction, deduction, observation, or application of principles. The premises underlying these methods are (1) that a person learns to think by thinking and (2) that knowledge gained through self-discovery is more meaningful, permanent, and transferable than knowledge learned from teachers using expository techniques.

The strategies presented in this module are not easy to implement. To use them effectively and without classroom control problems requires your conviction and careful preparation. Even with firm conviction and careful preparation there may need to be a period of trial and error in implementation before you perfect your implementation. Yet, discovery, problem solving, and inquiry are important teaching tools and are absolutely worth your effort, time, and the potential frustrations that can occur for the beginning teacher who deviates from the traditional teacher-centered, expository methods.

SUGGESTED READING

Barell, J. *Teaching for Thoughtfulness*. White Plains, NY: Longman, 1991.

Baron, J., and Steinbert, R. J. *Teaching Thinking Skills: Theory and Practice*. New York: Freeman, 1987.

Bateman, W. L. *Open to Question*. San Francisco: Jossey-Bass, 1990.

Beyer, B. K. *Practical Strategies for the Teaching of Thinking*. Newton, MA: Allyn & Bacon, 1987.

Bobcock, S. S., and Schild, E. O. *Simulation Games in Learning*. Beverly Hills, CA: Sage, 1968.

Bransford, J. D., and Stein, B. S. *The Ideal Problem Solver*. New York: W. H. Freeman, 1984.

Chance, P. *Thinking in the Classroom*. New York: Teachers College, Columbia University Press, 1985.

Costa, A. L. (ed.). *Developing Minds: A Resource Book for Teaching Thinking*. Alexandria, VA: ASCD, 1985.

Educating Americans for the 21st Century. Washington, DC: The National Board Commission on Pre-College Education in Mathematics, Science, and Technology, 1983.

Grant, G. E. *Teaching Critical Thinking*. New York: Praeger, 1988.

Heiman, M., and Slomianka, J. (eds.). *Thinking Skills Instruction: Concepts and Techniques*. Washington, DC: National Education Association, 1987.

Heitzmann, W. R. *Educational Games and Simulations*. Rev. ed. Washington, DC: National Education Association, 1987.

Jones, K. *Simulations: A Handbook for Teachers and Trainers,* 3rd ed. revised. New York: Nichols, 1987.

Raths, L. E.; Wasserman, S.; Jonas, A.; and Rothstein, A. *Teaching for Thinking,* 2nd ed. New York: Teachers College, Columbia University Press, 1986.

Resnick, L. B. *Education and Learning to Think*. Washington, DC: National Academy Press, 1987.

Sternberg, R. J. "Teaching Critical Thinking: Eight Easy Ways to Fail Before You Begin." *Phi Delta Kappan* 68(6):456–459 (February 1987).

Sternberg, R. J., and Lubart, T. I. "Creating Creative Minds." *Phi Delta Kappan* 72(8):608–614 (April 1991).

Wassermann, S. "Teaching for Thinking: Louis E. Raths Revisited." *Phi Delta Kappan* 68(6):460–466 (February 1987).

Whimbey, A., and Lockhead, J. *Problem Solving and Comprehension,* 4th rev. ed. Hillsdale, NJ: Erlbaum, 1984.

POSTTEST

Short Answer

1. List two advantages of inquiry over expository methods.

   _____

   _____

2. List two disadvantages of inquiry over expository methods.

   _____

   _____

3. Should students be free to challenge each other's thinking?

   _____

4. Should students be allowed challenge the book?

   _____

5. Describe the steps in problem solving.

   _____

   _____

   _____

6. Name two criteria that can be used to test the suitability of a problem, according to this module.

   _____

   _____

7. Students have difficulty finding projects to do. Give at least two suggestions for helping students find them.

   _____

   _____

8. Is it ordinarily good policy to publish class survey results outside the school?

   _____

9. What devices can you use to make objective the recording of observations?

   _____

   _____

10. What techniques are recommended in order to standardize interviews?

    _____

    _____

11. Explain how to conduct a case study.

    _____

    _____

    _____

12. Tell how to conduct a Socratic dialogue.

    _____

    _____

    _____

    _____

13. What is the difference between a controlled discussion and a true discussion?

    _____

_____

_____

14. How does conducting a value-clarifying discussion differ from conducting a controlled discussion?

_____

_____

_____

_____

15. Outline the procedure for conducting role-playing.

_____

_____

16. Why use simulations?

_____

_____

17. What procedures would you use for launching and carrying out student research projects in your classes?

_____

_____

_____

_____

_____

18. Describe the distinguishing characteristic of discovery teaching.

_____

_____

19. Describe the procedure for carrying out a moral dilemma discussion.

_____

_____

_____

20. Name three procedures used in traditional approaches to teaching moral values.

_____

_____

_____

21. How would you use a value sheet?

_____

_____

22. List four questions to consider before you select a controversial issue to teach.

_____

_____

_____

_____

23. Distinguish among the following terms: fact, concept, generalization.

_____

_____

_____

24. Describe how inquiry teaching differs from discovery teaching.

_____

_____

_____

25. Describe specifically how you would teach a generalization in your field.

_____

_____

_____

26. Describe the IDEAL method of problem solving.

_____

_____

_____

_____

27. Identify ten thinking skills.

_____

_____

_____

_____

_____

28. Describe how you would teach each of the thinking skills identified in number 27.

_____

_____

_____

_____

_____

_____

_____

_____

_____

_____

29. According to this module, there are a number of processes involved in true inquiry. Identify those that are "idea-building" processes.

_____

_____

_____

_____

30. According to the discussion of inquiry as presented in the module, which of the inquiry processes requires the highest level of mental operation?

_____

_____

_____

MODULE 11
Reading, Writing, and Study Skills

RATIONALE

Regardless of the subject or grade level that you teach, you should be interested in helping your students develop their skills in reading, writing, and studying. Since the release of two publications in particular, *Becoming a Nation of Readers* and *The Writing Report Card*, all teachers, particularly those of middle and junior high schools, have been encouraged to help students develop reading, writing, and studying skills.[1]

These skills go hand-in-hand, one reinforcing the other. Research indicates that from a quarter to a third of secondary school students cannot read their textbooks. Furthermore, research also indicates that when reading skills are inadequate or minimal, students waste time, become frustrated, and lose interest, often starting a cycle that blocks further learning. Data on school dropouts reveal that more than three times as many poor readers as good readers drop out of school before graduation. The public has rightly become concerned as stories about reading scores have made the front pages of newspapers. Families know that reading achievement is used as a predictor of success in academic work, on college admission examinations, on civil-service tests, and in career placement and upgrading.

The rationale of the ongoing Right to Read program is based on the recognized gap between student needs and student accomplishment. As educators, we must accept this challenge to help all our students develop functionally adequate skills in reading, writing, and studying. At the same time, recognizing the value of effective reading, we must work to increase every student's performance to the highest possible level. We must help them to continue on a lifelong process, making a major contribution to their growth and development and to the richness of their lives.

This module primarily addresses the reading process, elaborating on techniques and activities designed to improve reading. We hope the material will provoke you to further thought and study on what more you can do to help your students achieve reading and writing competency.

SPECIFIC OBJECTIVES

At the completion of this module, you should be able to:

1. Identify the major features of the reading process.
2. Describe the content teacher's responsibility for teaching reading.
3. Describe the content teacher's responsibility for encouraging writing skill development.
4. Describe the content teacher's responsibility for helping students develop their study skills.
5. Describe activities for building vocabulary.
6. Describe the major aspects of reading comprehension.
7. Characterize good homework assignments.
8. Describe procedures for the use of textbooks and study guides.
9. Identify the features of good questions to accompany reading.
10. Describe the steps in effective study.
11. Explain scanning and skimming, and describe their uses.
12. Distinguish among recreational reading, critical reading, and imaginative reading.
13. Describe the features of critical reading and problem solving.
14. Identify the special features of reading maps, charts, graphs, and diagrams.
15. Distinguish among various types of problem readers.

---

[1]Richard Anderson et al., *Becoming a Nation of Readers: The Report of the Commission on Reading* (Urbana, IL: Center for the Study of Reading; Washington, DC: National Academy of Education, 1985); Arthur N. Applebee et al., *The Writing Report Card: Writing Achievement in American Schools* (Princeton, NJ: National Assessment of Education Progress, 1986).

16. Plan activities to include directed reading, supervised study, and diagnosis of reading difficulties.

17. Describe the reading inventory and Cloze procedures.

What Kind of Reader Are You?

In an important sense, you already know a good deal about reading. Yet, before you undertake to help others, it should be useful to examine your reading habits as well as your general ideas about reading. What kind of reader are you? Slow and plodding or rapid and superficial, word-for-word or idea-to-idea, absorbed or impatient, easily distracted or off in another world? You have been reading for many years. Within each day you may read a considerable variety of things: notes, signs, letters, information on boxes, a newspaper or two, a magazine, part of a book. Because you take reading for granted, you may never have stopped to evaluate yourself as a reader. The following sets of questions will not measure your reading ability, but will help you explore your habits, experiences, knowledge, and ideas before you read the rest of the module. Before you commit yourself to a mental answer to each set of questions, reread the set. Stop at each set and let your thoughts wander in many directions before continuing with the next set.

1. When you first picked up this book, did you look through the table of contents? Did you see how the entire book was organized? Did you read the module headings? Were you curious about any special features?

2. Did you open the book at random or choose a section in which you were interested? Did you sample any of the module's content? How quickly did you read it? How carefully and how critically? On the basis of your first impressions, did you decide how much you would get out of this book? Do you always rely on your own judgment or sampling, or do you usually consider someone else's opinion, a friend's, a teacher's, a librarian's?

3. Do you read everything at the same speed or with the same attention to individual words? Have you ever tried to speed up your reading? What were the results? Have you tried to read mainly for ideas, rather than for specific facts to remember?

4. What happens when you come across words of which you may not be too sure? Do you skip them and expect to figure out the gist of what you are reading from the parts that you do know? Do you look up unfamiliar words in a glossary or dictionary? Do you try to fit the meaning in the passage?

5. When you finish reading a new selection, passage, or chapter, do you think over what you have read or do you just go on to the next reading? If you stop to think it over, do you jot down notes on what you have read or discuss it with other people?

6. Are you satisfied with the way you have done homework? Are you efficient or are you slow and impatient with yourself? Do you have good study habits or would you like to improve them? How would you try to achieve higher stages of self-discipline?

7. When you encounter statistics, graphs, or charts, do you skip them or do you spend time studying them? What is their real value to you? What was the author's purpose in using them?

8. Do you continue serious reading mainly in the area of your school major? Are you satisfied with your present reading interests?

9. How well do you read instructions on tests, in books, in recipes, on hobby materials, or similar sets of directions?

10. Have you enjoyed reading fiction, poetry, plays, and other forms of imaginative writing? Have any books had an effect on the way you think or feel about life, other people, yourself, the world, or the future?

11. How quickly do you find numbers in a directory; dates and events of a person's life; specific facts in newspapers, reference books, or textbooks?

12. Are you easily distracted when you read, or do you concentrate enough to forget the place or time or your other responsibilities? What factors can make the difference?

13. Where do you look for the main ideas in books, newspapers, and magazine articles? What makes it possible to remember more content more readily?

14. Do you review for tests by reading over the entire material for which you are responsible? Does reviewing make you nervous or pressured, or are you reassured by refreshing your memory?

15. Have you read material with which you disagreed? Were you bothered by the facts, the author's opinions, the bias, the tone, the language, the attitudes, values, and beliefs? How did it affect your reading? Did you take any action? Did you work out your own viewpoint, using evidence collected through research? Have you ever changed your mind as a result of reading?

16. How would you sum up your own purposes in reading? Should teachers read in special ways, for themselves, for preparing their teaching materials, and procedures for anticipating their students' reactions?

Since there are no right or wrong answers for this exercise, there is no score. But the areas touched on and the problems raised in this survey will give you insight into the discussion and procedures that follow. The way you explored your own habits, experience, and knowledge will help you apply your answers to the problems of reading and study techniques. It should be clear from the items included that all of us can continue to improve our reading for the rest of our lives.

Every Teacher Is a Teacher of Reading

Consciously or unconsciously, every teacher is a reading teacher. No reading takes place without content, and the content that teachers must use is their own subject-matter area. Although severe problems require the help of a reading specialist, the subject-matter teacher will be thwarted in reaching the learning goal if students are unable to read the textbook or the written materials assigned for study. The subject-matter teacher as the resident expert in the content field has learned the concepts and specialized vocabulary to be mastered, the materials and activities to be used, the sequences of growth and maturation and the kinds of learning to be measured and evaluated. However, if the subject-matter teacher fails to help all students unlock the messages contained in the written words, the students will be condemned to rely solely on the oral presentations in class and ultimately emerge as impaired learners.

Different content requires different reading styles and approaches, a fact that becomes especially apparent when the student leaves the elementary grades. Within a single school day, the student may confront equations, diagrams, and problems of mathematics; the technical vocabulary, detailed data, and causal explanations of science; the chronological or thematic presentation of events and the interpretations of social studies; the imaginative or expository literature of English; and a host of other specialized reading materials. No one teacher handles them all, but all teachers must be prepared to make their contributions to students' progress in the context of their own disciplines.

Some misguided teachers exercise this obligation as teacher of reading with considerable reluctance. They exhibit the attitude that the teaching of skills such as reading, "which should have been learned in the lower grades," is beneath their dignity and beyond the call of duty. Such teachers eventually find themselves flying in a tiresome holding pattern with many of their students in great need. They have failed to learn a significant fact about educational systems, which is that not all students make identical progress each year. It should have been impressed early upon them that when children start grade one there is a minimum of three years of difference among them in readiness for learning. Some are on target at age six and ready. Some are precocious and already one year or more advanced in their skills. Some, too, are slower in maturing and are at least one year or more behind. From grade one onward, the amount of separation in achievement among these groups progresses annually, so that by grade five, for example, there may be five years of difference among those who started at the same age and same time. Consider this: "By the junior high school years this overall spread is estimated to be approximately two thirds the mean age of the grade group. A group entering the seventh grade is approximately twelve years of age. Two thirds of this figure is eight. Consequently, the spread in achievement is from third grade to the eleventh."[2]

The Reading Process

Reading is an active process; it does not happen to the student and it is not done for the student. Since it requires attention or a favorable attitude or set, it is not mechanical. An aroused interest or a felt need starts it and keeps it going. The reader's feeling of purpose is the motivating and effective sustaining force. Basically, reading is a thinking process, since its central aspect is extracting meaning from print. The essential unit of meaning is the idea, the concept, the thought, the image, or the statement. Meaning does not emerge from an arbitrary string of words, but from words in relationship. The sum total of these relationships makes up the context of the reading material, and only within a context do words (or other symbols) have meaning. Understanding and enlarging contexts is the reader's major goal. Finally, reading is a developmental process, changing with the ideas, concepts, or operations that increase in depth and scope with the reader's life experience.

Reading is not an isolated skill. It is one of the four major communication skills: listening and speaking (oral skills), and reading and writing (written skills). Only after a child has achieved success in the oral realm can the child learn to read. Of course, all the language skills are related and in this hierarchic scheme reading becomes the third component of language mastery.

The organization of the reading program in the elementary school, after the readiness stage has been reached in kindergarten and early first grade, reflects the organization of this hierarchy. Developmental programs are begun that provide systematic instruction to classes, to small groups, and to individuals. Functional programs that use resource materials from all parts of the curriculum are scheduled. Recreational reading programs are devised that focus on reading for personal enjoyment. Enrichment reading programs are explored in an effort to further expand reading experiences to other language arts areas. Remedial programs are developed to keep pace with the needs that are revealed as students progress through all of these programs.

In the middle and upper elementary grades there is special emphasis on cultivating study skills, such as locating information (e.g., through an index or table of contents, in reference books and in tables and charts) and organizing ideas (e.g., with notes, outlines, and summaries). These developmental programs are sequentially arranged to (1) reinforce and extend those desirable reading skills and appreciations acquired in previous years and (2) develop new skills and appreciations as they are needed to comprehend and enjoy advanced and complex forms of written communications. Among the abilities included in those developmental reading programs extended into the secondary schools are:

☐ Getting the central idea

☐ Selecting the significant details

☐ Understanding words in context

☐ Following directions

---

[2]John I. Goodlad, *School Curriculum and the Individual*. (Waltham, Mass.: Blaisdell Publishing, 1966), p. 6.

☐ Answering specific questions

☐ Determining relationships

☐ Drawing conclusions

☐ Predicting outcomes

☐ Outlining and summarizing

☐ Determining the author's purpose and mood

☐ Understanding figurative language

☐ Evaluating ideas

☐ Understanding graphic material

☐ Increasing speed

☐ Adjusting speed to purpose and content

☐ Using reference material

Whether or not a highly structured developmental reading program in which the entire faculty becomes involved during specified periods in reading instruction will exist in your school, you should feel responsible for attending to the reading and learning needs of your students in your subject, at least in the areas of vocabulary development, improving comprehension, and in developing reading flexibility.

Remedial classes in most schools are usually taught in special sessions or in reading laboratories—generally by a reading specialist. The focus of this instruction is usually upon individual difficulties experienced by individual students. Some students may be just latent learners who need a little more time for mastery while others may be plagued by deepseated and serious blockages that require the expertise of the skilled practitioner to eliminate.

Building Vocabulary

Success in working with vocabulary building often hinges upon the interest in word growth and development shown by the teacher. Enthusiasm exhibited by you for an apt phrase or a descriptive adjective can be "caught" by your students especially if the student response is acknowledged and rewarded. It helps to condition students to savor the language to which they are exposed so that their progress can be accelerated.

Direct and indirect student experiences are major sources of new words for students. Drawing upon such experiences in the classroom and encouraging students to use the vocabulary that they have already mastered and to listen to and appropriate what they hear others use enables students to apply new meanings to words already known.

A major hurdle for beginning teachers is the finding of the middle way in introducing new words. Avoid the assumption that everyone knows every word: knows what it looks like, what it sounds like, what it means in the particular context used in the text, and what it means in other contexts. Also avoid the belaboring of definitions of words beyond the appreciation of anyone except the belaborer, as well as the elaboration of nuances beyond the current need for study.

Effective teachers are accustomed to using the following techniques in their systematic attempt to expand knowledge of vocabulary:

1. *Provide appropriate context for new words.* The dictionary defines only certain limits within which a word may range. Selecting the appropriate meaning is the skill that has to be developed. Note how the context brings out the meaning in each of the following sentences:

    a. Jake is a *pugapoo*. His mother was a cute little black poodle, his father a feisty, sandy-haired pug.

    b. He was a *rock hound* who loved to wander through the desert hunting for interesting rocks and semiprecious stones.

   c. The *savannah*, a flat grassy plain, stretches from here to there.
   d. He was a true hero—a *Lochinvar* out of the west.
   e. *Orcs* are nasty, despicable, foul-mouthed, foul-breathed, dirty, murderous goblins.
   f. He drove forward about a *league*, five miles in our reckoning.[3]

2. *Teach key words.* Key words or "stopper" words to be encountered by the student in new assignments or units should be taught by the teacher prior to the assignment. These may be precisely the words with multiple meanings so that the specific meaning in the new material must be gleaned, obviously from the context. Attend to both the oral and visual mastery of these stopper words you are focusing on. Use the chalkboard to list such words and get all students to attend to the configuration of the word. Skip about the class with the questions you ask that require oral pronunciation of stopper words. Above all, provide positive reinforcement with your commendation for students who attempt to use words under study in oral responses to questions in the classroom.

3. *Utilize word-attack devices.* To develop understanding of word meanings, various word attack devices can be used. If there are roots, prefixes, and suffixes that can be pinpointed, these can be separated and analyzed. Long words can be divided into easy-to-manage syllables. Sounding out the words, placing the proper stress, hearing and recognizing the auditory components call into play other senses used in learning. Syntactical clues can be clarifying aids, such as the endings: *-ed*, which probably indicates a verb; *-ly*, which usually indicates an adverb; or *-ist*, which generally indicates a person who does or is something. Marks such as capital letters, articles, auxiliary verbs, and prepositions are also helps to decide the function of words. The way a word is used in a sentence, or in its relationship with other words, often will supply a broad hint to its meaning.

4. *Teach the use of printed aids to reading.* These include marginal notes, parenthetical definitions, headings, footnotes, summaries, and punctuation marks such as commas, periods, and the like.

5. *Encourage and teach use of the dictionary.* "When a student learns to make appropriate and frequent use of the dictionary, he is strengthening his power to keep his vocabulary growing for life."[4] Perhaps the key word in this statement is *appropriate*. The dictionary is a resource with which students need help. Among the necessary dictionary-use skills for vocabulary growth are the following:
   a. Using guide words.
   b. Selecting the best-fitting meaning.
   c. Recognizing differences in meaning.
   d. Figuring out pronunciation by proper use of the key.
   e. Syllabication, stresses, and blending.
   f. Relating the meaning to word derivation.
   g. Using information about nuances of meaning among synonyms.
   The teacher who provides experience with any or all of these skills, to a whole class, to small groups, or to individual students, contrasts sharply with the one who merely says, "Look it up in the dictionary." Of course, there are times when students must be told to "look it up" when the inquiries about the same word are repeated often, or when the request appears to indicate a laziness on the part of the student. The teacher response should be based upon the goal of developing a self-sufficient inquirer rather than on the petulance of the instructor, though. A quick way to kill a budding interest in word growth is to make the quest too tedious or time consuming.

---

[3]Leonard H. Clark and Irving S. Starr, *Secondary and Middle School Teaching Methods*, 6th ed. (New York: Macmillan Publishing Co., 1991), p. 304.

[4]Ellen Lamar Thomas and H. Alan Robinson. *Improving Reading in Every Class*, abridged ed. (Boston: Allyn & Bacon, Inc., 1972), p. 33.

6. *Utilize word slips or vocabulary notebooks.* Recording words on a word slip or in a vocabulary notebook, if the practice is connected with the other activities, may be the task that sets the student on the road to independent vocabulary growth. On small slips of paper or in a notepad, he or she records the word and the sentence in which it was used. When convenient, he or she looks it up and lists the meaning that fits the context. The pronunciation should be recorded if it presents a problem, and the derivation may be helpful in remembering the meaning. Some find 3×5 index cards useful, while others use bookmarks to write down the word, which they later transfer with the sentence to a notebook for full treatment.

Some teachers who use these techniques fail to carry their efforts far enough. The goal is the absorption of the new definition into the oral vocabulary of the student. Often, the leap is not made from notebook to mind, and mastery is never quite ensured. To avoid such a fate for your efforts, make use of the work that is done by students:

☐ Periodically, examine their collections of words and volunteer appropriate comments.

☐ Occasionally, schedule a quiz on contextual meanings of several of the words that have been recorded.

☐ Conduct short sessions, such as the last 10 minutes of a class before the bell, devoted to contests in word recognition, word spelling, word definition or words collected in the notebook.

ENCOURAGE Wide READING

"The most important means of vocabulary development is wide reading. This is at once the most painless and the most rewarding way of building one's vocabulary. In wide reading the student not only meets many new words in different fields but also becomes familiar with their different meanings in a variety of contexts."[5] With increments of contact or meaning at repeated encounters, the students gradually incorporate the words into their vocabulary. The competent reader who practices this independently can be encouraged or praised by the teacher for acquiring unfamiliar words. The reluctant reader needs the teacher's help in finding books or magazines that deal with the reader's interests. He or she needs to be shown the delights and freedom that potentially come from unlocking the message of the book.

Sanford Patlak, a physical education instructor and coach, succeeds in involving students in reading all kinds of books on sports. He learns the students' reading levels and discusses their individual interests. From this large, carefully acquired and readily available supply, he recommends books appropriate in content and reading ease. When students return books, he manages to chat informally, a practice they carry over to their own interaction. His encouragement, guidance, and enthusiasm make reading continuous and habit-forming for some otherwise reluctant readers.[6]

Have you always been or ever been a wide reader? Did any teacher ever take the time to find out where you were on the reading scale or endeavor to interest you in some special book that that teacher treasured? It is not so difficult a project to adopt and it is loaded with benefits for the caring teacher who tries it. More than anything else it reveals to a student a caring attitude on your part and hence works toward encouraging your student in efforts to improve.

If you have not been an extensive reader, begin now. Your reluctance may have stemmed from the difficulties you have had with the printed word. Now that you are older and are focusing on material designed for early youth, some of the previous

[5]Ruth Strang, Constance M. McCullough, and Arthur E. Traxler, *The Improvement of Reading*, 4th ed. (New York: McGraw-Hill, 1967), p. 241.

[6]H. Alan Robinson and Ellen Lamar Thomas, eds., *Fusing Reading Skills and Content* (Newark, Del.: International Reading Association, 1969), pp. 81–88, and Ellen Lamar Thomas and H. Alan Robinson, *Improving Reading in Every Class*, abridged ed. (op. cit., pp. 301–307).

difficulty may have lessened. Enjoy it! Profit from it! Remember your experiences as you emerge from your previous alienation to print so that you can recapture your feelings and delights as you work with "reluctants" whom you discover in your classroom.

It has been said that there is more new vocabulary to learn in a first course in high school biology than in a first course in high school French. There is enough accuracy in that statement to give any teacher pause for thought. The plaguing part about assuming responsibility to change the situation is the lack of time: there just are not enough minutes in any period to attend to all the words you could possibly dwell upon. The solution of this problem for you will depend upon your ability to select the most salient, or significant, or prevalent, or key words in the context of your goal.

Improving Comprehension

You read in order to understand, regardless of what you read and whether you read for information or for pleasure. Some writers distinguish three levels of comprehension: (1) reading the lines, (2) reading between the lines, and (3) reading beyond the lines.[7] This is a useful analysis, which we shall follow in this module.

Reading the Lines

Reading the lines refers to the literal meaning of the material, clearly the most basic level, without which no other is possible. When we noted earlier that about one-third of secondary school students could not read their textbooks, we meant that they could not comprehend the material, even on this literal level. Whether the words, sentence structure, concepts, or any combination of these creates the problem of comprehension—or whether the students' training, ability, or background is involved—must be determined by the teacher. Through direct and indirect questions, the teacher informally diagnoses students' problems and checks the diagnosis by experimenting and observing responses. Then the teacher can use alternate texts, varied reading assignments, and different guide questions to assist students with this level. Prereading and postreading discussions are essential to provide stimulus and reassurance. Reading the lines is usually tested by questions such as: What is the author telling us? What evidence is the author giving for the statements? What does the sentence (paragraph, selection, chapter, book) mean?

Beginning teachers must be aware of the necessity to adjust their thinking to the array of abilities in any group that they address. They must avoid making the error sometimes made by teachers, referred to earlier, of assuming that all students are at grade level on all topics and with all skills. Although students may be on step in some areas, the chances of finding this situation as a regular routine are slim.

Textbooks present special difficulties for those students who may not be quite ready when particular topics arise for study. No one text can meet the reading needs of all students at the same time. Therefore it seems only sensible for each teacher to exercise good judgment in making assignments in the classroom.

Experienced teachers often resort to the use of a number of texts as well as differentiated assignments when suitable materials are on hand. Beginners will work toward this end and begin early the collection and cataloging of materials to facilitate an early attempt at following in this direction.

Reading Between the Lines

The second level, reading between the lines, is one in which the reader "recognizes the author's intent and purpose, interprets the thought, passes judgment on his statements, searches for and interprets clues . . . , distinguishes between fact and opinion, and separates his own ideas from the author's."[8] The reader also judges the merit of

---

[7]Strang, McCullough, and Traxler, op. cit., pp. 11–12.

[8]Ibid., p. 12.

the author's evidence or sources. This is obviously a mature level of reading, requiring thinking and experience. Reading between the lines involves answering such questions as: Why do you think the author wrote this? What does this mean to you? Do you agree or disagree with it? Why? Can you separate the facts from author opinions? Do the opinions seem to follow logically from the facts? Are you convinced by the author's facts, evidence, and judgments, or do you have opinions that are different? In what ways are your sources of evidence different from the author's?

The most prevalent error regarding the teaching of this skill appears to be in making assignments. Students are not prepared by the teacher to perform the task that is set for them. The purpose for the activity is not clearly established, and hence the reading is done without adequate orientation, without the proper motivation, and without, the stimulation that should accompany the start of an interesting activity. One activity (among a host of others) that has proved helpful calls for teachers to elicit predictions about the content to be read. Each student records what he or she thinks is about to happen or what he or she feels the main idea of the author will be or what the supporting data for the generalization of the chapter will be. After the reading the accuracy rate of each student is judged by contrasting their own predictions against the consensus of the class resulting from the study.

Reading Beyond the Lines

Reading beyond the lines "involves deriving implications, speculating about consequences, and drawing generalizations not stated by the author."[9] The process of analysis also leads to a new synthesis by the reader whose initiative and originality lead to new insights and to reflection on the significance of the ideas. This goal is perhaps the highest and most difficult to attain; yet, some aspects of it are within reach of the more mature students. Teachers can offer such questions as: If what the author says is true, what additional conclusions not mentioned in the selection can we draw? What other reactions can we or other people have to the same material, and why? If things had been different from ways mentioned by the author, how would this have changed our viewpoint? What changes can be expected to occur if things continue as the author predicts? What changes would you like to see, and why? How would they become possible? Why are these alternatives important? To whom? What new directions of thinking has this reading started for you?

Reading imaginative literature, especially drama and poetry, commonly involves reading beyond the lines.

Methods for Improving Comprehension

Devices that will help students improve comprehension include the following.

Provide Background Experience.   The same kinds of experience listed under Building Vocabulary apply here with great force. The nonreading experiences—trips, talks, films, recordings, and television—may help supply a background of concepts, familiar information, and prior learning that makes new learning easier and more enjoyable. "To achieve full comprehension, the reader must know not only the semantic and structural meaning, but he must have had some experience related to the author's ideas."[10] In practical classroom terms, this quotation signifies that the teacher must investigate the students' backgrounds—in life experience as well as in reading—before assigning new reading. Besides specific vocabulary, the students need a preview of the basic concepts to be encountered and assistance in recognizing the value and relevance of the new material. What themes they will meet and what importance they may have in their lives—as students, as adolescents, as citizens, as human beings—

---

[9]Ibid.

[10]Ibid., p. 11.

are a natural introduction. Questioning to elicit background and to establish direction and purpose is part of the teacher's contribution to the students' success in reading.[11]

Give Fully Developed Homework Assignments.   You may remember assignments of the type, "For tomorrow, read Chapter 14 and answer questions 1–4 at the end of the chapter." Whether the assignment was on the board or was dictated by the teacher, it was assumed that all or most students would read the material, write full answers to the questions, and be adequately prepared to participate in the next lesson. The teacher may have been relying exclusively on these assumptions for the next day's activities. In the light of knowledge of the reading process and of student needs and abilities, this kind of assignment should be evaluated.

No reason is given for doing the assignment. Presumably, the teacher knows the sequence, or this may be the next chapter in the text. Since no subject or topic is mentioned, no frame of reference is suggested. No stimulus to thinking—especially the problem-solving variety—no arousal of curiosity, no attention-grabbing or interest-generating activity appears. The only student experience tapped by this assignment is the knowledge that the routine requires simple obedience. If the material were interesting in itself, students might be self-motivated. Yet, only a few minutes of class time and some imagination are all that is needed to develop a dramatic, challenging, provocative, or stimulating start to the homework assignment. For a long-term assignment, such interest-stimulating motivation is indispensable. Similarly, assistance with major concepts, varied sources of material, and suitable problems for projects should be included when needed as integral parts of assignments and assignment making. Assignments should also anticipate problems in reading and provide for them in matters such as student interest, background or experience, new concepts, vocabulary, structure, and tone. Differentiated assignments can individualize learning. By imaginatively adopting the student's point of view and building assignments creatively from there, the teacher can really reach the learner. Attention paid to the manner of making assignments will pay dividends, indeed. Make sure the student knows why he or she should do the assignment, that is, how it fits into the ongoing study and what he or she can expect to be able to do with the new knowledge once gained. Intelligence of this sort can serve as a motivation for completion of the study and also as a self-testing procedure when the student tries to determine if the assignment has been completed.

Teach Students How to Use Their Textbooks.   In the subject-matter areas, some schools still use a single textbook for all students in the same grade level, although in recent years more schools have begun to vary the books according to ability levels of students and other considerations. Whether or not your school uses one or many textbooks, though, most of the time the books you must use have been selected by others. Having inherited these hand-me-downs, you will be obliged to determine how well they will serve your classes. Is the material organized in a way best suited to inform or satisfy the students? Is the presentation readable, comprehensible, and adequate? A teacher can say one textbook is better than another only when the teacher applies these questions to specific classes and students. Hence, some teachers use different textbooks for different groups within the same class. So long as areas of common learning are included, there is a basis for whole-class discussion. There may be other advantages. If different groups or individuals have undertaken supplementary work, different sources are essential.

Spending time on cooperative examination of textbooks pays dividends to the teacher and to the class. A review of the textbook prior to any assignment can include the following:

☐ The table of contents, for overall scope of treatment and organization as well as for detail.

---

[11]David L. Shepherd, "Reading in the Subject Areas," in *Reading for All*, ed. by Robert Karlin (Newark, Del.: International Reading Association, 1973), pp. 173–179.

☐ The preface, foreword, and introduction for statements of purpose and use as well as acknowledgment of assistance.

☐ The major parts, chapter headings, instructions, and summaries.

☐ Problems for solution or study.

☐ Special aids, such as illustrations, diagrams, footnotes, and reference materials.

☐ Appendices, glossaries, and indexes.

Because these features are underutilized by most students, you should plan to teach the parts of a book, making use of available textbooks. The skills needed for mastering this material appear later in this module in the discussion of flexibility. Planning a session on problems of the organization and features of textbooks is both natural and rewarding.

Utilize Study Guides and Questions.   A valuable device for the detailed reading of chapters is the study guide. In some respects, a study guide is an elaboration of the assignments, with questions as the core and suggested readings as aids to finding answers. Organized according to content—thematic, chronological, conceptual, logical—the guide should include both easy and difficult reading, basic and enriched materials. The questions set one or more of the following tasks for the student: (a) following directions; (b) grasping details or facts; (c) finding the main thought; (d) recognizing relationships of time, place, cause and effect, and motives and reactions; (e) drawing inferences or extracting implied meanings; (f) anticipating outcomes; (g) recognizing tone, mood, and intent; (h) drawing comparisons and contrasts; (i) making generalizations; and (j) evaluating or judging according to acceptable criteria.

As in all questioning, whether oral or written, used in class or in connection with outside reading, the teacher must make sure that

☐ Questions are definite and clear.

☐ Questions aim at recognizable, meaningful, and attainable goals.

☐ Questions are challenging and thought provoking.

☐ Questions are adapted to the background, abilities, needs, and interests of the students.

Formulating good questions is worth all the time and effort a teacher can give. Eventually, the students learn to develop their own questions—the stage at which purpose and direction reflect the concerns close to them (see Module 8, which treats questioning). It is the study guide, with its major questions, allowance for a selection of specific subdivisions, and provision for varied resources, including multiple readings, that is an ideal vehicle for individualizing education.

Use Directed Reading Lessons.   Sometimes, textbook material is difficult because of the nature of the topic, the age and relative inexperience of the students, the vocabulary and concepts, or some combination of these factors. The teacher may plan a directed reading lesson in which the techniques discussed in the Building Vocabulary and Improving Comprehension sections are combined with the experience of reading the selection in class. To conduct a directed reading lesson:

1. Prepare students by going over new vocabulary and ideas and by reviewing old material and experiences so that they can see the relationships between the new and the old.

2. Have students skim the selection and look at pictures, headings, and so on.

3. Help students formulate questions about the selection to be read, for instance:
   a. What should a student try to find out when studying the selection?
   b. Is this the kind of selection that must be studied carefully?
   c. How does this selection connect with other lessons studied in the past?

Three or four questions are quite enough. Too many questions may confuse and discourage the students. The questions should be student made rather than teacher made, if at all possible.

4. Let students read the selection to themselves.

5. Discuss the reading. By using questions, help them see the relationships among the facts presented and also relationships to what has been learned previously.

Teaching How to Study

Writers who for many years have observed and experimented with students' study habits have generally agreed on the main features of efficient study skills. The list of admonitions about how to study, which has resulted from their efforts, however, is as long as your arm. It contains almost as many different entries as the number of researchers who have looked into the process of study. The most widely circulated list contains suggestions such as the following:

☐ Establish a study routine for yourself. Make a schedule indicating time and place, and on cue assume your study position in the study environment.

☐ Start working immediately. Have your study materials all ready to go before you start your routine.

☐ Space your learning prudently. Take short breaks when fatigue sets in or your attention begins to stray.

☐ Study actively. React to your reading. Recite orally to yourself.

☐ Vary your study technique to suit the subject you are studying and the purpose of your study.

☐ Avoid rote memorization. Strive instead for comprehension, and put recall into your own words.

☐ Put the brief notes that you write into your own words. Avoid rewriting the text.

One group of researchers distilled its findings until it emerged with a system made up of six basic steps. The researchers named it the PQ4R system. "PQ4R is a package of techniques that should be effective in improving the reading of chapter-length materials when the student's purpose is thorough understanding of the content. . . . The steps in the procedure are Preview, Question, Read, Reflect, Recite, and Review."[12] Studies have shown that even top honors students benefit from studying and using these techniques. Since study skills are usually the haphazard result of trial and error, all students need help. Expository, informational materials in any subject area can be the basis for "how to study" sessions, with steps being worked on separately before the total approach is attempted. Let us examine each of the steps more closely.

Preview

This step provides for an overview or survey of the material: "How does an author help you learn in just minutes what a chapter will contain? How can you make the best use of these clues? What are the advantages in making an advance survey?" Brief practice under teacher guidance can help make this step automatic. Experience with the parts of a textbook can serve as a useful preliminary. Headlines, subtitles, introductory paragraphs, and summaries are invaluable for a picture of overall content. Questions that students prepare independently—mentally at least—may touch on their own background, their expectations, the type of material, its relative difficulty, the

---

[12]Thomas and Robinson, op. cit., p. 70. The authors acknowledge their debt to Francis P. Robinson, Donald E. P. Smith, and Thomas F. Stanton. (This procedure is a refinement of the *SQ3R*. In SQ3R the steps are Survey, Question, Read, Recite, and Review. They correspond closely to the PQ4R steps—Preview, Question, Read, Reflect, Recite, and Review.)

sequence and structure of presentation, and the author's purpose and main ideas. Since different subject areas have special features, some flexibility is needed, but all study materials should be treated with this overview, survey approach. The 5 minutes spent previewing an easy chapter or the 15 minutes spent on a difficult one are well spent. They provide the student with "an accurate map of the rugged terrain."

QUESTION

As in all reading comprehension, this is the crucial step. Ways of helping students acquire this skill include turning headlines into questions; formulating main ideas as questions; searching for deeper, more probing questions than the surface ones; and pretending to be the teacher and asking questions that might be used in class or on examinations. Anticipating possible answers is frequently helpful in both the actual reading and in leading to more and deeper questions.

Read and Reflect

When students start with questions, they must read to find answers. This involves looking for meaning with full attention and at a speed adapted to the difficulty of the passage, sometimes pausing completely. The tasks enumerated in the section on textbooks cover the kind of reading vital to effective study. All aspects of reading the lines, reading between the lines, and reading beyond the lines are important. Reflecting is not a separate step but an essential component of the reading step. Since study is more than memorization and more than preparing for a class discussion or a test, this emphasis makes information "the *foundation* for higher-level thought."[13] Recognizing how important and useful the knowledge is, the student becomes a "studier," a thinker rather than a repository of facts.

RECITE

This step is really a self-reciting operation. No matter how many times a student rereads a difficult chapter or passage, that student does not understand until able to answer in his or her own words the question: What have I read here? Some experts advise looking away from the printed material or covering it, at least half the time. One suggestion to students from Thomas and Robinson: " 'See it! Say it! Hear it! Draw or write it!' is a four-way reinforcement. The variety itself helps you recall. The change of pace—eyes, voice, ears, pencil—keeps you alert and increases absorption."[14] Through this technique, instead of a semipassive memorization, the student turns half-learned to fully learned material. The student selects because the student understands what is important. Only as an aid does the student make notes, choosing one or more of the marking and note-making techniques: marginal lines, underlining, see-through coloring, marginal mininotes, numerals, asterisks, question marks, check marks, capsule summaries, quick outlines in shorthand, notebook jottings, and others. Whatever keeps the student mentally active and not copying absentmindedly or semiautomatically may be helpful. If to this note making the student adds the processes of his or her own reflections, interpretations, evaluations, and brainstorming, the student is making full and meaningful use of the self-reciting step. Since developing good habits in this area requires work and students may have acquired such ineffective methods as repeated rereading and excessive underlining, the teacher must teach this step directly and provide sufficient practice.

REVIEW

Think of your own experiences with forgetting, or perhaps consult a psychology textbook with material on short-term memory, long-term memory, retention, and recall. Whatever shape the curve of forgetting takes, we all personally experience the decay of learning. To counteract some of this, we reread both immediately after completing

---

[13]Ibid., p. 79.

[14]Ibid., p. 94.

a chapter and after a period of time. Review helps us regain a broad, overall view of the chapter and helps us check on important details. Spacing review over a day or a longer period dramatically increases retention, yet requires shorter times for each successive rereading. Only this arrangement makes "quick review" an effective, meaningful exercise.

In the beginning of the year, it is a useful practice to walk your students through a study session or two. Begin by selecting a section in your text on which to focus. Having preread the section yourself, determine just what you would want your students to learn from their study of it. Note the caliber of the words used in the text and mark for further explanation or attention those words that might prove difficult for various groups of students in your class.

When your exploration has been completed, set the stage for the work of your students. Lead them to see how the section you intend to start will fit into the scheme of learning they have been following. Announce the purposes for their reading and give some direction to their quest. Have them skim through the section, looking at the pictures, paragraph headings, and so on. Supplying a study guide at the outset that tells the student what to do and how to do it will be a great boon for all, but especially for slower students.

The post-reading discussion of the section should reveal many things to you about the quality of reading your students are capable of and the nature of some of the difficulties that will hinder their future study efforts. You should be able to develop a clearer picture of those most ready for independent study and those still needing some kind of crutch, and you should discover what kinds of problems are most disconcerting to those who have difficulties in performance. Conclusions about differentiating future assignments are often the result of this kind of end analysis of study. Sessions of this sort should be repeated frequently throughout a semester as you pass from one unit to the next. Your judgment about the difficulties inherent in upcoming lessons or units should be juxtaposed with your knowledge of the abilities of the various students in your class to help determine the frequency and nature of future supervised study periods. At some point in the year it may be necessary for you to conduct 10-minute supervised periods such as this on almost a daily basis until you are sure that your students have learned how to get where they want to go.

Supervising Study

Since studying is an individual activity, some teachers neglect to plan for it in class, the library, laboratory, or resource center. Yet that is the only way to supervise it. On the basis of observation of students' habits, the teacher recognizes their individual needs, provides appropriate materials and assignments, offers help with questions and procedures, checks on understanding, and evaluates progress. The time spent on this kind of individualized, supervised study will be a major contribution to students' reading skills and their learning.

Developing Flexibility in Reading

Look through a typical page of a textbook in social studies, science, mathematics, English, business education, music, or a foreign language. You will recognize the need for building vocabulary and improving comprehension. Consider the students as they move from one classroom to another or undertake homework assignments. Besides adjusting to diverse content, they must also shift gears in their rate and style of reading. In these, the teacher must help both by direct teaching and by providing varied practice. Obviously, textbooks cannot be read as though they were light fiction; yet, some people seem fascinated with record-breaking reading speeds. Since speed reading is definitely not for most schoolwork, the question should be: In what ways and for what purposes should reading speeds be varied?

Scanning

Scanning, the most rapid reading method, is used to locate specific items of information: a name, an address, a date, a phrase. Used with directories, dictionaries, indexes, tables, maps, and columns, this form of search involves having an image or word clearly in mind, so that an entire body of material can be scanned or reviewed quickly without the reader having to understand or to perceive all the words. Sometimes the single words or facts for which the reader is looking seem to pop out of the context. Exercises in any subject can be easily devised by the teacher. Use the simple experience involving class examination of a textbook. Since students must consult many resources quite rapidly, this skill is essential.

Good readers will naturally adapt their reading approach to the type of reading they are asked to do and the purpose they have in mind. Poorer readers tend to read everything in the same fashion—slowly, laboriously, inefficiently. Teachers must supply specific practice and instruction if they hope that such students will learn how to vary their rate.

Skimming

Skimming, another rapid form of reading, is used to survey the content of a book, chapter, or article for such purposes as getting the gist of the material, its general structure or plan, or the facts bearing on a particular problem. The eyes seem to float down the page, lighting on main ideas or significant phrases or words. Besides its usefulness as a rather close sampling during initial reading, skimming is also useful for quick review. The preview step in the study-skills procedure lends itself to skimming. Teacher-created exercises for finding answers to questions about main points are a typical use of this technique.

Recreational or Light Reading

Recreational or light reading is the fairly rapid form of reading you use when the material is easy or fast-moving and the main purpose is entertainment or passing the time pleasantly. Readers have no problem recognizing the type of material or situation for which this technique is appropriate. Most frequently this category includes the reading of narrative, biographical, or journalistic material. The humorous and the sentimental also fall within its range.

Self-starters will have no difficulty in your class with this kind of reading. All others, though, will need your guidance, encouragement, enthusiasm, participation, and leadership. Lacking assurance about what to read and, perhaps, unsure of their power in reading, some students do not know where to begin. Like adults, though, who hear about and then read best-sellers for pleasure, students will try to get on the bandwagon that has been set rolling by an interesting or respected teacher. "Being-in-the-know" will form the motivation for some students who want to be able to respond to teachers' queries about books that were highlighted in class.

For other students, reading recommended books will supply topics for conversation with a teacher they admire and like. Some adolescents are fearful of conversation with adults, especially teachers, because they are unsure about what topics to address. For many students, a teacher who is willing to talk about the reading they have done is a delightful person. Without such a person around, they have almost nothing to do with the reading they have done and almost no reason for spending time doing it.

Close Reading of Imaginative Literature

Close reading of imaginative literature is sometimes confused with recreational or light reading, both traditionally lumped together as Reading or Literature and assigned by the English or language teacher. Although enjoyment remains the major aim, the more artistic or more complex material requires a mature response, depending on "imaginative entry" into fiction, drama, or poetry.[15] Among other tasks, close reading develops

---

[15] Dwight L. Burton, "Teaching Students to Read Imaginative Literature," in *Teaching English in Today's High Schools*, ed. by Dwight L. Burton and John S. Simmons (New York: Holt, Rinehart and Winston, 1970), pp. 90–105.

perception of meaning, interpretation of character motivation and interaction, and evaluation of structure and effect. Learning to read better is a lifelong activity, since the fusion of emotional and intellectual responses and the cultivation of sensitivity and insight remain a challenge to even the most highly skilled readers. Special problems are perhaps best handled by English and language teachers. Ideally, the abilities involved should become the property of all students.

Critical Reading

Critical reading is another example of the slow, careful reading that requires mature cognitive processes. Since its main purpose is developing independent thinking and skills in analysis and judgment, the process has numerous components. The reader first has to recognize what the author is saying. Then the reader weighs the evidence for reliability, accuracy, and representativeness; tries to separate opinion from fact; and identifies the viewpoints and biases of the writer. In analyzing the material, the reader checks the author's assumptions and logic and traces the relationship between the evidence, assumptions, and conclusions. The critical reader detects fallacies and recognizes the way the author intends the reader to draw inferences. The reader is alert to propaganda devices or emotional appeals. Sensitive to tone, style, and diction, the reader is critical in the most alert and positive way. Through reading experiences in the subject-matter areas, the student meets the challenge of the open marketplace of ideas and grows in intellectual maturity.

Some Special Aspects of Reading

Research

No new reading skills or rates are needed for research, but it does require an effective use of scanning, skimming, study, and critical reading.

Problem Solving

This involves a combination of skills and rates similar to reference work. It may be required in almost any subject-matter area. In science, mathematics, and social studies it may be especially necessary to focus on a problem, separate the relevant from the irrelevant, make the problem manageable, attack it with appropriate resources and processes, work out the pattern of explanation, and present the solution. Most careful reading and rereading are essential at every stage.

Reading Maps, Graphs, Charts, Tables, Diagrams, and Illustrations

A procedure to use when dealing with these aids to learning is to insist upon the reading by the students of the title and any legend that is attached. Not reading these appears to be the prime stumbling-block in students' quest for understanding the information contained in such visuals. Preparation for this step will, of course, include the teaching of such concepts as latitude and longitude, scale, finding directions, reading elevations, recognizing key symbols, and the like. Student focus can be enhanced by supplying pointed questions that will give them some reason to examine the aid and track down the information requested. For example: How many inches represent a hundred miles on this map? What two countries border Spain? How many state parks are shown? Where is Cleveland in relation to Cincinnati? How many miles is Chicago from Denver?

Graphs and tables will have to be taught in a similar basic way. Students tend to skip devices of this sort because they do not know how to use them. Demonstrations by you on the vast amount of information that can be gleaned from such devices will help some to lay the groundwork. Thereafter, until conviction sets in, motivation to attend to such data should be supplied by your pointed questions to which students must search for answers.

Readability Formulas

As a rule none of these procedures will be effective unless the reading level of the textbook matches the reading level of the students. Use a technique such as the Dale-

Chall readability formula or the Fry readability graph to estimate the grade level of the text. To use these formulas is not difficult. For instance, the procedure for the Fry technique is to:

1. Determine the average number of syllables in three 100-word selections taken one from the beginning, one from the middle, and one from the ending parts of the book.

2. Determine the average number of sentences in the three 100-word selections.

3. Plot the two values on the Fry readability graph (Figure 11.1). Their intersection will give you an estimate of the text's reading level at the 50 percent to 75 percent comprehension level.[16]

Practice use of the Fry readability graph by doing Exercise 11.1.

FIGURE 11.1   Fry Readability Graph

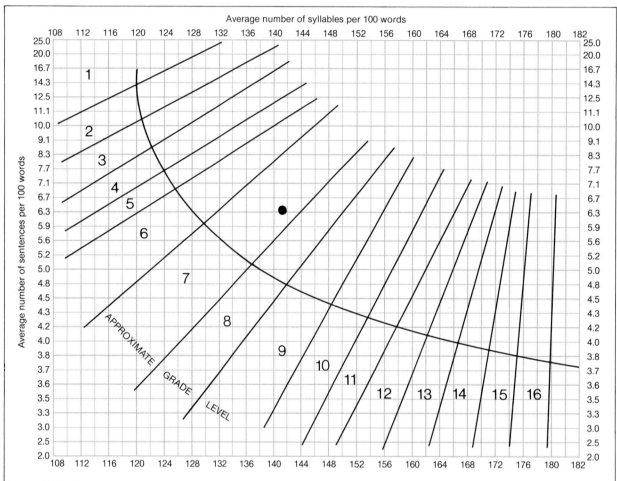

DIRECTIONS:
Randomly select 3 one hundred word passages from a book or an article. Plot average number of syllables and average number of sentences per 100 words on graph to determine the grade level of the material. Choose more passages per book if great variability is observed and conclude that the book has uneven readability. Few books will fall in gray area but when they do grade level scores are invalid.

Count proper nouns, numerals, and initializations as words. Count a syllable for each symbol. For example, "1945" is 1 word and 4 syllables and "IRA" is 1 word and 3 syllables.

EXAMPLE:	SYLLABLES	SENTENCES	
1st Hundred Words	124	6.6	
2nd Hundred Words	141	5.5	
3rd Hundred Words	158	6.8	
AVERAGE	141	6.3	READABILITY 7th GRADE (see dot plotted on graph)

---

[16]Edward Fry, "A Readability Formula That Saves Time," *Journal of Reading* (April 1968), 11:587.

EXERCISE 11.1   PRACTICE COMPUTATION OF READING LEVEL USING THE FRY FORMULA
A Self-Check Exercise

For a text in which you find that three 100-syllable passages contain 130, 145, and 149 words and 7, 9, and 11 sentences, respectively, what would be the reading level?

Answer Key

Your answer should be grade 6, computed in this way:

$$\frac{130 + 145 + 149}{3} = \frac{424}{3} = 141 \text{ syllables}$$

$$\frac{7 + 9 + 11}{3} = \frac{27}{3} = 9 \text{ sentences}$$

By plotting 141 and 9 on the graph, you find that the intersection of the two points falls in the area designated as approximately grade level 6. Presumably, then, the book would be suitable for most sixth-graders.

Since these formulas give only the technical reading level of the book, you will have to interpret the results by subjectively estimating the conceptual reading level of the work. To do so, consider your students' experience with the subject, the number of new ideas introduced, the abstraction of the ideas, and the author's external and internal clues. Then raise or lower the estimated level of difficulty.

To tell how well your students can read the text, use the Cloze technique, or an informal reading inventory. The Cloze technique that was first described by Bormuth in 1968 has since appeared in a number of versions.[17] From your textbook select several typical passages so that you will have a total of 400 to 415 words or so. Delete every eighth word in the passage except for the words in the first and last sentences, proper names, numbers, and initial words in sentences. It will be helpful if you eliminate 50 words. Duplicate the passages with 10 to 15 space blanks replacing the eliminated words. Pass out these "mutilated" readings to the students. Ask them to fill in the blanks with the most appropriate words they can think of. Collect the papers. Score them by counting all the words that are the exact words in the original text and by dividing the number of correct responses by the number of possibles.[18] (Fifty blanks makes this division easy.)

$$\text{Score} = \frac{\text{Number of correct responses}}{\text{Number of possibles}}$$

You can assume that pupils who score better than 50 percent can read the book quite well, students who score between 40 and 50 percent can read the book at the instructional level, and pupils who score below 40 percent will probably find the book frustrating.

To conduct a silent reading inventory, ask the students to read four or five pages of the text, and then give a 10-item quiz on what they have read. You can consider the text too difficult for any student who scores less than 70 percent on the quiz. Similarly, to conduct an oral reading inventory, have the student read a 100-word passage. The text is too difficult for any student who stumbles over and misses more than 5 percent of the words.[19]

Problem Readers

Types of Problem Readers

All teachers should know about the different kinds of problem readers to recognize those who can be helped in regular classes and those who need special treatment. Readers have numerous individual differences, but almost all can be helped to improve. Therefore, subject matter teachers along with reading specialists and English teachers share the responsibility for helping problem readers.

Slow Learners. Slow readers may be slow learners who, because of a below-average rate of maturation, need relatively easy materials with which they can cope. These materials should contain the basic or common learnings agreed upon as essential to the subject. Instruction should feature spaced repetition and adequate explanation. Work should be planned for small groups or individuals who need encouragement. Slow learners respond to teachers who show patience and understanding. Students can overcome the social or emotional problems acquired as a result, perhaps, of unfavorable comments by previous teachers or of their recognition that other students work on more difficult material.

---

[17]J. Bormuth, "The Cloze Readability Procedure," *Elementary English* (April 1968), 45:429–436.

[18]Some persons recommend that only exact words be counted; others would allow exact synonyms. We suggest that you not count synonyms or verbs of different tense. *See* N. McKenna, "Synonymic Versus Verbatim Scoring of the Cloze Procedure," *Journal of Reading* (November 1976) 20:141–143.

[19]*See* M. S. Johnson and R. A. Kress, *Informal Reading Inventories* (Newark, Del.: International Reading Association, 1965).

Underachievers. Able readers can work below their capacity for some reason. Building interests is fundamental and can be done by connecting reading with activities in which they are successful. Within the subject-matter area, practice in skills that are inadequately developed can move them from present levels to higher levels of performance. Variety of materials (textbooks, supplementary resources, homework assignments, and individualized projects) plus encouragement can help build their confidence and achievement. Such readers can recognize their problems, set their own purposes, and increase their voluntary reading.

Culturally Different Readers. Culturally different, economically impoverished, or educationally disadvantaged readers may have difficulty because of language or language variety differences, home or environmental conditions, or previous educational experiences. Since most school materials are sources of difficulty to these students, special programs offer the best remedy. To be sure, building vocabulary, improving comprehension, and developing flexibility are the same reading objectives as for all readers, but special knowledge, training, and expertise are needed for effective teaching of these students. The subject-matter teacher should work with the reading specialist in order to outline the concepts, which should be handled sequentially, and to identify materials that will stimulate progress by these students.

Bright-but-Bored Readers. Although bright or gifted students may not be thought of as problem readers, many have poor reading and study habits. Frequently, they need help overcoming boredom or distraction by being offered materials that are varied, absorbing, intellectually challenging, and rewarding. The rapid readers can benefit from instruction in study skills, from critical and imaginative reading that requires interpretation and evaluation, and from creative reading. Encouraging them to plan a balanced program with reading, social experiences, outdoor and recreational activities, and unscheduled time helps them place their reading progress in a reasonable perspective and enables them to reach a higher level of achievement.

Learning-Disabled Readers. Students with emotional, visual, auditory, and neurological problems require individual diagnosis and treatment. Teachers should be alert to the need to identify such students and to guide them to those specialists who can provide help.

Helping Problem Readers

Often the difficulty with problem readers is not so much that they cannot read as that they will not read. If you can stimulate these students to want to read, some of your problems will be solved. Try to sell reading in your subject to them. Do everything you can to make reading assignments exciting and interesting. Read interesting assignments to them. Discuss the reading with them. Provide variety.

Many students can read much better than their class performance and their opinions of themselves indicate. Moreover, they may know much more about the subject than you realize or they think they do. Try to discover and harness these abilities and knowledge. Utilize discussions in which they tell of their own experiences. Initiate brainstorming sessions in which students tell you as many words about the topic to be studied as they can think of. Ask students to predict what the author will say about the topic, and then let them read the selection to see if they were right. Provide study guides that show students what to look for in the assignment before they start reading. In the guide use easy recognition questions. The more successes you can provide the students, the sooner they will learn to read on their own.

Show students how! Teach the vocabulary and how to decipher the meaning of new words. Show them how to locate the main ideas and supporting ideas in their reading. Demonstrate how to identify and use the author's organization pattern.

In short, arouse their interests, encourage them, and show them how.

Writing Across the Curriculum

Regardless of the subject or grade level you teach, you must be interested in helping your students develop their skills in reading and in writing. This is especially the case for teachers of middle schools, where "writing across the curriculum" has received particular attention since the 1986 publication of *The Writing Report Card*. Since that report, increased attention has been given to the encouragement of all teachers to participate in helping students develop their writing and reading skills. In all subject areas—and with students of all ability levels—students are encouraged to write and teachers are encouraged to diagnose and prescribe based on student writing errors. Many schools have cross-curriculum reading and writing programs that are coordinated by the English departments. *The Writing Report Card* reported that results of a coordinated effort are superior to traditional writing sequences in workbooks and front-of-the-room English or language-arts teaching, and that students who use the process techniques of planning, revising, and editing produce superior written products.

Word processors and computers with word-processing programs have also proved helpful. With these aids, students can make extensive revisions without copying material by hand. This freedom from hand copying allows students to focus on the skill of revising and not on the labor of copying and recopying by hand. With this freedom, students can concentrate on responding to instruction.

SUMMARY

This module attempts to show you how to improve your own reading skills, but primarily how to help students learn to read, study, and write more effectively. After all, everyone who teaches must be a teacher of reading, writing, and study skills.

Reading is an active process in which people attempt to extract ideas, concepts, thoughts, or images from the pattern of words set forth on the printed page. The reader's major goal is always to understand and enlarge contexts. It is to this end that all must direct their reading skills and activities. To help students become proficient, you as the teacher must be able to help them with each of the major subdivisions of reading skills and activities: building vocabulary, improving comprehension, and developing flexibility.

To build students' vocabulary it is recommended that you: (1) provide students with many experiences, (2) encourage wide reading, and (3) teach vocabulary directly. Direct teaching of vocabulary requires you to: (1) provide appropriate contexts, (2) teach the key or "stopper" words, (3) utilize word attack devices, (4) encourage and teach the use of the dictionary, and (5) utilize word slips or vocabulary notebooks.

There seem to be three levels of comprehension: reading the lines, reading between the lines, and reading beyond the lines. To help students learn to read at the highest level, you should: (1) provide background experience, (2) give fully developed homework assignments, (3) teach students how to use their textbooks, (4) utilize study guides and questions, (5) use directed reading lessons, and (6) teach students how to study by the PQ4R method (Preview, Question, Read, Reflect, Recite, and Review).

To develop flexibility in their reading, you should teach students to adjust their speed and style of reading to their reading objectives and the type of material to be read. Some reading should be scanned, some skimmed, some read lightly, some read closely, some studied, and some read critically. Frequently, a combination of methods is desirable or necessary.

You will find that problem readers in your classes will include slow learners; underachievers; culturally, economically, or educationally disadvantaged students; bright students who do not read as well as they should; and students with learning disabilities. Each of these should be treated in a special way in order to give them optimum help.

The following is a summary of guidelines for the things middle and secondary school teachers can consider to improve students' skills in reading, writing, and studying:

1. Use essay test items, homework, and in-class assignments that require expository writing. Read what students write and write your own positive and prescriptive comments on their papers.

2. Encourage students to reread material; use oral readings in the classroom.

3. Provide instruction in word meaning. Studies show that students who receive instruction in word meanings have greater mastery of those meanings than those who receive no instruction in word meaning.[20] Teach meanings about the difficult words in selections before students read the selection: this increases comprehension of that selection.[21]

4. Plan activities before reading a selection to activate students' background knowledge. The relationship between background knowledge and comprehension is positive. The more background knowledge a reader has—that is, related to the text—the greater the comprehension of the text.[22]

5. Provide direct instruction in helping students identify main ideas in text material where the ideas appear in different places in the paragraphs. Help students infer main ideas when the ideas are not stated directly or clearly. In grades five and six, students seem to be able to select main ideas from paragraphs on worksheets, but they often have difficulty in transferring this skill to find main ideas in text materials.[23] When students are working in cooperative learning groups they can participate in different activities, such as: select the topic for a paragraph, select the main idea from several choices given, select main ideas from text materials. Students may work at a task suitable to their abilities. They may locate the main idea at the beginning, middle, or end of a paragraph taken from a text; or determine that the main idea is not stated and should be inferred from selected paragraphs; or determine which details from a paragraph support some information from the main idea; or write the details on a graphic web with the main idea recorded in the center of the web and record the details on strands that radiate out from the center of the web.[24]

6. Model the process of making inferences with materials on the students' instructional reading levels. The ability to make inferences is one of the skills that differentiates good readers from poor readers. As part of your direct instruction, you will need to integrate a student's prior knowledge with the text before reading the material and ask questions that call for information inferred by the student.[25]

7. Teach critical reading skills to all—including disadvantaged and below-grade-level readers. Disadvantaged students in middle school grades were given instruction in critical reading, and after the instruction, were just as capable of reading critically as their advantaged peers.[26]

---

[20]Isabel L. Beck et al., "Effects of Long-Term Vocabulary Instruction on Lexical Access and Reading Comprehension," *Journal of Educational Psychology* 74(3):506–521 (Spring 1982).

[21]Edward K. Kaneenui et al., "Effects of Text Construction and Instructional Procedures for Teaching Word Meanings on Comprehension and Recall," *Reading Research Quarterly* 17(2):367–388 (Winter 1982).

[22]R. Scott Baldwin et al., "Effects of Topic Interest and Prior Knowledge on Reading Comprehension," *Reading Research Quarterly* 20(4):497–508 (Spring 1985).

[23]Barbara Taylor et al., "A Comparison of Students' Ability to Read for Main Ideas in Social Studies Textbooks and to Complete Main Idea Worksheets," *Reading World* 24(1):10–15 (Fall 1985).

[24]James F. Baumann, "Children's Ability to Comprehend Main Ideas in Content Textbook Reading," *Reading World* 2(2):322–331 (Spring 1983).

[25]Betty C. Holmes, "A Confirmation Strategy for Improving Poor Readers' Ability to Answer Inferential Questions," *The Reading Teacher* 37(1):144–148 (October 1983).

[26]Barbara K. Clark and Barbara C. Palmer, "Reading and the Disadvantaged: Some Myths and Facts," *Reading World* 21(10):208–212 (Fall 1982).

8. Encourage students to make mental images before they read. Studies show that visualization training does increase the comprehension of some students.[27]

9. Plan instruction in outlining and in note taking to help increase students' mastery over content material. Students who outline increase their learning[28] and those who take notes increase their comprehension and recall of materials.[29]

10. Promote a writing and reading interaction in the classroom, for these are processes that complement each other. The reading comprehension of good writers is better than that of average writers, and better writers do more free reading than those with lesser writing ability.[30] Students of middle school grades who receive training in writing summaries have greater comprehension and retention when they apply that skill as they read.[31]

SUGGESTED READING

Anderson, R., et al. *Becoming a Nation of Readers: The Report of the Commission on Reading.* Urbana, IL: Center for the Study of Reading; Washington, DC: National Academy of Education, 1985.

Barr, R., and Sadow, M. *Reading Diagnosis for Teachers.* 2nd ed. White Plains, NY: Longman, 1990.

Barr, R., et al. (eds.) *Handbook of Reading Research, Volume II.* White Plains, NY: Longman, 1991.

Bragstad, B. J., and Stumpf, S. M. *Study Skills and Motivation: A Guidebook for Teaching,* 2nd ed. Boston: Allyn & Bacon, 1987.

Brown, R. G. *Schools of Thought.* San Francisco: Jossey-Bass, 1991.

Carr, E., et al. "Using Cloze for Inference Training with Expository Text." *The Reading Teacher* 42(6):380–385 (February 1989).

Carroll, J. B. "The National Assessments in Reading: Are We Misreading the Findings?" *Phi Delta Kappan* 68(6):424–430 (February 1987).

Devine, T. G. *Teaching Study Skills: A Guide for Teachers.* 2nd ed. Boston: Allyn & Bacon, 1987.

Heller, M. F. *Reading-Writing Connections.* White Plains, NY: Longman, 1991.

Kellough, R. D., and Roberts, P. L. *A Resource Guide for Elementary School Teaching: Planning for Competence,* 2nd ed. Chapter 11. New York: Macmillan, 1991.

Moore, D. W., and Moore, S. A. *Developing Readers and Writers in the Content Areas: K–12.* White Plains, NY: Longman, 1986.

Purvis, A. C., and Niles, O. *Becoming Readers in a Complex Society.* Chicago: National Society for the Study of Education, University of Chicago Press, 1984.

Tonjes, M. J. *Secondary Reading, Writing, and Learning.* Boston: Allyn and Bacon, 1991.

Weinstein, C. E., and Mager, R. E. "The Teacher of Learning Strategies," in Merlin C. Wittrock, ed., *Handbook of Research on Teaching,* 3d ed. New York: Macmillan, 1986.

---

[27]Robert J. Tierney and Jones W. Cunningham, "Research on Teaching Reading Comprehension." In *Handbook of Reading Research,* ed. by David Pearson (New York: Longman, 1984).

[28]Wayne H. Slater, "Teaching Expository Text Structure with Structural Organizers," *Journal of Reading* 28(8):712–718 (May 1985).

[29]Thomas H. Estes and Herbert C. Richards, "Habits of Study and Test Performance," *Journal of Reading Behavior* 17(1):1–13 (Fall 1985).

[30]Timothy Shanahan, "The Impact of Writing Instruction on Learning to Read," *Reading World* 19(3):357–368 (Spring 1980).

[31]Karen D'Angelo Bromley, "Precise Writing and Outlining Enhance Content Learning," *The Reading Teacher* 38(4):406–411 (January 1985).

POSTTEST

Short Answer   In the following test, select from each group of four statements the one that is most accurate. State the reasons you believe your choice is best. Then explain the shortcomings or inadequacies of the other statements.

1. a. Reading is most important for impressing people socially.
   b. Reading is essential to success in every subject-matter area, except strictly physical activities.
   c. Reading is valuable because it may help in getting better jobs in later life.
   d. Reading is the major means for controlling the environment.

   _____
   _____
   _____
   _____
   _____
   _____

2. a. Reading is the responsibility of the English teacher.
   b. Reading can be developed only by reading specialists.
   c. All subject-matter teachers are responsible for reading improvement.
   d. Reading skills cannot be taught because they depend mainly on the native ability of students.

   _____
   _____
   _____
   _____
   _____
   _____

3. a. Repeated drill on graded word lists is the best way to learn new vocabulary.
   b. Acquiring vocabulary depends mainly on understanding the contexts in which words appear.
   c. Key words should first of all be looked up in a dictionary.
   d. The meaning of words is more clearly explained by roots, prefixes, and suffixes than by their use in sentences.

   _____
   _____
   _____
   _____
   _____

4. a. Unlike other reading, textbook mastery mainly involves "reading the lines" and memorizing them.
   b. All textbooks are equally satisfactory for learning study skills.
   c. When a school uses a single textbook for each grade, all students should be expected to learn the same content.
   d. A variety of textbooks should be used to allow for individual differences among students.

   _____
   _____

_____

_____   _____

_____

_____

5. a. If a teacher wants to discuss a subject in class the next day, every student has
      to do the same homework assignment.
   b. Homework assignments should be varied according to the abilities of students.
   c. Long homework assignments are a good way to make students read rapidly.
   d. Good homework assignments do not have to involve student interests.

_____

_____

_____

_____

_____

6. a. Reading with numerous questions in mind is the best way to check on compre-
      hension.
   b. Questions to guarantee comprehension should keep close to the literal meaning
      of the reading material.
   c. The most helpful questions are those that appear at the end of each chapter in
      a book.
   d. Questions in study guides are needed mainly by the slowest students.

_____

_____

_____

_____

7. a. Almost all students need help in developing effective study skills.
   b. As long as students pass tests, we can assume that they know how to study.
   c. Study skills develop naturally over a period of time as a student matures.
   d. All the steps in studying can be mastered with one good explanation by the
      teacher.

_____

_____

_____

_____

8. a. Scanning means reading very carefully to seek out each important word.
   b. Scanning is reading quickly with the mind set on finding specific information,
      such as a date, a formula, or any important fact.
   c. Scanning is very quick reading that helps the reader decide whether to reread
      the material more carefully.
   d. Scanning is done by sweeping the eyes back and forth over the words to test
      speed or eye movements.

_____

_____

_____

_____

_____

_____

9. a. Skimming involves looking for phrases to underline or to memorize.
   b. Skimming means reading very quickly to pick out a word or idea here and there.
   c. Skimming allows for reading every other sentence.
   d. Skimming uses "floating down" the page to find main ideas and key phrases.

_____

_____

_____

_____

_____

10. a. Critical reading means judging how much fact and how much opinion an author has included, how much bias and how much fairness the author shows.
    b. Critical reading involves deciding whether an author's style is appropriate to the material.
    c. Critical reading refers to judging whether one writer or one book is better than another.
    d. Critical reading means using personal taste to decide what the student would like to read and report on.

_____

_____

_____

_____

_____

_____

11. a. Maps, charts, graphs, tables, and illustrations are included to help people who cannot read the text.
    b. Maps and other graphic aids are used to decorate pages so that they do not have only straight text.
    c. Maps and other graphic aids usually include material that is not in the text.
    d. Maps and other graphic aids are usually important additions to the visual and conceptual content of a text.

_____

_____

_____

_____

12. a. Except for a few special cases, most people read as well as they are able.
    b. Every reader can learn to become a better reader by applying interest and effort.
    c. Because we do a great deal of reading to succeed in school or to get along in life, we automatically learn to become better readers.
    d. By continuing to increase our reading rate and the variety of reading material we become better readers.

_____

_____

_____

_____

_____

_____

13. a. A student who scores 60 percent on a silent reading inventory can be considered a capable reader.
    b. A student who stumbles on no more than 10 percent of the words in an oral reading inventory can be considered a capable reader.
    c. A student who scores better than 60 percent on a Cloze procedure can be considered a capable reader.
    d. A student who scores better than 145 on the Fry chart is a capable reader.

_____

_____

_____

_____

_____

14. a. To help slow readers, use very challenging materials.
    b. To help slow readers, concentrate on intensive drill.
    c. To help slow readers, feature spaced repetition and adequate explanation.
    d. To help slow readers, concentrate on critical reading and problem solving.

_____

_____

_____

_____

_____

15. a. When reading maps or charts, one should first preview the materials to ascertain their general nature and relevance to other material.
    b. When dealing with underachieving readers, it is usually best to concentrate on a single textbook approach.
    c. When building a study guide for slow readers, you should emphasize probing questions.
    d. When teaching students research skills, you should abandon the PQ4R approach and substitute the SQ3R approach.

_____

_____

_____

_____

_____

MODULE 12
Providing for Individual Differences

Need for a Variety of Materials

Teaching Homogeneously Grouped Classes

The Academically Talented

The Academically Slow

Guidelines for Teaching Students Who Indicate Willingness to Try

Guidelines for Teaching the Recalcitrant Learners

The Culturally Different

The Socioeconomically Deprived

Ethnic Groups

The New Immigrants

Working with Handicapped Students

SUMMARY

SUGGESTED READING

POSTTEST

No one is exactly like anyone else. Even indentical twins are not identical in all respects. In spite of the similarity in their genetic background, environmental factors beginning even before birth shape each twin differently. And for most people, the differences in genetic structure eliminate the chances of anyone's being an exact duplicate of anyone else. Brothers and sisters may have family resemblances; tenth-graders may have some traits in common, as do members of honors sections, teacher credential candidates, and college professors; yet each one is an individual and looks and behaves differently from everyone else.

The ways in which individuals differ are manifold. Not only are there differences in physical appearance but also in personality traits and cultural backgrounds. Some of your students will be quick and some slow; some academically talented, others less so; some socially skillful, some socially inept; some eager, some phlegmatic; some interested in your subject, some not; some female, some male; some friendly, some hostile; some from socioeconomic or cultural backgrounds similar to yours, others from quite different backgrounds.

Some of these differences may be of no importance as far as school is concerned: whether a student's eyes are blue, grey, or brown does not really matter. Other differences are extremely important for teaching, because what is good education for one person may not be good for another. Therefore, in this module we present some of the differences in students that you should consider in your teaching; some ways of finding out important characteristics of individual students; some of the curricular and organizational schemes that have been invented to provide for differences in students; and strategies and tactics that you can use in your own classes, not only to cope with the problems of individual differences but also to use these differences to enhance student learning.

RATIONALE

At the completion of this module, you should be able to:

1. Describe ways in which administrators attempt to provide for individuals. Among the plans you should be able to describe are:
   a. Curriculum tracks
   b. Tracks, streams, and homogeneous groups
   c. Promotion schemes, including continuous promotion, minicourses, half-yearly and term promotion, and nongraded plans
   d. Curriculum provisions including electives, minicourses, and extracurriculum
   e. Use of teaching aides, learning centers, and modular schedules

2. Summarize the arguments for and against the use of plans featuring the principle of homogeneous grouping.

3. Describe how to conduct such strategies and tactics as:
   a. Differentiating the assignment
   b. Using grouping within the classroom
   c. Conducting the class as a laboratory
   d. Units
   e. Contracts
   f. Learning activity packets
   g. Special assignments
   h. Individualizing instruction
   i. Special help
   j. Laboratory classes
   k. Continuous progress plans
   l. Self-instructional devices
   m. Study guides
   n. Self-correcting material
   o. Machines for teaching
   p. Distance learning

SPECIFIC OBJECTIVES

q. Small groups and committees
r. Independent study
s. Acceleration of bright students
t. Projects

4. Describe methods by which you can make time for individual instruction.

5. Design a learning-activity center.

6. Describe approaches for teaching certain homogeneous groups, such as
   a. Academically talented students
   b. Slow learning students
   c. Students from disadvantaged backgrounds
   d. Learning handicapped students
   e. Students of different cultural and ethnic origins

MODULE TEXT

NECESSITY OF PROVIDING FOR DIFFERENCES IN STUDENTS

Students differ in many ways: physical characteristics, interests, intellectual ability, motor ability, social ability, aptitudes of various kinds, background, experience, ideals, attitudes, needs, ambitions, dreams, and hopes. Having long recognized the importance of these individual differences, educators have made many attempts to develop systematic programs of individualized instruction. In the 1920s there were the "programmed" workbooks of the Winetka Plan. The 1960s brought a multitude of plans, such as IPI (Individually Prescribed Instruction), IGE (Individually Guided Education), and PLAN (Program for Learning in Accordance with Needs). The 1970s saw the development and growth in popularity of individual learning packages, such as the SIP (Self-Instructional Package) discussed in Module 4 and the IEP (Individualized Education Program) for handicapped learners that resulted from Public Law 94-142, passed by Congress in 1975 and put into effect in 1978. Although some of these efforts did not survive the test of time, others met with more success; some have been refined and are still being used. Public Law 94-142 was refined by Congress in the 1980s. By the 1990s, some schools were reporting success in the use of IEPs for all students, not just for handicapped learners.

Furthermore, for a variety of reasons (e.g., modality preferences, information-processing habits, motivational factors, and physiological factors) all persons learn in their own ways and at their own rates. Interests, background, innate and acquired abilities, and a myriad of other influences shape how and what a person will learn. No two students ever learn exactly the same thing from any particular learning experience.

As discussed in Module 1, there is growing interest today in the psychological factors of learning and in the possibility of matching students to instructional treatments. A second and perhaps related area that has demanded attention—just as important as individual learning styles—is the increase in the number of students from diverse cultural backgrounds whose primary language is not English. Only recently have educators recognized and addressed the importance of cultural diversity. The recognition and acceptance of students from a great variety of backgrounds are central to the concept of multicultural education. The goals of multicultural education are to:[1]

1. Recognize the strength and value of cultural diversity.

2. Develop human rights and respect for cultural diversity.

3. Give legitimacy to alternative life choices.

4. Provide social justice and equal opportunity for all.

5. Develop a society where political power is equally distributed among members of all ethnic groups.

---

[1] C. Sleeter and C. Grant, "An analysis of multicultural education in the United States," *Harvard Educational Review* 57(4): 421–44 (1987).

The variety of individual differences among students requires that teachers find teaching strategies and tactics to accommodate those differences. The teaching credential authorizes you to teach in any public school in a state and in many states demands that you be prepared to teach in a school that is ethnically, culturally, linguistically, and socioeconomically diverse. A teacher whose preparation occurs exclusively among students of a background similar to that of the teacher may not be prepared to teach in a classroom of such diversity. In order to be able to teach students who are different from you, you need to develop skills in:

☐ Establishing a classroom climate in which all students feel welcome.

☐ Providing a classroom environment in which all students feel they can learn.

☐ Involving students in democratic decision-making.

☐ Building upon students' learning styles.

☐ Adapting to students' skills levels.

☐ Using techniques that emphasize cooperative learning and that deemphasize competitive learning.

To address the diversity of individual students in your classroom, individualized instruction is imperative. In practice, though, many techniques used by teachers to address this diversity are simply techniques by which teachers (1) manipulate course content so that it is easier for some students and more difficult for others, (2) give some students more work than they give others, or (3) allow some students to progress more or less rapidly than others do. For example, a teacher will frequently double or triple the normal amount of homework given to middle school students if those students are in a class identified as a gifted and talented education (GATE) class. Those students in time may "burn out" and become alienated to formal education.

True individualization of instruction requires a quite different approach. The emphasis should be on the development of each person to his or her fullest potential—with the accent not on the differences but on the development. Therefore, individualized teaching goals and subject matter should vary from student to student, according to the unique characteristics of each individual. Although difficulty and speed are considerations, the principal thrust should be on providing all students with the curriculum best suited for each of them individually.

Knowing the Student

To provide adequately for individual differences, you must know something about your students' strengths, weaknesses, interests, goals, backgrounds, and attitudes. You cannot expect to provide for differences you know nothing about. To find out this information, teachers have a great number of tools available, including observation, conferences, questionnaires, test results, and the cumulative record folder. These are described in Module 6.

In this quest for knowledge about the student, keep in mind that learners vary according to which sensory portal (i.e., learning modality) each student prefers using or is especially adept at using. The primary choices are auditory, visual, tactile, and kinesthetic. And, of course, how a student prefers to learn and how that student learns best may not be the same—modality preference and modality adeptness may not be the same. Because most secondary and middle school students neither have a preference nor a strength for auditory reception, teachers might be advised to limit their use of the lecture method of teaching. Middle and secondary school students tend to prefer and to learn best by being physically active—that is, through tactile or kinesthetic experiences. They prefer to learn by touching objects, by feeling shapes and textures, and by moving things around. In contrast, sitting and listening are difficult for these students. Dependence on the tactile and kinesthetic modalities decreases with maturity. Some students are visual learners who can read easily and rapidly and can visualize what they are reading about.

Most people eventually become somewhat proficient with each of these learning styles, even developing an ability to switch from one to the other according to mood or some other variable. Since most of your students will not have reached this point, it will be necessary for you to know which style each prefers most often as well as to provide opportunities for each student to learn using the mode that suits that student best in the learning activity of the day. Another of the tasks of a teacher is to help students develop skills in the different ways of learning.

Often the best thing for a teacher to do is to get out of the way of the learner and let the student proceed unhindered. Since the student is the agent of his or her own learning, the more actively engaged the student is in a task, the more effective a producer of learning the student will become. In the past teachers were often known to impede learning by insisting on adhering slavishly to some well-established classroom procedure. They would feel threatened if students deviated from the pattern or schedule. Of course, good judgment always comes into play, for sometimes a teacher must impose his or her will. The intention here is solely to free new teachers from the compulsion to pontificate rather than teach or control rather than create a learning environment.

Some students are comfortable with beginning their learning in the abstract, whereas others feel the need to begin with the concrete. Some prosper while working in groups, whereas others prefer to work alone. Some are quick in their studies, whereas others are slow and methodical and cautious and meticulous. Some can sustain attention on a single topic for a long time, becoming more absorbed in their study as time passes. Others are slower starters and more casual in their pursuits but are capable of shifting with ease from subject to subject. Some can study in the midst of music, noise, or movement, whereas others need quiet, solitude, and a desk or table. The point is that students vary in not only their skills and preferences in the way knowledge is received, but also in how they mentally process that information once it has been received.

Anthony Gregorc classifies learners according to whether they prefer to begin with the concrete or the abstract and according to whether they prefer random or sequential ordering of information.[2] As a result, his learning-style delineator has four categories: (1) concrete sequential, (2) concrete random, (3) abstract sequential, and (4) abstract random.

Concrete sequential learners prefer direct, hands-on experiences presented in a logical sequence. These learners work well with workbooks, computer programs, and other forms of programmed instruction. Concrete random learners prefer more wide-open, exploratory kinds of activities, such as games, role-playing, simulations, and independent study. Most middle and secondary school students are better at one of these two categories of concrete learning than at either category of abstract learning.

Abstract sequential learners are skilled in decoding verbal and symbolic messages, especially when presented in logical sequence. These learners learn well by reading and listening to lectures. Abstract random learners can interpret meaning from nonverbal communications and consequently do well in discussions, debates, and media presentations.[3]

The trap the teacher should avoid is to regard all students who have difficulty or who do poorly in school as being alike. In a culture such as ours that values quantity, speed, and measurement, it is easy to make the mistake that being a slow learner is the same as being a poor learner. The perceptive teacher understands that slowness may be simply another style of learning, with potential strengths of its own. Slowness can reflect many things—caution, a desire to be thorough or a meticulous style, a great interest in the matter at hand. To ignore the slow student or to treat all slow students

---

[2]Anthony Gregorc, "Learning and Teaching Styles—Potent Forces Behind Them." *Educational Leadership* (January 1979), pp. 234–36.

[3]Adapted from Robert Heinich, Michael Molenda, and James D. Russell, *Instructional Media,* 3rd ed. (New York: Macmillan, 1989), p. 398. By permission of Macmillan Publishing Company.

as though they were victims of some deficiency is to risk discouraging those who have deliberately opted for slowness and thus limiting their learning opportunities.

An obligation of the teacher is to recognize that students have different ways of receiving information and different ways of processing that information. These differences are unique and important, and they are what the teacher should address in his or her teaching. Thus, you should try to learn as much as you can about how each student learns and processes information. But because you can never know everything about your students, the more you vary your teaching strategies, the more likely you are to reach more of the students more of the time.

Administrative Provisions

Schools have traditionally tried to provide for the differences among students through administrative means, such as by providing different types of schools for persons with different goals. For example, in medieval times, the clerk-to-be was educated in a monastery or church school, whereas the would-be knight was apprenticed as a page to an influential knighted lord. In seventeenth-century Massachusetts, the minister-to-be went to Harvard for academic training, whereas the tradesman was schooled in a private venture school or as an apprentice.

Today, there continues to be an attempt to provide different types of schools for persons with different needs or goals. There are magnet schools, fundamental schools, middle schools, private schools, church-affiliated schools, trade schools, continuation high schools, and so on.

Curriculum Tracks

The practice of providing different routes for students with different vocational and academic aims continues. Some school systems provide different schools for youths planning for different vocations, but in most school systems, these differences are accommodated by offering a variety of curricula in comprehensive high schools. By a judicious selection of courses or curricula, students can prepare themselves for entrance to a college or for a specific vocation. If students wish neither four-year college nor vocational preparation, they can select a general program of high school studies. The offering of a choice of curricula is probably the most common administrative or organizational method of providing for individual differences at the high school level. Although the choice of curriculum may begin in middle school or junior high school, it usually begins at the high school. Such choice is infrequent at lower grade levels.

Tracks or Streams

Some school systems are organized on the basis of student ability. For instance, one sequence might be for honors students, a second sequence for college preparatory students, a third sequence for general students, and a fourth sequence for slow learners. These different sequences—sometimes called tracks or streams—may differ from one another in difficulty and complexity of content, rate of student progress, and methods of instruction. Thus, the students in a mathematics honors group may move to the study of calculus in the twelfth grade, while a slow group might never go beyond the development of basic computational skills.

Homogeneous Groups

Tracks or streams are, in effect, a type of homogeneous grouping. **Homogeneous groups** are formed by dividing students into class sections, according to some criterion or a combination of criteria. Usually the criteria are a combination of ability and past academic success. Other criteria are gender (e.g., boy's physical education), educational-vocational goals (e.g., business English or college preparatory English), or just interest. In any case, the reasons for forming homogeneous groups are to provide for the differences in students and to make teaching more efficient and perhaps easier. Theoretically, when classes are grouped homogeneously, it is easier to select content and methods that will be suitable for all students in that group.

To a degree, homogeneous grouping works. When all the students in an advanced mathematics class are bright, interested, motivated, and self-confident, no doubt teaching them is easier. And it is easier to find content and methods suitable for everyone in a class if the group is homogeneous. Nevertheless, homogeneous grouping is not necessarily the answer to the problem of addressing individual differences in students.

In the first place, homogeneous groups are not truly homogeneous; they are merely attempts to make groups similar, according to certain criteria. Girls' physical education classes are homogeneous in that they are limited to girls, but all girls are not alike physically, mentally, emotionally, socially, or in terms of their interests and skills in physical education. Even if a school were to have a section of girls' physical education in which all the girls were interested in physical fitness or in sports, there would still be great differences in the characteristics and capabilities of the girls. All homogeneous grouping does is to reduce the heterogeneity of classes; it makes certain aspects of the problem of providing for individual differences in students a bit more manageable.

You should remember that last point. Many teachers teach as though they believe their classes really are homogeneous. Do not be one of those teachers. Always keep in mind that a homogeneous class is one in which your school administrators have tried to reduce the spread of one or more student characteristics. Other characteristics will run the full gamut of possibilities, just as in heterogeneous classes. In classes grouped according to ability and academic history, the range of academic ability may be reduced, but the range of interest, ambitions, motivations, and goals is probably just as wide as in any other class. Even the range of ability in a high-ability class may be quite large — a 30-point range in IQ in such a class would be quite usual. Similarly, a slow class may consist of students who have learning difficulty because of a lack of innate ability, students who have learning difficulty because of their background in or out of school, students who have learning difficulty because of poor self-esteem, and students who could learn easily if they tried. No matter how much a school attempts to homogenize classes and no matter what plan of grouping is used, you as the teacher will always face the problem of providing for differences in individual students. Homogeneous grouping can reduce some problems but never can eliminate them all.

Homogeneous grouping brings with it several built-in problems of its own. One of these is the danger that in ability-grouping schemes the less-talented students and those with learning difficulties may not get the attention they deserve. Teachers who teach "slow classes" often feel frustrated. Many of them seem to feel that being asked to teach classes of slow learners is somehow demeaning: after all, they are subject-matter specialists and to spend their talents on the less-than-bright is to waste those talents. This teacher attitude defeats the purpose of ability grouping. If you feel this way, perhaps you should not go into teaching. All who wish to teach should be willing to adapt their teaching to their students.

Another danger of homogeneous grouping is that the content and methods used will not be those best suited for the students being taught. Frequently, classes of bright students are hurried through their courses without any real mind-stretching experiences. Of course, bright students usually learn more quickly, but just learning more of the same is hardly the way to develop their talents to the fullest. Perhaps even more dangerous is the common practice of watering down academic courses for slow students. The result is dull, drab, boring teaching day after day. If you teach homogeneously grouped classes, you should adjust your content and your teaching strategies to the students so that the classes will be productive experiences for them, as they master skills and learn concepts worthwhile to them now and in the future.

In practice, the less academically inclined students are more often short-changed than are other students. When courses are merely watered-down versions of academic courses, their classes may not only waste their time but actually be harmful to them. The courses are seldom structured so that these students can capitalize on the strengths they have. Instead, the assumption is that these students cannot learn. Because little is expected of them, they do little. There is often little fun, or success, or relevancy to provide motivation. In the classes in which students most need hands-on experiences to challenge and motivate, there is no challenge and little motivation. Furthermore, these students have little chance to learn from the interaction with their more talented or motivated peers. Students learn a great deal from one another. Consequently, slow learners benefit from associating with talented and motivated peers, who in turn can learn from the slow learners. In many instances, the classes for slow students have become educational ghettos—simply a continuation of the educationally deprived environments in which they often live outside school. There is no student in a public school who cannot learn if given the proper classroom environment, opportunity, and encouragement.

One practice that helps perpetuate the problems inherent in teaching is the division of students into classes of, perhaps, about 30 students. For administrative purposes, students are divided into categories based upon age and assigned to these classes. Teachers are appointed to instruct a certain number of classes daily. Unconsciously, such teachers begin thinking in terms of the entire number in each group. Progressive sequences are designated for study, and specific levels of mastery are earmarked for those subjects that are developmental in nature. Expectations are established for each student in each class for quarterly or annual achievement, based on the amount of content in the subject and the time to be allocated for its mastery. The teacher who forgets that individuals differ will fall easy prey to the "class" dilemma and tend to think only in terms of group achievement.

Explore your thoughts about homogeneous grouping by working through Exercise 12.1.

Promotion Schemes

The old-fashioned techniques of skipping grades and of retaining students in the same grade for another year are other administrative devices used to provide for differences in student ability. Years ago, in order that the period skipped or repeated might not be too long, city systems instituted half-year courses. Under this sort of plan, students were promoted every half year. Today, some systems schedule half-year and quarterly courses and even short minicourses.

Continuous Progress.   Continuous progress (or continuous promotion) plans consist of dividing the course work of the curriculum into modules. When a student completes one module, that student is ready to go on to the next. Usually, the students are issued learning activity packets that contain the instructions and materials for studying the module so that individual students can work through the modules alone, at their own pace. Theoretically, at least, continuous progress plans are an excellent means of providing for individual differences. Students who are not ready to move on when the class moves on are not forced to do so, and students who finish the module quickly are not forced to wait for others to catch up. Furthermore, not all students must follow the same order of units. Not only may a student change the order of the modules, but the student can, in effect, build a personal sequence or course by electing to skip certain modules or select additional modules different from those designated for the other students. In theory (though seldom in practice), students by their choices of modules can have courses and curricula specially tailored to meet their needs.

Continuous progress programs, most common in continuation high schools, are programs where promotion is based on readiness. Students are promoted to the next step or grade when they are ready. The difficulty preventing a more widespread use of this concept is that schools are graded. At the end of a school year, students go on to the next grade, whether they are ready or not, though in recent years some states and districts have mandated standards to regulate whether an individual student is promoted or not.

A promising development of recent years is the use for all students of Individual Education Programs (IEPs), which originally were used with special-needs students.

This is truly an attempt to develop an individualized program of instruction for every student. The use of IEPs could be combined with the concept of continuous progress programs for promotion.

Nongraded Schools.   The continuous progress program works well with the concept of a nongraded school. In a nongraded school, students are not placed in courses because they are in a certain grade but because they have reached a certain level of academic proficiency or achievement. In such a program, a class might consist of students from throughout the total school population who are proficient in a particular subject, rather than being limited to students from a particular grade.

Curriculum Provisions for Individual Differences

In addition to the various curricula, tracks, or streams that can be found in comprehensive schools, curriculum builders try to provide for individual differences by developing a diversity of courses and programs, extending from the humanities to vocational subjects and even including extracurricular activities. To give students an adequate opportunity to study in areas that appeal to them, a variety of electives are built into the program. A good selection of electives allows students to pursue special interests and explore special bents. They allow students to add both breadth and depth to their courses of study. Even further variety is offered by the extracurriculum, which allows students to elect activities for the experience and fun provided.

Three additional innovations provided by the administration of some schools may make it easier for teachers to provide for individual differences: (1) the introduction of adult teacher aides, (2) the establishment of learning centers in the school and in classrooms, and (3) the adoption of flexible, modular daily schedules.

Use of Teacher Aides

Teacher aides can help teachers provide independent and individualized study. By using adult aides to supervise classroom management and to help with time-consuming chores, teachers have more time to work with individuals and small groups. Among the tasks that aides can do to help individualize the instruction are:

☐ Help students as they practice.

☐ Help students with their seatwork.

☐ Help follow up.

☐ Tutor individual students.

☐ Supervise and help small groups of students.

☐ Assist in laboratory preparation and activities.

☐ Assist students who have special learning difficulties or whose native language is not English.

☐ Supervise students who are working in learning-activity centers.

School-Home Connections

The beginning of the final decade of the twentieth century saw educators embracing the idea of rekindled partnerships among the home, school and community in order to promote the success of students in school. Although many teachers do effectively involve parents and guardians in their children's school work, most families still have little positive interaction with the schools that their children attend. Elsewhere in this text are suggestions about ways the teacher can communicate with parents (or guardians) and thus effect an individualization of a student's learning. Some of these are to make time for parent conferences, to write positive notes home about a student's learning or behavior, and to include an assignment folder that must be signed weekly by a parent or guardian.

Some states, districts and local schools have adopted formal policies about home and school partnerships. According to Zelma P. Solomon, "Any school can be more successful if parents are productively involved in their children's education. Any student

EXERCISE 12.1   ABOUT HOMOGENEOUS GROUPING

The purpose of this exercise is to learn more about the advantages and disadvantages afforded by grouping students homogeneously. Answer the following questions and then share your responses with those of your classmates.

1. For secondary school and middle school learning of your field, do you personally favor homogeneous grouping? Explain why or why not.

2. Do you think homogeneous grouping is democratic? Explain why or why not.

3. Is it fair for bright students to sit in the same classes as slow students?

4. Is it fair for slow students to be relegated to slow sections?

5. Describe recent research you can find that supports or rejects the notion of homogeneous grouping.

6. Describe any teaching techniques supported by research that can aid in the learning of both bright and slow students in a heterogeneously grouped class.

can be more successful if schools link comprehensive parent involvement programs to curricula. . . ."[4] School and administrative efforts to foster parent involvement include student-teacher-parent contracts; weekly calendars and folders that include the student's record and that are sent home each week; home visitor programs; and workshops for parents. Some schools have initiated homework hotline programs where students and parents can get help by phone on homework.[5]

Learning-Activity Centers

A **learning-activity center** is a special station located in the classroom where an individual student (or a group of two, if student interaction is necessary for the center) can quietly work and learn at his or her own pace.[6] All materials needed by the student are provided at the learning-center station, including clear instructions for operation. A familiar example is the personal computer station.

As devices for individualizing the instruction, learning-activity centers provide value in two ways for students working at the center: (1) the student is giving more time and attention to the learning task, and (2) the student is likely to be engaging his or her most effective learning modality.

Learning-activity centers are of three types:

1. *Direct-learning center*, where performance expectations are specific.

2. *Open-learning center*, where the goal of the teacher is to provide opportunity for enrichment, motivation of interest, and creative discovery.

3. *Skill center*, where the focus is on the development of a particular skill, such as microscope manipulation.

Although in all cases the primary reason for using a learning-activity center is to individualize the instruction, there are other specific reasons you might want to use this concept in your classroom:

□ To provide multisensory experiences to enhance learning.

□ To provide enrichment experiences.

□ To provide a special place for students to review, perhaps for a student who has been absent or who has fallen behind the rest of the class.

□ To provide further opportunity for creativity and discovery.

□ To provide a special place for students with special needs, such as a student with a learning handicap.

□ To provide special opportunities for students to learn from learning packages that utilize special equipment or media of which a limited quantity may be available for use in your room, such as a computer or a laser videodisc player.

Designing a Learning-Activity Center. To set up a learning-activity center in your classroom, you can be as elaborate and creative as your time and resources allow. Here are guidelines for designing a center:

□ Materials in the center should be safe for student use.

□ The specific learning objectives and instructions for use of the center should be clearly posted and understandable to the student user. A cassette or videotape is sometimes used for this purpose.

□ The center should be attractive to the students.

---

[4]Zelma P. Solomon, "California's Policy on Parent Involvement," *Phi Delta Kappan* 72(5):359–362 (January 1991), p. 362.

[5]For a description of partnership programs see the special section "Parent Involvement" in *Phi Delta Kappan*, volume 72, number 5, January 1991.

[6]This section on learning-activity centers is adapted from R. D. Kellough and P. L. Roberts, *A Resource Guide for Elementary School Teaching: Planning for Competence*, 2d ed. (New York: Macmillan, 1991), pp. 170–71. By permission of Macmillan Publishing Company.

☐ The center should be easily supervised by you or an aide.

☐ The purpose of the center should be clearly understood by the students. Note well: centers should never be used for punishment!

☐ Topics for the center should be related to the ongoing program, perhaps as review, remediation, or enrichment.

☐ The center should contain a variety of activities geared to the varying abilities and interest levels of the students. A choice of two or more activities at a center is one way to provide this.

☐ All materials to be used at the center should be available, and their use clearly understood by the student user.

☐ The self-instructional package (see Module 4) is quite effective when designed to be used at a learning-activity center.

Try your hand at designing a learning-activity center by doing Exercise 12.2.

Flexible Schedules

Schools that have adopted flexible modular scheduling are those schools that felt stymied by the rigidity of the five-, six-, or seven-period day. They concluded that the usual 45-, 55-, or 60-minute periods in such a scheduled day are both too short and too long. Such periods often provide more minutes for instruction than are reasonably usable for the teaching goals of that hour. At other times such periods are too short to permit goal satisfaction, as when a group needs to do research, take a field trip, or view a long film. In contrast, modular schools establish as a base period an amount of time that represents the smallest number of minutes that can be effectively utilized. In such a schedule, for example, a period can be as short as one module (say, 15 minutes), in which students can meet for such things as attendance taking and other school business. Periods can be extended by linking as many "mods" as the instruction goals seem to indicate as being necessary. In a similar fashion, the size of the student group can be modified from 3–10 students (known as a small group) to 10–20 students (middle group) to 60–120 students (large group)—the size determined by the nature of the instruction planned. During the day, or during the week, not all periods have the same length or meet in the same sequence.

In some degree, flexible schedules have been in existence for about 50 years. Perhaps you attended a school with some kind of flexible schedule. In the schedule shown in Figure 12.1, the school day is divided into 15-minute modules. According to this schedule, on Monday the seventh-graders are free to go to the learning center during modules 1–3 and also during modules 16–19, their lunch hour. During modules 4–6, 7–9, and 13–15, they meet in regular (middle) class-size groups, but in modules 10–12 and 20–22 they all meet together for large-group instruction in science or in language arts. On other days the students follow much the same pattern, except that they meet in regular-size classes for science and language arts and have large-group instruction for social studies on Thursday. Unstructured but supervised time for independent study in learning centers is available to them every day.

In practice, undisciplined and lesser-motivated students are those who seem to have the most difficulty with flexible modular schedules, and these are the same students who have the most difficulty with traditional school schedules. A flexible schedule without quality individualized attention to the individual needs of all students seems to be of no value in addressing the needs of at-risk students.

Differentiated Schools

Although specialized schools for students with special interests, abilities, or talents have always been in existence, the interest and implementation in special high schools grew during the 1980s, especially within large metropolitan school districts. The plan is called **magnet schools**. Within a large district, separate high schools would be given special functions and identities. For example, one school functions as a funda-

EXERCISE 12.2   DESIGNING A LEARNING-ACTIVITY CENTER

Select a specific grade level, topic, and purpose, and design a classroom learning-activity center. Bring your completed design to class to share with your colleagues (or take a video picture of students using your center). Using an instrument designed by you and the criteria discussed on pages 371–372, evaluate the effectiveness of your learning-activity center. Share the evaluation with your colleagues.

Monday	Mods 1–3	Unstructured or unassigned time. The student has the option of reporting to any of the six learning centers. In addition, the library is available, as well as the student center.
	Mods 4–6	Social Studies Middle Group
	Mods 7–9	Spanish
	Mods 10–12	Science Large Group
	Mods 13–15	Math Middle Group
	Mods 16–19	Unstructured (lunch included here)
	Mods 20–22	Language Arts Large Group
	Mods 23–26	Clubs and Activities
Tuesday	Mods 1–3	Science Middle Group
	Mods 4–6	Unstructured
	Mods 7–9	Spanish
	Mods 10–12	Physical Education
	Mods 13–14	Math Small Group
	Mods 15–18	Unstructured (includes lunch)
	Mods 19–21	Language Arts Middle Group
	Mod 22	Unstructured
	Mods 23–26	Clubs and Activities
Wednesday	Mods 1–2	Social Studies Small Group
	Mods 6–9	Unified Arts
	Mods 10–12	Music
	Mods 13–15	Math Middle Group
	Mods 16–18	Unstructured (includes lunch)
	Mods 19–20	Language Arts Small Group
	Mods 21–22	Unstructured
	Mods 23–26	Clubs and Activities
Thursday	Mods 1–3	Unstructured
	Mods 4–6	Social Studies Large Group
	Mods 7–9	Spanish
	Mod 12	Unstructured
	Mods 13–15	Science Middle Group
	Mods 16–18	Unstructured (includes lunch)
	Mods 19–20	Language Arts Small Group
	Mods 21–22	Unstructured
	Mods 23–26	Clubs and Activities
Friday	Mods 1–3	Physical Education
	Mods 4–6	Music
	Mods 7–9	Science Middle Group
	Mods 10–12	Math Middle Group
	Mods 13–19	Unstructured (includes lunch)
	Mods 20–22	Language Arts Middle Group
	Mods 23–26	Clubs and Activities

FIGURE 12.1
A Flexible Schedule

mentals school, another specializes in science and technology, another specializes in business and industry, and yet another specializes in the performing arts. While the principal purpose in creating specialized high schools within a large district is to provide for the special talents and interests of individual students, the magnet schools theoretically also provide a mechanism for racial desegregation. In some cases, magnet schools have perhaps enhanced the opportunities for special funding from either state or private sources. The continuation high school is yet another type of special high school, one that provides for special needs of individual students, perhaps those who must work or who for one reason or another have found it impossible to continue in a regular high school.

Differentiating Assignments

In the ordinary lesson, there is usually no reason why every student should have to do exactly the same activities, even though the lesson objectives may be the same for every student. Consequently, the teacher can provide for differences in ability and interest by differentiating the assignment, such as specifying different learning activities for different students or groups of students, perhaps on the basis of learning styles and modalities. For example, to accomplish the same learning objective one group of students may read and discuss, whereas another group may participate in a simulation or some other more concrete activity. After group study, these separate learning groups could then share what they had learned with the other groups.

Differentiating Length and Difficulty

Another way to differentiate by assignment is to divide the class into groups or committees and then assign work according to length and difficulty. You might, for instance, divide your class into three groups. One group could be assigned readings in a somewhat difficult text and asked to respond to some difficult problems. A second group could read less-demanding selections and be assigned easier problems. The third group's reading assignment could be extremely easy, with no real problems to confront it at all. In this case, all students are studying the same thing but at different levels of difficulty. Usually such groupings can be done after completion of the first three to six weeks of school on the basis of achievement in the first unit of study. The groupings, then, are not foisted upon the class as an outside judgment about student ability but are agreed upon after discussion of the most appropriate way to achieve upcoming goals. Each student exercises responsibility for selecting the group to which to belong based on record achieved. Errors in judgment about placement are readily rectifiable as the unit progresses if there is flexibility of movement from one group to another.

Differentiating Type of Work

You can also differentiate assignments by allowing students to do different types of work to achieve the learning objectives and thus capitalizing on the different interests and abilities of the students. Perhaps some students might learn best through art, others through reading, others through discussion, and others through drama. There is no reason why everyone should do the same thing. What is important is that students achieve the understandings, skills, and attitudes of the learning objectives.

For example, not everyone needs to learn about the antebellum South by writing essays and answering questions. Students may pursue their study in different ways, and then share their work with others in the class. Talented students might produce illustrations of life in the South; a student interested in mechanical drawing might draw a layout of the plantation; a student interested in foods might investigate the menus of the era, a student engineer might construct a cotton gin; a student choreographer could score and dance a ballet in the *Gone with the Wind* motif; a young poet could contribute lyric poetry, or an ode or two.[7]

Although differentiating assignments by giving different ones to small groups and committees of students is relatively easy, there is no reason why differentiation cannot be done on a more individualized basis. Usually, the procedure is to give students a number of options, from which they select their own individual activities. A good way to offer these options is in a study guide issued to the students at the outset of a course or unit.

You can also differentiate within a single lesson. For example, in a mathematics lesson, you might assign certain students problems 1, 4, 5, and 8, while others do problems 2, 3, 6, 7, 9, and 10. Frequently, math teachers add some difficult exercises to challenge the more capable students. Usually, however, you will find that in order

---

[7]This possible scenario was adapted by the authors from one originally published in Leonard H. Clark and Irving S. Starr, *Secondary and Middle School Teaching Methods*, 4th ed. (New York: Macmillan, 1981), p. 103. By permission of Macmillan Publishing Company.

to differentiate among your students in a meaningful way, you need a longer block of time than just a single lesson. Ordinarily, the differentiated assignment should be a long assignment covering a period of several days or even weeks.

Yet another way of differentiating to accomplish the same learning objectives is to provide self-instructional packages (see Exercise 4.1 in Module 4) that have been prepared for individual students according to their individual prior understandings and accomplishments. Although each self-instructional package is designed to accomplish the same learning objective, the packages are written at varying levels of cognition and with varying activities, based on learning styles and modalities as well as on the level of understanding expected. A beginning teacher, however, likely has little time to individualize instruction by preparing several self-instructional packages on the same topic. That would be a good activity for instructors from a department to work on cooperatively during in-service workdays.

Homogeneous Groups Within the Classroom

Another way to differentiate in a class is to establish homogeneous groups. Grouping can be accomplished in several ways:

1. Divide the class into groups on the basis of prior achievement in the subject.
2. Divide the class in accordance with expressed student interests.
3. Divide the class according to goals, where students interested in the same goal work together as a group.
4. Divide the class into groups according to needs, such as students who require remediation work.

Differentiation of class assignments to meet the needs of these various groups can be accomplished by varying the length, difficulty, and content of the assignments. There is no need for groups with different interests or goals to study exactly the same content. To conduct several groups in one class is hard work—but then no one ever said that good teaching is easy. Actually, using groups is often less difficult than trying to teach the unready in a whole-class situation. The practice of trying to teach the entire class at one time often compounds the problems inherent in group teaching and only exacerbates a teacher's problems the longer it is continued. Many teachers who have "burned out" probably tried to teach as if all students in the class were of the same ability, interests, and experiences.

The technique used in providing individualized instruction to groups of varying size and skill levels is known as **multilevel teaching**.[8] It is accomplished through one of two ways:

1. Using the same materials to teach different objectives.
2. Using different materials to teach the same objectives.

To work successfully with homogeneous groups within the classroom, the essentials are:

☐ To be sure that each student has something worthwhile to do.
☐ To encourage students to participate in both planning and implementing plans for the group work.
☐ To supervise the group carefully, always being sure that every group gets its share of your attention, guidance, and help.

The use of written assignment sheets and study guides may help the groups keep on task.

Homogeneous groups should be kept fluid and flexible. That is, moving from any group to another should be based on conclusions about subject mastery, learning goals,

---

[8]N. Peterson, *Multilevel Teaching* (Lawrence, KS: Bureau of Child Research, University of Kansas, 1979).

and a student's personal development. Groups that are formed only once a year can become stultifying to learners who catch on, who achieve the learning goals for particular sessions of instruction, or who become motivated to progress but cannot leave their group for another. To maintain flexibility in group work, the following steps should be taken when using multilevel teaching:[9]

1. Define the objective for each skill and the sequence of steps necessary to teach each of these objectives.

2. Pretest each student to determine his or her entry level for a particular objective. This pretesting will be used in determining the groups in which students are placed.

3. Prepare data sheets for recording performance during group work.

4. Select materials that are easy to manipulate and adapt.

5. Present instructional tasks and record responses and other relevant information. These can be items presented in the group's assignment sheets or study guides.

6. Analyze the data after each group session.

Conducting the Class as a Laboratory

Another way to differentiate is to conduct the class as a laboratory. This approach is best served by long-term assignments, as in the unit plan. In the laboratory, students work under the guidance of the teacher either in small groups or as individuals. No student is necessarily working on the same project as any other student at any particular time. Rather, one group may be working on a group project; one group may be setting up a demonstration; some students may be doing research for individual projects; some students may be participating in the preparation and implementation of a simulation; one or two students may be working in a learning-activity center; and some students may be studying required or optional readings. The laboratory period is a work period.

Although there is no set procedure for teaching by the laboratory method, when you conduct a laboratory you should try using a procedure similar to the following. Provide a general study guide, unit of work, or learning packet that outlines exactly what is to be accomplished in the unit. The activities may be required or optional. Let students select activities from the study guide, or allow them to suggest activities themselves. Once you have approved their individual plans, let the students execute those plans. They may search for information in pamphlets, books, or magazines or on computers or laser videodiscs. They may confer with one another and assist one another. Help, guide, and supervise the students as they execute their plans:

1. Observe students to diagnose their study and work habits.

2. Show students where and how to locate information.

3. Demonstrate how to use the tools of learning.

4. Clarify assignments.

5. Help students redefine their goals for study.

6. Suggest methods for attacking problems.

7. Discuss errors in their thinking and procedures.

8. Help students summarize their work.

As a means of providing for individual differences, laboratory classes have many merits. When properly executed, they allow students to work on individual learning sequences that are theirs alone and within their preferred learning styles and modalities. The loose structure allows students to work at their own speeds. The swift or more able can move as quickly as they wish without waiting for the slow, and the slow do not have to push themselves unreasonably to keep up with their swifter peers. There

---

[9]Adapted from Kim and Kellough, p. 190. By permission of Macmillan Publishing Company.

is no need for all students to do the same thing in a laboratory setup. The students, under guidance, can select the activities they feel will be most useful, because students learn in different ways. However, unless the laboratory method is given a form, as in the unit, contract, or modular approach, the laboratory can become chaotic and the learning experiences of the students will prove meaningless.

For the laboratory method to work best, the classroom should be set up as a learning laboratory. The more fully equipped the room, the better. The students should have easy availability to a classroom library of pertinent books and other reading materials, to audiovisual equipment, and to plenty of work space. Most of this material should be kept in the classroom permanently. For instance, overhead projectors, other types of projectors, VCRs, and computers should be either assigned as permanent equipment or on long-term loan. Books can be borrowed from the main school library for the duration of the course or unit. All of this material and equipment should be set up so that it is readily available to the students when they need it. Always remember that for safety and classroom control, foot traffic should be kept to a minimum. Figure 12.2 illustrates a classroom laboratory in a suburban New Jersey high school.

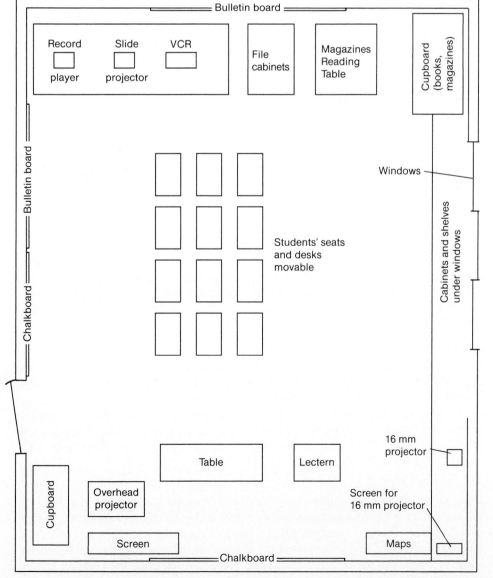

FIGURE 12.2
A Classroom Laboratory

Special Assignments for Special Students

Another way to differentiate the assignment is to give special assignments to special students. These special assignments can be done as part of the regular classwork, in addition to the regular classwork, or instead of the regular classwork. For example, in a certain English class the teacher noticed that one of the students, though quite bright, was having a great deal of trouble with ordinary classwork, primarily because the student had not learned basic writing skills. Consequently the teacher found special materials aimed at correcting the student's problem, wrote a special study guide, and put the student to work on correcting the problem on a part-time basis. In that same class, the teacher recognized that a brilliant student found the normal work boring because it was too easy. The teacher took this student off the ordinary course work and substituted a series of assignments from a literature course given in a nearby liberal arts college. The student did very well at this college-level work, which took the place of the ordinary high school work for an entire term.

Students should be expected to work on such special assignments both during class time and out of class as homework. You can work with special students during the class period if you conduct the class as a laboratory or have small-group and individual study sessions. You can also work with them during nonteaching periods or during the hours before and after school.

Cooperative-Learning Groups

Another way to differentiate assignments is by the use of cooperative-learning groups. (The use of cooperative groups of three to six students with mixed abilities is discussed in Modules 8 and 9.) Cooperative-learning groups can be helpful in individualizing instruction because: (1) slower students are helped by their peers, (2) cooperation rather than competition is stressed, (3) brighter students learn from facilitating the learning of others in their group, and (4) a group feeling is created that serves to improve individual feelings of self-worth and confidence.

Units, Learning Activity Packets, and Contracts

Units, contracts, and learning activity packets are specialized versions of differentiated assignments. They differ from one another only in detail.

Unit Teaching

In many schools, a unit is simply a topic about which a number of lessons are grouped. For instance, a teacher of English who has been teaching lyric poetry for a couple of weeks might say that she is teaching a unit on lyric poetry, even though her teaching consists of nothing more than a series of unrelated lessons having to do with lyric poetry. A true unit of instruction is a planned sequence of lessons designed to achieve the broader goals and understandings of the unit. Units consist of sequential daily lessons. Units are the sequential building blocks of course content and activities.

Learning Activity Packets

Learning activity packets (which include instructional learning packets, learning modules, instructional modules, learning packets, and the specialized type presented in Module 4, the self-instructional packet) are usually developed in much the same way as are units. They are really an adaptation of the unit idea to meet the demands for individualized instruction, independent study, student acceptance of the responsibility for more of their own learning, and continuous progress plans. They differ from units in that they place more emphasis on the individual.

The Contract Plan

Units and learning modules (previous section) can be set up as contracts. In a contract, the student agrees to do a certain amount of work of a certain quality during a specified period of time. Teachers frequently forget to specify that the student must meet both the requirements of quality and quantity. Quality control is sometimes quite difficult when teaching with the contract idea. (The procedure for using the contract plan is explained in Module 4.)

Individualizing Instruction

The ideal way to provide for individual differences is to provide each student with a tailor-made curriculum and lessons. Since every student is different, every student should ideally have a different curriculum and different learning experiences. At present, unless a school is equipped with the most modern programs, this ideal method is beyond most teachers' means. Differentiated assignments, units, and modules provide only partial differentiation for individuals or small groups, though modules may offer a good approach to the ultimate goal. This section considers techniques that allow teachers to concentrate on individual instruction.

Special Help

Undoubtedly, the most common way to individualize instruction is to teach students on a one-to-one basis through the special help that most teachers give to students who need assistance. Teachers have always given special help to those who seem to need it and probably always will, no matter how sophisticated teaching methods or tools become. Students who are having difficulties and students who are doing well both need special help. At times, all that is needed is to give a student a pat on the back, or encourage a student to continue, or suggest a new line of attack. Often, to be of any real benefit, the special help will entail tutoring or devising special instruction aimed specifically at correcting a student's faulty learning. Sometimes a teacher just helps a student with some task the student finds difficult. Perhaps the most interesting type of tutoring comes when you help a student work on a difficult, advanced, independent project. To really help the student who is having academic difficulty or the student who needs special guidance to forge ahead independently requires that you give them individualized assistance. The teacher, as either tutor or guide, must teach students individually.

Some teachers provide what they call "brown-bag lunch" assistance to students who meet with them in their classrooms at lunch time. During this time the teacher provides individual help on homework or any other problem for which the student seeks the teachers' help or advice.

Continuous Progress Courses

The continuous progress course combines a laboratory approach with the use of learning activity packets or learning modules. Even if a school is not organized according to the continuous progress plan, you can arrange your own courses according to the plan. (This procedure is discussed in Module 4.)

Use of Self-Instructional Devices

Learning activity packets are self-instructional devices (see Exercise 4.1 in Module 4). They consist of the materials to use, instructions on how to use them, and self-correcting exercises through which students can instruct themselves. Self-administering and self-correcting materials of this sort make it much easier to individualize instruction. That each student has directions, materials, and self-correcting exercises frees both students and teacher from the necessity of a lockstep education. A teacher need not spend so much time telling what to do, how to do it, or giving and correcting exercises and tests. The time saved can be used to design self-instructional programs that fit individual student needs, learning styles, and learning modalities, as well as to provide individual attention to the student working through the material.

Study Guides. Study guides are useful for individualizing instruction regardless of whether they are part of a module, unit, or contract. Special study guides that provide explicit instructions on how to implement individual assignments or special projects can be very useful. A good special study guide will inform students how to begin, explain the objectives, present questions and problems to guide their thinking, and point out things to look for. Exactly what it should contain, of course, depends upon the activity for which it is designed, but it should enable the student to function for varying periods of time without direct assistance from the teacher. (Special study guides are discussed more fully in Module 4.)

Self-Correcting Materials.   Self-correcting materials, exercises, and tests can relieve a teacher of much busy work. As with the self-check exercises used in this textbook, self-correcting materials are used for diagnosis and practice. Do not use them for calculating term marks or for deciding whether a student has passed a unit or module. Mastery tests and similar teacher-administered and -corrected evaluative instruments should be used for that purpose. If self-administered, self-correcting materials are used for marking, too much responsibility is placed on the students, possibly tempting them to be dishonest.

In making self-administering, self-correcting exercises and tests, put the answers on a separate sheet of paper, or print them upside down or on the back side of the test or in a file in the classroom. Even when it makes no difference, few people have enough willpower to resist the temptation to peek when the answers are easily available. As you completed the self-check exercises in this book, did you resist peeking at the answers before you should have? Whatever arrangement you decide on, be sure that the students write their answers on separate sheets. Do not let them write on the text or exercise itself; then you can use the exercises or tests for other students and other classes. Some teachers believe that the best procedure is to keep all test and exercise papers on file so that students can obtain them whenever they are needed; other teachers pass them out with the study guide.

Machines for Teaching.   Many media devices are useful as self-instructional devices. The language laboratory, for instance—which is little more than a tape recorder or combination of tape recorders—is used for practice of pronunciation and pattern drills in a foreign language. There is no reason that this device cannot be used for practice in spoken English, dictation in business courses, and similar exercises. Some machines can play a number of tapes at once so that different students can practice different exercises at the same time.

The most sophisticated machines for self-instruction are computers and computer programs. By means of computer-assisted instruction (CAI) and computer-managed instruction (CMI) it is possible to adjust students' instruction to their peculiar needs, abilities, and rates of learning. (The use of programs and computers is described in Modules 13 and 14.)

If you do not have such sophisticated equipment, you can get much the same effect by giving tapes to students and letting individual students use the tape recorder whenever it is free. Although tape recorders are concerned only with verbal communication, they can still be used for any number of individualized lessons. Students can listen to different tapes, just as they read different books and articles. Exercises and lessons can also be put on tape for individual consumption. Teachers can dictate lessons and instructions into the tape recorder. The resultant tape can be played by individual students in class or during free or unscheduled periods or while in the learning-activity center. The tape will tell them what to do, ask them questions, and give them information. If they find the assignment difficult, they can repeat the playing of the tape or portions of the tape until they are satisfied. In order that the recorders not be too noisy, students should wear earphones while listening.

Many English departments employ the tape recorder for help in critiquing student composition efforts. Teachers discovered that covering student papers with red pencil markings created negative feelings about writing. They also discovered that writing at length their critical reaction or constructive suggestions on each student paper was time consuming and impersonal. Many, however, found out that dictating a commentary on an individual student's tape was not only easier but also much more intimate and rewarding to the students, who listened to the playback privately before the next class period on composition. They discovered that many students who previously had not bothered to read the written critique were willing and eager to listen to the teacher observations when delivered on tape.

The 8-mm, self-loading, individual-viewing film projector can be used in much the same way, except that the film to be used must ordinarily be purchased. Many schools now will not have the 8-mm projector available, because they have not retained their popularity with teachers. Homemade lessons can, however, be prepared for the 35-mm slide projector. Prepare a sequence of slides that tells your story. If you wish to go to the trouble, you can make captioned slides or tape record a commentary to go with the slides. Otherwise, you can copy a commentary for the students to read as they view the slides. Individual viewing of slides can be arranged easily by placing a screen of white cardboard close to the projector, such as is often done for learning-activity centers. With a little experimenting, you will be able to project a small but clear image that makes for fine individual viewing. If possible, use a machine that allows you to preload your slides in trays for automatic or semiautomatic viewing. Be sure the slides are numbered so that the students will not get them mixed up. Also, mark the slides at the top right corner so that students will load them into the machine right-side up.

Filmstrip and 16-mm film projectors will probably require that you use commercial materials rather than your own tailor-made lessons, though you can make your own filmstrips if you have available a special half-frame camera. (Procedures for individualizing with the use of these films and filmstrips are described in Module 14.)

Outside of the writing board and the overhead projector, perhaps the VCR is one of the most widely used media sources in today's classroom, and the video-camera is an outstanding tool for preparing individualized instructional programs. The teacher can prepare self-instructional packages that incorporate the use of video tapes, and students in the learning-activity center can play these tapes as they study their individualized instructional programs. Students also can plan and record lessons on videotapes for the teacher to view later.

Perhaps the most sophisticated self-instructional devices are computers and computer programs. In their most sophisticated versions—computer-assisted and computer-managed, and with interactive laser videodiscs—they have tremendous potential for individualizing instruction. (More is discussed about these tools in Module 13.)

Distance Learning. Although newer instructional technologies such as computers and interactive videodiscs have captured more attention recently, older mechanisms such as television still provide opportunities for addressing the individual needs of students. As defined today, distance learning is the application of telecommunications and electronic devices to enable learners to receive instruction that originates from some distant location.[10] Satellite television broadcasting is an outgrowth of former correspondence and television courses. Perhaps the best tested of all self-instructional devices is the correspondence course. It has been used with success for many years. Many of the current broadcast courses, both radio and television, are excellent. Distance learning can be used to offer individual student instruction that otherwise would not be available to them. Students with special needs should be encouraged to make use of these kinds of courses. Use them just as you would any other learning activity package.

Using Small Groups and Committees for Individualizing Instruction

To individualize instruction, a teacher might want to divide the class into groups or committees according to ability, interest, need, learning styles or modalities, or task to be completed. Homogeneous grouping and the use of cooperative learning groups have already been discussed; the groups may or may not all study the same topic. Sometimes it is better if they do not.

In any sort of group or committee instructional activity there should be an agreed upon time for termination of the activity, and when that time has been reached each of the groups or committees performs the culminating activity that it has prepared. In this fashion all students experience the psychic satisfaction of having contributed to the overall growth of the class.

---

[10]At Keene Junior High School, Keene, New Hampshire, educators have created an interactive, distance-learning system by combining video and microwave technologies. For a description of this distance learning program *see* Elliot Washor and Deborah Couture, "A Distance Learning System That Pays All Its Own Costs," *T. H. E. Journal* 18(5): 62–64 (December 1990).

The following steps provide an outline suitable for most small-group and committee work. Not all of the steps will apply to all small-group and committee work. Feel free to adapt them as needed:

1. Choose a group leader and a group recorder.

2. Define the group task.

3. Establish the group objectives.

4. Set up a plan.
   a. What tasks must be done?
   b. What material and/or equipment must be secured?
   c. How will information be shared among the committee members?
   d. What records or notes need be kept?
   e. Who will do each of the various tasks?
   f. When will each task be done?
   g. What are the time limits for the entire group activity?

5. Implement the group plan.

6. Share the results with each other.

7. Plan how to report the group's findings.

8. Present the report.

Independent Study

One of the goals of education is to help students learn to work independently; consequently, students should have practice in working independently. Independent study is one way to teach students to become self-sufficient, self-directing, and responsible. When the independent study concerns things that are important and interesting to the student (as it always should), it has an excellent motivating effect. To conduct independent study well, however, is a difficult task. The teacher has to steer a course between too much guidance and too little guidance; the one hinders the student's independence, whereas the other ends in chaos.

In conducting independent study, the teacher should practice the following precautions:

1. The independent study should be appropriate. Students tend to bite off too much or wander off into irrelevant areas. Sometimes they wish to do things for which the school does not have the proper facilities, equipment, or material. Try not to let students choose studies that they are going to have to give up before they finish. Study guides and learning activity packets eliminate much of this danger, but they tend to confine students to preplanned topics that sometimes may not be appropriate for the needs of the individual student.

2. Students tend to choose topics that are too broad. The teacher needs to provide guidance to the student who is selecting a topic for an independent study so the student can experience success and not get bogged down because the topic was too general. If, for example, the student selects the topic of "evolution," the teacher will want to have a brainstorming session with that student to narrow this down to some aspect within that broad concept.

3. In the beginning, have the student map out quite definitely what the student hopes to accomplish and how it will be accomplished; at this point, it may be wise to require the student to prepare a written agenda or plan to which you can react and give a final approval. If the independent study plan follows a study guide, available computer program, or learning activity packet, much of the problem can be alleviated, though it may still be wise for the student to decide on a time schedule and agenda.

4. Keep a running check on the student's progress. All teachers know how easy it is to put off term papers and other independent study projects. By checking, you can also catch potential difficulties, correct errors, and help misguided students to get

back on the track before it is too late and they become discouraged. Schedule conferences with each student doing independent study so you will be sure that you check on each student sufficiently and not neglect anyone. Also strive to be available to students—let them know you welcome their requests for advice and guidance.

Acceleration

Some students can move more rapidly through courses than others. Such acceleration is possible if a teacher prepares units or learning packets in advance. A teacher can allow students to accelerate in traditional classes by giving them special assignments, or, more frequently, by letting students move through the ordinary assignments more rapidly. If you do not have this year's work entirely mapped out, there is probably no reason why the student should not follow your plan from last year. If you have a syllabus or curriculum guide, then the planning for accelerating the exceptional student is relatively easy. Another easy way is to let students work through the readings and exercises of a good textbook or workbook. Or you might draw upon items and exercises from other textbooks or workbooks.

Evaluating an accelerated student's work can be something of a problem. The work the student is doing is beyond the call of duty. The student could just be doing what the rest of the class is doing—and for top grades! And yet, to acknowledge shoddy work with high grades is not only to encourage poor scholarship but also to validate study habits that will eventually hurt a student's academic growth. Procedures for grading accelerated work should be carefully explored with a student before the work is begun. The emphasis should be placed on the quality of the work done as well as the quantity, with the due dates clearly delineated as well as the penalties for failure to meet clearly stipulated and agreed-upon deadlines. To save building extra tests, you might have students demonstrate what they have learned by writing summaries of the topic or by making an oral presentation to the rest of the class. Test banks also can be very helpful in this situation.

Projects

The project (also discussed in Module 10) is a form of independent study in which an individual or a small group of students attempt to produce something, such as a map, a model, a booklet, a paper, or a report. At one time the term *project* referred to something having tangible value (such as a vase or a lamp) or some article made for use or as a present. The motivational power of this form of study was thought to derive from its similarity to real life (i.e., adult life), where the need for the product supplies the motivation for the work to be done.

Students should do projects because they want to and because the product of their effort seems valuable to them. Therefore, they should decide whether to do a project, what project to do, and how to do it. You, as their teacher, should limit yourself to advising and guiding students so that their projects will be successful. Projects laid out by teachers are not really projects; they are assignments. Use the following procedure when you include projects in your teaching:

1. Stimulate ideas by providing lists of things students might do (see Exercise 10.4), by asking former students to tell about past projects, by suggesting readings that might give students ideas for projects, or by using class discussion to explore possible projects.

2. Let students reject the idea of doing a project. Students who do not wish to do a project should be allowed to do something else.

3. Assist students in selecting projects for which they are likely to experience success, which means topics that are narrow enough to be clearly understood by the student. It also means topics for which they have available the necessary materials, equipment, and other resources.

4. Let students plan the procedure they will follow. Help them with their planning.

5. Guide students as they proceed with their plan.

6. Allow students to share the progress and outcomes of their project study with other students. The worth inherent in this form of study derives not only from individual contributions to the tangible product but also from the learning that can result from the experience and the sharing of that experience.

7. Evaluate the students' work in terms of quality, the quantity of time spent, and the knowledge acquired.

Making Time for Individual Instruction

Individualized instruction is an extremely time-consuming way of teaching. Unless you are willing to relinquish center stage and allow students to accept much of the responsibility for their own learning, it is an impossible way to teach. To help students make the right decisions, you must provide them with self-instructional materials, study guides, learning packets, and self-administering and self-correcting tests and exercises. And you must also ensure that necessary materials, resources, and equipment are readily available. When these provisions are made, students can move ahead without waiting for you. Without the necessary materials and equipment, you will never find time to do all the work that needs to be done with each individual student.

Arrangements also must be made for students to help each other. Young people can and do learn from their peers. Bright students can help the slower students, though perhaps more effective is to let the average or slow student who has mastered a concept or skill help students who have not yet done so. Be careful, however, that you do not exploit your successful students.

If you keep your classes informal, as in the laboratory-type class, you will find that you have much more time to do important things than if you keep to formal classes. Still, no matter what approach you use, you will be busy.

Accepting Different Evidence of Accomplishment

If to provide for individual differences you arrange for students to learn in different ways, you must allow for different evidences of student progress and achievement. Of course, every student should attain the major goals. But if you allow some students to learn through verbal symbolization and others to learn from more concrete activities, then in estimating student accomplishment you should consider the levels of learnings that are associated with the different learning activities.

Need for a Variety of Materials

To provide for individual differences there must be a variety of things for students to do. A single textbook course will no longer suffice. The teacher needs materials suitable to the variety of interests, ability levels, learning styles, and modalities. Not only do you need a variety of materials, but also you need them to be where the students can get them when needed. The classroom suitable for truly individualized instruction must be full of attractive and usable materials, readily available for student use. Such a classroom would in itself be a resource center—truly a laboratory for learning.

The time for you to start preparing for the creation of this type of classroom is now, before you begin to teach. To wait until you meet your first class of students will unnecessarily inhibit you from reaching your goal. If you have not already started a filing system to preserve pictures, charts, handouts, and so on, then start now. (You may want to return to Exercise 2.6, in which you began to build your own resource file.) Down the road, you may need to edit your resource file to keep it to a manageable size, but to delete some of the items you have collected is easier than to have to find the precise one that you neglected to save.

Exercise 12.3 will help you begin thinking about the ideal classroom.

Teaching Homogeneously Grouped Classes

In many schools, students are grouped homogeneously, sometimes by a deliberate plan of ability grouping, sometimes by incidental selection as the more academically talented students select the more academically rigorous courses, and sometimes by a

EXERCISE 12.3   DESIGNING AN IDEAL CLASSROOM

Your purpose for this exercise is to think about and then design an ideal—but plausible—classroom for the subjects and grade levels you intend to teach. Think about the type of classroom activities you want to concentrate on using and about the materials and equipment that you would like to have on hand. This is supposed to be a fun exercise for you, one in which you can dream and create. Then, lay out in detail that dream classroom of yours, complete with exterior dimensions, window and door locations, and everything else that you would need to make it your ideal classroom. Include:

1. Your name
2. Subject and grade level for which the classroom is designed
3. Date

Upon completion of your ideal classroom share your design with your classmates, explaining to them the rationale of all its inclusions.

combination of the two. Varying your course content and methods of teaching according to the type of class you have will make your teaching more effective.

The Academically Talented

Since most teaching methods were first invented for use with academically talented and motivated students in mind, you can use any methods presented in this book when teaching such students. You should always try to make the work interesting and challenging, to give the talented students plenty of opportunity to exercise their talents, and to move the course briskly. The following specific suggestions will be of help:

☐ Challenge the talented to think and dig deep into a subject. Use problem solving, inquiry, and open-ended assignments. Insist that students dig deep into the subject. Hold them to a high level of analysis and critical thinking.

☐ See that high academic standards are maintained, not allowing sloppy thinking or sloppy work. Hold the students responsible for disciplined thinking and work.

☐ Don't hold these students back in their work. Give them opportunity to move on to more interesting or challenging material. They should not have to repeat what they already know or have done.

☐ Be sure they are well grounded in the academic skills.

☐ Provide maximum responsibility for their own work, letting them plan and evaluate. Encourage their independent study and research.

☐ Use high-level materials, including original sources, advanced textbooks, and appropriate reading levels.

☐ Use the seminar discussion strategy in which students present and criticize original papers or reports and discuss topics in depth. Be sure that their discussions hew to a high level of criticism and thinking.

☐ Involve the students in inviting guest speakers to class and in planning interesting and relevant field trips.

☐ Familiarize yourself with special off-campus programs that are specifically designed for the gifted and talented and encourage your students to get involved. Although special programs may be expensive, scholarships are often available.[11]

☐ Try to provide these students with opportunities to work with the latest media and audiovisual materials available for learning in your subject field.

The Academically Slow

Slower learners in middle and secondary school classes are typically of two different types of students: (1) those students who try to learn but simply need more time to do it, and (2) those students who are capable but do not try, referred to variously as underachievers, recalcitrant, or reluctant learners.[12] Teaching strategies that work well with those who do try do not necessarily work well with those students who do not try—making life difficult for a teacher who has a class of 30 students, half who try and half who do not. It is worse still for a teacher who has a class of 30 students that includes some who try but have difficulty, one or two gifted learners, and some who seem unwilling to try.[13]

Guidelines for Teaching Slow Students Who Indicate Willingness to Try. The following guidelines may be helpful when working with a slow student who is willing to learn:

1. Emphasize basic communication skills, such as speaking, listening, reading, and writing.

---

[11]Excellent programs are available for talented junior high and senior high school students at Johns Hopkins University, California State University at Sacramento, and the University of North Texas at Denton.

[12]This section adapted from Kim and Kellough, pp. 190–192. By permission of Macmillan Publishing Company.

[13]Richard D. Kellough, "The humanistic approach: An experiment in the teaching of biology to slow learners in high school—an experiment in classroom experimentation," *Science Education* 54(3):253–62 (1970).

2. Help these students improve their reading skills, such as pronunciation, word meanings, and comprehension.

3. Teach content in small sequential steps with very frequent (at least four during one class period) comprehension checks.

4. Vary your instructional strategies often (about every 10 minutes), and use a variety of audiovisual and games materials to engage the visual, verbal, and kinesthetic.

5. Through frequent use of individual positive reinforcement, attend to increasing individual students' sense of personal worth.

6. If you are using a single textbook, be certain that the reading level is adequate for individual student use, or else discard it and rely on materials that you prepare specifically for these students.

7. You probably should not rely upon successful completion of out-of-class student homework unless the assignments are carefully made to ensure student success. Maximize the use of in-class on-task work and the use of cooperative learning, with your close monitoring of individual student progress. You will be moving around the classroom much of the time, and a rule of thumb is that if by the end of the school day your calf muscles do not ache, then you haven't been mobile enough in the classroom.

8. At the beginning of the semester, learn as much about each of the students as you possibly can.

9. Be less concerned with content coverage than with the students' successful understanding of content that is covered, and with their developing self-concepts. Content knowledge testing, if used at all, is used only as an indicator of progress being made. Grading may be necessary but is largely irrelevant. Check with a school administrator about the possibility of using credit/no credit grading or "therapeutic" grading if you think either would be more suitable to your purposes.

10. Use cooperative learning for slow learners who need specific remediation.

11. Individualize the learning as much as possible.

Guidelines for Teaching the Recalcitrant Learners.   For working with the recalcitrant learners you can use many of the same guidelines recommended for the slower learners, except that you should understand that the reasons for their educational behaviors may differ. Slower learners are simply slower to learn, but they can learn and are willing to learn. Recalcitrant learners may be slow, or they may even be gifted. Frequently they have inadequate self-concepts about learning and personal problems that simply distract them from their school work. Because of personal problems, many have a long history of poor attention to schoolwork habits. Consider the following guidelines:

1. Make clear your classroom behavior rules (CBRs) at the beginning, and show that you intend to enforce them.

2. At the beginning of the semester, learn as much about each of the students as you possibly can, but be cautious in how you do this because many of these students will suspect any indication of a genuine interest in them shown by you or any other adult. Be businesslike, trusting, genuinely interested, and patient.

3. Early in the semester, with the help of adult volunteers, work out an individual education program (IEP) with each individual student.

4. Help these students improve their studying and learning skills, such as concentrating, remembering, and comprehension. Mnemonics, for example, is a device these students positively respond to.

5. Teach content in small, sequential steps with very frequent (at least four during one class period) comprehension checks.

6. Use a variety of audiovisual and simulation materials to engage the visual, verbal, and kinesthetic, especially designed to engage students in active learning as afforded by inquiry and real problem solving.

7. Through frequent use of individual positive reinforcement, help increase each individual student's sense of personal worth. This can be accomplished in a variety of ways, such as special tutoring for individual students by adult volunteers from the community and by group class meetings designed to diminish individual anxieties, angers, and frustrations.

8. If you are using a single textbook, be certain that the reading level is adequate for individual student use, or else discard it and rely on materials that you have prepared specifically for these students.

9. You should not rely upon successful completion of out-of-class student homework unless the assignments are carefully made to ensure student success. Maximize the use of in-class on-task work and the use of cooperative learning, with your close monitoring of individual student progress.

10. Be less concerned with content coverage than with the students' successful understanding of content that is covered, and with their developing self-concepts. Content knowledge testing, if used at all, is used only as an indicator of progress being made. Grading may be necessary but is largely irrelevant. Check with a school administrator about the possibility of using credit/no credit grading or "therapeutic" grading if you think either would be more suitable to your purposes.

11. Forget about trying to use traditional teaching techniques, such as lecturing; rather, individualize the learning as often as you possibly can. With the combined use of their IEPs, individual student contracts, and self-instructional packages, you have a sure-fire direction for success with these at-risk students. But their programs will take considerable amounts of your time and energy to prepare and implement.

The Culturally Different

Students from poverty areas or from ethnic minority groups are often products of cultures quite different from the middle-class culture to which most teachers belong.[14] That their cultures should be so different is not surprising, for the United States is a country of many cultures, many of which result from ethnic heritage — African American, Cuban American, Puerto Rican American, Italian American, Polish American, Native American, Jewish American, Iranian American, Filipino American, Chinese American, Mexican American, French Canadian American, and so on. California students, for example, represent more than 70 language groups and dozens of nations.[15] Some inner-city California school systems are trying to cope with student bodies made up of students who speak 40 to 50 different languages.

Other cultural groups are the result of economic differences. The cultures of the upper class, the middle class, the urban poor, and the rural poor differ considerably even when they are all white, Anglo-Saxon, and protestant, for people who live in poverty seem to develop a culture of poverty and families from the upper class seem to develop a culture quite different from that of middle-class families.[16] In fact, the various cultures are frequently more a product of socioeconomic factors than of ethnic factors.

Let us now examine some of the educational problems of the children of poverty — the socioeconomically disadvantaged.

The Socioeconomically Deprived

Students from the lowest socioeconomic classes are individuals. We often think of them as deprived — and of course to be poor is not an advantage. Poverty deprives people of many of life's amenities and opportunities, but not all poor people are deprived.

---

[14]This section from Clark and Starr, pp. 357–66. By permission of Macmillan Publishing Company.

[15]Laurie Olsen, "Crossing the Schoolhouse Border: Immigrant Children in California." *Phi Delta Kappan* (November, 1988) 70:211–18.

[16]Oscar Lewis, *Current* (December, 1966), pp. 28–32.

Children of the poorest socioeconomic classes and of racial and ethnic minorities may be the recipients of warm support from parents and grandparents in their extended families and of a rich cultural heritage, of pride of race and ethnicity, skills of coping and self-reliance, and, to them, a most satisfactory lifestyle. Be careful not to make overquick judgments concerning who is or is not deprived.

Many students from poor neighborhoods are truly deprived, however. Among them are boys and girls:

Whose homes are hovels, shacks, or run-down tenements;

Whose homes are really the streets;

Whose homelife is barren and abusive;

Who have never lived in homes where there were books, magazines, and other cultural amenities, or where people enjoyed reading;

Whose family members are illiterate;

Who never have had occasion to hear, not to say learn, standard English;

Whose families consist of single parents living on the edge of despair and defeat;

Who lack any sort of desirable guidance and help at home;

Who lack any reputable adult figures to pattern their lives after;

Whose education has been interrupted by frequent moves to escape arrest as illegal aliens or as migrant workers;

Whose families cannot supply adequate food and clothing;

Who, in sort, live lives that are just plain miserable!

Fortunately these youths frequently have much more potential than surface appearances indicate. They deserve more from their schools than faint-hearted teaching. The following paragraphs include suggestions that may make the task easier.

1. Often the handicap that is holding back a deprived youth may be the inability to read well. Sometimes simply adjusting the reading level of the material to be studied may make the difference between student learning and student frustration. Make every effort to bring the students' reading abilities up to par as quickly as possible. Until this objective has been achieved, try to find easy reading material suitable for the age and interest levels of the students. Use a variety of reading materials. Use multiple readings in laboratory fashion rather than the single textbook. Use adult material of low reading level. (Certain metropolitan newspapers are written for adult readership at quite low reading levels, for instance.) In addition use materials other than reading matter: tapes, recordings, videotapes, films, and pictures. Where no suitable reading matter is available, prepare your own. Paraphrase difficult reading matter so that the poor readers can read it. Try to make it informative, interesting, and adult but easy to read and understand. Strive for clarity. Use short, direct sentences and basic everyday words, and keep the text clear, to the point, and sparsely worded. Provide the students with good intellectual food, but do not overload your text with too many ideas.

2. Use simple language in the classroom. Worry less about the words students use and the way they express themselves and more about the ideas they are expressing. Let them use their own idioms without carping overmuch on grammar, syntax, and the like. However, take care to use proper English yourself. Do not conduct classes in dialect.

3. Be sure the work laid out for the deprived students is realistic. Forget about covering the subject and concentrate on teaching well. The best procedure seems to be to pick a theme or topic and divide it into short segments. In teaching these segments seek out much feedback in order to be sure that the students learn the essentials of each segment before they move on to the next one. Because attendance of poor students is likely to be sporadic, try to individualize their assignments so that they can pick up where they left off and move through the course in an orderly fashion even when they have been absent excessively. Use laboratory techniques, individual

instruction, and individual help. Adjust the subject content to the needs of the students. Because many of them are physically oriented, they enjoy working on concrete projects. Begin at the students' level and then move toward the more abstract and academic.

4. In giving assignments, make directions clear and explicit. You can often help students tremendously if you will only show them how to study. This is especially true when teaching children from poverty-stricken environments.

Assignments should not only be realistic in length and difficulty, they should also be realistic with respect to the experience, needs, and expectations of the students. Students from poverty areas need a curriculum that seems valuable to them and is close enough to their own lives to have meaning. They profit from learning from people at home and in the community. They need to learn about themselves.

5. Try to capitalize on students' interests and point out the practical value of what is to be learned. Take advantage of their belief in the usefulness of the fundamentals, the vocational, and the scientific. Let them read the sports page, science fiction, or anything else that will get them started. This is no time for intellectual snobbery.

A discussion that is centered on topics with which the students have some firsthand familiarity can be a lively, informative, thought-provoking learning experience. When, at Jersey City's Snyder High School, one of the "difficult" classes discussed ways to improve the city, the students had an opportunity not only to express themselves in full discussion but also to think seriously about problems of some importance to themselves personally. Poor adolescents, like other students, manufacture their own concepts. They will build on them most effectively if they learn by means that emphasize thinking and creativity.

This illustration points up the fact that classes for "deprived" youth should be interesting, relevant, and active. Role-playing and dramatic presentations are often very successful. In Central High School, Newark, New Jersey, for instance, a Black Studies class noted for its high rate of absenteeism showed an amazing amount of potential talent when it rehearsed, read, and videotaped a short play. At least one student who was believed to be a nonreader showed that she could not only read but read dramatically when the occasion seemed worthwhile.

Other teachers have achieved good results from having students create a class book out of their own writing. A junior high school teacher in an extremely difficult slum area uses student-designed and -executed bulletin boards and displays very effectively. Classes that feature games are usually popular as well as classes that make use of the various media. Classes that use a variety of materials are always likely to be more interesting than textbook recitations. Books should probably always be thought of as aids to learning, but they should not be the be-all and end-all of instruction in classes in which students do not read well.

6. Make sure that each student has real success. Everyone needs the feeling that comes from succeeding in doing something worthwhile. Poor adolescents do not have such feelings in school often enough. One way to provide them with the opportunity to experience such feelings is to encourage them to help each other with troublesome assignments and to work together in cooperative learning groups. Such arrangements provide students with allies and coworkers with whom they can share both the work and the responsibility. Because they are not alone in the learning endeavor, they can look to other students for support, and so the fear of failure or of appearing foolish is not so pressing. Students frequently learn better from other students, and as a result both the helper and the one being helped are rewarded with a feeling of success and importance.

7. Physical activities are useful in classes of lower socioeconomic-status students. Acting out scenes or role-playing can sometimes be very effective, particularly in teaching history or interpreting literature. The tendency of students from the lower socioeconomic classes to be physically oriented also makes it likely that they will take favorably to teaching machines and other gadgetry. Give them plenty of chances to learn by doing, for such activities will ordinarily be much more successful than lecturing and other primarily verbal techniques.

8. From the preceding paragraphs, you can readily see that students from poverty areas, just as other students, benefit from taking the responsibility for charting and conducting their own learning activities. Teachers tend to do too much for students when we should encourage them to do things themselves. Try to involve students in the planning and executing of the lessons. If you start with something familiar to them, they are usually competent enough to take a large share in the decision making if they have a little help and guidance.

9. Poor adolescents need to have opportunities to create and to learn to think. Problem-solving activities that are consistent with the ability levels and experience of the students seem to be excellent for these students.

10. Open-ended questions and discussions can also be used with good results. To make them most effective, you should learn to conduct discussions as conversations. The ordinary teacher-centered discussion is liable to be more like an inquisition than a conversation. That is too bad, because it tends to stop students from thinking. Instead, use unstructured discussions of real problems. Unstructured discussions may help you understand the students and help them learn how to express themselves. In selecting problems to study, (a) be sure the problems seem real to the students, and (b) be sure to pick problems they will accept. Sometimes they do not recognize problems as problems. Sometimes they do not want to. In such cases you may get them to see the truth by challenging their thinking. The Socratic method is useful for this purpose. Use it to pursue the faulty thinking of individual students. In doing so, be careful to let each student keep his self-respect. On the other hand, do not force students into discussions they would rather avoid. There is no point in discussing what they already know too much about.

11. Respect both the students and their culture. Accept the students as persons, and let them know by your behavior that you are on their side. Because of unfortunate past experiences, the students will sometimes need a great deal of convincing. Try to overcome the hostility by deeds, not words. Do not talk down to the students. Do not be condescending. Do not demean yourself. Tend to your teaching and concentrate on getting the material across. If you convince the students that you respect them and are trying your best to teach them, you may find that their hostility will be replaced by loyalty and respect.

12. If students have not learned basic skills because of failure in the earlier grades, help them learn those skills. You should expect to do a considerable amount of remedial teaching.

13. Be firm, strict, and definite, but not harsh. Harsh measures may seem to work on the surface, but as a rule they make it more difficult to carry out any meaningful communication or real learning. Firmness, definiteness, and strong control are absolute necessities, however, especially in the first few weeks of classes when the students will test you to find out what they can get away with.

14. Because deprived youths may be disaffected and suspicious, you must make an extra effort. Use the same techniques for both poor and affluent youth, but change the tactics to allow for differences in the situation. Avoid watering down courses and course requirements; doing so may lead to further educational deprivation. Do provide intensive remedial techniques wherever needed and make the coursework relevant to the lives of the students.

15. Be sure the course content has meaning to the students and relates to their lives and interests. Be sure the content helps the students to understand themselves and their role so that they can learn how to function in society. Do not put this at a low how-to-do-it level but at a high enough level so that they can understand what is really involved. Give them real work. Do not feed them pap. If the students cannot do the work required of them, substitute work they can do but make it something respectable.

16. Avoid boring the students but do use plenty of repetition, review, and drill to develop skills, proper habits, and firm knowledge.

Ethnic Groups

The school population includes numerous students from racial and ethnic minorities. In recent years, this diversity has been enriched by waves of immigrants, particularly those coming to escape troubles in Asia and in Latin America. This influx of immigrants, while enriching life in the United States, also greatly increases the problem of supplying an appropriate education for all American youth.

Every ethnic group has its own culture. Some of these cultures are somewhat similar to the culture of poverty described in the preceding section of this module, partly because the ethnic groups and the lower socioeconomic groups tend to overlap. Do not, however, make the mistake of thinking that because a student is a poor immigrant he or she follows the pattern of the culture of poverty.

All ethnic cultures are rich, but each is different. These differences may be difficult to understand unless you take steps to learn about them and respect them. If you do not do so, you may find teaching your students difficult because cultural differences result in different ways of learning. For example, unlike most middle-class white American students, black children tend to spend time setting the stage before starting to work on their lessons. Instead of getting to work immediately, they are inclined to take time to look over the assignment, check the lesson material, and ask questions. This cultural trait tends to reduce the amount of time they spend on task. Some teachers take this delay as a sign of misbehavior, but it is not intentionally so, and in some cases may make the students' studying a better organized procedure.[17]

Similarly, urban poor black youth may not do well in rigidly structured classes with fixed time schedules. They do much better in informal, loosely structured class arrangements. In such classes, they work best together cooperatively at their own pace, preferably focusing on general principles and ideas rather than on detail. Furthermore, they believe that, no matter how successful or unsuccessful they have been, their efforts should be recognized. Another black cultural trait to which you should adjust is their preference for oral over written communication. They generally learn best from listening, and they perform best when speaking. Also their oral communication is more likely to be dramatic, artistic talk such as is often heard from their clergy rather than the direct, concise straightforwardness that schools advocate. These differences in communication can cause a conflict between the school instruction and the students' learning style that may require you to adjust your teaching style in order to attain an optimum learning environment.[18]

You need also to be acquainted with the mores and taboos of the culture from which your students spring. Things that you do as a matter of course, without thinking, may appear gauche, impolite, or disrespectful to people of other cultures. Poor black students, for instance, often expect to be called by name rather than a nickname. A black student may consider persons who address him as Jim or Jimmy, rather than James, to be disrespectful. They believe that the use of nicknames should be reserved for intimates only. Similarly, be aware of the meaning of gestures, signs, and body language. To cross one's fingers as middle-class Americans do to entice good luck or to ward off bad luck is considered obscene by Southeast Asians, for instance. Students from some cultural groups, such as certain Native Americans, believe that to strive to be singled out for distinction or praise in class is bad manners. For you to single out a student for special praise or recognition could be most embarrassing for that student.

Become familiar with the meaning of the symbols and superstitions peculiar to some cultures. For a Vietnamese to dress in white is a sign of mourning, for instance. If you can recognize their signs and symbols and show respect for their taboos and customs, your life with students from other cultures can become considerably easier.

---

[17]Shirl E. Gilbert and Geneva Gay, "Improving the Success of Poor Black Children." *Phi Delta Kappan* (October, 1988), *133*:137.

[18]Ibid.

Do not, however, assume that the supposed characteristics of an ethnic group are common to all members of that group. Remember that individuals in every ethnic group can differ from one another. Avoid making unwarranted generalizations based on students' race or language. Not all Asian parents, for instance, fit the stereotypes often given them (i.e., quiet, submissive, reserved, and cooperative). The old saying that "one man's meat is another man's poison" is just as true for other ethnic groups as your own. Everyone has likes and dislikes. Socioeconomic status, place of origin, religion, and so on, all have their influence on individual beliefs, values, and notions about correct behavior. Class differences are as great in minority ethnic and racial groups as in the mainstream society. A poverty-stricken immigrant is not usually the same sort of person as a prosperous American physician, even though they may spring from the same race and nationality. In a New Jersey suburb, for instance, parents revolted at a program set up to introduce youngsters to American schools. The prosperous representatives of Japanese firms living in New Jersey with offices in New York City did not appreciate what they considered a lesser program for their children and made their feelings known not only at the school but also in the statehouse. Remember also that people from Asian or from Latin American countries may be from different nationalities. Again, in metropolitan New Jersey, in one school there occurred clashes between Cubans and Puerto Ricans who did not empathize with one another very well. Cubans are not Puerto Ricans or Mexicans, and Japanese are not Chinese or Vietnamese, any more than Americans are Canadians, French are Germans.

Obviously, to make your teaching efficient and effective, your teaching strategies must be compatible with the students' cultural background. Therefore make it a point to learn as much as you can about that culture. To that end talk to other more experienced school personnel and to interested laypersons. They can not only give you tips on what you should know but also may be able to suggest helpful reading. Take advantage of every opportunity, for the need for studying your students' culture is worth every effort. Esther Lee Yao suggests that if you are dealing with Asian immigrant youth, you can learn about the local Asian community by visiting local Asian businesses and by attending local Asian festivities. The businessowners and festival attendees will usually be glad to explain the high points of their world to you if properly approached.[19]

You can also learn much from parents of your students. However, when speaking to parents, be very polite and politic. Be careful to use language that could not be interpreted detrimentally—for example, say "unfamiliar with American customs" rather than "rude" and "uninterested" rather than "lazy." It is also helpful if you can become familiar with their body language. Also, when you are talking to Asian parents about their children, you would be wise to describe the students' strengths before you bring up any weaknesses or proposals for remediation and requests for support.[20]

You can also learn a great deal from the students themselves. Talk with them. Let them present their experience in the world as topics for themes and talks. In one class, the students put together a booklet about their experiences. These experiences sometimes make excellent firsthand resource information for social studies classes, especially if your students are recent immigrants.

One important step that you can take in your attempts to understand your students and their cultures is to become very familiar with your own ethnic background and the characteristics of your culture. Perhaps, if you become more familiar with the culturally learned opinions, attitudes, and assumptions of your own cultural group, your understanding of other cultural beliefs will improve.

Whenever feasible, you should try to incorporate ethnic materials to bolster your teaching; to help students come to grips with the pluralism of modern American society;

[19]Esther Lee Yao, "Working Effectively with Asian Immigrants' Parents." *Phi Delta Kappan* (November, 1988), *70*:223–225.

[20]Ibid.

and to eliminate racial, cultural, and ethnic bias. In most up-to-date school systems the curriculum builders have provided curriculum materials for teachers' use. The point is to use such materials judiciously so as to eliminate bias and stereotyping. In every course students should have opportunities to show pride in their roots and to make the most of their talents.

You should also make yourself familiar with the language of the groups. If your students are Spanish speaking, learn basic Spanish. If they speak a dialect of the ghetto, learn it. Do not worry so much about the words students use and the ways they express themselves as about the ideas they are expressing. Let them use their own idioms without carping on grammar, syntax, and the like. Do, however, try to help them master the skills of standard English. Your own instruction should be in excellent but simple standard English.

Otherwise, your basic strategies for teaching culturally different students should not differ greatly from good teaching of any other students.

The New Immigrants.   The major problem for recent immigrants and some other ethnic groups is the language barrier. In 1980 more than half the students in New York City lived with parents whose native tongue was not English. Yet, standard English is a virtual necessity in most American communities if a person is to become vocationally successful and enjoy a full life. Further, language is the most important medium by which students new to the United States can integrate their former lifestyle with the new to them Americanism they are now facing. This language problem places a heavy burden on teachers. Learning to communicate reasonably well in English takes an immigrant youth at least a year, probably more; some authorities say three to seven years. Their early English is seldom good enough for them to cope with school classes. Even then it becomes necessary for teachers to adjust their teaching considerably to allow for students' lack of facility in English.

Language problems make it quite difficult to know where to place immigrant students. How do you handle a student who has very little comprehension in English but who is a whiz in calculus? Intelligence tests are not much help. They are built on the supposition that the student understands English and American ways. Students probably should not be pulled out of the regular program to attend special classes unless absolutely necessary, but they need bilingual support, which the school should supply.

In laying out courses for ethnic students, take care that the course work seems relevant to them. However, when dealing with immigrant students from war-torn areas, be cautious. Course content can sometimes be too relevant—too close to home—and concern things that the students would do better to forget than to discuss or investigate. Immigrant children who have suffered the traumas of war, revolution, and terrorism should not have to live through it again in your classes. If a situation is not threatening, students are usually quite willing to investigate. Your problem is to encourage them, not to discourage them by bringing up their traumatic past or by making them appear foolish or stupid as they face your abstraction.

Parents of immigrant children are ordinarily truly concerned about their children. They are often troubled about the direction in which the American schools seem to be taking their children. The value systems, manners, moral standards, traditions, and social behavior that the children are learning in school so often do not conform to those the parents hold dear. They would be glad to help you and other teachers do well by their children. Sometimes their educational goals seem to be set extremely high. Unfortunately, they often do not know enough about American customs and education in order to help their children much. If you solicit their help, they may do all they can to help, and perhaps you and they can fill each other in as you go along.

Working with Handicapped Students

In Public Law 94-142, the Education for All Handicapped Children Act, Congress mandates that all students have the right to a full and free public education. The legislation requires the least restrictive environment for special students—the hard of hearing, the deaf, the speech impaired, the visually handicapped, the mentally handi-capped, the emotionally disturbed, and the orthopedically impaired. It has placed em-phasis on mainstreaming and a normalized environment for all students.

In effect, this means that you must be, part of your time, a special education teacher. Basically, special education teaching is not very different from ordinary teach-ing, except that it requires more care, better diagnosis, greater skill, more attention to individual needs, and greater understanding of the students. Yet, the challenges of teaching handicapped persons in the regular class are great enough so that to do the job right, you need additional specialized training far beyond the scope of this book. Before you get far into your teaching career, you should take courses in teaching the handicapped in regular classrooms.

Because of its concern for problems of the handicapped, Congress has decreed that an Individualized Educational Program (IEP) be devised for each handicapped student. According to law, each IEP should be made up by a team of specialized personnel, parents, and classroom teachers yearly. It should contain (1) a statement of the student's present educational levels, (2) the educational goals for the year, (3) specifications for the services to be provided and the extent to which the student should be expected to take part in the regular program, and (4) the type, direction, and evaluative criteria for the services to be provided. Consultation by special and skilled support personnel becomes essential in all mainstream models. The consultant works directly with teachers or with students and parents. You should have an active role in the preparation of these specifications for the handicapped students assigned to your classes as well as the major responsibility for carrying them out.

Some general guidelines for working with handicapped students within the frame-work of the regular class are:

1. Maintain a consistent approach. Students find themselves very frustrated when they cannot depend upon teacher reactions to their responses.

2. Define objectives in behavioral terms.

3. Adapt and modify materials and procedures to the special needs of the handicapped. Children with cardiac conditions can be umpires in baseball games. A child who cannot sit still for longer than 10 minutes might require a change in learning activity every 10 minutes.

4. Reward approved and acceptable behavior and generally ignore unacceptable be-havior.

5. In planning lessons, break complex activities into simple components, move from the known to the unknown, let slower children learn through interesting and real experiences.

6. Anticipate. Watch for signs of restiveness, frustration, anxiety, unwillingness to work. Change assignments on an individual basis, if necessary.

7. Provide for as much student success as you can. Handicapped children have not usually experienced much success. Give them activities and experiences that ensure success and some mastery.

SUMMARY

The individualization of instruction requires that you provide opportunities for students to work toward different goals, to study different content, and to work in different ways. Just to vary the rate or amount of work the students do is not enough. A list of fifteen techniques and methods you might use follows. Each of these methods or techniques has been described somewhere in this module. As you go through the list, see if you can describe how to carry out each of the techniques.

1. Vary your tactics and techniques in classes according to the abilities and personality characteristics of your students.

2. Run your class as a classroom laboratory.

3. Utilize the facilities of the library or resource center.

4. Utilize small-group instruction.

5. Differentiate your classwork and homework assignments.

6. Give special assignments to individual students or small groups.

7. Use individual or group projects.

8. Encourage independent study.

9. Use the unit method and unit assignments.

10. Use self-instructional materials such as self-correcting assignments, learning packets, computer-assisted instruction, and distance learning.

11. Give students special help.

12. Use the contract plan.

13. Use a continuous progress scheme. (You can run your course on a continuous progress plan even if the plan has not been adopted schoolwide.)

14. Use minicourses.

15. Use a variety of textbooks, readings, and other materials.

SUGGESTED READING

Baca, L. M., and Cervantes, H. T. *The Bilingual Special Education Interface.* Santa Clara, CA: Times Mirror/Mosby, 1984.

Banks, J. A., and Banks, C. A. M. *Multicultural Education: Issues and Perspectives.* Needham Heights, MA: Allyn & Bacon, 1989.

Blake, H. E. *Creating a Learning-Centered Classroom.* New York: A & W Visual Library, 1977.

Bloom, B. S. "The search for methods for group instruction as effective as one-to-one tutoring." *Educational Leadership* 41(8):4–18 (May 1984).

Epstein, J. L. "Paths to Partnership." *Phi Delta Kappan* 72(5):345–349 (January 1991).

Fenstermacher, G. D., and Goodlad, J. I. *Individual Differences and the Common Curriculum,* Eighty-second Yearbook of the National Society for the Study of Education, Part I. Chicago: The University of Chicago Press, 1983.

Gearheart, B. R., and Weishahn, M. W. *The Exceptional Student in the Regular Classroom.* Santa Clara, CA: Times Mirror/Mosby, 1984.

Hardman, M., et al. *Human Exceptionality.* 3d ed. Needham Heights, MA: Allyn & Bacon, 1990.

Hiemstra, R., and Sisco, B. *Individualizing Instruction.* San Francisco: Jossey-Bass, 1990.

Knapp, M. S., and Shields, P. M. "Reconceiving Academic Instruction for the Children of Poverty." *Phi Delta Kappan* 71(10):753–758 (June 1990).

Kulik, J. A. "Individualized systems of instruction." In H. E. Mitzel, ed. *The Encyclopedia of Educational Research.* 5th ed. New York: Macmillan, 1982.

Rose, M. *Lives on the Boundary.* New York: Penguin, 1989.

Stanley, J. C. "A better model for residential high schools for talented youths." *Phi Delta Kappan* 72(6):471–473 (February 1991).

Tuttle, F. B. *Gifted and Talented Students: What Research Says to the Teacher.* Rev. ed. Washington, DC: National Education Association, 1983.

Want, M. C., and Wahlberg, H. J., eds. *Adapting Instruction to Individual Differences.* Berkeley, CA: McCutchan, 1985.

Wright, J. D. *Teaching the Gifted and Talented in the Middle School.* Washington, DC: National Education Association, 1983.

POSTTEST   **Short Answer**

1. What does true individualization of learning entail?

   _____

   _____

   _____

   _____

2. Give a theoretical justification for homogeneous grouping.

   _____

3. Explain the meaning of the following statement: homogeneously grouped classes are not homogeneous.

   _____

4. What arguments are there against homogeneous grouping?

   _____

   _____

5. Describe the supposed merits of continuous promotion.

   _____

   _____

   _____

6. What is the principal reason for the introduction of minicourses?

   _____

7. What is the advantage of a learning center or a learning-activity center?

   _____

   _____

8. Explain at least two ways that you could differentiate an assignment.

   _____

   _____

9. What is meant by the term *classroom laboratory*?

   _____

   _____

10. Explain why the unit approach is recommended for providing for individualization.

    _____

    _____

11. Why is the learning activity package a good instrument for individualizing instruction?

    _____

    _____

12. Explain the essential difference between a learning contract and a learning activity package or unit.

    _____

    _____

13. Why are study guides used in individualizing instruction?

    _____

    _____

14. For what would you use self-correcting materials?

_____

15. How can you make time for working with individual students?

_____

_____

16. What difference in teaching style does homogeneous grouping require of you?

_____

_____

17. What should be contained in an IEP?

_____

_____

18. List five suggestions for teaching the academically talented.

_____

_____

_____

_____

_____

19. Describe recent research regarding the use of homogeneous grouping in schools.

_____

_____

_____

_____

20. Would it be advantageous, or even feasible, for a teacher to develop Individual Educational Plans (IEPs) for every student? Why or why not?

_____

_____

_____

_____

21. Describe the purposes for which you could design a learning-activity center.

_____

_____

_____

_____

22. Describe ways the school and teacher can effectively involve parents or guardians in their child's education.

_____

_____

_____

_____

PART V
Preparing and Using
Instructional Aids

Part V, consisting of two modules, facilitates your selection and use of specific instructional aids by:

□ Providing guidelines for the selection and use of nonprojected instructional resources.

□ Providing guidelines for the selection and use of projected instructional resources.

□ Providing guidelines for the selection and use of printed materials.

□ Providing guidelines for the use of visual display materials.

□ Providing ideas for sources of teaching materials.

What you do speaks so loudly, they can't hear what you say.
—Ralph W. Emerson

I've finally come to the conclusion that computers are smarter than people. Not once have I ever seen one jogging.
—Bob Orben

MODULE 13
Nonprojected Instructional Aids

RATIONALE

Long ago, when humankind was young and writing had not yet been invented, men and women taught their children by means of very simple tools. Telling children what they should know was a very important teaching technique, but there were other teaching and learning methods, too. Children learned to hunt by practicing with spears, by throwing sticks, and by simulating hunts of simulated animals. Parents taught geography by maps drawn in the sand and religion by pictures drawn on the walls of caves. The history, customs, and lore of a group were portrayed by dance and drama. From the very earliest times, teachers have depended on diverse teaching tools to make their teaching interesting and effective.

Today, teachers still depend on a variety of teaching tools to make their teaching interesting and effective. In some respects, though, modern teaching tools are much more sophisticated than those of old. Yet, we use our new tools for the same purposes and in much the same ways that our ancestors did: to make things clear, to make instruction real, to spice up the learning process, and to make it possible for students to teach themselves. Teaching would be impossible without some instructional aids, including printed materials, three-dimensional objects, and flat aids on which to write or display materials. This module is about these kinds of aids, called nonprojected visual aids. The projected visual aids, those that require electricity and that project material onto screens, are presented in the next module.

We begin this module with a discussion of textbooks. Although the most common of all teaching tools used in schools in this country, textbooks are not always chosen wisely or used effectively. Other printed materials, such as workbooks, can be a way to awaken thought and interest when used well but can be a source of tedium when used poorly. Sometimes the most useful of printed materials are teacher-made exercises and study guides as well as supplementary reading material.

If you are to teach effectively, how to get the most out of the various printed materials available will be one of the most pressing problems for you to solve. Similarly, you will have to master the use of display materials. Bulletin boards, pictures, charts, and similar displays often make the difference between students' understanding and not understanding.

When teachers create their own visual aids, audiovisual aids, and teaching devices (such as the self-instructional package presented in Module 4), they can raise their teaching from the humdrum of dispensing information to the excitement of experimenting with new ideas. This and the module that follows both end with suggestions about where and how to procure materials of instruction—after all, if you do not have it, you cannot use it.

SPECIFIC OBJECTIVES

At the completion of this module, you should be able to:

1. Explain the pros and cons of textbook use.
2. Describe recommended procedures for using textbooks.
3. Describe how to teach with multiple readings.
4. Describe criteria to consider when selecting textbooks.
5. Describe how other printed and duplicated materials may be used in your teaching.
6. Explain how to use display devices, including a writing board, a bulletin board, a flannel board, and charts and graphs.
7. Describe several sources for procuring free or inexpensive printed materials.

MODULE TEXT

Textbooks

Of all the materials of instruction, the textbook has had the most influence on teaching content and method. For many teachers, it has been the "be all and end all" of their instructional life. This is unfortunate because, properly used, the textbook is merely one of many teaching tools. It should not be revered as the ultimate word. As a tool, the textbook is an aid, a means to an end. Do not let it dominate you. You, not the textbook, are supposed to be the master.

Although textbooks are only teaching tools, they can be of great value, particularly to beginning teachers. You will find them very helpful in your planning, because they: (1) provide an organization or structure for the course; (2) provide selection of subject matter that can be used as a basis for determining course content and determining emphases; (3) provide a certain number of activities and suggestions for teaching strategies and tactics; and (4) provide information about other readings, sources of information, audiovisual and other aids, and other teaching materials and teaching tools.

You will also find that a textbook can make an excellent base for building interesting, high-order learning activities (discussion, inquiry, research activities) that call for critical thinking and other higher mental processes. On the other hand, textbooks are far from being the ideal tool some teachers take them to be. They have many faults. As used by many teachers, they assume too large a place in the classroom and in curriculum making. Their construction is often too rigid to allow them to fit in easily in today's enlightened classroom situation: they are sometimes dull; they discourage the reading of more profitable materials; they are often superficial; and above all they do not allow for differences in students' talents, interests, and goals. Uncritical users have a tendency to build their whole course around their text, modifying class activities to conform to the time needed for text analysis.

To get the most out of your textbooks and to avoid their weaknesses, you should:

☐ Become familiar with the textbook before you use it.

☐ Use the textbook in your planning as a source of structure if it seems desirable to do so, but do not let yourself become chained to the book.

☐ Use the text as only one of many materials and activities. Use other readings, simulation, role-playing, discussion, films, and pictures.

☐ Use problem-solving approaches in which the text is but one source of data.

☐ Use only those parts of the book that seem good to you. Skip the other parts, and rearrange the order of topics if you think it desirable. In other words, adapt the text to your pupils and their needs.

☐ Use additional or substitute readings to allow for differences in students.

☐ Provide help for students who do not read well.

☐ Teach students how to study the text and to use the parts of the text, such as table of contents, index, headings, charts, graphs, and illustrations.

☐ Use the illustrations, charts, graphs, and other aids included in the textbook in your teaching. Build lessons around them; study them.

☐ Encourage critical reading. Compare the text to source materials and other texts. Test it for logic and bias.

☐ Teach vocabulary.

☐ Incorporate the textbook into a multiple-text teaching strategy.

Introducing the Textbook

Because students seldom know how to use their texts efficiently and effectively, Cartwright has suggested that on the first day before they begin to read, you introduce students to the textbook in a lesson in which you and they discuss the following:[1]

1. *The title page.* What information does it give? When was the book written? Has it been revised? Who is the publisher? Where was it published? Do these indicate any likelihood of bias?

---

[1]William H. Cartwright, *How to Use a Textbook*, How to Do It Series, no. 2, rev. ed. (Washington, DC: National Council for the Social Studies, 1966).

2. *The preface.* What does the author claim he or she intended to do? What was his or her purpose?

3. *Table of contents.* How much weight is given to various topics? How can we use the information contained in the table of contents to help us study the text?

4. *The list of maps, charts, and illustrations.* What is the importance of these devices? How can one use them to aid study? Choose examples of each—maps, charts, tables, graphs, illustrations—and have pupils find essential information in them.

5. *Appendix.* What does *appendix* mean? What is it for?

6. *Index.* Use drill exercises to give pupils practice in using the index. These can be made into games or contests.

7. *Glossary.* What is a glossary? Why is it included? Utilize exercises that call for looking up words and then using them in sentences.

8. *Study aids at the ends of chapters.* How can study questions be used? Which are thought questions? Which are fact questions?

9. *Chapter headings, section headings, paragraph leads, introductory overviews, preliminary questions, and summaries.* What are the purposes of each of these? Use exercises that call for getting meaning from aids such as these without reading the entire text.

Selecting the Textbook

Because textbooks play such a large part in most classes, they should be selected carefully. In many schools textbook selection is made by a committee of teachers, and in some states the selection is made from a list of textbooks that has been approved by a statewide textbook adoption committee. In some schools, the teacher is free to choose whatever textbook that teacher wants. No matter what the selection process used, the text should be tested according to certain criteria. Exercise 13.1 provides the criteria and an opportunity for you to examine student textbooks against those criteria.

Item 29 of Exercise 13.1 concerns the reading or readability level of the textbook. Sometimes the reading level is supplied by the textbook publisher. If not, you can apply selections to a readability formula presented in Module 11 (see Exercise 11.1). A simple method for discovering whether a textbook is too difficult for the students is to ask them to read selections from it aloud. If they can read the selections without stumbling over many of the words and can tell you the gist of what has been said, you can feel confident that the textbook is not too difficult.

Multitext and Multireadings Approaches

Expressing a dissatisfaction with the single-textbook approach to teaching, some teachers have substituted a multitext strategy, in which they use one set of books for one topic and another set for another topic. This strategy provides some flexibility, though it really is only a series of single texts.

Other teachers—usually the more knowledgeable and proficient—use a strategy that incorporates many readings for a topic during the same unit. This multireading strategy gives the students a certain amount of choice in what they read The various readings allow for differences in reading ability and interest level. By using a study guide, all the students can be directed toward specific concepts and information, but they do not have to all read the same selections. To implement this type of multireading approach:

1. Select your instructional objectives.

2. Solicit the help of your school librarian. Generally, school librarians are quite willing to help you put a list of readings together.

3. Select a number of readings that throw a light on your objectives. Be sure there are several readings for each objective. Provide for variation in students' reading levels and interests as you make your selections.

EXERCISE 13.1 TEXTBOOK SELECTION CHECKLIST

The purpose of this exercise is to provide a form for your textbook selection process. Locate several textbooks used in a middle or secondary school course you intend to teach, and then review the textbooks with these criteria. (You will want to duplicate this form so you have a copy for each book reviewed.)

	Excellent 5	Good 4	Adequate 3	Problems 2	Poor 1	NA 0
A. Textbook						
1. Author(s) respected in field.						
2. Published by a respected company.						
3. Table of contents logically sequenced.						
4. Teacher's manual available.						
5. Testing materials available.						
6. Binding will hold up to use.						
7. Font (print) size for ease of reading.						
8. Page headers for quick reference.						
9. Free from excessive printing errors.						
10. Photographs (and other graphics) current.						
11. Graphics well displayed.						
12. References current and thorough.						
13. Relevant exercises provided.						
14. Latest edition has recent copyright.						
15. Clear and interesting writing style.						
B. Format						
16. Important ideas explained and defined.						
17. Difficult ideas visually represented.						
18. Chapter objectives provided.						

	Excellent 5	Good 4	Adequate 3	Problems 2	Poor 1	NA 0
19. Chapter summaries provided.						
20. Relevant resources provided.						
21. Useful research projects suggested.						
22. Useful and complete index provided.						
23. Useful glossary provided.						
C. CONTENT						
24. Content logical and complete.						
25. Meets course objectives.						
26. Concepts presented accurately.						
27. Footnotes (if any) useful to reader.						
28. Proper mix of cognitive question types.						
D. READING						
29. Appropriate readability level.						
30. Levels of abstraction appropriate.						
31. Material presented in an interesting way.						
32. Stereotypes avoided.						
33. Sexist and racist language avoided.						
34. Concrete examples of abstract concepts.						

SUBTOTALS _____

Textbook _____ TOTAL SCORE = _____

Author(s) _____

Publisher _____

Most Recent Copyright Date _____

Date of review _____ Reviewer _____

From E. C. Kim and R. D. Kellough, *A Resource Guide for Secondary School Teaching: Planning for Competence*, 5th ed. (New York: Macmillan, 1991); pp. 103–104. By permission of Macmillan Publishing Company.

4. Build a study guide that directs the students toward the objectives, and suggest readings appropriate to each objective.

5. Let the students select what they will read to meet the provisions of the guide.

Other Print Materials

The number and amount of printed materials suitable for instruction is almost infinite. Besides textbooks, there are other books, periodicals, pamphlets, and brochures. Many of these are available without cost or for only a small fee. Newspapers and magazines are excellent sources of reading matter for every one of the subject fields. They are also excellent sources of materials for bulletin boards. You should start now making a collection of things you might use, if you have not already done so. Once you have begun teaching, student and student committees can be utilized to do the gathering. Gathering materials is discussed later in the module.

Paperbacks

The paperback revolution of several decades ago opened up a great reservoir of fairly inexpensive reading matter for use in classes. Paperbacks make the multireading approach practicable. They also "make it possible to read primary sources rather than snippits, and both extensively and intensively rather than being exposed only to a single textbook account. With inexpensive paperbacks it is much easier to provide pupils with opportunities to analyze and compare works, a practice which is almost impossible if one uses only the ordinary textbook or anthology."[2]

Workbooks

Many schools use workbooks in their classes. Sometimes educators scoff at workbooks on the grounds that they encourage rote learning and discourage creative thought. These allegations hold true when the workbooks are limited to narrow fact questions and when the learning exercises require only that students search the text for pat answers, like dogs sniffing about the yard for a bone. Nevertheless, well-made workbooks can be useful tools. The learning activity packets that are so highly recommended by modern theorists are really a variation of the workbook. So are the duplicated exercises that are so often prepared by teachers. Well-written workbooks in the hands of skillful teachers can prove most effective as aids to learners. They are susceptible, to be sure, to abuse from the lazy teacher who uses them as a replacement for imagination and leadership. Even the best of aids loses its effectiveness when thoughtlessly overused or when no one bothers to follow up or check for the accuracy of written-in responses. Conscientious teachers:

☐ Try to find workbooks that emphasize thinking and problem solving rather than simple rote learning.

☐ Follow up the workbook assignments. They correct them. They use their exercises as bases for next steps.

☐ Use workbook assignments as a springboard for higher learning.

☐ Let students work on different exercises or different workbooks. There is no advantage in everyone's doing the same workbook exercises at the same time. However, if students are using workbooks not designed to accompany their text or syllabus, then cut and edit the workbook exercises so that they do match the course.

Duplicated Materials

The teaching tools used most by teachers are perhaps the duplicated materials they run off and give out to their students. These materials may be dittoed, mimeographed, or copied. Often they are prepared from commercially produced masters. More frequently, perhaps, they are teacher-made, typed or written by the teacher, and then reproduced. No matter what mode of production you use, you should make every effort to be sure that the copy given to the students is clear, attractive, and free from errors.

One of the most common types of duplicated material consists of duplicated exercises prepared by the teacher. All that has been said about workbooks applies to these exercises as well. When using them, you should consider the advisability of using answer sheets so that you can save the duplicated material and use it again. Sometimes teachers require pupils to retain their exercises and answer sheets in a notebook. The result is a sort of combination workbook and review book that can be helpful to both teacher and students. It has the advantage of being written for the class and course being taught and thus contains material the teacher wants included.

As you have already learned, springboards are materials or activities that, it is hoped, will be jumping-off places for student inquiry, investigation, or discussion. Among the materials used for springboards are films, film clips, and videotapes. Most consist of duplicated or printed reading matter, sometimes purchased from commercial sources, but more often homemade. Among the homemade springboard material you can make are descriptions of real or imagined situations that should arouse the curiosity of the students, case studies, historical accounts, news items, stories, and anecdotes. When you select material to be duplicated as a springboard, keep in mind the objective of arousing the student's interest and stirring up open-ended questions.

Among the most common uses of duplicated materials for instruction is the study guide (also discussed in Modules 4 and 12). Study guides are especially useful for students who are working alone or in small groups in individualized, laboratory-type classes; for students involved in special assignments, independent study, research activities, or supplementary assignments; and for such special activities as field trips and movie or TV watching. Their purpose is to provide students with directions and suggestions for carrying out the activity and to pose questions and problems that will provoke thought along the lines of the designated study. As self-instructional devices they tend to free students to inquire without the constriction of marking time until the teacher has an opportunity to attend to their status or achievement. Among the elements that may be found in a study guide are a statement of purpose, directions to follow, questions to answer, problems to solve, things to do, answer sheets, suggested reading, and suggested follow-up activities. An example of a special study guide follows:

SPECIMEN ACTIVITY GUIDE OR JOB BREAKDOWN

Project: Screwdriver—Wooden handle
Part: Handle—Hard maple
        Size $1\frac{1}{4}''$ sq. $\times$ 4″

1. Layout diagonals both ends.
2. Drill center holes.
3. Drill one end $\frac{31}{64}$ diameter $\times$ $1\frac{11}{16}$ deep.
4. Assemble ferrule and wood.
5. Turn $1\frac{1}{16}$ diameter entire length.
6. Turn $\frac{1}{4}$-inch radius knurled end.
7. Mill six grooves equidistant .050 deep.
8. Turn $\frac{1}{2}$-inch radius.
9. Sandpaper wooden surfaces only.
10. Get instructor's approval.

Prepare your own springboard study guide by doing Exercise 13.2.

EXERCISE 13.2   PREPARATION OF A SPRINGBOARD STUDY GUIDE

Review the material on springboards and study guides as presented in Modules 4 and 10. On separate paper prepare a springboard and general study guide for a unit you will likely teach. Think carefully about your conclusions and the organization of your guide so that it is clear, attractive, and useful. Upon completion, share your study guide with your classmates for their feedback about it.

If you wanted to copyright your springboard study guide, describe how you would go about doing that.

Copyright Law for Use of Printed Material

As a teacher you need to be aware of the laws regarding use of copyrighted printed materials. Your local school district may provide a copy of district policies. From section 107 of the 1976 Federal Omnibus Copyright Revision Act, here are some basic guidelines for the use of printed materials:

Permitted uses—you may make[3]

1. Single copies of: a chapter of a book; an article from a periodical, magazine, or newspaper; a short story, short essay, or short poem whether or not from a collected work; a chart, graph, diagram, drawing, cartoon, or an illustration from a book, magazine, or newspaper.

2. Multiple copies for classroom use (not to exceed one copy per student in a course) of: a complete poem if less than 250 words; an excerpt from a longer poem, but not to exceed 250 words; a complete article, story, or essay of less than 2,500 words; an excerpt from a larger printed work not to exceed ten percent of the whole or 1,000 words; one chart, graph, diagram, cartoon, or picture per book or magazine issue.

All permitted copying must bear an appropriate reference (i.e., author, title, date, source, publisher).

Prohibited uses—you may not

1. Copy more than one work or two excerpts from a single author during one class term.

2. Copy more than three works from a collective work or periodical volume during one class term.

3. Reproduce more than nine sets of multiple copies for distribution to students in one class term.

4. Copy to create or replace or substitute for anthologies or collective works.

5. Copy "consumable" works, e.g., workbooks, standardized tests, answer sheets.

6. Copy the same work from term to term.

Display and Display-Type Devices and Materials

There are infinite ways to display information and materials for students to see. Projected techniques are discussed in Module 13. In this section, other devices and materials are discussed. In using all of them, the following general and rather obvious rules apply: They should be clearly visible; be attractive; catch the eye; be simple, clear, and to the point; have a center of interest; and avoid clutter and confusion.

Writing Board

They used to be slate blackboards. Today, your classroom most likely will have either a board that is painted plywood (chalkboard), a magnetic chalkboard, or a white or colored (light-green and blue are common) multipurpose board on which you write with special marking pens. The multipurpose board can be used as a projection screen, to which figures cut from colored transparency film will stick; the board will often have a magnetic backing. Whichever type you have, here are guidelines for using the classroom writing board:

1. Use colored chalk (or marking pens) to visually highlight your "board talk," a strategy particularly beneficial for students with learning difficulties.

2. Start each class with a clean board, and at the end of class do not leave until you have cleaned the board for the teacher who follows you in this classroom—simple professional courtesy.

3. Print neatly, clearly, and orderly, beginning at the far left and large enough that all can see.

---

[3]E. C. Kim and R. D. Kellough, *A Resource for Secondary School Teaching: Planning for Competence*, 5th ed. (New York: Macmillan, 1991), p. 301. By permission of Macmillan Publishing Company.

4. Use the board to record student contributions. Print the name of the contributor, because that is a strong, positive reinforcer when a student is recognized thus by the teacher.

5. Rather than giving instructions orally, print them on the board.

6. Above the board you may find clips for hanging posters, maps, and so on. Use them.

7. Keep your own personal supply of chalk (or pens) with you at all times.

8. Do not block the view of your board writing, and do not write with your back to your audience.

9. If you have a lot of material to put on the board, do it prior to class, or better yet, put the material on transparencies and use the overhead projector rather than the chalkboard.

10. Plan, practice, and execute your board writing so that it is neat, legible, organized, and visible to all in the class.

Bulletin Boards

Bulletin boards are, or should be, instructional tools. You should treat them as such, not as classroom decorations. They can be used to motivate, interpret, supplement, and reinforce. To be useful teaching tools, they must be kept up to date and aimed at the objectives of the unit being taught. The following are a number of suggestions for effective use of bulletin boards:

1. Bulletin boards should be carefully planned. In planning the board, select one of the instructional aims of the unit and gather material suitable for that aim. Pick out the most desirable materials until you have only what seems to be the best of the lot. Resist the temptation to use too much material. Then sketch out a plan for presenting the material you have selected. In your plan try to do the following:
   a. Make the display tell a story.
   b. Have a center of interest (only one central idea or theme to a board).
   c. Use lines or arrows to draw the viewer to the center of interest.
   d. Be sure it is visible and eye-catching. Be sure captions and pictures are large enough to strike the eye. Keep captions brief and clear.
   e. Utilize questions, action, and drama to attract attention.
   f. Provide for plenty of white space. There should be no solid blocks of material and no clutter. Again, resist the temptation to use too much. A few well-selected items will have more impact than a large hodgepodge.
   g. Consider using unusual materials, such as three-dimensional objects, combining the bulletin board with a table display, or other devices to give the bulletin board zip. Color, variety, and humor add spice. To build a mood, coordinate the colors to the ideas or atmosphere you wish to present.

2. Turn the planning and preparation of the bulletin boards over to a pupil committee. You might have a competition to see who prepares the best board.

3. Be sure the materials are secured firmly and neatly. Consider the use of invisible fastening, such as bulletin board wax or adhesive plastic, or loops of masking tapes with the adhesive side out. Fasten one side of the loop to the material and the other to the wall. Or use double-faced adhesive tape, or tape tack units. These consist of a thumbtack stuck through a piece of adhesive tape with the adhesive side out. Fasten the tape to the material and fasten it to the bulletin board. Sometimes, fastening with brightly colored thumbtacks makes the display more interesting.

4. To be sure that the bulletin board stays up to date, keep a calendar or schedule for changing it.

5. Start a collection of bulletin board materials. Encourage pupils to bring in materials for your collection.

Charts

Charts can be used for displays just as bulletin boards are, but, as a rule, they are better suited for explaining, illustrating, clarifying, and reinforcing points in specific lessons. Among the many types of useful charts are lists, graphs, organizational charts, flowcharts, pictorial charts, diagrammatic presentations of cause and effect and other relationships, multicolumned lists showing contrast or comparison, and time charts and time lines. In general, the principles previously mentioned concerning the use of chalkboards and bulletin boards also apply to the use of charts. Clarity, simplicity, and dramatics are essential considerations. At the risk of a certain amount of repetition, consider the following suggestions:

1. Most of the charts used in classrooms should be the work of students who have found out the information, planned how to represent it, and executed the plan themselves.

2. Charts should be planned ahead. Sketch out the chart on a piece of paper before beginning the chart itself. Pencil in the details of the chart lightly before inking them in.

3. Make the chart simple. One major point is quite enough for a chart.

4. Make the chart clear. Avoid confusing detail. Do not crowd it. Use symbols one can understand.

5. Make charts eye-catching. Use colors and pictures.

6. Make charts forceful. Emphasize a central idea.

7. Be sure charts are visible. Make letters and symbols large enough. Leave plenty of white space so the message stands out.

8. Keep everything in proportion. Be careful of spacing.

9. Avoid too much printing and writing. Let the chart tell its own story. To avoid too much printing on the chart, use a legend and keyed symbols.

Graphs

Since graphs are a specialized type of chart, the suggestions for making and using graphs follow those for constructing and using charts. In addition, the following tips may prove valuable:

1. Keep the graph in proportion. This is particularly important.

2. Don't try to show too much on the same graph. If you wish to show several phenomena, use several graphs.

3. Be sure to select units that fit your idea and your paper. In making pie graphs (circle graphs), note that one percent $= 3.6°$ ($100\% = 360°$).

4. Be sure there is a common baseline for all phenomena represented. Have the baseline start at zero.

5. Be sure the total to which individual items are compared is shown.

6. Use color coding to show contrast, comparisons, or growth. Be sure the key tells exactly what each symbol represents.

7. Be sure to credit your sources.

8. Be sure the title is brief but clear.

Flip Charts

Flip charts are used frequently in schools, sales meetings, and television studios. They are really series of charts, set on a tripod, to illustrate points in the lesson. Certain map sets and series of biological charts are examples of commercially prepared flip charts. Homemade flip charts can be made on large pads such as those artists use for sketching. All you do is prepare a series of charts on the pages of the pad so that you can flip the pages over as you need them. They should be used the most in middle and secondary schools.

The simplicity of the flip chart's design makes it possible to move back and forth easily from chart to chart as one desires. Separate charts, arranged in order on top of each other and mounted on an easel or even stood on a chalk tray, can be used in exactly the same way, though they are usually a little more difficult to manage physically.

Flannel Boards

Flannel boards and their close relatives—felt boards, hook-and-loop boards, and magnetic boards—have many of the advantages and uses of chalkboards. They are best used for immediate presentations rather than for displays over a long period of time. In some ways, they are not as flexible or useful as chalkboards; in others they are more so. They do have several advantages:

1. You can prepare the material to be presented in advance.
2. The material to be presented can be saved to be used again.
3. They can be used very dramatically. Just slap the material up for all to see at the propitious moment and drive home your point. It is probably this feature that makes advocates claim that flannel boards are 50 percent more effective than chalkboards.
4. They are especially useful for showing change and development, because it is so easy to add or to subtract from the display without the disturbance that erasing creates. This also makes them excellent for reinforcing points. Just put up or take off the appropriate word, caption, or picture to make your point.

Making a Flannel Board.   To make a flannel board is very easy. Simply cut a piece of plywood or similar board to the desired proportions. Then cover the plywood with suede, or long-napped flannel, nap side out. Stretch it tight, and tack or staple it to the board. The result should give you a smooth, tight, nappy surface to which light sandpaper-backed paper figures and the like will adhere.

Making Flannel Board Display Materials.   To prepare flannel board display materials is also easy. First, select the materials you wish to display. These might be pictures cut out of magazines, student drawings, homemade graphs, diagrams, captions, figures or letters made of flannel cloth, felt, or some similar material. Strips of yarn may be used to make letters, to show relationships, or simply for decoration. Whether construction paper, cardboard, or cloth, the material used should be lightweight. If too heavy, it will fall off the board. It may be necessary to back flimsy material with construction paper to give it body. Next, prepare the materials so they will stick to the board. You can do this by any of the following procedures.

☐ Glue (not paste) pieces of sandpaper, sand side out, to the back of the picture or figure. It is not necessary to cover the entire back. Sandpaper at the corners or strips crossed on the center of the back will usually do, but do not be too stingy.

☐ Cover the back of the material with rubber cement. Sprinkle sand on the rubber cement while it is still wet. Let dry.

☐ Using a brush and long strokes, cover the back of the material with water glass (sodium silicate). Sprinkle with sand while still wet.

☐ Paint the back of the letter or figure with oil-based paint. Spray or sprinkle the wet paint with flocking. If the letters or figures are made from felt, flannel, roughened construction paper, oilcloth, blotting paper, or light sponge, they do not need any sandpaper backing. Just press them on the flannel board as is.

When laying out the design for your flannel board, keep in mind the suggestions for the effective use of bulletin boards listed in the preceding section.

Felt Board and Hook-and-Loop Boards

Felt boards are simply flannel boards made with felt rather than flannel. Stiff felt-backed dining room table pads make excellent felt boards. Hook-and-loop boards are the commercially prepared boards used by speakers, salespersons, and television studios. They are made of the type of materials used for Velcro fasteners. They are somewhat more dependable than homemade flannel boards. They are used in exactly the same manner as flannel boards.

Magnetic Boards

Magnetic boards are also used in the same manner as flannel boards. These boards are made of thin sheets of iron or steel-based metal to which materials are attached by means of small magnets. To make a magnetic board, you simply cut the sheet of metal to the desired size, paint it with automobile enamel or blackboard paint, and either nail it to a wooden frame or tape the sharp edges so that they will not cut the fingers. Galvanized iron screening, stapled or tacked to a wooden frame, also makes a satisfactory magnetic board. Materials for displaying on a magnetic board can be made simply by gluing the materials to small magnets with heavy-duty glue or mending cement. If the magnetic board is enameled, write on it with a grease pencil; if painted with chalkboard paint, write on it with chalk. Many families use magnetic boards to post notices and reminders.

Pictures and Posters

A picture is worth a thousand words, it is said, so teachers should use them effectively and save some breath. Pictures make excellent tools for clarifying and illustrating what you wish to teach. They make good springboards for inquiry. They can be used for sparking interest in the topic. Sometimes an entire lesson can be built around a single picture.

In using pictures, there are no special techniques necessary. As in any other teaching, the teacher should try to guide the students. One of the best ways to do so is to ask questions that will guide students into interpreting. Another is to point out what students should look for and to explain its significance. The teacher must also be careful to use only pictures that are pertinent and useful. You must avoid showing students pictures just for the sake of showing them. Also, avoid passing pictures around the room while the class is in progress. When the students are looking at the pictures, they are no longer paying attention to the class instruction. It is better practice to use the opaque projector.

Finally, do not forget that most pictures in textbooks were put there because the author thought they shed light on the content being studied. Detailed study of the pictures in the texts, using controlled discussion, or open-ended questioning techniques may prove to be very rewarding.

When selecting a picture to show to the class, keep in mind the following criteria. A picture should be suitable for the purpose, make an important contribution to the lesson, be accurate as to authenticity, be easy to understand, be interesting, and be easily visible to the entire class.

Posters have somewhat of an advantage over other pictures for display and instructional purposes. They are usually large and striking. Commercially printed or prepared posters can be used in the same manner as other pictures. Making posters can be an interesting, worthwhile student activity. If you wish to use poster-making as one of your activities, do the following:

1. Discuss the possibilities with students.
2. Discuss the criteria of good poster-making.
   a. Aim at getting one idea across.
   b. Use as few words as possible.

    c. Make key words stand out. Use contrast, size, or color for this purpose.

    d. Keep the design simple.

    e. Leave plenty of white space.

3. Have students block out their designs on a sheet of paper, and get teacher approval of the design.

4. Let the students execute their own designs.

Sources of Teaching Materials

Ingenious teachers can find almost limitless supplies of teaching materials available from a host of sources. Much of this material is free for the asking, and other material is available for a small fee. To find out what is available, turn to your local curriculum guides and resource units, as well as to those of other schools and communities. Among publications that may prove helpful are the journals of professional organizations and the publications from your state department of education. Many educational periodicals list and review new materials. In addition, there are a number of reference works that specialize in listing instructional materials. Among those that you might find useful for nonprojected materials are:

☐ *Annual Paperbound Book Guide for High Schools.* New York: Bowker.

☐ Aubrey, R. H. *Selected Free Materials for Classroom Teachers*, 6th ed. Belmont, CA: Fearon-Pitman, 1978.

☐ *Bibliography of Free and Inexpensive Materials for Economic Education.* New York: Joint Council on Economic Education.

☐ Civil Aeronautics Administration, *Sources of Free and Low-Cost Materials.* Washington, DC: U.S. Department of Commerce.

☐ *Educators' Guide to Free Audio and Visual Materials.* Randolph, WI: Educators' Progress Service.

☐ *Educators' Guide to Free and Inexpensive Teaching Materials.* Randolph, WI: Educators' Progress Service.

☐ *Educators' Guide to Free Social Studies Materials.* Randolph, WI: Educators' Progress Service.

☐ *Educators' Guide to Free Teaching Aids.* Randolph, WI: Educators' Progress Service.

☐ *Free and Inexpensive Learning Materials.* Nashville, TN: Division of Surveys and Field Services, George Peabody College for Teachers.

☐ *Index to Multi-Ethnic Teaching Materials and Teaching Resources.* Washington, DC: National Education Association.

☐ *Materials List for Use by Teachers of Modern Foreign Languages.* New York: Modern Foreign Language Association.

☐ Mathies, L. *Information Sources and Services in Education.* Bloomington, IN: The Phi Delta Kappa Educational Foundation, 1973.

☐ *New Educational Materials.* Englewood Cliffs, N.J.: Citation Press.

☐ *Sources of Free and Inexpensive Pictures for the Classroom.* Randolph, WI: Educators' Progress Service.

☐ *Textbooks in Print.* New York: Bowker.

☐ U.S. Government Printing Office. Thousands of publications. Catalogs available.

☐ *Using Free Materials in the Classroom.* Washington, DC: Association for Supervision and Curriculum Development.

☐ Woodbury, M. *Selecting Instructional Materials*, Fastback 110. Bloomington, IN: Phi Delta Kappa Educational Foundation, 1978.

The following periodicals are a sampling of those that carry information about instructional materials and how to procure them:

The English Journal

Journal of Business Education

Journal of Home Economics

Journal of Physical Education and Recreation

Learning

The Mathematics Teacher

Media and Methods

Music Educators' Journal

School Arts

The Science Teacher

Social Education

Social Studies

COMMUNITY AS A RESOURCE

The community itself may be the best of all the resources available to you. It can provide places and things to see first-hand in the field, and it can provide speakers and materials of instruction for use in the classroom. To take advantage of the many community resources available, every school needs a community resource file. If your school does not have one, you should collect information about resources yourself and record it on 5 × 8 cards. A central file would be more efficient, but a file of your own is usually well worth the effort. In it there should be such information as the following:

1. Possible field trips.
   a. What is there?
   b. How is location reached?
   c. Who handles arrangements?
   d. Expense involved?
   e. Time required?
   f. Other comments?

2. Resource people.
   a. Who are they?
   b. How can they help?
   c. Addresses?

3. Resource material and instructional materials obtainable locally.
   a. What is it?
   b. How is it procured?
   c. Expense involved?

4. Community groups.
   a. Names and addresses?
   b. Function and purpose?
   c. Type of thing with which they can help?

5. Local businesses, industries, and agencies.
   a. Name?
   b. Address?
   c. Key personnel?

SOURCES OF FREE AND INEXPENSIVE MATERIALS

As mentioned, much material is available without cost. Pictures are available in a multitude of magazines. Commercial houses and government agencies have reams of printed material they would like to give you, and sometimes also samples, filmstrips, and other audiovisual materials. All that is required to obtain these materials is a letter of request. In your letter, state who you are, what you are asking for, and why you want it. Write your letter on official school stationery. Sometimes, it is useful to have students write the letter. If you have students do this, be sure to check over the letters to see that they meet the standards of good letter writing, and countersign them so that the recipients will know the request is valid.

Once you get the material, you must examine it carefully before using it with students. Some items will turn out to be useless and others so overladen with bias or sales pitch that they are impossible to use. In evaluating materials, use such criteria as the following:

☐ Will the material really further educational objectives?

☐ Is it free from objectionable advertising, propaganda, and so on?

☐ Is it accurate, honest, free from bias (except when one wishes to illustrate dishonesty and bias, of course)?

☐ Is it interesting, colorful, exciting?

☐ Does it lend itself to school use?

☐ Is it well made?

Exercise 13.3 will help you begin a collection of free and inexpensive materials.

SUMMARY

Effective classroom teaching is impossible without the help of instructional aids. This module has presented and discussed a variety of kinds of aids that do not depend upon electricity for their use—textbooks, workbooks and other printed material; the writing board; and display materials, such as the bulletin board. In addition, this module and the one that follows end with suggestions about where and how to procure free and inexpensive instructional materials. The next module continues your study of instructional aids by focusing your attention on those that require electricity to project sight and sound—the audiovisual tools of instruction.

SUGGESTED READING

Copyright Law: What Every School, College and Public Library Should Know. Skokie, IL: Association for Information Media and Equipment, 1987. Videotape.

Heinich, R.; Molenda, M.; and Russell, J. D. *Instructional Media.* 3d ed. New York: Macmillan, 1989.

Talab, R. S. *Copyright and Instructional Technologies: A Guide to Fair Use and Permissions.* 2d ed. Washington, DC: Association for Educational Communications and Technology, 1989.

EXERCISE 13.3 COLLECTING AND EVALUATING FREE MATERIALS

The purpose of this exercise is to start your collection and evaluation of free and inexpensive teaching materials. From one of the resources listed in this module, select one free material that is offered to teachers, send for it on official school stationery, and when it arrives share the material with your colleagues. Evaluate all materials using the following criteria.

1. Name of free material:

2. Source of free material:

3. Will the material further your educational objectives?

4. Is the material free from objectionable advertising, propaganda, etc.?

5. Is the material accurate, honest, and free from bias?

6. Is it interesting, colorful, exciting?

7. Does it lend itself to school use?

8. Is it well made?

Short Answer

1. The textbook should not dominate your teaching. How should you use it?

   _____

2. In selecting a textbook, what should you look for?

   _____

   _____

   _____

   _____

3. How does one conduct a multitext approach?

   _____

   _____

   _____

   _____

   _____

   _____

   _____

   _____

   _____

   _____

4. What has been the great advantage of the paperback?

   _____

5. In selecting a workbook, what particularly should you look for?

   _____

   _____

   _____

6. What sort of things can you use for springboard material?

   _____

   _____

7. What is the purpose of a study guide?

   _____

   _____

8. In speaking of writing boards and bulletin boards, it is recommended that you leave plenty of white space. What is meant by white space? Why should you leave plenty of it?

   _____

   _____

9. Flannel boards are supposedly much more effective than writing boards. Why?

   _____

10. How do you make the material to put on a flannel board?

    _____

    _____

    _____

11. How can you get the most benefit out of a bulletin board?

    _____

12. How can you make a bulletin board or chart forceful?

_____

_____

_____

_____

13. What is a flip chart?

_____

_____

14. How do you use it?

_____

_____

15. Why use pictures in your teaching? Why not pass them around the room during a class?

_____

_____

_____

16. What would you include in a community resource file?

_____

_____

_____

17. Experts warn against the overuse of a single textbook. Explain why.

_____

_____

_____

18. Where could you turn to find out about teaching material that might be suitable for your teaching?

_____

_____

19. Describe what you should look for when deciding whether material that you have obtained free is suitable for use in your teaching.

_____

_____

_____

_____

MODULE 14
Projected and Recorded Instructional Aids

RATIONALE

SPECIFIC OBJECTIVES

MODULE TEXT

Audiovisual Aids

Uses of Audiovisual Aids

General Guidelines for Using Audiovisual Aids

Selecting the Proper Audiovisual Aid

Preparing for the Audiovisual Aid

Guiding the Audiovisual Activity

Following up Audiovisual Activities

Projection and Projectors

Operating Projectors

The Opaque Projector

The Overhead Projector

Preparing Transparencies

Mounting Transparencies

Making a Transparency Overlay

Masks

Slides and Filmstrips

Using the Slide Projector

Slide-Loading Procedure

Preparing a Slide Program

Use of Filmstrips

Projection Procedure for Filmstrip

Making a Filmstrip

Film Loops

Films as a Teaching Tool

Procedures for Showing Instructional Films

Silent Film

Individualizing Instruction

Using General-Purpose Commercial Films

Television

Instructional Television

General and Educational Television Programs

Physical Arrangements for Television Classes

Tape Recorders and Other Players

Audio Recordings

Video Recordings

Videodiscs

Multimedia

Computers and Microcomputers

Computer-Assisted Instruction (CAI)

Computer-Managed Instruction (CMI)

Copyright Laws Regarding Use of Recordings and Projected Visuals
Making Your Own Materials
SUMMARY
SUGGESTED READING
POSTTEST

This module continues the study of instructional tools, focusing on how to use those audiovisual aids that depend upon electricity to project sight and sound and to focus images on screens. The aim of this module is not to teach you how to operate modern pedagogical technology but to help you develop a philosophy for using it and to provide some strategies for using these instructional tools in your teaching.[1]

By the end of your study of this module you will have command of a general strategy for the use of audiovisual aids, and will be able to recite, in general, something about the various types of audiovisual aids available to you and how to use them in your teaching.

RATIONALE

At the completion of this module, you should be able to:

1. Explain the benefits of using audiovisual aids.
2. Explain the virtues and uses of overhead projectors, opaque projectors, slide projectors, and filmstrip projectors.
3. Explain how to make and use transparencies, flip-ons, overlays, and masks.
4. Describe how to prepare a slide program.
5. Describe the general procedures for presenting instructional films.
6. Describe how to adapt slide projectors, filmstrip projectors, and film projectors for individual or small-group instruction.
7. Describe how to use commercial and public broadcasting television to enhance classroom instruction.
8. Explain the recommended procedure for conducting instructional television classes.
9. Describe procedures for using taped recordings and records.
10. Describe uses and resources for computers and microcomputers in teaching.
11. Describe uses and resources for laser videodiscs in teaching.
12. Describe ways to mix instructional media.
13. Explain the criteria for selecting audiovisual instructional aids.
14. Describe general principles for the effective operation of projectors.
15. Explain the ways in which one might make use of commercial films for instruction.
16. Explain the pros and cons of silent and sound films and videotapes.
17. Demonstrate awareness of the copyright laws regarding the use of projected visuals.

SPECIFIC OBJECTIVES

Audiovisual Aids

Certain teaching tools that rely upon sight and sound fall into the category commonly known as audiovisual aids. Included in this general category are such teaching tools as charts, models, pictures, graphs, maps, mock-ups, globes, flannel boards, writing boards, and all of the other tools discussed in the previous module. Also included in the general category of audiovisual aids are those devices that require electricity for their operation—projectors of various sorts, computers, sound recorders, video recorders, laser videodisc players, computers, and so forth. This module is about the selection and use of tools of this second group, the ones that require electricity to project sight and sound and that focus images onto screens.

MODULE TEXT

---

[1]The word *technology* encompasses both machines and techniques—a technique for individualizing instruction is as much a part of educational technology as a teaching machine. The word *medium* refers to any intermediate agency, means, instrument, or channel. A lecture, a movie, a television show, a newspaper, and a photograph are all media by which persons can transmit ideas to other people. You should be careful not to confuse *technology* with gadgetry and *medium* with the mass media. Each word has a broader meaning. Furthermore, you should remember that *medium* is singular and *media* plural—there is no such thing as *a* media, only a medium.

These instructional tools are aids to teaching. It is important to remember that their role is to aid you, not to teach for you. You must still select the objectives, orchestrate the teaching plan, evaluate the results, and follow up the lessons. If you use audiovisual aids prudently, your teaching will benefit.

Uses of Audiovisual Aids

The main effort of any teacher in instruction is to make the message clear—communicate the idea, capture the content, clarify the obscure for the learners. Hence, teachers almost universally rely on the spoken word as their primary medium of communication. Most of the day is filled with explanation and discourse, to the point that the teaching profession has been accused of making words more important than reality—perpetuating a culture of verbalism in the schools. Teachers use definitions, recitations, and—perhaps too often—rote memory in the quest of the goals for the day.

To rely on verbalism is to rely on communication through abstract symbolization. symbols (in this case, letters and words) may not always communicate what is intended. Audiovisual aids can serve to facilitate communication and understanding by adding depth to the learning, thus making the learning less abstract. Utilizing the concept that one picture is worth a thousand words, such aids attempt to clarify the presentation as well as to intensify the image by doubling the number of senses through which the information is communicated to the learner—that is, sound plus sight. Instead of just description, these aids create visual images to accompany the script. In communicating the definition of the word *escarpment*, for example, imagine how much more vivid, effective, and complete the students' understanding would be when pictures or slides or films are used than if words were used alone. With the addition of visuals, an empathy for the word can be developed; a "eureka" phenomenon can be produced in place of the boredom of memorizing a bare-bones definition that satisfies only the verbal need for understanding. Consider a presentation of the concept of air pressure in lecture form versus an actual demonstration or a visual presentation of the crushing of a vacuumized can by the power of the atmosphere. Consider a recitation by a teacher about the nature of Elizabethan Theatre versus a graphic illustration with an actual wood model or a computer rendering of London's Globe Theatre.

Aids not only can help clinch the achievement of educational goals but also can be exciting, thus enhancing lessons being taught. When properly utilized, aids can make graphic and thrilling what might have remained pedestrian and routine. They can add color to a presentation, help motivate some students to attend to the instruction, and serve to reinforce the learning that has already taken place.

Sometimes you may hear teachers express the opinion that the use of audiovisual aids sugarcoats learning and thus is educationally undignified. Do not be misled by that opinion. Remember, your job is to teach so that students learn, and any device that will help you achieve that end must be considered. The use of audiovisual aids is an essential for making teaching effective.

General Guidelines for Using Audiovisual Aids

Like any other boon to progress, audiovisual aids must be worked with if they are to yield what is expected. The mediocre teacher who is content to get by without expending additional effort will in all likelihood remain just that, a mediocre teacher, despite the excellent quality of whatever aids he or she chances to use. Because the mediocre teacher fails to rise to the occasion and hence presents poorly, that teacher's lesson results in being less effective and less impressive than it could have been. The effective teacher makes the inquiry about audiovisual aids and expends the effort needed to implement them well for the benefit of the students. The effective teacher will capitalize on the drama made possible by the shift in interaction strategy and enhance the quest for knowledge by using vivid material. Such teaching involves four steps:

1. Selecting the proper audiovisual aid.
2. Preparing for the audiovisual aid.

3. Guiding the audiovisual activity.

4. Following up the audiovisual activity.

Selecting the Proper Audiovisual Aid. Care must be exercised in the selection of an audiovisual aid for use in the classroom. A poor selection, an inappropriate aid, can turn an excellent lesson into a disappointing fiasco. An audiovisual aid that projects garbled sound, outdated pictures, or obscure or shaky images will not be met with delighted response from the class. An aid that is too difficult to present, takes too long to set up, or is not suitable for the age level will dampen the enthusiasm of a class as quickly as a boring lesson.

In the selection process, then, the effective teacher follows an inquiry routine similar to this:

1. Is the contemplated aid suitable? Will it help to achieve the objective of the lesson? Will it present an accurate understanding of the facts in the case? Will the aid highlight the points that the teaching has underscored? Will it work with the equipment used in the school?

2. Is the audiovisual aid within the level of understanding of the class? Is it too mature? too embarrassing? too dated?

3. Is the audiovisual aid lucid in its presentation? Is it clear in its images and sounds?

4. Is the audiovisual aid readily available? Will it be available when needed?

The best response for most of these questions can come after a careful previewing of the aid. Sometimes, because of existing conditions, this dry run is not possible. However, the best way to discover how inadequate the catalogue descriptions are of films, filmstrips, videotapes, and records—or the condition in which the product has been left by previous users—is to try them out yourself under practice conditions.

Preparing for the Audiovisual Aid. To use audiovisual aids with maximum effectiveness usually will require preparation of two types: psychological and physical. From the psychological standpoint, students have to be prepped for the utilization of the aid and coached on how best to profit from its presentation. Films, filmstrips, recordings, and pictures will require that you spend some time setting the scene. You will need to make clear the purpose of the activity, suggest points to look for, present problems to solve, and, in general, clue your students about potential dangers that may mislead them.

From the physical standpoint, preparation pertaining to the machine to be used, the equipment involved, and the arrangement of the classroom furniture will have to be attended to. Sometimes, as with the use of the chalkboard, the preparation is minimal. All that may be necessary may be the identification of the aid and a brief recitation concerning the use you intend to make of it, other than making sure of a satisfactory supply of chalk and erasers. At other times, however, as when the morning or afternoon sun affects the visibility, each section of the classroom will need to be checked, as well as the focusing dials of the apparatus for appropriate sharpness of images and the amplitude dials for clarity of voice sound. In the absence of preparation, bedlam can ensue. The missing chalk, the borrowing and lending of board erasers among the students, or the absence of an extension cord can spell defeat for even the best audiovisual aid. The double-checking of the action-readiness of the projector and the arrangement in sequence of the slides to be used are vital to success.

Guiding the Audiovisual Activity. The purpose of audiovisual teaching tools is not to replace teaching but to make teaching more effective. Therefore, you cannot expect the tool to do all the work. You should, however, make it work for your purposes. You will have to highlight in advance the usage of those things that you want to be remembered most completely. You may have to enumerate the concepts that are developed or to illustrate relationships or conclusions that you wish to be drawn. You may have to prepare and distribute a study guide or a list of questions for students to respond to, to stop the presentation periodically for hints or questions, or maybe even to repeat the entire performance to ensure a more thorough grasp of particulars.

Following up the Audiovisual Activity.   Audiovisual presentations that are allowed just to lie there upon completion squander valuable learning opportunities. Some discussion should ensue that is pointed and directed toward closure. The time for such postmortems should have been a vital part of the preparation for the use of the aid. Upon completion of the use of the aid, students are now permitted to and indeed expected to engage in responding to the sets of questions proposed in the preview activity. Points that were fuzzily made should be clarified. Questions that were not answered should be pursued in depth. Deeper responses that go beyond the present scope of the inquiry should be noted and earmarked for further probing at a later date. Quizzes, reviews, practice, and discussions all can be used to tie loose ends together, to highlight the major concepts, to clinch the essential learnings. The planned, efficient use of the aid helps create the atmosphere that audiovisual presentations are learning opportunities and not purely recreational activities.

PROJECTION AND PROJECTORS

Projection machines make it possible to bring into the classroom experiences in a vivid form that otherwise could only be talked about. For example, a film on Egypt can re-create for students aspects of life in a distant land or ancient culture that they might be exposed to in no other way. Such machines also enable a teacher to project the image of an artifact, a picture, or a book page on a screen in such a fashion as to be discernible to all at the same time without interrupting the flow of the class that occurs when students must pass objects from hand to hand about the room. Among the most common and most useful kinds of projectors available for teachers' use are the opaque projector, the slide projector, the filmstrip projector, the overhead projector, and, of course, the 16-mm film projector. Modern technology has improved these machines so that despite their growing sophistication and multiplicity, they have been almost "defanged." Attention has been devoted to making more simple the running procedure for each in order to diminish the risk of error in operation.

OPERATING PROJECTORS

This module lacks the space to dwell at length on how to run the various machines used as teaching aids. Each has its own idiosyncrasies peculiar to its own make and model. The hands-on approach in which you cultivate a familiarity with a strange machine and develop your dexterity in handling it by actually going through the motions and manipulating its parts is the mode of study recommended by this module of study. However, there are a few general principles that you ought to keep in mind any time you are confronted with a machine with which you are unfamiliar:

1. Handle it. Push its buttons and learn what happens. Dissipate your anxiety about your personal affliction of awkwardness in the presence of such a robotical monster. Gain familiarity with the vernacular about the machine; say the words, and aim to increase your at-easeness when near it. Whatever facility you develop beforehand will stand you in good stead on D-days, when the students are present or when mayhem is imminent in a class that is teetering on the brink of boredom while waiting for the show to begin or to continue.

2. One of the first interviews you should conduct in each new school you join after your career has been launched is with regard to the audiovisual equipment possessed by that school. It may be severely dated and markedly different from what you have been exposed to in practice. The generalities that you have collected, however, should see you through to success, especially if you have set aside your awe of the mechanical and strengthened your confidence in yourself.

3. Your first move in greeting audiovisual machines should be to read the directions supplied. The more difficult machines usually have the directions printed somewhere

on the casing. These directions will show how the machine's operations differ from others of the same ilk—such as how, specifically, to thread the film—even though the principles are always more or less the same.

4. Projectors all have to be focused. Focusing is done by adjusting the distance from the light source to the lens and/or the lens to the screen. In a slide projector or a movie projector, the light source is in back and the lens in front. In an overhead projector, the light source is on the bottom and the lens is on top. The light passes from the light source through a slide or transparency (frame) and through the lens to the screen. What you have to do is to move the lens back and forth (or up and down in the case of the overhead) until you get a clear picture. Usually the best technique is to move from a blur through a sharp focus until the image starts to blur again and then turn back to the point of sharpest focus. The image can also be brought into focus by moving the projector toward or away from the screen. This fact is important to remember when you find that you cannot move the lens far enough to focus the image sharply.

The point stressed here is that no matter what projection machine with which you have to deal, you focus it by establishing the proper distance between the lens and light source and the lens and screen. You look in turn how to plug the set in, how to turn the set on, and how to adjust the distance to get a sharp picture.

The Opaque Projector

The opaque projector (see Figure 14.1) is a most convenient teaching tool. It usually requires a dark room that may be difficult to effect. Since the model used loads from underneath, if the size of the object projected should be bulky, it may let light seep out. Bringing the picture into sharp focus can also be tricky. Once you get the hang of focusing it, though, you will find this machine can be used to meet many of your classroom needs. The enlarged image that you desire of a picture or of a printed page, or of a test paper, or of a three-dimensional object can be projected onto a film screen, or on a white wall or even on a chalkboard. A distinctive feature of the opaque projector

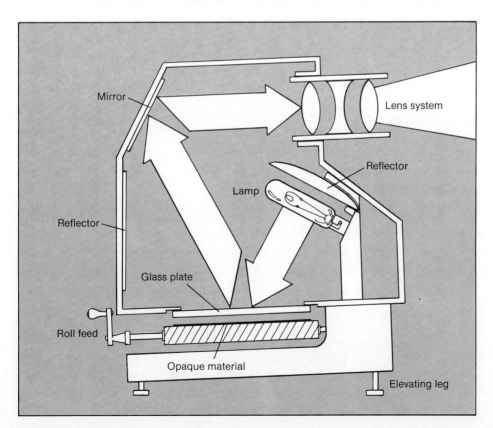

FIGURE 14.1
Opaque Projector, Cutaway View (Courtesy of Robert Heinich et al. *Instructional Media*, 3rd ed., New York: Macmillan, 1989, p. 154. By permission of Macmillan Publishing Company.)

is the presence of a **platen**—a shelf at the base of the machine that can be lowered or raised—on which is placed the item to be projected. A handle or a crank is provided for this operation. When the platen has been returned to its closed position, after loading, it is held by springs to keep the picture or object to be viewed immobilized. When showing pictures from textbooks or the like, a piece of heat-resistant glass can be placed across the open book to flatten its surface and thus improve the focus of the screen picture. Objects that may be damaged by heat should not be used in older models of this projector. In addition, objects made of metal may become hot to handle after they have been in the machine and should be touched with care. In the classroom you use this projector for the following purposes:

☐ Project pictures and other opaque materials that are too small for students to see easily from their seats. This practice eliminates the necessity for passing such material around the class. It also allows everyone a chance to see the material at once and gives you a chance to point out details and clear up questions while everyone can see.

☐ Enlarge maps and project them on a suitable surface to trace the boundaries, rivers, and other features represented.

☐ Project student work so all students can see it as you discuss it. This is an excellent device to show students good work or to allow students to react to one another's work.

☐ Project illustrative material in student reports. Often, shy students do well at reporting when they can use projection as a support.

☐ Project work on the writing board for evaluation and correction.

☐ Project illustrative material for lectures and teacher or student talks.

☐ Project illustrative drawings onto the writing board, from which tracings can then be made for a variety of purposes.

The great advantage of the opaque projector is that it projects the image of the real thing. You need not prepare a slide or a transparency. All that you need to do is to place the material to be projected on the bed of the projector, turn the projector on, and focus it. Focusing objects such as the pages of a book that will not lie flat may be something of a problem, but usually with patience you will obtain clear images on the screen. Some opaque projectors are equipped with built-in pointers that show up on the screen; these pointers can be manipulated by a handle on the front of the projector to point to a detail of whatever is being shown on the screen.

The Overhead Projector

In use since the early 1960s, the overhead projector is one of the most versatile of teaching tools available today (Figure 14.2). Every classroom should have one standard overhead projector, just as every classroom should have a writing board. There are four general types of overhead projectors:

1. Standard projectors.
2. Portable projectors, which can be easily hand-carried from room to room.
3. Rear-projection systems, which allow the teacher to stand off to the side rather than between the audience and the screen.
4. Video overhead projectors, which use color cameras to send images to TV monitors.

Many schools now utilize rear-projection systems and video overhead projectors, and computer technology has increased the versatility of the overhead even more greatly. For space reasons discussion here must be limited to the standard overhead projector.

The overhead projector can be used in full daylight. It allows you to point things out or to make notations from the front of the room without losing eye contact with your students, as you typically must do when you turn your back on the class to write on a writing board. You also do not block the view of the students when you use a

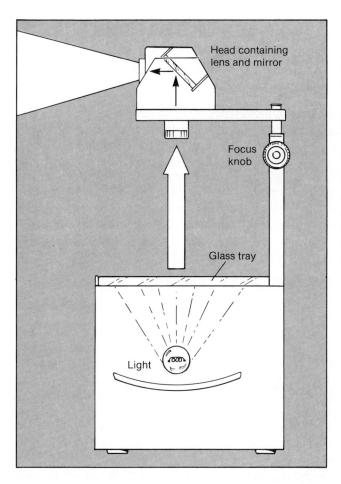

FIGURE 14.2
Overhead Projector. An overhead projector consists of a glass-topped box that contains a light source and a vertical post mounting a head that contains a lens. To use it, place an acetate transparency on the glass top (some overhead projectors are equipped with acetate rolls to use as transparencies), switch on the light, and adjust the focus by moving the head, which contains the lens, up and down.

projector. In addition, the overhead projector allows you to prepare material ahead of time and save it for use again and again. With the help of flip-ons (overlays), you can easily show development and changes and compare and contrast. An overhead projector can be used to record the progress of a discussion. Finally, the overhead projector can both make your teaching more effective and reduce the amount of time you must spend on time-wasting chores such as copying material onto a writing board.

These are a few ways in which the standard overhead projector may be used:

1. Write on the transparency as on a chalkboard while the class proceeds. When the time comes to move on, just roll up the acetate or take a new blank sheet. In this way, you do not have to erase and so can come back to reconsider, if necessary.

2. Emphasize specific points in a lesson by projecting them as they come up in class.
   a. Write points on the transparency as you go along.
   b. Flip on preprinted materials at propitious moments.
   c. Uncover blocked-out preprinted material as the points come up. To keep preprinted material out of sight, simply cover it with opaque material until the proper moment.

3. Present pictures, drawings, diagrams, outlines, printed matter, and maps.

4. Project an outline form. Fill it in as you go along.

5. Project an outline. Cover it. As you proceed, uncover the points as they are made.

6. Reproduce or enlarge maps.

7. Project grids for graphing.

8. Project silhouettes.

9. Project tests and quizzes.

10. Correct tests, quizzes, and papers. Project the correct answers by writing on the transparency. Transparencies made on spirit duplicators are excellent for this purpose because you can also make duplicate copies. It is then possible for the teacher to go over something projected on the screen or board while the students follow along on their own copies.

Preparing Transparencies.   Overhead projectors project images in the same way that film projectors and slide projectors do, by shining light through a transparent film or glass. They will not project opaque substances except to make silhouettes. Transparencies may be bought readymade. Many excellent ones are for sale by the various supply houses; however, they are extremely easy to make. Even though the transparencies you make may not be as finished as those commercially made, you will probably find that your own homemade transparencies are more effective for your purposes. After all, when you make your own, you can tailor them to your own needs, something a stranger cannot do, no matter how expert. You can make satisfactory transparencies for overhead projection by the following methods:

1. By using a Polaroid or copy camera. (Polaroid sells a special film for this purpose).

2. By drawing or writing directly on acetate. Usually a frosted acetate, frosted side up, seems to work better for this purpose than smooth, clear acetate. Use India ink, drawing ink, transparent color pencils, felt tipped pens, or grease pencils (china marking pencils) for writing directly on acetate. If you wish to project in color, remember to select an ink or pencil that is translucent. Opaque inks and pencils project only in black, or in silhouette. Grease pencils (china marking pencils) work very well, but the pencils sold by supply houses specifically for making transparencies may be better. If you use felt-tipped pens, check to see whether the ink and the acetate are compatible. Sometimes the ink of the felt-tipped pens will not stick to the acetate. Impromptu transparencies can be made by writing or drawing while the transparency is on the machine. You can make up a transparency as the class progresses, for instance, by recording on a transparency the important points made in a discussion. For more finished transparencies, the following procedure is recommended:
   a. Sketch the transparency on a sheet of paper.
   b. Cover the paper with the acetate transparency sheet.
   c. Trace the sketch. Use drawing ink.
   d. Add color if you wish. Use translucent colored inks, felt-tipped pens, or transparent color pencils.
   e. Spray with a clear plastic to give permanence.
   f. Mount the transparencies, if you wish.

3. By making transparencies on spirit master duplicating machines. If you wish, the machine will make color transparencies. The technique for making such transparencies includes the following:
   a. Make a spirit master as you would for any other duplicating. Use color if you wish to project in color.
   b. Place the spirit master on the duplicating machine and run through two or three sheets of paper to be sure it is working properly.
   c. Take a sheet of frosted acetate, frosted side up, and hand feed it through the duplicator.
   d. Spray the resulting transparency with a clear plastic.
   e. Mount the transparency if you wish. A clear sheet of plastic placed over the transparency face when mounting will give it additional protection.

4. By making transparencies on several types of copying machines. With these machines, you can make transparencies from books or from single sheets of printed or typed material. The capabilities of the machines differ according to their design and the copying process used. Consequently, you should become familiar with a

machine's capabilities and the technique for operating it before attempting to make transparencies.

5. By lifting pictures from magazines and similar sources if the paper of the magazine is clay-coated. Probably the easiest of several ways to lift a picture is the following method, which uses clear Contact paper:

   a. Test the paper to see if it is clay-coated. To do this, wet your finger and rub it along the border of the picture. If a greyish white substance rubs off on your finger, the paper is clay-coated.

   b. Cut a piece of Contact paper to fit the picture. Contact can be purchased in any home-center, wallpaper or hardware store, variety or five-and-ten-cent store.

   c. Place the picture face up on a flat surface.

   d. Remove the protective covering from the Contact and place the Contact on the picture, sticky side down.

   e. Bind the Contact to the picture. Rub from top to bottom and left to right. Use a straight edge or a rolling pin. Be sure you get a good bond all over; you should have no air bubbles or creases when you get through.

   f. Place the Contact with the picture bonded to it in a pan of water.

   g. Add a teaspoon of detergent and let soak for at least half an hour.

   h. Remove the picture and Contact from the water. Slowly and easily pull the paper (picture) from the Contact. Do not rush this step. Be sure to leave the picture and Contact in the water long enough before you try to separate the picture from the paper. If the picture does not come clean, the transparency will be worthless.

   i. Wipe off any residue of paper or clay with a soft wet rag or a piece of cotton.

   j. Blot off any excess moisture with a paper towel.

   k. Let dry.

   l. Spray with clear plastic.

   m. Mount.

Mounting Transparencies.   If you wish, you can mount your transparencies. Mounting transparencies has certain advantages when it comes to preserving and storing them, though in some cases the added length and width makes them difficult to transport and file. Mounts are necessary if one intends to attach flip-ons to the transparency. Otherwise, except for certain machine-made transparencies that are very thin, mounting is not an absolute necessity.

Making a Transparency Overlay.   A transparency overlay is one that you can flip on to another so as to change the detail being presented. Thus, if the basic transparency was an outline map of Europe, for example, one flip-on might show the national boundaries prior to 1914, another the boundaries in 1921, another in 1940, and another in 1990. Or the basic transparency might show the formula: $2 + 2 = \square$ and the overlay shows the answer: 4. By adding the overlay to the basic transparency you can show the complete formula: $2 + 2 = 4$. This is illustrated in Figure 14.3. Or if we wish to show the variation of a phenomenon during the first quarters, we could combine overlays of a graph as in Figure 14.4.

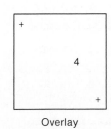
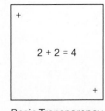

Basic Transparency   Overlay   Basic Transparency plus Overlay

FIGURE 14.3
Transparency with Overlay

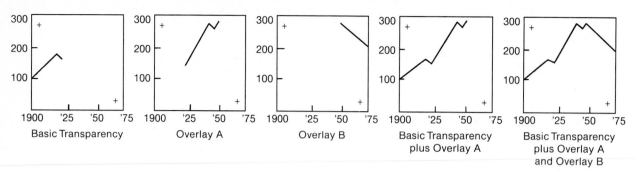

FIGURE 14.4
Transparency with Several Overlays

You make overlays or flip-ons for transparencies in exactly the same way that you make the transparencies. You can just lay them on top of the basic overlay, if you wish, but usually it is better to hinge them to the basic transparency's mount. Separate overlays tend to get mixed up and to mix you up. Hinges can be purchased or made out of a piece of tape (Figure 14.5).

Use register marks (+) at the top left and bottom right corners of the basic transparency and each overlay so that you can match them up properly and easily, as shown in Figure 14.6. When the + marks on the overlay fit exactly over the + marks on the basic transparency, the two are properly aligned.

Masks.   Masks are opaque overlays that block out a portion of the transparency so it will not be projected. You can make a mask by laying a piece of paper over the area not to be shown, or you can hinge a piece of light cardboard or plastic so that it will cover the area you wish to block off. The latter procedure is advantageous when one wishes to use the transparency again and again. Masks are useful for heightening the dramatic impact of the information to be shown by the transparency during the class.

Review the use of overhead projectors by doing Exercise 14.1.

FIGURE 14.5
Graph Presented with
Hinged Overlays

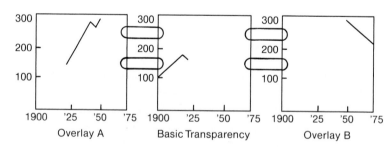

FIGURE 14.6
Overlay Line-Up Technique

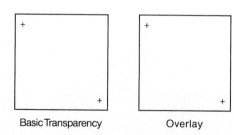

EXERCISE 14.1   THE USE OF OVERHEAD PROJECTORS
A REVIEW

The purpose of this exercise is to provide a review of important points that have been discussed thus far in this module. Answer each of the following questions and then share your responses with your classmates. Discuss any differences with your course instructor.

1. If you were faced with a new overhead projector you had never seen before, how would you go about focusing it, once you had found out how to turn it on?

2. If the projector were a filmstrip projector rather than an overhead projector, what difference in focusing would you expect?

3. Suppose you have never before used an opaque projector. You have loaded a picture on the tray, turned on the projector, and removed the lens cover. You have an image on the screen, but it is not in focus. How do you focus it?

4. Suppose you want to present an outline of a lecture point by point as you proceed through the lecture.

   a. How could you do it with an overhead projector?

   b. How would you go about making an impromptu transparency?

   c. What type of pencil must you use in making a transparency if you wish to project in color?

Slides and Filmstrips

Slides and filmstrips are variations of the same medium. Most of what can be said about one of them also applies to the other. In fact, many filmstrip projectors are also slide projectors and vice versa. This section treats them as different media, but remember that they are closely related.

Using the Slide Projector.   For educational purposes, 35-mm slides are available in great abundance. Commercially produced slides can be purchased through school supply houses and photography and other stores. Other slides can be obtained from students, friends, neighbors, and relatives. It is quite possible to make your own slides. With a little practice, you can learn to copy pictures, book pages, documents, and maps with a 35-mm camera. Photographs you take of scenes and events may be excellent teaching aids. You may even find use for your vacation photos. Techniques to use in copying documents and taking other pictures can be found in photographic manuals and works on instructional media.[2]

Slides of flat visuals (magazine pictures, photographs, maps, etc.) can be easily made with a device known as the Kodak Ektagraphic Visualmaker and a Kodak Instamatic camera.[3] With the use of this device no specialized skills are necessary to make perfect 35-mm slides. With the sophistication of computers and specialized equipment, slides can also be generated from computer programs, but the expense of the equipment for this technology is still beyond the means of most school districts.

Slides may be used in a number of ways. An effective technique is to use single slides to illustrate important points or concepts. Another technique is to arrange a series of slides into a slide program, as in a filmstrip. If you wish, you can prerecord your own commentary and sound effects and synchronize them with the slides, although for most class purposes this is not necessary. Slide projection can also be adapted for individual or small-group use, such as in a learning activity center. For individual or small-group viewing, the image can be projected onto a sheet of white cardboard no larger than the projector itself. Some teachers place white paper in a cardboard box and project into it, thereby shielding the image from outside light and keeping it from distracting other students.

Slide projection is excellent for illustrating, clarifying, motivating, and summing up, as well as for introducing study, discussion, or research. Projecting two or more pictures at once makes it possible to show comparisons and contrast. Use slides as springboards. Encourage students to build slide programs and illustrated reports as individual or small-group projects. This technique is an excellent way to make concepts and facts clear and to stimulate thinking.

Slide-Loading Procedure.   To load slides into slide carriers or trays, position the slides in this way:

1. Face the screen.
2. Hold the slide so that it reads normally. (In most cases, commercially processed slides will carry the company trademark on the side of the slide that faces the projection screen.)
3. Invert the slide, so that the image is upside down, and insert the slide into the tray slot.

Thumb spots help orient slides for projection. Traditionally, the spot is placed in the top right-hand corner of the slide on the side that is away from the screen when the slide is in position for loading.

---

[2]*Copying*, Eastman Kodak Publication M1 (Rochester, NY: Eastman Kodak Co., 1969); *How to Make Good Pictures*, Eastman Kodak Publication AW1 (Rochester, NY: Eastman Kodak Co.); *Producing Filmstrips and Slides*, Eastman Kodak Publication S–8 (Rochester, NY: Eastman Kodak Co., 1969); Robert Heinich et al., *Instructional Media*, 3rd ed. (New York: Macmillan, 1989).

[3]*Simple Copying Techniques with a Kodak Ektagraphic Visualmaker*, Eastman Kodak Publication S–40 (Rochester, NY: Eastman Kodak Company).

Preparing a Slide Program.   Slide programs are quite easy to prepare. Students can and do make excellent programs. Basically, this is the procedure:

1. Decide on your objectives.
2. Decide on the points you want to make.
3. Select slides that will make your points. Use slides that are technically good, though it sometimes is necessary to use a slide that is photographically less than good.
4. Arrange these points into an outline or scenario.
5. Arrange the slides in sequence according to the scenario.
6. Make title and commentary slides, or prepare an oral or written commentary.
7. Place the slides into the projector tray. Be sure they are in proper sequence. If you will be using a single-slot projector, place the slides in order and number them. Even though you will not be using a slide tray, the slide tray is the best place to keep your slides in order.
8. Plan a commentary, if you think one is needed. If you plan a written commentary, make copies so everyone can see it. This type of commentary is good for small-group and individual work. If you plan an oral commentary, you or someone else may read or give the commentary as the slides are shown. This procedure is most common. If you wish, you can tape record your comments. When you do, be sure to include some sort of signal on the audiotape so that the operator will know when to go to the next slide. If you have the proper equipment, it is quite easy to produce a taped program in which the slides are changed automatically by an electronic signal, but such sophistication is not really necessary.

Use of Filmstrips.   Filmstrips are, in effect, a series of slides strung together on a roll of film. They may be used in much the same way as slide programs. In fact, sometimes it may make for more effective teaching if you treat frames as individual slides. Studying an individual frame alone, even for an entire period, has much to recommend it. Studying single frames or short sequences may be more interesting and effective than viewing the entire filmstrip. Many filmstrips come with recorded commentary and sound effects. They may be impressive, but perhaps you would rather provide your own commentary as the filmstrip progresses. To run through an entire filmstrip without stopping for discussion or sharing of ideas usually makes the class monotonous. For this reason, you should be very careful when selecing sound filmstrips. Unless they are unusually well done, they may be boring. In any case, when using the silent filmstrip you should try to involve the students as much as possible. With slower students, allow them to read the captions of silent filmstrips. Stop periodically to discuss the implications of the pictures. You may want to let one of the students run the projector, which would relieve you of that chore and make at least one student interested.

   Filmstrips are excellent for small-group and individual work. Use individual screens or screens in boxes. You may, or may not, want to give students study guides to use as they view the filmstrips individually. Such study guides make it possible for students to study completely on their own. With some filmstrips and slide programs, study guides are not really necessary because directions, problems, and other instructional matter that you would expect in a study guide appear on the filmstrip.

Projection Procedure for Filmstrips.   When ready for showing, the filmstrip should be in a roll with the lead end on the outside and the tail of the film in the center of the roll. Face the screen and hold the filmstrip so that the title reads normally. Keep the same surface toward the screen, invert the filmstrip, and insert the end downward into the threading slot, pushing gently while you turn the film-advance knob slowly until the sprocket wheels engage the perforations along the edges of the filmstrip. When the focus frame or title appears, take time to frame it properly by working the framing lever or knob until you see only one complete frame on the screen. Then focus the picture by moving the lens forward or back.

Making a Filmstrip.   It is possible to make filmstrips, but to do so requires special equipment or special skills. Ordinarily, what you must do, in effect, is to make a slide program and then have an audiovisual person turn it into a filmstrip with special equipment. If one has good slide projection equipment, making filmstrips hardly seems worthwhile. The slide program will do almost everything the filmstrip can do. If you wish to make filmstrips, however, you can find detailed instructions in various texts.[4]

Film Loops

The single-concept loop film projector is a simple video device that should not be overlooked. It requires no threading or rewinding. Plastic, self-contained cartridges are inserted into a slot in the rear of this unit and the program is viewer ready. The cartridge is foolproof because it can only be inserted in the correct, ready-to-show position. A focus knob, a framer, and an elevation level are the only controls. Three-to-fifteen minute films are available in most subject areas and at most grade levels. Such films illustrate one concept or idea and often are used to introduce a problem without trying to solve it or to demonstrate a technique or procedure for performing some task.

Loops of this type are commercially prepared on 8-mm film. Local programs, that is, sequences produced by you or someone in your school on this kind of film are easy to make. All that is needed is an easy-to-operate 8-mm camera, normal classroom lighting, and a self-made plan to follow. You can compose and produce film loops that meet with your specifications and are germane to the topic you are teaching in precisely the way you desire.

Films as a Teaching Tool

Films, including video cassettes, can be one of the most useful of all teaching tools. They can be used to arouse interest, to change students' attitudes, to clarify students' concepts, to stimulate thinking, to summarize, to reinforce learning, to demonstrate, and to bring vividly into the classroom much that could otherwise only be talked about. They make wonderful springboards for further learning. And with the increase in the availability in schools of video cameras, recorders, and video players, students and teachers can use this film technology to make their own videos. This section discusses both instructional films made for use in the classroom and general purpose or entertainment films or videos.

Despite this usefulness, there are several disadvantages to the use of films. Some films are irrelevant, and some could give students faulty or misleading notions about a topic. Films may emphasize elements that you do not want emphasized in your course; unless on video cassette, films are not very adaptable because it is difficult to excerpt what you want. Films may be difficult to get exactly when you need them. Finally, they require special provisions for projection.

Many classic films are now available on video cassettes or on laser videodisc. Your school audiovisual center may have many available for your use. The discussion that follows concerns the use of instructional films that come as video cassettes or as standard 16-mm films.

Procedures for Showing Instructional Films.   Instructional films are those designed for instructional use in the classroom. They range from presentations of literary masterpieces to short sequences on how to use a certain piece of equipment. Since they are instructional tools, you should usually select films that are pertinent to your teaching objectives, using the films when these objectives are the basis of the content to be shown. The biggest hitch in the utilization of films concerns their availability and your planning. With effective use of long-range planning and early ordering of films, you should be able to make your instruction close to the expected arrival of the film requested.

---

[4]In such texts as Jerold E. Kemp's *Planning and Producing Audiovisual Materials,* or technical manuals such as Eastman Kodak's *Producing Filmstrips and Slides,* Publication S–8.

If you cannot get the film you want when you want it, it is usually better either to adjust your calendar to the related content when you can get the film or to skip the film altogether. In some cases, however, films are of enough general interest that they can be used at almost any time during the year. If possible, the film should be previewed by you before showing it to the class.

Once the projector has been set up and threaded, it is wise to double-check to see that everything is working. Film projectors are quite rugged as a rule, but in the school situation they usually get a maximum of use and a minimum of maintenance. Checking the equipment, therefore, is essential.

You would be wise to learn to troubleshoot the minor difficulties likely to occur in the different machines you have available. With 16-mm projectors many of the common difficulties can be corrected easily and quickly if you are familiar with the equipment. You ought to be able to change the fuses and lamps and to determine when a machine is not threaded properly. With older machines, it is important to understand the type of loops and tension required in threading, though in newer self-threading machines such matters are not so critical.

Once you are ready to start, introduce the film. Be sure that the students know what they are supposed to be doing. Unless you make a point of this, they may think of the movie simply as entertainment. Let them know what they should look for and what questions to think about. In some cases, you may want to give them a study guide to follow. Then as soon as everyone is ready, start the movie and keep quiet. Do not make comments while the movie is running. If you must interrupt for some purpose, stop the machine, say what has to be said, and restart it. To talk while the movie is in progress is silly. All you do is interrupt the film. Besides, no one can hear you. Usually the need for comment can be anticipated and taken care of by your introduction to the film. On the other hand, do not be afraid to stop the film for class discussion or explication if it seems advisable. By so doing, you may make instructional films much clearer. Movies that present a story, however, probably should not be interrupted, because interruptions may destroy the film's impact.

Upon completing the movie, follow it up. Discussion of what was presented is always in order. Written work, tests, problems, reading on the topic, and practice of a skill demonstrated in the film are also useful. The point is to make sure that the students profit from the showing. If there is no adequate follow-up, films will become mere recreation. Sometimes the follow-up will show the necessity for seeing the movie again. This is often true when teaching skills. Then you may want to stop the film, have the student practice, and then show the film again.

Introducing, setting up, and following up films, if done well, are likely to be time consuming. Consequently, you should be careful to allow yourself plenty of time for the introduction, showing, and follow-up, as well as any emergencies that may occur. If a film breaks, wind the film around the takeup reel several times, mark the break with a slip of paper, and continue with the showing. This procedure will allow you to continue with the presentation and yet notify the audiovisual or film library people of just where the break is. Do not try to repair the break yourself. Amateur, extemporaneous, hasty splicing—or attempts to pin, paper clip, or tape broken film together—only make it more difficult for the next user of the film.

Think about how you would introduce a film by doing Exercise 14.2.

Silent Film.   In this age of sound, you may tend to forget how valuable silent films can be. The visual impact may be all that is needed. Sometimes it is better to be able to provide your own commentary. There are times when you would do well to turn off the sound on sound films and use your own or student commentary. Furthermore, silent films lend themselves to techniques in which teachers emphasize and clarify by stopping the film and repeating vital sequences as they explain and amplify the film presentation.

Individualizing Instruction.   Films can be used for small-group and independent study, as was pointed out in Module 12. Single-concept films and 8-mm cartridge projectors

EXERCISE 14.2   INTRODUCING A FILM
Critiquing an Introduction

The following description is what actually occurred in a seventh-grade science class. Read the description and write a critique of the procedure (introduction to the film) used by the teacher of that class. After you have written your critique share it with others in your class.

> On Monday of the final week of a three-week unit on the planets, the teacher told the class that today they would view a film about the outer planets. The teacher then told the students that the pictures in the film were taken by the *Voyager* spacecraft mission and that the students should take notes during the film, because after the film they would be given an open-note quiz about the film. The quiz would count toward their grades. After this introduction the film was started.

Critique:

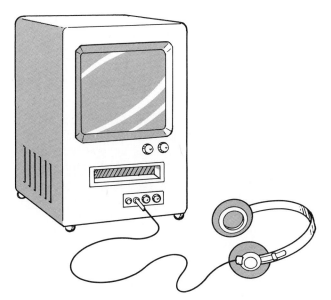

FIGURE 14.7
8-mm Cartridge Projector
Suitable for Individual
Viewing

are excellent for this purpose. Single-concept films are excellent because they concentrate on the single concept. The 8-mm cartridge machines are ideal for individual work, because they are so easy to use, as illustrated in Figure 14.7. Any student can insert the cartridge and operate the machine. Because the screen is part of the machine, there is no problem of devising a screen for individual projection.

Standard 16-mm equipment can also be used for small-group and individual work. To prepare a 16-mm machine for small-group work, connect earphones to a junction box plugged into the speaker output. Use a sheet of white paper or a cardboard box for a screen. If you put the group viewing the film in a corner of the classroom and the students use earphones, they can watch movies to their hearts' content without disturbing anyone. This is shown in Figure 14.8.

A similar technique can be used to prepare a 16-mm projector for independent study:

1. Load the film and thread the projector.
2. Plug earphones into the speaker outlet.
3. Arrange a sheet of paper, or use a box for a screen.

White-lined cardboard box

FIGURE 14.8
16-mm Projector Set up for
Individual Viewing

4. Give students directions in a written guide. Instruct them about how to turn on the machine, run it through, and stop it at the end of the film. A good technique is to have the students stop the film before it is completely run out and then back it up to the starting point so that the projector will be ready for the next user before the machine is turned off. This technique may not be necessary if the machine is self-threading. However, using it may save some confusion.

Using General-Purpose Commercial Films.   The commercial cinema can be a considerable instructional aid, especially in English, foreign language, and social studies courses. Films playing in local theaters can be used as a basis for oral and written reports. Films that all can see, such as those shown in school or at theater parties, make excellent bases for discussion and other exercises and reports.

To be aware of new films that you might use in connection with your teaching, you ought to scan the notices of coming attractions and read the reviews in newspapers and magazines. Students can do much of this type of work for you. Let them tell the class about appropriate films that they have seen or seen reviewed. Theater managers will usually be glad to cooperate with you. They can tell you when they expect to show recommended films. Sometimes, if they have reason to expect a good house, they can arrange for a showing of film classics and other requested films, and for special showings of regularly scheduled films. Film classics are also available in 16-mm for use in schools. These 16-mm films may be either feature length, abridged, or short subject. Showing feature-length films may create something of a schedule problem. This problem can be avoided by scheduling the movie after hours or in episodes. Scheduling movies is not a great problem in schools that have truly flexible schedules. Many excellent films, fit for classroom use, are available from the governmental agencies and from Chambers of Commerce, industry, and travel services. Often these movies are better for your purposes than the usual instructional films. You can find out about them by writing to the agencies concerned. For information about films available, see such references as *Educator's Guide to Free Films.*[5]

Among the strategies teachers use in order to utilize commercial films are:

1. Announce films that are coming to town or on television, and discuss how they might contribute to the course.

2. List films as optional activities. Have on the writing board or bulletin board a list of films in local theaters or TV that would be useful for optional activities such as oral or written reports.

3. Arrange theater parties for exceptional movies.

4. Discuss films that all students have had a chance to see.

5. Assign exercises and reports, such as the following, based on *The Bridge Over the River Kwai*, a classic movie that reappears on television from time to time: "Map out a route for the railroad from Bangkok to Rangoon, using a large-scale map. Draw a series of map overlays, showing the positions of the various armies in Southeast Asia during the period from the fall of Burma on. Make a terrain map, showing the terrain, vegetation, and principal obstacles. Where did the Japanese actually put their railroad? Would you select the route they did?"[6]

6. Utilize such activities as the following:
   a. Terrain study.
   b. Climate and weather study.
   c. Study of strategy and tactics.
   d. Study of people of the area—religion, economy, social customs.
   e. Map study of campaigns.

[5]Randolph, Wis.: Educator's Progress Service.

[6]Adapted from Leonard H. Clark, "Social Studies and *The Bridge Over the River Kwai*," *School Paperback Journal*, 2:18–20 (Oct. 1965).

   f. Study of important individuals.

   g. Placing of the event into the context of history. Of what importance was it? What led up to it? What resulted from it? What if it had never come off?

   h. Checking the movies against other sources to see if they present the event, period, or characters accurately. For instance, the movie *Becket* presents Thomas Becket as the leader of the Anglo-Saxon cause. Was he really?

   i. Dramatic criticism.

   j. Comparison of the picture with the book.

   k. Study of architecture, art, or customs as shown in the movie.

Television

Everyone in the United States knows that television is a powerful medium. Its use as a teaching aid, however, may present scheduling, curriculum, and physical problems that some school systems have not been able to handle.

For purposes of professional discussion, television programs can be divided into three categories: instructional television, educational television, and general commercial television. Instructional television refers to programs specifically designed as classroom instruction; educational television, to programs of public broadcasting designed to educate in general, but not aimed at classroom instruction; general commercial television programs include the entertainment and public service programs of the television networks and local stations.

Instructional Television

As just noted, television is not always used well in schools. Probably in utopian circumstances, television should not be used for classroom instruction, but rather should be reserved for supplementing ordinary curricula and instruction. Nevertheless, sometimes instructional television that takes on the role of classroom instruction is necessary in circumstances in which courses cannot be successfully mounted, because they are beyond the capabilities of the local resources, staff, and facilities. By using television well, schools can offer students courses that otherwise would be impossible. In other school systems, because of a desire for economy or in an attempt to bring the students in touch with master teachers and the very best teaching, instructional television courses have been introduced as substitutes for the regular courses.

Where instructional television courses have been introduced, the fact that the television class is taught by a master television teacher does not relieve the classroom teacher of any teaching responsibilities. He or she must plan, select, introduce, guide, and follow up, as in any other course. Otherwise, the television teaching will leave the students with learning gaps and misunderstandings. In spite of the marvels of television and other machines, students still need the personal guidance of all teachers. To use instructional television properly, you should follow a procedure similar to the following:

1. Prepare for the telecast.
   a. Study the advance material. If possible, preview the telecast.
   b. Arrange the classroom.
   c. Prepare and distribute materials and supplies as needed.
   d. Discuss the lesson to be viewed. Fill in any necessary background. Teach any vocabulary necessary.

2. Guide the learning.
   a. Circulate to help students, if necessary.
   b. Observe student response. Note signs of lack of understanding or misunderstanding.

3. Follow up.
   a. Question and discuss.
   b. Reteach and clarify as necessary.

    c. Use the telecast as a springboard to new experiences involving student partici-
       pation, creativity, problem solving, and critical thinking.
    d. Tie to past and future lessons and experiences.

This same procedure also holds for supplementary programs that are used to fill out, deepen, and enrich the day-by-day instruction.

GENERAL AND EDUCATIONAL TELEVISION PROGRAMS

In addition to instructional television programs, there are general and educational programs that you can utilize in your teaching: regular commercial programs, special events, and general cultural, educational, informational, and enrichment programs of the Public Broadcasting System and independent educational television stations. Both public broadcasting stations and commercial stations offer a multitude of programs that can be used to supplement and enrich your teaching. Probably the foremost examples include news programs, news specials, and interview programs such as "Nightline" and the "MacNeil-Lehrer Newshour." Such programs can be excellent sources of material for use in all sorts of courses, not only, as you might surmise, for courses in the social studies. For example, every day the weather map and the radar patterns shown on the weather report portion of the local news give you ammunition for the study of highs, lows, air currents, and the reading of weather maps. Science editors report on new developments in science almost every day and bring attention to important science knowledge in their science news specials. Stock market reports are basic to the study of business and economics courses.

    Ordinary commercial programs may turn out to be the best sources of all. All radio dramas occur in time and place and are subject to dramatic and literary criticism. They can be used to establish historical and literary concepts. You have already seen how movies can be used for such purposes. What would make a better subject for the study of plot or characterization (or lack of it) than many of the weekly television dramas? Music is omnipresent. Even commercials can be used—they give almost unlimited opportunities for the study of logic, propaganda, and rhetoric.

    Educational television courses, such as those given by public broadcasting stations or by colleges and universities on commercial stations, often include lectures, demonstrations, and background information that is usable for high school courses. Although these courses may be aimed at adults pursuing college credit, they are usually not too difficult for many secondary school students.

    To find what programs you might use that are telecast locally, you might consult such references as the local newspaper, news and television magazines, the local television guide, professional journals, and television station and network publicity releases. Sometimes you can obtain helpful information about future programs suitable for school use by writing to the stations or networks.

    Television studios do not ordinarily adapt their schedules to those of the secondary schools. This problem may be met in several ways. One solution is to tape programs for replay during the class period. Attention should be paid, however, to copyright laws (discussed later in this module). Another solution is to ask students to watch the telecast at home. This solution is fraught with problems because not everyone will be able to watch that television program. Some may not have television sets available (the family may not own one), some may have an adult in the house who wants to watch another show at that time, and some may not have the time available to watch that show. Consequently, you should make such assignments selectively to certain individuals or committees who will report what they have seen and heard. Sometimes, when a major event is to be telecast on several networks, you might do well to ask different students to watch different channels so that they can compare the coverage. For instance, the difference in opinions of various commentators on a presidential message might be quite revealing. In any case, the assignments made to the students must be clear and must be followed up. You might find it helpful to list the assignments, questions, and projects on the bulletin board.

Physical Arrangements for Television Classes

When using television in the classroom, you should make sure that everyone can see and hear sufficiently well. The following are guidelines for the physical arrangement of the classroom:[7]

1. Use large-screen (at least 21-inch) television monitors with front directional speakers.
2. Place the monitors so that each student has an unobstructed line of sight.
3. The screen should not be more than 30 ft from any student.
4. The set should be about 5½ ft from the floor (that is, about the same height as the teacher's face).
5. The vertical angle of sight from any student to the set should never be more than 30 degrees; the horizontal angle, never more than 45 degrees.
6. The room should be kept lighted so that students can see to write notes.
7. No glare should reflect from the screen. To reduce glare you can:
   a. Move the set away from windows.
   b. Tilt the set downward.
   c. Provide the set with cardboard blinders.
8. The sound should come from front directional speakers.
9. Students should have adequate surface space for writing.
10. To allow for quick, easy transition from the telecast, television classrooms should be fitted with adequate audiovisual equipment, display space, filing and storage space.

Tape Recorders and Other Players

Audio Recordings

You will find that tape recordings, CDs, and records are also excellent media for many purposes. In addition to bringing music, speeches, plays, and other dramatic devices to the class, they can be used to support other media. (What would movies and television be like without the background of sound tracks?) Audiotape can also be used to record your own performance so that no one can criticize your work. Such recording is essential in the study of language and speech.

Audiotapes or cassettes can be used as supplements to workbooks and textbooks in any classroom or as powerful primary sources of information within a course. It is possible, for example, to build a language laboratory around a storage and retrieval system of cassette tapes. Stored tapes can also be used as learning resources in: literature or drama courses; in laboratory experiments for detailed instruction; learning activity centers, as exciting supplements in the progress of a lesson where opinions of experts in the field under study are needed for decision making; and in musical appreciation.

Video Recordings

Videotaped programs can do about everything that the older 16-mm films can do. In addition, videotape makes it possible to record student activities, practice, special projects, and the like. It gives students a marvelous opportunity to see and hear themselves in action.

---

[7]Clark and Starr, 6th edition, p. 388. By permission of Macmillan Publishing Company.

Videodiscs

Laser videodiscs and players for classroom use are now reasonably priced, with an ever-increasing variety of disc topics for middle and secondary school subjects.[8] There are two formats of laser videodisc: (1) freeze-frame format (CAV—Constant Angular Velocity, or Standard Play) and (2) non-freeze-frame format (CLV—Constant Linear Velocity, or Extended Play), and both will play on all laser disc players. Laser videodiscs play on videodisc players, which are quite similar to VCRs and just as easy to operate. Discs are visual archives or visual databases, presenting large amounts of information that can be easily retrieved, reorganized, filed, and controlled by the user with the remote control that accompanies the player. Each side of a double-sided disc stores 54,000 separate still-frames of information. Visuals, both still and motion sequences, can be stored and then selected for showing on a television monitor or programmed onto a computer disk for an individualized presentation. More than a thousand titles of laser videodiscs are available for educational use. Your school district audiovisual center probably has a number of titles already; for additional titles you can refer to the latest edition of the *Videodisc Compendium*.[9]

Multimedia

You should use different media to reinforce one another. You will do so naturally some of the time, such as when you write on the overhead projector to illustrate a problem you are discussing. But you should make an effort to combine media in ways that will make your teaching effective and exciting. You can do so by using different media in sequence or by using them simultaneously. The essential ingredient is that the media support one another and the instruction.

For instance, you might want to show a picture of a scene, then a map of the area, and then a taped narrative describing what travel was like. Or you might present all three simultaneously: as the taped narrative plays, you could point out features referred to by the narrative on both the map and the picture. In teaching the westward movement, for instance, you could project a map of the West on the writing board and then with colored chalk trace routes west on the board, as you project pictures of the terrain and other features on an adjacent screen. Techniques using two or more screens can be both interesting and informative. For instance, while you hold a picture on one screen, you can flash a series of closeups on another. Or you could present a schematic on one screen and a picture of the real thing on another, or a picture on one screen and pictures about it on another. Similarly, such presentations could be combined with the use of models, real objects, or sound tracks. Almost anything will serve as long as the media used support each other and the objectives of instruction. However, if the media are incompatible and do not complement each other, they may confuse rather than clarify.

Computers and Microcomputers

During the 1980s educational technology in the use of computers expanded tremendously, and it continues to do so. Computers can assist instruction by carrying out such chores as drill and practice activities. The computer can not only present the drill exercise but also score it immediately and prescribe corrective instruction when necessary. The computer can also prescribe individualization by preassessing students' knowledge, presenting them with the information they need, and evaluating their progress. With the advent of classroom computers, there may almost be nothing the machine cannot do if the teacher is aware of its potential and has the appropriate software programs available.

---

[8]The state of Texas, for the 1991–1992 school year, became the first state to allow its public schools to use state textbook funds to purchase certain videodiscs as an option to textbooks. Others are certain to follow that precedent.

[9]Compiled by Emerging Technology Consultants of St. Paul, MN.

Computer-Assisted Instruction (CAI)

Computer-assisted instruction (CAI) is the term used to describe the use of computers for instructional tasks. In computer-assisted instructional techniques, the student interacts with lessons that are programmed into the computer system. These programs (the software) come packaged in the form of disks, cassette tapes, and cartridges. Software packages for computer-assisted instruction use a variety of interactive instructional methods, and often a single program will use a combination of several—drill and practice, tutorial, gaming, simulation, discovery, and problem solving are the common modes of interaction. Figure 14.9 compares the methods used in computer-assisted instruction.

Unfortunately, many classrooms still are without computers, and others may have only one available. Often when such is the case, the computer is used by the teacher solely as a visual aid. When only one or two computers are available for classroom use the teacher must be creative in deciding for what, how, and when and by whom they will be used. In part, this decision is governed by the availability of software. Some schools have a computer laboratory that houses a number of computers so that a teacher can either take an entire class or send a few students for special computer work. Find out how and what computers are used in your local schools, especially in your discipline, and share those findings with others in your class.

Computer-Managed Instruction (CMI)

Rather than providing direct instruction, **computer-managed instruction (CMI)** uses the computer to manage information about the progress of instruction by maintaining student records of performance. Essentially, the computer-managed instructional system can maintain records of student performance, administer diagnostic tests, score them, prescribe follow-up steps, and monitor student progress. Although CMI is still in its developmental stages, there is growing interest in its use, specifically as a tool to aid in individualizing instruction.

Copyright Laws Regarding Use of Recordings and Projected Visuals

Off-Air Videotaping

You should keep in mind these laws regarding videotaping:[10]

Permitted Uses—You may:

1. Request your media center to record the program for you if you cannot or if you lack the equipment.
2. Retain a videotaped copy of a broadcast (including cable transmission) for a period of 45 calendar days, after which the program must be erased.
3. Use the program in class once during the first 10 school days of the 45 calendar days, and a second time if instruction needs to be reinforced.
4. Have professional staff view the program several times for evaluation purposes during the full 45-day period.
5. Make a limited number of copies to meet legitimate needs, but these copies must be erased when the original videotape is erased.
6. Use only a part of the program if instructional needs warrant (but see the next list).
7. Enter into a licensing agreement with the copyright holder to continue use of the program.

Prohibited Uses—You may not:

1. Videotape premium cable services such as HBO without express permission.
2. Alter the original content of the program.

---

[10]Heinich, p. 431.

Methods	Description	Role of Teacher	Role of Computer	Role of Student	Applications/ Examples
Drill-and-Practice	Content already taught Review basic facts and terminology Variety of questions in varied formats Question/answer drills repeated as necessary	Arranges for prior instruction Selects material Matches drill to student Checks progress	Asks questions "Evaluates" student responses Provides immediate feedback Records student progress	Practices content already taught Responds to questions Receives confirmation and/or correction Chooses content and difficulty level	Parts of a microscope Completing balance sheets Vocabulary building Math facts Product knowledge
Tutorial	Presentation of new information Teaches concepts and principles Provides remedial instruction	Selects material Adapts instruction Monitors	Presents information Asks questions Monitors responses Provides remedial feedback Summarizes key points Keeps records	Interacts with computer Sees results Answers questions Asks questions	Clerical training Bank teller training Science Medical procedures Bible study
Gaming	Competitive Drill-and-practice in a motivational format Individual or small group	Sets limits Directs process Monitors results	Acts as competitor judge scorekeeper	Learns facts/ strategies/skills Evaluates choices Competes with computers	Fraction games Counting games Spelling games Typing (arcade-type) games
Simulation	Approximates real-life situations Based upon realistic models Individual or small group	Introduces subject Presents background Guides "debriefing"	Plays role(s) Delivers results of decisions Maintains the model and its database	Practices decision making Makes choices Receives results of decisions Evaluates decisions	Troubleshooting History Medical diagnosis Simulators (pilot/ driver) Business management Laboratory experiments
Discovery	Inquiry into database Inductive approach Trial and error Tests hypotheses	Presents basic problem Monitors student progress	Presents student with source of information Stores data Permits search procedures	Makes hypotheses Tests guesses Develops principles/rules	Social science Science Food-intake analysis Career choices
Problem Solving	Works with data Systematizes information Performs rapid and accurate calculations	Assigns problems Checks results	Presents problem Manipulates data Maintains database Provides feedback	Defines the problem Sets up the solution Manipulates variables Trial and error	Business Creativity Troubleshooting Mathematics Computer programming

FIGURE 14.9

Utilization of Various CAI Methods (Source: Heinich, p. 360. By permission of Macmillan Publishing Company.)

3. Exclude the copyright notice on the program.

4. Videorecord in anticipation of a request for use—the request to record must come from an instructor.

5. Retain the program, and any copies, after forty-five days.

Computer Software

You should also pay attention to the laws concerning computer software:[11]

Permitted Uses—You may:

1. Make a single back-up or archival copy of the computer program.

2. Adapt the computer program to another language if the program is unavailable in the target language.

3. Add features to make better use of the computer program.

Prohibited Use—You may not:

1. Make multiple copies.

2. Make replacement copies from an archival or back-up copy.

3. Make copies of copyrighted programs to be sold, leased, loaned, transmitted, or given away.

Making Your Own Materials

Many teachers enjoy making their own teaching materials. Besides the duplicated materials so common in elementary and secondary school classes, teachers make slides, transparencies, tapes, and all sorts of audio and visual teaching aids. Doing so can be a great deal of fun and satisfaction. It also has the advantage of giving you the material you want, not what some professor or publisher thinks you want. Suggestions for making teaching aids are presented elsewhere in this text and in a number of references. The following is a sampling of publications on the production and use of such materials:

Anderson, Ronald H. *Selecting and Developing Media for Instruction.* New York: Van Nostrand Reinhold Company.

Brown, James W., and Richard B. Lewis. *AV Instructional Technology Manual for Independent Study,* 5th ed. New York: McGraw-Hill Book Company, 1977.

Bullard, John R., and Calvin E. Mether. *Audio-Visual Fundamentals: Basic Equipment Operation and Simple Materials Production,* 2nd ed. Dubuque, Ia.: William C. Brown Company, Publishers, 1979.

Eastman Kodak Publications, 343 State Street, Rochester, NY 14650.

 Adapting Your Tape Recorder to the Kodak Carousel, SC-1.
 Applied Color Photography Indoors, E-76.
 Audio-Visual Projection, S-3.
 Basic Copying, AM-2.
 Basic Developing, Printing, and Enlarging, AJ-2.
 Color Photography Outdoors, E-75.
 Composition, AC-11.
 Copying, M-1.
 Effective Lecture Slides, S-22.
 Good Color Pictures—Quick and Easy, AE-10.
 Making Black and White Transparencies for Overhead Projection, S-17.
 Planning and Producing Visual Aids, S-13.
 Producing Slides and Filmstrips, S-8.

Goudket, Michael. *Audiovisual Primer,* rev. ed. New York: Teachers College Press, 1974.

Green, Lee. *Teaching Tools You Can Make.* Wheaton, Ill.: Victor Books, 1978.

[11]From a December, 1980, Congressional amendment to the 1976 Copyright Act.

Heinich, Robert, et al. *Instructional Media*, 3rd ed. New York: Macmillan, 1989.

McClure, Larry, Sue Carol Cook, and Virginia Thompson. *Experience-Based Learning: How to Make the Community Your Classroom.* Portland, Oregon: Northwest Regional Educational Laboratory, July 1977.

Minor, Edward O. *Handbook for Preparing Visual Media,* 2nd ed. New York: McGraw-Hill Book Company, 1978.

Minor, Edward O., and Harvey R. Frye. *Techniques for Producing Instructional Media*, 2nd ed. New York: McGraw-Hill Book Company, 1977.

Oates, Stanton C. *Audio Visual Equipment: Self Instructional Manual*, 4th ed. Dubuque, Iowa: William C. Brown Company, 1979.

University of Texas at Austin, Instructional Media Center (VIB), Austin, Texas.
Better Bulletin Boards.
Designing Instructional Visuals.
Educational Displays and Exhibits.
Instructional Display Boards.
Models for Teaching.
The Overhead System
The Tape Recorder.
Using Tear Sheets.

SUMMARY

In this and in the previous module we have presented and discussed a variety of tools that you can use. When used wisely, these tools will help you to reach more of your students more of the time. Middle and secondary school teachers must meet the needs of a variety of students—linguistically and culturally different, the poor readers and good readers. The materials presented in these two modules should be of help. The future will undoubtedly bring technological innovations that will be helpful to the teacher—laser videodiscs, computers, and telecommunications equipment have only marked the beginning of a revolution for teaching. By the year 2000, new instructional delivery systems made possible by microcomputers and multimedia workstations will likely fundamentally alter the role of the classroom teacher.[12]

To help the teacher analyze and to understand the effects of his or her instructional efforts, and to help students understand the results of their learning efforts, the teacher needs to know how to measure and to evaluate those instructional and learning efforts; that is the topic of the next module.

SUGGESTED READING

Bitter, G. G., and Camuse, R. A. *Using a Microcomputer in the Classroom.* 2d ed. Englewood Cliffs, NJ: Prentice Hall, 1988.

Caissy, G. A. "Evaluating educational software: A practitioner's guide." *Phi Delta Kappan* 66(4):249–50 (December 1984).

Copyright Law: What Every School, College and Public Library Should Know. Skokie, IL: Association for Information Media and Equipment, 1987. Videotape.

Green, L. *501 Ways to Use the Overhead Projector.* Littleton, CO: Libraries Unlimited, 1982.

Heinich, R.; Molenda, M.; and Russell, J. D. *Instructional Media.* 3d ed. New York: Macmillan, 1989.

Horn, R. V. "Laser videodiscs in education: Endless possibilities." *Phi Delta Kappan* 68(9):696–700 (May 1987).

Johnson, J. *Electronic Learning: From Audiotape to Videodisc.* Hillsdale, NJ: Lawrence Erlbaum, 1987.

---

[12]Royal Van Horn, "Educational Power Tools: New Instructional Delivery Systems," *Phi Delta Kappan* 72(7):527–533 (March 1991).

Kemp, J. E., and Smellie, D. C. *Planning, Producing, and Using Instructional Media.* 6th ed. New York: Harper & Row, 1989.

Miller, J. K. *Using Copyrighted Videocassettes in Classrooms, Libraries, and Training Centers.* 2d ed. Friday Harbor, WA: Copyright Information Services, 1988.

Talab, R. S. *Copyright and Instructional Technologies: A Guide to Fair Use and Permissions.* 2d ed. Washington, DC: Association for Educational Communications and Technology, 1989.

Turner, S., and Land, M. *Tools for Schools: Applications Software for the Classroom.* Belmont, CA: Wadsworth, 1988.

Short Answer

POSTTEST

1. Describe how audiovisual aids help to reduce a reliance on verbalism.

2. What should be your basic considerations when selecting an audiovisual aid?

3. When focusing a projector what is the basic principle to take into account?

4. If you have a set of small prints that you want students to see and study, what is the most efficient way of presenting them to your students?

5. Describe the advantage of running off a transparency and a ditto sheet of an evercise on a spirit master.

6. Can it be done?

7. Describe the essential difference between an opaque projector and an overhead projector.

8. It has been said that the overhead projector is the teacher's best friend. What is so good about this kind of projector?

9. Describe how you would go about making a hand-drawn colored transparency.

10. Describe how a transparency overlay or flip-on is used.

11. Describe the purpose of a mask when used with an overhead projector.

12. Describe how you could adapt a slide projector for individual or small-group viewing.

13. Identify the guidelines for preparing a slide program.

14. What should you do if a 16-mm film breaks?

_____

15. What can you do to ensure that students understand that films used in the class-room are for instruction, not for entertainment?

_____

16. Many people think that films are the audiovisual aid par excellence, but they have many disadvantages. Identify three of them.

_____

_____

_____

17. Once a film showing is completed and the machine is turned off, what should you, the teacher, do next?

_____

18. How might you utilize in your instruction commercial films showing at local theaters or on television?

_____

19. Give an example of a multimedia presentation.

_____

20. Describe two uses of the microcomputer in education.

_____

_____

21. When might it be preferable to use a silent film or filmstrip for instruction?

_____

_____

22. What advantage does a slide program have over a filmstrip?

_____

23. Describe two ways that you could use Public Broadcasting or commercial television programs for classroom use.

_____

_____

24. Which audiovisual devices can be used to individualize instruction?

_____

25. Describe the difference between computer-assisted instruction and computer-managed instruction.

_____

_____

26. For a classroom teacher, which of the following is permissible by law without obtaining permission from the copyright holder? _____
    a. Make multiple copies of a computer program.
    b. Record a video program and keep the tape for up to one year.
    c. Record a premium cable channel program.
    d. Make a copy of a computer program to give to a colleague.

PART VI
Preparing for Measurement, Evaluation, and Grading

Part VI, consisting of two modules, assists you with:

□ Understanding the process of measurement.

□ Understanding the purposes for grading.

□ Understanding the methods for grading.

□ Providing tools for measurement.

□ How to prepare and score tests and other evaluative instruments.

□ Reporting achievement.

Babe Ruth's record of 714 home runs will never be forgotten. But how many of us know that the Babe struck out 1330 times, a record unapproached by any other player in the history of baseball?

—Harold Helfer

Children need models more than they need critics.

—Joseph Joubert

MODULE 15
Measurement and Evaluation

RATIONALE

Evaluation is an integral part of the educational scene. Curricula, buildings, materials, specific courses, teachers, supervisors, administrators, equipment—all must be appraised in relation to student learning, the ultimate goal of the school. When gaps between anticipated results and achievement exist, attempts are made to eliminate those factors that seem to be limiting the educational output, or in some other way to improve the situation. Thus, educational progress occurs.

To learn effectively, students must know how they are doing. Similarly, to be an effective teacher, you must be informed about what the student knows, feels, and can do so that you can build on student skills, knowledge, and attitudes. Therefore you need continuous feedback indicating student progress and problems in order to plan appropriate learning activities. If this feedback tells you that progress is slow, you can provide alternative activities; if it indicates that students have already mastered the desired learning, you can eliminate unnecessary practice. In short, evaluation provides a key for both effective teaching and learning.

The importance of continuous evaluation mandates that you know the principles and techniques of evaluation and measurement. This module will explain some principles of evaluation and show you how to construct and use tests and other evaluative techniques. We define the general terms related to evaluation, consider what makes a good test, relate the criteria to standardized and teacher-made tests, suggest procedures to use in test construction, point out the advantages and disadvantages of different types of test items, and explain the construction and use of other evaluative devices and techniques.

SPECIFIC OBJECTIVES

At the completion of this module, you should be able to:

1. Define evaluation and measurement, indicating two specific differences between the terms.
2. Explain the distinction between a norm-referenced test and a criterion-referenced test, and give an example of the appropriate use of each.
3. List five criteria for selecting a test, and cite a purpose for each criterion.
4. Set up a table of specifications for a unit test, and classify five items in correct cells in the table.
5. Cite five different uses of test results.
6. Give four different types of objective questions, and indicate one advantage and one disadvantage of each type.
7. Specify four guidelines for a teacher preparing an essay test.
8. Define percentile, stanine, and grade equivalence, and explain a use of each.
9. Demonstrate two devices by which you might ensure objectivity in your evaluation of a product or process.
10. Diagram a teaching model and indicate where evaluation is utilized.

MODULE TEXT

A Teaching Model

When Bob Hernandez begins his daily trip to his job, his usual route is Lincoln to Main, Main to College, and College to the parking lot beside Central High School. Since construction has started on the new highway, Bob sometimes has to change his route. If the Lincoln-Main intersection is blocked, he goes on Washington to Lake Street and then over to Main. In the fall, when the family is still staying at the cottage, his drive to work takes him in a southeasterly direction instead of the northwest route he takes from home. Occasionally, he has an errand, mailing a package or returning a book to the library. Again his trip is adjusted to the situation. How are such revised routes planned? Often with little conscious effort, since the driver is familiar with the area, knows where he is going, where he is, and what must be accomplished en route.

If Bob Hernandez is driving in a city unfamiliar to him, he plans his route more carefully, using a map or specific directions provided by someone who is acquainted with the area. In such a situation, he may recognize another possibility. Without a street number, sign, or other recognizable clue, he may not know when he reaches his destination. So the final target, which is obvious in a familiar situation (going to work), may not be so easily determined in a strange or unfamiliar setting.

The teacher's plans for the educational journeys of the students in a class require answers to the same basic questions: Where are we going? Where are we now? How do we get where we are going? How do we know when we get there?

These are questions that must be considered in educational evaluation. The answers provide the teacher with the basis for working with individual students and with groups. Since in the never-static educational setting the answers are ever-changing, the teacher continuously assesses and adjusts flexible plans to the new situation.

The basic question of goals—or "where are we going"—is in a broad sense determined by society. State requirements and limitations, school board policies, curricula, and courses of study usually evolve with input from all segments of the community. Major factors considered include the society, the students, the school, and the future. The purpose and philosophy of the school distilled from the collected efforts of all of these forces provide the broad objectives for the teacher (the where). Guidelines in each course of study provide the framework within which the teacher will make selections of content and strategies (the what and how). For those who believe that process is a crucial goal of education, the strategies relate to objectives. If one objective is that the student will be able to demonstrate a rational method of attacking a new problem, then a problem-solving approach must be implemented in the classroom. If, however, the objective is the rote memorization of tribal lore or the accumulation and retention of a wide variety of facts about the world in general, a different approach will be called for. The teacher, in selecting specific objectives and activities appropriate for the situation, exerts considerable influence on the learning environment and helps determine where we are going.

"Start where the student is" is a pedagogical cliché. Nevertheless, the statement emphasizes the need to know where we are before we can make reasonable plans for progress. A student who reads at the third-grade level is not going to be able to cope successfully with a social studies text written on the seventh-grade reading level. A student who does not comprehend percentage is not ready for interest problems. A diagnostic test is one tool for determining where we are. Other evaluation procedures can also provide information about skills and understanding, such as reading a paragraph and giving an oral summary to indicate comprehension, driving a golf ball to demonstrate the skill, and writing a description of a picture to reveal how well the student can write a paragraph. Students are frustrated and do not progress educationally when they are bored by tasks that they have already mastered as well as by tasks that require skills or knowledge they do not have. Information about a student's achievement provides a basis for appropriate planning to stimulate further development.

Information about where we are going (objectives) and where we start (achievement and attitude of students) enables the teacher to propose several plans for reaching the goals. Students, for example, may work as individuals or in groups on common goals or on specific individualized objectives. Selection and implementation of a plan and of appropriate learning activities require continuing evaluation to check on progress and to adopt strategies to promote the desired student behavior. When student feedback indicates satisfactory attainment of objectives, the teacher moves to a new unit, problem, or content area and develops another learning cycle. In the learning cycle (Figure 15.1) evaluation is critical. It establishes the starting point, provides data on progress, and indicates arrival at the destination. A teacher must recognize the need for good evaluation and measurement and must develop skill in preparing effective instruments.

FIGURE 15.1
Learning Cycle

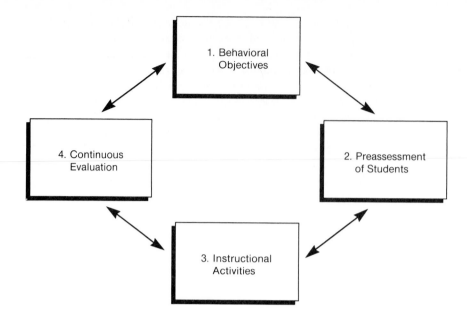

Evaluation and Measurement

The terms *evaluation* and *measurement* are related. Measurement refers to quantifiable data and relates to specific behavior. Tests and the statistical procedures used to analyze the results are the emphases in measurement. Evaluation includes measurement data plus other types of information, such as anecdotal records and written and oral performance ratings. Evaluation also involves a value judgment factor. A teacher may share the information that May Grisso received the top score in East High School on the College Entrance Examination Board Scholastic Aptitude Test (SAT); this statement refers to measurement. However, when the teacher adds that May has not been an outstanding student in the English program at East, evaluation has occurred. Measurement is descriptive and objective, whereas evaluation involves information from varied sources including subjective value input.

Assessment and appraisal are two other terms often used. Both of these suggest going beyond the quantifiable information to a personal interpretation or evaluation. The National Assessment of Educational Programs is dealing with measurement in specific content areas for ages nine, thirteen, seventeen, and for adults.[1] Since this testing covers the United States and is expected to provide data to improve the curriculum, the use of assessment as a synonym for evaluation seems appropriate.

Tools for Educational Measurement

Over the years teachers have used four basic approaches for assessing pupil progress:

1. The oral test, which survives as the "orals" given to candidates for advanced degrees and in casual classroom questioning.
2. The observation of student performance.
3. The examination of samples of the products of student activity.
4. The written test with which we are all so familiar.

Criterion-Referenced and Norm-Referenced Instruments

The instruments used in any of these approaches may be criterion-referenced or norm-referenced. **Criterion-referenced** tests, sometimes called mastery tests, are de-

---

[1]For their 1988 report, see "Education," *Time* 131(25):79 (June 20, 1988).

signed to check whether or not the learners have met the basic objectives of a learning segment. Their object is to determine whether or not students can or cannot perform at a set standard. They are, in effect, what the astronauts call "go—no go" instruments. They are not designed to sort out the best from the average or the less than average but to determine whether or not individuals have met the standard. If students do not meet the standard, presumably they should be given more opportunity to learn the concept or skill, or be failed. They are not particularly tied into age and grade-time-schedules as are other tests, because they take into consideration that not all students will progress at the same rate or be at the same level at the same time. In this kind of testing it is the mastery that is sought, and time is a variable instead of the reverse. Programmed materials, continuous progress courses, and some competency-based curricula rely on such instruments.

Norm-referenced tests, on the other hand, are designed to compare pupils with each other and to determine each individual's standing. They are useful when the concern is communication of information about students to parents, colleges, or employment agencies. They reflect the influence of our competitive social structure. And because most citizens have been exposed to their *modus operandi,* they are understood fairly well by patrons of the school. They facilitate the process, for example, of selecting the six most accurate math students in a grade or in deciding into which reading group to place a new student when he or she joins a class. They also are relied upon as predictors of future success, as, for example, when selections are made for admissions after the college aptitude exams have been administered. It is expected that those who score highest will be most likely to succeed in advanced classes. Since some items in norm-referenced tests are easy and some are difficult by design, it is possible to list students' results in a continuum from highest to lowest and examine specifically where each stands with regard to the other test-takers.

For instance, you might use a norm-referenced test to determine a student's reading level. The individual's score in relation to the group may be expressed in various ways. Percentile rank is commonly used. If Jenny Chang's reading score is at the 35th percentile for tenth-graders, then 35 of 100 tenth-graders who took the test scored below Jenny. Another frequently used system for representing relative performance is stanines. This standard nine-point scale was developed during World War II as a simple and usable norm. A single digit from a low of 1 to a high of 9 indicates where the individual score falls in relation to the group (Figure 15.2). Jenny Chang's reading score at the 35th percentile rank can also be described as being in stanine 4.

Similarly, grade equivalents are sometimes used to represent the relative performance of students on a test. This method is expressed in two numbers; for example, 9.4 shows the arithmetic average (mean) of students in the fourth month of the ninth grade. The calendar year is divided into ten parts, nine representing the school year and one for summer vacation. Jenny Chang's grade equivalent of 8.2 indicates, according to the test, that as a tenth-grader she reads as well as the average student in the second month of the eighth grade.

These three methods of expressing scores are used to indicate how an individual score compares to the group. Percentile and grade equivalent are perhaps more easily understood by parents and teachers. The stanine and other standard scores are more useful because the difference between steps remains the same. They are all examples of norm-referencing. Techniques for calculating and interpreting such scores will be discussed in a following section of this module.

Probably both criterion-referenced and norm-referenced tests have a place in secondary schools today. The teacher, recognizing the differences in purpose and use,

Stanine	1	2	3	4	5	6	7	8	9
Percentile	1–4	5–11	12–23	24–40	41–60	61–77	78–89	90–96	97–100

FIGURE 15.2
Comparison of Percentiles and Stanines

must select or construct the appropriate type. As a rule, norm-referenced tests better lend themselves to ordinary school marking systems, whereas criterion-referenced tests are more useful for diagnosis, individualizing instruction, and determining student competency.

Types of Tests

Pedagogical tests differ both in form and purpose. Let us look at a sampling of the different types of tests commonly used by classroom teachers. Remember, this list is not an exhaustive study of testing. You will come across other types of tests in your teaching.

Achievement tests are designed to measure the student's level of accomplishment: how much a student has learned about a subject area or a segment of that subject. They are usually commercially prepared and are accompanied by charts and manuals to assist in scoring and interpreting student results.

Teacher-made tests are commonly achievement tests prepared by the teacher to measure student learning in a specific area. A pretest is given prior to planned instructional activities. The pretest should provide information about student background that is pertinent to the content and should help the teacher plan more efficiently, in the light of the student strengths and weaknesses revealed by the test. Prerequisite skills and concepts that have not been acquired can be incorporated in the plan. Unnecessary duplication can be eliminated. Students with expertise in the area can be utilized in the instructional program. A posttest is given at the end of instruction to indicate student achievement at that point. The difference between pretest and posttest scores gives an indication of student growth.

A standardized test is one prepared with careful research by testing experts so that the instrument represents desirable test characteristics. A test manual that is usually available provides information about administering the test, scoring it, and interpreting results. Norms also are provided as a basis for comparison to a large group or population. These tests are useful for assessing such qualities as students' intellectual abilities, academic achievement, attitudes, interests, and aptitudes. As a rule they give one a single score or measurement level by which one can estimate the differences among individuals and changes in knowledge, behavior, interests, and the like, for an individual over a period of time.

An objective test is one that can be scored consistently; the answers are either right or wrong. This type of test is probably most frequently used in schools. True-false, multiple-choice, and matching are examples of types of questions used on objective tests.

Essay tests require original student responses to a question and are considered subjective measures. Different people may react differently when scoring responses in a test of this sort. The same person scoring on two or three occasions could arrive at two or three different scores. Often the answers cannot be considered right or wrong, but involve such value judgment as "more logical," "better evidence," or "more important point."

Speed tests include time as a factor in the test. This should be applied only when the time involved in the performance is critical. Typing tests are commonly timed.

Power tests are those that allow the student sufficient time to respond to the items. A teacher should provide time for 90 percent of the students to complete a test in which time should not be considered as a part of the test.

A diagnostic test is specifically designed to determine the students' deficiencies. A readiness test is constructed to find out whether the student has the understanding, skills, and, sometimes, motivation to go to the next level.

A performance test is designed to indicate the level at which the student can accomplish a specific skill, usually psychomotor in emphasis. The physical education programs utilize these tests, such as in shooting baskets or in executing a tennis serve. Vocational education uses performance tests frequently, also. To make objective the observation of performance of this sort, teachers frequently turn to rating scales or checklists.

STANDARDIZED TESTING

Standardized tests are useful for assessing such qualities as students' intellectual abilities, academic achievement, attitudes, interests, and aptitudes. They are used both to measure the differences among individuals and to determine changes in an individual's knowledge, behavior, interests, emotions, and the like over a period of time. They are common tools for determining a person's mental ability, suitability for employment, special aptitudes, career placement, personality deviation, grade placement, college admission, and so on. They are especially useful for surveying broad areas of achievement. They are called standardized tests because, after being carefully prepared, they have been given to a large presumably representative standardizing group of persons whose test scores have been treated statistically to set up norms by which to judge the meaning of individuals' test scores.

Some standardized achievement tests, for instance, can tell a teacher how the achievement of individual students or classes compares with that of students in the country at large, whereas other standardized achievement tests can be used to point out an individual student's strengths and weaknesses for diagnostic purposes. They are seldom valuable for determining student progress in a particular course, however, for they usually do not sufficiently reflect the objectives and content of specific courses. Personality, character, aptitude, and intelligence tests that reflect students' inclinations and potentials are also excellent diagnostic tools.

In general, standardized tests fall into three basic categories: general intelligence and achievement tests, attitude and personality tests (including projective tests), and interest and aptitude tests.

General Intelligence Tests.   General intelligence tests are the oldest type of standardized tests. They were invented at the turn of the century in attempts to find ways to identify children's learning potential. Perhaps the most important step in this movement was the development by Binet and Simon of tests by which to identify feebleminded or retarded children for the French government. From these tests and their revisions by Lewis M. Terman come the concepts of mental age and intelligence quotient (IQ). By mental age the testers meant a person's score on a test of mental ability expressed in terms of the average chronological age of persons whose score was the same as his: for example, if a boy's mental test score is equal to that of the average nine-year-old, his mental score is 9, no matter what his chronological age may be. The intelligence quotient, which was derived from the mental-age concept for the Stanford-Binet test (Terman's 1916 revision of the Binet-Simon test), was the ratio of the mental age, as defined by the tests, and the chronological age. Until the 1960s it was indicated by the formula

$$IQ = \frac{MA}{CA} \times 100.$$

Since the 1960s, however, the IQ scores of the Stanford-Binet tests, and many other tests, have been reported as deviation IQs in which the IQ is reported as a standard score whose mean is 100 and whose standard deviation is 16.[2]

The Stanford-Binet test and the Wechsler Intelligence Scale for Children (WISC) and the Wechsler Adult Intelligence Scale (WAIS), which have been widely used in recent years, are individual tests. They are time-consuming to give and require the services of a highly skilled professional to administer, score, and interpret. Since World War I, however, when the U.S. Army invented the pencil-and-paper Army Alpha group

---

[2]Some test developers have used other standard deviations, ranging from about 5 to 20, in defining their deviation IQs.

test to test the intelligence of recruits, many group intelligence tests have been published. Among them are such well-known tests as

- California Test of Mental Maturity
- Henman Nelson Tests of Mental Ability
- Kuhlmann-Anderson Tests
- Lorge-Thorndike Intelligence Tests
- Terman-McNemar Test of Mental Ability
- School and College Ability Tests (SCAT)
- Scholastic Aptitude Test (SAT)
- Graduate Record Examination (GRE—a combination of intelligence and achievement tests)
- Miller Analogies Test
- College Entrance Examination Board tests (CEEB—frequently called the College Boards)

In addition, textbook houses and test publishers have published a great number of group tests aimed at measuring student achievement in various subject fields. Some of the commonly used achievement tests are the California Achievement Tests, the Metropolitan Achievement Tests, and the Iowa Tests of Educational Development.

Interest and Aptitude Tests.   Interest and aptitude tests are useful for diagnosis and for counseling students. They include vocational aptitude and interest tests such as the Differential Aptitude Test, the Strong Vocational Interest Blank, and the Kuder Preference Record. These tests can give teachers and counselors insights into the abilities and interests of students and the probabilities of their potential success in various careers and vocations.

Personality Tests.   Personality tests are basically tools for school psychologists and counselors, though they can provide valuable information for teachers also. They include paper-and-pencil tests, drawing tests, and rating scales, as well as situational tests and projective techniques for evaluating personality or emotional problems. Among the many well-known personality tests that are ordinarily used in counseling students with serious adjustment and learning problems are the Minnesota Multiphasic Personality Inventory (MMPI), the Rorschach Ink-blots, the Thematic Apperception Test (TAT), and the California Psychological Inventory. Administration and interpretation of these tests should be left to experts.

References.   Information concerning the various standardized tests can be found in such works as the Mental Measurement Yearbooks[3] and Levy and Goldstein's *Tests in Education*[4] and such journals as *Education Index, Psychological Abstracts, Review of Educational Research* and *Educational and Psychological Measurement.*

Characteristics of a Good Test

The teacher who is constructing a test or selecting a test for use must be concerned about some basic characteristics: validity, reliability, objectivity, usability, and discrimination. Validity, the most important, refers to whether the test measures what it is supposed to measure. The key questions concerning validity are:

- Does the test adequately sample the content area?
- Does the test involve the cognitive, affective, and psychomotor skills that are important to the unit?

---

[3]O. K. Buros, *Mental Measurement Yearbook* (Lincoln, Neb.: University of Nebraska Press, various cumulative editions).

[4]Philip Levy and Harvey Goldstein, *Tests in Education* (Orlando, Fla.: Academic Press, 1984).

□ Does the test relate to all the behavioral objectives for the unit?

Standardized tests involve more complex analysis of validity when results are used for prediction.

Reliability refers to the consistency of results (for instance, a scale is reliable if it always records ninety pounds when one weighs a 90-pound object on it). Test results may not be consistent because of test conditions, poorly designed or worded questions, errors in scoring, and a number of other chance variables. Human errors, such as errors in grading or errors in reading questions, are inevitable. However, instrument-centered errors as well as student-centered errors are taken into consideration by some of the statistical treatments. When you are selecting a standardized test or producing different forms of a test to administer to several sections of a class, you should investigate this concept further.

Objectivity refers to freedom from subjective judgments for both the teacher and student. This characteristic implies careful attention in the construction of items and in the selection of the form of items for the test.

Usability refers to the practical aspects of time and resources required for the test, compared to the value of information obtained. An essay test, for instance, may be easily prepared by the teacher, but the time involved in grading the test for 28 students may make such a test impractical. Although the preparation of an objective-type test requires more time initially, the grading is relatively quick and easy. Sometimes grading tests involves rather strict time limits because reports on students are due at a specified time, such as at the end of a semester. Cost or equipment required may eliminate the consideration of certain standardized tests.

Discrimination refers to the ability of a test to separate students on the basis of how well they perform on the test. Discriminating power is not a factor in a criterion-referenced test. However, in tests given to determine the individual's position in the group, the differentiation ability of the test is crucial. The teacher should make an item analysis of tests to determine the difficulty and discriminatory power of each item as a basis for revising the test. The use of computers in many schools facilitates item analysis, but since the procedure involves only counting and dividing, the teacher untrained in statistics can handle it. Quite specific guidelines for the difficulty and discriminating power of the items in a well-constructed test are available in textbooks of educational measurement.

Constructing the Instrument

The first step in constructing a measurement instrument is to make an evaluation plan. In this plan, make provisions to:

1. Test all desired outcomes. Before the teaching of the unit, determine the objectives of the unit, define them as specific student behavior, outline the unit content, and draw up a table of specifications that will show the objectives, the content, and the number or weight of the test items to be given in each area.

2. Build the test when the unit is being constructed.

3. Be sure that you test all objectives in proportion to their importance. Following a table of specifications should ensure that the test has the proper balance.

4. Be sure the items are of the proper degree of difficulty. Include some easy items for the slowest students so they will not give up before even trying. Arrange the items from easiest to most difficult so as not to discourage the less able.

5. Be sure the instructions give students all the information they need in terms they can understand.

6. Be sure the items are clearly worded. The reading level must not be too difficult; the grammar, vocabulary, and usage must be appropriate for your purpose.

7. Allow time to write good items and criticize the plan. Try it out once.

8. Keep the mechanics simple. For instance, do not mix types of test items.

9. Plan for easy scoring.

Classroom tests and testing programs can and do occasionally have disadvantages or negative side effects. For example, test programs may impede the teaching process by so dominating the school program that instruction becomes totally geared toward tests. This domination is sometimes particularly harmful when standard tests are used as an integral part of the school system's evaluation program. Tests can become, in the eyes of the students, just a series of opportunities to fail, and teachers are likely to corrupt their courses and teach for the test so as to be sure that their students do well. Similarly, passing tests and getting good marks may become so important to students that they are concerned only with marks and not with learning. Cheating and unethical or immoral attitudes often result from overemphasis on testing and test results, too. Sometimes testing can interfere with students' wholesome growth in other ways. Tests can be harmful to students when the tests are used to categorize students as successes or failures, or when test results are considered the final word on a learner's abilities, aptitudes, and prospects, or when they are the only means of communication between the school and the home.

Attaining Validity

To be sure that your test measures what is supposed to be measured, you should construct a table of specifications. This two-way grid indicates behavior in one dimension and content in the other (Figure 15.3). In this grid, behavior relates to the three domains: cognitive, affective, and psychomotor. Cognitive domain, involving mental processes, is divided, according to Bloom's taxonomy, into six categories: (1) simple memory or knowledge, (2) comprehension, (3) application, (4) analysis, (5) synthesis (usually involves an original product in oral, written, or artistic form), and (6) evaluation. (See Module 3 for a fuller explanation of the domains.)

The teacher examining objectives for the unit decides what emphasis should be given to the behavior and to the content. For instance, if vocabulary development is a concern for this class, then probably 20 percent of the test on vocabulary may be appropriate, but 50 percent would be unsuitable. This planning enables the teacher to design a test to fit the situation, rather than a haphazard test that does not correspond to the objectives either in content or behavior emphasis. Since knowledge questions are easy to write, tests often fail to go beyond that level even though the objectives state that the student will analyze and evaluate. The sample table of specifications for a unit in World Literature on Understanding Others indicates a distribution of questions on a test. Since this test is to be an objective test and it is so difficult to write objective-type items to test syntheses and affective and psychomotor behaviors, this table of specifications calls for no test items in these areas. If these categories are included in the unit objectives, some other additional evaluative devices must be used to test learning in these categories. The teacher could also show the objectives tested, as indicated within parentheses in Figure 15.3. Then, a check on inclusion of all objectives is easy.

Essay or Objective Tests

Although performance tests are frequently used to test students' skills, written essay and objective tests are the types of tests most frequently used to test students' knowledge. These two types of tests have a number of similarities and differences, and advantages and disadvantages, as shown in Figure 15.4. You should bear these characteristics in mind when deciding whether to use an objective-type or essay-type test in a specific situation.

Building Objective-Type Tests

To make tests more objective, test builders have invented several types of so-called objective test items, which, when properly used, tend to reduce the amount of sub-

CONTENT	BEHAVIORS								TOTAL
World Literature	Cognitive						Affective	Psychomotor	
Understanding Others	Knowledge	Comprehension	Application	Analysis	Synthesis	Evaluation			
I. Vocabulary Development		3 (1,2)	2 (2)						5
II. Individual Selections			1 (8)	2 (7)		2 (7)			5
III. Literary Forms and Style	1 (3)		1 (3)	1 (6)		2 (6)			5
IV. Comparison of Culture	2 (4, 5)			3 (4)					5
V. Comparison of Values	3 (5)			1 (5)		1 (8)			5
TOTAL	6	3	4	7		5			25

FIGURE 15.3
Table of Specifications

jectivity and human error, particularly in the scoring.[5] The following paragraphs give examples of a number of different types of objective test items, with some suggestions that should help you in constructing such items.

Essay

Student organizes his own responses with minimal restrictions.

Student uses his own phrases, words, and expressions in responding.

Student responds to a very few items.

Student spends most of his time thinking and then writing.

Quality of test is largely determined by person doing the grading.

Test is relatively easy to build.

Test is very difficult to grade.

Test encourages bluffing.

Test can be used to measure the achievement of goals that are measurable by a written test.

Test can be used to encourage pupils to learn (facts, concepts, principles, and so on).

Test can be used to stimulate either convergent or divergent thinking.

Objective

Student operates on an almost completely structured task.

Student selects the correct response from a limited number of alternatives, or recalls a very short answer.

Student responds to a large number of items.

Student spends most of his time reading and thinking.

Quality of test is determined by the test constructor.

Test is very difficult to build.

Test can be graded quickly and easily.

Test encourages guessing.

Test can be used to measure the achievement of goals measurable by a written test.

Test can be used to encourage students to learn (facts, concepts, principles, and so on).

Test can be used to stimulate either convergent or divergent thinking.

FIGURE 15.4
Characteristics of Essay and Objective Tests (Source: Joseph F. Callahan and Leonard H. Clark, *Foundations of Education*, 2d. ed. (New York: Macmillan Publishing Co., 1983), p. 238. By permission.)

---

[5]Some writers classify all objective-type items as short-answer items. What we call short-answer items they call unstructured free-choice items.

Supply (Short or Completion) Items. Supply test items, such as short answer or completion items, require the student to recall the correct answer. They differ from recognition list items, such as true-false or multiple-choice items, in that the student must actually supply the answer rather than select one from a set of alternatives. For example:

SHORT ANSWER ITEM

Give the name of the author of the short story "The Beggar."

COMPLETION ITEM

The name of the author of "The Beggar" is _____
(Anton Chekov)

The advantages of these items include the reduction of student guessing and ease of construction. Dangers include emphasis on recall of a specific word or factual detail that is not essential; subjectivity in grading when unanticipated responses, legibility, and spelling are involved; neglect of higher cognitive behaviors; and focus on rote memory. Suggestions for writing short answer items include:

☐ Design the items so that there is sufficient information to indicate clearly one correct response.

☐ Avoid copying statements directly from textbooks.

☐ For completion items, put the blank at the end or near the end of the statement.

☐ Try to develop items that require the student to go beyond the knowledge level.

☐ Avoid ambiguous statements.

☐ Provide sufficient space for writing the answer.

True-False Items. True-false items are declarative sentences that the student marks as true or false statements. For example:

A right triangle is necessarily a scalene triangle. (False)

One advantage of true-false items is the wide sampling of content possible in a short time. The choice between alternate answers is a realistic task for the student since he often must make such decisions in the real world. The items are relatively simple and time-saving to construct. Grading is easy. On the other hand, the fact that guessing is encouraged by the 50-50 chance of success is a disadvantage. Another disadvantage is that there is danger of overemphasis on details and on the lowest level of the cognitive domain when writing true-false items. Further, brief statements that are completely true or false are hard to phrase. Although these items are not suitable for controversial content, they can be useful for stimulative or instructional tests. Some suggestions for constructing these test items include:

☐ Use statements related to significant objectives.

☐ Write statement clearly and precisely, avoiding ambiguities.

☐ Use positive statements; avoid negative statements since they tend to confuse students.

☐ Avoid specific determiners, such as *never, all, often,* or *usually,* which frequently identify a statement containing them as true or false.

☐ Try to develop items that require more than knowledge for responses.

☐ Do not use statements directly from the text.

☐ Make true and false items similar in length.

☐ Do not overload test with either true or false statements.

☐ Arrange a random pattern of correct responses.

☐ Provide a simple method for indicating responses, so grading is accurate.

Matching Items. Matching items consist of two sets of terms to be matched to show some indicated relationship. Literary titles may be matched with authors; definitions, with words; geographic names, with locations; dates, with events; statements or examples, with principles; people, with identification; symbols, with terms; causes, with effects; parts, with units to which they belong; short questions, with answers. For example:

In the blank provided, indicate the correct solution for the equation by marking the letter of the answer. Use a letter only once.

_____ 1. $2x + 3 = 7$. A. $x = 9$.
_____ 2. $4x = x + 9$. B. $x = 7$.
_____ 3. $6x - 7 = x - 2$. C. $x = 5$.
_____ 4. $9 - 4x = 2 - 3x$. D. $x = 4$.
_____ 5. $\frac{2}{3}x = 6$. E. $x = 3$.
F. $x = 2$.
G. $x = 1$.
H. $x =$ Correct answer is not listed.

[Correct answers are 1–F; 2–E; 3–G; 4–B; 5–A.]

Another format for matching items is providing a list of terms or phrases that are then applied to a series of items. For example:

Each of the following statements is a sentence. Decide whether the sentence is simple, compound, complex, or compound-complex. Then put the letter corresponding to the correct choice in the blank at the left.
A. Simple.
B. Compound.
C. Complex.
D. Compound-complex.

_____ 1. During the summer, many families plan vacation trips, and the national parks are crowded.
_____ 2. If you want a cabin in Yosemite during July, your reservation must be made months in advance.
_____ 3. Camping is a popular and economical way of traveling.
_____ 4. A family that camps must plan carefully for a pleasant trip.
_____ 5. Preparing your own meals is an important economy.

[Correct answers are 1–B; 2–C; 3–A; 4–C; 5–A.]

The matching of items is a means of checking student recognition of relationships and associations. Many items can be handled in a short period of time. However, the emphasis is usually on knowledge. A teacher may have difficulty finding content that is appropriate and providing plausible incorrect responses.

Suggestions for constructing matching test items include:

□ Limit alternatives in a set to 10 or 12; more can be very confusing and time-consuming for students.

□ Each set should be homogeneous.

□ Include two or three extra choices from which responses can be chosen. This practice decreases the possibilities of guessing.

□ Arrange choices in a sequential order, such as alphabetically, or in time sequence.

□ Put all of both sets on the same page so the student does not have to turn from page to page.

□ Make directions clear and specific. Explain how matching is to be done and whether responses are used more than once.

□ Keep the response items short. Otherwise, student time is used in searching through responses.

Multiple-Choice Items.   Multiple-choice items provide a statement or question and a number of possible responses. The student selects the correct or best response. There is a possibility of measuring not only knowledge, but comprehension, application, analysis, and evaluation with multiple-choice items. Guessing is substantially reduced with careful construction of responses so that the undesired ones seem plausible. For most test writers this is the preferred type of test item. For example:

_____ 1. An individual is most likely to receive a severe sunburn in the middle of the day because
      a. we are slightly closer to the sun at noon than at any other time.
      b. when the sun's rays fall directly on a surface, more energy is transmitted than when the rays fall obliquely on the surface.
      c. when the sun is directly overhead, the rays pass through less filtering atmosphere than when the sun is lower in the sky.
      d. the air is warmer at noon than at other times of day.

[Correct answer is b.]

Suggestions for constructing multiple-choice items include:

□ Arrange the possible responses in a vertical list to help the student see his or her choices.

□ Provide four or five choices.

□ Be sure all responses would seem plausible to students who do not know the correct response.

□ Be sure every choice has grammatical consistency with the question or incomplete statement.

□ Make the correct answers about the same length and vocabulary level as the others.

□ State the problem or question clearly in the introduction so the choices are as brief as possible.

Situation Items.   Situations followed by statements to be checked or classified can be set up to measure various cognitive levels. For example:

Bill Collins planned a large garden to help cut down food expenses for his family. He purchased a quantity of ladybugs and placed them in the garden area. Check statements that are good reasons for his action.

_____ 1. Ladybugs are colorful insects.
_____ 2. The ladybug improves the fertilization of tomatoes and squash.
_____ 3. Ladybugs encourage cross-pollination of sweet corn.
_____ 4. The ladybug is a natural enemy of aphids.
_____ 5. Many gardeners want ladybugs in their gardens.
_____ 6. The garden yield may be increased when ladybugs are in the area.
_____ 7. Ladybugs help control certain insect pests.

[Correct answers are 4, 6, 7.]

Items of this type are difficult to build. These situations are often difficult to present briefly, and providing appropriate ways for the student to respond may challenge the ingenuity of the teacher. A summary of formats, difficulties, and recommended uses of the various objective-type items is shown in Figure 15.5.

Guidelines for Preparing an Objective-Type Test.   When building an objective-type test, let the following be your guidelines:

□ Be sure the directions are clear and complete.

□ Be sure your testing emphases are consistent with your teaching emphases.

FIGURE 15.5
An Overview of Objective-Type Items (Source: *Measuring Educational Outcomes* by Bruce W. Tuckman, © 1975 by Harcourt Brace Jovanovich, Inc. Reprinted by permission of the publisher.)

Type	Format	Sample Item	Difficulty in Writing	Difficulty in Scoring	Measure of	Recommended Use
Unstructured	Free Choice	What form of economic system is most often instituted in African and Asian countries following independence?	Easiest (6)	Can be difficult	Recall of knowledge	One-time/one-class testing
Completion (Fill-in)	Free Choice	The form of economic system most often instituted in African and Asian countries following independence is	5	Can be difficult	Recall of knowledge	One-time/one-class testing
True-False (Yes-No)	Fixed Choice	The form of economic system most often instituted in African and Asian countries following independence is socialism. TRUE FALSE	3	Easy	Recognition of knowledge	Multi-group/ repeated testing
Other Two-Choice	Fixed Choice	Circle those African and Asian countries that have introduced socialism upon achieving independence. INDIA GHANA ZAÏRE CHINA SOMALILAND LIBYA	4	Easy for small groups but more difficult for larger ones	Classification of facts	One-time/one-class testing
Multiple Choice	Fixed Choice	Upon achieving independence, the majority of Asian and African countries turned economically to (A) capitalism. (B) laissez-faire. (C) socialism. (D) mercantilism.	2	Easy	Recognition of knowledge or comprehension (or occasionally of higher levels)	Multi-group/ repeated testing
Matching	Fixed Choice	Match the countries to the economic systems. (1) Capitalism (2) Communism (3) Socialism (4) Isolationism a. South Africa b. Sri Lanka c. Ghana d. Madagascar	Most difficult (1)	Easy for small groups but more difficult for larger ones	Recognition of knowledge or comprehension	Change of pace

475

☐ Be sure that the test is neither too long nor too short. Everyone, or nearly everyone, should be able to finish it.

☐ Set up a simple, clear system of responses, easy to answer and easy to correct.

☐ Put the easiest items first and the most difficult toward the end so that pupils will not get discouraged and give up before finishing.

☐ Group items by type; do not intermix true-false, matching, arrangement, multiple-choice, and situation questions.

☐ Ask only one question at a time. There should be no cross references between questions. Each item should stand alone—independent and unified.

☐ Do not provide options; all students should take the same test.

☐ Ask important questions; avoid trivial questions and trick questions.

☐ Keep the items clear.

☐ Avoid the use of vague, qualitative terms such as *seldom, often, most, far, near, much, few.*

☐ Use correct grammar.

☐ Avoid double or triple negatives.

☐ Avoid difficult, arcane vocabulary, gobbledygook, and jargon.

☐ Consider providing a mix of different types of test items to make the test more reliable.

Building Essay Tests

Since objective questions do not provide students an opportunity to organize ideas or show their creativity, such questions limit students' freedom of response. Essay questions are so named because students respond in an essay form that varies in length from a sentence or two to many pages. Essay questions are suitable for assessing learning at the higher cognitive and affective levels. To reduce the element of student guessing, the questions must be clear and specific. Because writing responses to essay questions is time-consuming, the number of essay questions you can use in a test is severely limited. This fact makes it difficult to cover all the objectives.

Although the essay test takes less time to construct than the objective test because it involves fewer questions, the scoring of essay tests is time-consuming, and consistency of scoring is hard to maintain.

You should prepare your students to take essay tests. In your preparation, you should: (1) discuss the meaning of such terms as compare, contrast, and illustrate; (2) develop suitable responses to sample questions; (3) stress the importance of the careful reading of questions; (4) stress the planning of responses; (5) conduct activities in which the students practice how to attack essay questions; and (6) consider such bothersome elements as padding answers, proofreading, and legibility.

Examples of essay questions are:

Discuss the essay test as a measure of achievement.

Compare essay and objective tests in relation to the following factors: (a) validity, (b) reliability, (c) usability, (d) discrimination, and (e) objectivity.

Suggestions for constructing essay questions include:

☐ Expected student answers should relate to significant content and behavior, as indicated in the table of specifications and objectives.

☐ Phrase the items clearly and specifically so the students know what is expected of them.

☐ The number and complexity of the questions should be reasonable for the time limits so the students can demonstrate their achievement.

☐ The questions should pose interesting and challenging problems for the student.

□ If spelling, grammar, and writing style are to be scored, students should be informed about how much these factors will influence the scoring.

□ All students should write on the questions given. This increases reliability.

□ The point value of the questions should be indicated.

Performance Tests, Checklists, and Scales

As you have seen, a performance test consists of observing a learner performing a certain behavior or evaluating the product of the behavior. The test could, of course, include both the process and the product. To set up a performance test you must:

1. Specify the performance objective.

2. Specify the test situation.

3. Set the criteria for judging the excellence of the process and/or product.

4. Make a checklist by which to score the performance or product. (This checklist is simply a listing of the criteria you established in step 3. It would be possible to use a rating scale, but ordinarily a rating scale makes scoring too complicated.)

5. Prepare directions in writing, outlining the situation, with instructions for the students to follow.

For example, this is a checklist for map work:

Check each item if the map comes up to standard in this particular category.

_____ 1. Accuracy.
_____ 2. Neatness.
_____ 3. Attention to details.

Skillful teachers also use checklists to ensure objectivity in their observation of student behavior. Usually a rating scale is more suitable for this purpose. An example of a rating scale is shown in Figure 15.6. To prepare a rating scale you must:

□ Specify just what behavior you wish to observe.

□ Describe the behaviors so that you can recognize and judge them.

□ Decide what weight to give to each behavior.

□ Design the rating scale. Ordinarily, a five-point scale will be most satisfactory. More points tend to make the scale confusing; fewer points are too limiting. An odd number of points makes it possible to record a middle position.

□ Label the points on the scale to make them clear.

Scoring Tests

Correcting Objective Tests

Objective tests can be designed so that students answer the items directly on the test or on answer sheets. In some schools, teachers may have facilities for checking tests by machine. Then, of course, the tests should be set up to use answer sheets. If you do not have machine scoring available, you may still wish to use answer sheets to save time and effort when marking tests. If answer sheets are used, they should be arranged

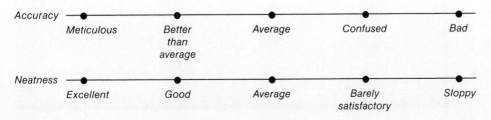

FIGURE 15.6
An Example of a Rating Scale for Map Work (Check the spot on each continuum that is most descriptive of the student's work.)

so that the student can move easily from the test to the answer sheet. One way to do this is to make the columns on the answer sheet correspond with the pages of the test.

For many teachers, marking on the test paper is an advantage because the test can be returned to the student and used for teaching those areas not mastered. To simplify marking, teachers should have all answers arranged at the left side of the page. Some teachers then simply take an extra copy of the test to make their key and fill in all responses correctly. The key can then be placed against the test and the answers compared. Often, it is easier to cut off the text of the test so that the key will be a strip that can be laid along either side of the answers on the test being corrected. This makes it easier to correct answers listed on the left side of the page, if the scorer is right-handed. Some teachers find it easier to score by simply checking all correct items, that is, items that agree with the key. Others prefer to mark the wrong answers.

Keys can also be prepared to fit over the answer section of a test with cutouts for the students' answers. These keys are known as masks (Figure 15.7). Keys can be prepared either to fit over this section with cutouts for the students' answers or to place beside the students' responses. Keys that indicate correct responses should be accurately prepared and written in colored ink so the key is easily identified. All possible answers should be included in the key. Use of a colored pencil to mark incorrect responses speeds the counting of errors.

Scoring Essay Questions

Scoring essay questions is difficult since it requires much time and involves subjectivity. You can make your handling of this task more effective by following certain procedures:

1. Write out a model answer when you construct the item. Sometimes, as you attempt to respond to your own questions, you will see some of the ambiguities and can improve the question.

2. Assign points to the various subparts of the response. In doing so, consider how many points will make an answer excellent, acceptable, or unacceptable.

3. Score each test anonymously so that the identity of the student is not a factor.

4. Score the same test questions at the same time for all the students; for example, read and score all answers for question 1 before you start reading the responses to question 2.

5. Consider the use of a two-step scoring procedure. In this procedure, reading the answers and rating the responses into three categories (excellent, acceptable, poor) is the first step. Rereading and scoring points is the second step. Some teachers

FIGURE 15.7
An Example of a Mask

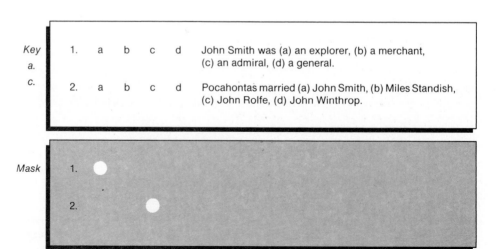

prefer to assign points on the first reading. However, sorting followed by scoring gives one a chance to add unpredicted responses to the point array before the actual scoring.

6. Read each set of answers through without interruption when possible. Fluctuations in the feelings and attitudes of the reader are lessened when no external interference occurs.

7. Try to disregard irrelevant factors. If neatness is not a criterion, then it should not influence scores. When handwriting is not a part of the objective measured, then handwriting should not be a factor.

8. Finally, if essay tests are used, teachers are obligated to score the tests with as much reliability and objectivity as possible. The questions that are carefully designed can provide information about students' achievements, which helps the teacher plan for students' growth and evaluate the teacher's own instructional activities. Good questions can also stimulate the student to find relationships, synthesize ideas, apply concepts, and evaluate a variety of materials.

EVALUATING THE TEST INSTRUMENT

Educational evaluation is not complete unless you evaluate the tests and other instruments you use. The variables considered when evaluating a test instrument include validity, discriminating power, difficulty, reliability, and usability.

Validity

How well does the test measure what you wanted to measure? Does the content of the test measure the content of the instruction? Does it cover all of the instructional objectives? Is the emphasis on the objectives in the test proportional to that in the instruction?

Discriminating Power

Discriminating power refers to how effectively the item differentiates between the students who did well and those who did poorly on the test. One procedure for determining a test's discriminating power is an item analysis using the upper 25 percent and lower 25 percent of the scores.[6] Perfect discrimination of an item would mean that all the students in the upper quarter answered correctly and all in the lower quarter answered incorrectly. Such precise differentiation between groups seldom occurs. The difference between the number of students in the upper group who answer the test item correctly and the number of students in the lower group who answer the item correctly is divided by the number of students in both groups. For example:

Of 100 scores, the top 25 include 20 correct responses on item A; the low 25 include 8 correct responses on the same item.

$$\text{Index of Discrimination} = \frac{20 - 8}{50} = \frac{12}{50} = .22+$$

The index varies from $+1.00$ to -1.00. Positive 1 indicates complete differentiation in the desired direction. Any negative value indicates the item discriminates in the wrong direction and is therefore unsatisfactory. Any discriminatory values above $+0.40$ are considered good. The range $+0.40$ to $+0.20$ is called satisfactory. Teacher-made tests that are norm-referenced should have more than half of the items with an index discrimination of $+0.40$ or above, and another 40 percent of the items with a satisfactory index. No items should have a negative index.

---

[6]Technically it would be better to use the top 27 percent and bottom 27 percent, but for practical purposes in the classroom situation the uppermost and lowest quarters will suffice.

Difficulty

Another type of item analysis determines item difficulty. Basically, the level of difficulty of an item is determined by the percentage of students who have answered the item correctly. It can easily be calculated. First, tabulate the number of students who correctly answered the question and divide by the number of students who tried to answer. Then, multiply by 100 to change the quotient to a percent. For example:

Nineteen of the 25 students who responded to a question answered it correctly.

$$\text{Item Difficulty} = \frac{19}{25} \times 100 = 76.$$

For norm-based tests, the items answered correctly or incorrectly by all or most of the students contribute little to determining the norms. In fact, the level of difficulty should be near 50 percent. One recommendation is that only items in the 40 to 70 percent range should be included in a test.

Neither the item difficulty nor discriminating power apply to criterion-referenced tests. Responses on criterion-referenced tests will indicate whether or not individual students know or can do what they are supposed to have learned. If the lesson or unit has been well taught, it is possible that 80 percent or more of the students will have answered all of the items right. Discrimination among students and difficulty factors of items are largely irrelevant for this type of test. If the items show whether or not the objective has been attained, they are good items.

Reliability

Do the test results concur with the results of other tests and evaluations? One way to check is to rank the performance of the students on your various tests. If the results of the new test are consistent with the other tests, presumably the tests are reliable. In the example (Figure 15.8), presumably Test III is reliable because its results seem to be consistent with those of Test I and Test II.

Usability

Is the test too long or too short? Is it too hard or too easy? Is it easy to score? Did the students find the directions clear?

General Suggestions

File of Test Items

Tests should be analyzed and revised by the teachers. Reusing the same tests encourages cheating. But using the good questions of a test, eliminating or improving the poor items, and adding new items produce a better test than writing all new items.

Keep a file of your good questions as a convenient way of improving tests. To construct a test item file, put the question on one side of a file card and information about the item on the reverse side. File the question by unit, problem, or some other

FIGURE 15.8
Checking the Reliability
of a Test

Student	Rank Order in		
	Test I	Test II	Test III
A	1	1	1
B	2	3	2
C	3	4	4
D	4	2	3
E	5	5	6
F	6	6	5

convenient classification. These cards can then be pulled, sorted, and used as a basis for a new test. Since frequent short tests may be important for feedback to both teacher and student, you can use them to develop the test item file rapidly. Then questions for a unit test or semester examination will be readily available. Objective questions and essay questions from your test file may be combined in the same test. If the equipment is available, test files can be built in a computer data-storage bank as well. The questions could then be pulled from the data bank when it is time to make the test. The computer will randomly select questions from a data bank, or it will make several alternative tests from the data bank using the same data bank of questions. Begin your file of test questions by doing Exercise 15.1.

FREQUENCY OF TESTING

Since tests can fulfill different purposes, when a test should be given depends on the purpose. Before making realistic plans for instructional activities, a teacher must know the level of student achievement. This information can be obtained through testing. To work with individual students effectively, a teacher needs a diagnosis of the deficiencies of the student. Testing can provide this information. Effective learning requires feedback to the student that testing can provide. Grades or reports on progress of students ordinarily include some test results as a part of the evaluation. Students want information about their capabilities and talents to help them make vocational and educational choices. Testing can provide some data for these decisions. In the appraisal of materials, teaching strategies, and programs, test results are one source of data. Each of the purposes mentioned suggests when the test results can be used. Continuous evaluation means tests are given as the data from the testing are needed.

CHEATING

You can discourage cheating by clarifying what the behavioral objectives are and how the objectives will be evaluated. A teacher should give the students information about time allowance for the test, the type of test, its purpose, and the general content. Use other means of evaluation to provide more opportunities for students who do not perform well under the pressure of a test situation. Keep alert while the test is given, discourage student communication, and circulate to see how the students are progressing. Such awareness tends to hamper some of the tactics often used in cheating.

If several sections of a class are to take the test, you should vary some of the questions. Perhaps the multiple-choice sections may remain the same, but you should vary the true-false and essay questions. You might, for instance, prepare three different forms of the test. Sometimes each class could use a different form; other times, one third of each class might use one form. A variety of approaches in different tests will show students that the teacher wants to be fair. In individualized instruction, group tests are eliminated; personal growth becomes a motivation and eliminates the purposes of cheating.

SUMMARY

This module has indicated that testing is an integral part of a teaching model. Criterion-referenced and norm-referenced tests both have a place in the school. Validity, reliability, usability, discrimination, and objectivity are discussed as they relate to teacher-made tests. Advantages and disadvantages of types of objective items (supply, true-false, matching, and multiple-choice) are presented. There are suggestions for writing good items of each type. How to construct and score essay questions is also considered. To ensure that the objectives are adequately covered both from the content and behavior dimensions, the use of a table of specifications is recommended. Since tests are such an important part of the teaching-learning situation, as well as the general educational scene, the teacher must purposefully work to develop skills in test construction and utilization. Accountability requires that the responsible teacher collect data on the effectiveness of teaching. Test results are an important part of these data.

Cheating is a persistent problem whenever group testing is done. Teachers can minimize the problem by using tests as an integral part of the instructional program and including other sources of information in grading. Cheating is discouraged by teacher circulating and sensitivity to the problem.

SUGGESTED READING

Cangelosi, J. S. *Designing Tests for Evaluating Student Achievement.* White Plains, NY: Longman, 1989.

Cangelosi, J. S. *Evaluating Classroom Instruction.* Chapter 2. White Plains, NY: Longman, 1991.

Cirn, J. T. "True/false versus short answer questions." *College Teaching* 34(1): 34–37 (Winter 1986).

Ebel, R. L., and Frisbie, D. A. *Essentials of Educational Measurement.* 5th ed. Needham Heights, MA: Allyn & Bacon, 1991.

Gronlund, N. E. *How to Construct Achievement Tests.* 4th ed. Needham Heights, MA: Allyn & Bacon, 1988.

Gronlund, N. E., and Linn, R. L. *Measurement and Evaluation in Teaching.* 6th ed. New York: Macmillan, 1990.

Lorber, M. A., and Pierce, W. D. *Objectives, Methods, and Evaluation for Secondary Teaching.* 3d ed. Chapter 8. Englewood Cliffs, NJ: Prentice Hall, 1990.

EXERCISE 15.1 PREPARING TEST QUESTIONS

For a secondary or middle-school course that you intend to teach, practice writing test questions, then have your questions critiqued by your classmates for clarity and accuracy. Prepare two test items for each type. On separate paper prepare the answer for each question.

Subject and grade level for which these items are prepared: _____

1. Essay-type questions:

2. Short-answer questions:

3. True-false items:

4. Matching items:

5. Multiple-choice items:

6. Situation items:

7. Completion-sentence items:

8. Performance-test items:

Multiple Choice Insert the correct answer in the space provided.

_____ 1. A criterion-referenced test is constructed so that
   a. each student will attain a perfect score if the student has mastered the objectives.
   b. the student will be compared to other students and his or her position in the group determined.
   c. the test measures what it is supposed to test or meets the criterion established.
   d. the deficiencies of a student are located in a specific area of behavior.

_____ 2. Evaluation and measurement are defined so that
   a. the terms are synonymous.
   b. evaluation includes measurement.
   c. measurement includes evaluation.
   d. measurement and evaluation are not directly related.

_____ 3. The items on a true-false test are _least_ likely to
   a. measure complex cognitive behavior.
   b. encourage guessing.
   c. cover a quantity of material in a short time.
   d. take a reasonable amount of teacher time for constructing and checking.

_____ 4. Supply (completion or short answer) items should be constructed
   a. with the blank at the beginning for easy grading.
   b. with hints such as the first letter of the term to limit responses.
   c. with several blanks so the student has several chances to respond correctly.
   d. with emphasis on important content so the item is worthwhile.

_____ 5. Which teacher comment about scoring easy tests will improve the reliability of the test?
   a. "I like to read all the student's answers at one time to get an overview of what he or she knows."
   b. "I can do a better job of scoring when I don't know whose paper I'm reading."
   c. "The time it takes to separate test papers item by item is time I could use more profitably for other purposes."
   d. "I can tell how much a student knows by scanning his paper."

_____ 6. In a model of teaching, testing is essential in
   a. preassessment of students.
   b. implementation of instructional plans.
   c. evaluation of learning.
   d. both a and c.

_____ 7. Multiple-choice items are superior to matching and to true-false items for some purposes because they
   a. save teacher time in construction and grading.
   b. decrease the number of questions the student can answer in a specified time.
   c. measure cognitive processes beyond memory.
   d. increase student choices in the test situation.

_____ 8. Student scores on standardized tests can be expressed in terms of
   a. percentile rank.
   b. stanine.
   c. grade equivalent.
   d. all of these.

If the following table of specifications is set up for a unit on short stories in ninth-grade English, indicate the appropriate placement of the tally for each question listed. Put the letter(s) of the correct cell in the blank. Use the highest cognitive level involved.

CONTENT	COGNITIVE BEHAVIOR					
Vocabulary	Knowledge A	Comprehension D	Application G	Analysis J	Synthesis M	Evaluation P
Literary Style	B	E	H	K	N	Q
Elements of the Short Story (Plot, Characters, Setting, Theme)	C	F	I	L	O	R

_____ 9. Ten items listing synonyms to be matched with 10 of 13 words given.

_____ 10. What effect on the reader is expected when the author tells the story in the first person?
   a. The reader is an observer of the action.
   b. The reader identifies with the author.
   c. The reader gets a broad insight into the motivation of all characters.
   d. The reader quickly perceives the theme of the story.

_____ 11. Compare the "Tell-Tale Heart" with "The Fugitive" in regard to
   a. point of view.
   b. setting.
   c. plot.

_____ 12. At the end of "Split Cherry Tree," Pa feels that Professor Herbert is a "fine man" because
   a. Professor Herbert had a good education.
   b. Professor Herbert respected the gun Pa carried.
   c. Professor Herbert treated Pa as a worthy individual.
   d. Professor Herbert displayed his intelligence to Pa.

_____ 13. Select the best story you read and defend your selection, using four criteria for a good short story.

Check   Check the purposes for which teacher-made tests can be appropriately constructed.

_____ 14. Diagnosing student instructional needs.

_____ 15. Indicating level of student achievement.

_____ 16. Predicting vocational success.

_____ 17. Indicating psychological problems.

_____ 18. Determining effectiveness of teaching.

_____ 19. Showing whether instructional objectives have been attained.

_____ 20. Measuring the effectiveness of an experimental program.

Matching   Match the correct test characteristic (a through h below) with the question asked about the test. Use a term only once.

_____ 21. Does the test measure what is supposed to be measured?

_____ 22. Can the test be constructed, administered, and scored conveniently?

_____ 23. Are the results consistent?

_____ 24. Do the test results show the different achievement levels of the students?

_____ 25. Are results affected by the student or the scorer?

a. Comprehensiveness.
b. Correlation.
c. Discrimination.
d. Efficiency.
e. Objectivity.
f. Reliability.
g. Usability.
h. Validity.

_____ 26. A student whose test score falls at the fiftieth percentile would be in which stanine band?
  a. 1
  b. 3
  c. 5
  d. 7
  e. 9.

_____ 27. To ensure objectivity in your observation of a pupil's performance
  a. use norm-referenced instruments.
  b. use criterion-referenced instruments.
  c. use stanine scoring.
  d. use a checklist.

_____ 28. In building an essay test
  a. provide students with several choices of questions.
  b. relate the questions to the specifications in a table of specifications.
  c. give equal credit to all items in the essay test.
  d. provide students with opportunities for extra credit questions.

Short Answer   Complete the model of a learning cycle by filling in the blanks.

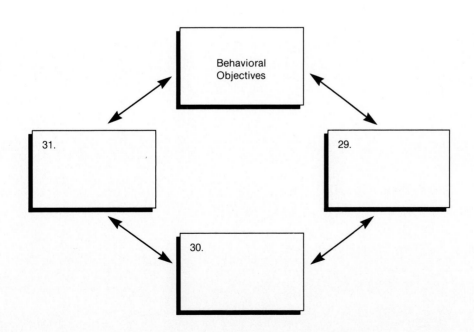

29. _____

30. _____

31. _____

List four uses of test results.

32. _____

33. _____

34. _____

35. _____

MODULE 16
Grading

Grading is time-consuming and frustrating for most teachers. What should be graded? Should marks represent student growth, level of achievement in a group, effort, attitude, general behavior, or a combination of these factors? What should determine grades—tests, homework, projects, class participation, group work, or all of these? How can individualized instruction be graded? These are just a few of the questions that plague the teacher when decisions about grades must be made.

The report card that records the grades assigned may be one of the few communications left between the school and the student's home. Unless, however, the teacher and the school have clearly determined what grades represent and unless such understanding is periodically reviewed with each set of new parents, the report card may create unrest and dissatisfaction on the part of parents and students and prove to be an alienating device. The grading system, then, instead of informing the parents may separate the home and the school, which have a common concern—the best development of the student.

The development of the student encompasses growth in the cognitive, affective, and psychomotor domains. Consequently, paper-and-pencil tests provide only a portion of the data needed to indicate student progress. Different methods of evaluation must be utilized to determine how the student works and what he or she can produce. The teacher needs a repertoire of means of assessing learner behavior and progress.

Although grades have been a part of the secondary school for only 100 years, they have become entrenched. Both parents and students have come to expect evaluations. Some critics suggest that the emphasis in school is on getting a high grade rather than on learning.

There have been complaints about subjectivity and unfair practices. As a result, a variety of systems for evaluation has evolved. When teachers are aware of alternative grading systems, they may be able to develop grading processes that are fair and effective for particular situations.

This module considers the purposes of grading. The differences between criterion-referenced and norm-referenced grading are examined. Some practices in evaluating tests, themes, and other student products and student procedures are suggested. Self-evaluation is discussed along with pros and cons of peer evaluation. We will scrutinize some of the problems involved in grading in such situations as individualized instruction or contract teaching. Practices in grading are discussed.

At the completion of this module, you should be able to:

1. Indicate purposes accomplished by norm-referenced grading and by criterion-referenced grading.
2. Set up a frequency distribution for a set of test scores and estimate the stanines.
3. Explain three criteria for an effective grading system.
4. Discuss grading in relation to the normal curve, individualized instruction, themes, homework, and class discussion.
5. List and describe instruments for evaluating the behavior and products of secondary students.
6. Indicate specific reasons for helping middle and secondary school students develop self-evaluation skills.
7. Construct a rating scale for some activity or product appropriate to a content area, such as cookies in food class, laboratory procedures in a chemistry class, group discussion in social studies.
8. Explain three means of evaluating affective objectives.
9. Demonstrate how a teacher might set up a point system for grading a class at the end of six weeks.
10. Select appropriate answers to the posttest with no more than three errors.

MODULE TEXT

Grading and Evaluation

Grading is a tedious task that many teachers dread. The aversive reaction of teachers results from a number of factors, including:

- □ Lack of clarity about what grades represent.

- □ Inability to communicate student behavior—such as content mastery in the cognitive domain, study skills, affective response—with a symbol.

- □ Parent and student confusion about the communication.

- □ Guilt about subjectivity in determining grades.

- □ Concern that grades may adversely influence student behavior, vocational or employment opportunities, and further educational goals.

Evaluation is a requisite in effective learning. Unless learners know how they are progressing, they cannot make the modifications necessary to achieve the goal. They may be practicing incorrect procedures; for example, in spelling a student may be learning incorrectly a word that he or she miscopied. Feedback is necessary to keep the learner on target. When a student is performing well, the positive reinforcement facilitates learning.

Evaluation and grading are not synonymous. Evaluation implies the collection of information from many sources, including measurement techniques and observation. These data are then the basis for value judgments for such purposes as diagnosing learning problems, recommending vocational alternatives, and grading. Grades are only one aspect of evaluation and are intended to communicate educational progress to both parents and students. Some questions that must be considered by individual teachers and schools are:

- □ What should be the criteria for marking—comparison with a group, self-development, or both?

- □ What kinds of experiences are involved—academic achievement, attitudes, study patterns, personal habits, or social behavior?

- □ What consideration should be given to the psychological effect of grades on students? For instance, will a student who is consistently unsuccessful become convinced that he or she is worthless or inadequate? Will the student give up the ghost and refuse to even try any longer? Will the student who is academically talented and receives high grades with little effort become satisfied with mediocrity?

- □ What form of marking is best for communicating—a percentage plan, a letter or number system, pass/fail, a written description, several grades (one for achievement, one for social skills, and one for study habits), or a combination of these?

FIGURE 16.1

Guidelines for Report Card Marks (Source: Fairfax, Va., County Public Schools. *Grading and Reporting to Parents: Intermediate and Secondary*, pp. 6–8. Reprinted by permission. Note that Fairfax County uses a plus letter system. Other school systems may use either no plus or minus, or both plus and minus letter marking systems.)

Mark		Criteria	Percentage
A	Thorough mastery of subject matter	—Demonstrates outstanding achievement and mastery of subject area —Goes beyond the goals established for the class in achievement and contribution —Achieves maximum growth in relation to the established objectives —Is self-directed in his/her attainment —Evidences understanding and appreciation of the fundamental concepts of the subject area —Exercises superior ability in problem solving and in arriving at logical conclusions —Shows originality in the preparation of assignments —Expresses ideas clearly both orally and in writing	94–100

Mark		Criteria	Percentage
B+	Above average, good consistent effort	—Demonstrates scholarship and achievement well above the class average —Does his/her assignments thoroughly and accurately and occasionally contributes creatively —Is growing into leadership in the development of class and individual goals	90–93
B		—Does independent work in addition to the required assignment	84–89
C+	Average achievement	—Achieves the objective developed for the average of the class —Is responsible and participates in class activities —Evidences normal growth at grade level in relation to his/her capacities and skills —Frequently requires individual direction and supervision —Achieves sufficient subject matter mastery to enable him/her to proceed to advanced high school work in the subject —Is alert, interested, and participates in class activities —Tries consciously to finish each project or assignment within the	80–83
C		time limits allowed	74–79
D+	Below-average achievement	—Frequently falls below the level of achievement of which he/she is capable —Seldom completes an undertaking without teacher direction and encouragement —Evidences little growth other than that developed through class association —May be irregular in attendance and generally fails to make up the work he/she has missed —Quality of work is poor, though he/she may have made efforts to improve	70–73
D		—Shows little interest in the class and rarely contributes	64–69
F	Poor work, lack of comprehension	—Infrequently completes assignments requiring extended interest and development —Rejects teacher assistance and leadership —Evidences capacity to undertake many of the class activities but refuses to take part —Puts forth no effort though he/she has limited ability —Received an "incomplete" and has done nothing to warrant its change within time allowed —Has excessive unexcused absences —Fails to meet the minimum requirements of the course	Below 64 No credit
I	Incomplete	—Fails to complete daily work, reports, tests, examinations, assignments, etc.	No credit
P	Pass	—Completes daily work, reports, tests, examinations, assignments, etc., in a satisfactory manner	In lieu of A,B,C,D,F
WP/ WF	Withdraw/Pass Withdraw/Fail	—(See Withdraw/Pass-Withdraw/Fail section, page 35)	No credit

The school system or the individual school in which you will teach has, undoubtedly, its own procedure for grades. This procedure is the one that you must use. One of your first professional obligations will be to inquire about, to study, and to adapt your thinking about grading to the procedures used in the school and in your department. An example of the approach of one school system can be seen in Figure 16.1, which is a copy of a page extracted from the *Program of Studies Handbook of the Fairfax County Public Schools* in Virginia. It serves as a guide for all of the intermediate and secondary teachers in that county school system. However, there are always means of adapting a system; for example, student conferences can always be used to supplement any grades, parent conferences by phone or in person can be individually scheduled, or descriptions of student work and progress can be written as letters to parents to explain grades.

Probably the greatest benefit of any grading system is that teachers must establish criteria and priorities. Someone must decide just what student behavior is important in the learning situation and what the criteria for effective performance are to be. The decisions may be made by the teacher, by students, or through a cooperative effort. All students should know exactly what the decisions are, and the decisions should definitely be reflected in the learning activities and evaluation. Behavioral objectives must be carefully selected and clearly stated as a basis for effective learning.

CRITERION-REFERENCED AND NORM-REFERENCED GRADING

There are two basic approaches to grading. One is similar to norm-referenced measurement and the other to criterion-referenced measurement, treated in Module 15.

In norm-referenced grading, the aim is to reveal how the individual compares to the other students in the group under instruction or with the larger groups who have taken a particular test. It is useful when communicating information about students to parents and colleges or employment agencies. In criterion-referenced grading the aim is to communicate information about an individual's progress in knowledge and work skills in comparison to that student's previous attainment or in the pursuit of an absolute, such as content mastery. Criterion-referenced grading is featured in continuous-progress curricula, competency-based curricula, and other programs that focus on individualized education.

The philosophy of these two approaches is different. Norm-referenced grading reflects a competitive social structure. The grade is assigned to indicate how a student compares with other students. The top grade, usually A, generally means that the students receiving that grade have learned the content better than most other students in the class. The lowest grade, F or U in many scales, shows that the student has done poorly and has achieved less than others in the class. In general, the system assumes that the group of students approximates a normal distribution or bell-shaped curve. Such a distribution of marks follows a pattern of a similar number of As and Fs and of Bs and Ds. In the curve shown in Figure 16.2, As and Fs each represent 7 percent of the students, Bs and Ds each represent 24 percent, and 38 percent of the students receive Cs. In other situations, the allocation may be 5 percent for As and Fs, 15 percent for Bs and Ds, and 60 percent for Cs. Many other allocations of grades on the normal curve have been used by teachers to fit certain groups.

One problem that frequently occurs when using norm-referenced grading is what to do with students in the high academic track. Should all receive As and Bs? If a wider grading scale is used for them, does it represent the students' achievement accurately for college entrance? For example, does C in an advanced English class mean the same

FIGURE 16.2
Possible Distribution of Marks

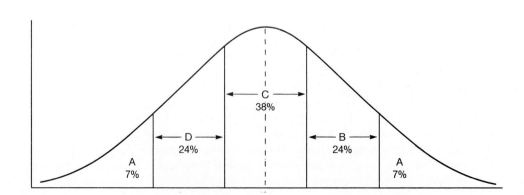

level achieved by a student getting C in an average class? Probably the achievement in the advanced class represents more complex content and more sophisticated activities by students. To counteract the grade effect of a more difficult curriculum, some schools have special procedures for indicating advanced work on transcripts sent to colleges or to prospective employers. The same kinds of difficulties may arise with students from other academic tracks. Employers may interpret grades so that expectations for performance are unrealistic. Then, of course, the school is blamed. Grades often have an effect extending beyond the school.

Criterion-referenced or competency-based grading is based on whether or not a student achieves the specified objectives for the course. The objectives must be clearly stated to represent important student outcomes. This approach implies that effective teaching and learning result in high grades (As) for most students. In fact, when a mastery concept is used, the student must accomplish the objectives before being allowed to proceed to the next learning task. The philosophy of teachers who favor criterion-referenced procedures recognizes individual potential. Such teachers accept the challenge of finding teaching strategies to help students progress from where they are to the designated level. Instead of wondering how Juan compares with Ted, the comparison is between what Ted could do yesterday and what he can do today, and how well these performances compare to the set standard.

Most school systems use both norm-referenced and criterion-referenced grading. In beginning typing classes, for example, a certain basic speed and accuracy are established as criteria. Perhaps only the upper third of the advanced typing class is to be recommended for advanced secretarial courses. The grading for the beginning class might appropriately be criterion-based, but grading for an advanced class might better be norm-referenced. Sometimes both kinds of information are needed. A report card for a junior high student in the eighth year of schooling might indicate how that student is meeting certain criteria, such as an A grade for addition of fractions. Another entry might show that this mastery is expected at sixth-grade level. Both criterion- and norm-referenced data may be communicated to the parents and students. Appropriate procedures should be used: a criterion-referenced approach to show whether or not the student can accomplish the task, and a norm-referenced approach to show how well that student performs compared to others. Sometimes, one or the other is needed; other times, both are required.

Interpreting Standardized Test Scores

To interpret standardized test scores and to understand other norm-referenced marking systems, one needs a basic knowledge of elementary descriptive statistics. So, as time permits, dig into one or more of the references listed at the end of the module. The statistics that will most concern you, however, are the normal curve, measures of central tendency, measures of variability, and derived scores.

The Normal Curve

The normal curve has already been discussed. It is a bell-shaped curve, bilaterally symmetrical with a single peak in the center, representing a distribution of scores in which most scores cluster in the middle and other scores are distributed evenly toward the two ends. Such a distribution is typical of physical or behavioral traits and aptitude or intelligence test scores in the general population or large groups. (See Figure 16.2.)

Not all score distributions are normal, of course. If most of the scores are clustered toward one end of the curve, the curve is said to be skewed (Figure 16.3). Such skewing may indicate that the test was too hard (Figure 16.3A) or too easy (Figure 16.3B) for the group being tested, or that the group was not a really normal one. On the other hand, skewed test-score distributions may be useful for discriminating among gifted students or low-ability students. Skewed distributions are rather typical of class-size groups.

FIGURE 16.3
Skewed Curves

A   B

MEASURES OF CENTRAL TENDENCY

The central tendency or "average" of a group of scores can be indicated statistically in three ways:

1. The mean, or arithmetical average, is determined by dividing the sum of the scores by the number of scores, such as:

$$M = \frac{\Sigma X}{N}$$

when M is the mean, X is the raw score, N is the number of scores, Σ (sigma) means the sum of or to add, and ΣX is the sum of the scores.

For instance, the mean of 17, 18, 25 would be 20:

$$M = \frac{\Sigma X}{N} = \frac{17 + 18 + 25}{3} = 20$$

This measure is important because it is used as the basis for computing other statistical values.

2. The mode is the score that occurs most frequently in a distribution. Although it is the easiest to determine (you only have to look at the scores and select the one that occurs most often), it is likely to be quite misleading, particularly when the distribution of the scores is skewed.

For instance, in the distribution 50, 45, 45, 45, 35, 30, 25, 15, 10, the mode is 45, but the mean is only 33.33.

3. The median is the middle point in the distribution. If there is an odd number of scores, the median is the middle score; or if there is an even number of scores, the median is halfway between the two middle scores. This value is very useful because it is easy to calculate and gives a good indication of the central tendency, particularly when the distribution is skewed. In fact, the median often gives a more realistic indication of central tendency in skewed distributions than the mean does. For the set of scores $X = 10, 15, 20, 25, 80$, for instance, the median is 20, but the mean is 30. In such a situation the unrepresentative high score causes the mean to be less dependable than the median.

MEASURES OF VARIABILITY

Measures of variability indicate how much the scores in a distribution vary. The most obvious one, the range, that is, the difference between the highest and the lowest scores in the distribution, gives one a rough estimate of the variability of the distribution, but does not help one understand the variability of the scores within the distribution very well. The standard deviation corrects that defect, for it gives quite an accurate picture of the variation of the scores within a distribution—the larger the standard deviation, the greater the variability.[1]

To compute a standard deviation you use the following formula:

$$\sigma = \sqrt{\frac{\Sigma(X - M)^2}{N}}$$

---

[1]Standard deviation is indicated by σ, s, or SD, depending upon the material being used.

FIGURE 16.4
Calculation of Standard Deviation

X	M	(X – M)	(X – M)²
33	23.6	9.4	88.36
28	23.6	4.4	19.36
24	23.6	.4	.16
23	23.6	– .6	.36
22	23.6	–1.6	2.56
21	23.6	–2.6	6.76
20	23.6	–3.6	12.96
18	23.6	–5.6	31.36
$\overline{189}$ = ΣX			$\overline{161.88}$ = Σ(X – M)²

$$M = \frac{\Sigma X}{N} = \frac{189}{8} = 23.6$$

$$\sigma = \sqrt{\frac{\Sigma(X - M)^2}{N}} = \sqrt{\frac{161.88}{8}} = \sqrt{20.24} = 4.5$$

in which X is one raw score, M is the mean for a set of scores, and N is the number of scores in the set. The procedure is relatively simple. For instance, to calculate the standard deviation of the following set of scores: 20, 22, 33, 18, 21, 28, 24, and 23, one would complete the following steps.

1. Prepare a table with the headings X, M, $(X - M)$, and $(X - M)^2$ as in Figure 16.4.
2. List the individual scores under column X.
3. Determine the mean of the scores and place that figure in column M. (In this case the mean will be 189 ÷ 8 or 23.6).
4. Subtract the mean from each score and place the result in the column labeled $(X - M)$.
5. Square each entry in column $(X - M)$ and place the results in column $(X - M)^2$.
6. Add the numbers in column $(X - M)^2$ to find $\Sigma(X - M)^2$.
7. Substitute the appropriate values into the formula and solve the equation.

The standard deviation is closely related to the normal curve. In a normal distribution about 68 percent of the scores fall in the area between +1SD and –1SD (i.e., 34 percent of the scores fall between the mean and +1SD and 34 percent of the scores fall between the mean and –1SD), whereas about 13.5 percent of the scores fall between +1SD and +2SD and another 13.5 percent fall between –1SD and –2SD and only about 2 percent fall between +2SD and 3SD or between –2SD and –3SD (Figure 16.5).

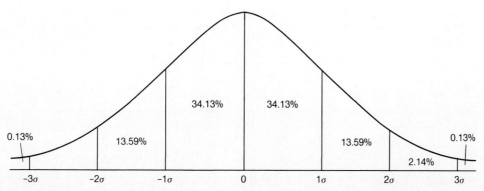

FIGURE 16.5
Percent of Cases Falling Within Standard Deviations in a Normal Curve

DERIVED SCORES

Test scores may be reported either as raw scores or as derived scores. A raw score is the number of the student's correct responses on a test. A derived score is a raw score that has been modified so as to make interpretation easier. Common types of derived scores include percentile ranks, standard scores (including T scores and stanines), deviation IQ scores, and age-grade scores. These types of scores are particularly useful for reporting the results of standardized tests and assessing the relative achievements, abilities, and aptitudes of students. Figure 16.6 shows how these various scores interrelate.

Percentile Scores.   Percentile scores indicate the percentage of persons in the distribution whose scores fall at or below a given raw score. For example, a student having a percentile score of 25 scored as well as or better than 25 percent of those taking the test. The 50th percentile is the median and in a normal distribution also the mean.

Percentiles are easy to use and compute. They can be used with any type of test. Since they show where the individual student stands in comparison with the other students in the group, they are excellent tools for comparing a person's performance on different tests.

FIGURE 16.6

A Normal Curve Showing (1) Percentage Distribution of Scores, (2) Standard Deviations, (3) *z* Scores, (4) *T* Scores, (5) Deviation IQ Scores, (6) College Entrance Examination Board Scores, (7) Stanine Scores, and (8) Percentile Ranks. (Source: Joseph F. Callahan and Leonard H. Clark, Foundations of Education, New York: Macmillan Publishing Company, 1983, p. 235).

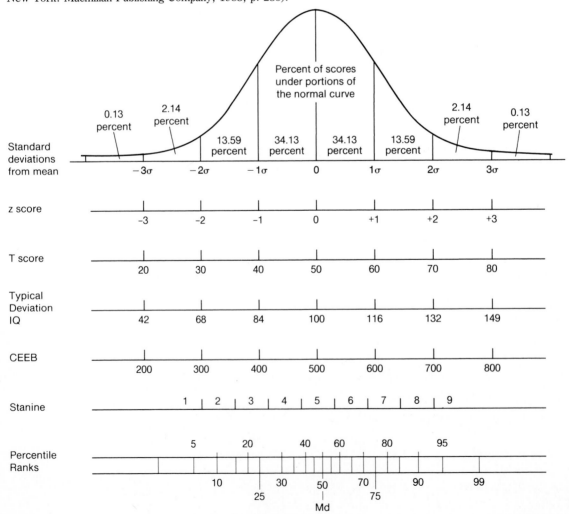

Percentage Scores.   Do not confuse percentile ranks with percentage scores. Percentage scores are simply raw scores expressed in terms of the percentage of correct responses. Thus, if a student gets 25 items right on a 50-item test, the percentage score would be 50. Fifteen right on a 20-item test would give a student a percentage score of 75.

Standard Scores.   Standard scores express individuals' scores in terms of their distance, in standard deviations, from the mean. Thus, if a student's score should fall one standard deviation above the mean, the student standard score would be +1. If it should fall a half standard below the mean, it would be −0.5. Standard scores of this sort are called *z* scores. They are computed by the formula:

$$z = \frac{X - M}{\sigma}$$

where X is a particular raw score, M is the mean for a set of scores, and σ is the standard deviation for that set of scores. By substituting in the formula of the example shown in Figure 16.4, a student whose raw score was 24 would have a *z* score of .088:

$$z = \frac{X - M}{\sigma} = \frac{24 - 23.6}{4.5} = .088$$

Note that the positive *z* scores indicate raw scores above the mean, negative *z* scores indicate raw scores below the mean, and a *z* score of 0 indicates a raw score at the mean. Sometimes, in order to eliminate numbers and decimal fractions, test workers designate the mean by the value 100 (or 5, or 10) and express the deviation from the mean as a multiple of the standard deviation.

T Score.   The *T* score is an example of the practice of transforming standard scores so as to eliminate negative numbers and decimal fractions. *T* scores report exactly the same information as *z* scores except that the mean is expressed as 50 and each standard deviation is equal to 10. The formula used to compute a *T* score is:

$$T = 10z + 50$$

Therefore, if a *z* score was +1.5, the corresponding *T* score would be 65.

$$T = 10 \times 1.5 + 50 = 15 + 50 = 65$$

CEEB Scores.   Other examples of the use of standard scores are the scores reported in the Army General Classification Test and the College Entrance Examination Board (CEEB) tests. The CEEB scores are computed by the formula:

$$CEEB = 100z + 500$$

The Deviation IQ.   The deviation IQ is also a standard score with a mean of 100 and standard deviations ranging from 5 to 20 depending on the intelligence test used. Because of this fact, when interpreting deviation IQs, you must know not only the IQ reported but also the standard deviation of the test used.

Stanine Scores.   Stanine scores that consist of nine one-half standard deviation bands centered on the mean are another example of test scores based on standard deviations. To compute stanine scores you use the following procedure:

1. Find the mean of the raw scores.
2. Find the standard deviation of the raw scores.
3. Measure one-quarter standard deviation down from the mean and one-quarter standard deviation up from the mean to establish the limits of stanine 5 (the middle stanine).
4. Find the limits of stanine 1 through stanine 4 and for stanines 6 to 9 by measuring down or up one half standard deviation for each stanine.

However, a shortcut method for estimating stanine scores is described later in the discussion of grading techniques.

Age-Grade Scores.   Age-grade scores are another device for reporting standardized-test results. An age score reports test performance in terms of the typical performance of persons of that age. Similarly, grade scores report test results in terms of the grade level for which this performance is average. Thus, an age score of 10 would indicate that a student's achievement is equivalent to that of the average 10-year-old even if that student is 17, and a grade score of 10 would indicate that student's performance to be typical of the average tenth-grader even though that student is only in grade 7.

Teacher-Made Instruments

Classroom testing serves several purposes. Teachers use classroom tests to determine how well the various students have achieved and how far they have progressed. Teachers also use classroom tests for diagnostic purposes. Class test scores indicate what the students have learned well and what they have not learned. Analysis of test scores may show that some content has not been well taught and so should be reviewed in future lessons or that certain students have not learned well and need remedial help. Teachers also use tests for motivating students, for guidance purposes, and for instructional devices. Tests can also be used to detect and define students' curricular needs and so establish bases for planning and revising course content and curricula.

Unfortunately, classroom tests sometimes have negative side effects. Some schools and classes, for instance, may become too test dominated. As a result, teachers may teach for the test rather than for real student learning. Similarly, overemphasis on tests and marks may cause students to aim at grades rather than knowledge. As a result of these emphases they may try to attain high marks by such unethical methods as cheating. Sometimes tests have deleterious effects on student morale, personality, and motivation. Students who often fail their tests may so lose self-esteem that they no longer see any point in trying to learn anything. As a result, they may drop out of the class literally or figuratively. Those who remain physically present may no longer attempt assignments, pay attention, study, or, in general, expend energy on what they take to be a useless, impossible waste of time and effort. Failure after failure is no reward. Tests can also be harmful to students when they are used to categorize students as successes or failures; or when test results are considered the final word on a student's abilities, aptitudes, and prospects; or when they are the only means of communication between the school and the home.

Assigning Grades to Tests

After a teacher-made test has been given and scored, it should be used as an instructional tool. Students can be helped to note their errors and discover how to avoid them in the future. In criterion-based situations, successful students are moved to the next level or sequence while those who have been unsuccessful are recycled for further study and efforts. With norm-referenced results, though, more than a raw score or the number correct will be required to serve your purpose. Further analysis of the data will be necessary to supply the information needed for student evaluation. Figure 16.7 illustrates how you might record raw scores from a test so that you will be enabled to make the kinds of judgments required of you.

Rank, Order, Range, and Mode

Assume, for example, that you have administered a 100-point test to a class of 25 students. The number of correct responses on each test paper is looked upon as the raw score for that paper. The scores in Column 1 of Figure 16.7 represent the raw scores without regard to any order—just as you finished scoring them. Column 2 contains the same scores that have been arranged in order from highest to lowest (rank order). Here you can readily note which was the lowest score and which was

FIGURE 16.7
Frequency Distribution

Unarranged	Arranged	Step Interval of 1		Step Interval of 3		Step Interval of 5	
Column (1)	(2)	(3)		(4)		(5)	
Score	Score	Score	f	Score	f	Score	f
45	97	97	1	96–98	1	95–99	1
76	92	92	1	93–95	0	90–94	2
86	90	90	1	90–92	2	85–89	5
60	89	89	1	87–89	2	80–84	3
80	87	87	1	84–86	3	75–79	3
86	86	86	2	81–83	0	70–74	3
59	86	85	1	78–80	3	65–69	1
49	85	80	3	75–77	3	60–64	2
97	80	77	1	72–74	2	55–59	2
80	80	76	1	69–71	1	50–54	1
73	80	75	1	66–68	1	45–49	2
90	77	73	2	63–65	0	$N = 25$	
85	76	70	1	60–62	2		
77	75	68	1	57–59	2		
61	73	61	1	54–56	0		
87	73	60	1	51–53	1		
75	70	59	1	48–50	1		
68	68	57	1	45–47	1		
70	61	51	1	$N = 25$			
51	60	49	1				
80	59	45	1				
87	57	$N = 25$					
92	51						
57	49						
73	45						
$N = 25$	$N = 25$						

the highest, as well as the difference between the two (the range) and the most frequent score (the mode, the score appearing most often). In this test, the mode was 80.

Frequency Distribution Table

For some purpose you may have in mind, it may be easier to arrange your data in a frequency distribution table by grouping like scores, as in column 3 of Figure 16.7. Each score is listed only once. Each column that begins with f indicates how many times each score was made.

When the number of cases is large, the data can be arranged with larger step intervals (such as 3 or 5) to make your chart more manageable. In the fourth column, with a 3-step interval, the interval 45–47 includes the scores 45, 46, 47. In the fifth column, the interval 45–49 includes the scores 45, 46, 47, 48, 49.

Mean and Median

The mean of these scores is the arithmetical average compiled by adding up all the test scores and dividing by the number of test takers. In Figure 16.7, the sum of the scores is 1,846; the number of scores is 25; the mean for this test then is 73.84.

To find the median, the middle score, take the number of scores (25), add 1 and divide by 2. (The reason you add 1 is to find the pivotal score.) The middle score of this distribution is the thirteenth from either top or bottom. If you count the tallies from either end, you will find the median score to be 76:

$$\text{Median} = \frac{(N + 1)}{2} \text{ th score in order of size when } N \text{ is the number of cases}$$

The median is also the 50th percentile. This means simply that one-half or 50 percent of the scores fall above and one-half or 50 percent of the scores fall below the median.

INSPECTION METHOD

This organization of information will enable you to make some descriptive statements about the entire class and to compare individuals within the group. You may make further use of this arrangement of scores to help you assign grades by the inspection method. Natural breaks in the listing are noted and used in determining letter grades.

Figure 16.7, for example, notes that a spread of 5 points exists between the score of 97 and the score of 92. The score of 92 could thus be used as the upper limit for grade B. The next large gap occurs between the scores of 80 and 85; hence, 80 could be the upper limit of grade C. The next large gap occurs between 61 and 68; and following that, the next large gap is between 51 and 57. This arrangement could produce the following grade distribution:

Grade A	97–up	One score, A
Grade B	85–92	Seven scores, B
Grade C	68–80	Ten scores, C
Grade D	57–61	Four scores, D
Grade F	45–51	Three scores, F

PERCENTAGE METHOD

In some schools the percentage method of arriving at grades is used. A predetermined percent of the possible score for a test, homework, or other assigned material is set up for each grade. For instance, 94 percent may be set as a matter of schoolwide policy as the lower limit for an A grade, as in Fairfax (Figure 16.1). In the same manner 64 percent may be set as the low limit for a passing grade of D. In a school in which three grades are given (Satisfactory, Unsatisfactory, and Fail) the cutting percentages will be announced by administrative policy. Needless to say, there is a wide variation among school systems in the percentages used because it is relatively easy to standardize. Using the Fairfax County method, the distribution noted above would become:

Grade A	96%	one score of A
Grade B	86%–95%	six scores of B
Grade C	75%–85%	seven scores of C
Grade D	70%–74%	three scores of D
Grade F	69%–less	eight scores of F

STANINES

Standard scores also can be used for grading. Instead of the 5-point system of letter marks traditionally used to turn raw scores into grades, some teachers have begun using a more defensible system known as the stanine system (Standard Nine). They divide the tested population into nine groups (stanines) instead of five. With the ex-

FIGURE 16.8
Distribution of Scores on English Test

SCORE	FREQUENCY
25	1
24	3
22	4
20	5
19	2
18	3
15	1
14	2
13	2
10	1
9	1
	$N = 25$

	Lowest	Lower	Low	Low Average	Average	High Average	High	Higher	Highest
Stanine	1	2	3	4	5	6	7	8	9
Percentage of Scores	4	7	12	17	20	17	12	7	4

FIGURE 16.9
Approximation of Scores in Each Stanine

ception of stanine one (the lowest) and stanine nine (the highest) these groups are spaced in units of half a standard deviation.

Percentages of the class group that fall within each of the nine stanine classifications for a normal population are shown in Figure 16.9. A useful characteristic of stanines is the equal distance between steps. Like percentile ranks, stanines report test performance in terms of the student's relative position in some known group. The middle score, the median, is the one to start with in setting up a stanine chart.

Note that in Figure 16.8 the median score is 20. It falls in the stanine 5 category in Figure 16.9 and has been labeled average. The other scores are located in stanines by using the percentages provided in this table. In stanines 4 and 6, for example, the percentage of students is seen to be 17 (17% of 25 − 4.25) or 4 students. In stanines 3 and 7, the percentage is seen to be 12 percent and the number of students is 3. In stanines 2 and 8 the percentage is seen to be 4 percent (1 student). Figure 16.10 illustrates how letter grades might be allocated to the stanine subgroups. Note that stanines 4, 5, and 6 are designated average; stanines 7, 8, and 9 are designated high categories.

Try your hand at frequency distribution and grading by working through Exercise 16.1.

Observation Techniques

The learner progresses most efficiently when he or she knows what the goals are, how he or she is progressing toward those goals, and what behavior changes are needed for their achievement. Continuous evaluation, then, is needed for this process to occur. Tests, if well constructed and appropriately used, provide some of the measurement data. But student performance, in addition to paper-and-pencil testing, is another source of information about student learning. For example, skill in making foul shots can be appraised only by an actual demonstration on the gym floor. Threading the

FIGURE 16.10
Allocation of Grades to Stanine Subgroups

Distribution Score Frequency		Progress Grade	Explanation
25–1	—Stanine 8 ⎫	B or A	A 20% of 25 = 5, 5 scores should be in Stanine 5.
24–3	—Stanine 7 ⎭	B	B Score 20, the median, has a frequency of 5.
22–4	—Stanine 6 ⎫	C	17% of 25 = 4.25, 4 scores should be in Stanines 4 and 6.
20–5	—Stanine 5 ⎬		Score 22 has a frequency of 4 but we must combine 18
19–2 ⎫	—Stanine 4 ⎭		and 19 for a frequency of 5.
18–3 ⎭			12% of 25 = 3, 3 scores should be in Stanines 3 and 7.
15–1 ⎫	—Stanine 3 ⎫		Score 24 is no problem, but scores 14 and 15 must be combined.
14–2 ⎭			
13–2	—Stanine 2 ⎭	D	7% of 25 = 1.75, 2 scores should be in Stanines 2 and 8.
			Only 1 score remains for Stanine 8.
10–1 ⎫	—Stanine 1	F	4% of 25 = 1, 1 score should be in Stanines 1 and 9.
9–1 ⎭			Since 2 low scores remain, they would fall in Stanine 1.

sewing machine, preparing a lunch, and making a speech are other competencies that can be appraised only by student activities in real or simulated situations. Sometimes the final result or product is the focal point; at other times the procedure is important. The preparation of the soup, the sandwich, and the dessert for a lunch may each be appraised. But, at some point, there must be coordination of the procedures so that the hot soup and sandwich are ready to serve together and the dessert is available at the appropriate time. The evaluation of products and procedures is an integral part of the teaching-learning situation. Means for such evaluation must be planned and utilized to help the student learn.

Observation techniques are used in evaluating procedures and products. Problems arise in determining the major factors in the appraisal; distinguishing between quality levels; and establishing, quantifying, or marking steps. When students are presenting speeches to enlist support for some specific cause, should the basis for evaluation be the logic of the appeal, the speaker's poise and posture, the number of listeners who changed their point of view, the organization of the speech, or all of these? What is to be evaluated depends on the situation and corresponds to the objectives involved. These criteria for evaluation should be established by the teacher, students, or both before the students plan their speeches.

The Rating Scale.   Various methods of summarizing observations include rating scales, checklists, and anecdotal records. If, for instance, an oral report is prepared for social studies, a number of items might be included in the rating scale, as in Figure 16.11.

The rating scale might be prepared either by students, as they select the major criteria for good reports, or by the teacher. Preparing such an evaluation instrument can be a learning situation in which students analyze behavior and specify desirable aspects of the behavior. The scale might be used by the teacher, by the student presenting the report, or by the class.

Teachers should help students develop self-evaluation skills. Using a rating scale and comparing results with the teacher rating or with the class rating (average) could be a step in developing skills of self-analysis for the student. A student also might do a self-evaluation after reporting to the group and compare it with one done later after hearing an audiotape of the talk. For instructional purposes, the rating scale provides feedback to the student to help him or her improve performance. The evaluation may also be used by the teacher as input for the grading of the student.

The Checklist.   The checklist is another method for use in observing student behavior. Use it to note the presence or absence of student skills and understanding. It is particularly useful for recording characteristics of student behavior and for noting down skills that need further development. For some class activities it may be especially necessary that the checklist reflect the sequence of actions performed. If the students are working in small groups, such items as in Figure 16.12 might be included. The

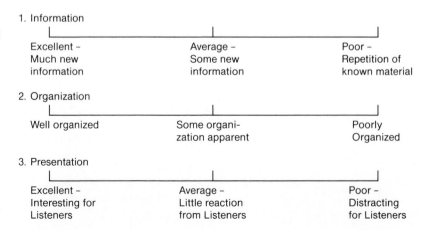

FIGURE 16.11
An Example of a Rating Scale

1. Information

| Excellent –
Much new
information | Average –
Some new
information | Poor –
Repetition of
known material |

2. Organization

| Well organized | Some organi-
zation apparent | Poorly
Organized |

3. Presentation

| Excellent –
Interesting for
Listeners | Average –
Little reaction
from Listeners | Poor –
Distracting
for Listeners |

EXERCISE 16.1   FREQUENCY DISTRIBUTION AND GRADING
A Self-Check Exercise

The purpose of this exercise is to practice what you have learned so far about grades distribution. An answer key follows. Suppose you gave a unit test to your class of 32 students. Their test raw scores were: 35, 32, 34, 28, 30, 27, 32, 24, 18, 30, 26, 10, 31, 24, 26, 30, 25, 21, 25, 31, 19, 25, 26, 20, 31, 20, 24, 30, 21, 18, 30, and 26.

1. Set up a frequency distribution table for this set of scores.

2. What was the median score on this test? _____

3. What percent of the scores would fall into each of the stanine bands?

4. What number of scores would you allocate to each band?

5. What scores would you allocate to each band?

6. What letter grade would you assign to each stanine band?

7. Share and discuss your answers with your classmates.

ANSWER KEY

The frequency distribution table:

RAW SCORE	FREQUENCY
35	1
34	1
32	2
31	3
30	5
28	1
27	1
26	4
25	3
24	3
21	2
20	2
19	1
18	2
10	1

$$N = 32$$

The median is 26.

The percentage of scores and the number of scores to be allocated to each stanine band would be:

STANINE	PERCENT		NUMBER OF SCORES
9	4%	of 32 =	1.28 (or 1)
8	7%	of 32 =	2.24 (or 2)
7	12%	of 32 =	3.84 (or 4)
6	17%	of 32 =	5.44 (or 5)
5	20%	of 32 =	6.40 (or 6)
4	17%	of 32 =	5.44 (or 5)
3	12%	of 32 =	3.84 (or 4)
2	7%	of 32 =	2.24 (or 2)
1	4%	of 32 =	1.28 (or 1)

Allocations of scores to the stanines must be approximated because we cannot use fractions and all the same scores must appear in the same stanine. Following are two sets of possible allocations of scores and corresponding letter marks based on the foregoing data.

STANINE	Possible Score Allocation	LETTER MARKS	Possible Score Allocation	LETTER MARKS
9	34–35	A	34–35	A
8	32		32	
7	31	B	31	B
6	27–30		28–30	
5	26	C	25–26–27	C
4	24–25		24	
3	20–21	D	19–20–21	D
2	18–19		18	
1	10	F	10	F

Behavior	Yes	No	Uncertain
1. Begins work promptly			
2. Explains his point of view			
3. Listens to others			
4. Is a leader sometimes			
5. Is a follower sometimes			
6. Keeps group working on the task			
7. Is pleasant to others in the group			
8. Makes worthwhile contributions			

FIGURE 16.12
An Example of a Checklist

checklist not only is a useful device for the teacher in observing behavior but also reminds students about their own activities.

Anecdotal Records.   Anecdotal records are simply brief, written statements of what has been observed. The anecdotal record should provide objective evidence about the procedure or product. Each anecdotal record is limited to recording a single situation. It can be useful to a teacher in understanding an individual student and planning for his or her learning.

When an anecdotal record is used, the teacher indicates that the characteristics of the procedure or product are not well enough defined to organize into a checklist or rating scale. Teachers who use anecdotal records for evaluation are compiling information instead of relying on memory. By regularly collecting and recording this information, they guard against the tendency to recall only recent data and critical incidents that might otherwise make evaluations unfair and biased. Sometimes, anecdotal records may not present data on all students. Unless you consciously plan to write for different students and include all of them, the anecdotes will usually deal with just the excellent and the poor students.

Log.   A log differs from an anecdotal record in that a log is a daily record. Using a log lends itself to ensuring that you are getting observations of all students. The log also might tend to show development patterns, since it is an ongoing record.

Teachers need to experiment with different ways of collecting information about student learning. When a variety of procedures is used, the teacher and students will be able to develop devices appropriate to specific situations.

Anecdotal records and logs are useful for evaluations of an informal nature. Tests, reports, projects, and products are formally evaluated. Questions asked during or outside of class, explanations to peers, listening, and unassigned contributions to the class (bringing a new book to class or a clipping for the bulletin board) are activities that are informally evaluated. These behaviors can be interpreted as responses in the affective domain.

Affective Domain.   Learning in the affective domain is particularly difficult to measure. Whenever a teacher communicates an attempt to evaluate such behavior, students can easily fake the responses. The teacher, however, must be aware of what influence the teaching has on the attitudes of students. Unless students retain or improve their attitudes toward the subject and toward school, the teacher is failing to do an effective job. Some of the student responses that should cause teachers to examine their objectives and learning activities include pain, fear, anxiety, frustration, embarrassment, boredom, and discomfort.[2] Although teachers ordinarily do not try to develop a system for grading these informal areas, they should evaluate the influence of their teaching in this area of feelings. Unsigned questionnaires provide considerable useful information. Course-related student behaviors that are indicators include the incidence of dropping class, absence, tardiness, submitting unrequired papers and projects, evidence of careful work on assignments, and volunteering for special activities.[3]

Interest in value education forces teachers to evaluate the affective behavior of the students with whom they work. Ingenuity is needed in developing and using various techniques for collecting data about student reactions. When a considerable amount of cheating takes place in testing situations, for example, or when intense student animosities are apparent in class discussions or in small-group work, or when assignments are regularly missed or a general fatigue is evident regarding good or poor performance in the class, a careful review and analysis of the total teaching-learning environment is undoubtedly being signaled for.

Grading Theme Papers

English teachers perhaps more frequently than any other group are concerned with the evaluating of student writing. Social studies, health, science, and even mathematics assignments also involve writing of reports or essays. Probably all teachers at some time evaluate written compositions of students. Many factors are involved in such evaluation and should be specified in accordance with the objectives.

These factors fall into two general categories, content and mechanics. Content encompasses ideas, organization, style, wording, and similar areas. Mechanics deal with grammar, punctuation, spelling, and neatness. Since to some students the two areas seem totally unrelated, teachers may choose to give an evaluation for each category. The symbol *A/C* on a theme graded by one English teacher indicates the paper to be excellent as far as ideas and style are concerned, but mediocre mechanically; the grade preceding the slash represents content, and the grade following the slash represents mechanics. Some teachers give specific values to mechanical errors to encourage the student to proofread carefully. Reflection upon the tendency of some students to repeat endlessly the same mistake in written work has led some teachers to attach penalties to repetition of previous errors. The goals of this procedure are to encourage proofreading, to cultivate pride in the final product, and to magnify the error of letting mediocre efforts suffice. In English classes where this system is followed, not all errors are penalized alike. Errors in areas previously studied (and supposedly mastered), such as capitalization, for example, are assumed to be due to carelessness. Such errors are penalized moderately as a motivation toward more careful writing. Errors in areas currently under study are penalized more severely in an effort to motivate more study and additional mastery of new concepts. Some teachers work out guidelines with their students similar to the following in their quest for improvement in writing:

☐ *Major errors.* Run-on or fragmentary sentence; muddled sentence.
　(One such error reduces mechanics grade a letter.)

☐ *Serious errors.* Nonagreement of subject and verb; nonagreement of pronoun with antecedent; lack of antecedent; incorrect word.
　(Three of these reduce grade a letter.)

☐ *Minor errors.* Misspelling, errors in capitalization, punctuation mistakes.
　(Five of these reduce grade a letter.)

These classifications change as students develop more skill in mechanics. The classifications or penalties may change each semester or each grading period.

---

[2]Robert F. Mager, *Developing Attitude Toward Learning* (Palo Alto, Calif.: Fearon, 1968), pp. 49–57.
[3]Ibid., pp. 79–81.

When objectives are improved proofreading and sensitivity to mechanical errors, the teacher may use assigned theme papers in proofreading activities before final evaluation of the themes. For example, a group of students may exchange themes and read them to catch any spelling errors and then exchange again and read for capitalization and punctuation accuracy. These activities not only provide student opportunities for learning but also assist the teacher in correcting errors.

Since grading content and style is much more subjective than checking mechanical errors, the teacher should frequently provide models of well-organized and interesting writing. The selection of student writing for use as models is helpful to the teacher and is a reward system for students. Student judgment of style and content can be cultivated through use of models and through peer grading of themes (without names, of course). If students read several themes and rank them according to content, important aspects of writing style can be emphasized and illustrated. Teachers of all content areas can use these same approaches to improve student writing: models, discussion, peer sharing, and evaluation of written work.

Teachers may not evaluate all student themes with the same emphasis. On some occasions, a paragraph may be written for a specific purpose — perhaps to explain how to do a task. Mechanics may not be graded at all. The teacher should indicate to the class what objectives are involved in the student writing and in the evaluation. Teacher time, student interest, and needs are several factors to be considered. Grading themes is time-consuming. A teacher must determine whether the time required in such effort pays off in student progress. Unless the students get feedback on their writing within a reasonable time and learn from the teacher evaluation, for instance, the teaching is probably inefficient. Sometimes it is wise to set up a system for correcting themes. One system that seems to be advantageous is to ask students to write on alternate lines and then to insert corrections on the blank lines. This arrangement facilitates checking; when a student is required to rewrite the entire theme, the teacher must reread the entire theme, and often finds new errors in the process. Giving a second grade for the correction of mechanical errors may be desirable.

Occasionally, it may be useful to evaluate themes as you circulate around the classroom while the students are writing. By reading as students are producing the composition, the teacher may be able to offer suggestions and correct some errors on the spot. Such a strategy provides variety and utilizes teacher time for individual problems. Help in organizing themes while writing may result in important learning for the student.

Evaluation of Individualized Instruction

Individualized instruction requires individual evaluation and grading. Teachers have found no one way to deal effectively with the variety of starting levels, speed of learning, motivation, distractions, projects, and activities. In a continuous-progress curriculum, when diagnostic tests are given and assignments are developed to provide the learning experiences the student needs to progress in the subject area, each student may be doing lessons that are different from those of all other students in the group. How then should the progress of individual students be evaluated?

Sometimes the student and teacher can together establish goals for the individual. These goals may be the basis for a progress grade. The report might also include the norm level of this work. Marvin may be working in general mathematics on basic multiplication facts. Since he is accomplishing the objectives for his learning tasks, his progress is good. However, the task is one that an average fourth-grader masters. Marvin's evaluation should probably include both his learning and the level of the task. The evaluation of a student who works quite slowly should show his or her growth and give some indication of his work pattern. Can such information be most satisfactorily communicated to students, parents, other schools, and employers by letter grades, written comments, or some other system? Each school using individualized instruction must consider this problem as it evolves its philosophy of grading, and each teacher must adapt the procedures used in the classroom to that philosophy. Some commercially prepared systems (such as IPI) have totaled the number of concepts involved in the whole math curriculum.[4] When they report, they need merely indicate the current achievement for norm groups such as "20–30 packets completed by successful students. Lupe has completed 25 packets and thus has 5 more to finish before semester's end." Since in these systems progress is continuous, no difficulty is caused by routine slowness. When the current target has been achieved, the student merely goes on to the next. Lupe, for example, would start on Packet 26. Even over year-ends and year beginnings if Lupe has not mastered Packet number 30, she will pick up in the new year where she left off and work on that sequence until Packet 30 has been mastered.

CONTRACTS

Contracts are another individualized approach that teachers utilize. Contracts may be set up for the class with basic requirements for a passing grade, and options for higher grades. A six-week contract in U.S. history might include such options as:

D
{
Read text assignments.
Attend class.
Get at least 50 percent on three tests given.
}

C
{
In addition to the previous requirements, participate in class discussion.
Report to class on one current event related to each of three content sections.
}

B
{
In addition to the previous requirements, read a book from the list provided, and participate in a panel discussion to share ideas from the book with the class.
}

A
{
In addition to the previous requirements, plan and carry out an individual project, such as study of a community agency or investigation of a specific problem. This project must be approved by the teacher.
}

In this approach each student makes a selection of the grade aimed for and writes a personal contract. The teacher must be aware of quality in this arrangement. Each contract should include time limits and criteria for satisfactory work. The choice by students, as well as timing and quality level, provide for individual differences.

Other uses of contracts may involve more student planning. Groups of students may prepare learning packages that include objectives, resources, activities, and tests. Then, individual contracts may be written regarding the use of these learning packages, their evaluation, or the production of additional packages. Some teachers prefer to use contracts for independent study. The student then will be planning his or her own objectives, activities, resources, and evaluation. In these situations some teachers establish a range of grades or values that become possible for those who opt to go this independent route. A maximum number is established—10 points, for example—to be added for acceptable work, or an increase of one letter grade for an A/B on the special project. The same caution, of course, applies here regarding judgment of value of work submitted as was previously pointed out. Unless the quality of the work meets the specifications agreed upon at the outset of the activity, full credit will not be awarded to it. The situation to be avoided is permitting students to expect the maximum of reward for spotty or inferior production merely because they have done something extra.

Teacher assistance is important in the contracts that are more student-centered. Guidance in setting reasonable objectives and in selecting appropriate activities helps the student recognize his or her own strengths and limitations. Students also recognize

---

[4]Individually Prescribed Instruction (IPI) is a program designed to teach arithmetic, reading, and sciences for grades K–6. Subjects are broken into sequences of major cognitive objectives and programmed learning units are provided for each objective. Progress is monitored on the basis of present and past performance.

some of the opportunities and limitations of their environment. Providing for specific evaluation in the contract is important because when the bases for grading are established, misunderstandings are less likely to arise. Usually both self-evaluation and teacher evaluation should be included in the grading plan for contracts. (See Modules 4 and 12 for additional discussion concerning contracts.)

Self-Evaluation

Self-evaluation is an important goal of the school as well as one aspect of the evaluation process. Effective persons, according to perceptual psychologists, have a positive self-concept. They must think well of themselves, recognizing their capabilities and accepting their limitations. To achieve such self-understanding requires not only having experienced success but also guidance in self-analysis. To meet these needs, teachers should provide opportunities for students to seriously consider what they have learned, how much they have progressed, and what learning styles they have developed. One procedure is the use of rating scales, portfolios or checklists. These instruments emphasize the criteria for evaluation. They give students a means of expressing their feelings to the teacher, and give the teacher another input of data to use in evaluation. A follow-up conference, in which teacher ratings and self-ratings are compared and explained, can be mutually beneficial. Probably a joint evaluation should be the final result of such a conference.

Any of the devices developed for evaluating student products and procedures can be utilized for self-evaluation. In addition, you can construct specific instruments to encourage self-evaluation. The student may compare responses made early in the school year with those made near the end of the school year. Such comparison may provide the student with information previously not recognized about his or her own growth. Items similar to the following may be used:

Check appropriate responses. If other terms should be added, write them in the blanks.

1. My assignments are turned in
   a. promptly.
   b. late.
   c. on time.
   d. occasionally.
   e. never.
   f. _____ .
2. My classmates in general consider me
   a. a friend.
   b. a nobody.
   c. a person to ridicule.
   d. an enemy.
   e. _____ .
3. I consider myself to be
   a. intelligent.
   b. one who has difficulty learning.
   c. average in intelligence.
   d. the smartest in the class.
   e. the slowest student in the class.
   f. _____ .
4. My work in school represents
   a. the best I can do.
   b. enough to get by.
   c. my preferences; I do what I enjoy.
   d. as little effort as possible.
   e. whatever will keep the teacher satisfied.
   f. whatever keeps my parents satisfied.
   g. _____ .

Open-ended questions may also provide information to students and teachers. Examples: What have you learned in class this week that you can use outside of school? What have you learned about yourself during this unit?

Some students prefer to let the teacher do the evaluating. The teacher, however, has a responsibility to encourage self-evaluation. Only when individuals recognize their strengths can they utilize their full potential. As human beings they have limitations they should consider realistically as they set their own personal goals. Teachers who accept each student as an individual whose unique capabilities must be encouraged contribute to the development of adolescents. This acceptance, plus successful experiences, gives the student a basis for developing and maintaining self-respect and a feeling of worth. Such a positive self-concept is not only an educational goal in itself but is a prerequisite for maximum learning. Self-evaluation is an essential ingredient of the school program and should be implemented by each teacher.

Grading and Reporting

The first step in grading for report cards is to formulate an evaluation plan. This plan should spell out exactly what will be evaluated and what the relative importance of each factor will be. It should be established prior to the teaching so that both the teacher and the students understand the importance of the various activities. A teacher may, for example, in considering plans for six weeks in biology, decide that important activities are: (1) class participation, (2) homework assignments, (3) tests (three in number), (4) laboratory performance, and (5) special projects. The importance of these may be established by points, weights, or percentages. The teacher may arbitrarily select a number of points or the appropriate weights, as in the following example:

	POINTS	WEIGHT	PERCENTAGE
1. Class participation	150	3	30
2. Homework assignments	50	1	10
3. Tests	150	3	30
4. Laboratory performance	100	2	20
5. Special projects	50	1	10
	500		100

This decision indicates that tests and class participation will receive equal emphasis; laboratory work is one-fifth of the grade; homework and special projects together are considered as important as laboratory work.

Then the teacher must plan the appraisal in each area. Evaluation of class participation cannot be done fairly at the end of six weeks without periodic information. The teacher should sample the class participation throughout the grading period. For example, the discussion on Tuesday of the first week might be evaluated in classes 1 and 2, on Wednesday in classes 3 and 4, and on Thursday in classes 5 and 6. The schedule could be rotated so that the appraisal of discussion would provide a good sample of student behavior. Students who were absent or did not contribute might be deliberately involved in the next evaluation. The teacher should use a system of evaluation that considers the quality as well as the frequency of participation. Marking should be done as soon after class as possible so that the situation is recalled.

Teachers evaluate homework in different ways. Some simply check to see whether the assignment has been done. Others spot-check assigned work. Perhaps question 2 is used as the basis for grading one assignment, and then questions 1 and 6 are used next time. Sometimes teachers have students check their own work. Since the purpose of discussing assigned work in class is to increase learning, the correcting of papers before they are turned in may have merit. Procedures probably should be varied. But you should always keep in mind that homework may be the effort of a student, a group of students, a parent, or some other person. Some teachers encourage cooperative study and prefer short, frequent quizzes for the appraisal of daily work by someone.

However they arrange it, effective teachers respect the adage that insists on never assigning anything that is not going to be checked.

Evaluating laboratory performance and special projects would involve such evaluation instruments and procedures as ratings, checklists, or logs. Points from these evaluations would necessarily be totaled for each student. Then a frequency distribution could be made and grades assigned by inspection, or by some other procedure, such as using stanines. Teachers should consider the time involved in the procedures and attempt to simplify their work.

Grading Example

Let us consider an example from a biology class. Ms. Babashoff, the teacher, has elected to use a five-point scale. She finds that one of her students, Sue Lightfoot, has the following weighted evaluations:

	Evaluation	Weight		
1. Class participation	5	×	3	= 15
2. Homework	4	×	1	= 4
3. Tests	3	×	3	= 9
4. Laboratory performance	5	×	2	= 10
5. Special projects	2	×	1	= 2
			Total	= 40

The frequency distribution for the class is:

Total Frequency Scores

47–1
45–2
42–3
41–1
40–5
36–3
35–1
34–4
29–2
27–2
25–3
18–1   **The median is 34.**
17–1
15–2
13–2
$N = 33$

The teacher now applies the grading system of her school to this distribution. There is no absolute way to decide how grades should be allocated. Considering the total situation, the teacher makes the choices that seem most reasonable. Expect to discover that the process of grading is a time-consuming, subjective endeavor. Exercise 16.2 will give you some practice in application of grades from a frequency distribution table.

Grading Systems

The most popular grading system appears to be the use of letter grades in a five-point scale: A, B, C, D, F or U. Some schools use numbers 1, 2, 3, 4, and 5 rather than letters. Often descriptive phrases are used to explain the letter marks, such as A equals outstanding achievement or D equals minimum achievement. Sometimes letter grades are combined with the percentage system. Then, percentage cutoffs are used for the letter grades, such as: A, 95–100, or D, 70–76. In some schools, the five-point scale is modified, adding plus (+) or minus (−) to the letters to indicate the upper area or lower area of the letter grade's range. This modification, in effect, changes the five-point scale to a thirteen-point scale.

Percentage grading systems, which were formerly popular, are used less frequently today. It was assumed that teachers could discriminate more clearly the amounts of student progress or differences if they had more specific calibrations to use in their measuring device. Such attempts proved rather futile, however, because few if any teachers could defend the fine distinctions in the schoolwork of students that the percentage system required. It was also assumed that grades of this sort prepared students for the competition they would meet in the adult world because in order to achieve they would have to vie with other students. Motivation to succeed would happen in a natural fashion and serve to augment learning. The failure or disinclination of some students to respond to the stimulus of marks and grading has caused this system of grading to give way to other systems in recent years.

The trend has seemed to be toward a marking system that provides broad areas to indicate general information about individual achievement in comparison to the pattern of the group. However, more schools seem to be trying to develop grading procedures that show the progress of individual students. In general, school marking systems have not provided adequately for the presence of individual differences among students. Students in the typical graded school have been grouped more on a basis of chronological age and time in class than on ability or aptitude. The fact that the manifold differences existing among them is not permitted to modify expectations for each has complicated the teacher's life.

Arriving at the Grade

The following excerpt describes how one school system helps support each teacher's approach to arriving at marks for work done:[5]

> Teachers provide written instructional objectives and evaluation measures to each student at the beginning of the course. The student is given continual feedback on the quality of work as it relates to the course objectives.
>
> Each teacher develops a percentage based and/or letter based evaluation design best-suited to his or her class for arriving at the quarter grade and the final grade. This design must explicitly indicate how the quarter grade is determined (e.g., the weighting of the tests, assignments, etc.). A copy of this design is placed in the grade book and the information is given to students and parents at the beginning of the course.
>
> Teachers use their judgment on individual tests or assignments in determining the weight of test items and the procedures for scoring tests appropriate for a specific class or subject area.
>
> Grading begins with the individual and with his or her achievement and not with a preconceived pattern. Any system or curve which predetermines the number or distribution of grades tends to be unrealistic and unfair and is not used. Because the art of test making is imprecise at best, this guideline does not preclude teachers' adjusting raw scores or using commercially prepared tests and their results when determining class grades. The county-mandated testing program results are not used in assigning individual student grades. The "curve" of normal distribution should not be used in arriving at grades.
>
> Quizzes, tests, examinations, essays, homework, or papers are evaluated and/or graded, returned promptly, and reviewed with the student before the next related test is administered.
>
> Grades reflect all marks recorded, and each piece of work or each assignment may be valued according to the individual teacher's grading rationale. To emphasize the professional judgment of the teacher in determining quarter, semester and final grades, the following caveat is offered. There may be circumstances in which the collective quarter marks show a definite trend (ascending or descending) in a student's achievement. When these circumstances occur, a modification of a strictly "numerical" or "letter" average may be a more accurate evaluation of the overall work of the student. For example, students overcoming difficulties during the early part of a grading period should not be penalized for their initial performance; and students enjoying early success and

---

[5]*Program of Studies Handbook,* Fairfax County Public Schools, Virginia, pp. 7–8.

EXERCISE 16.2   ASSIGNING GRADES
FROM A FREQUENCY DISTRIBUTION

In this exercise, you will practice application of grades from a frequency distribution table and then compare your response with some ideas of experienced teachers and with your classmates. Refer to the frequency distribution scores for Ms. Babashoff's biology class (in the section of the text headed Grading Example).

1. What grades (A, B, C, D, and F) would you assign to the distribution given in that example?

2. Compare your list with these possible grades for the biology class, as provided by an experienced teacher:

SCORES FREQUENCY

Scores		
47–1 } A		If biology is a course for select students:
45–2		$40-47 = A$
42–3		$25-36 = B$
41–1 } B		$13-18 = C$
40–5		
36–3		If stanines are estimated:
35–1		$45-47 = A$
34–4 } C		$41-42 = B$
29–2		$25-40 = C$
27–2		$15-18 = D$
25–3		$13 = F$
18–1		
17–1 } D		
15–2		
13–2 F		
$N = 33$		

3. Discuss both the grades you assigned and the grades assigned by the experienced teacher with your classmates.

expecting to let this success "average out" should have this "letting down" reported as unsatisfactory performance. The same consideration should be given when determining the final course grade.

A student should be considered to be doing passing work when the marks received indicate a general level of acceptable achievement and a general pattern of acceptable responses. Careful consideration should be given all work. Failure or success on one test or one assigned task (e.g., a book report or notebook) should not be sufficient basis for failing or passing of the course or the grading period.

The teacher conducts frequent and ongoing evaluations in determining a quarter grade. *The teacher is required to use one mark per week in determining a grade, but is encouraged to use at least two marks per week.* These marks can reflect formal or informal tests or quizzes, classroom or lab participation, teacher observation, homework, special assignments, etc. Weekly evaluation encourages class attendance and consistency in study habits.

All nine-week grades and final examination (evaluation activity) grades are used in determining the year's grade. For semester courses, the semester grade is the final grade. For quarter courses, the quarter grade is the final grade. In courses for which the acquisition of a specific skill is the primary terminal objective (e.g., typing) the teacher's grading design will reflect student evaluation in reference to instructional objectives.

The above guidelines are offered to assist teachers in arriving at a grade; however, the grade given reflects the teacher's professional evaluation of student achievement and must be clearly justifiable by the teacher.

Written Evaluations

An alternative calls for written evaluations instead of letter or numerical grades. As utilized by many of the schools today, this plan makes it possible to report not only individual student achievements but also their strengths, areas needing improvement, social skills, and study habits as well. Such evaluation is more meaningful to parents and students. It also requires careful consideration by the teacher of the individual as a person. However, writing such reports is so time-consuming for the teachers that it may become a vague statement with trite phrases, especially if the teacher tries to write many of these reports at one sitting.

Two-, Three-, Five-Mark Systems

Some schools are using pass-fail grading; they report only if the student's work is passing or failing, satisfactory or unsatisfactory. The rationale to support such a system is that it creates a better learning atmosphere. Fewer anxieties and less competition reduce cheating, and yet students work to meet the objectives. Disadvantages include the lack of stimulation for certain students, the possibility that the evaluation will be neglected, and the fact that excellence goes unrecognized or unrewarded. Because of these disadvantages, some school systems have introduced a three-category system: Honors/Pass/Fail. In an attempt to gain the advantages of both systems, some school systems use both grading systems. In such a plan, for instance, the required courses might be graded with the usual letter grades, but the student might have an option to request pass-fail grading for an elective course.

In addition to subject grades, report cards often include information regarding attitude and habits. A conduct grade to represent social and personal behavior in the school environment has generally been discontinued. Each teacher evaluates the students in regard to their personal and social traits. Frequently, these are reported with coded numbers. The numbers may represent specific behaviors such as: (1) study habits are good, (2) assignments are incomplete or unsatisfactory, or (3) improvement in work is evident.

Another way of including evaluation in social and study skills is a five-point scale, ranging from 1—Student initiates opportunities to learn and displays excellent study habits to 5—Student is apathetic, uncooperative, and disturbs others. All parties touched by this communication system must understand and accept the parameters within which resulting marks are effective. It must be recognized by all that each mark given will be a judgment call and as such is subject to some error. Each interpreter of the grade must accept that a 4 or a 2 on this scale represents an impression by the teacher of the student's participation—not a concise, specific hard number of responses made comparing favorably or unfavorably with the responses from the rest of the class. When separate symbols are used to distinguish achievement from other student behaviors, and all parties accept the guidelines established, communication between the teacher, the student, and the home is facilitated.

Whatever grading system is used, certain essential elements should be included in the evaluation process:[6]

☐ Learning objectives should be clearly understood in advance, with criteria for measurement and levels of performance.

☐ The teacher should communicate meaningfully, either in written or oral form to the student, in discussing with the student his or her strengths, weaknesses, and suggestions for improvement with respect to the objectives of the course.

☐ The student should be involved in self-evaluation of strengths and weaknesses and should plan improvement in meeting the course objectives as well as personal learning goals.

☐ Time is needed for the teacher and student to share perceptions and engage in a discussion of each other's evaluation.

School report systems usually include periodic grading (six or nine weeks), semester grades, and averages for the year. These stipulated marking times necessitate that the planning and use of evaluation procedures be continuous. Interim reports to parents should be used whenever one notes a change in a student's general behavior. Improved performance, as well as less favorable trends, should be reported to the student and to the home. The school can encourage students greatly by commendations for progress. In some communities, contacts between the home and school always involve problems. Positive reinforcement can help students and help produce amicable school-community relations.

Testing Goals

The tendency to forget the reason for testing or evaluating or grading is ever present for teachers. Busy teachers sometimes can become preoccupied with the process and lose almost complete sight of the product and/or the purpose. They begin to test to get a mark or a grade for reporting purposes, and thus students start giving little thought to the material that has been learned or that yet remains to be mastered. One of the goals of teaching is keeping the student aware of the goals of teaching so that the student can alter study procedures to fit his or her needs. When the student is appropriately motivated, he or she should seek such information in the quest of a learning goal. Teachers can supply such guidance only when they have available the appropriate data on which to base their counsel. The fact that these data can also be used for communicating to parents and others about student progress should be looked upon as a plus but must always be kept in its place as a helping technique rather than as an ultimate purpose.

SUMMARY

Since evaluation is an integral factor in the teaching-learning process, you must aim to include the following in your teaching performance:

1. Utilize a variety of instruments to appraise the behavior of students and to focus on the development of the individual. Keep students informed of their standing and progress. Return tests promptly, review the answers to all questions, and respond to inquiries about marks given. Writing the frequency distribution of the

---

[6]Glenys G. Unruh and William M. Alexander, *Innovations in Secondary Education*, 2d ed. (New York: Holt, Rinehart and Winston, 1974), p. 49.

scores on the board will enable each student to see where he or she is and to interpret that score in relation to the rest of the class.

2. Use appraisal procedures continuously so as to contribute to the positive development of the individual student. Such an emphasis requires that the evaluation be important to the student and related to what he or she considers important. Effective evaluation is helping the student know his or her competencies and achievement. It encourages further learning and the selection of appropriate tasks. Some teachers give a short quiz every day for this purpose, whereas others achieve the same end by periodic unannounced short tests. Full period tests are reserved for the end of a chapter, or unit, and also the end of a quarter or semester.

3. Adapt the marking system of the school to your situation. When you set your own standard and grade each student in relation to it, you are said to be using an absolute system of grading. When you use the normal curve or a predetermined percentage in each category as the basis for awarding grades, you are said to be using a relative system. Of the two, the absolute system that incorporates your judgment of a student's progress more properly places emphasis on individual evaluation.

4. Avoid using grades as a threat or overstressing them for motivational purposes. It is legitimate to consider as tentative the grade you arrive at after consideration of the factual data you have accumulated. Consideration of extenuating circumstances, such as sudden illness in class, prolonged absence for a serious matter, and so on, should then take place before making the grades permanent. Adjusting a borderline mark into the higher alternative in the light of some classroom performance is indeed defensible. Almost never, though, is it prudent to award a lower grade to a student than that student has already earned on the basis of the objective evidence at hand.

5. Consider your grading procedures carefully, plan them, and explain your policies to the students. The various factors to be considered in arriving at a grade and the weight accorded to such things as homework, written assignments, and oral class contributions should all be explained before study is begun.

6. Involve the students, whenever feasible, in setting up criteria and establishing the relative importance of activities. Such cooperative planning is a learning experience for students and encourages self-evaluation. It is important that students understand the directions on any test you give. Before permitting students to begin, make sure to explain any ambiguities that result from the terminology used. Base your tests on the important material that has been taught. Your purpose in giving the test, of course, is not to trap or confuse the student but to evaluate how well he or she has assimilated the important aspects of learning.

7. Incorporate continuous evaluation in your learning activities to be sure that students are aware of their progress. The goals of tests administered should serve as a challenge, but they should be attainable. Goals set too high or tests made up of questions that are too hard discourage students and so diminish the motivational factor. Goals set too low, with questions that are too easy, encourage disregard of the subject matter that is taught and perpetuation of a lackadaisical approach to study.

8. Strive for objective and impartial appraisal as you put your evaluation plan into operation. Do not allow personal feelings to enter into a grade. Whether you like or dislike a student, the grade you give should represent the student's level of achievement based on the same objective standard used for all.

9. Try to minimize arguments about grades, cheating, and teacher subjectivity by involving students in the planning, reinforcing individual student development, and providing an accepting, stimulating learning environment. Remain alert while students are taking a test. Do not occupy yourself with other tasks at your desk such

as reading a book or marking papers while a test is in progress. Circulate, observe, present at least a psychological deterrent to cheating by your demeanor, but be sure not to distract.

10. Keep accurate and clear records of test results so that you will have an adequate supply of data on which to base your judgmental decisions about grades. Sufficient data of this sort are especially helpful when final grades are called into question or when students or parents require information in depth.

SUGGESTED READING

Cangelosi, J. S. *Designing Tests for Evaluating Student Achievement.* White Plains, NY: Longman, 1989.

Ebel, R. L., and Frisbie, D.A. *Essentials of Educational Measurement.* 5th ed. Needham Heights, MA: Allyn and Bacon, 1991.

Gronlund, N. E. *How to Construct Achievement Tests.* 4th ed. Needham Heights, MA: Allyn and Bacon, 1988.

Gronlund, N. E., and Linn, R. L. *Measurement and Evaluation in Teaching.* 6th ed. New York: Macmillan, 1990.

Lorber, M. A., and Pierce, W. D. *Objectives, Methods, and Evaluation for Secondary Teaching.* 3d ed. Chapter 8. Englewood Cliffs, NJ: Prentice Hall, 1990.

POSTTEST

Multiple Choice   Select the best answer to complete the statement and put the correct letter in the blank at the left.

_____ 1. In setting up a frequency distribution the teacher begins by
    a. listing all scores.
    b. arranging scores from low to high.
    c. finding the middle score.
    d. tabulating scores.

_____ 2. Use of the normal curve in grading implies that the teacher
    a. has an average class.
    b. will know how many A, B, C, D, and F grades to give.
    c. will make judgments about assigning grades.
    d. is using a fair and impartial system.

_____ 3. If a teacher wants three tests to have equal weight,
    a. the raw scores must be changed to standard scores.
    b. the raw scores are simply added for a total score.
    c. each test score is assigned a letter grade that is translated to points and the points are totaled.
    d. each test score should be expressed as percentage correct and the three should be added.

_____ 4. An advanced class received the following scores on a science test: 29, 16, 20, 23, 28, 25, 11, 15, 26, 17, 20, 23, 27, 25, 23, and 19. What is the median?
    a. 26
    b. 15
    c. 23
    d. 21

_____ 5. An effective grading system is *least* likely to
    a. be limited to academic achievement.
    b. include evaluation of a variety of student behaviors.
    c. be able to provide criterion- and norm-referenced grades.
    d. provide information about the achievement of objectives.

_____ 6. Student products and processes are evaluated by
    a. one of the following devices: a rating scale, checklist, anecdotal record, log.

b. teacher, student, and peers.

c. the criterion established in the behavioral objective.

d. the procedure and individuals appropriate to the intent of the objective.

_____ 7. Homework is an important phase of learning activities in many classes and consequently should be

a. carefully graded by the teacher.

b. utilized for learning.

c. occasionally collected and spot-checked.

d. considered as a major.

_____ 8. When contracts are used in a class, the major purpose of evaluation is to

a. grade the students.

b. consider whether the student accomplished the amount of work he selected.

c. determine the quality of student achievement.

d. increase self-analysis and development through individual goals and criteria.

_____ 9. Class participation can be graded easily and fairly

a. at the end of the grading period.

b. by a plan of daily grading.

c. by a planned schedule of grading each class.

d. by keeping anecdotal records.

_____ 10. Students learn best when they are

a. reminded of their shortcomings so that they are more realistic in setting goals.

b. accepted as worthy individuals and are encouraged to undertake challenging tasks.

c. homogeneously grouped and are encouraged to work together on similar tasks.

d. heterogeneously grouped and are encouraged to work together on similar tasks.

Check   A group from the Student Council of Walton High School studied grading systems. Its report to the Advisory Committee included a statement of purpose for grading. Read the following statements and check those that provide valid reasons for grades.

_____ 11. Teachers can control student behavior with grades.

_____ 12. Colleges and employers can get information about students.

_____ 13. Grades give a student information about his or her progress.

_____ 14. Grades replace learning as a motivation for students.

_____ 15. Grades encourage continuous evaluation of student learning.

Analyze   Mr. Taylor decided to use a weight system for six-week grades. The four items selected were class participation, tests, group project, and assignments. He decided that the most important phase of the learning activities was class participation, which should be half of the grade. The group project and tests were of equal value, but the assignments were half as important as the tests. Set up a system of weights for Mr. Taylor to use. Put the appropriate number in the blank.

_____ 16. Class participation.

_____ 17. Tests.

_____ 18. Group projects.

_____ 19. Assignments.

Indicate in the blank provided which of the following situations require:
- a. criterion-referenced grades.
- b. norm-referenced grades.
- c. both kinds of evaluation.
- d. neither type of evaluation.

_____ 20. To select students for continuing the study of French from French II classes.

_____ 21. To find students to do special projects in their special interests for biology.

_____ 22. To assign a transfer student to the appropriate English class in a three-track English program (slow, average, advanced).

_____ 23. To choose students for competition in the state science tests.

_____ 24. To select an appropriate learning package for individualized instruction in geometry.

_____ 25. To decide whether a student should go to the next level of instruction in a continuous progress general science curriculum.

PART VII
Becoming a Professional

The single module of Part VII provides information about and guidelines for:

☐ The laboratory experiences of teacher preparation.

☐ The student teaching experience.

☐ Getting a job.

☐ Growing in the profession.

The mediocre teacher tells. The good teacher explains. The superior teacher demonstrates. The great teacher inspires.

—William A. Ward

I find that a great part of the information I have was acquired by looking up something and finding something else on the way.

—Franklin P. Adams

MODULE 17
Becoming a Professional

RATIONALE

To become a truly professional teacher you must cultivate a wide repertoire of teaching skills and an understanding of when and how to use them in the teaching-learning situations you encounter.

To master this type of know-how, it will be necessary to learn much more of the theory behind the various methods than we have been able to discuss in these modules. To become more proficient, teachers take many different routes, such as graduate study, workshops, independent study, curriculum committee work, action research, and professional conferences. The essential point is that all of them are working to improve teaching competencies. You are never too old to learn in the teaching profession. And you are never old enough to let yourself become locked into a rigid teaching style. You should always be ready to renew and revamp your style. Who knows, you may find a revised style more comfortable, and new strategies and tactics may make you more interesting. While you are still in training, it would be helpful for you to observe as many different teachers as you can to note the many different styles and strategies in action. You should also avail yourself of every opportunity that presents itself to try out various techniques and examine your performance in them.

Professional laboratory experiences provide an opportunity for you to become familiar with various teaching methods and life in school by actually observing and working with students and teachers in classrooms. It is this portion of the program that gives reality to teacher education.

In a sense, the professional laboratory experiences—particularly student teaching—are the culmination of your teacher education. But teacher education does not stop when you begin to teach. In addition to learning from experiences in school and classroom, you should also upgrade your skills and understandings by professional growth activities of various sorts. It is not too early to become familiar with these opportunities now.

This module briefly examines professional laboratory experiences and suggests ways to make them profitable. It also discusses ways by which you may examine and evaluate your own teaching, both in your laboratory experiences and later in your own classes, so that you can correct your shortcomings and build on your strengths. Finally, the module examines some of the methods you can use to grow professionally, starting now.

SPECIFIC OBJECTIVES

At the completion of this module, you should be able to:

1. Explain the purposes of the laboratory experiences of teacher preparation.
2. Describe the characteristics and roles in teacher preparation of the three types of professional laboratory experiences.
3. Explain what student teachers can do to make their student-teaching experience pleasant and profitable.
4. Describe procedures for analyzing and evaluating your lessons and teaching procedures.
5. Describe the suggestions made in this module for growing in the profession.

MODULE TEXT

Professional Laboratory Experiences

Professional laboratory experiences include the portions of your college or university program in which you observe classroom teachers in the act of teaching, participate in the conducting of classes, teach simulated classes and minilessons, microteach, and teach real classes in the student teaching or internship experience.[1] This module con-

---

[1]*Internship* can sometimes refer simply to student teaching by another name, or it can sometimes refer to a longer or more independent and paid apprenticeship period. In this module, the term *student teaching* refers to both concepts.

siders observation, participation, and student teaching experiences that occur in secondary and middle schools.

Unless you are different from most persons preparing to be teachers, your professional laboratory experiences will have the greatest impact of all your college experiences. These experiences are real, often exciting, and full of opportunities for creative learning and application of what you have learned. They provide a milieu in which you can experiment with different styles and strategies and develop skills in the various techniques of teaching.

Observation

Most programs for teacher preparation provide opportunities to observe teachers and students in the public schools. Often, a portion of the observation will occur in a middle school, and then in a junior or senior high school, and then sometimes in alternative schools. Programs may also allow students to observe how other students teach, as well as provide demonstration lessons. This variety of observation can give you insights into relations between students and teachers; the various backgrounds of students you will teach; and the effects of different teaching strategies, different instructional materials, and different styles of teaching. The more different styles you observe, the better will be your understanding of the potentials of the various approaches.

Some ways to make your observation profitable include:

☐ Concentrate on watching the students in the classrooms. Note the range of differences in appearances, abilities, and interests that appear in a single class. Note how students react to different teaching approaches. Which teaching techniques and materials excite their interest and which engender boredom? Follow a student's schedule all day long. How does it feel to go through the routine of being a middle or secondary school student today? (It may be quite different from what you remember.) Try to think of ways that you as a teacher could make the classes more enjoyable and profitable.

☐ Observe the ways different teachers handle their classes. How do they get their classes started? How do they bring their classes to a conclusion? How do they develop the important points? How do they create interest? How do they get students involved in their own learning? How do they provide for differences in students? What techniques for motivation, probing, discovery, inquiry, closure, and reinforcement are used? How do students respond to the various tactics? What procedures are used to establish and maintain classroom control?

☐ Observe the climate of each class. What seems to be the cause of the climate? Is the class teacher-centered or student-centered? Is the class diffusely structured or centrally structured? Is the student morale high or low, and what seems to be the cause for the state of the morale?

☐ Give particular attention to the manner in which the teachers implement various strategies and the students' responses to each of the strategies.

Participation

In student teaching, after a period of observation and participation, the teacher trainee gradually begins to take over some of the classes and other duties that make up a teacher's load, under the supervision of one or more cooperating teachers as well as a college supervisor. The experience is expected to develop into a genuine simulation of teaching reality. The cooperating teacher, the professional of record, always retains ultimate responsibility for what happens in the classroom, but the intent is for the student teacher to assume as much responsibility as possible—as though the class were fully his or hers to lead. The legal, instructional, and pedagogical ramifications of this activity are such that only a simulation of reality is possible. But the greater the effort to approximate the real thing and the greater the sensitivity to the goals of the activity on the part of everyone concerned, the more rewarding the student teaching experience will be. For most teacher candidates, student teaching is the capstone of their teacher preparation program. It can be both exciting and rewarding. It can also be both difficult and trying.

STUDENT TEACHING

Perhaps the first thing to remember about student teaching is that, like observation and participation, it is intended to be a learning experience. It is in student teaching that the beginning teacher first applies the theories and techniques learned in college classes to real teaching situations. Here you will have an opportunity to try out various strategies and techniques so as to begin to build a wide repertoire of teaching skills and to develop an effective, comfortable teaching style.

Student teaching is also a time of trial and error. Do not be discouraged if you make mistakes or your lessons do not go well at first. If you were already a skilled teacher, you would not need the practice. Making mistakes is part of the learning process. Use them as a means for improvement. With the help of your cooperating teacher and supervisor, try to analyze your teaching to find what steps to take to do better next time. Perhaps your execution of the strategies and techniques was faulty; perhaps you used a strategy or technique inappropriate for the particular situation. Such errors can be quite easily remedied as you gain experience.

As a general rule, errors of omission are often worse than errors of commission. The latter generally reflects faulty judgment or inexperience. They do, however, just as often confirm an indication of good will, commendable effort, and a willingness to try. The worst omission errors most often stem from lack of zeal: failure to devote enough time to planning adequately, neglect of previewing audiovisual equipment, lack of research on the topic of presentation, and the like.

In this connection, do not be quick to reject a teaching strategy or technique that fails for you. As you become more skilled in using various strategies and techniques, you will find that all have their uses. Do not allow yourself to become one of those boring teachers who can teach in only one way. Instead, if a strategy or technique does not work for you, examine the situation to see what went wrong. Then try it again in a new situation after brushing up your technique and correcting your faults.

Since student teaching is a time for learning and for getting the mistakes out of your system, it is important not to become discouraged. Many student teachers who do miserably for the first weeks blossom into excellent teachers by the end of the student-teaching period. On the other hand, if things seem to go well at first, do not become overconfident. Many beginners, too soon satisfied with the seeming success of early classes, become complacent and doom themselves to mediocrity. In any case, examine your classes to see what went well and what went wrong. Then try to correct your faults and capitalize on your strengths.

After your initial anxiety and nervousness wear off, use your student teaching as an opportunity to try out new strategies and techniques. Avoid becoming a clone of the cooperating teacher or a replica of the old-time teacher who gave lectures, heard recitations, and sometimes did very little else. But work out the new approaches and techniques you wish to try with your cooperating teacher before you try them. Usually the cooperating teacher can show you how to get the most out of your new ventures and warn you of pitfalls you might encounter.

Make haste slowly as you try new methods and approaches. Things will go more smoothly if you continue with the same strategies and tactics to which the class is accustomed. Students used to a particular style may not readily adapt to innovations. This reluctance is especially bad when the teacher confronts students with quick changes in the length and difficulty of homework assignments or an abrupt switch from prescriptive, didactic methods to discovery and inquiry approaches.

Sometimes the cooperating teacher may think it necessary to veto what seems to you to be your best ideas. Usually there is a sound basis for the veto. It may be, in the cooperating teacher's view, that these ideas will not serve the objectives well, or they may require time, money, or equipment not available to you, or violate school policy, or seem unsuited to the age and abilities of the students. Sometimes your ideas may be rejected because they conflict with the cooperating teacher's pedagogical and philosophical beliefs or prejudices. Whatever the objection, you should accept the decision gracefully and concentrate on procedures the cooperating teacher finds acceptable. After all, the classes and the instruction are the cooperating teacher's responsibility.

Furthermore, you need to become a master of many techniques. If you master the techniques and style your cooperating teacher recommends now, you will have begun to assemble a suitable repertoire of teaching skills. Later, when you are teaching your own classes, you can expand your repertoire by trying out other strategies and styles you find appealing.

To be successful in student teaching requires more study and preparation than most students think possible. To do the job, you must know what you are doing, so pay particular attention to your planning. Bone up carefully on the content of your lessons and units and lay them out carefully step by step. Leave nothing to chance. Check and double-check to be sure you have your facts straight, that your teaching strategies and tactics will yield your objectives, that you have the necessary teaching materials on hand, that you know how to use them, and so on. It is most embarrassing when you find you cannot solve the problems you have given to the students, or cannot answer the students' questions, or cannot find the equipment you need, or cannot operate the projector. So try to be ready for any contingency. As a rule, you should ask your cooperating teacher to approve your plan before you become committed to it. If the cooperating teacher suggests changes, incorporate them into the plan and try to carry them out.

Planning lessons and units for student teaching is no easy task. To become really sure of your subject matter and to think out how to teach it in the short time available during your student teaching is asking a lot of yourself. Therefore, prepare as much as you can before the student teaching period begins. Try to find out what topics you will be expected to teach and master the content before you report for your student teaching. Then when you start student teaching you can concentrate on planning and teaching, confident that you have a firm understanding of the content. Many students have botched their student teaching because they had to spend so much time learning the content they never had time to learn how to teach! Remember, middle and secondary school classes are not replicas of college classes. The content of what you must teach will probably be quite different from what you have been studying in college lately. You will need time to master it. If you take the time before your student teaching starts, you will have a considerable advantage.

Because student teaching is difficult and time demanding, most teacher education institutions recommend that student teachers not combine student teaching with other courses or outside work. If you have to work to eat, you must, but very few people are able both to hold down a job and perform creditably in their student teaching. Outside jobs, additional courses, trying to master inadequately learned subject content, and preparing classes are just too much for one ordinary person to do well at the same time. It is true that many successful teachers have moonlighted on outside jobs or on course work for advanced degrees. It is also true that many undergraduate students have maintained high grades with a full load of college courses and at the same time have worked full time in the evenings. But the student teaching experience is so unique in the many demands that it makes on a student teacher's time as to be virtually impossible for you to perform in a superior fashion if you bog yourself down with outside responsibilities at this crucial early part of your career.

Usually student teaching starts with a few days of observing. This gives you a few days to get ready for actually teaching. Use this time to become familiar with the classroom situation. Get to know the students. Learn their names. Borrow the teacher's seating chart and study it and the students as the class proceeds. In this way you will learn to associate names with faces and also have some inkling of the sort of persons with whom you will soon be dealing. Learn the classroom routines and other details of classroom management. Familiarize yourself with the types of teaching, activities, and assignments that the class is used to so that you can gradually assume the classroom teaching responsibility without too much disruption. Remember, at first students are likely to resent too much deviation from what they have come to expect.

In your observation of the efforts of your cooperating teacher in the act of teaching, keep in mind the following topics and questions:

□ *Aims.* What were the aims of the lesson? How did the teacher make the students aware of them? Were the aims achieved?

□ *Homework.* Did the teacher make a homework assignment? At what point in the lesson was the assignment made? How did the assignment relate to the day's work? How was the assignment from the previous day handled? How did the teacher deal with students who failed to submit completed work? How much time did the teacher spend on the assignment for the next day? Did the students appear to understand the assignment?

□ *Review.* How much of the period was devoted to review of the previous lesson? Did the teacher make any effort to fit the review into the day's lesson? How did the teacher conduct the review—question and answer, student summarization of important points?

□ *Methods.* What various methods were used by the teacher in the day's lesson? Did the teacher lecture? For what length of time? How did the teacher shift from one method to the next? How did the teacher motivate the students to attend? Was any provision made for individual differences among the students? Was any provision made for student participation in the lesson? Were the students kept busy during the entire period? Did any disciplinary problems arise? How did the teacher dispose of them?

□ *Miscellaneous.* Was the teacher's voice pleasant enough to listen to? Did the teacher have any distracting idiosyncratic habits? Were lighting and ventilation adequate? What system did the teacher use for checking attendance?

□ *Evaluation.* How could this lesson have been improved?

Relations in Professional Laboratory Experiences

When you take part in professional laboratory experiences in school, you are in a rather odd position. In a sense, you are neither teacher nor student; yet, in another sense, you are both teacher and student. Many college students have found this position trying. Therefore, included here are a number of suggestions that may make your life a little more pleasant during your laboratory experiences. Although these suggestions apply to observation, participation, and student teaching experience, they are somewhat loaded toward student teaching, the most difficult of the professional laboratory experiences. These suggestions are not meant to be preachy. Rather, they are conclusions drawn from years of observing and trying to help student teachers. It is hoped that they will point out some of the pitfalls in student teaching and ways to make this experience a success.

In professional laboratory experiences your relationship with your cooperating teacher is critical. You should concentrate on keeping these relationships friendly and professional.

Whether you like it or not, student teaching—and to a lesser degree, observation and participation—is a job as well as a learning experience, and the cooperating teacher and college supervisor are your bosses. Ordinarily, you can expect them to be nice bosses who will not only strive to help you in every way they can but will also be tolerant of your mistakes. They are bosses, however, and must be treated as such.

They will have pretty high expectations of you. Not only will they expect you to have an adequate command of the subject to be taught, they will also expect you to have the following:

1. A basic understanding of the nature of learners and learning.

2. A repertoire of teaching skills and some competence in them.

3. A supply of instructional materials.

4. An adequate understanding of the process of evaluation and some skill in its techniques.

Do not disappoint them. You should check yourself in each of these areas. If you believe yourself deficient in any of them, now is the time to bring yourself up to par. Student teaching is too hectic to take time out for learning and collecting what you already should have learned and collected.

Your colleagues in the school will also expect you to be a professional—a beginning professional, it is true, but a professional just the same. You will be expected to do your job carefully without carping, criticizing, or complaining. Carry out instructions carefully. Keep to the routines of the school. If next week's lesson plans are due at the department head's office before the beginning of school Friday morning, make sure that they are there. Be prompt with all assignments. Never be late or absent unless previous arrangements have been made. Pay attention to details. Fill out reports, requisitions, and so on, accurately and on time. Be meticulous in the preparation of your unit and lesson plans. Never approach a class unprepared. Be sure you know your content and exactly how you plan to teach it. Nothing upsets cooperating teachers more than classes that do not go well because the student teacher was not sufficiently prepared.

Build a reputation for being responsible and dependable by carrying out your assignments faithfully and accurately. Sometimes student teachers fail because they do not understand what their responsibilities are or how to carry them out. Study the teacher's handbook, observe the cooperating teacher, and heed the cooperating teacher's instructions so that you will know just what to do and when and how. If you are uncertain about what to do or how to do it, ask, even though it may embarrass you to admit ignorance. It is much better to admit you do not understand than to keep quiet and reveal it.

Be a self-starter. Teachers, principals, and college supervisors are impressed by evidences of initiative. Volunteer to do things before you have to be asked. Willingly take on such tasks as reading papers and correcting tests. Take part in cafeteria supervision, extracurricular activities, attendance at PTO meetings, and the like. Participating in such activities will give you experience and expertise in these areas of the teacher's job and will also indicate to your colleagues that you are a professionally minded person who does not shun the nitty gritty.

Remember that you are being evaluated all the time that you are student teaching, so try to be just a little more accurate, a little more prompt, a little more precise, a little more dependable, and a little more willing than in other college activities.

During your professional laboratory experiences you are a guest of the school in which you are observing, participating, or student teaching. Your place in the school is not a right, but a privilege. Behave in a way that will make you and succeeding student teachers welcome. As quickly as you can, adapt yourself to the culture of the school and conform to the mores of the school as they apply to teachers. Do not stand on your rights—as a guest of the school you may not have many—but concentrate on your responsibilities. Try as soon as possible to become a member of the school staff and to set up pleasant relationships with your cooperating teacher and other colleagues.

Refrain from criticizing the school, its administration, or its teachers. Be particularly careful about what you say to teachers and other student teachers. If some things in a situation bother you, seek the advice of your college supervisor before you do anything drastic. If there is to be any friction, let the college supervisor absorb the sparks. It is his or her job to see that everything runs smoothly and that you get the best learning experience possible in your laboratory experience.

Do not under any circumstances discuss school personnel with the students. Often students tell student teachers how much better they are than their regular teachers. Do not respond to such bait. To allow yourself to discuss a teacher's performance and personality with a student can lead only to trouble.

Professional laboratory experiences, particularly student teaching, throw students and cooperating teachers into a closeness that can be greatly rewarding and also extremely difficult. From the point of view of the cooperating teacher, the student teaching period presents a threat in several ways. To allow a newcomer to interfere in the smooth running of the class is risky. More than one teacher has had to work extra long hours to repair the damage done to a class by an incompetent student teacher. Teachers who are insecure may find the presence of any other adult in their classes threatening; the presence of a student teacher critically observing the teacher's work can be particularly disturbing. So avoid any appearance of opposing or competing with the cooperating teacher. Consult with him or her before you undertake anything and follow his or her advice and instructions carefully. If you believe those instructions or advice are wrong, your only recourse is to consult with the college supervisor.

Above all, listen to what the cooperating teacher tells you! Many teachers (and college supervisors as well) complain that student teachers do not listen to what they are told. Often student teachers do not listen because they are so caught up in their problems that they find it difficult to concentrate on anything else. They may be too busy justifying their behavior or explaining away what has gone amiss in their classes to hear someone else's criticism. Although it may require some effort, try to hear what the cooperating teacher has to say and follow through on the suggestions. Teachers find it exasperating when student teachers carry on in unwanted ways in spite of the teacher's long and detailed instructions or explanations of what should be done.

As with any public figure in the community, you can expect that you and your performance will be discussed by students as well as the parents in the community. Usually, the students' comments are far removed from the teacher's ears but sometimes chance remarks are caught as you walk through the halls or as students are leaving the room. Let them not turn your head because often these remarks are quite flattering. At the same time, guard against that feeling of depression that usually follows derogatory statements about your efforts or intentions. Whether you are praised or denounced, try to assume an objective attitude and use the comments for the inherent value they may possess. Remind yourself that you cannot always be all things to all people, nor should you even try to be. Your personality, the school regulations, and the classroom procedures will not let you be equally appealing to or effective with all of your students. You must expect that in the process of upholding your standards you will leave an occasional student dissatisfied. Only by keeping your reactions under control will you be able to preserve a positive feeling for your job.

Relationships with Students

Your relationships with students may make or break you in a laboratory situation, so try to make them as friendly and purposeful as possible. Students like teachers who treat them with respect and whom they can respect. Therefore, treat them courteously and tactfully but at the same time require of them standards of behavior and academic productivity reasonably close to those established by the regular teacher. Show that you have confidence in them and expect them to do well. Let them know you are interested in them and in their activities.

The best way to earn the students' respect and liking is to do a good job of teaching and to treat all students fairly and cordially. Do not, however, become overfriendly. Be friendly, not chummy. Your role is not to be a buddy, but to be a teacher. Seek respect rather than popularity. Remember that you are an adult, not a kid. The students will respect and like you more if you act your age and assume your proper role.

Analysis of Teaching

The examined life is always better than the unexamined life, philosophers tell us. If you know yourself, there is little doubt that the knowledge is beneficial to you as a teacher. Therefore, those who wish to become really professional should examine themselves and their teaching every once in a while. By so doing, it may be possible to detect weaknesses in your classroom behavior and teaching techniques that you can remedy and to discover unrealized strengths on which you can capitalize. This section of the module discusses a number of methods by which to examine your own teaching behavior in the classroom. Most of the procedures you will study here are rather simple methods of analyzing or evaluating teaching. It is hoped that they will not only give you a basis for examining your own teaching but will also serve as a means for reviewing some of the strategies and tactics discussed in earlier modules.

Analyzing Your Lessons

To make the most of your student teaching, you should occasionally stop to examine your lessons. The simplest way to do this is to stop and think back over a lesson and ask yourself how it went and why. Usually, it is best to pick good lessons to examine so that you can see what you are doing well. The practice is good for the ego and tends to reinforce your good traits. From time to time, you will want to examine classes that failed, to see if you can figure out why they did not go well. If you are having trouble with a class, such an analysis may help you spot the difficulty and correct the errors that you may have been making.

In this type of analysis, as you review your lesson, ask yourself such questions as: What went well? What went badly? Why? What could I have done to improve the lesson? Next time, how should I handle this type of class? A questionnaire, such as that portrayed in Figure 17.1, should prove helpful in this reviewing of your procedures. Rating scales and checklists are also useful, but probably not as useful as the open-ended questionnaire. Figure 17.2 is an example of a rating scale used in rating the teaching experiences of student teachers. Figure 17.3 is a rating scale devised by a group of prospective student teachers as a means of rating their teaching during student teaching. Perhaps you could develop a better one yourself.

Another way to check on your teaching is to consider at what level your students have learned. According to Bradfield and Moredock, there are five levels of performance. These levels are set forth in Figure 17.4. Ideally, the students should attain the highest levels of learning in your units. Examine your teaching. Is it the type that should bring students to this high level of learning? Or does it handcuff them to the lower levels?

FIGURE 17.1
Self-Analysis of a Lesson.

Use this form to analyze the class you thought went best this day.

1. Do you feel good about this class? Why or why not?
2. In what way was the lesson most successful?
3. If you were to teach this lesson again, what would you do differently? Why?
4. Was your plan adequate? In what ways would you change it?
5. Did you achieve your major objectives?
6. Was the class atmosphere pleasant, productive, and supportive?
7. Were there signs of strain or misbehavior? If so, what do you think was the cause?
8. How much class participation was there?
9. Which students did extremely well?
10. Were there students who did not learn? How might you help them?
11. Were the provisions for motivation adequate?
12. Was the lesson individualized so that students had opportunities to learn according to their abilities, interests, and needs?
13. Did the students have any opportunities to think?

FIGURE 17.2
Criteria for an Educational
Experience (Source: J. A.
Vanderpol, Jersey City
State College, unpublished
manuscript.)

Column 1—insert *M* for much, or *S* for some, or *L* for little, or *N* for none.
Column 2—insert *A* for all children, *M* for most children, *F* for few children, *N* for no children.
Column 3—list specific next steps the teacher will take to improve the learning experience.

	1	2	3
1. What intellectual experiences were involved?			
a. Information-getting (fact-finding and compiling)?			
b. Organizing facts into own patterns (reasoning)?			
c. Judging, evaluating, applying criteria?			
d. Problem-solving (inventing criteria)?			
e. Creative thinking?			
(cf. also item 9)			
2. Did the learning experience utilize emotional powers?			
a. Wholesome and self-expressive interest in the ideas or end-product of the work?			
b. Wholesome and self-expressive interest in the activity?			
c. Wholesome and self-expressive interest in the persons or group?			
3. Did the learning experience give opportunity for realistic relating by each child?			
a. to individual peers?			
b. to peer groups?			
c. to teacher and other adults?			
4. Did the learning experience promote realistic self-esteem?			
a. Awareness of own feelings?			
b. Recognizing own purposes or goals?			
c. Finding ways to effectively fulfill "a" or "b"?			
d. Realistic awareness of effect of powers and imitations?			
e. Realistic awareness of effect of own words and behavior upon others?			
f. Increased awareness of what he wants from situation to situation (i.e., of own self-expressive interest)?			
g. Realistic viewing of own competences (present and in near future)?			
h. Realistic, independent ideas of self-worth?			
i. Realistic awareness of learnings needed next?			
5. Did the learning experience promote improved behaviors in significant life situations?			
a. Family?			
b. Social groups?			
c. Civic competences?			
(1) Voting			
(2) Study of public problems			
(3) Organizing action groups			
6. Did the learning experience involve choosing?			
a. Ability to make critical choice?			
b. Ability to explain and support choice?			
c. Consideration of the consequences of own decision upon self and upon others?			

	1	2	3
7. Did the learning experience improve understanding of how own mind works?			
a. Such mind-needs as "who, how, what, why, when, where, so what"?			
b. Basic outlines or structures of ideas (peg ideas) into which many future ideas will be organized?			
c. Logical reasoning patterns such as "if. . ., then. . ." thinking; or of "Are there any alternative answers"?			
d. Examining evidence or making careful generalizations or asking for needed "date"?			
e. Recognizing own bias or error or mistaken idea?			
f. Considering what thoughts, feelings, and actions will be changed in the future?			
g. Applying the new learning or idea to many situations or kinds of ideas?			
h. Increased readiness for "more of same" ideas or activities?			
8. Did the learning experience promote realistic concepts of others?			
a. Awareness of others' feelings?			
b. Recognizing others' purposes or goals?			
c. Finding ways to effectively fulfill "a" or "b"?			
d. Realistic awareness and acceptance of others' powers and limitations?			
e. Realistic expectations from others?			
f. Realistic awareness of effect of own words and behaviors upon others?			
g. Increased awareness of what he "wants" from situation to situation?			
9. What intellectual skills or competences have been forwarded?			
a. Speaking skills?			
b. Writing skills?			
c. Reading skills?			
d. Arithmetical skills?			
e. Eye-hand muscular coordination?			
f. Discriminating discussion skills?			
10. Did each student experience a feeling of achievement?			
11. Did the experience provide for teacher-student conferences and constant re-evaluations?			

FIGURE 17.3
Rating Scale Designed by
Teaching Interns

Rate yourself: 5, 4, 3, 2, 1 (5 is best)

1. Did I look O.K.?
2. Did I sound O.K.?
3. Did I make my point?
4. Was I clear?
5. Did I make them think?
6. Is my questioning technique O.K.?
7. Is my writing-board work O.K.?
8. Is my audiovisual O.K.?
9. Did the lesson develop logically?
10. Overall rating:

Another way to upgrade your teaching is to examine your lesson plans. Presumably, the better your lesson plans, the better your teaching will be. Perhaps the form included as Figure 17.5 will help you to evaluate your plans. With a little adjustment, it could be used to evaluate unit and course plans. When using this form, remember that all the characteristics may not be necessary for every lesson plan, but in the long run teachers whose lessons do not meet these criteria cannot be fully effective.

FIGURE 17.4
Levels of Performance
(Source: James M. Bradfield
and H. Stewart Moredock,
*Measurement and Evaluation
in Education,* New York:
Macmillan Publishing Co.,
1957, p. 204.)

Level	Performance
I	*Imitating, duplicating, repeating.* This is the level of initial contact. Student can repeat or duplicate what has just been said, done, or read. Indicates that student is at least conscious or aware of contact with a particular concept or process.
II	*Level I, plus recognizing, identifying, remembering, recalling, classifying.* To perform on this level, the student must be able to recognize or identify the concept or process when encountered later, or to remember or recall the essential features of the concept or process.
III	*Levels I and II, plus comparing, relating, discriminating, reformulating, illustrating.* Here the student can compare and relate this concept or process with other concepts or processes and make discriminations. He or she can formulate in his own words a definition, and can illustrate or give examples.
IV	*Levels I, II, and III, plus explaining, justifying, predicting, estimating, interpreting, making critical judgments, drawing inferences.* On the basis of understanding of a concept or process, student can make explanations, give reasons, make predictions, interpret, estimate, or make critical judgments. This performance represents a high level of understanding.
V	*Levels I, II, III, and IV, plus creating, discovering, reorganizing, formulating new hypotheses, new questions, and problems.* This is the level of original and productive thinking. The student's understanding has developed to such a point that he or she can make discoveries that are new to him or her and can restructure and reorganize knowledge on the basis of the new discoveries and new insights.

1. The Objective
   a. The objective is clearly stated.
   b. The objective is measurable.
   c. The objective is pertinent to the unit and course.
   d. The objective is worthwhile.
   e. The objective is suitable to the students' age and grade level.
   f. The objective can be achieved in the time alloted.
   g. The objective can be attained in different degrees and/or amounts.
   h. The objective is relevant to the students' lives.

2. The Procedure or Suggested Activities
   a. The suggested activities will stimulate students' thinking.
   b. The suggested activities will produce the objectives.
   c. The procedure is outlined in sufficient detail to be followed easily.
   d. The procedure allows for individual differences.
      (1) choice in required work
      (2) optional work for enrichment
      (3) encouragement of initiative
   e. The activities in the procedure are interesting and appealing enough to arouse student motivation.
   f. The activities relate to
      (1) the aims of the students
      (2) the needs of the students
      (3) work in other courses
      (4) extracurricular life
      (5) out-of-school life
      (6) community needs and expectancies.

FIGURE 17.5
Form for Evaluating Lesson Plans

Audio and Video Feedback

Both audio- and videotapes of your classes can be a great help to you as you examine your teaching and personality. Although at first the presence of the tape recorder or camera may make you nervous and self-conscious, the feeling will soon wear off. Then the camera or recorder can get a good record of how you look and sound as you teach. You can and should use this record as a basis for detailed analysis of your teaching, but just listening to and seeing yourself may give you important insights into your own teaching behavior. If your self-observation is done thoughtfully and critically, it will, of course, be more rewarding than if it is superficial. Using a simple questionnaire in which you ask yourself such questions as the following may make your self-observation more useful:

What are my best points?

What points are fairly good?

What points are not so good?

Are my explanations clear?

Do I speak well and clearly?

Do I speak in a monotone?

Do I slur my words?

Do my sentences drop off so that ends are difficult to hear?

Do I involve everyone in the class or do I direct my teaching only to a few?

Are my questions clear and unambiguous?

Do I dominate class discussions?

Do I allow certain students to dominate the class?

FIGURE 17.6
Types of Teaching
Activities Checklist (Five-
Second Interval Tallies)

TEACHING OPERATION	Tallies
Motivating Planning Informing Leading discussion Disciplining Counseling Evaluating Other	

According to one analysis, there are seven major types of teaching operations: motivating, planning, informing, leading discussion, disciplining, counseling, and evaluating. One way to evaluate your teaching would be to check on a form, such as that shown in Figure 17.6, the type of teaching you were doing every five seconds in one of your classes. In this form an eighth category has been added for operations that do not seem to fit into any of the seven listed.

A usually more profitable use of the recording device is to apply interaction analysis techniques to recording of your own teaching. Such self-evaluation may be more illuminating than simple critical listening to your recordings or hearing the criticisms and comments of an observer.

INTERACTION ANALYSIS

There are a number of methods by which one can analyze the student-teacher interaction in a class. All of these methods require the services of either an observer or an audio- or video-recorder. Interaction analysis is valuable because it gives you an indication of just who is doing the talking in the class. From it you can learn whether or not the class is teacher-dominated or student-dominated, free and open or repressive, and whether the teaching style is direct or indirect—in short, the classroom atmosphere and type of learning that is going on. As a rule of thumb, you can safely assume that when classes are satisfactory, the following take place:

1. The interaction will show that students actively participate at least half of the time. (Teachers who find themselves to be talking more than half the time should check their procedures.)

2. As far as possible, every student participates in some way. (Classes that are dominated by a few students are not satisfactory.)

3. A good share of the class time is given over to thoughtful, creative activity rather than to mere recitation of information by either teacher or students.

Interaction analysis schemes vary from the simple to the complex. Some, such as the Flanders system, require that the observation be done by trained observers and that upon completing the observation, the observer arranges findings into a matrix from which one can tell not only what happened but what the atmosphere of the class was. Such systems can give you an excellent picture of the interaction in the classroom that may lead to important insights into your own teaching. If you tape-record the class, it is possible to apply the analysis to the class without the use of an outside observer. Therefore, it would be advantageous for you to learn how to use this system of interaction analysis. Unfortunately, there is not enough space to go into the procedure in detail in this module.

Even though they are not so useful as the more sophisticated methods, simple interaction analysis techniques can be truly helpful. The picture they give is not as clear, but they will show up glaring faults and give indications of more subtle elements of the classroom interaction and atmosphere.

Probably the simplest type of classroom interaction analysis is for an observer to mark down on a sheet of paper every time the teacher talks and every time a pupil talks, such as:

T P T T T P T T T P P T T

This record shows how much the teacher talks as compared to how much the students talk, although it will not show how long they talk. If you tape-record your class, you can do this analysis yourself.

A more complex refinement of this technique is for an observer to sit at the back of the class and to record the number of times each person speaks. This technique gives you a much clearer picture of what is happening in the class. The disadvantage of this technique is that it requires an outside observer. Neither audio- nor videotapes of the type teachers could procure in the ordinary classroom situation would be usable for such an analysis. Figure 17.7 is an illustration of the tallying by this method of interaction analysis. In this figure, the teacher is represented by a circle, and the students by squares. Exercise 17.1 will help you think about this figure.

Another version of the form of analysis just described is for the observer to record who is talking every five seconds. This variation of the tallying approach has the advantage of showing what persons are interacting and how much they talk, though it does not give as complete a picture as the Verbal Interaction Category System (V.I.C.S.) or Flanders analysis system.

Some supervisors use a simplified version of the Flanders system that does not require the use of a matrix. In this version of the system the observer simply records, at regular intervals, whether the teacher or a student is talking, and the nature of the talk. Flanders has divided the talk into 10 categories. Teacher talk he has divided into talk designed to influence students indirectly and talk designed to influence students directly. Under indirect influence teacher talk he includes 4 subcategories:

1. Talk in which the teacher accepts the student's feelings in a nonthreatening manner.
2. Talk in which the teacher praises or encourages the student's performance or behavior.
3. Talk in which the teacher accepts, uses, or builds on the student's ideas.
4. Talk in which the teacher asks questions designed to elicit ideas.

In direct influence teacher talk Flanders includes:

5. Lectures and teacher talks in which the teacher presents information and ideas.
6. Orders, commands, and gives directions that students are expected to follow.
7. Criticizes student behavior, reprimands, and gives explanations justifying class procedures.

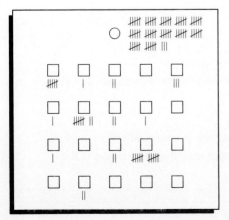

FIGURE 17.7
A Form for Interaction
Analysis

FIGURE 17.8
Interaction Analysis Check
Sheet

	Category	Tallies
Teacher Talk	Accepts Feeling Praises or Encourages Accepts or Uses Ideas of Students Asks Questions Lectures Gives Directions Criticizes	
Student Talk	Student Response Student Initiation	
	Silence or Confusion	

Student talk in this type of instruction analysis is limited to two categories:

8. Student responses to the teacher.

9. Student-initiated talk.

This type of interaction analysis also provides for a 10th category for times when no one is speaking or if there is a confusing babble as at the beginning or end of a class period or during laboratory or small-group discussion sessions.[2]

To record the interaction according to this simplified version of the Flanders system use a form such as that shown in Figure 17.8.

Evaluating Specific Teaching Techniques

Evaluating Your Discussions

To improve your skill in using class discussions, you should analyze the discussions that you lead. It is possible to do this in armchair fashion, but it would be more productive to react to a tape recording of the discussion. A self-evaluation form, similar

FIGURE 17.9
Self-Evaluation Form for
Discussion Leaders

A.

1. Did I have a legitimate objective?

2. Were the objectives suitable for the discussion technique?

3. Did I get good participation?

4. Did I encourage participation or did I tend to cut people off?

5. Did I keep from letting people dominate?

6. Did I encourage the shy, timid, etc.?

7. Did I keep the group to the subject?

8. Did I domineer or dominate?

9. In what did I best succeed?

10. In what was I least successful?

11. Did I solicit evocative questions and tentative solutions?

12. Did I summarize conclusions or positions so as to follow through and tie the discussion together?

B.

1. Identify the techniques that seemed to make the discussion effective.

2. Identify the techniques that seemed to detract from the effectiveness of the discussion.

---

[2]Edmund J. Amidon and Ned A. Flanders, *The Role of the Teacher in the Classroom* (Minneapolis, MN: Paul S. Amidon and Associates, 1963), p. 15.

EXERCISE 17.1   REVIEWING INTERACTION ANALYSIS

The purpose of this exercise is to check your comprehension of the meaning of interaction analysis. Answer each of the following questions, then compare your responses with your classmates. Resolve any differences.

1. If a classroom analysis of one of your typical classes consists almost entirely of Ts, what would it show about your teaching?

2. Does this analysis indicate that perhaps you should consider changing your style? Why or why not?

3. Do the tallies in Figure 17.7 give you any inkling about the style of the teacher in that class?

4. Do the tallies in Figure 17.7 tell you anything about class participation?

5. With respect to the tallies in Figure 17.7, what generalizations can you make about that class?

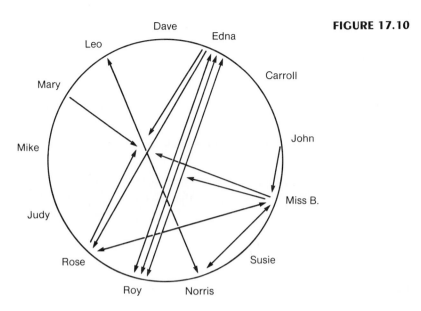

FIGURE 17.10

to the one presented as Figure 17.9, should be very helpful for spotting your weaknesses and building your strengths in leading discussions. Flowcharts that depict the course of the discussion may be even more useful. Preparing the flowchart can be entrusted to a student observer since the technique for preparing one is so simple. If the class is arranged in a circle, preparing the flowchart is easier; it is slightly less so if the class is arranged as a hollow square; but when the class is arranged in rows, making the chart becomes quite difficult. (Discussions are difficult to conduct when the students are in rows, too.) All the observer does is to make an arrow from the speaker to the person to whom he or she is speaking each time anyone speaks. A direct reply to a speaker can be noted by a double-headed arrow. Comments or questions that are directed to the group rather than to an individual are indicated by arrows that point to the center of the circle or square. An example of a flowchart showing a portion of a class discussion appears as Figure 17.10.

Figure 17.11 shows another device used to analyze class discussions. In this technique, a recorder simply tallies the number of times each person talks. There is no indication of the conversational interchanges, so this type of record does not give you as complete a picture as the flowchart does.

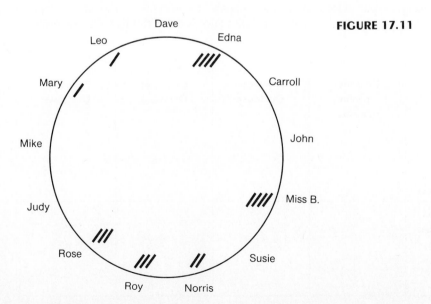

FIGURE 17.11

Questions

Questions are among the teacher's most important tools; it is important to learn how to use them well. To check on your questioning technique, you might record and observe yourself (see Module 8). Among the things you might observe are:

☐ What sorts of questions do I use?

☐ Are my questions clear?

☐ Do I ask one question at a time or do I confuse students by asking two or more questions as one?

☐ Do I ask real questions, or are my questions whiplash questions that start out as statements and then suddenly convert into questions, such as: "The point that the author was trying to get across is what?" Whiplash questions are not really fair because they give students the wrong set.

☐ Do my questions require students to use their knowledge, information, and ideas?

☐ Do I direct my questions to students or to the class as a whole?

☐ Do I wait until I have finished asking my question before calling on someone to answer it?

☐ Do I follow up my questions with probing questions to ferret out ideas, understandings, and thinking?

Most questions in a typical class are aimed at eliciting memorized facts and information. When teachers ask high-order questions, the questions are likely to be convergent questions rather than divergent or evaluative questions. Review Module 8 if you cannot remember what these are. To find out what type of questions you and your students use, a form similar to that presented as Figure 17.12 can be helpful. To use the form, an observer simply checks the appropriate column each time the teacher asks a question.

Analysis of Test Results

Analysis of students' test results can give one an inkling of the success of your teaching, providing the tests are properly designed and written. For test results to be of value for the analysis of your teaching success, the teaching objectives must be carefully defined and each test item must be aimed at a teaching objective. Once you have given and corrected the test, to analyze the test you must set up a chart that indicates what objective each test item tests, and what items each pupil got right, as in Figure 17.13. Such a chart would show you how effectively you taught by indicating how well you achieved each of your objectives. In the example, for instance, if the small sample is any indicator, the teacher evidently was quite successful with objective 1 and not so

FIGURE 17.12
A Form for Analyzing Questions

	Cognitive Memory Questions	Convergent Questions	Divergent Questions	Evaluative Questions
Teacher Questions				
Student Questions				

Key: + = correct response; 0 = incorrect response

Objective	Item	Joe	Julia	Jamaal	Juanita	Jean	Josie
1.	1	+	+	+	+	+	+
	2	+	0	+	+	+	+
	3	+	0	0	+	+	+
2.	4	+	0	0	0	0	+
	5	+	+	+	0	0	0
	6	0	+	0	+	0	0

FIGURE 17.13
Example of Test Item Analysis Form

successful with objective 2. This type of analysis is also an excellent tool by which to diagnose the progress of the various students in the class.

Student Evaluation

You can learn much from the students' opinions of your teaching. Just watching their reactions will be enlightening. An eager, enthusiastic, attentive class is a good sign; an apathetic, inattentive, antagonistic class is not. Another method by which to gather student evaluations is to use a simple questionnaire or opinion sampling. Some teachers make a practice of collecting such data at the end of the school year, but if you are to capitalize on the information, perhaps it would be better to collect it earlier in the year. Whenever you do it, make sure that the evaluations are entirely anonymous. To preserve anonymity, use check sheets rather than handwritten comments. Sometimes, however, students will react well to open-ended, free response questions if the questions ask for constructive criticism concerning ways to make the course more effective.

Growing in the Profession

Surveying Employment Prospects

Early in your teacher preparation program you should start thinking about your first job and your career in teaching. If you have not done so already, you should investigate the job market. At the moment this is being written, there appears to be a change settling in regarding the availability of jobs. The decline in student enrollments of the 1970s and early 1980s precipitated a drastic reduction in the number of candidates interested in a teaching career. Of late, however, it appears that the demand has caught up with and in many cases has surpassed the supply of teachers, which had seriously dwindled. Salaries in teaching are rising. Several states have made teaching and teacher preparation items of immediate concern.

Similarly, you should try to pick courses that will prepare you for the subject matter you are likely to have to teach in middle or secondary schools. Courses in writing, composition, and American literature are more likely to be useful to beginning English teachers than Gothic literature, for instance.

In times of tight employment it may be wise to consider the advisability of seeking a graduate degree or working as a substitute teacher for a year or two. Both of these experiences will make you more hirable. Being a substitute teacher has the added advantage of giving you an inside track when opportunities in the system open up.

Take advantage of the facilities of your college placement service early. You will probably find them anxious to coach you on ways to find, apply for, and obtain jobs, and also to tell you how you can best prepare for the jobs that are becoming available. Similarly, education professors are usually anxious to coach students on such matters as finding job opportunities, writing letters of application, securing favorable recommendations, job interviewing, preparing for the types of jobs available, and so on. The sooner you become knowledgeable in these areas, the better chances you will have of finding congenial employment when the time comes.

You should, as soon as you can, become familiar with the certification requirements of the state or states in which you hope to teach, just as you should become familiar with the college graduation requirements. Usually you can be confident that your college program will meet the local certification requirements for your major. Studying the certification requirements may show you how to become certifiable in more fields and in other parts of the country.

Professional Memberships

Become familiar with the teacher associations in your field as early as you can. Organizations such as The National Council of Teachers of English, The National Council for the Social Studies, and the National Council of Teachers of Mathematics publish journals and monographs that can help you become familiar with what is going on in the teaching field. They also provide opportunities for fellowship with leading teachers and supervisors. As a rule, local affiliates of these organizations welcome teacher education students to their meetings. These meetings provide opportunities to meet important professionals and to learn about the most recent developments in the teaching field.

The local affiliates of the teachers' unions (The American Federation of Teachers and the National Education Association) also provide opportunities for students to become involved in professional activities. You may find joining the union's student affiliate or attending the state or national meetings especially profitable. State and regional conventions in particular can give beginners a superb view of new professional materials and technology available. There is hardly a supplier of educational materials or equipment that does not exhibit at these conventions.

Keeping Up

Once you have begun to teach, do not become complacent. After a period of teaching some teachers become bored, frustrated, and discontented. This phenomenon attacks teachers who do not grow with the profession and so atrophy. Teaching is interesting and exciting if you approach it that way. Try to keep it so by keeping up with what is going on and by becoming active in the professional organizations. Attend workshops, institutes, and conventions that present the new methods and materials of your profession. Take graduate courses that will help you better understand your subject, your pupils, and methods of teaching. Take interest in the students and their activities. Involve yourself in curriculum revision. In short, keep yourself professionally and personally alert and active. You should begin this process now!

Try to grow personally as well as professionally. Keep your mind sharp by staying interested in many things and by becoming more expert in your field. Deepen your appreciation for your work and guard against letting it become a secondary occupation. You may find it necessary to combine your teaching with other work—either part-time work or homemaking—but do not let the other work take away from your teaching. Keep abreast of developments in your field through refresher courses, professional reading, or advanced graduate study. No matter how you do it, keep moving forward with your development of your own personality and your mastery of professional skills. Arrange to visit other teachers and interact with them about what accounts for their success. Keep yourself on the alert for new ways of doing things, new approaches to your students and your subject. Therein lies the excitement of your new profession— reaching a point of competency in your teaching, engaging in activities that bring about successful learning, and finding outlets for your creative juices that will benefit your students. Thus equipped, involve yourself in curricular revision and in short keep yourself professionally alert and alive.

HAIL AND FAREWELL

Working through these modules may have made it seem that teaching is a difficult, arduous profession. Maybe so, but it is also rewarding. Teaching done well is never dull. It can be great fun. Besides, it is important. Working with young minds will keep you on your toes. It also gives you an opportunity to influence the shaping of the future.

Teaching is a profession to be proud of. We welcome you to it!

Farber, B. A. *Crisis in Education: Stress and Burnout in the American Teacher.* San Francisco: Jossey-Bass, 1991.

Goddard, R. E. *Teacher Certification Requirements: All Fifty States.* 4th ed. Sarasota, FL: Teacher Certification Publications, 1986.

Moran, S. W. "Schools and the beginning teacher." *Phi Delta Kappan* 72(3):210–213 (November 1990).

Perrone, V. *A Letter to Teachers.* San Francisco: Jossey-Bass, 1991.

Check In the following, check the appropriate answers according to the module text.

1. Check those of the following that the cooperating teacher will expect you to have when you come to do your student teaching.

  _____ a. A command of the subject to be taught.

  _____ b. Expertise in many teaching skills.

  _____ c. A supply of instructional materials.

  _____ d. An adequate understanding of the evaluation process.

  _____ e. A well-developed teaching style.

2. To make a favorable impression on your cooperating teacher and supervisor,

  _____ a. Prepare very carefully.

  _____ b. Go right ahead with your plans without asking advice.

  _____ c. Show your expertise by criticizing the school's procedures.

  _____ d. Learn and follow the school routines.

  _____ e. Be prompt at all assignments.

  _____ f. Listen to what you are told.

  _____ g. Study the content before the class period begins.

Multiple Choice Write the letter of the most appropriate answer in the space provided.

_____ 3. When you get right down to it, college supervisors and cooperating teachers are your

  a. colleagues.

  b. assistants.

  c. bosses.

  d. collaborators.

_____ 4. As a student teacher, you are

  a. a member of the school staff.

  b. only a student.

  c. a guest of the school.

  d. on your own.

_____ 5. Most college teacher education students find that the most difficult part of their teacher education program is

  a. Theory courses.

  b. Microteaching.

  c. Participation (practicum).

  d. Student teaching.

_____ 6. To make your participation experience profitable, you should

  a. engage in as many types of experiences as you can.

  b. spend the entire period conducting classes.

  c. spend the entire period observing.

  d. focus on getting to know the students.

_____ 7. Basically, student teaching is supposed to be

  a. a testing experience.

  b. a learning experience.

  c. a trial experience.

  d. a full-fledged teaching experience.

Short Answer

8. Suppose you should try out a new teaching technique and it fails miserably for you. What should you do, according to this module?

   _____

   _____

9. According to Bradfield and Moredock, what is the highest level of teaching?

   _____

   _____

   _____

   _____

10. List four of the eight criteria for the objective included in the form for evaluating lesson plans.

    _____

    _____

    _____

11. What is the purpose of recording and playing back your lessons?

    _____

    _____

12. An interaction analysis shows that most of the class consisted of teacher-initiated talk in which the teacher gave students information and asked narrow memory questions. If this class is typical of this teacher's style:
    a. is she a direct or indirect teacher?
    b. is her style a most effective one?

    _____

    _____

    _____

13. A simple interaction analysis tally shows the following: T T T T T P T P T P T T T P T T P T T P T P T P T P.
    a. What does this show about the class?
    b. Is the class good or bad?

    _____

    _____

    _____

14. List six things you would look for in evaluating a discussion.

    _____

    _____

    _____

    _____

    _____

15. The flowchart of a discussion shows that there are only a few arrows from the teacher's position and all of these point to the center of the diagram. How would you interpret this phenomenon?

    _____

    _____

    _____

16. Why should you avoid using whiplash questions?

_____

_____

17. In what ways are cognitive memory questions, convergent questions, and divergent questions different?

_____

_____

_____

_____

_____

18. In an item analysis, we find the following:

Objective	Item	A	B	C	D	E	F
	1	+	+	+	+	+	+
1	2	+	+	+	+	+	+
	3	+	+	0	+	+	0
	4	0	0	+	0	0	0
2	5	0	0	0	0	0	0
	6	+	0	+	0	+	0

(Pupil columns: A B C D E F)

Assuming that this excerpt is typical of the entire test item analysis, what does it tell you?

_____

_____

_____

19. Identify and explain three ways that you can prepare yourself to be more hirable.

_____

_____

_____

20. Explain why this module recommends that you join a professional organization in your teaching field.

_____

_____

_____

_____

POSTTEST ANSWER KEYS

1. b, h, c	11. √	21. c	31. a
2. a, f	12.	22. a	32. c
3. e	13. √	23. c	33. d
4. b	14. √	24. b	34. c
5. d, g	15. √	25. c	35. a
6. √	16.	26. b	36. c
7. √	17. √	27. d	37. a
8.	18. c	28. b	38. d
9. √	19. a	29. b	39. d
10. √	20. a	30. c	40. a

1. a. Teachers have not really thought through what they are trying to do.
   b. Teachers have not thought about how they ought to do it so their teaching becomes inconsequential, irrelevant, and dull.

2. a. What should my objectives be?
   b. How should I try to achieve these objectives?

3. a. What do I want to accomplish?
   b. How can I accomplish it?
   c. Who is to do what?
   d. When and in what order should things be done?
   e. When will things be done?
   f. What materials and equipment will I need?
   g. How will I get things started?
   h. How shall I follow up?
   i. How can I tell how well I have accomplished my goals?
   j. Why?

4. Teachers do not ask themselves: why should the students have to study and learn this?

5. a. The curriculum.
   b. Nature of the learners.
   c. What do you have to work with?
   d. Nature of the community.
   e. What the community expects.
   f. The nature of the subject matter.

6. Will it contribute to the achievement of the objectives?

7. Does it contribute to the objectives?

8. a. Suggested objectives.
   b. Suggested content.
   c. Suggested learning activities.
   d. Suggested reading.
   e. Suggested audiovisual and other materials of instruction for a course or curriculum.

9. It makes the coordination of teaching and learning activities easier.

10. It provides not only content, but a basis for organizing the course units and sequence.

11. The only real difference is that the team must plan together. This may cause some difficulty because you may have to give in to the group's wishes even when you do not want to and you must execute your part of the group plan even when it does not please you.

12. Probably the best argument is that it seems to promote favorable motivation and attitudes.

13. A resource unit lists objectives, teaching procedures, materials, and so on, that a teacher might use when building a plan for a particular teaching unit.

14. A textbook can be used to give your course its basic outline and to form the basis of various units and lessons. It should not be the be-all and end-all of one's teaching, however.

15. a. It produces well-organized classes.
   b. It helps to produce a purposeful class atmosphere.
   c. It helps to reduce discipline problems.
   d. It ensures that you know the subject.
   e. It tends to make classes more effective.

MODULE 3

1. C	2. B	3. D	4. X
5. X	6. C	7. X	8. B
9. A	10. A	11. B	12. B
13. B	14. B	15. B	16. A
17. A*	18. B	19. A	20. B
21. G	22. G	23. S	24. G
25. S	26. S	27. G	
28. C	29. C	30. B	31. B
32. ( )	33. (√)	34. (√)	35. (√)
36. 4	37. 3	38. 2	39. 6
40. 1	41. 5		
42. c			
43. d			
44. b			
45. a			
46. B C A S X R		47. B C A S X R	
48. B A S X R		49. B A S X R	
50. A			

51. A criterion-referenced behavioral objective is one that specifies the standards of behavior required.

52. a. They prepare a clear objective for your teaching.
   b. They provide definite bases for evaluation.

53. Terminal behavior is the behavior of the learner at the completion and as a result of the instruction.

54. A covert objective is one in which the learner activity cannot be observed directly.

---

*If you predict or realize without indicating to someone else your prediction or realization, the activity is covert; if you write down or tell the prediction or realization, it is behavioral.

55. The taxonomies give a framework by which to structure your teaching so that it covers the more important types of learning.

56. a. Who?
    b. Does what?
    c. Under what conditions?
    d. How well?

57. For what purpose?

58. It is impossible to observe activity in the affective domain directly.

59. Descriptive objectives that describe the result of learning are most useful to describe general aims and goals. Since they represent covert activity they are not really useful as specific objectives except perhaps in the affective domain.

60. Specific objectives should support the more general objectives and goals.

61. A general objective, or educational goal, aim, or purpose.

62. Behavioral objectives usually make the best specific objectives.

63. Level 5, Perfection and maintenance of the psychomotor domain.

64. Level 3, Valuing of the affective domain.

65. Level 4, Analysis of the cognitive domain.

66. Level 2, Comprehension of the cognitive domain.

67. Level 3, Valuing of the affective domain.

68. Level 2, Comprehension of the cognitive domain.

69. Level 3, Application in the cognitive domain.

MODULE 4

1. a	2. a	3. d	4. d
5. d	6. a	7. b	8. c
9. b	10. c	11. d	12. a

13. Both.

14. Yes.

15. Yes, if you think it advisable.

16. Either. It is up to you. The trend at the moment is to favor behavioral objectives for everything.

17. Any four from the following:
    a. It is pertinent to the course.
    b. It centers on some major underlying issue, problem, or theme.
    c. It is not too difficult, too big, or too demanding of time or resources.
    d. It is relevant to students' lives and to the community.
    e. It is suitable to students' interests and abilities.

18. Pick four from the following:
    a. They really contribute to the larger (general) objectives of the course or unit.
    b. They should be clear to you and to your students.
    c. They should be specific enough.
    d. They should be achievable in the time and with the resources available.
    e. They should be worthwhile and seem worthwhile.
    f. They should allow for individual differences, that is, attainable in different amounts and in different ways.

19. a. Activities that motivate.
    b. Activities that tie in with past units and other course work.
    c. Planning activities.

20. a. No. They can schedule themselves during the laboratory sessions.
    b. No. They do not all have to read the same material to solve the problems, for instance.

21. The learning packet is designed more for independent, individual self-study.

22. None, really.

23. Note the requirements for 1, 2, 3, and 4 on the study guide. Then have the student indicate which level he intends to shoot for.

24. a. Problems to be solved.
    b. Activities to do.
    c. Directions for finding information needed to solve problems and for doing the activities.
    d. Optional, related activities from which to select.
    e. Information concerning readings and materials.

25. a. Rationale including overall objectives and reasons that this learning is worth study.
    b. Specific objectives.
    c. Directions for carrying out the activities to be included in the module.
    d. Materials needed for the module or directions for obtaining them.
    e. Measuring devices, such as pretests, progress tests, and posttests.

26. a. The course should be psychologically organized.
    b. The course should be compatible with the available resources.
    c. The course plan should lend itself to retention and transfer.
    d. The course content, organization and instruction should contribute to the achievement of the course objective.
    e. The course content, organization, and teaching strategies should reflect the nature of the discipline.

27. a. Determine the objectives.
    b. Determine the course content including topic, sequence, and emphasis.
    c. Decide on the time allotment.
    d. Determine basic strategies, major assignments, and materials.

28. There are more than three possibilities. Your module text mentions the following. Take your pick.
    a. The value of the learning needs to be pointed out.
    b. The ways the learning can be used needs to be pointed out.
    c. The learning should be thorough. It is better to learn a lesser amount thoroughly than a lot superficially.
    d. The student should have occasion to draw generalizations and apply them.
    e. There should be many opportunities for renewal of the learning.

29. The steps are
    a. Prepare overall course objectives.
    b. Determine the sequence of modules.
    c. Prepare general and specific objectives for the modules.
    d. Select content and learning procedures for the modules.
    e. Prepare learning packet for the modules.

30. a. Introduce course and planning.
    b. Set up limits.
    c. Set up criteria for topic selection.
    d. Select topics.
    e. Select problems to be studied in each unit.
    f. Make final decisions by discussion and consensus procedures.

31. The self-instructional package is designed to teach one small piece of content well, and in a time duration of approximately 50 minutes. Other types of learning packages usually are designed to cover more content and to take more student time. In addition, the self-instructional package is designed with one student in mind and written specifically for that student.

32. a. Specific purpose, e.g., remediation, enrichment, etc.

b. Maximum student time required about 50 minutes.

c. Write with individual student in mind.

d. Incorporate frequent learning comprehension checks.

e. Incorporate all three learning modalities.

MODULE 5

1. F. "The best laid plans of mice and men gang aft agley."

2. T. Not necessarily detailed written plans, but plans. Otherwise how do they know what to do and how to do it?

3. F. You must have more than subject matter in your head. The lesson plan outlines what and how to teach. In the beginning you had better have both a written objective and procedure.

4. T. You will develop your own style anyway. It would be nice if it should be appropriate to you.

5. F. Why not?

6. F. Not after several years.

7. T. Bring them up to date and smooth out the wrinkles.

8. F. Not really. There is no single most important element. If your overall conception is no good, the lesson plan will not save it.

9. T. Course or unit goals are usually general. Lesson plan objectives should be specific.

10. F. That is a class period. A lesson begins when you begin it and ends when you end it.

11. F. If it is a good one, why not?

12. T. Use the one that suits you and your purposes best.

13. F. This one is iffy. Probably you could find something better to do as a follow-up, but studying in class under supervision is an excellent thing.

14. T. If you have made a careful plan, it is usually best to stick with it, but you should never marry a set plan until death do you part.

15. F. Should be in outline format.

16. F. Not every lesson needs one, but most of them do.

17. F. Usually not. They are usually general unit objectives.

18. F. An outline is much more usable.

19. T. Absolutely. That's one reason for writing out plans.

20. T. A strong conclusion can clinch closure.

21. F. You ought to have an outline of the content, but it does not necessarily have to appear here.

22. F. Some classes need only a simple outline, e.g., classes featuring a film or laboratory work sessions.

23. T. Most plan books are just layout sheets.

24. T. In some schools plans for the week must be submitted the previous Friday. Those may be only layouts.

25. T. Absolutely. Why would anyone want to throw away a good thing?

26. F. Not necessarily. There are several acceptable formats.

27. F. Most plans do need introduction, development, and conclusion sections, but some lessons are simply parts of units or long-term plans.

28. T.

29. T. Of course. Lest you forget.

30. F. All teachers should write detailed lesson plans.

31. The method should be such that it helps achieve the objectives.

32. Use it to give focus to your lesson. It can be featured in the introduction, the body, or conclusion of the lesson, but wherever it is located, it should be the central idea that binds the lesson together.

33. The reasons include:
    a. To form a firm base for your lesson, i.e., clarifying what you hope to do and how you hope to do it.
    b. To give yourself security during the lesson.
    c. To have a reminder in case you forget or are distracted.
    d. To inform a substitute teacher what was planned for the lesson.
    e. To provide a base for self- or supervisor evaluation.

34. Review, introduce the next lesson.

35. At the most propitious moment, i.e, when it fits in best. Giving it at the beginning of the class may keep you from forgetting it or rushing it, but it may be more logical to give it at the end of class sometimes.

MODULE 6

1. R	6. R	11. R	16. X
2. R	7. X	12. R	17. R
3. R	8. R	13. X	18. X
4. X	9. R	14. R	19. X
5. X	10. R	15. R	20. R

21. All sorts of information. Test scores, academic record, home information, extra-curricular activities, and health information.

22. Reward.

23. A modern theory of motivation that says the effort a student is willing to spend on a task is a product of (1) the degree to which the student believes he or she can successfully complete the task (expectancy), and (2) the degree of value the student places on any reward received for task completion.

24. Betty did not achieve Objective 1. The other students did.

MODULE 7

1. X	6. R	11. R	16. R
2. X	7. X	12. R	17. R
3. R	8. R	13. R	18. R
4. X	9. R	14. R	19. X
5. R	10. R	15. X	20. R

21. Classes need order, quiet, and discipline. When anything goes (which is what the French phrase means), discipline, order, quiet, and learning go too.

22. Make the students aware of the advantages of high standards and the disadvantages of low standards. Value-clarifying techniques may help.

23. Tiresome, boring, irrelevant teaching and courses.

24. Sounds ridiculous. Try to be firm, fair, and friendly.

25. No. Rigid rules may cut down on your options too much. A few simple ones would be much better.

26. It is easier to relax after being strict than to try to become strict after being relaxed. Start off being strict and you will usually fare better.

27. Permissive teaching is supportive teaching that helps students learn and think. It is not repressive; neither is it a free-for-all. All student behavior must be correct and within the limits established by the rules. In laissez-faire teaching anything goes. The result usually is chaos, not learning.

28. Desired student behavior should be steadily recognized and reinforced. Reinforcement of good conduct and of academic work can be done in many ways, such as with the use of verbal praise, public recognition, symbolic rewards, privileges, and material rewards. Behavior that is reinforced is that behavior most likely repeated. Praise is a form of reinforcement but may not always function in that way. Generally, praise should be private, simple, and specific to the action being praised. Whole class praise is usually ineffective in accomplishing anything.

29. Mobility and proximity in the classroom, demonstrated with-it-ness and overlapping behavior, use of nonverbal gestures and eye contact, teacher on-task behavior and promptness, teacher use of silence when students are working silently, effective modeling of those behaviors expected of students, and there are many more.

30. Movement management is a process of keeping the class moving forward smoothly and briskly without interruption and digressions.

31. Rhetorical verbal questions; loud, public verbal reprimands; any punishment that hurts student's feelings or that embarrasses student; nonpurposeful detention; punishment of entire class for action of one or a few; extra academic work; lowering of academic grade; physical activity such as pushups (unless a PE class); writing as punishment; corporal punishment of any sort.

MODULE 8

1. d   3. c   5. b   7. a
2. a   4. b   6. a

8. Yes. The module suggests the following:
   a. State purpose.
   b. Be logical.
   c. Include clues to development.
   d. Avoid attempting too much.
   e. Begin with an interest catcher.
   f. Provide for repetition.
   g. Provide for real and rhetorical questions.
   h. Be as short as reasonably possible.
   i. Include humor.
   j. Give examples.
   k. Summarize at end.
   l. Tell what you are going to tell them, tell them, and tell them what you told them.

9. Convergent questions are narrow-range questions that solicit a correct answer; divergent questions are broad and open-ended questions that have no singularly correct answer; input questions are those that involve knowledge input and recall of that knowledge; processing questions require a higher level of mental operation than input, requiring that the learner process the knowledge obtained; application questions are at the highest level of mental operation, requiring the student to apply knowledge to new situations.

10. Reword, rephrase, come back again.

11. Of course.

12. Of course. The open text recitation is one of the best techniques.

13. Any of the following may help: make questions interesting, use thought-provoking questions, carefully plan your questions, de-emphasize rote learning, keep the

content meaningful, follow questions with discussions of implications, use open text recitation.

14. The teacher may be tempted to talk too much. The teacher may think that because he or she has told it, the students know it.

15. An advance organizer is a brief presentation, either written or not, describing the main ideas of the coming lesson. It establishes a student mind set.

16. Plan your questions and their wording. Ask the question first, before calling on a student. Allow at least 3 seconds of student think time before expecting a response. Be prepared to wait even longer, as long as 9 seconds. Call on an individual if necessary. Ask for clarification if necessary. Build upon student responses. Give equal attention to all students. Hold equal expectations of all. Build your questions into a sequence, beginning with low-level and progressing to higher levels of mental operation. Allow student questions. Build upon those as well. Help your students word their questions. Help them understand assumptions being made in their questions. Use questioning to develop student skill in metacognition. Use Socratic questioning when appropriate. And there are many more.

17. Much the same as number 16. Students can work in teams, as described in the module, where one student observes and reports on the thinking of another.

18. Facts are just that, facts, isolated bits of information that are accepted truths. Concepts are attempts to organize the world of objects, facts, and events into a smaller number of categories. Concepts are usually single words, such as the concept of *democracy*. Processes are those skills by which we learn and organize our learning. The processes (as identified in this module, e.g., classifying, ordering, hypothesizing, inferring, etc.) are the same, regardless of the subject field.

19. This question is open-ended, and subject to discussion.

20. This question is open-ended, and subject to discussion, but generally when knowledge of facts is important for an understanding of concepts and generalizations.

MODULE 9

1. d	2. d	3. b	4. c
5. a	6. d	7. c	8. a
9. c	10. b	11. a	12. b
13. c	14. d	15. c	16. b
17. a	18. a	19. d	20. d

MODULE 10

1. a. Good motivating qualities.
   b. Teaches and offers practice in intellectual skills.
   c. Results in more thorough learning.
   d. Involves students.

2. a. Costly in time.
   b. Costly in effort.
   c. Sometimes lead to mislearning.
   d. Not very efficient.

3. Of course.

4. Why not?

5. Check back to the text for the answer. Basically, the steps are as follows:
   a. Become aware of the problem.
   b. Look for a solution.
   c. Test out solution to see if it will work.

6. a. Is it pertinent to course objectives?
   b. Is it relevant to students' lives?

    c. Is it feasible (time, materials, abilities)?

    d. Is it worthwhile?

7. a. Provide lists.

    b. Class discussion.

    c. Describe past projects.

    d. Bring in former students.

8. No.

9. a. Rating scales.

    b. Checklists.

    c. Standardized directions for observing.

10. a. Set procedure required of all interviews.

    b. Standard list of exactly worded questions used by all interviewers.

11. Turn back to the module and check your answers against the explanations.

12. Turn back again. Socratic dialogue is mostly a matter of asking leading questions until you get the student to arrive at the conclusion you wanted him or her to reach.

13. Basically that it is controlled by the teacher and so teacher-dominated. True discussions are free and open ended.

14. Value-clarifying discussions are very open, free from leading questions, preaching, or teacher judgments.

15. Refer to module text to see if your answer checks with it. Basically the procedure is

    a. Pick the situation.

    b. Select the cast.

    c. Be sure students understand the situation.

    d. Brief the audience.

    e. Stage the role playing.

    f. Repeat with reversed roles or different players if it seems desirable.

    g. Follow up.

16. They are fun. They make clear difficult concepts and procedures. They give practice.

17. Again, see the module text and compare your answer with it. Basically the procedure is:

    a. Decide on goals or problem.

    b. Define problem.

    c. Allocate tasks.

    d. Gather materials and equipment.

    e. Gather the data.

    f. Review and analyze the data.

    g. Draw inferences.

    h. Report findings and conclusions.

18. The student arrives at the conclusion or generalization rather than having it told to him or her.

19. Present the students with a dilemma. Conduct a discussion about the dilemma in which you use thought-provoking and probing questions if necessary to stimulate thought but keep the discussion open, nonjudgmental, and nonauthoritative.

20. Pick from the following:

    a. Example (modeling).

    b. Persuasion.

    c. Limiting choice.

    d. Inspiration.

    e. Citing dogma and religion.

    f. Appeal to conscience.

    g. Exhortation (telling them what to believe).

21. Use it to clarify students' values and beliefs about issues. Present the issue; have students fill out value sheet; follow up by class discussion, small-group discussion, reading selected sheets or portions of sheets to class, read them privately with comments but no grade, have committee select sheets representing various positions to be read to the class.

22. Select from the following:
    Is the topic relevant to the course?
    Are the students knowledgeable and neutral enough?
    Is it worth the time and effort?
    Do we have sufficient material?
    Can the topic be discussed without upsetting the students or the community?

23. Facts are isolated bits of information that are accepted truths. Concepts are attempts to organize the world of objects, facts, and events into a smaller number of categories; they are major ideas that share a common set of attributes. Whereas concepts are usually one word, understandings (principles, theories, and laws) are statements that are derived from facts and concepts.

24. Whereas discovery is the result of knowledge-seeking, inquiry is an open-ended and creative-thinking process of seeking knowledge. As teaching strategies both involve students in active problem-solving and decision making. The difference between the two strategies is with who identifies the problem, the amount of decision-making done by the students, and in the level of mental operation. In inquiry, students more often identify the problem to be solved, make more of the decisions about how to collect data and about when there is sufficient data. In inquiry problem solving there is a higher sophistication of mental operation required, specifically those in the "idea-using" processes of the inquiry cycle as described in the module.

25. Generalizations (laws, principles, and theories) can provide springboards for further study, for there are undoubtedly always exceptions to statements of generalization. Your first decision in teaching toward student understanding of a generalization is whether to do it deductively (from concrete to abstract) or inductively (from the abstract to the concrete). A deductive approach, which is more traditional, follows the learning theory of Robert Gagné, for which a hierarchy of tasks are identified that lead the learner from simple to complex learning. An inductive approach would begin by having students identify what they already know about the abstract generalization. Students would categorize what they know and look for patterns and relationships; hypothesize about what they do not know; and explore those unknowns through their own active problem solving, discovery, and inquiry. This is the guideline that should direct your own specific response to this question.

26. *I*dentification of problem (I), *de*finition of problem (D), *e*xploration of possible ways of solving the problem (E), *a*ct on a problem solving strategy (A), *l*ooking for effects (L).

27. Recognizing, identifying, defining. Finding evidence. Observing accurately and without prejudice. Interpreting and reporting results. Detecting faulty arguments, bias, reasoning, etc. Seeing relationships. Choosing among alternatives. Drawing inferences and conclusions. Analyzing. Making connections between what is known and new ideas.

28. Begin by teaching them directly, by modeling the skill and then guiding students through practice of the skill. Finally, students should be encouraged to apply this new skill to new situations.

29. Explaining, generalizing, inferring, interpreting data, making analogies, and synthesizing.

30. Idea-using processes: applying, controlling variables, defining operationally, hypothesizing, model building, and predicting.

The most accurate statements are:

1. b	2. c	3. b	4. d
5. b	6. a	7. a	8. b
9. d	10. a	11. d	12. b
13. c	14. c	15. a	

For supporting reasons and for explanations of the limitations or inaccuracy of the other statements, reexamine the module at appropriate points.

1. True individualization entails a tailor-made curriculum for each student, not just a change of pace or varying amount of content to be covered. It narrows the span of ability or achievement in a class so that everyone is able to profit from the same presentation. It diminishes the need for so much remedial instruction and individual attention.

2. Theoretically, it makes it easier to pick content and methods suitable for everyone.

3. There is always a spread of characteristics in a homogeneously grouped class. Besides, all the characteristics, other than those reduced by the grouping process, run the entire gamut found in the population.

4. They tend to be written off. Teachers give up on them. Teachers concentrate on the uninteresting and unchallenging content and presentation, because they conclude that poor students can't keep up. Missing is the spark of vitality from student responses often supplied by the brighter students.

5. Everyone can move through the curriculum at his or her own pace. No one is forced to move on before being ready or to wait for others to catch up.

6. To provide for more variety, and to circumvent the failure attributed to long periods of time spent on units that fail to capture the imagination of the student.

7. It provides a place for students to work on their own with all the materials they need readily available.

8. a. Give some students more work and others less.
   b. Give some students more difficult work and others easier.
   c. Use committees and small-group work.
   d. Individualize.
   e. Give totally different assignments.

9. A classroom laboratory is arranged so that the materials and equipment are readily available for students to work individually and in groups, or on a variety of assignments or projects, under guidance.

10. The bulk of the work is done in a laboratory situation in the true unit. Not all students are expected to attend at the same time to what the teacher is saying. Not everyone does the same thing in the same way.

11. It allows students to work individually on different units at the same time as well as allowing for laboratory-type procedures. It is a self-teaching instrument that frees the student to establish his or her own pace of learning.

12. The feature of *quid pro quo*. In the contract, the student specifies the scope and depth of his or her inquiry. In the packet, the student demonstrates mastery of the content in the fashion requested.

13. They give the student direction and structure so that the student can work without constant recourse to the teacher for direction.

14. Practice, diagnosis, and study, but not for marks.

15. Use study guides, self-correcting materials, student tutors and proctors, and laboratory teaching.

16. Not much, just that you adapt the content, materials, and methods to the group.

The basic approach should be about the same, but adapted to students' talents, interests, abilities, and goals.

17. Students' present educational levels. Year's educational goals. Specifications for services to be provided; extent students should be in regular programs. Type, direction, and criteria for the services.

18. Pick from the following:
    a. Encourage the talented to think and to understand their thinking processes. Use problem solving, inquiry, and open-ended assignments. Insist that students dig into the subject. Hold them to a high level of analysis and critical thinking.
    b. See to it that the talented maintain high academic standards. Do not accept sloppy thinking or sloppy work. Force them to discipline themselves and their thinking.
    c. Do not hold them back or stand in the way of their learning. Give them a chance to move on to the new, the interesting, and the challenging. Do not make them repeat what they already know.
    d. Be sure they become well grounded in academic skills.
    e. Give them lots of responsibility for their own work. Let them plan and evaluate. Encourage independent thought, study, and research.
    f. Use high-level materials: original sources, college textbooks, and adult materials.
    g. Use the seminar discussion strategy in which students present and criticize original papers or reports and discuss topics in depth. Be sure that their discussions hew to a high level of criticism and thinking.

19. Recent research indicates that it doesn't work as expected.

20. Yes, if time permits.

21. Provide multisensory experiences for enrichment and remediation for further creativity and discovery, for special needs students, and for special equipment.

22. Various ways schools and teachers have attempted to involve parents and guardians in their children's education is to use folders of records, a calendar of activities, assignments that are sent home each week, homework telephone hotlines, parent workshops, etc.

MODULE 13

1. The textbook helps to organize student learning, but should be only one of many instructional tools. Teachers sometimes use many reading resources, rather than a single textbook. In using their textbook or other reading materials students should be encouraged to practice the PQ4R approach.

2. The module lists thirty-four items. Basically, it should present the relevant content interestingly, logically, and accurately at a reading level that is compatible with that of the students.

3. Select a number of readings that will lead to the instructional goals. Let the students under guidance read those things that will best suit them. Although they read different things, since the readings all lead to the goals, the students should emerge with the concepts. A study guide will help the students in their study. The readings should have as much spread in interest, reading level, and so on, as is feasible to provide for the students' differences.

4. The greatest advantage has been their inexpensiveness, which allows one to use multitexts, introduce original pieces, mark up books, and so on.

5. Most important, try to find something that encourages thinking. Avoid workbooks that are cut and dry. Otherwise, use the same criteria as for other books and materials.

6. Almost anything, including anecdotes, stories, case studies, pictures, films, filmstrips, histories.

7. To guide students so that they can study alone without being tied to the teacher's apron strings.

8. White space is blank space. Leave white space so what you want to stress will stand out.

9. They are more dramatic.

10. Attach sandpaper, felt, or flannel, or Velcro fasteners to light material such as paper. See the module text for the details.

11. Use it as a teaching tool.

12. Have a central focus without clutter that draws the eye toward what you want to show off. Use eye catchers and lines to draw attention to the center of interest. There should be plenty of white space and no clutter.

13. A flip chart is a big pad of charts that one can flip back and forth as needed.

14. You flip the pages to the proper place, talk about it, and then flip to the next page.

15. Pictures give life to dull classes and reality to abstract descriptions, but when you pass them around the room, they distract students from the lesson.

16. People, places, things, directions, persons to contact, and any other information on local resource persons, materials, and places to visit.

17. Among the reasons you might cite are: they have only a single point of view, they have only a single reading level, they are too rigid, they are too dull, they do not allow for students' individual differences, they are likely to be superficial, and they discourage students from reading more profitable works.

18. Among the many sources of information are curriculum documents, resource units, educational periodicals, and the reference works listed in this module.

19. When evaluating the suitability of free materials you should look for whether the material meets your learning objectives, whether it treats ethnic groups and genders fairly, whether it is free from objectionable advertising or propaganda, its accuracy, whether the material is interesting and attractive for student use, and its durability.

MODULE 14

1. By showing students the real thing or a representation of the real thing, the students see or hear it rather than words about it.

2. Is it suitable to do the job you want it to do? Other considerations pale before this one.

3. The distance between the lens and light source must be properly adjusted.

4. Use the opaque projector. With it you can blow up the pictures so all can see and study them.

5. You can show the material on the screen or board while students work with copies at their seats.

6. Of course.

7. Overhead projectors project only transparent (translucent) material. An opaque projector projects the image of opaque materials.

8. It is versatile, can be used in a lighted room, takes only a second to prepare, can be used as a chalkboard and for many things.

9. That depends upon how fancy you want to make it. A quick, temporary transparency can be made by drawing on the frosted plastic with a grease pencil or felt-tipped pen. To draw a more finished project, follow the procedure outlined in the module text.

10. Lay it on top of the basic transparency to add new information, or take it off to subtract information.

11. It blocks out part of the transparency you do not want pupils to see now.

12. Run it on a small screen or box. Use earphones if it is a sound program.

13. To do a good job is quite a lengthy process. Check your answer against the module text.

14. Wrap the film around the take-up reel a few times, mark the break with a slip of paper, and continue with the show. *Do not* try to tape or pin the film together.

15. Lots of things. Require notes; give quizzes; introduce it well; use study guide, follow-up, discussion, and assignments, for example.

16. Some movies are pretty awful—boring, irrelevant, or incorrect. Students tend to think of them as entertainment. Movies may emphasize what you would rather not emphasize. They are not very adaptable. They require special arrangements to get them when you need them.

17. Follow up. What else?

18. See special films. Use them as optional activities, assign activities for theater parties, bases for committees, or individual reports.

19. Music plus pictures, maps plus pictures, tape plus pictures, board plus screen, or two screens—or any other combination you think of.

20. The microcomputer can be used to individualize instruction, conduct drill and practice, give immediate feedback, present learning programs, and the like. It can provide both computer-assisted instruction and computer-managed instruction, if the software is available.

21. If you want to explain things yourself or stop the film to go into detail on a particular point, or when the sound film is incorrect, distracting, or boring.

22. In slide programs the sequence can be varied to suit your needs, if you do not use canned commentary. It is much easier to put together a slide program than it is to construct a filmstrip.

23. One could assign viewing for homework, videotape progress, assign different channels to different students, use viewing as an extra or optional activity, or if the occasion permits, watch the program in class.

24. Most of them. Slides, filmstrips, 8mm and 16mm films, overheads, audio- and videotapes, records (with earphones) are all easily adapted for individual viewing and listening even if you do not have individual equipment.

25. CAI (Computer-Assisted Instruction) is programmed software that puts the student in contact with pretests, facts, instruction, and responses. It provides drill and practice exercises, or tutors under the control of the student until the point of mastery has been reached. CMI (Computer-Managed Instruction) is software that does all the record keeping when attempting individualized instruction. It manages the instruction, i.e., keeps track of test gains made, indicates next sequential step to take, and provides reports that can be used when grouping students for instruction.

26. None.

MODULE 15

1. a	8. d	15. √	22. g
2. b	9. A or D	16.	23. f
3. a	10. K	17.	24. c
4. d	11. O	18. √	25. e
5. b	12. L	19. √	26. c
6. d	13. R or Q	20.	27. d
7. c	14. √	21. h	28. b

29. Preassessment of students.

30. Instructional activities.

31. Continuous evaluation.

32–35. Pick from the following:
   a. Placement.
   b. Determine readiness.
   c. Grading.
   d. Diagnosis.
   e. Promotion.
   f. Setting goals.
   g. Determine what to do next.
   h. Judge the effectiveness of one's teaching.

MODULE 16

1. b	5. a	9. c	13. √
2. c	6. d	10. b	14.
3. a	7. b	11.	15. √
4. c	8. d	12. √	

16. 5
17. 2 } any other numbers in same relationship, such as
18. 2
19. 1

{ 10
4
4
2 } or { 50
20
20
10 }

20. a	22. b	24. d
21. d	23. b.	25. a

MODULE 17

1. a, c, d. Expertise in many teaching skills is asking too much at this stage; you have not had a chance to start developing teaching style yet.

2. a, d, e, f, g. Ask advice to keep from making unnecessary blunders; criticizing the school shows not your expertise, but your boorishness.

3. c

4. c

5. d

6. a

7. b

8. Examne the incident to see what went wrong and then try again.

9. One that includes all the lower level plus creating, discovering, reorganizing, and formulating new hypotheses, new questions and problems; in short, the level of original and productive thinking.

10. The objective should be clearly stated, measurable, pertinent to unit and course, worthwhile, suitable to age and grade level, achievable, attainable in different degrees and/or amounts, and relevant to the students' lives.

11. So you can get a picture of what you and your teaching are like.

12. a. Direct
    b. Probably not as effective as it would be if it were more indirect.

13. a. Teacher did most of the talking.
    b. Can't tell. Probably the teacher talks too much.

14. Select from good objectives, objectives obtainable by discussion techniques, good participation, teacher drew students out, teacher did not let anyone dominate, teacher kept group on the topic, teacher did not dominate, teacher used evocative questions and tentative solutions, teacher summarized well when needed, and teacher tied the discussion together in summary.

15. Teacher runs a good discussion, does not dominate, and draws out the class.

16. Whiplash questions are really incomplete sentences. They tend to confuse. They do not induce the proper set for answering questions.

17. Cognitive memory questions are narrow memory questions calling only for recall of information. Convergent questions are narrow thought questions that call for coming to a correct solution. Divergent questions are broad, open-ended thought questions for which there are probably no single correct answers.

18. The students seem to have achieved objective 1 but missed objective 2. If objective 2 is important, it probably should be retaught.

19. Choose from (a) become certifiable in more than one subject, (b) pick courses that will prepare you to teach middle and high school courses, (c) seek a graduate degree, (d) do substitute teaching, (e) take advantage of the college or university placement service, (f) learn the skills of job procurement.

20. Basically so you can learn about new developments in the field at meetings or by reading their journals and monographs and so you can meet leaders and knowledgeable practitioners in your teaching field.

Glossary

Accountability. The concept that an individual is responsible for his or her own behaviors and should be able to demonstrate publicly the worth of the activities carried out.

Advance Organizer. Preinstructional cues used to enhance retention of materials to be taught.

Affective Domain. The area of learning related to interests, attitudes, feelings, values, and personal adjustment.

AFT. One of two national teachers' unions, the American Federation of Teachers.

At-Risk. General term given to students who show a high potential for dropping out of formal education.

Behavioral Objective. A statement describing what the learner should be able to do upon completion of the instruction, and containing four ABCD ingredients: the *a*udience (learner), the *b*ehavior, the *c*onditions, and the *d*egree (performance level).

Brainstorming. A teaching strategy where judgments of the ideas of others is forbidden, and used to create a flow of new ideas.

Classroom Control. The process of influencing student behavior in the classroom.

Classroom Management. The teacher's system of establishing a climate for learning, including techniques for preventing and handling student misbehavior.

Cognition. The mental operations involved in thinking.

Cognitive Domain. The area of learning related to intellectual skills, such as retention and assimilation of knowledge.

Competency-Based Instruction. See *performance-based instruction.*

Comprehension. A level of cognition that refers to the skill of understanding.

Computer Literacy. The ability at some level on a continuum to understand and to be able to use computers.

Computer-Assisted Instruction (CAI). Instruction received by a student when interacting with lessons programmed into a computer system.

Computer-Managed Instruction (CMI). The use of a computer system to manage information about learner performance and learning-resources options in order to prescribe and control individual lessons.

Convergent Thinking. Thinking that is directed to a preset conclusion.

Cooperative Learning. An instructional strategy that uses small groups of students working together and helping one another on learning tasks, stressing support for one another rather than competition between each other.

Criterion. A standard by which behavioral performance is judged.

Criterion-Referenced. Standards are established and behaviors are judged against the preset standards, rather than against behaviors of others.

Critical Thinking. The ability to recognize and identify problems and discrepancies, to propose and test solutions, and to arrive at tentative conclusions based on evidence.

Deductive Learning. Learning that proceeds from the general to the specifics.

Direct Intervention.   Teacher use of verbal reminders or verbal commands to redirect student misbehavior, as opposed to the use of nonverbal gestures or cues—that is, indirect intervention.

Discipline.   In teaching, the process of controlling student behavior in the classroom. An archaic term that has been largely replaced by the terms *classroom control* or *classroom management.*

Discovery Learning.   Learning that proceeds in this sequence: identification of a problem, development of hypotheses, testing of hypotheses, arrival at conclusion.

Divergent Thinking.   Thinking that expands beyond original thought.

Eclectic.   Utilizing the best from a variety of sources.

Educational Goal.   A desired instructional outcome that is broad in scope.

Empathy.   The ability to understand the feelings of another person.

Exceptional Child.   A child who deviates from the average child in any of the following ways: mental characteristics, sensory ability, neuromotor or physical characteristics, social behavior, communication ability, or in multiple handicaps.

Feedback.   In interpersonal communication, information sent from the receiver to the originator that provides disclosure about the reception of the intended message.

Goal, Course.   A broad generalized statement telling about the course.

Goal, Instructor.   A statement telling what the instructor intends to do.

High School.   See *secondary school.*

Holistic Learning.   Learning that incorporates emotions with thinking.

Inductive Learning.   Learning that proceeds from the specifics to the general.

Inquiry Learning.   Like discovery learning, except that the learner designs the processes to be used in resolving a problem. Inquiry learning requires higher levels of mental operation than does discovery learning.

Instructional Module.   Like the self-instructional package (SIP), any free-standing instructional unit that includes these components: rationale, objectives, pretest, learning activities, comprehension checks, posttest.

Integrated Language Arts.   Teaching reading, writing, and spelling, not as separate subjects, but as an unsegregated whole combined with thinking, experiencing, and emotional considerations.

Intermediate Grades.   Grades four through six.

Intern Teaching.   Like student teaching, except the intern teacher usually is paid a salary.

Internalization.   The extent to which an attitude or value becomes a part of the learner.

Intervention.   See *direct intervention.*

Intuition.   Knowing without conscious reasoning.

Junior High School.   See *secondary school.*

Learning.   A change in behavior resulting from experience.

Mainstreaming.   Placing an "exceptional child" in a regular classroom for all or part of his or her learning.

Mastery Learning.   The concept that a student should master the content of one lesson before moving on to the content of the next.

Metacognition.   The ability to think about, understand, and to develop your own thinking and learning.

Micro Peer Teaching.   Teaching a limited objective for a brief period of time to a group of 8 to 10 peers, for the purpose of evaluation and improvement of particular teaching skills.

Middle School.   Schools that have been planned for students ranging in age from 9 through 14, and generally have grades five through eight, with grades six through eight being the most popular organization, although many varied patterns exist. For example, a school might include grades seven and eight and still be called a middle school. Although middle schools vary considerably in organization, generally the fifth and sixth grades are each self-contained (each class has one teacher for all or most of the day), while seventh and eighth grades are departmentalized, that is, students in these higher grades may meet each day for a homebase class and then go to other rooms and teachers for other subjects.

Multicultural Education.   A deliberate educational attempt to help students understand facts, generalizations, attitudes, and behaviors derived from their own ethnic roots as well as others. In this process the students should unlearn racism and biases and recognize the interdependent fabric of our human society, giving due acknowledgment for contributions made by all its members.

NEA.   The oldest and largest of two national teacher's unions, the National Education Association.

Norm-Referenced.   Individual performance is judged relative to overall performance of the group.

Overlapping.   The teacher's ability to attend to several matters at once.

Paraprofessional.   An adult who is not a credentialed teacher but works in the classroom with and under the supervision of a credentialed teacher.

Performance Objective.   See *behavioral objective.*

Performance-Based Instruction.   Instruction designed around evaluating student achievement against specified and predetermined behavioral objectives.

Positive Reinforcer.   Encouraging desired student behaviors by rewarding those behaviors when they occur.

PQ4R.   A study strategy where students preview the reading, create questions, read to answer the questions, reflect, recite, and review the original material.

Probationary Teacher.   An untenured teacher. After a designated number of years teaching in the same district, an untenured or probationary teacher upon rehire usually receives a tenure contract.

Psychomotor Domain.   Classification of learning locomotor behaviors.

PTO.   School organization of parents and teachers.

Realia.   Real objects used as visual props in teaching, such as political campaign buttons, plants, memorabilia, and so on.

Reliability.   In measurement, the consistency with which an item is measured over time.

Secondary School.   Traditionally any school housing students from grades seven through twelve. Those secondary schools housing grades seven, eight, and sometimes nine are termed junior high schools; schools housing grades twelve, eleven, ten, and sometimes nine are termed high schools.

Simulation.   An abstraction or simplification of a real-life situation.

SQ3R.   A study strategy where students survey the reading, create questions, read to answer the questions, recite the answers, and review the original material.

Student Teaching.   The field experience component of teacher education where the teacher candidate practices teaching children under the direct supervision of a credentialed teacher and a college or university supervisor.

Teaching Style.   The way a teacher teaches, that teacher's distinctive mannerisms complemented by his or her choices of teaching behaviors and strategies.

Tenured Teacher.   After serving a designated number of years in the same district as a probationary teacher, upon rehire the teacher receives a tenure contract, which means that the teacher is automatically rehired each year thereafter, unless the contract is revoked by either the district or the teacher and for specific and legal reasons.

Terminal Behavior.   That which has been learned as a direct result of instruction.

Think Time.   See *wait time.*

Validity.   In measurement, the degree to which an item measures that which it is intended to measure.

Wait Time.   In the use of questioning, the period of silence between the time a question is asked and the inquirer does something, such as repeats the question, or calls upon a particular student, or answers the question him- or herself.

With-it-Ness.   The teacher's ability to timely intervene and redirect potential student misbehavior. Equivalent to the old adage, "having eyes in the back of your head."

NAME INDEX

Adams, Franklin P., 523
Ahanahan, Timothy, 353n
Alexander, William M., 518n
Amidon, Edmund J., 540n
Anderson, Richard, 330n
Anderson, Ronald H., 455
Applebee, Arthur N., 330n
Aubrey, R. H., 420

Baldwin, R. Scott, 352n
Barbe, Walter, B., 18n
Baum, Robert, 289n
Baumann, James F., 352n
Beck, Isabel L., 352n
Beyer, Barry K., 289n
Blakeslee, Thomas R., 12n
Bloom, Benjamin, 67, 67n, 70, 70n, 108, 215
Bormuth, J., 349n
Bradfield, James M., 536n
Bransford, J. D., 288n
Briggs, Leslie, 67n
Bromley, Karen D'Angelo, 353n
Brophy, Jere E., 57n, 166n, 187n, 188n
Brown, Duane, 174n
Brown, James W., 455
Bruner, Jerome, 292n
Bullard, John R., 455
Buros, O. K., 468n
Burton, Dwight L., 344n
Burton, William H., 316n

Callahan, Joseph F., 471n, 498n
Carroll, John, 108
Cartwright, William H., 407n
Charles, C. M., 192n, 195n
Clark, Barbara K., 352n
Clark, David L., 54n
Clark, Leonard H., 97n, 225n, 259n, 303n, 335n, 376n, 391n, 411n, 448n, 451n, 471n, 498n
Cook, Sue Carol, 455
Costa, Art, 31, 232n, 288n, 289n
Couture, Deborah, 383n
Cunningham, Jones W., 353n

Dewey, John, 288, 288n, 294
Disney, Walt, 1
Dunn, Rita, 12n

Einstein, Albert, 31
Emerson, Ralph W., 403

Emmer, Edmund T., 195n
Estes, Thomas H., 353n

Feather, N., 166n
Flanders, Ned A., 540n
Fry, Edward, 346n
Frye, Harvey R., 455

Gagné, Robert M., 67n, 288, 288n, 292n
Gay, Geneva, 395n
Gerould, Katharine F., 163
Gilbert, Shirl E., 395n
Glasser, William, 192n
Goldstein, Harvey, 468n
Good, Thomas L., 57n, 166n, 187n, 188n
Goodlad, John I., 333n
Goudket, Michael, 455
Grant, C., 362n
Green, Lee, 455
Gregorc, Anthony, 364, 364n
Gunter, Mary Alice, 17n
Guthrie, W. K. C., 313n

Hanson, R. J., 17, 17n
Harmin, Merrill, 318n
Harrow, A. J., 74, 74n
Heinich, Robert, 364n, 431n, 433n, 441n, 454n, 456
Helfer, Harold, 459
Holmes, Betty C., 352n
Hotchkiss, Phyllis Riley, 17n

Jackson, Roberta M., 291n
Johnson, M. S., 349n
Johnson, Rita, 108
Johnson, Stuart, 108
Joubert, Joseph, 459

Kaneenui, Edward K., 352n
Kaplan, Sandra N., 289n
Karlin, Robert, 339n
Keller, Fred, 108
Kellough, Richard D., 5n, 107, 107n, 108, 187n, 292n, 324n, 371n, 378n, 389n, 410n, 415n
Kemp, Jerold E., 443n
Kim, Eugene C., 5n, 187n, 292n, 324n, 378n, 389n, 410n, 415n

Kimball, Roland B., 316n
Klopfer, Leopold E., 6n
Kounin, Jacob S., 191n
Krathwohl, David R., 70, 70n
Kress, R. A., 349n

Levy, Philip, 468n
Lewis, Oscar, 391n
Lewis, Richard B., 455

Mager, Robert F., 508n
Masia, Bertram B., 70, 70n
Mathies, Lorraine, 420
McClure, Larry, 455
McCullough, Constance M., 336n, 337n, 338n
McKenna, N., 349n
Mether, Calvin E., 455
Michaels, J. W., 178n
Minor, Edward O., 455
Molenda, Michael, 364n
Moredock, H. Stewart, 536n

Oates, Stanton C., 455
Olsen, Laurie, 391n
Orben, Bob, 403

Palmer, Barbara C., 352n
Patlak, Sanford, 336
Peale, Norman Vincent, 163
Pearson, David, 353n
Peterson, N., 377n
Popkewitz, Thomas S., 307n

Raths, Louis E., 318n, 319n
Resnick, Lauren B., 6n
Richards, Herbert C., 353n
Roberts, P. L., 371n
Robinson, Francis P., 341n
Robinson, H. Alan, 335n, 336n, 341n, 342n
Russell, James D., 364n
Ruth, Babe, 459

Shepherd, David L., 339n
Silver, H. F., 17, 17n
Simmons, John S., 344n
Simon, Sidney B., 318n
Slater, Wayne H., 353n
Slavin, Robert E., 192n

SUBJECT INDEX